The Environmental Case

Translating Values into Policy

Judith A. Layzer
Middlebury College

CQ PRESS

A Division of Congressional Quarterly Inc.
Washington, D.C.

CQ Press
1255 22nd Street, N.W., Suite 400
Washington, D.C. 20037

(202) 822-1475; (800) 638-1710

www.cqpress.com

⊗ The paper used in this publication meets the minimum requirements of the American National Standard for Information Sciences—Permanence of Paper for Printed Library Materials, ANSI Z39.48-1992.

Printed and bound in the United States of America

05 04 03 02 01   5 4 3 2 1

Typeset by Sheridan Books, Ann Arbor, Michigan

Cover designed by Naylor Design

Maps redrawn by Laris Karklis

Library of Congress Cataloging-in-Publication Data

Layzer, Judith A.
    The environmental case : translating values into policy / Judith A. Layzer.
        p. cm.
Includes bibliographical references and index.
    ISBN 1-56802-726-5 (alk. paper)
    1. Environmental policy—United States—Case studies. I. Title.
    GE180 .L39 2002
    363.7′056′0973—dc21

                                                        2001008233

For Jean and David Layzer,
with love, gratitude, and admiration

Contents

**Part 2   History, Changing Values, and
Natural Resource Management**

Part 3   Addressing Commons Problems

Part 4   Anti-Environmental Backlash Prompts New Approaches

Preface

The idea for this book emerged while I was a graduate student in political science at the Massachusetts Institute of Technology (MIT) in the mid-1990s. My adviser, Stephen Meyer, and I were developing his new course in environmental policy, and, after searching extensively for material that would convey the drama and fascination of environmental politics to undergraduates, we made an important discovery: although there were quite a few informative and readable texts on the history, substance, and efficacy of environmental policymaking, few described environmental politics in action. I set out to craft a set of case studies because, after all, everyone loves a good yarn. My hope was that I could write these cases in such a way that readers would be riveted but would also glean from them essential lessons about American environmental politics and policymaking. My primary goal, then, was not to assess policies from a normative perspective but to familiarize readers with the processes by which environmental policies are made, from the way we decide which problems are worthy of the government's attention to how we choose to address those problems.

Once the number of cases reached a critical mass, I began to think about a semester-long series. Thus, the organization of the book as a whole emerged as I added cases that captured new aspects of politics or policy, such as a new object of concern (wetlands or species extinction, for example) or a novel political dynamic (such as the backlash against environmentalism or collaborative approaches to decision making). The division between pollution and natural resources was an obvious one; the other division—between common property resources and new solutions—was less obvious but was chosen to reflect changes in environmental policy concerns and approaches. In revising the cases for publication and in responding to the universal advice of reviewers, I incorporated a more explicit analytic framework based on John Kingdon's model of the policy process. I also made more transparent the major themes raised in each case. Of course, in doing so, I viewed the material through a particular lens—that of political science and, more specifically, one that focused on the role of problem definition in policymaking, as eloquently articulated by Deborah Stone in her book *Policy Paradox*.

Although I imposed a clear structure, I tried to keep each case sufficiently self-explanatory that economists, sociologists, historians, and others interested in using the book in their courses would not feel confined by my interpretation. Moreover, I sought to make the cases accessible not only to students and scholars but to activists, policymakers, and ordinary people as well. Each case contains a wealth of fascinating characters and events and provides a foundation for more in-depth study of the issues raised. Taken as a whole, they provide a portrait of U.S. environmental policymaking, from the local to the international levels, that should be valuable to anyone concerned about the environment.

ACKNOWLEDGMENTS

Writing this book would not have been possible without the support of both MIT and Middlebury College. MIT funded the initial development of the cases, and Middlebury generously provided funds for research assistants—both directly and through the Environmental Studies program. In addition, many people labored to bring the book to fruition. Stephen Meyer, who supported the writing of the cases, has been consistently enthusiastic and has continued to use them in his classes. The undergraduates—first at MIT and then at Middlebury— who pilot-tested the cases gave enormously helpful feedback on them. Several Middlebury students provided research assistance, particularly Katrina O'Brien, Sarah Weston, and Jess Widay. Lee Rowland spent a summer working cheerfully and tirelessly, tracking down sources and information for the book. Colleagues Christopher Bosso (Northeastern University) and Christopher Klyza (Middlebury College) read and made insightful comments on parts of the book. I am also grateful to reviewers Gordon Bennett (University of Texas at Austin), Mark Lubell (Florida State University), Stuart Shulman (Drake University), and Stacy VanDeveer (University of New Hampshire), all of whom gave extremely detailed and thoughtful feedback on the manuscript.

At CQ Press, acquisitions editor Charisse Kiino handled the original manuscript with great professionalism and an infectious optimism about its prospects. Manuscript editor Lynn Whittaker pointed out unclear passages and trimmed my prose with care and delicacy, so any remaining ambiguity or wordiness is solely my responsibility. Managing editor Ann Davies and production editor Belinda Josey diplomatically engineered a tight production schedule, patiently tolerating my penchant for last-minute editing. Finally, Debra Naylor gets credit for the cover design.

In addition to those who contributed directly, many others helped by making my life wonderful while I was working on the book. Foremost among those are my lifelines: Christine Dunlap, Molly Goodwin, Elizabeth Phillips, Melissa Shufro, and Elizabeth Swan. Bill Rodriguez provided insightful editorial commentary on early drafts and cheered me on when I nearly became discouraged. Carolyn Layzer helped by reading chapters with her usual enthusiasm and more generally by being my most loyal fan. Deborah Stone and Jim Morone have been generous beyond measure—with friendship, advice, encouragement, and a wonderful summer hiatus in Brookline, for which I am eternally grateful. My colleagues at Middlebury have encouraged me throughout this process, sympathizing with the long nights and weekends that invariably come with trying to finish a book. I am especially grateful to two people who will not see *The Environmental Case* in print: Richard Marius, with his outsized passion, taught me to write sparingly and well; and my sister, Daryl Layzer, showed me through her own grace and dignity how to live every day and take nothing for granted. Finally, this book is dedicated to my parents, who instilled in me a passion for thinking, learning, and educating. By providing freedom and security in equal measure, they enabled me to take this circuitous but remarkable journey.

Introduction

Environmental politics concerns "how humanity organizes itself to relate to the nature that sustains it."[1] Environmental controversies have erupted over such diverse issues as preserving wilderness, saving endangered species, protecting or restoring ecosystems, cleaning up toxic dumps or spills, reducing pollution, conserving energy, developing new energy sources, introducing new technologies, ameliorating changes in the global climate, and ensuring an equitable distribution of environmental hazards. These kinds of issues have assumed positions of primacy in American politics, alongside the more conventional social, budget, and foreign policy concerns. While the policy process has many generic features, environmental policymaking has a host of distinct attributes and thus warrants its own analytic niche. The goal of this book is to provide a conceptual framework for students of environmental policymaking that illuminates the general attributes of the American political system as it grapples with this particular object of public action.

This introductory chapter begins with an explanation of two critical features underlying U.S. environmental politics. It then describes the major actors—policymakers, advocates, experts, and the media—and introduces key concepts that help explain the process by which environmental policy is made. The result is a general framework for analyzing the process, elements of which will be examined more closely in the subsequent cases. The chapter concludes by explaining the rationale behind the selection, organization, and presentation of the twelve case studies in this volume. Each case is interesting in its own right but was chosen because it offers important lessons for anyone who wants to understand why environmental policy controversies turn out the way they do.

TWO CRITICAL FEATURES OF U.S. ENVIRONMENTAL POLICYMAKING

Understanding environmental policymaking begins with a recognition of its two critical features. First, environmental policy disputes are, at heart, contests over values. Although to the casual observer, these conflicts appear to revolve around arcane technical issues, nearly every one involves a more fundamental disagreement over how human beings ought to interact with the natural environment. Second, even though environmental disputes are grounded in conflicting values, the participants in environmental policy contests rarely make value-based arguments. Instead, they define problems in terms of the science, economics, and risks associated with environmental issues. Let's examine each of these features in more detail.

The Clash of Values at the Heart of Environmental Policymaking

The participants in environmental debates are divided into two broad camps based on entrenched differences in their beliefs about the appropriate relationship between humans and the natural environment. While each side incorporates a range of perspectives, for analytic purposes we can categorize them as environmentalists and cornucopians. Because value differences divide participants, environmental policy conflicts are rarely resolved by appeals to reason; no amount of technical information is likely to convert adversaries in such disputes.[2]

One Category: Environmentalists. Environmentalism is not a single philosophy but a congeries of beliefs with several roots. Environmental values, in one form or another, have been a feature of American culture and politics since before the arrival of white settlers on the North American continent. In fact, many contemporary environmentalists root their own values in the spiritual beliefs of Native Americans.[3]

Most historians, though, date the origins of American environmentalism to the late eighteenth- and early nineteenth-century Romantics and Transcendentalists, an elite group of artists and writers who celebrated wild nature as a source of spiritual renewal and redemption. They believed that only by preserving untrammeled wilderness could we ensure that landscapes remained to replenish the weary soul. In the 1830s, George Catlin, a painter who traveled frequently in the West, was the first to plead for the establishment of a national park to preserve land in its "pristine beauty and wildness" for future generations.[4] Twenty years later, Henry David Thoreau deplored the wholesale clearing of land for farming and moved to a cabin at Walden Pond in search of a more "simple" and "natural" life. Thoreau also emphasized the importance of preserving wild nature for building character; in his famous essay "Walking," he wrote: "Hope and the future for me are not in lawns and cultivated fields, not in towns and cities, but in the impervious and quaking swamps."[5] Later in that century, John Muir, founder of the Sierra Club and an ardent and prolific advocate of wilderness preservation, described nature as a "window opening into heaven, a mirror reflecting the Creator."[6] A century later, the federal government embedded the preservationist philosophy in such laws as the Wilderness Preservation Act (1964), the Wild and Scenic Rivers Act (1968), and the National Trails Act (1968).

A second type of environmental concern, conservationism, accompanied the Progressive movement that emerged at the turn of the twentieth century. Unlike preservationists, who wanted to set aside swaths of undisturbed nature, conservationists were utilitarians who advocated the prudent use of natural resources; as historian Samuel Hays points out, conservationists adhered to the "gospel of efficiency."[7] Conservationists were intent on managing the nation's coal, oil, timber, grassland, and water according to scientific principles to ensure their availability in the long run. (Importantly, most of the "science" at the time was geared toward increasing natural resource yields; a broader focus on ecosystems would come later.) Conservationists like Gifford Pinchot, for example, deplored the wasteful cut-and-run logging practices of private timber companies, fearing that American industrialists would appropriate and squander the nation's natural resources unless government stepped in and planned for their orderly exploitation. It was this concern that drove the federal government to set aside forest reserves and create the Forest Service in 1905 to manage them for the public benefit.

While strains of preservationist and conservationist thought pervade contemporary environmental debates, a divergent strand of environmentalism emerged after World War II, one more concerned with pollution and the interdependence of human beings and nature than with preserving pristine natural areas or managing natural resources responsibly. The scientific discipline of ecology, which focuses on the study of living organisms and their environment, is the primary wellspring of modern environmentalism.[8] In the late 1940s, naturalist Aldo Leopold sowed the seeds of the contemporary environmental movement with his book, *A Sand County Almanac,* which developed an ecologically based "land ethic" based on principles of interrelatedness and stability. According to Leopold, "All ethics rest upon a single premise: that the individual is a member of a community of interdependent parts."[9] "A thing is right," he continued, "when it tends to preserve the stability and beauty of the biotic community. It is wrong when it tends otherwise."[10]

Another philosophical foundation of mainstream environmentalism is the limits-to-growth thesis espoused by Donella Meadows and her coauthors in 1970. Based on a mathematical method called system dynamics, this perspective recognized the importance of relationships and feedback loops in complex systems.[11] According to the limits-to-growth argument, the human population is outrunning the earth's capacity to support it. Adherents of this view generally are not opposed to economic growth altogether; rather, they aspire to growth that is "sustainable"—that is, growth that does not come at the expense of future generations. An unregulated market system is thus anathema because it invariably leads to unsustainable levels of production and consumption.

Finally, deep ecologists distinguish themselves from the mainstream environmentalists, whose environmental beliefs they regard as superficial. Deep ecology is ecocentric: whereas anthropocentric perspectives treat human beings as morally superior to other forms of life on the basis of our capacity for language and complex thought, ecocentric perspectives treat the world as "an intrinsically dynamic, interconnected web of relations in which there are absolutely no discrete entities and absolutely no dividing lines between the living and the nonliving, the animate and the inanimate, or the human and the nonhuman."[12] As this passage makes clear, deep ecology adopts a premise of "biospherical egalitarianism"—that is, the inherent and equal value of all living things. Moreover, deep ecologists believe that human quality of life depends on maintaining a deep connection to, rather than simply a respectful relationship with, other forms of life. It is worth noting that deep ecology is *not* logically derived from ecology; nor does it depend for substantiation on the results of scientific investigation.[13] Rather, as philosopher Arne Naess explains, "To the ecological field worker, the equal right to live and blossom is an intuitively clear and obvious value axiom."[14]

A Second Category: Cornucopians. In contrast to environmentalists, cornucopians[15] (or Prometheans[16]) place a preeminent value on economic growth. The term *cornucopian* suggests abundance and limitlessness and thus contrasts sharply with environmentalism. Adherents of this perspective fear that environmental restrictions threaten their own economic well-being or the economic well-being of their community.

Cornucopians have unlimited confidence in humans' ability to devise technological solutions to resource shortages.[17] For them, what appear to be limits to economic expansion are not; rather, our potential for growth is bounded only by our ingenuity. Best known among the cornucopians are economists Julian Simon and Herman Kahn, who say "we are confident that the nature of the physical world permits continued improvements in humankind's economic lot in the long run, indefinitely."[18] A theme of the cornucopian literature is that the kinds of doomsday forecasts made by environmentalists never come to pass. While resource shortages may arise in the short run, the lesson of history, according to Simon and Kahn, is that "the nature of the world's physical conditions and the resilience in a well-functioning economic and social system enable us to overcome such problems, and the solution usually leaves us better off than if the problem had never arisen."[19]

In addition to being technological optimists, cornucopians value individual liberty—defined as the freedom to do as one wishes without interference—above all else. Some proponents of this philosophy contend that environmentalists are actually socialists disguising their rejection of markets and preference for government control over the means of production as a concern about the environment.[20] Cornucopians criticize environmental regulations not only for limiting individual freedom but also for consuming resources that would otherwise be used productively out of the economy.[21] They believe ensuring that individuals can pursue material prosperity is the best way to protect the environment because they think that affluence leads to demands for better health and a cleaner environment.[22] The role of government, in such a world view, is simply to assign property rights in the earth's resources and let the market dictate allocations of the goods and services that flow from these resources.

Cornucopians regard their perspective as logical, rational, and optimistic; in contrast, they see environmentalists as sentimental and irrationally pessimistic. In particular, they eschew philosophies that elevate plants, animals, and nonliving creatures to the level of human beings, adopting instead a view of the world in which "people may not sit above animals and plants in any metaphysical sense, but clearly are superior in their placement in the natural order." Thus, "decent conditions must be provided for all of the former before there can be long-term assurance of protection for the latter."[23]

In short, the fault line between environmentalists and cornucopians arises out of different world views. Environmentalists are a diverse lot, ranging from those who believe that all life has value to those who yearn for simpler, less harried times to those with practical concerns about the impact of pollution on human health or the economy. There are also many varieties of cornucopians: some place a higher value on economic growth than they do on the aesthetic or moral importance of the natural world; others are avid outdoorsmen who have more faith in individuals' than in government's ability to protect natural amenities. However, the heterogeneity of environmentalism and cornucopianism should not obscure the importance of the fundamental value differences underpinning environmental controversies. Only by recognizing the importance of such differences can we understand why environmental policymaking is rarely a matter of recognizing a problem and devising a solution. Moreover, the extent to which participants' values diverge is the best clue to how intractable a conflict will be: controversies that involve consensual values like human health are typically less polarized than disputes over ecology, where value differences are vast and often irreconcilable.

How Participants Define Problems to Gain Support

Because the values of participants on both sides are entrenched, environmental politics consists largely of trying to gain the support of the previously unaware and undecided rather than trying to convert the already committed. As political scientist E. E. Schattschneider famously observed: "the outcome of every conflict is determined by the extent to which the audience becomes involved in it."[24] To attract sympathizers, advocates define problems strategically in ways they think will resonate with a majority of the public.[25] Defining a problem in politics is a way of simplifying a complex reality; it involves framing information to draw attention to some elements of a problem while obscuring or minimizing others.[26] Problem definition also entails explaining cause and effect, identifying victims and villains, and assigning responsibility for remediation.[27]

By changing which aspect of a problem the public focuses on, advocates can raise (or lower) its visibility and thereby get it onto (or keep it off) the political agenda.[28] Participants in an environmental policy controversy compete ferociously to provide the authoritative explanation for a problem because "causal stories are essential political instruments for shaping alliances and settling the distribution of benefits and costs."[29] Participants also compete to project the problem's consequences because they know that fear of loss or harm is likely to galvanize the public. In addition to facilitating alliances and raising public awareness, by authoritatively defining a problem advocates can limit the range and type of solutions the public and policymakers are likely to see as plausible. As Schattschneider also pointed out, "The definition of the alternatives is the supreme instrument of power."[30]

When polled, a large majority of Americans profess their support for environmental values,[31] making baldly anti-environmental rhetoric generally unacceptable in political discourse.[32] As a result, cornucopians know they must define environmental problems in ways that make their points in subtle and indirect ways, rather than proclaiming anti-environmental values. The competition between environmentalists and cornucopians to define an environmental problem thus revolves around three attributes: the scientific understanding of the problem; the economic costs and benefits of addressing the problem; and the risks associated with action or inaction. Because each of these is speculative, advocates can choose assessments and projections that are most consistent with their values. They then "frame" that information—using symbols, metaphors, numbers, and causal theories—to emphasize either environmental or economic risk, depending on their policy objectives.

Translating Scientific Explanations into Causal Stories. The first battleground in any environmental controversy is the scientific depiction of cause and effect. Rather than simply providing an authoritative explanation, science leaves considerable latitude for framing because, as a general rule, the scientific understanding of an environmental problem is highly uncertain. Most scientific research on these problems involves practitioners in multiple disciplines, many of which are relatively young, working at the frontiers of scientific knowledge. More importantly, few environmental problems can be simulated in laboratory experiments: they involve complex interactions among factors for which it is difficult or impossible to control. Thus, in the early stages of research, a wide range of uncertainty surrounds explanations of the problem's causes and consequences. Over time, the boundaries of that uncertainty are likely to narrow. Because observational data are likely to be consistent with more than one theory, however, it may take a long time for scientists to converge on an explanation; in the meantime, scientists are likely to prefer theories that are consistent with their own values.[33]

An example of the process of building scientific knowledge is the way that scientific understanding of atmospheric ozone depletion has advanced since the 1970s. The stratospheric ozone layer absorbs UV-B radiation, thereby regulating the earth's temperature and protecting plants, animals, and people from excessive radiation. During the 1970s, scientists developed several theories to explain the observed reduction in stratospheric ozone over the poles. Some scientists were concerned about aircraft emissions of nitrogen oxides; others suggested that nitrogen-based fertilizers or fallout from nuclear weapons tests might be the primary culprits. Over time, a theory advanced by chemists Sherwood Rowland and Mario Molina in 1974 superseded the others and gained broad acceptance. Rowland and Molina proposed that chlorine-containing compounds, such as chlorofluorocarbons, destroy the ozone layer through a series of complex, solar-induced chemical reactions. As researchers learned more about stratospheric chemistry, estimates of ozone reduction became more accurate and the mechanisms by which it occurs more accurately specified.[34]

Unfortunately, the time period within which scientists converge on and refine an explanation is likely to be considerably longer than the time available to policymakers for choosing a solution. This is because the identification of a potential problem by scientists prompts the mobilization of interests that are concerned about it and demand a governmental response. The norms of scientific investigation—particularly those of deliberate and thorough study, rigorous peer review and criticism, and forthright expression of uncertainty—create opportunities for proponents of new policies, as well as for defenders of the status quo, to portray the problem in ways that are compatible with their own values and policy preferences. In most cases, advocates of more protective environmental policies publicize the worst-case scenarios theorized by the science, overstate the certainty of scientific knowledge, and press for an early and stringent—or precautionary—policy response to avert catastrophe. In contrast, opponents of more protective environmental policies emphasize the uncertain state of current knowledge or, if there is a strong scientific consensus that an environmental problem is genuine, highlight dissenting views within the scientific community.[35]

Shifting Attention to the Economic Costs and Benefits. As the scientific consensus explaining an environmental problem becomes more firm, advocates then turn to economic arguments to define the problem. In particular, cornucopians emphasize and environmentalists downplay the economic costs of policies to address the problem. Like scientific explanations of cause and effect, the costs of regulation are highly uncertain, and projections vary widely depending on the assumptions used and the time horizon considered. For example, analysts disagree on the number of jobs likely to be lost as the direct result of an environmental regulation and diverge even more dramatically on the number of collateral jobs—in restaurants, banks, and other service industries—that will disappear. They make different assumptions about future levels of economic growth; the extent and pace of technological adaptation to a regulation; and the likelihood and extent of offsetting effects, such as the establishment or growth of new industries. As is true of scientists, given a choice among equally defensible assumptions, economists are likely to select premises that reflect their values; thus, it is not surprising that industry projections of costs associated with a regulation tend to be much higher than projections made by environmentalists, with government estimates typically in the middle.[36]

In addition to debating projections of the cost of environmental policies, competing parties disagree over the desirability of benefit-cost analysis (BCA) as a decision-making tool. BCA entails determining the ratio of monetary costs to benefits of addressing a problem; by implication, government should undertake a program only if its benefits outweigh its costs—that is, if the BCA ratio is greater than one. In the past twenty-five years, economists have developed a host of increasingly sophisticated techniques for assessing the benefits and costs of environmental policies. Nevertheless, many environmentalists contend that BCA is a political device for slowing the growth of regulation rather than a genuine analytic tool. They point out that estimates of the prospective costs and benefits of environmental protection are inherently biased against environmental protection because judgments about environmental benefits, such as the value of a saving wilderness or reducing the likelihood or severity of asthma attacks among sensitive populations, are difficult—if not impossible—to quantify, whereas immediate and tangible costs naturally accrue in dollars. Moreover, they argue, using BCA as a decision rule eliminates questions of ethics and morality from the political calculus.[37] Regardless of how it is derived or how accurately it reflects a program's value, the number generated by a BCA constitutes a powerful frame because, as Deborah Stone observes, numbers have an aura of credibility and technical neutrality and therefore carry a great deal of political weight.[38]

Dramatizing the Risks of Action or Inaction. Finally, like scientific knowledge about a problem and the economic costs of addressing it, perceptions of the risk associated with it are subject to framing. People do not assess risk based on objective analysis of statistical evidence; rather, they employ heuristics, or inferential rules—what political scientist Howard Margolis calls "habits of mind."[39] Psychologists have identified some inferential rules they believe shape the average person's perception of risks. Using the "availability" heuristic, for example, people judge an event as likely or frequent if instances of it are easy to recall. Thus, they overestimate the risk of dramatic and sensational events, which tend to get media coverage, while underestimating the risk of unspectacular events.[40] Many psychologists also believe that the public incorporates factors besides expected damages—the measure used by experts—into their assessment of risk. Among those factors are: whether the risk is taken voluntarily, its immediacy, its familiarity, the extent of control one has over the risky situation, the severity of the possible consequences, and the level of dread the risk evokes.[41] Some of these factors may explain why environmentalists are more successful at drawing attention to problems whose effects appear immediate, dramatic, and catastrophic than to those whose impacts are more remote and mundane.

Psychologists have found that other aspects of the way risk is framed can have a dramatic impact on risk perceptions as well.[42] First, people value the same gains differently, depending on the reference point. For instance, they value the increment from $10 to $20 more highly than from $110 to $120. Second, people are more concerned about losses than they are about gains of the same amount—they fear losing $10 more than they value gaining $10. Third, people overweight low probabilities and underweight moderate and high probabilities; so they fear rare events more than common ones. Recognizing the importance of these elements of framing to the way the public perceives risk, both sides in an environmental contest define the problem as a loss from an already low status quo and overstate the likelihood of low probability but potentially disastrous outcomes: environmentalists tend to depict catastrophic environmental or human health risks of inaction, whereas cornucopians typically minimize environmental risks while focusing attention on dramatic economic risks.

In sum, the hallmark of a successful environmental policy campaign is the ability of its organizers to craft the dominant problem definition around the scientific explanation, the costs of regulation, and the risks associated with inaction. The side that succeeds in defining the problem has an enormous advantage in politics because the way people think and talk about a policy problem shapes what they are willing to do about it. As Deborah Stone observes, "Political fights are conducted with money, with rules, with votes, and with favors, to be sure, but they are conducted above all with words and ideas."[43]

MAJOR ACTORS IN ENVIRONMENTAL POLICYMAKING

The actors who have an impact on environmental policymaking are found both inside and outside government. Governmental decision makers must choose whether to address an environmental problem and, if so, how. Advocates on both sides try to influence those decisions, adjusting their tactics to reflect the arena within which decisions are being made. Their success depends heavily on both the support of experts and the media's coverage of the issue.

Decision Makers in the Government

Foremost among the decision makers in the national environmental policymaking process are the president and members of Congress who formulate legislation, the executive branch administrators who interpret and implement those laws, and the courts that review both the laws and their implementation by agencies. In various combinations these actors determine whether, in response to a challenge launched by advocates, environmental policy becomes more protective or more permissive or simply remains the same. In making those decisions, policymakers are influenced by their values; however, they are also responsive to the incentives and constraints created by their institutional settings.

Legislative Actors. Legislative actors—the president and Congress—decide which problems government will address and formulate the basic goals of public policy. In making such decisions, members of Congress are deeply concerned with the views of their constituents because, whether they are environmentalists or cornucopians at heart, they must be reelected if they hope to pursue their policy goals. Reelection concerns prompt legislators to support policies that distribute benefits to their constituents and oppose policies that threaten to impose on them direct, visible costs. Electoral considerations also create incentives for legislators to avoid positions likely to provoke controversy and to take positions they expect will garner them credit.[44] But members of

Congress are concerned with more than simply holding office; most also want to make good public policy and attain the respect of their peers.[45]

Moreover, unlike rank-and-file members of Congress, the president and congressional leaders face powerful incentives to take on public policy issues of national—rather than simply district- or state-level—concern. The president, because he is elected by a national constituency and wants to establish a legacy, is likely to be attentive to broad public policy goals. Similarly, legislative leaders are looking for opportunities to demonstrate their leadership skills; moreover, their visibility both among the public and the political elite tends to elicit a sense of responsibility for public affairs.[46] Both the president and congressional leaders have considerable resources with which to promote policy change. The president can initiate change by sending Congress a bill, using the bully pulpit to persuade the public that change is worthwhile, or issuing an executive order. Congressional leaders can expedite a bill's passage by orchestrating negotiations and by forging legislative coalitions.

For both leaders and rank-and-file legislators, then, the key constraint is an issue's *salience*—whether the public cares about it.[47] Neither the president nor congressional leaders are likely to expend political resources on an issue unless they perceive it to be widely salient; similarly, to calculate wiggle room on an issue, rank-and-file legislators must ascertain its salience among their constituents. For politicians trying to assess constituent opinion about an environmental issue, one straightforward indicator is polling data. (According to Riley Dunlap, "the mere expression of supportive opinion in a scientific survey or informal poll . . . can be a vital resource" for groups hoping to bring about or block policy change.[48]) While it can convey broad public preferences, however, survey evidence can be misleading; the wording of questions and the order in which they are asked can yield vastly different responses. Moreover, district- and state-level polling on individual issues is often not available. Most importantly, though, it is hard to ascertain the salience of an issue from survey data because surveys have difficulty detecting how much people actually care about a problem or the extent to which abstract values translate into support for concrete proposals.

Given the unreliability of survey data, politicians rely on a host of other indicators of an issue's salience. Because they tend to get media coverage, rallies and protests have been a mainstay of political activists; such public demonstrations are the simplest and most direct way for people with few political resources to transmit their concerns to elected officials. Other activities such as phoning, writing letters, and sending emails and faxes also convey salience. Complicating the analysis is the fact that creating the perception that an issue is salient is not a one-way street that runs from the public to politicians; legislators who want to promote a particular policy use "crafted talk" to shape their constituents' views.[49]

Administrators. Although usually less visible than legislators, administrators also play a critical role in environmental policy because they implement the laws passed by Congress. Doing so involves choosing the models and projections that underpin administrative regulations, devising the regulations themselves, and monitoring and enforcing compliance. Throughout this process, administrators have substantial discretion to modify policy goals.[50] In exercising their discretion, they bring considerable political resources to bear, including their longevity, expertise, and established relationships with organized interests and key members of Congress.

Whether they are environmentalists or cornucopians, administrators' propensity to pursue environmentally protective goals is constrained in several ways. One of the key factors that limit administrators' discretion is the agency's mission and organizational culture.[51] "Mission" refers to the agency's original mandate, while "organizational culture" refers to the norms and standard operating procedures that have evolved over time. Some agencies, such as the Forest Service and the Bureau of Land Management, were founded to conserve natural resources for human consumption. For a long time, such agencies were staffed by professionals, such as foresters and range managers, whose expertise lay in maximizing natural resource yields. As a result, those agencies' decisions historically emphasized resource extraction—often at the expense of environmental protection. In contrast, the Environmental Protection Agency (EPA) was created to serve environmental protection goals, so the orientation of its professionals and standard operating procedures reflect this disposition. As a result, the EPA's decisions tend to be relatively protective, often imposing substantial costs on industry.

Agencies do not simply act according to their missions and organizational cultures, however; the preferences of an agency's organized clientele, the nature and extent of its congressional oversight, and the direction given by the president and his political appointees also constrain bureaucratic choices.[52] Organized interests dissatisfied with an agency's behavior can appeal directly to sympathetic members of Congress who in turn exert pressure on agency officials. The president imposes his will on agencies by appointing directors whose views are consistent with his own. Thus, when implementing their statutory mandates, agency officials must navigate cautiously to avoid antagonizing powerful interests and their allies in Congress or the White House. Failure to do so almost always moves the battle to the courts.

The Judiciary. The federal courts have the authority to review agency decisions to determine whether they are consistent with congressional intent and thus can circumscribe an agency's ability to pursue protective or permissive policies. The Administrative Procedures Act allows courts to invalidate decisions that lack "substantial evidence" or are "arbitrary and capricious." Moreover, many environmental statutes allow the courts to strike down agency decisions if they cannot discern a reasonable connection between the action and the supporting record. The courts increased the potential for environmental litigation substantially when, in the early 1970s, they expanded the concept of "standing" to permit almost any group to challenge agency regulations in federal court, regardless of whether its members are directly affected by the agency's activities.[53] Congress also encouraged environmentalists' use of the courts by inserting provisions in environmental laws explicitly granting citizens and citizen organizations the right to sue not only polluters that violate the law but also agencies that fail to implement or enforce their statutory mandates with sufficient zeal.

Like legislators and administrators, judges may be environmentalists or cornucopians, but they face institutional constraints when evaluating an agency's decisions: they must base their reasoning on precedent, as well as on the wording and legislative history of a statute. There has been considerable debate over how closely to scrutinize agency decisions—in particular, whether to examine the reasoning or simply the procedures followed—but regardless of the standard applied, the courts habitually require agencies to document a comprehensible justification for their decisions.[54] Thus, litigation has become "an especially potent resource for making transparent the values, biases, and social assumptions that are embedded in many expert claims about physical and natural phenomena."[55]

State and Local Decision Makers. While this discussion so far has focused on national policymaking, the politics of an issue depends in part on whether it is addressed at the local, state, regional, or national level. Although there are many similarities among them, each of these arenas has distinctive features. For example, environmental interests may be disadvantaged at the state and local levels because those officials tend to be concerned, above all, with economic development and are much more constrained than federal officials by the need to attract and retain industry.[56] Moreover, many states and most local governments do not have the sophisticated technical capacity necessary to analyze complex environmental problems and therefore to distinguish among effective and ineffective solutions. Finally, environmentalists are often more influential at the national level than at the state or local levels because they lack the resources to fight on fifty or more fronts at once. Making the analysis even more complicated is the fact that environmental policymaking almost always involves more than one government level: because the United States has a federalist system of government, national policies are often implemented by regional, state, or local entities. And political events at one level sometimes affect decisions made at another: local activism may eventually prompt a national response.

Actors Outside the Government

While politicians, administrators, and judges make environmental policy decisions, actors outside of government shape the context in which those decisions are made. In particular, organized interests that advocate for particular solutions play a major role because they make strategic choices about which venue to compete in, selecting the one they expect will be most hospitable to their goals.[57] Having chosen the arena, they select from a variety of tactics to influence governmental decision making. Critical to the success or failure of their efforts are experts, who provide the arguments and empirical support for advocates' positions, and the media, which may promote, reject, or modify the frames imposed by advocates.

Advocacy Organizations. Like governmental decision makers, advocates generally fall into one of two camps: environmentalists, who support more environmentally protective policies, and cornucopians, who endorse less restrictive environmental policies. Advocacy groups on both sides are diverse in terms of funding sources and membership.[58] Some rely heavily on foundations or even the federal government for funding, while others raise most of their money from individual members. Some of the national environmental organizations, like the Sierra Club and the Wilderness Society, are well established; community-based environmental groups, in contrast, may be more ephemeral, springing up to address a single problem and then disbanding. Similarly, a host of long-standing organizations, such as the National Association of Manufacturers, oppose efforts to make environmental policies more protective, while myriad local groups have formed to prevent incursions into private property rights.

Although individual groups tend to specialize, advocates are most potent when they form broad coalitions. Such coalitions are often fleeting: they are united by common policy goals, but connections among them may not last beyond a single policy battle. However, the cohesiveness of a coalition over time is a key determinant of its political effectiveness. Coalitions that cannot maintain a united front tend to fare poorly, particularly in the legislative arena.[59]

As important as building coalitions is choosing whether to fight in the legislative, administrative, or judicial arena and deciding on the appropriate tactics for defining a problem in that venue. Advocates know that the perception that a problem is salient is a key determinant of whether elected officials will attend to it. Thus, while conventional tactics such as lobbying legislators and contributing money to a political campaign remain important means of exercising influence in the legislative arena, "outside lobbying"—that is, raising public awareness of issues and stimulating grassroots mobilization—has become an increasing prominent advocacy tool.[60] Because much of the public has only a vague understanding of individual environmental issues and relies on cognitive shortcuts and cues to know what to think,[61] advocates rely heavily on stories and symbols to define problems in ways that raise their salience. By contrast, in the administrative and judicial arenas, public opinion plays a lesser role and reasoned argument a larger one. To persuade bureaucrats and judges to adopt their preferred solution, advocates need to muster more sophisticated theoretical and empirical evidence in support of their definition of a problem.

Experts. Advocates rely on experts and the research they generate to buttress their claims about the causes and consequences of an environmental problem. In environmental politics, experts include scientists, economists, lawyers, and policy analysts with specialized knowledge of environmental problems and policies. They reside in academic departments, think tanks, foundations, interest groups, and government agencies. They are at the center of what political scientist John Kingdon calls "policy communities," where solutions to public policy problems are devised and the technical justifications for those solutions developed. Both the public and policymakers tend to give greater weight to the views of experts than to those of outright advocates; as political scientist Benjamin Page and his coauthors observe, "Their credibility may be high because of their actual or portrayed experience and expertise and nonpartisan status. It is not unreasonable for members of the public to give great weight to experts' statements and positions, particularly when complex technical questions affect the merits of policy alternatives."[62]

Of course, experts are not neutral purveyors of "facts." As explained earlier, most policy-relevant questions are "trans-scientific"—that is, they involve value judgments based on uncertain science.[63] For example, policymakers might ask an expert to ascertain a "safe" level of benzene in the environment. In making such a calculation, a chemical industry scientist is likely to make benign assumptions about benzene's hazards, consistent with her cornucopian values; in contrast, an academic scientist is likely to adopt more precautionary premises consistent with her environmental values.[64] Similarly, an industry economist is likely to make more pessimistic assumptions about the economic effects of benzene regulations than is a government or academic economist.

The Media. Finally, the media—television, radio, newspapers, news magazines, and, more recently, the Internet—are critical to determining the success or failure of competing advocates' efforts to define a problem. Writing nearly eighty years ago, Walter Lippman likened news coverage to "the beam of a searchlight that moves restlessly about, bringing one episode and then another out of darkness into vision."[65] Evidence is steadily accumulating to suggest that "the media may not only tell [the public] what to think about, they may also tell us how and what to think about it, and even what to do about it."[66] For most people the media are the only source of information about the environment, so what the media choose to focus on and the nature of the coverage are crucial to shaping public opinion.[67] Scholars have also found that the way the media frame issues significantly affects how the public attributes responsibility for problems.[68] (Of course, people are not mere sponges for views expressed in the press; they make sense of the news in the context of their own knowledge and experience.[69])

Because the media have such a profound impact, the way they select and portray the news can have serious consequences for problem definition. Above all, the media focus on stories that are "newsworthy"—that is, dramatic and timely. Sudden, violent risks and disasters with immediate and visceral consequences—such as oil spills, floods, and toxic releases—are far more likely to make the headlines than are ongoing problems like species loss.[70] Furthermore, because journalists face short deadlines, they rely heavily on readily available information from stable, reliable sources—such as government officials, industry, and organized interest groups—and the complexity of environmental science only reinforces this tendency.[71] Finally, in presenting the information gleaned from such sources, most reporters attempt to balance competing points of view, regardless of the relative support for either side; few journalists provide critical analysis to help readers sort out conflicting claims.[72] In their quest for balance, however, journalists tend to overstate extreme positions.[73] Even a balance of alarming and reassuring claims "unavoidably conveys uncertainty and foreboding."[74]

Media coverage of environmental issues also affects policymakers, not just through its impact on the public but directly as well. Although there is little evidence that media-aroused public opinion is a strong force for policy change, news stories can prompt an elite response, even in the absence of a strong public reaction.[75] This is probably because, while media coverage rarely arouses an instantaneous, major change in public opinion, policymakers (and particularly legislators) worry that media coverage *will* affect public opinion over time and so act preemptively. The relationship between the media and policymakers is not unidirectional, however. Policymakers influence the media as well as react to it; in fact, policymakers are often more aware of their own efforts to manipulate media coverage than of the media's influence on their policy choices.[76]

THE ENVIRONMENTAL POLICYMAKING PROCESS

Many scholars have found it useful to model the process by which advocates, experts, the media, and decision makers interact to create policy as a series of steps:

- agenda setting—getting a problem on the list of subjects to which policymakers are paying serious attention;
- alternative formulation—devising the possible solutions to the problem;
- decision making—choosing from among the possible alternatives the approach that government will take to address the problem;
- implementation—translating a decision into concrete action; and
- evaluation—assessing those actions for their consistency with a policy's goals.[77]

Distinguishing among these steps in the policymaking process can be useful analytically. At the same time, scholars generally acknowledge that in reality the process is rarely that orderly or systematic.

That the policymaking process is not linear does not mean it is inexplicable; in fact, John Kingdon has developed a fruitful model that captures its key attributes.[78] Kingdon portrays policymaking as a process in which people in and around government are concentrating on a set of problems; policy communities made up of experts, journalists, and bureaucrats are initiating and refining proposals; and political events—such as a change of administration or an interest group campaign—are all occurring simultaneously.[79] In general, policymakers—both legislative and administrative—engage in routine decision making. Wary of major change, with its unpredictable fallout, they tend to prefer making incremental modifications to existing policies.[80] A substantial departure from the status quo is likely only when hospitable political conditions come together with a compelling problem definition and an available solution. Such a convergence rarely just happens, however; usually a policy entrepreneur must link a solution to a problem when a window of opportunity opens. And even if all the elements are aligned and policy does change, a problem is never finally solved; each decision is simply one more step in a never-ending contest.[81]

Windows of Opportunity and Major Policy Change

Major policy changes are likely to occur only when a window of opportunity opens for advocates to push their pet solutions.[82] In environmental policymaking, a window may open as the result of a legal decision that forces legislators or administrators to reexamine a policy. A crisis or focusing event—such as an oil spill or the release of a major scientific report—can also open a window of opportunity by providing powerful new evidence of the need for a policy and briefly mobilizing public opinion. A recurring window of opportunity for a policy choice is turnover of key personnel—such as a change in congressional committee chairmanships, Speaker of the House, Senate majority leader, president, or agency director—which can alter the dynamics of an issue substantially. More mundane events, such as a legislative reauthorization or a regulatory rulemaking deadline, may also open windows of opportunity.

Once the window has opened, policy may or may not change. Although some objective features define a policy window, advocates must recognize it to take advantage of it. Even if they accurately perceive a policy window, advocates have a limited time within which to capitalize on the opportunity because such windows stay open only briefly. A policy window may close because the participants in a policy debate feel that they have addressed the issue by making a decision or enacting a policy. Alternatively, participants may fail to get action, in which case they may be unwilling to invest further time, energy, political capital, or other resources in the endeavor. Finally, public attention may be diverted by newsworthy events in other arenas, causing a window to close prematurely. Opponents of policy change recognize that policy windows open infrequently and close quickly and that both participants and the public have limited attention spans, so when a window opens they try to delay action by studying an issue or by another expedient until the pressure for change subsides. As Kingdon observes, supporters of the status quo try to take advantage of the fact that "the longer people live with a problem, the less pressing it seems."[83]

The Role of Policy Entrepreneurs in "Softening Up" and "Tipping"

Given the relative advantage held by supporters of the status quo, it is clear that advocates of policy change must do more than simply recognize a policy window; in order to take advantage of a political opportunity, advocacy groups must recruit one or more policy entrepreneurs to promote their cause. Policy entrepreneurs are individuals willing to invest their political resources—time, energy, reputation, money—in linking a problem to a solution and forging alliances among disparate actors in order to build a majority coalition.[84] Policy entrepreneurs must be adept at discovering "unfilled needs" and linking them to solutions, willing to bear the risks of investing in activities with uncertain consequences, and skilled at coordinating the activities of individuals and groups.[85] A policy entrepreneur must be ready to "ride the wave" when a policy window opens[86]; she must have lined up political allies, prepared arguments, and generated favorable public sentiment in preparation for the moment a decision-making opportunity presents itself.

Among the most important functions a policy entrepreneur performs while waiting for a policy window to open is "softening up" the policy communities whose endorsement is so important to the credibility of a policy solution, as well as the larger public. Softening up involves getting people used to a new idea and building acceptance for a proposal.[87] Policy entrepreneurs have a variety of means by which to soften up policy solutions: they can give speeches, write scholarly and popular articles, give briefings to policymakers, compose editorials and press releases, and teach the new approach in classrooms. Over time, a consensus often emerges, particularly within a policy community, around a short list of ideas for solving a problem. Eventually, there is a broader convergence on an idea whose time seems to have come, a phenomenon known as "tipping." At the tipping point, support for an idea is sufficiently widespread that it seems to take on a life of its own.

To affect policymaking, solutions that have diffused throughout the policy community and the public must catch on among decision makers as well. The process by which this happens is interesting: participants in a policy debate typically begin by staking out an extreme position and holding fast to it. At this point, the bargaining and persuasion among coalitions commence, and participants try to build consensus by dealing in as many interests as possible. Once it becomes apparent that one side is going to prevail, however, the remaining participants recognize that if they do not get on the bandwagon, they will have no say in the final decision. As Kingdon observes, "Once an issue seems to be moving, everybody with an interest in the subject leaps in, out of fear that they will be left out."[88]

CASE SELECTION

The cases in the chapters that follow not only introduce a variety of environmental issues, but they are fairly representative of the environmental policymaking process. They cover problems from all regions of the country; offer examples of local, national, and international politics; and are indisputably of great concern to those who attend to this policy area. All of the cases illuminate the impact of participants' values and issue framing. In addition, each case highlights a small number of more particular attributes of environmental policymaking, expanding on various aspects of the brief depiction of the process above. As a whole, then, the cases provide a relatively comprehensive foundation for understanding the way the American political system handles environmental issues. The cases are organized into four general categories of problems.

Tackling the Issue of Pollution

When the issue of pollution burst onto the national political scene in the 1960s and early 1970s, the public responded with overwhelming interest in and concern about dirty air and water as well as toxic waste. Chapter 2, which describes the formation of the EPA and the passage of the Clean Air and Clean Water Acts, depicts the impact of widespread public mobilization on the legislative process. The case makes clear that when political leaders perceive an issue as being very much on the public's mind, they often compete to craft a strong legislative response. Agencies trying to implement laws forged under such circumstances, however, are likely to encounter a host of practical obstacles. Chapter 3, which relates the story of toxic waste dumping at Love Canal, reveals the extent to which local and state governments resist confronting pollution issues. It also demonstrates the impact of media coverage on politics: alarming news stories can prompt citizen mobilization, and coverage of local groups' claims in turn can nationalize an issue and produce a policy response. In addition, this chapter makes clear that scientific experts can rarely resolve environmental policy controversies and may, in fact, exacerbate them. The final case in this section, "Government Secrets at Rocky Flats" (chapter 4), explores the government's role in polluting the environment. In particular, the case examines the military's use of national security to conceal sloppy environmental practices; the impenetrable relationship that developed between a government agency and its private contractors; and the governmental response to exposure and the public's demands for environmental cleanup.

Reforming Natural Resource Management Policies

Natural resource issues have a much longer history in American politics than do pollution issues; in fact, the distinctive feature of natural resource policymaking in the United States is that it is critically shaped by the legacy of past policies. The first chapter in this section, chapter 5, details the dynamics of the controversy over drilling for oil in Alaska's Arctic National Wildlife Refuge, illuminating the particularly intractable nature of conflicts between wilderness and natural resource development. It also draws out the way competing advocates use language—particularly symbols and metaphors—to define problems. Chapter 6, which deals with federal grazing policy, takes up one of the nation's least publicized natural resource issues: how to manage the arid rangeland of the West. This case provides an opportunity to observe not only the impact of past policies on current decision making but also the ways that failure by advocates to arouse public concern about an issue helps to perpetuate the status quo. In contrast, chapter 7—"Jobs vs. the Environment: Saving the Old-Growth Forests of the Pacific Northwest"—shows that attracting public attention to a natural resource concern using legal leverage and outside lobbying campaigns can overwhelm historically entrenched interests and change both the course of policymaking on an individual issue and an agency's approach to decision making more generally.

Addressing Commons Problems

Common property resources, such as the oceans and the global atmosphere, present policymakers with a unique challenge because addressing these issues is severely hampered by the free-rider problem. That is, "individuals have little or no incentive to . . . work for a collective good, since they will receive the benefits if others work for it and succeed in obtaining it (hence the term 'free ride')."[89] The fisheries and climate change cases throw these concerns into particularly sharp relief. Chapter 8, the case of overharvesting the New England groundfish, illustrates the way that government's efforts to manage a commons can exacerbate the free-rider problem, particularly when regulated interests dominate the regulatory process. In addition, the case outlines some of the novel approaches that governments are exploring to manage common-property resources more effectively, as well as the cultural sources of resistance to adopting such solutions. Chapter 9 examines one of the most complex and divisive commons problems facing the world today: climate change. The case reveals how the lack of an overarching global authority impedes efforts to address the threat of global warming and explains how domestic politics has prevented leaders in the United States from acting more aggressively on this issue.

Reshaping Politics Through Novel Approaches and Solutions

The first case in this section, chapter 10, takes up the backlash against environmentalism that, although it began in the 1970s, flowered in the mid-1990s. This case illuminates the difficulties politicians face in ascertaining an issue's salience as well as the tools proponents of protective policies have for resisting policy reversals. Partly in response to the backlash, but also to critiques from within the environmental movement, some policy entrepreneurs began exploring new ways to address environmental problems. Thus, the main theme underlying each of the remaining cases is that changing the problem-solving approach or offering novel solutions to address a problem can reshape the politics of that problem. Sometimes leaders can break a political logjam simply by offering a different policy tool, as was done with tradable sulfur dioxide permits in the case of acid rain (chapter 11). Alternatively, changing the institutional structure within which a decision is made can have dramatic effects: as the case of the California gnatcatcher and habitat conservation plans (chapter 12) illustrates, new approaches to solving a problem can make possible otherwise inconceivable solutions. Finally, in chapter 13, the Everglades restoration case demonstrates the ways in which demands by scientists and environmentalists for ecosystem-level solutions, as well as the need to coordinate the activities of multiple agencies, has created a new kind of collaborative environmental politics. At the same time, as all of the cases in this final section make clear, many of the same political forces evident in previous cases are at play regardless of the decision-making approach adopted or the type of solution crafted. Institutionalized ideas and practices continue to limit the pace of policy change, and underlying value differences among participants remain, so the ability to define problems continues to be a critical source of influence.

GETTING THE MOST OUT OF THESE CASES

This chapter has provided a cursory introduction to the burgeoning field of environmental politics and policymaking. The cases that follow deepen and make concrete the concepts introduced here, highlighting in particular the way that participants use language to define problems in ways consistent with their values. As you read, you will notice similarities and differences among cases. I encourage you to look for patterns, generate hypotheses about environmental politics, and test those hypotheses against the other instances of environmental policymaking that you study, read about in the newspaper, or become involved in. Questions posed at the end of each case may help you think more deeply about the issues raised in it and generate ideas for further research.

Notes

1. John S. Dryzek and David Schlosberg, eds., *Debating the Earth: The Environmental Politics Reader* (New York: Oxford University Press, 1998), 1.
2. This point is made about policy controversies more generally in Paul A. Sabatier, "An Advocacy Coalition Framework of Policy Change and the Role of Policy-Oriented Learning Therein," *Policy Sciences* 21 (1988): 129–168.
3. See, for example, Black Elk, "Native Americans Define the Natural Community," in *American Environmentalism*, 3d ed., ed. Roderick Frazier Nash (New York: McGraw-Hill, 1990), 13–16. Critics argue that environmentalists have romanticized Native Americans and other early peoples, pointing out that they too were capable of hunting species to extinction; that the Indians of eastern North America deliberately influenced the range and abundance of countless other wild plant species through their food-gathering and land-use practices; and that Native Americans made great use of fire and, in doing so, altered the landscape on a sweeping scale. They contend that much of what we now see as "natural" is in fact the result of human alteration during earlier time periods. See, for example, Stephen Budiansky, *Nature's Keepers: The New Science of Nature Management* (New York: Free Press, 1995).
4. George Catlin, "An Artist Proposes a National Park," in *American Environmentalism*, ed. Nash, 31–35.

5. Henry David Thoreau, "The Value of Wildness," in *American Environmentalism,* ed. Nash, 36–39.

6. Quoted in Roderick Nash, *Wilderness and the American Mind,* 3d ed. (New Haven: Yale University Press, 1982), 125.

7. Samuel Hays, *Conservation and the Gospel of Efficiency* (Cambridge: Harvard University Press, 1959).

8. Peter Bowler explains that while a distinct science of ecology emerged in the 1890s, ecology did not flower as a discipline until the 1960s with the proliferation of environmental concern. See Peter Bowler, *Norton History of Environmental Sciences* (New York: Norton, 1992).

9. Aldo Leopold, *A Sand County Almanac* (New York: Oxford University Press, 1948), 239.

10. Ibid., 262.

11. Donella Meadows et al., *The Limits to Growth* (New York: Universe, 1972).

12. Robyn Eckersley, *Environmentalism and Political Theory* (Albany: State University of New York Press, 1992), 49.

13. Arne Naess, "The Shallow and the Deep, A Long-Range Ecology Movement: A Summary," *Inquiry* 16 (1983): 95–100.

14. Ibid., 95.

15. Dryzek and Schlosberg coin the term *cornucopians* in *Debating the Earth.*

16. Prometheus stole fire from Olympus and gave it to humans. To punish him for this crime, Zeus chained him to a rock and sent an eagle to eat his liver, which in turn regenerated itself each day. Thus, the term *Prometheans* suggests a belief in the endless regenerative capacity of the earth.

17. Wildavsky and Dake provide another label: *hierarchists.* They say: "Hierarchists . . . approve of technological processes and products, provided their experts have given the appropriate safety certifications and the applicable rules and regulations are followed. In hierarchical culture, nature is 'perverse or tolerant.'" See Aaron Wildavsky and Karl Dake, "Theories of Risk Perception: Who Fears What and Why?" *Daedalus* 119 (fall 1990): 41–60.

18. Julian L. Simon and Herman Kahn, *The Resourceful Earth* (New York: Blackwell, 1984), 3.

19. Ibid.

20. Mary Douglas and Aaron Wildavsky, *Risk and Culture* (Berkeley: University of California Press, 1982).

21. See, for example, Aaron Wildavsky, *But Is It True?* (Cambridge: Harvard University Press, 1995).

22. See, for example, Michael Fumento, *Science Under Siege* (New York: Quill, 1993), 370; Wildavsky, *But Is It True?*

23. Gregg Easterbrook, *A Moment on the Earth* (New York: Viking, 1995), 649.

24. E. E. Schattschneider, *The Semisovereign People* (New York: Holt, Rinehart, and Winston, 1960), 189.

25. Political scientists use a variety of terms—problem definition, issue definition, and issue framing—to describe essentially the same phenomenon. Although I use the terms interchangeably, I refer readers to Deborah Stone's *Policy Paradox,* whose discussion of problem definition and its political impact is the most precise I have found. See Deborah Stone, *Policy Paradox: The Art of Political Decisionmaking* (New York: Norton, 1997). See also David Rochefort and Roger Cobb, eds., *The Politics of Problem Definition* (Lawrence: University Press of Kansas, 1994).

26. Donald A. Schon and Martin Rein, *Frame Reflection: Toward the Resolution of Intractable Policy Controversies* (New York: Basic Books, 1994).

27. Stone, *Policy Paradox.*

28. Frank R. Baumgartner and Bryan D. Jones, *Agendas and Instability in American Politics* (Chicago: University of Chicago Press, 1993).

29. Stone, *Policy Paradox,* 2–3.

30. Schattschneider, *The Semisovereign People,* 68.
31. Gallup poll release, "Environmental Concern Wanes in 1999 Earth Day Poll," wysiwyg://19/http://www.gallup.com/poll/releases/pr990422.asp; Willett Kempton, James S. Boster, and Jennifer A. Hartley, *Environmental Values in American Culture* (Cambridge: MIT Press, 1995); Everett Carll Ladd and Karlyn H. Bowman, *Attitudes Toward the Environment* (Washington, D.C.: AEI Press, 1995).
32. Riley E. Dunlap, "Public Opinion in the 1980s: Clear Consensus, Ambiguous Commitment," *Environment,* October 1991, 10–22.
33. Ernst Mayr, *This Is Biology: The Science of the Living World* (Cambridge: Harvard University Press, 1995).
34. While a few skeptics continue to challenge theories of ozone depletion, by the early 1990s, most climatologists accepted the conclusions of the World Meteorological Association that "anthropogenic chlorine and bromine compounds, coupled with surface chemistry on natural polar stratospheric particles, are the cause of polar ozone depletion." See Larry Parker and David E. Gushee, "Stratospheric Ozone Depletion: Implementation Issues," CRS Issue Brief for Congress, No. 97003 (Washington, D.C.: Congressional Research Service, January 16, 1998).
35. On occasion, roles are reversed. For example, scientists have been unable to detect a relationship between electromagnetic fields (EMFs) and cancer. In this case, proponents of EMF regulation are the ones citing minority scientific opinions.
36. Eban Goodstein and Hart Hodges, "Polluted Data," *American Prospect* 35 (November–December 1997): 64–69.
37. Stephen Kelman, "Cost-Benefit Analysis: An Ethical Critique," in *The Moral Dimensions of Public Policy Choice,* ed. John Martin Gillroy and Maurice Wade (Pittsburgh: University of Pittsburgh Press, 1992), 153–164.
38. Stone, *Policy Paradox.*
39. Howard Margolis, *Dealing with Risk: Why the Public and the Experts Disagree on Environmental Risk* (Chicago: University of Chicago Press, 1996).
40. Paul Slovic, Baruch Fischhoff, and Sarah Lichtenstein, "Rating the Risks," in *Readings in Risk,* ed. Theodore Glickman and Michael Gough (Washington, D.C.: Resources for the Future, 1990), 61–75.
41. Slovic et al., "Rating the Risks." Howard Margolis rejects this explanation for differences between expert and public assessments of risk. He argues instead that the difference turns on "habits of mind"; in particular, in some cases, the public stubbornly perceives only the costs of a technology or activity and is unable to see the benefits and therefore cannot make the appropriate trade-off between the two. See Margolis, *Dealing with Risk.*
42. Amos Tversky and Daniel Kahneman, "The Framing of Decisions and the Psychology of Choice," *Science* 211 (January 30, 1981): 453–458.
43. Stone, *Policy Paradox,* 34.
44. David R. Mayhew, *Congress: The Electoral Connection* (New Haven: Yale University Press, 1974).
45. Richard Fenno, *Congressmen in Committees* (Boston: Little, Brown, 1973).
46. Timothy J. Conlan, Margaret Wrightson, and David Beam, *Taxing Choices: The Politics of Tax Reform* (Washington, D.C.: CQ Press, 1990); Martha Derthick and Paul J. Quirk, *The Politics of Deregulation* (Washington, D.C.: Brookings Institution, 1985).
47. John W. Kingdon, *Congressmen's Voting Decisions,* 3d ed. (Ann Arbor: University of Michigan Press, 1989).
48. Riley Dunlap, "Public Opinion in Environmental Policy," in *Environmental Politics and Policy,* ed. James P. Lester (Durham: Duke University Press, 1989), 87.
49. Lawrence R. Jacobs and Robert Y. Shapiro, *Politicians Don't Pander: Political Manipulation and the Loss of Democratic Responsiveness* (Chicago: University of Chicago Press, 2000).

50. Jeffrey L. Pressman and Aaron Wildavsky, *Implementation* (Berkeley: University of California Press, 1984).

51. James Q. Wilson, *Bureaucracy* (New York: Basic Books, 1989).

52. Herbert Kaufman, *The Administrative Behavior of Federal Bureau Chiefs* (Washington, D.C.: Brookings Institution, 1981).

53. "Standing" is the right to bring a lawsuit. Historically, the courts have granted standing to anyone who can demonstrate that he or she is personally affected by the outcome of a case. The 1972 case, *Sierra Club v. Morton*, laid the groundwork for the subsequent broadening of the courts' interpretation of the standing requirement.

54. Sheila Jasanoff, *Science at the Bar: Law, Science, and Technology in America* (Cambridge: Harvard University Press, 1995); David M. O'Brien, *What Process Is Due? Courts and Science-Policy Disputes* (New York: Russell Sage, 1987).

55. Jasanoff, *Science at the Bar*, 20.

56. Paul Peterson, *City Limits* (Chicago: University of Chicago Press, 1981).

57. Baumgartner and Jones, *Agendas and Instability*.

58. For an extensive discussion of the funding, membership, tactics, and goals of major environmental interest groups, see Ronald G. Shaiko, *Voices and Echoes for the Environment* (New York: Columbia University Press, 1999).

59. Gary Mucciaroni, *Reversals of Fortune: Public Policy and Private Interests* (Washington, D.C.: Brookings Institution, 1995).

60. Ken Kollman, *Outside Lobbying: Public Opinion and Interest Group Strategies* (Princeton: Princeton University Press, 1998).

61. Shanto Iyengar argues that "people are exquisitely sensitive to context when they make decisions, formulate judgments, or express opinions. The manner in which a problem of choice is "framed" is a contextual cue that may profoundly influence decision outcomes. See Shanto Iyengar, *Is Anyone Responsible? How Television Frames Political Issues* (Chicago: University of Chicago Press, 1991), 11.

62. Benjamin I. Page, Robert Y. Shapiro, and Glenn R. Dempsey, "What Moves Public Opinion," *Media Power in Politics*, 3d ed., ed. Doris A. Graber (Washington, D.C.: CQ Press, 1994), 132.

63. Alvin Weinberg, "Science and Trans-Science," *Minerva* 10 (1970): 209–222.

64. Frances M. Lynn, "The Interplay of Science and Values in Assessing and Regulating Environmental Risks," *Science, Technology, and Human Values* 11 (spring 1986): 40–50.

65. Walter Lippman, *Public Opinion* (New York: Macmillan, 1922), 229.

66. Maxwell McCombs and George Estrada, "The News Media and the Pictures in Our Heads," in *Do the Media Govern?*, ed. Shanto Iyengar and Richard Reeves (Thousand Oaks, Calif.: Sage Publications, 1997), 247.

67. Maxwell E. McCombs and Donald L. Shaw, "The Agenda-Setting Function of the Press," in *The Emergence of American Political Issues: The Agenda-Setting Function of the Press* (St. Paul, Minn.: West Publishing, 1977), 89–105; Fay Lomax Cook et al., "Media and Agenda Setting Effects on the Public, Interest Group Leaders, Policy Makers, and Policy," *Public Opinion Quarterly* 47 (1983): 16–35.

68. Shanto Iyengar, "Framing Responsibility for Political Issues," in *Do the Media Govern?*, ed. Iyengar and Reeves, 276–282.

69. Marion R. Just et al., *Crosstalk: Citizens, Candidates, and the Media in a Presidential Campaign* (Chicago: University of Chicago Press, 1996).

70. Michael R. Greenberg et al., "Risk, Drama, and Geography in Coverage of Environmental Risk by Network T.V.," *Journalism Quarterly* (summer 1989): 267–276.

71. Herbert Gans, *Deciding What's News* (New York: Pantheon, 1979); Dorothy Nelkin, *Selling Science*, rev. ed. (New York: Freeman, 1995).

72. Nelkin, *Selling Science*.

73. Eleanor Singer, "A Question of Accuracy: How Journalists and Scientists Report Research on Hazards," *Journal of Communication* 40 (autumn 1990): 102–116.

74. Alan Mazur, *A Hazardous Inquiry: The Rashomon Effect at Love Canal* (Cambridge: Harvard University Press, 1998), 123.

75. Doris A. Graber, *Mass Media and American Politics,* 5th ed. (Washington, D.C.: CQ Press, 1997). Graber points out that the relative dearth of evidence supporting theories of media-generated public opinion and policy changes is probably the result of using insufficiently sophisticated methods to detect such effects, not the absence of effects.

76. John Kingdon, *Agendas, Alternatives, and Public Policies,* 2d ed. (New York: Harper-Collins, 1995).

77. See, for example, Charles O. Jones, *An Introduction to Public Policy,* 2d ed. (North Scituate, Mass.: Wadsworth, 1984).

78. Kingdon, *Agendas.*

79. Kingdon suggests that these three activities, or streams, proceed independently of one another. Gary Mucciaroni argues that changes in problem definition, solutions, and political conditions are actually quite closely linked. See Mucciaroni, *Reversals of Fortune.*

80. As Charles Lindblom, Aaron Wildavsky, and others have described incrementalism, decision makers tinker with policies at the margin rather than engaging in a comprehensive reexamination of each issue. See Charles E. Lindblom, "The Science of Muddling Through," *Public Administration Review* 14 (spring 1959): 79–88; Aaron Wildavsky, *The Politics of the Budgetary Process,* 3d ed. (Boston: Little, Brown, 1979).

81. Stone, *Policy Paradox.*

82. Kingdon, *Agendas.*

83. Ibid., 170.

84. Ibid.

85. Michael Mintrom and Sandra Vergari, "Advocacy Coalitions, Policy Entrepreneurs, and Policy Change," *Policy Studies Journal* 24 (1996): 420–434.

86. Kingdon, *Agendas.*

87. Ibid.

88. Ibid., 162.

89. Stone, *Policy Paradox,* 218.

Recommended Reading

Kingdon, John W. *Agendas, Alternatives, and Public Policies.* 2d ed. New York: Harper-Collins, 1995.

Rosenbaum, Walter A. *Environmental Politics and Policy.* 5th ed. Washington, D.C.: CQ Press, 2002.

Stone, Deborah. *Policy Paradox.* New York: Norton, 1997.

CHAPTER 2

The Nation Tackles Pollution

The Environmental Protection Agency and the Clean Air and Water Acts

At the turn of the twenty-first century, Americans take for granted the importance of federal laws aimed at reducing air and water pollution. Yet thirty years ago, the federal government was virtually uninvolved in pollution control. That changed abruptly when, on July 9, 1970, President Richard Nixon established the Environmental Protection Agency. Shortly thereafter, Congress approved two of the nation's most far-reaching federal environmental laws: the Clean Air Act of 1970 and the Federal Water Pollution Control Act of 1972, commonly known as the Clean Water Act. Both laws shifted primary responsibility for environmental protection from the states to the federal government and required federal regulators to take prompt and stringent action to curb pollution.

This surge in environmental policymaking in the early 1970s was not a response to a sudden deterioration in the condition of the nation's air and water. In fact, while some kinds of pollution were getting worse in the late 1960s, other kinds were diminishing as a result of municipal bans on garbage burning and the phasing out of coal as a heating fuel.[1] Instead, this case reveals the profound impact that redefining, or framing, an issue can have on policymaking. As political scientists Frank Baumgartner and Bryan Jones observe: "[If] disadvantaged policy entrepreneurs are successful in convincing others that their view of an issue is more accurate than the views of their opponents, they may achieve rapid success in altering public policy arrangements, even if these arrangements have been in place for decades."[2]

This is true because when redefining the issue raises its salience—as manifested by widespread public activism, intense and favorable media coverage, and marked shifts in public opinion polls—politicians respond. In particular, a legislator who seeks a leadership role must take positions that appeal to more than a local constituency and demonstrate a capacity to build winning coalitions. Because his constituency is national, the president—or anyone who aspires to be president—is the one most likely to embrace issues that promise broad public benefits; the president is also best equipped, in terms of political resources, to forge a winning coalition for a major policy change. Thus, it is hardly surprising that competition among presidential candidates has been the impetus behind some of the nation's most significant environmental policies. Rank-and-file legislators are also moved by highly salient issues: they jump on the bandwagon in hopes of gaining credit—or at least avoiding blame—for addressing a problem about which the public is intensely concerned.

This case also shows how a focusing event—in this instance, Earth Day—can open a window of opportunity for a leader to promote policies that policy entrepreneurs have linked to the newly popular framing of an issue. The implementation of an ambitious new policy often encounters serious practical obstacles, however. While legislators are responsive to public enthusiasm about an issue, agencies must cater to "multiple principals"—that is, they must appease the president and the congressional committees that oversee and fund them.[3] In addition, they must grapple with the demands of organized interests: agencies depend on the cooperation of those they regulate because they have neither the resources nor the personnel to enforce every rule they issue; moreover, organized interests provide agencies with political support in Congress.[4] The process of implementing environmental legislation is particularly complicated because the agencies administering it operate in a highly fractious interest group setting whose members have a propensity to take their disagreements with the agency to court. Thus, regardless of provisions aimed at ensuring compliance with their lofty goals, policies that depart dramatically from the status quo rarely achieve the targets set forth in the legislation.

BACKGROUND

Until 1970, a patchwork of local, state, and federal laws and institutions aimed to reduce pollution in order to protect public health. Beginning in the mid-1950s, the federal government expanded its funding and advisory roles in pollution control, but the emphasis on state-level design and enforcement persisted. Because state and local officials were deeply concerned about fostering economic development and because environmental activists in most states had insufficient clout to challenge economic interests, this arrangement meant that few states undertook serious pollution control programs.

Air Pollution

The earliest concerns about air pollution in the United States arose in response to the smoke emitted by factories that accompanied industrialization. Chicago and Cincinnati enacted the nation's first clean air laws in 1881. Chicago's ordinance declared that "the emissions of dense smoke from the smokestack of any boat or locomotive or from any chimney anywhere within the city shall be . . . a public nuisance."[5] By 1912, twenty-three of twenty-eight American cities with populations greater than 200,000 had passed similar laws, but these ordinances did little to mitigate air pollution.[6] During World War II, Los Angeles initiated the nation's first modern air pollution program in response to a public outcry about the odors of a wartime industrial plant. The city also placed severe curbs on oil refineries and backyard incinerators. Soon thereafter, in 1948, toxic smog in Donora, Pennsylvania, killed 20 people and sickened almost 6,000, afflicting 43 percent of the city's population.[7] Similar incidents occurred in London and New York in the early 1950s.

In the mid-1950s, after these and other air pollution episodes attracted widespread media coverage, the federal government began to buttress state efforts with financial and research assistance. In 1955, Congress authorized the Public Health Service, a bureau within the Department of Health Education and Welfare (HEW), to conduct air pollution research and to help states and educational institutions train personnel and carry out research and control. Upon taking office in 1961, President John F. Kennedy asserted the need for an effective federal program.

Then, in November 1962, a four-day inversion produced an air pollution episode in New York that caused the death of an estimated eighty people.[8] The event rekindled public interest in pollution control legislation; in response, Congress passed the Clean Air Act of 1963, which expanded HEW's authority to enforce existing state laws, encouraged the development of new ones, and regulated interstate air pollution. Two years later, the Motor Vehicle Air Pollution Control Act required HEW to establish regulations controlling emissions from all new motor vehicles. And in 1967, Congress passed the Air Quality Act, which required the National Air Pollution Control Administration, a small division within HEW, to designate regional air quality control areas, issue air quality criteria, and recommend pollution control techniques. By 1970, however, the federal government had designated less than one-third of the metropolitan air quality regions projected in the statute, and no state had established a complete set of standards for any pollutant.[9]

Water Pollution

The federal government involved itself in controlling water pollution as early as the late nineteenth century, but—as in the case of air pollution—legal authority belonged almost entirely to states and localities. In 1899, Congress passed the Rivers and Harbors Act prohibiting dumping of refuse that might impede travel in any navigable body of water. In 1912, Congress passed the Public Health Service Act, which authorized studies of waterborne diseases, sanitation, sewage, and the pollution of navigable streams and lakes. Finally, the 1924 Federal Oil Pollution Act prohibited ocean-going vessels from dumping oil into the sea. These laws were largely ineffectual, however, and by the 1940s every state had established its own agency responsible for controlling water pollution. The powers of these agencies varied widely, and states had no recourse when upstream users polluted rivers that crossed state borders.[10]

In an effort to create a more coherent water pollution policy, Congress passed the Federal Water Pollution Control Act in 1948. This law directed the surgeon general of the Public Health Service (PHS) to develop a comprehensive program to abate and control water pollution, administer grants-in-aid for building municipal waste treatment plants, conduct research, and render technical assistance to states. The law authorized the surgeon general to enforce anti-pollution measures in interstate waters, but only with the consent of the affected states.[11] The PHS was unable to manage the federal water pollution program to the satisfaction of either conservation groups or Congress, however, and President Harry Truman further hampered the law's implementation by preventing the agency from distributing loans to states and localities for sewage treatment plants.

Hopeful of redirecting and strengthening HEW's efforts, Congress transferred responsibility for water pollution control from the surgeon general to his superior, the secretary of HEW, with the Federal Water Pollution Control Act of 1961. The new law extended federal enforcement to all navigable waters, not just interstate waters, and called for an increase in appropriations for municipal treatment plants. Four years later, Congress went even further with the Water Quality Act of 1965, which officially created a separate Federal Water Pollution Control Administration (FWPCA) within HEW. The act gave the states until June 30, 1967, to develop individual water quality standards for drinking water, fish and wildlife, recreation, and agriculture on their interstate navigable waters. Finally, the bill established an explicit national goal: the "prevention, control, and abatement of water pollution." The following year, Sen. Edmund Muskie, D-Maine, proposed, and Congress passed, a bill that created a $3.5 billion sewage treatment plant construction fund.[12] Despite this expansion in federal jurisdiction, however, three consecutive bureaucratic reorganizations hampered the FWPCA's ability to exercise its statutory authority, rendering its efforts more apparent than real.

THE CASE

Although the pace of federal air and water pollution control legislation accelerated during the 1960s, the laws passed in the early 1970s marked a substantial departure from the past because the federal government preempted the states and assumed primary responsibility for cleaning up the nation's air and water, instituting strict new pollution control standards. The impetus for this change was not a sudden or dramatic increase in the scale of the problem, but rather a widespread redefinition of the pollution problem—sparked by environmental writers such as Rachel Carson—and the consequent emergence of environmental protection as a popular national cause. Public concern about pollution outran the incremental responses of the 1960s and culminated at the end of the decade in a massive Earth Day demonstration. That event, in turn, opened a window of opportunity for advocates of strict pollution control policies. Politicians, recognizing the popularity of environmentalism, competed for voters' recognition of their environmental qualifications.

Environmentalism Becomes a Popular Cause

In 1962, Rachel Carson published *Silent Spring*, the book that many credit with lighting the fuse of the modern environmental movement. The *New York Times*'s Philip Shabecoff later described the impact of Carson's work:

What Carson did in *Silent Spring* . . . was to present the scientific evidence in clear, poetic, and moving prose that demonstrated how the destruction of nature and the threat to human health from pollution were completely inter-twined. . . . The book synthesized many of the concerns of the earlier con-servationists and preservationists with the warnings of new environmental-ists who worried about pollution and public health. It made frighteningly clear that they were all skeins of a large web of environmental evil settling over the nation and the world. . . . She combined a transcendentalist's pas-sion for nature and wildlife with the cool analytical mind of a trained scien-tist and the contained anger of a political activist. She touched an exposed wound.[13]

On the *New York Times* bestseller list for thirty-one weeks, Carson's book ignited a firestorm of environmental activism and was soon followed by an avalanche of anti-pollution literature, including Paul Ehrlich's book *The Popu-lation Bomb.*

Then a series of highly publicized disasters hit. A Union Oil Company well blew out six miles off the coast of Santa Barbara, California, and for several weeks, oil leaked into the Pacific Ocean at the rate of 20,000 gallons a day, pol-luting twenty miles of beaches. Cleveland's Cuyahoga River, heavily polluted with industrial chemicals, burst into flames. Mercury scares frightened people away from seafood, and coastal communities closed beaches when raw sewage washed up on shore.

Calls for environmental awareness in response to these episodes fell on receptive ears. The population was becoming younger and better educated: between 1950 and 1974, the percentage of adults with some college education rose from 13.4 percent to 25.5 percent.[14] Demographic change was coupled with a streak of unprecedented prosperity as the nation's economy rocketed out of World War II. The emerging generation, finding itself in the midst of this boom, began to worry about the pollution that accompanied rapid growth and urbanization. One indication of the growing public interest in environmental issues during this time was the explosion of citations under the heading "envi-ronment" in the *New York Times* index. In 1955, the word was not even indexed; in 1965, it appeared as a heading but was followed by only two citations; by 1970, however, there were eighty-six paragraphs under the heading.[15]

Earth Day 1970

The heightened environmental awareness of the 1960s culminated on April 22, 1970, in the national celebration of Earth Day. The demonstration was the brainchild of Sen. Gaylord Nelson, D-Wisc., who had a long-standing interest in the environment. After meeting with biologist and environmental popular-izer Paul Ehrlich, Nelson conceived of an environmental teach-in to raise pub-lic awareness and hired Dennis Hayes, a twenty-five-year-old Harvard Law School student, to organize the event on a budget of $125,000.[16] Interestingly, the established preservation-oriented groups such as the Sierra Club, the Audubon Society, and the National Wildlife Federation played little or no role in Earth Day. In fact, as Shabecoff points out, they were surprised by and unprepared for the national surge in emotion.[17]

The absence of such mainstream groups notwithstanding, Earth Day was a resounding success—an outpouring of social activism comparable to the civil rights and Vietnam War protests. The *New York Times* proclaimed, "Millions Join Earth Day Observances Across the Nation." *Time* magazine estimated that 20 million people nationwide were involved.[18] Organizers claimed that more than 2,000 colleges, 10,000 elementary and high schools, and citizens' groups in 2,000 communities participated in festivities.[19]

Citizens in every major city and town rallied in support of the message. For two hours New York City barred the internal combustion engine from Fifth Avenue, and thousands thronged the fume-free streets; in Union Square, crowds heard speeches and visited booths that distributed information on such diverse topics as air pollution, urban planning, voluntary sterilization, conservation, and wildlife preservation. In Hoboken, New Jersey, a crowd hoisted a coffin containing the names of America's polluted rivers into the Hudson. In Birmingham, Alabama, one of the most polluted cities in the nation, the Greater Birmingham Alliance to Stop Pollution (GASP) held a "right to live" rally. Washington's chapter of GASP passed out forms that pedestrians could use to report buses emitting noxious fumes or smoke to the transit authority.

Students of all ages participated in an eclectic array of events. Fifth graders at the Charles Barrett Elementary School in Alexandria, Virginia, wrote letters to local polluters. Thirty girls from Washington Irving High School in New York, collected trash and dragged white sheets along sidewalks to show how dirty they became. University of New Mexico students collected signatures on a plastic globe and presented it as an "enemy of the earth" award to twenty-eight state senators accused of weakening an environmental law. At Indiana University female students tossed birth control pills at crowds to protest over-population. And at the University of Texas in Austin, the campus newspaper came out with a make-believe April 22, 1990, headline that read: "Noxious Smog Hits Houston: 6,000 Dead."

Although it was the target of most Earth Day criticism, even the business community jumped on the Earth Day bandwagon in an effort to improve its image. Rex Chainbelt, Inc., of Milwaukee announced the creation of a new pollution control division. The Reynolds Metal Can Company sent trucks to colleges in fourteen states to pick up aluminum cans collected in "trash-ins" and paid a bounty of one cent for two cans. And Scott Paper announced plans to spend large sums on pollution abatement for its plants in Maine and Washington.

Politicians also tried to capitalize on the Earth Day fervor. Congress stood in recess because scores of its members were participating in programs: Sen. Edmund Muskie addressed a crowd of 25,000 in Philadelphia; Sen. Birch Bayh spoke at Georgetown University; Sen. George McGovern talked to students at Purdue University; and Sen. John Tower addressed oilmen in Houston. Most

Table 2-1
Public Opinion on Air and Water Pollution, 1965–1970

Q: Compared with other parts of the country, do you think the problem of air/water pollution in your area is very serious or somewhat serious?

Year	Sample Size	Air (%)	Water (%)
1965	2,128	28%	35%
1966	2,033	48	49
1967	2,000	53	52
1968	2,079	55	58
1969	NA	NA	NA
1970	2,168	69	74

Source: John C. Whitaker, *Striking a Balance: Environment and Natural Resources Policy in the Nixon-Ford Years* (Washington, D.C.: AEI, 1976), 8. Reprinted with the permission of The American Enterprise Institute for Public Policy Research, Washington, D.C.

audiences greeted politicians with suspicion, however. University of Michigan students heckled former interior secretary Stewart Udall until he promised to donate his $1,000 speaker's fee to the school's environmental quality group. Protestors at a rally held by Sen. Charles Goodell of New York distributed a leaflet calling his speech "the biggest cause of air pollution." And organizers in the Environmental Action Coalition refused to allow politicians on their platform at all to avoid giving Earth Day a political cast.

The Polls

Public opinion polls confirm that Earth Day marked the emergence of environmentalism as a mass social movement in the United States. Before 1965, pollsters did not even deem pollution important enough to ask about, but by 1970 it had become a major electoral force. As Table 2-1 shows, over the five-year period leading up to Earth Day the increase in public awareness of air and water pollution is striking: survey data gathered between 1965 and 1969 reflect public recognition of pollution, but most people do not identify it as a high priority issue. Then, between the summer of 1969 and the summer of 1970, the public's concern reached a tipping point, and the issue jumped from tenth to fifth place in the Gallup polls. By 1970, the American public perceived pollution as more important than race, crime, and teenage problems (see Table 2-2). In December 1970, a Harris survey showed that Americans rated pollution as "the most serious problem" facing their communities. According to another Harris poll, conducted in 1971, 83 percent of Americans wanted the federal government to spend more money on air and water pollution control programs.[20]

Writing in the spring of 1972, poll editor Hazel Erskine summed up the rapid growth of the environmental issue this way: "A miracle of public opinion has

Table 2-2
Most Important Domestic Problems, 1969 and 1971

Q: Aside from the Vietnam War and foreign affairs, what are some of the most important problems facing people here in the United States?

Problem	May 1969 Survey	May 1971 Survey	Significant Changes
Inflation, cost of living, taxes	34%	44%	10%
Pollution, ecology	1	25	24
Unemployment	7	24	17
Drugs, alcohol	3	23	20
Racial problems	39	22	−17
Poverty/welfare	22	20	2
Crime, lack of law and order	15	19	4
Unrest among young people	6	12	6
Education	5	8	3
Housing	NA	6	NA

Source: John C. Whitaker, *Striking a Balance: Environment and Natural Resources Policy in the Nixon-Ford Years* (Washington, D.C.: AEI, 1976), 8. Reprinted with the permission of The American Enterprise Institute for Public Policy Research, Washington, D.C.

been the unprecedented speed and urgency with which ecological issues have burst into the American consciousness. Alarm about the environment sprang from nowhere to major proportions in a few short years."[21] According to historian Samuel Hays, this shift in public opinion was no transient phase but reflected a permanent evolution associated with rising standards of living and human expectations. "Environmental politics," he claims, "reflect major changes in American society and values. People want new services from government stemming from new desires associated with the advanced consumer economy that came into being after World War II."[22]

Politicians Respond

The emergence of broad-based public support for pollution control empowered proponents of more stringent policies, who pressed their demands on Congress and the president, citing the polls and Earth Day as evidence of the salience of environmental problems. To promote more ambitious policies, they capitalized on the competition between President Nixon and aspiring presidential candidate Edmund Muskie for control over the issue of environmental protection. The candidates, in turn, became increasingly ambitious in their proposals.

Creating the Environmental Protection Agency. Reflecting their perception of the issue's low salience, neither of the two presidential candidates in 1968 made the environment a campaign focus. Republican Richard Nixon and Democrat Hubert Humphrey both concentrated on issues of peace, prosperity, crime, and inflation. Only one of the thirty-four position papers and statements published in the compendium *Nixon Speaks Out* covers natural resources and environmental quality; in another Nixon campaign publication containing speeches, statements, issue papers, and answers to questions from the press, only 5 of 174 pages are devoted to the environment, natural resources, and energy.[23] Nixon staff members do not recall even one question to the candidate about the environment.[24] The Humphrey campaign was equally silent on the subject.

Yet by 1970, Nixon had grasped the growing salience of environmental protection and begun staking out his position. In his State of the Union address in January 1970, Nixon made bold pronouncements about the need for federal intervention to protect the environment, saying:

> Restoring nature to its natural state is a cause beyond party and beyond factions. It has become a common cause of all the people of this country. It is the cause of particular concern to young Americans because they more than we will reap the grim consequences of our failure to act on the programs which are needed now if we are to prevent disaster later—clean air, clean water, open spaces. These should once again be the birthright of every American. If we act now they can.[25]

Nixon went on to assert that the nation required "comprehensive new regulation." The price of goods, he said, "should be made to include the costs of producing and disposing of them without damage to the environment."[26] Then, on February 10, Nixon delivered a Special Message to the Congress on Environmental Quality in which he outlined a thirty-seven-point program encompassing twenty-three separate pieces of legislation and fourteen administrative actions.[27] On July 9, the president submitted to Congress an executive reorganization plan that proposed the creation of the Environmental Protection Agency (EPA) and consolidated a variety of federal environmental activities within the new agency. The EPA's principal functions were to establish and enforce environmental protection standards; conduct research; gather and evaluate pollution information; strengthen environmental protection programs; recommend policy changes; and help control environmental pollution.[28]

Ironically, the original impetus for the EPA came not from the environmental community but from a commission appointed by President Nixon to generate ideas for streamlining the federal bureaucracy. The President's Advisory Council on Executive Organization, known as the Ash Council, was composed primarily of business executives; however, the council's staff comprised several environmental policy entrepreneurs. At first, council head Roy Ash favored vesting responsibility for both natural resources and pollution control in a single "super department," the Department of Natural Resources. But council staff worried that such a plan would force environmentalists to compete with better-organized and -financed natural resource development interests. They proposed instead an independent agency with jurisdiction over pollution control.[29] Council members also favored establishing an executive agency because creating a regulatory commission would require legislative action and would thus open up the council's proposals to congressional politics. Furthermore, the council preferred the scientific and technical nature of executive agency decision making, whereas they were concerned that commissions tended to be dominated by legal and adjudicative experts.[30]

President Nixon did not accept all of the Ash Council recommendations for the EPA, but he retained the central idea: to create an agency devoted to comprehensive environmental protection. The presidential message accompanying Reorganization Plan Number Three clearly reflects the pervasiveness of defining pollution using ecological ideas:

> Despite its complexity, for pollution control purposes, the environment must be perceived as a single, interrelated system. Present assignments of departmental responsibilities do not reflect this interrelatedness. . . . This consolidation of pollution control authorities would help assure that we do not create new environmental problems in the process of controlling existing ones.[31]

The Senate was hospitable to Nixon's proposal and introduced no resolution opposing it.[32] In spite of the objections of some prominent members, the House did not pass a resolution opposing the reorganization either, so on December 2, 1970, the EPA opened its doors.

The Clean Air Act of 1970. One of the first tasks of the new agency was to implement the Clean Air Act Amendments of 1970. This was a particular challenge for the fledgling bureau because this new legislation was much more than an incremental step beyond past policy experience; in fact, it was a radical departure from the approach previously taken by the federal government. Instead of helping the states design air pollution programs, the EPA was now to assume primary responsibility for setting air quality standards and for ensuring that the states enforced those standards.

Congress and the president had begun work on the 1970 Clean Air Act months before the Nixon administration established the EPA. Recognizing the rising political cachet of environmentalism and wanting to launch a preemptive strike against Senator Muskie—his likely rival for the presidency—Nixon sent air pollution legislation to Congress in February 1970. Under the bill, HEW would issue stringent motor vehicle emissions standards and improve its testing procedures and regulation of fuel composition and additives. For stationary sources (that is, factories and electric utilities), the bill established national air quality standards, accelerated the designation of air quality control regions, and set national emissions standards for hazardous pollutants and selected classes of new facilities.[33]

The administration's proposal fared well in the House of Representatives. Under the guidance of Rep. Paul Rogers, D-Fla., the Commerce Committee's

Subcommittee on Public Health and Welfare marked up the bill, and the full committee reported out a somewhat stronger version than the original. On June 10, the full House passed the bill by 374–1.

The Senate received the administration bill less warmly because in that chamber Nixon's rival, presidential hopeful Muskie, was the undisputed champion of the environmental cause. On March 4, shortly after President Nixon submitted his bill to the House, Muskie introduced an alternative, the National Air Quality Standards Act of 1970. His objective at the time was to prod agencies to strengthen their implementation of the 1967 act, rather than to initiate a radically different policy. Muskie had spent his Senate career characterizing pollution control as a state responsibility; as he understood it, the problem lay not in the design of the program but in its administration.[34] Over the summer, however, Muskie changed his tune. He asked the Public Works Committee's Subcommittee on Air and Water Pollution to draft a new set of amendments containing stringent new provisions including national, rather than regional, standards for major pollutants.

Senator Muskie's sudden change of heart was a clear attempt to reestablish his dominance in the environmental area. Despite his considerable record, not only Nixon but some prominent environmental advocates had challenged Muskie's commitment to environmental protection. A highly critical report by a Ralph Nader study group, released in May of 1970, singled out the senator as a weak and ineffectual sponsor of clean air legislation. The report, entitled *Vanishing Air,* assailed Muskie as

> the chief architect of the disastrous Air Quality Act of 1967. That fact alone would warrant his being stripped of his title as "Mr. Pollution Control." But the Senator's passivity since 1967 in the face of an ever worsening pollution crisis compounds his earlier failure. . . . Muskie awakened from his dormancy on the issue of air pollution the day after President Nixon's State of the Union message. . . . In other words, the air pollution issue became vital again when it appeared that the President might steal the Senator's thunder on a good political issue.[35]

Media publicity of the Nader report's charges put Muskie on the defensive. The Senate's environmental leader felt compelled to "do something extraordinary in order to recapture his [pollution control] leadership."[36]

In the end, Muskie's subcommittee drafted an air pollution bill more stringent than either the president's *or* the House of Representatives'. It called for nationally uniform air quality standards that ignored economic cost and technological feasibility considerations and were based solely on health and welfare criteria; it required traffic control plans to eliminate automobile use in parts of some major cities; and it mandated a 90 percent reduction in automotive emissions of carbon monoxide, hydrocarbons, and nitrous oxides by 1975. In a clear manifestation of the burgeoning popularity of environmental protection, senators got on the bandwagon and endorsed this version of the clean air bill unanimously (73–0) on September 21, 1970.[37]

The House-Senate conference that ensued was unusually protracted, involving at least eight long sessions over a three-month period. The Senate's eight conferees held an advantage over the five from the House because Muskie's prolonged attention to pollution issues had attracted several qualified and committed staffers who had amassed considerable expertise. As a consequence, the final conference report more closely resembled the Senate rather than the House version of the bill.

On December 18, both chambers debated and passed the conference version, and on December 31, President Nixon signed the Clean Air Act of 1970. Its centerpiece was the requirement that the EPA set both primary and secondary national ambient air quality standards.[38] The states were to submit state implementation plans (SIPs) outlining a strategy for meeting primary standards by 1975 and secondary standards "within a reasonable time." If the EPA determined a SIP to be inadequate, it had to promulgate a plan of its own. The act also targeted some polluters directly: it required automobile producers to reduce the emissions of new cars by 90 percent by 1975, and it required the EPA to set new source performance standards for all major categories of stationary sources.

The highly symbolic language, goals, and structure of the 1970 Clean Air Act clearly reflect the public's attentiveness to the problem of air pollution and its demand for federal action. As Helen Ingram points out, the new law

> set far more ambitious air pollution control goals, which were to be accomplished more quickly and under a more demanding regulatory regime than could possibly have been projected from previous policy evolution. . . . The understanding of clean air changed significantly through the legislative process in 1970. The pragmatic, functional definition of air quality, restricted to what was economically and technologically feasible, was abandoned, and clean air was legislated a fundamental national value.[39]

The Clean Water Act of 1972. President Nixon made not only air pollution but water pollution legislation a pillar of his February 10, 1970, Special Message to Congress on Environmental Quality. When Congress failed to address water pollution in that legislative session, the president moved administratively, using the permit authority granted by the Refuse Act of 1899 to control industrial pollution of waterways. By executive order, Nixon directed the new EPA to require industries to disclose the amount and kinds of effluents they were generating before they could obtain a permit to discharge them into navigable waters.[40] When a polluter failed to apply for a permit or violated existing clean water regulations, the EPA referred an enforcement action to the Justice Department.

Neither the permit process nor the enforcement strategy was particularly effective at ameliorating water pollution, however. While the president endorsed the permit program, Congress was not pleased at being circumvented; state agencies were angry that federal rules superseded their own regulations; and many industries were furious at the sudden demands for discharge information.[41] Thus, by July 1, 1971, when the first 50,000 applications from water-polluting industries were due, only 30,000 had arrived, and many of those contained incomplete or inaccurate information. The enforcement process, which relied heavily on the overburdened federal court system, was slow and cumbersome.[42] Finally, in December 1971, a district court in Ohio dealt the permit program its final blow: it held that the EPA had to draft an environmental impact statement for each permit issued in order to comply with the National Environmental Policy Act (NEPA).[43]

While the EPA muddled through with its interim program, Congress began to debate the future of water pollution policy. In February 1971, President Nixon endorsed a proposal to strengthen a bill he had submitted to Congress the previous year. In it he increased his request for annual municipal waste treatment financing from $1 billion to $2 billion for three years and established mandatory toxic discharge standards. In addition, he requested authority for legal actions by private citizens to enforce water quality standards.

Refusing to be upstaged by the president, Muskie seized the opportunity to offer even more stringent legislation. The Senate began hearings in February, and eight months later Muskie's Public Works Committee reported out a bill: the Federal Water Pollution Control Act Amendments. Much to the administration's dismay, the price tag for the Senate bill was $18 billion, three times the $6 billion cost of Nixon's proposal. Moreover, the administration found unrealistic the overarching objectives of the Senate bill: that "wherever attainable, an interim goal of water quality which provides for the protection and propagation of fish, shellfish, and wildlife and provides for recreation in and on the water should be achieved by 1981" and that "the discharge of all pollutants into navigable waters would be eliminated by 1985." Finally, the administration considered the Senate bill inequitable, claiming that it imposed a disproportionate burden on industry by singling out in particular those that could not discharge into municipal waste treatment facilities. Nevertheless, on November 2, 1971, the Senate passed the bill unanimously by a vote of 86–0.

After failing to shift the Senate position, the administration retrained its sights on the House deliberations, with some qualified success: the House reported out a bill similar to the one proposed by the administration. In contrast to the Senate version, the House bill retained the primacy of the states in administering the program. Despite their initial differences, the House–Senate conferees—after meeting forty times between May and September 1972—produced a bill that both sides could live with. In another extraordinary display of unanimity, the Senate passed the conference bill by 74–0, and the House approved it by 366–11.

The compromise was too stringent for the administration, however. It retained the fishable, swimmable, and zero-discharge goals, as well as the financing provisions, that were so objectionable to the president. Furthermore, the bill's timetables and total disregard for economic costs offended the White House. So, in a tactical maneuver, Nixon vetoed the Clean Water Act on

October 17, the day that Congress was scheduled to adjourn for the year. To Nixon's chagrin, Congress responded with unusual alacrity: less than two hours after the president delivered his veto message, the Senate voted to override the veto by 52–12.[44] The next afternoon the House followed suit by a vote of 247–23, and the Clean Water Act became law.

The New Environmental Regulations. The Clean Air and Clean Water Acts reflected the prevailing definition of pollution, in which industrial polluters (not consumers) were the villains, and citizens (and only secondarily the environment) were the unwitting victims. They also reflect the public's skepticism of both corporations' willingness and government bureaucrats' ability to address pollution. Concerns about "regulatory capture," whereby agencies become subservient to the industries they are supposed to monitor, had preoccupied academics for years, but in 1969, political scientist Theodore Lowi popularized the concept in his book *The End of Liberalism.* Lowi criticized Congress for granting agencies broad discretion in order to avoid making hard political tradeoffs. He argued that agencies, operating out of the public eye, strike bargains with the interest groups most affected by their policies, rather than making policies that serve a broader national interest. Led by policy entrepreneur Ralph Nader, reformers disseminated the concept of regulatory capture. Two reports issued by Nader's Center for the Study of Responsive Law, *Vanishing Air* in 1970 and *Water Wasteland* in 1971, attributed the failures of earlier air and water pollution control laws to agency capture. More important, they linked that diagnosis to Nader's preferred solution: strict, action-forcing statutes, reasoning that unambiguous laws would constrain bureaucrats' ability to pander to interest groups.

Members of Congress got the message. In addition to transferring standard-setting authority from the states to the federal government, the Clean Air and Clean Water Acts employed novel regulatory mechanisms—such as strict deadlines, clear goals, and uniform standards—that both constrained the EPA's discretion and limited polluters' flexibility. For example, the Clean Air Act gave the EPA thirty days to establish health- and welfare-based ambient air quality standards. The states then had nine months to submit their SIPs to the EPA, which had to approve or disapprove the SIPs within four months of receipt. The agency was to ensure the achievement of national air quality standards no later than 1977. Similarly, the Clean Water Act specified six deadlines. By 1973, the EPA was supposed to issue effluent guidelines for major industrial categories; within a year it was to grant permits to all sources of water pollution; by 1977, every source was supposed to have installed the "best practicable" water pollution control technology; by 1981, the major waterways in the nation were to be swimmable and fishable; by 1983, polluting sources were to install the "best available" technology; and two years later all discharges into the nation's waterways were to be eliminated.

Congress also sought to demonstrate its commitment to preventing regulatory capture by incorporating public participation into agency decision making and thereby breaking up regulated interests' monopoly. For example, the Clean Water Act required the EPA to solicit public opinion in writing and implementing regulations. In addition, the legislature encouraged public participation by explicitly granting citizens the right to bring a civil suit in federal court against any violator or "against the administrator [of the EPA] where there is alleged a failure of the administrator to perform any act or duty under [the Clean Air Act] which is not discretionary." As political scientist Shep Melnick explains:

> Previous statutes had required citizens wishing to sue administrators to show that they had suffered direct, concrete harm at the hands of an agency. Almost all the regulatory laws passed in the 1970s, though, authorized "any citizen" to file suit against administrators either for taking unauthorized action or for failing to perform "nondiscretionary" duties. Some statutes even reimbursed litigants in such suits for their trouble. When combined with detailed statutes these opportunities for judicial review provided fledgling environmental and consumer groups with powerful resources within the regulatory process.[45]

Finally, the Clean Air and Water Acts of the early 1970s reflected impatience with market forces and a desire to spur the development of new pollution control technology as well as to encourage firms to devise innovative new production processes. The new laws included provisions that forced technology in three ways: by prompting the development of brand new technology, by encouraging the use of available but not-yet-used technology, and by forcing diffusion of currently used technology within an industry. The motor vehicle provisions of the Clean Air Act, for example, forced the development of a brand new technology: the catalytic converter. When Congress was debating the 90 percent emissions reduction, the automobile manufacturers contended they did not have the technology to meet those standards, but Muskie responded with a flourish that such a dramatic reduction was necessary to protect human health, so companies would have to devise a solution. (As it turned out, car makers were able to meet the standards relatively easily.) The Clean Water Act, on the other hand, pushed polluters to adopt technology that was already available but not widely used during the first stage. In the second stage, however, the act required firms to meet standards achievable with the best technology available, even if it was not in use at the time.

Implementation: Idealism Tempered

The Clean Air and Water Acts were sufficiently grandiose that they would have presented a challenge to any agency, but they were particularly onerous for a brand new one comprising staff from all over the federal government. Not surprisingly, because of the short time frame for implementing these laws, combined with the haste in which the agency was designed, the EPA did not attain the ideal of interrelatedness outlined by President Nixon; instead, different offices continued to manage pollution in different media. Nor did the EPA fulfill the mandates of the Clean Air and Water Acts to virtually eliminate pollution in the nation's air- and waterways. Although born in a period of great idealism, the EPA had to survive in the constrained world of practical politics: it had to establish relationships with and reconcile the demands of the president and Congress, and it had to navigate a course in a sea of influential interest groups, state and local officials, the media, and the public. In all of these endeavors, the EPA was vulnerable to lawsuits because the statutes compelled it to act quickly and decisively, despite a dearth of scientific and technical information on which to base, and—more importantly—with which to justify, its decisions.

Setting a Course. The new EPA was an organizational nightmare, as it comprised

> an uneasy amalgam of staff and programs previously located in 15 separate federal agencies. EPA had a total budget of $1.4 billion and programs previously located in 15 different places, ranging geographically from a floating barge off the Florida coast to a water quality laboratory in Alaska. In Washington, D.C. alone there were 2,000 employees scattered across the city in 12 separate office buildings.[46]

The first EPA administrator, William Ruckelshaus, was a lawyer and former Justice Department official. He was confronted with the awesome tasks of coordinating the disparate offices of the new agency (it lacked a headquarters until 1973), establishing a set of coherent priorities, and carrying out the statutory mission of regulating polluters. From the outset, Ruckelshaus balanced his own approach against the conflicting preferences of Congress and the White House.

Although President Nixon created the EPA and introduced pollution control legislation, he was more of a political opportunist than a genuine environmentalist. He regarded environmentalism as a fad, but one that promised political rewards: "Elected with only 43 percent of the popular vote in 1968, Nixon needed to take bold steps to expand his ideological base in order to be reelected in 1972."[47] In truth, Nixon was hostile toward the federal bureaucracy and, as biographer Stephen Ambrose notes, wanted "credit for boldness and innovation without the costs."[48] Thus, Nixon instructed White House staff to scrutinize the EPA's activity, sought to block its rulemaking, and introduced legislation to reduce its authority. Most notably, he established a "quality of life" review under the Office of Management and Budget (OMB) to assess the legal, economic, and budgetary implications of EPA regulations—a mechanism that, by 1972, "had become an administration device for obstructing stringent regulations, as the environmental groups had originally feared."[49]

Several members of Congress, on the other hand, exhibited a genuine zeal for environmental protection. Members of the House and Senate subcommittees with jurisdiction over pollution control encouraged Ruckelshaus to enforce the law vigorously. Senator Muskie, in particular, was dogged in his efforts to train national attention on pollution control and thereby hold the EPA's feet to the fire. His subcommittee held frequent hearings requiring Ruckelshaus to explain delays in setting standards. Other members on related committees were more conservative; for example, Rep. Jamie Whitten, D-Miss., chairman of the House Appropriations Subcommittee on Agriculture, Environment, and Consumer Protection, controlled the agency's purse strings and was a vocal opponent of strong environmental regulations.[50]

Squeezed between supporters and detractors in Congress and the White House, Ruckelshaus tried to build an independent constituency that would support the EPA. To establish credibility as an environmentalist and earn public trust, he initiated a series of lawsuits against known municipal and industrial violators of water pollution control laws. To reinforce his efforts, he promoted the agency in the media, giving frequent press conferences, appearing on talk shows, and making speeches before trade and business associations. According to John Quarles, EPA's first assistant administrator for enforcement:

> Ruckelshaus believed in the strength of public opinion and public support. The organized environmental movement had been formed because of public pressure and Ruckelshaus responded instinctively to that pressure. He did not seek political support for his actions in the established structures of political power. He turned instead directly to the press and to public opinion. . . . In doing so, he tied the fortunes of EPA to public opinion as the only base for political support.[51]

Ruckelshaus had to do more than file lawsuits and woo the media, however; he had to promulgate a series of regulations to meet statutory deadlines, notwithstanding the paucity of scientific and engineering information. Compounding the technical obstacles, the targeted industries resisted agency rulemaking. Although it had been ambushed by the regulatory onslaught of the late 1960s and early 1970s, business quickly adapted to the new political order. Between 1968 and 1978, the number of corporations with public affairs offices in Washington rose from one hundred to more than five hundred.[52] Corporations began to emphasize government relations as a fundamental part of their missions. They hired articulate and politically sophisticated CEOs; they encouraged stockholders and employees to make political donations and communicate with their members of Congress; and they contributed heavily to political action committees (PACs). Corporations also began giving generously to conservative think tanks, such as the Heritage Foundation, the Business Roundtable, and Stanford's Hoover Institution. Those think tanks in turn generated research in support of business goals. In short, polluters continued to dominate environmentalists at the implementation stage; with its almost bottomless resources, industry was able to challenge regulations administratively and in the courts.[53]

Implementing the Clean Air Act. Reflecting their newfound clout, the industries especially hard hit by regulation—automobile, steel, nonferrous smelting, and electric power—all succeeded in winning delays from the EPA.

The automobile manufacturers were among those the Clean Air Act singled out most directly.[54] Before the passage of the 1966 National Traffic and Motor Vehicle Safety Act, the automobile was completely unregulated by the federal government. Yet only four years later, the Clean Air Act required car makers to cut emissions of carbon monoxide, nitrogen oxides, and hydrocarbons by 90 percent within five years. Producers immediately applied for a one-year extension of the deadline, contending that the technology to achieve the standards was not yet available. Ruckelshaus denied their petition on the grounds that the industry had not made "good faith efforts" to achieve the standards. The manufacturers then took their case to the U.S. Court of Appeals for the District of Columbia, which overturned Ruckelshaus's decision, saying that the agency needed to give economic factors greater weight. Later that year, Ruckelshaus conceded and granted a one-year extension.

The power companies, automobile manufacturers, and coal and oil producers next saw a window of opportunity to weaken the Clean Air Act requirements in the energy crisis of 1973–1974. Threatening widespread economic dislocation, these energy-related industries pressured Congress and the president into passing the Energy Supply and Environmental Coordination Act of 1974. The act included another one-year extension for hydrocarbon and carbon monoxide emissions and a two-year extension for nitrogen oxide emissions. When a controversy arose over the health effects of acid emissions from catalytic converters, EPA administrator Russell Train (Ruckelshaus's successor) granted the auto manufacturers a third extension.[55]

The delays in achieving automotive emissions standards left the EPA in an awkward position, however: because of the extensions, states could not rely on cleaner cars to mitigate their pollution problems and would have to reduce dramatically the *use* of automobiles (a politically unappealing prospect). Acknowledging the enormity of their task, Ruckelshaus granted seventeen of the most urbanized states a two-year extension on the transportation control portion of their implementation plans, giving states until 1977 to achieve air quality standards.[56] Although most state officials were pleased, disgruntled environmentalists in California filed suit in federal court to force the EPA to promulgate a transportation control plan (TCP) for Los Angeles. The plaintiffs charged that the Clean Air Act compelled the EPA to draft a plan for any state whose own plan the agency disapproved, not to grant extensions. The court agreed and ordered the agency to prepare a TCP for Los Angeles by January 15, 1973.

The pollution problem in Los Angeles basin was so severe that, in order to bring the region into compliance with air quality standards, the EPA had to write a transportation control plan that included gas rationing and mandatory installation of emissions control devices on all cars. Needless to say, such measures were unpopular. Public officials who were supposed to enforce the plan ridiculed it: Mayor Sam Yorty called it "asinine," "silly," and "impossible."[57] State and local officials clearly believed that their constituents supported clean air in the abstract but would not give up their cars to get it.

Contributing to the agency's credibility woes, just two weeks after Ruckelshaus announced the Los Angeles TCP, a federal court found in favor of the Natural Resources Defense Council (NRDC) in its suit to overturn the two-year extensions for states' compliance with the air quality standards. To Ruckelshaus's chagrin, the court ordered him to rescind all seventeen extensions. The states again were faced with a 1975 compliance deadline to be achieved without the benefit of cleaner cars.

Thus, in late 1973, the EPA produced a spate of TCPs for states whose own TCPs the agency had rejected. State officials immediately challenged the plans in court, and in some cases judges were sympathetic, finding that the EPA plans lacked sufficient technical support. But many of the plans went unchallenged, and by spring 1974, the EPA was in another quandary: it had promulgated numerous TCPs the previous year, but the states were not implementing them. While EPA lawyers believed they had the legal authority to require out-of-compliance areas to institute transportation controls, it was not clear how they would force recalcitrant states to do so, and the agency lacked the administrative apparatus to impose the control strategies itself. Ruckelshaus decided to try enforcing a test case in Boston, a logical choice since it already had an extensive mass transit system.

The backlash in Massachusetts was immediate and harsh, in part because the Boston plan was haphazard and incoherent—a reflection of the agency's lack of information. For example, one regulation required all firms with fifty or more employees to reduce their available parking spaces by 25 percent. The EPA planned to send enforcement orders to 1,500 employers but discovered that only three hundred of those on the list actually fit the category and many of those turned out to be exempt (hospitals, for example). In the end, only seven or eight of the twenty-five eligible employers responded to the EPA's request to cut parking spaces. As time went on, even northeast regional EPA officials became annoyed with the arbitrary assumptions and technical errors embedded in the Boston TCP. The carbon monoxide reduction strategy for the entire city, for instance, was based on an unusually high reading from an extremely congested intersection, and the ozone calculations were based on a solitary reading from a monitor that had probably malfunctioned.[58]

Ultimately, the city of Boston took the plan to court and won; the judge remanded the plan to the EPA for better technical justification. Eventually, a chastened EPA rescinded the Boston plan altogether and issued a replacement that dropped all mandatory traffic and parking restrictions, relying instead on stationary source controls and voluntary vehicle cutbacks. The EPA went on to abandon its attempts to force major cities to restructure their transportation systems, which in turn meant many remained out of compliance with air quality standards. By 1975, the statutory deadline, not one state implementation plan had received final approval from the EPA.

Implementing the Clean Water Act. Like the Clean Air Act, the Clean Water Act required the EPA to take on powerful industries armed only with scanty technical and scientific information. The law's cornerstone, the National Pollutant Discharge Elimination System, prohibited the dumping of any wastes or effluents by any industry or government entity without a permit. To implement this provision, the agency had to undertake a massive data collection task: it needed information about the discharges, manufacturing processes, and pollution control options of 20,000 different industrial polluters operating under different circumstances in a variety of locations.[59] To simplify its task, the EPA divided firms into 30 categories and 250 subcategories on the basis of product, age, size, and manufacturing process. The water program office then created an Effluent Guidelines Division to set industry-by-industry effluent guidelines based on the "best practicable technology" (BPT). The division collected and tabulated information on firms around the country. It found sufficient variation, however, to make generalizations about a single best technology highly uncertain. While the EPA wrestled with this problem, the NRDC sued the agency for delay. The court, finding in favor of the plaintiffs, forced the EPA to release guidelines for more than thirty industry categories and one hundred subcategories.

Although the permits granted to individual firms were supposed to be based on the BPT guidelines, the two were actually released simultaneously as a result of delay in issuing the guidelines. By the 1974 permit deadline, the EPA had issued more than half of the estimated 47,000 required permits; in other words, the agency dispensed permits to almost all of the "major" polluters before the guidelines had even appeared![60] Industry seized on this discrepancy to contest the permits in the agency's adjudicatory proceedings. In addition, major companies brought more than 150 lawsuits to challenge the guidelines themselves: the very day the EPA issued guidelines for the chemical industry, DuPont hired a prestigious law firm to sue the agency.[61] Ultimately, the EPA was forced to adopt a more pragmatic and conciliatory relationship with out-of-compliance firms. In response, disappointed environmental groups began to file suits against polluters themselves.

The 1977 Clean Air and Water Act Amendments

In 1977, under pressure from newly mobilized industry groups and with the public's attention elsewhere, Congress relaxed the stringent provisions of both the Clean Air and the Clean Water Acts. The 1977 Clean Air Act Amendments postponed the healthy air goals (that had to be achieved by 1975 under the 1970 act) until 1982. In areas heavily affected by car emissions, such as California, the act gave the states until 1987 to achieve air quality goals. The amendments also extended the deadline for 90 percent reductions in automobile emissions—originally set for 1975 and subsequently postponed until 1978—to 1980 for hydrocarbons and 1981 for carbon monoxide. Congress granted the EPA administrator discretionary authority to delay the achievement of auto pollution reduction objectives for carbon monoxide and nitrogen oxides for up to two additional years if he determined the required technology was not available. In addition, the amendments required that the EPA take into account competing priorities: it had to grant variances for technological innovation and file economic impact and employment impact statements with all new regulations it issued.[62] Moreover, the amendments gave the governor of any state the right to suspend transportation control measures that required gas rationing, reductions in on-street parking, or bridge tolls.[63]

The 1977 Clean Water Act Amendments similarly extended a host of deadlines. They gave industries that acted in "good faith" but did not meet the 1977 BPT deadlines until April 1, 1979, instead of July 1, 1977, to meet the standard. In addition, this amendment postponed and modified the best available technology (BAT) requirement that industry was supposed to achieve by 1983. It retained the strict standard for toxic pollutants but modified it for conventional pollutants.[64] This gave the EPA the flexibility to set standards less stringent than BAT when it determined that the costs of employing BAT exceeded the benefits. Finally, although the amendments retained the objective of zero discharge into navigable waters by 1985, the practical implications of that goal were few; the extension of the BPT target and the modification of the BAT target eliminated the connection between zero discharge and a specific abatement program. In short, while they did not explicitly delete the zero discharge goal, the 1977 amendments effectively abandoned it.[65]

Despite these rollbacks, the EPA continued to have formidable regulatory powers. In January 1978, shortly after Congress passed the amendments, President Jimmy Carter submitted his 1979 budget. Although he called for an overall spending increase of less than 1 percent over 1978, he requested an increase of $668 million for programs handled by the EPA.[66] That allocation reflected an important shift that had taken place at the EPA: in the months prior to the budget announcement, the agency had made a concerted effort to recast its image from that of protector of flora and fauna to guardian of the public's health. The move was partly to deflect a threatened merger of the EPA with other natural resources agencies, but it also reflected shrewd recognition of congressional support for programs aimed at fighting cancer.[67] The agency's PR campaign worked: by the end of the 1970s, the EPA had become the largest federal regulatory agency, employing over 13,000 people and spending $7 billion annually.[68]

OUTCOMES

As a result of White House obstruction, business resistance, and the sheer magnitude of the task, the EPA's accomplishments have been neither as dramatic nor as far reaching as the original air and water pollution statutes demanded. Moreover, a chorus of critics contends that what cleanup has been accomplished has come at a price far higher than necessary because regulations were poorly designed and haphazardly implemented. Nonetheless, the nation has made considerable progress in cleaning up air and water pollution.

On the one hand, in 1999, thirty-two areas with a combined population of 93 million people experienced more than two days a year during which the one-hour ozone standard was exceeded.[69] And the EPA continued to be well behind schedule in establishing emissions standards for air toxics, as required by Section 112 of the Clean Air Act. But, on the other hand, in the twenty-year period between 1979—when most air pollution controls were in place—and 1998, concentrations of carbon monoxide fell 58 percent; concentrations of nitrogen oxides dropped 25 percent; ambient levels of ozone (smog) dropped 17 percent; ambient levels of sulfur dioxide fell 53 percent; and airborne-led concentrations dropped 96 percent. Since 1989, the first year that monitoring networks were in place, concentrations of particulate matter of ten microns or less declined 25 percent.[70]

Nor has the nation realized the lofty objectives of the 1972 Clean Water Act. It is difficult to assess progress in ameliorating water pollution precisely because the EPA and the Council on Environmental Quality base their water quality indexes on only six pollutants, excluding such important sources of water degradation as heavy metals, synthetic organic compounds, and dissolved solids.[71] Moreover, according to the General Accounting Office (GAO), the states have assessed only about a third of total U.S. river miles, half of lake and three-quarters of estuarine square miles.[72] Of those, the EPA considers the water quality in about a third to be significantly impaired. Furthermore, the GAO has consistently found high levels of noncompliance with the discharge levels specified in their permits among both industrial and municipal polluters.[73]

More important from the perspective of many critics is that nonpoint source water pollution presents a significant and growing problem and continues to be virtually unregulated under the Clean Water Act. Nonpoint sources include farmlands, city storm sewers, construction sites, mines, and heavily logged forests; runoff from these sources contains silt, pathogens, toxic chemicals, and excess nutrients that can suffocate fish and contaminate groundwater. Nor does the act deal with groundwater, which supplies the drinking water for thirty-four of the one hundred largest cities.[74] In addition, loss of wetlands—which continued into the 1990s at the staggering rate of forty acres per hour—contributes to water quality problems.

Bearing in mind the deficiencies in measurement and the absence of controls on important pollution sources, water quality modeling by Resources for the Future suggests that the Clean Water Act has had only modest impacts on water quality. Since the act was passed in 1972, the number of river miles meeting swimmable, fishable, and boatable standards has increased by only 6.3 percent, 4.2 percent, and 2.8 percent, respectively.[75] On the other hand, many seriously polluted water bodies have been substantially cleaned up as a result of this law. Moreover, as of 1992, all sewage generated in the United States is treated before discharge.[76]

CONCLUSIONS

As this case makes clear, public attentiveness, especially when coupled with highly visible demonstrations of concern, can produce dramatic changes in politics and policy. Front-page coverage of Earth Day demonstrations in

1970 both enhanced public awareness of and concern about environmental problems and led elected officials to believe that environmental issues were highly salient. In response, aspiring leaders competed with one another to gain credit for addressing air and water pollution. Congress's near-unanimous support for the Clean Air and Clean Water Acts suggests that rank-and-file legislators also sought recognition for solving the pollution problem, or at a minimum got on the bandwagon to avoid blame for obstructing such solutions.

The Clean Air and Clean Water Acts that resulted from this process constituted a dramatic departure from the status quo in both the stringency and form of the nation's environmental policy framework. The command-and-control approach, which imposed uniform emissions standards on polluters, reflected the moral and political framing of the environmental issue: industrial polluters had caused the problem, and neither they nor government bureaucrats could be trusted to reduce pollution unless tightly constrained by highly specific standards and deadlines. The initial urgency of public concern and the immediacy of the legislative response meant that a fledgling EPA was destined to fail when it tried to implement the laws as written, however. It encountered hostility from the president, who wanted to weaken implementation of the law, as well as from its overseers in Congress, who berated it for failing to move more quickly.

Equally challenging was the need to placate polarized interest groups on both sides of the issue. Citizen suit provisions designed to enhance public involvement in the regulatory process resulted in a host of lawsuits by environmentalists trying to expedite the standard-setting process. At the same time, newly mobilized business interests used both administrative hearings and lawsuits to obstruct implementation of the new laws. Caught in the middle, the EPA tried to enhance its public image—first by cracking down on individual polluters and later by emphasizing the public health aspect of its mission. The agency hoped that by steering a middle course it could maintain its credibility, as well as its political support. Thus, on the one hand, the business backlash was effective: by the late 1970s, Congress had substantially weakened the requirements of the Clean Air and Water Acts. On the other hand, both laws survived, and both they and the EPA itself continue to enjoy broad public support.[77]

QUESTIONS TO CONSIDER

- Why did the federal government pass environmental laws in the early 1970s so markedly different in structure and content from those that came before?
- What are the strengths and weaknesses of the approach adopted in the Clean Air and Water Acts?
- How have the creation of the EPA and passage of the Clean Air and Water Acts in the early 1970s affected the environment and our approach to environmental protection in the long run?

Notes

1. Mary Graham, *The Morning After Earth Day: Practical Environmental Politics* (Washington, D.C.: Brookings Institution, 1999).
2. Frank R. Baumgartner and Bryan D. Jones, *Agendas and Instability in American Politics* (Chicago: University of Chicago Press, 1993).
3. Herbert Kaufman, *The Administrative Behavior of Bureau Chiefs* (Washington, D.C.: Brookings Institution, 1981); Kenneth J. Meier, *Politics and the Bureaucracy* (N. Scituate, Mass.: Duxbury Press, 1979), 70.
4. Francis E. Rourke, *Bureaucracy, Politics, and Public Policy*, 3d ed. (Boston: Little, Brown, 1976).
5. Clarence J. Davies III, *The Politics of Pollution* (New York: Pegasus, 1970).
6. Council on Environmental Quality (CEQ), *Environmental Quality: The First Annual Report of the Council on Environmental Quality* (Washington, D.C.: U.S. Government Printing Office, 1970).
7. John F. Wall and Leonard B. Dworsky, *Problems of Executive Reorganization: The Federal Environmental Protection Agency* (Ithaca: Cornell University Water Resources and Marine Sciences Center, 1971).
8. An inversion is an atmospheric condition in which the air temperature rises with increasing altitude, holding surface air down and preventing the dispersion of pollutants.
9. Gary Bryner, *Blue Skies, Green Politics: The Clean Air Act of 1990* (Washington, D.C.: CQ Press, 1993).
10. Davies, *The Politics of Pollution.*
11. Wall and Dworsky, *Problems of Executive Reorganization.*
12. Davies, *The Politics of Pollution.*
13. Philip Shabecoff, *A Fierce Green Fire: The American Environmental Movement* (New York: Hill and Wang, 1993), 109–110.
14. Marc K. Landy, Marc J. Roberts, and Stephen R. Thomas, *The Environmental Protection Agency: Asking the Wrong Questions*, expanded ed. (New York: Oxford University Press, 1994).
15. Charles T. Rubin, *The Green Crusade: Rethinking the Roots of Environmentalism* (Lanham, Md.: Rowman and Littlefield, 1998).
16. Graham, *The Morning After Earth Day.*
17. Shabecoff, *A Fierce Green Fire.* Although the environmental groups did not engineer Earth Day, their memberships had been growing in the 1960s, going from 124,000 in 1960 to 1,127,000 in 1972. See Robert Mitchell, "From Conservation to Environmental Movement: The Development of the Modern Environmental Lobbies," in *Government and Environmental Politics: Essays on Historical Developments Since World War Two*, ed. Michael Lacey (Baltimore: Johns Hopkins University Press, 1989), 81–113.
18. Kirkpatrick Sale, *The Green Revolution: The American Environmental Movement 1962–1992* (New York: Hill & Wang, 1993).
19. The following Earth Day anecdotes are assembled from reports in the *New York Times* and the *Washington Post*, April 23, 1970.
20. Mary Etta Cook and Roger H. Davidson, "Deferral Politics: Congressional Decision Making on Environmental Issues in the 1980s," in *Public Policy and the Natural Environment*, ed. Helen M. Ingram and R. Kenneth Godwin (Greenwich, Conn.: JAI Press, 1985), 47–76.
21. Hazel Erskine, "The Polls: Pollution and Its Costs," *Public Opinion Quarterly* 1 (spring): 120–135.
22. Samuel P. Hays, "The Politics of Environmental Administration," in *The New American State: Bureaucracies and Policies Since World War II*, ed. Louis Galambos (Baltimore: Johns Hopkins University Press, 1987), 23.

23. John C. Whitaker, *Striking a Balance: Environment and Natural Resources Policy in the Nixon-Ford Years* (Washington, D.C.: American Enterprise Institute, 1976).
24. Ibid.
25. "Transcript of the President's State of the Union Message to the Joint Session of Congress," *New York Times,* January 23, 1970, 22.
26. Ibid.
27. CEQ, *Environmental Quality.*
28. Ibid.
29. Richard A. Harris and Sidney M. Milkis, *The Politics of Regulatory Change: A Tale of Two Agencies* (New York: Oxford University Press, 1989).
30. Ibid.
31. CEQ, *Environmental Quality.*
32. Congress may not amend an executive reorganization proposal; it must approve or disapprove the entire package. To stop a reorganization, either chamber must adopt a resolution disapproving it within sixty days of its introduction.
33. Charles O. Jones, *Clean Air: The Policies and Politics of Pollution Control* (Pittsburgh: University of Pittsburgh Press, 1975).
34. U.S. Congress, Senate, *Congressional Record,* 91st Cong., 2d sess., March 4, 1970, S2955.
35. John C. Esposito, *Vanishing Air* (New York: Grossman, 1970), 270, 290–291.
36. Jones, *Clean Air,* 192.
37. Alfred Marcus, "Environmental Protection Agency," in *The Politics of Regulation,* ed. James Q. Wilson (New York: Basic Books, 1980), 267–436.
38. Primary standards must "protect the public health" by "an adequate margin of safety." Secondary standards must "protect the public welfare from any known or anticipated adverse effects."
39. Helen Ingram, "The Political Rationality of Innovation: The Clean Air Act Amendments of 1970," in *Approaches to Controlling Air Pollution,* ed. Anne F. Friedlander (Cambridge: MIT Press, 1978), 14.
40. An executive order is a presidential directive to an agency that enables the president to shape policy without getting the approval of Congress.
41. John Quarles, *Cleaning Up America: An Insider's View of Environmental Protection* (Boston: Houghton Mifflin, 1976).
42. Alfred Marcus, *Promise and Performance: Choosing and Implementing an Environmental Policy* (Westport, Conn.: Greenwood Press, 1980).
43. NEPA requires federal agencies to complete environmental impact statements before embarking on any major project.
44. Congress can override a presidential veto with a two-thirds majority in both chambers.
45. R. Shep Melnick, *Regulation and the Courts: The Case of the Clean Air Act* (Washington, D.C.: Brookings Institution, 1983), 8.
46. Arnold Howitt, "The Environmental Protection Agency and Transportation Controls," in *Managing Federalism: Studies in Intergovernmental Relations* (Washington, D.C.: CQ Press, 1986), 116.
47. Graham, *The Morning After Earth Day,* 31.
48. Quoted in ibid., 53.
49. Howitt, "The Environmental Protection Agency," 125.
50. Marcus, *Promise and Performance.*
51. Quarles, *Cleaning Up America,* 61.
52. The number of business-related PACs also increased from 248 in 1974 to 1,100 in 1978. See David Vogel, "The Power of Business in America: A Reappraisal," *British Journal of Political Science* 13 (1983): 19–43.
53. More than two thousand firms contested EPA standards within the first few years of its operation. See James T. Patterson, *Grand Expectations: The United States, 1945–1974* (New York: Oxford University Press, 1996).

54. The industry had mounted only weak resistance to Muskie's attacks on it. According to journalist Richard Cohen, Muskie later speculated that some industry leaders "could see what was coming" and therefore gave limited cooperation (or got on the bandwagon). The passive attitude of the car manufacturers probably also reflects its strong financial position at the time (imports represented only 13 percent of all U.S. auto sales) and its weak lobbying operation. General Motors, for example, did not even establish a Washington lobbying office until 1969. See Richard Cohen, *Washington at Work: Back Rooms and Clean Air* (New York: Macmillan, 1992).

55. Marcus, *Promise and Performance.*

56. Transportation control measures include creating bicycle paths and car-free zones, rationing gas, imposing gas taxes, building mass transit, establishing bus lanes, encouraging carpooling, and undertaking vehicle inspection and maintenance programs.

57. Quoted in Marcus, *Promise and Performance,* 133.

58. Howitt, "The Environmental Protection Agency."

59. Marcus, *Promise and Performance.*

60. The law required the EPA to grant permits to all industrial and government polluters, including 21,000 municipal sewage treatment facilities.

61. Marcus, *Promise and Performance.*

62. Recall that the original Clean Air Act did not allow the EPA to consider economic and technical factors.

63. Marcus, *Promise and Performance.*

64. Conventional pollutants are solids, biochemical oxygen demanding (BOD) pollutants, pH, and fecal coliform.

65. Marcus, *Promise and Performance.*

66. Dick Kirschten, "EPA: A Winner in the Annual Budget Battle," *National Journal,* January 28, 1978, 140–141.

67. Ibid.

68. Paul R. Portney, "EPA and the Evolution of Federal Regulation," in *Public Policies for Environmental Protection,* 2d ed., ed. Paul R. Portney and Robert N. Stavins (Washington, D.C.: Resources for the Future, 2000), 11–30.

69. Paul R. Portney, "Air Pollution Policy," in *Public Policies for Environmental Protection,* ed. Portney and Stavins, 77–123.

70. Portney, "Air Pollution Policy." Resources for the Future economist Paul Portney notes that we cannot attribute all reductions to policy alone; other factors, such as the rate and type of economic growth, prices, and even the weather, can affect air quality. On the other hand, as political scientist Walter Rosenbaum points out, the data also understate the significance of Clean Air Act achievements because they are not compared to what pollution levels would have been in the absence of regulation during a period (1970–1999) when the U.S. population increased by 33 percent and vehicle miles traveled grew by 140 percent. See Walter Rosenbaum, *Environmental Politics and Policy,* 5th ed. (Washington, D.C.: CQ Press, 2001).

71. Rosenbaum, *Environmental Politics.*

72. U.S. General Accounting Office, *EPA: Major Performance and Accountability Challenges,* GAO-01-257 (January 2001).

73. A. Myrick Freeman III, "Water Pollution Policy," in *Public Policies for Environmental Protection,* ed. Portney and Stavins, 169–213.

74. Council on Environmental Quality, *Environmental Quality: The Fifteenth Annual Report of the Council on Environmental Quality* (Washington, D.C.: U.S. Government Printing Office, 1984).

75. Freeman, "Water Pollution Policy."

76. Gregg Easterbrook, *A Moment on the Earth* (New York: Viking, 1995).

77. Americans continue to name air and water pollution as the world's most important environmental problems. Gallup poll release, "Despite Dire Predictions, Americans Have Other Priorities," http://www.gallup.com/poll/releases/pr010220.asp.

Recommended Reading

Graham, Mary. *The Morning After Earth Day: Practical Environmental Politics.* Washington, D.C.: Brookings Institution, 1999.

Landy, Marc K., Marc J. Roberts, and Stephen R. Thomas. *The Environmental Protection Agency: Asking the Wrong Questions,* expanded ed. New York: Oxford University Press, 1994.

Shabecoff, Philip. *A Fierce Green Fire: The American Environmental Movement.* New York: Hill and Wang, 1993.

Web Sites

Environmental Protection Agency, http://www.epa.gov.

CHAPTER 3

Love Canal

Hazardous Waste and the Politics of Fear

In the summer of 1978, Americans began to hear about a terrifying public health nightmare in Niagara Falls, New York. According to news reports, hundreds of families were being poisoned by a leaking toxic waste dump underneath their homes. Residents—plagued by cancer, miscarriages, and birth defects—were demanding to be evacuated and relocated. The episode, known simply as "Love Canal," became a national story because "it radicalized apparently ordinary people. [It] severed the bond between citizens and their city, their state, and their country."[1] Love Canal also shaped public attitudes about abandoned toxic dump sites—about the risks they pose and about government's responsibility for ensuring they are cleaned up. Finally, the incident was the catalyst for the nation's most expensive environmental law: the Comprehensive Environmental Response, Compensation, and Liability Act of 1980, popularly known as the Superfund Act.

The Love Canal case is important because it highlights the role of science and scientific experts in controversies over threats to human health. In such cases, public perceptions of risk dictate the political response, and experts contribute—often unwittingly—to public alarm and confusion. While scientists are fairly confident about the toxic effects of many chemicals in large doses, they are much more circumspect about the impact of prolonged exposure to small amounts of the same chemicals. Scientists base their risk assessments on animal bioassays, epidemiological studies, and cellular analyses, all of which yield highly uncertain results.[2] Because the results of such research do not translate directly into estimates of a chemical's carcinogenicity for humans, scientists can provide only educated guesses about those effects. Those estimates, in turn, are likely to reflect the experts' beliefs about the levels of risk to which the public *ought* to be exposed.[3] Under such conditions "technical expertise becomes a resource exploited by all parties to justify their political and economic views."[4] Further research may exacerbate political disagreements rather than resolve them.[5]

Although experts are uncertain about the risks posed by exposure to low levels of toxic chemicals, citizen groups formed in response to the apparent threats posed by toxic waste dumps and nuclear facilities—known as NIMBY (not-in-my-backyard) groups—have become commonplace. One critic describes them disparagingly:

Nimbys are noisy. Nimbys are powerful. Nimbys are everywhere. Nimbys are people who live near enough to corporate or government projects and are upset enough about them to work to stop, stall, or shrink them. Nimbys organize, march, sue, and petition to block the developers they think are threatening them. They twist the arms of politicians and they learn how to influence regulators. They fight fiercely and then, win or lose, they vanish.[6]

Initially, critics of the NIMBY phenomenon characterized such grassroots groups as emotional, uninformed, and unscientific; motivated by selfish interests, in particular by concern about property values; and unwilling to bear the costs associated with their lifestyles. As scholars have studied citizen opposition to noxious facilities, however, they have uncovered a more complex set of motives. Charles Piller argues that NIMBY groups unite disparate individuals to defy experts and technocrats who would impose risks on communities without consulting residents. According to Piller, members of NIMBY groups share a set of common characteristics: they perceive themselves as victims and are intensely focused on preserving their home environment.[7] Other studies have found that members of NIMBY groups think facilities in general impose serious health risks and are wary of government.[8] Still others emphasize that citizens' perceptions of risks take into account psychological, emotional, or social impacts of a facility on a community, whereas experts consider only the numerical probability of an accident.[9] In short, like members of more conventional environmental organizations, NIMBYists are deeply concerned with the impact of toxic substances and new technologies on human health; while the former are united for the longer term around shared ideals, however, the latter come together out of more immediate concerns and typically disband once the crisis passes.

The media play a major role in prompting NIMBY groups to form. Reporting on a risk mobilizes citizens in part because people assume that the more attention the media pay to a risk the worst it must be; according to psychologist Baruch Fischoff, "If scientists are studying it and the news reports it, people assume it must be worth their attention."[10] In addition, because media coverage emphasizes dramatic, newsworthy events, it is likely to be alarming, rather than calming. The media also amply NIMBY groups' political influence by covering of their activities. By focusing on human interest stories and anecdotes, the media create victims and assign responsibility for harm. When such stories involve human health threats, particularly to children, they appeal to highly consensual values and thus have enormous potential to resonate with the public. Media attention is effective not only because it galvanizes the larger public but because elected officials fear the consequences of negative publicity.[11] Critical media coverage may put policymakers on the defensive, forcing them either to justify a problem or act to solve it.[12] In addition, policymakers use the extent of media coverage as an indicator of public opinion on that issue.[13]

Publicity is often necessary to overcome state and local officials' resistance to addressing environmental problems. Those officials feel constrained by the need to foster economic development in order to retain high-income taxpayers.[14] In addition, because industry is mobile, they are cautious about taking on polluters for fear of alienating industries that employ citizens in the community.[15] Finally, they may be reluctant to intervene because they want to avoid financial responsibility for problems that promise to be costly to solve.

The story of Love Canal illustrates how experts, the media, and citizens interacted to overwhelm governmental resistance in the most famous hazardous waste crisis in U.S. history.

BACKGROUND

Love Canal is the site of a forty-acre chemical landfill in the city of Niagara Falls, New York. In the late nineteenth century, entrepreneur William T. Love received permission from the New York State legislature to build a canal that would divert the Niagara River away from the falls for about seven miles, dropping some 280 feet before it reconnected to the river. The canal, which would produce electricity while enabling navigation of the river, was the centerpiece of Love's scheme to construct a vast industrial city fueled by cheap and abundant hydropower.

Love dug a mile-long trench that was ten to forty feet deep and about fifteen feet wide, then built a factory and a few homes alongside it. But his dream collapsed in the mid-1890s when a financial depression caused investors to withdraw their support. In any case, the advent of alternating current allowing power to be transported over long distances rendered the notion of an industrial city near its power source less compelling. In a final blow, the U.S. Congress passed a law barring Love from diverting water from the Niagara because it wanted to preserve the falls. The abandoned canal soon became a popular fishing, swimming, and picnicking spot for residents.

In 1920, the canal was sold at public auction and became a municipal disposal site. Then, in 1942, the Niagara Power and Development Corporation gave the Hooker Chemical and Plastics Corporation permission to dispose of wastes in the abandoned canal, and in 1947 it sold the canal and sixteen acres of surrounding land to Hooker. Between 1942 and 1952, Hooker dumped 25,000 tons of toxic chemical wastes at the site, widening or deepening the canal at places to accommodate its needs.[16] Company officials were aware that the materials they were dumping were dangerous to human health; residents recall workers at the site had to rush to neighboring yards to wash their burns with water from garden hoses. As early as 1943, a letter to the *Niagara Gazette* claimed that the smell was unbearable and that the white cloud that came from the site "killed the trees and burnt the paint off the back of the houses and made the other houses all black."[17] A favorite game of neighborhood children was to pick up phosphorous rocks, throw them against the cement, and watch them explode. In the hot weather, spontaneous fires broke out, and noxious odors wafted through open windows of nearby homes.[18] Nevertheless, from the company's perspective, the site was ideal: it was large, lined with walls of thick, impermeable clay, and located in a thinly populated area. Furthermore, although Hooker took only minimal safety precautions—simply depositing drums or dumping the wastes directly into the pits and covering them with small amounts of topsoil—the company followed dumping practices legally acceptable at the time.

By 1952, the canal was nearly full. Hooker and the city of Niagara Falls covered the dumpsite with a protective clay cap and earth, and soon weeds and grasses began to sprout on its surface. In 1953, when city officials were looking for a plot on which to build a school, Hooker obliged them by transferring the sixteen-acre site to the Board of Education for a token fee of one dollar. At that time, Hooker issued no public or private warnings about the possible hazards posed by the buried chemicals. The company did, however, include in the deed a brief disclaimer that identified the wastes in a general way and excused it from liability for any injuries or deaths that might occur at the site. School board members toured the site with Hooker representatives and took test borings that showed chemicals in two locations only four feet below the surface. The school board—apparently unconcerned about any potential health threat and despite the misgivings of its own architect—began to build an elementary school and playground at the canal's midsection. When workers started to excavate and discovered chemical pits and buried drums, the board simply moved the school eighty-five feet north and installed a drainage system to divert accumulating water into the Niagara River.

Not long after the school was completed, the school board donated some property to the city so that it could build streets and sidewalks. Shortly thereafter, some homebuilders approached the school board about trading part of the Love Canal site for parcels the board wanted. At a meeting in November 1957, representatives of Hooker appeared and strongly opposed the trade, saying they had made clear at the original transfer that the site was unsuitable for any construction that required basements and sewer lines. The school board voted against the trade; nonetheless, developers began to build modest, single-family homes around the borders of the site. During construction, contractors cut channels through the clay walls lining the hidden canal and used topsoil from the canal surface for fill. Since the land the homes were on was not part of the original transaction between the school board and Hooker, the property owners' deeds did not notify them of chemicals buried in the adjoining land.[19]

In 1960, the school board gave the northern portion of the site to the city, and in 1961, it sold the southern portion at auction. By that time, the city had already installed streets paralleling and crisscrossing the canal. In the late 1960s, the state ran the LaSalle Expressway through the southern end of the site, necessitating relocation of a main street and uncovering chemical wastes that Hooker agreed to cart away.[20] By the early 1970s, the area around the canal was a working-class neighborhood; there were nearly one hundred homes on 97th and 99th Streets with backyards abutting a long, empty lot that should have been 98th Street but was really a chemical-filled trench (see Map 3-1).[21]

Map 3-1 Love Canal Emergency Declaration Area

Berghóltz Creek

Black Creek

91ST STREET

*93rd Street
School*

COLVIN BOULEVARD

Ring I

92ND STREET

93RD STREET

95TH STREET

102ND STREET

*LaSalle
Development*

**LOVE
CANAL**

Ring II

*99th
Street
School*

Ring II

Cayuga Creek

*LaSalle
Development*

Ring I

LASALLE EXPRESSWAY

Little Niagara River

Cayuga Island

LASALLE EXPRESSWAY

182

62

Berghóltz Creek

Niagara Falls

**Emergency
Declaration
Area**

*102nd Street
Landfill*

U.S.
CANADA

Tonowanda Channel

Grand Island

190

0   2
MILES

Emergency Declaration Area
(EDA) boundary

Ring I and Ring II; homes
immediately adjacent to
canal, which were destroyed

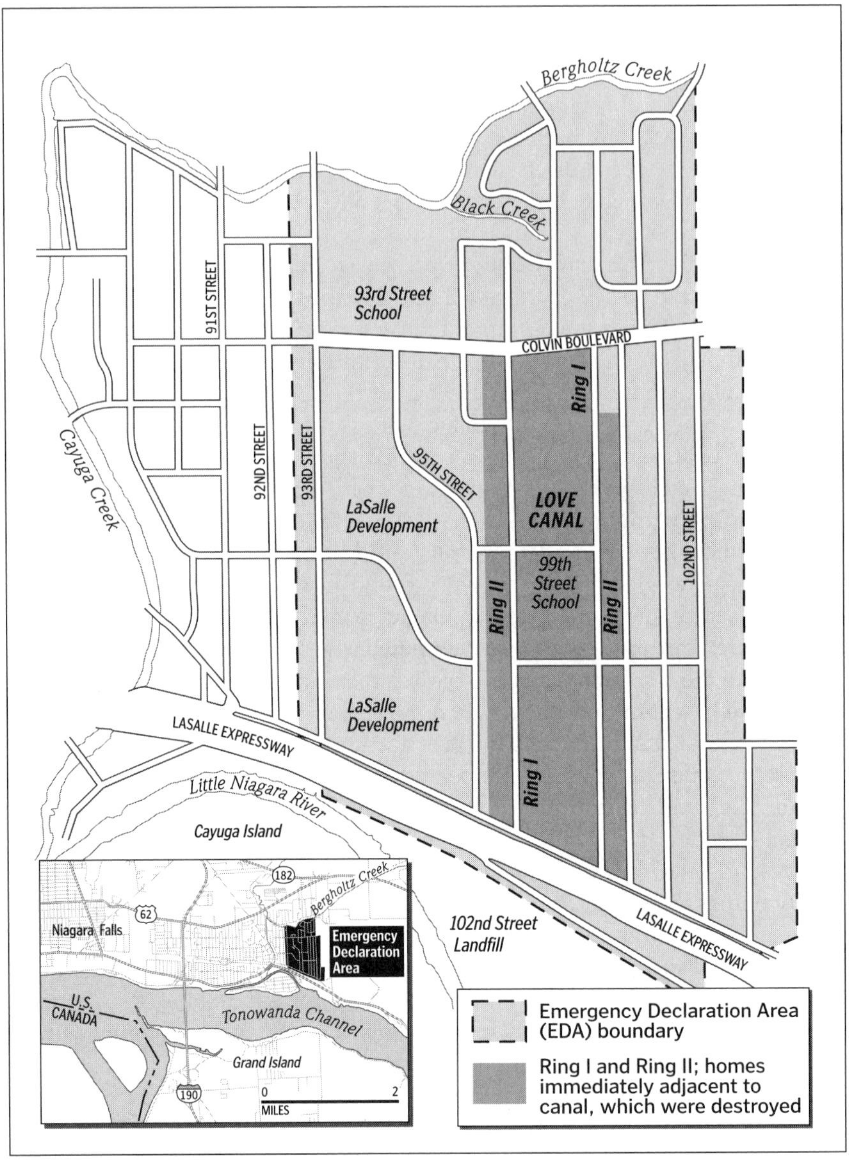

Source: New York State Department of Health, www.health.state.ny.us/nysdoh/
lcanal/lcdec88.pdf

Individual residents around the Love Canal site throughout the 1950s and 1960s complained to the municipal government about odors and odd afflictions, including rashes and respiratory problems, as well as oily black substances in basements and exposed, rusting barrels in fields around their homes. Members of crews building streets in the area complained of itchy skin and blisters. In 1958, Hooker investigated reports that three or four children had been burned by debris on their former property, but the company did not publicize the presence of the chemicals even after this incident, probably because it feared liability.[22] Municipal records indicate that, by 1969, building inspectors had also examined an area at or near the Love Canal dumpsite and reported that the conditions were hazardous, with holes in the surface of the field formed by rusting barrels collapsing and chemical residues left on the surface after rainwater had evaporated.[23] Still, the city took no action to investigate the problem further or to remedy it.

THE CASE

The early history of Love Canal reveals Americans' general faith in technology and complacency about chemical wastes during the postwar years, rather than venality on the part of municipal officials. Even in the 1970s, however, when it became apparent that there were potentially serious problems at the site, local officials continued to ignore them or tried to deal with them quietly, fearing not only the costs of cleanup but also the consequences of antagonizing a major employer and source of tax revenue. Addressing the possible hazards in the area promised to inflict economic consequences and tarnish the city's image. Only when the media began to pay attention to the issue, in turn prompting residents to mobilize and demand a solution, did elected officials respond.

The City of Niagara Falls Stonewalls

In the mid-1970s, when a prolonged period of wet weather dramatically changed the area's hydrology, visible signs of a problem at Love Canal began to appear. The LaSalle Expressway along the canal's southern end blocked the groundwater from migrating southward to the Niagara River. In 1976, the built-up groundwater overflowed the clay basin holding the waste and carried contaminants through the upper silt layer and along recently constructed sewer lines. From there it seeped into yards and basements of nearby houses.

Trees and shrubs in the area began to turn brown and die. The field covering the canal site turned into a mucky quagmire dotted with pools of contaminated liquid. One family became alarmed when they noticed their pool had risen two feet out of the ground. When they removed the pool, the hole quickly filled with chemical liquid, and soon their backyard was a wasteland. Local authorities pumped 17,500 gallons of chemical-filled water out of the yard in two days. After even the county's biggest waste disposal company refused to handle it, the waste was finally trucked to Ohio and poured down a deep-well disposal site.[24]

In 1977, Michael Brown, a reporter from the *Niagara Gazette,* became interested in Love Canal after hearing an eloquent plea for help from a resident at a public meeting. When Brown began to investigate, it became clear to him that both the city manager and the mayor of Niagara Falls were stonewalling residents who tried to contact them or to speak up in city council meetings. Brown quickly ascertained that city officials had been aware for some time that the situation was serious.

While making his inquiries, Brown also discovered that a fellow reporter, David Pollack, had documented the history of chemical dumping at Love Canal in October 1976. When Pollack got a private company, Chem-Trol, to analyze the sludge from some Love Canal basements, that company found toxic chemicals and determined that Hooker was their source. Pollack had also ascertained that early in 1976 the New York Department of Environmental Conservation (DEC) had begun testing houses around the canal site after they traced high levels of the pesticide Mirex in Lake Ontario fish to a dumpsite adjacent to the canal.[25] The DEC's investigation revealed that polychlorinated biphenyls (PCBs) and other highly toxic materials were flowing from the canal into adjoining sewers.[26] The DEC's study was proceeding slowly, however, because the agency lacked adequate funding, personnel, and equipment. Furthermore, the DEC got little cooperation: Hooker denied all responsibility, and municipal officials—uneasy about antagonizing the city's largest industrial employer and worried about the magnitude of the city's own liability—preferred to address the problem discreetly.

In April 1977, the city (with some funding from Hooker) hired the Calspan Corporation to develop a program to reduce the groundwater pollution at Love Canal. Calspan documented the presence of exposed, corroded drums and noxious fumes and notified officials that chemical contamination was extensive. That summer, the *Niagara Gazette* published a summary of the Calspan report and urged the city to undertake the cleanup project recommended by its consultants. The city declined, however, and the story was insufficiently dramatic to capture residents' attention. However, in September a municipal employee concerned about the city's inaction contacted the district's member of Congress, John LaFalce, and urged him to tour the area. Unable to get a response from the city manager, LaFalce asked the Environmental Protection Agency (EPA) to test the air in the basements along 97th and 99th Streets. In October, soon after LaFalce's visit, the regional EPA administrator wrote in an internal memorandum that, based on what he had seen, "serious thought should be given to the purchase of some or all of the houses affected."[27]

By April 1978, New York health commissioner Robert Whalen had become sufficiently concerned that he directed the health commissioner of Niagara County to remove exposed chemicals, build a fence around the dumpsite, and begin health studies of area residents.[28] The following month, the EPA released the results of its air sampling studies. At a public meeting at the 99th Street School, agency officials told residents that they had found benzene in the air of their basements. At this point, Michael Brown, shocked by the EPA's reports and disturbed by the unwillingness of local officials to acknowledge the seriousness of the problem, undertook his own investigation.

The Local Media Raise Residents' Concern

Brown's story in the *Niagara Gazette* on the benzene hazard claimed that there was a "full fledged environmental crisis" under way at Love Canal. With local and county authorities unwilling to investigate further, Brown conducted an informal health survey and found a startling list of residents' ailments—from ear infections and nervous disorders to rashes and headaches. Pets were losing their fur and getting skin lesions and tumors; women seemed to have a disproportionate incidence of cancer; and several children were deaf.[29]

By repeating residents' claims about their health problems, Brown's reporting enhanced their perceptions of the threats posed by the buried chemicals. Up until the spring of 1978, residents had been only dimly aware of the potential association between the fumes, the chemical wastewater, and their health problems. But as articles began to appear in the *Niagara Gazette* and then in the Buffalo papers that May and June, some local people became alarmed. Lois Gibbs, a resident of 101st Street since 1972, made a frightening connection: Gibbs's son, Michael, had begun attending kindergarten at the 99th Street School and had developed epilepsy soon afterwards. Gibbs contacted her brother-in-law, a biologist at the State University of New York (SUNY) at Buffalo, and he explained the health problems that could be produced by chemicals dumped in the canal. Gibbs tried to transfer Michael to a different school, but school administrators resisted.

Disconcerted, the normally reticent Gibbs started going door to door with a petition demanding that the city address residents' concerns about the school. Spending day after day talking with neighbors, she discovered that some homeowners, worried about declining property values, had formed a group to agitate for property tax abatement and mortgage relief. Gibbs also became deeply familiar with the health problems of canal area residents. To her,

> it seemed as though every home on 99th Street had someone with an illness. One family had a young daughter with arthritis. . . . Another daughter had had a miscarriage. The father, still a fairly young man, had had a heart attack . . . . Then I remembered my own neighbors. One . . . was suffering from severe migraines and had been hospitalized three or four times that year. Her daughter had kidney problems and bleeding. A woman on the other side of us had gastrointestinal problems. A man in the next house down was dying of lung cancer and he didn't even work in the [chemical] industry. The man across the street had just had lung surgery.[30]

Armed with this worrisome anecdotal evidence, Gibbs transformed herself into a highly effective policy entrepreneur. Although this was her first experience with political activism, Gibbs realized that she would need an organization behind her to wield any political clout. Following the strategic advice of her brother-in-law, she founded the Love Canal Homeowners Association (LCHA), which became the most visible and persistent of the citizen groups formed during this period. Gibbs devoted nearly all her waking hours to its activities. Her primary function was to promote a simple causal story—that Hooker had irresponsibly dumped dangerous chemicals that were making residents ill—and link it to her preferred solution: evacuation and compensation for all the families in the area.

Assessing (and Avoiding) Blame

The first response of government officials to LCHA activism was to assign responsibility to other levels of government. "It's a county health problem," said City Manager Donald O'Hara. "But if the state says the city has the authority to move them out and the people want to be moved, then we'll move them." Dr. Francis J. Clifford, the county health commissioner, responded: "Of course Don O'Hara says the responsibility is with the county. I'd say the same thing. The lawyers will fight it out."[31] Everyone hoped to pin the blame on the federal government, with its deep pockets, especially upon hearing of witnesses' claims that the U.S. Army had also dumped wastes into the canal in the early 1950s. But after a brief investigation, the Department of Defense denied those allegations.

In the meantime, the county did little more than install a couple of inexpensive fans in two homes and erect a fence through which children could still walk without knocking it over. The municipal government was equally dilatory: the city council voted not to spend public money for cleanup, since some of the site was owned by a private citizen living in Philadelphia. The city's tax assessor refused to grant any tax abatement on the homes, even though banks would not mortgage them and lawyers refused to title them.[32]

The city was also reluctant to pursue Hooker Chemical because it was an important employer and taxpayer in an area historically dependent on the chemical industry. At that time, Hooker employed about 3,000 workers from the Niagara area. The plant at Niagara Falls was the largest of Hooker's sixty manufacturing operations, and Hooker's corporate headquarters were there as well. Even more importantly, Hooker was contemplating erecting a $17 million headquarters downtown. Municipal officials were offering Hooker a lucrative package of tax breaks and loans as well as a $13.2 million mortgage on a prime parcel of land.[33]

Hooker itself maintained from the outset that it had no legal obligations with respect to Love Canal. The company retaliated against the negative press coverage with a concerted effort to redefine the problem: it launched a nationwide campaign involving thousands of glossy pamphlets and a traveling two-man "truth" squad to convince the media that the problems at Love Canal were not its fault. Hooker representatives emphasized that, in their view, the canal had been the best available technology at the time. The company, they said, was merely acting as a good corporate citizen, not admitting guilt, when it contributed money toward the city-sponsored Calspan study and volunteered to share cleanup costs.

The National Media Expand the Scope of the Conflict

Ordinarily, such a united front by industry and local officials would have squelched attempts at remediation; however, citizens' mobilization—combined with sympathetic media coverage of their complaints and demonstrations—enhanced their clout. Early August marked a turning point in the controversy because the arrival of *New York Times* reporter Donald McNeil on the scene transformed the issue from a local to a national one. In turn, national press coverage inflamed residents' passion and further escalated tensions.[34] Within a day of McNeil's first report on the situation, reporters from other national newspapers converged on Niagara Falls. The media's coverage of the ensuing confrontations was compelling because it conveyed the image of Hooker as at worst a malevolent and at best an irresponsible villain, while depicting residents as average—even virtuous—citizens and innocent victims.

As Gibbs and others organized residents, the New York Department of Health (DOH) was collecting blood samples, surveying residents, and testing air samples in homes. In early July 1978, residents received forms from the state indicating high levels of chemicals in their houses but providing very little information about what those levels meant. Then, on August 2, Commissioner Whalen announced the results of DOH's first large-scale health study of the area: researchers had found ten carcinogenic compounds in vapors in the houses at levels from 250 to 5,000 times as high as those considered safe. They also found that women living at the southern end of the canal suffered an unusually high rate of miscarriages and that their children were afflicted with an abnormally high rate of birth defects: a 29.4 percent miscarriage rate and five children out of twenty-four with birth defects. Four children in one small section of the neighborhood had serious birth defects, clubfeet, retardation, and deafness. The people who had lived in the area the longest had the most problems.[35]

Commissioner Whalen declared a public health emergency and concluded that there was a "great and imminent peril" to the health of the people living in and around Love Canal.[36] He urged people to take precautionary measures to avoid contamination but offered no permanent solutions. He was unwilling to declare the area uninhabitable, but he advised people to avoid spending time in their basements or eating vegetables from their gardens. Finally, he recommended that pregnant women and children under the age of two move out of the area.

On August 3, 150 residents—incensed by Whalen's announcement and fueled by the media coverage—met in front of their homes to collect mortgage bills and resolve not to pay them. They also planned to demand aid from the government or Hooker so they could relocate. Said one resident: "If they take my house, I owe $10,000 on it. I couldn't sell it for ten. They won't kick me out for two years, and that's two years' taxes and payments I save to find some-place else."[37] The following evening, the first families began leaving the con-taminated site, toting their cribs and suitcases past a scrawled sign that read: "Wanted, safe home for two toddlers."

Public meetings, which had been tense all summer, became increasingly acrimonious. Residents were frustrated because DOH scientists, in their attempts to conduct objective research, were reluctant to counsel fearful resi-dents about the results of their medical tests. Furthermore, the government officials to whom the scientists deferred in decision making refused to act, awaiting definitive study results and, more importantly, a clear assessment of financial culpability. At one packed meeting in a hot, crowded school audito-rium, sobbing young mothers stood up shouting out the ages of their children or the terms of their pregnancies and asked whether they would be moved out of their homes. Angry young fathers, still in the sweaty T-shirts they had worn to work in local chemical factories, stood on chairs and demanded to know what would happen to their small children if their wives and infants were moved.[38]

Media coverage was particularly well-timed for Love Canal residents because the governor of New York was facing an election in November 1978 and so felt compelled to respond to their increasingly publicized pleas. The state set up an office in a local school and provided rent vouchers, medical advice, and moving help for the thirty-seven families with pregnant women or infants under two years of age. Nor could the federal government ignore the spate of stories: on August 6, 1978, William Wilcox of the Federal Disaster Assistance Administration inspected the site at the request of President Jimmy Carter. The following day, the president declared an emergency at Love Canal and approved federal relief funds for the area.[39]

Shortly after this announcement, Governor Hugh Carey finally toured Love Canal for the first time. During that visit, he pledged to relocate and purchase the homes of the residents of 97th and 99th Streets—the 239 "inner ring" fam-ilies. Once these families were evacuated, he said, the state planned to raze the houses and the 99th Street School and begin a massive construction program to stop the leaching and seal the canal. The remediation plan, laid out in an engineering study sponsored jointly by the city and Hooker, called for ditches to be dug eight to ten feet deep along the periphery of the filled canal and drainage tiles to be laid and covered over. Chemical-laden water leaking out of the old clay canal bed would run down the tiles into a collecting basin, from which it would be pumped and taken for treatment or disposal.

The Outer Ring Residents Are Left Behind

The residents of the "outer ring" between 93rd and 103rd Streets were enraged by this solution, feeling that the state was ignoring their plight. They too had experienced health problems, and studies had detected high levels of chemicals in their homes as well. Under the supervision of Beverly Paigen, a biologist and cancer researcher who had been helping residents interpret the information they were receiving from the health department, the LCHA undertook a telephone survey to ascertain the pattern of illnesses in the historically wet drainage areas around the canal. But when Dr. Paigen analyzed the data and presented her results, complete with qualifying statements about her methodology, the DOH dismissed her findings, saying that the study was meaningless because it was put together by a "bunch of housewives with an interest in the outcome of the study."[40]

Frustrated, Lois Gibbs and the LCHA continued to press the state to relocate the outer ring families, fearing their political leverage would decline after the gubernatorial election in November. By this point, Gibbs had become adept at raising the salience of her cause: she orchestrated dozens of public demonstrations and rallies, wrote letters and made phone calls to officials, submitted to interviews on talk shows and news programs, and even testified before a congressional subcommittee. As a result, her version of events dominated national perceptions of the situation.

The state nevertheless continued to resist the idea of relocating the families who lived on the outskirts of the contaminated area. Groups of angry, outer ring residents began to picket the cleanup site and, on December 11, about fifty people braved twelve-degree temperatures to stop workers' cars attempting to enter the site. The police arrested six demonstrators obstructing traffic. Deepening residents' desperation, the state announced it had discovered dioxin at Love Canal. A *New York Times* report dramatized the lethal potential of dioxin, a byproduct of herbicide production, by noting that three ounces minced small enough into New York City's water supply could wipe out the city.[41]

To the disappointment of the LCHA, on January 29 the Federal Disaster Assistance Administration rejected an appeal from the state to reimburse it for the $23 million it spent removing the inner ring families and cleaning up the site. This decision increased financial pressure on state officials and made them even more reluctant to engage in a costly second relocation. The state's own experts were not cooperating, however; a blue-ribbon panel appointed by the governor concluded early in February that the area was hazardous, leading newly installed Health Commissioner David Axelrod to order that pregnant women and families with children under the age of two be removed temporarily from the area. This only fueled Gibbs's rage: she pointed out that if the area was dangerous for pregnant women and children, it posed a threat to everyone else as well.[42] Although twenty-four families moved, hundreds more remained in limbo. By this time, according to Gibbs, reporters were becoming impatient with the LCHA, and were beginning to ask, "If you're so afraid, why don't you just leave?" Residents replied that they were working people who had invested a lifetime of earnings in their homes. In any case, they asked, where would they go? What would they live on?

Experts vs. Citizens

For the families that remained, more uncertainty lay ahead. The $9.2 million cleanup effort encountered frequent delays as people raised safety concerns and public officials quarreled over new health studies. By August 1979, Love Canal residents had endured another long, hot summer made more oppressive by the fumes from the remedial construction site. For weeks people had been calling the LCHA office to say they were experiencing headaches, difficulty breathing, and burning, itching eyes. The DOH scheduled a public meeting for August 21, and residents again anticipated answers to questions about their health and their future.

Instead, what turned out to be the final meeting between residents and the Commissioner of Public Health did little more than clinch the antagonism between them. During the meeting, Dr. Axelrod acknowledged that the department had found dioxin in the soil, but said the remaining residents would have to deal with the risks on their own. With that, what little remained of residents' faith in scientific experts and government officials evaporated. Lois Gibbs says the officials "offered no answers, no useful information. The residents' confidence was shaken time and again. They didn't trust the safety plan or the construction plan or the health department officials. People were more frustrated when they left than when they arrived."[43] Sociologist Adeline Levine describes in vivid terms the deepening alienation of residents:

> The more that officials met with residents, the more negative feelings and relationships developed. When officials presented raw data, it confused people. When they tried to interpret the data in down-to-earth terms, describing risks as some number of deaths in excess of the usual number expected, people interpreted that to imply *their* deaths and their children's deaths. When they tried to calm people by saying that, despite all the serious possibilities, there was no evidence of serious health effects, the officials were seen as covering up, since no health studies had been done. Authorities trying to coordinate multiple governmental and private agencies were seen as wasting time in meetings. What the officials thought of as privileged advisory conferences were viewed as conclaves that excluded affected citizens. What officials saw as preliminary studies conducted to assess the situation were viewed by residents as wasting resources on repetitive research projects rather than doing something helpful. When they took action quickly or tried to do everything at once, for everyone, they overloaded facilities, made errors, and were faulted for bungling.[44]

At the end of August 1979, the Niagara Falls school board voted to close the 93rd Street School. Shortly thereafter, 110 families moved into hotels, taking advantage of an LCHA-initiated court settlement in which state officials agreed that, until the drainage ditches were complete, they would pay the hotel bills and a $13 per day meal allowance for those suffering medical problems because of fumes from the remedial construction site. The state emphasized that it was not paying for a permanent evacuation.

On November 6, the state finished construction of the multimillion-dollar drainage system at the dump site, and officials announced that the families could return to their homes. But a dozen of them refused. Challenging the cutoff of payments and asserting that their homes continued to be unsafe, the group vowed to stay at the motel until they were carried out.[45] As usual, Gibbs was hoping the motel sit-in would draw high-level attention to the situation facing the outer ring residents. She was well aware that Governor Carey had, in fact, already signed legislation authorizing the state to spend $5 million to buy up to 550 additional homes in the outer ring, most of them to the west of the canal, including her own house. The buyout had been mired in political squabbles and red tape, however, as local officials continued to resist responsibility for the problem.

Health Studies Breed Panic and More Publicity

By the end of 1979, money for relocating the outer ring families still was not forthcoming. As negotiations between the state and federal governments dragged on, skeptical residents feared that the public's interest was beginning to wane and that with it would go the pressure on politicians to act. But federal officials had unwittingly set in motion the catalyst that would change the fortunes of Love Canal residents irrevocably. In early 1979, the EPA—hoping to bolster its tarnished public image on dealing with hazardous waste—had created a Hazardous Waste Enforcement Task Force whose first assignment was to collect information about Love Canal. On December 20, the Department of Justice, relying on evidence gathered by the task force, filed a lawsuit on behalf of the EPA against Hooker Chemical, the City of Niagara Falls, the Niagara County Health Department, and the Board of Education of the City of Niagara Falls. The suit demanded $124.5 million, an end to the discharge of toxins in the Love Canal area, cleanup of the site, and relocation of residents if necessary. It was a landmark lawsuit because it asked the court to hold a private company retroactively liable for wastes it dumped many years ago in a site it no longer controlled.

To establish liability, however, the Justice Department had to prove that the health damages suffered by residents were linked directly to Hooker's wastes. Evidence had shown that the area was contaminated by toxic chemicals and that residents had unusually high rates of health problems, but to link those damages unequivocally to Hooker required further evidence. The Justice Department and the EPA hired Biogenics of Houston, headed by Dr. Dante Picciano, to investigate chromosomal damage among the residents, since such damage indicates exposure to toxic chemicals. The lawyers intended this to be a purely exploratory study that they could follow up with a full-blown epidemiological study if the results were positive.

From the outset, however, Picciano's work was flawed in ways that jeopardized its credibility. First, Picciano himself was a controversial figure; he had had a much-publicized falling out with his former employer, Dow Chemical, over his tests of that company's workers. Second, and more importantly, the study of Love Canal residents did not include a control group, apparently because the EPA did not wish to spend the time or money for one. And third, researchers selected study participants according to criteria that would maximize the chance of finding defects; that is, they intentionally chose people who had had miscarriages or other health problems. Nevertheless, in spring 1980, the study moved forward.

On February 24, 1980, more alarm bells went off when the EPA announced that air monitors in two houses several hundred yards from the fence around the canal had detected four suspected carcinogens: benzene, chloroform, trichloroethylene, and tetrachloroethylene. To residents' dismay, that disclosure merited only a few paragraphs in the Metro section of the *New York Times*. Similarly, only passing notice was taken of Attorney General Robert Abrams' filing, on April 28, of a lawsuit against the Occidental Petroleum Corporation and two of its subsidiaries, the Hooker Chemical Corporation and the Hooker Chemicals and Plastics Corporation, charging them with responsibility for the Love Canal disaster. With a presidential campaign in full swing, an influx of Cuban refugees, and the eruption of Mt. St. Helens, the focus of the national press had shifted.

Early in May, however, attention returned abruptly to Love Canal when Biogenics made the preliminary results of its study available. Dr. Picciano reported that he had found chromosomal aberrations in eleven of the thirty-six individuals tested. He concluded that eight of them had a rare condition called "supernumerary acrocentric fragments," or extra pieces of genetic material.[46] According to Picciano, such abnormalities should occur in only one person out of one hundred and might forewarn increased risk of miscarriages, stillborns, birth defects, or cancer. Nevertheless, he cautioned prudence in using this data in the absence of a control group.

On May 17, someone leaked the Biogenics story to the *New York Times*, and the EPA had to scramble to control the damage. The agency hastily scheduled a press conference in Niagara, preceded by private consultations with each of the residents in whom Picciano had detected abnormalities. The EPA set aside half an hour for each family with a doctor who would explain the results and answer questions. Following the individual sessions, EPA representatives gave local and national press conferences. Although officials were aware of the need for cautious interpretation of the study results, they were unable to control the ensuing media frenzy.

Love Canal residents were stunned by the news, and as White House officials held strategy meetings in Washington they became increasingly upset. Federal officials, recognizing the impact of the media coverage, raced to get the Biogenics study peer reviewed and decide on a course of action. In the meantime, the *New York Times* reported that Governor Carey and the White House were in an all-out feud over who would foot the bill for a large-scale relocation, which now appeared unavoidable.

At the LCHA offices on Monday, a crowd of anxious residents and the press gathered to await news of the government's next move. When the *Buffalo Evening News* reported that the "White House Blocks Love Canal Pullout," the crowd became agitated: people began stopping cars to spread the word, and one group set a fire in the shape of the letters "EPA" across the street. A few minutes later, a crowd of 200 blocked traffic on both ends of the street. Gibbs, hoping to defuse residents' ire, summoned the two EPA officials who were still in Niagara to address the crowd. Once they arrived at the LCHA offices, however, Gibbs refused to allow them to leave. For several hours, the residents held the officials hostage in their sweltering offices. Gibbs explained that they were simply protecting the officials from a potentially violent mob. She moved back and forth between the crowd and the hostages, assuring each that the situation was under control. Finally, the FBI threatened to rush the crowd. Three FBI agencies, four U.S. marshals, and six members of the Niagara Falls Police Department escorted the EPA officials from the LCHA office without further incident. Although it was resolved quietly, the episode left little doubt about residents' desperation.[47]

Figuring Out Who Will Pay

Ultimately it was the escalation of panic in Niagara Falls and across the nation—not the health studies, which continued to be inconclusive—that finally compelled politicians at the federal and state levels to support relocation for the remaining Love Canal homeowners. Officials had to work out the particulars, such as whether the move would be permanent or temporary and, most importantly, who would pay for it. Governor Carey, taking advantage of presidential election year politics, exerted continuous pressure on the Carter administration to finance a permanent move for residents living adjacent to the canal. He complained that the state had already shelled out $35 million for the initial evacuation and subsequent moves. Each day the press reported a new plea from the state to the federal government for relocation funds. Adding fuel to the fire, on May 21, the *New York Times* reported that a study had found nerve damage in twenty-eight of thirty-five Love Canal residents examined, whereas only two out of twenty in the Niagara Falls control group had similar ailments. Moreover, there was a qualitative difference in the nature of the impairment between the two groups.[48]

That afternoon, following media coverage of the latest study, President Carter declared a second federal emergency at Love Canal and urged the remaining families to move to temporary housing. The second Emergency Declaration Area was bound to the south by the LaSalle Expressway, to the east by uninhabited wooded wetlands, to the north by the Black and Bergholtz creeks, and to the west by 93rd Street (see Map 3-1). The relocation was intended to last up to a year, in order to give the EPA sufficient time to study the results of further medical tests of residents. The Federal Emergency Management Agency (FEMA) was to supervise the evacuation and relocation. When asked what finally prompted the federal government to act, EPA spokesperson Barbara Blum replied, "We haven't felt that we've had enough evidence before now."[49]

Five days after the president authorized the temporary relocation of 800 families, only 220 had registered for the move. Aware of their increasing leverage, many of the others said they would not leave until the government bought their houses. Residents also said they would refuse to participate in further health testing programs until an agreement was reached on the purchase of their homes. "We are not going to let the government use us as guinea pigs," said a spokesperson for the LCHA.[50] On May 23, Governor Carey presented a detailed plan for the resettlement and estimated the cost at $25 million, of which the state was committed to paying one-fifth. The tug-of-war between the governor and President Carter dragged on as the state continued to demand money, while federal officials insisted that federal laws did not permit the purchase of homes under an emergency program.

In mid-June, Governor Carey proposed that the federal government lend the state $20 million of the $25 million necessary to relocate outer-ring residents. While residents awaited a decision, controversy continued to swirl around the health studies. On June 14, nearly a month after the original Biogenics study's release, a scientific panel appointed by the EPA debunked its conclusions. Dr. Roy Albert of the New York University Medical Center, who headed the panel, called the results "indeterminate" and "really of no use."[51] Neither Dr. Albert nor Dr. Picciano would speculate as to why the two studies came up with such different results, but geneticists point out that everyone has some chromosome damage—possibly from viral infections, medical X-rays, or exposure to chemicals and medication—and that the examination of cells is extremely subjective.[52] Adding to the confusion, two days later the EPA released another scientific review, this time one that tended to support the Biogenics study. The second study group, headed by Dr. Jack Killian of the University of Texas, said "some individuals in the study had aberrations that were beyond the normal limits expected in 36 healthy people."[53]

On June 23, the DOH announced that in the early 1960s half the pregnancies of women living on a street bordering Love Canal had ended in miscarriage. That compared with a normal miscarriage rate of 15 percent. A compilation of state studies performed in 1978, when the state first declared a health emergency, the report described unusual numbers of miscarriages and birth defects, as well as reduced infant weight. The health effects had peaked in the neighborhood about twenty years earlier, the report said, within a decade of most of the dumping. The journal *Science* rejected the report for publication, however, saying it was statistically unsound.[54]

Throughout the summer, as experts debated the scientific merits of the health studies, the press perpetuated the causal story favored by Love Canal residents, portraying them as patriotic, working-class victims of corporate greed who had been abandoned by the government. "I can think of three or four [men] right off hand who say they'll never serve the country again for the simple reason that when they needed us, we were there," said one man. "Now they're turning their backs on us. It kind of makes you feel bad."[55] The *New York Times* ran such stories as "For One Love Canal Family, the Road to Despair" and "Love Canal Families Are Left With a Legacy of Pain and Anger." Journalists reported that, along with a sense of abandonment and isolation, many in Love

Canal were feeling a loss of control over their lives. "They realize that this loss of control stems from long-ago decisions to bury chemicals and then to build homes near that spot, not from decisions they made," said sociologist Adeline Levine. "Now control rests in large measure on the decisions on distant political figures."[56]

Touching on issues sure to elicit public sympathy, reporters noted that the disaster had particularly acute consequences for many of the area's children. They interviewed one young pediatrician who had helped to bring about the closing of the 93rd Street School because he had noticed in the mid-1970s that asthma and other respiratory diseases seemed to occur more frequently in Love Canal children than in his other patients. As the crisis unfolded, the children he saw began to manifest psychological problems, which he believed grew out of their intractable illnesses as well as the emotional hothouses in which they lived. "A lot of these kids are really upset that things might grow from their bodies, or that they might die prematurely," Dr. James Dunlop said.[57]

The Final Evacuation

The media portrait ultimately stirred a political response: in September 1980, despite the ongoing controversy over the health studies, President Carter signed an agreement to lend the state of New York $7.5 million and provide a grant of another $7.5 million to purchase the homes of the relocated residents. To repay the loan, the newly formed Love Canal Area Revitalization Agency (LCARA) planned to rehabilitate the abandoned area and resell the homes. On October 2, the president signed the bill that finally made concrete federal support for the Love Canal evacuation and renewal.

Ironically, a week later a five-member panel of scientists appointed by Governor Carey in June told the press that "inadequate" scientific studies might have exaggerated the seriousness of the health problems caused by toxic wastes. Of the Biogenics study the panel said: "The design, implementation, and release of the EPA chromosome study has not only damaged the credibility of the science, but exacerbated any future attempts to determine whether and to what degree the health of Love Canal residents has been affected." The panel described Dr. Paigen's nervous system study as "literally impossible to interpret . . . . It cannot be taken seriously as a piece of sound epidemiological research." After reviewing the government and private research from the previous two years, the panel concluded: "There has been no demonstration of acute health effects linked to exposure to hazardous wastes at the Love Canal site." It added, however, that "chronic effects of hazardous waste exposure at Love Canal have neither been established nor ruled out as yet in a scientifically rigorous manner."[58]

Residents reacted bitterly to these findings because they feared that the report might allow the government to back out of its agreement to buy area homes. But the panel's eminent chairman, Dr. Lewis Thomas of the Memorial Sloan-Kettering Cancer Center, responded to residents' denunciations, saying he believed that the anguish caused by the presence of chemicals and the possibility of future findings were reason enough not to live in the area.[59] In the end, the federal government did not renege on the buyout.

OUTCOMES

The crisis at Love Canal affected not only residents of the area but national politics as well, since the episode opened a window of opportunity for national policymaking. As Daniel Mazmanian and David Morell write, "Love Canal was one of those rare catalytic events, one of those seemingly isolated incidents that so often throws an entire nation into turmoil. This unpredictable turning point in the late 1970s bared both the sensitive chemophobic nerve lurking just below the surface of American public consciousness and the growing lack of trust in both business and government expertise."[60] After Love Canal hit the headlines, the media expanded the scope of the conflict by covering similar horror stories across the nation.

The Superfund Law

Members of Congress, sensitive to the furor caused by Love Canal, responded quickly with an ambitious new law that established a system for identifying and neutralizing hazardous waste dump sites. In early December, Congress passed the Comprehensive Environmental Response, Compensation, and Liability Act of 1980 (CERCLA)—commonly known as the Superfund Act—and on December 11, 1980, President Carter signed the bill into law. The EPA had been pressing Congress for a hazardous waste cleanup law for some time, but the specter of an incoming Republican president—and the closing of the window of opportunity opened by Love Canal—prompted congressional Democrats to get on the bandwagon and scale back their proposals sufficiently to garner majority support.[61]

The design of CERCLA clearly reflects the impact of Love Canal in defining the problem of abandoned hazardous waste dumps. To avoid the kind of delays experienced at Love Canal, the act authorized the EPA to respond to hazardous substance emergencies and clean up leaking chemical dump sites if the responsible parties fail to take appropriate action or cannot be located. To speed up the process, CERCLA established a $1.6 billion trust fund, the Superfund, financed primarily by a tax on petrochemical feedstocks, organic chemicals, and crude oil imports. Congress also responded to the issues of corporate responsibility that were so painfully obvious at Love Canal by instituting strict, joint, and several liability.[62] Strict liability means that any company that disposed of hazardous waste, even if it did so legally, is automatically liable for the costs of cleanup. Joint and several liability means that one party may be held responsible for the entire cleanup cost, even if it dumped only some of the waste. Such an approach transfers the burden of proof from the victims of toxic pollution to the perpetrators; it also creates a powerful incentive for companies to dispose of waste in a precautionary way or to reduce the amount they generate out of fear of future liability.

Congress passed CERCLA by an overwhelming majority. Although they had no real idea of the scope of the problem, members of Congress were clearly moved by the anecdotal evidence of human health effects from exposure to toxic waste and, more importantly, by public fears of such effects.[63] In passing Superfund, Congress ignored the wishes of the influential Chemical Manufacturers Association, which had opposed any cleanup legislation. By failing to get on the bandwagon as passage of the bill became imminent, the chemical industry missed an opportunity to weaken the law, which is one reason its provisions are so punitive.[64]

Legislators' unanimity in passing the Superfund law reflects not simply heightened public attention combined with the industry's failure to cooperate, but also the widespread perception that the nation's hazardous waste problem was serious but manageable: initial EPA studies had concluded that between 1,000 and 2,000 sites needed remediation at an estimated cost of $3.6 to $4.4 million. By the mid-1980s, however, it was obvious that the EPA had grossly underestimated the number of sites requiring cleanup. By 1986, the agency had identified more than 27,000 abandoned hazardous waste sites across the nation and had assigned almost 1,000 of the most dangerous to its National Priority List (NPL). In 1986, Congress passed the Superfund Amendments and Reauthorization Act, which increased funding substantially and tightened cleanup standards. By 2000, 757 of the 1,274 sites on the NPL had been cleaned up substantially.[65] However, the EPA anticipates adding about one hundred more annually, until the list reaches 2,100. The U.S. General Accounting Office estimates that cleanups under the law will cost the federal government about $300 billion and the private sector hundreds of billions more.[66]

The Remediation and Resettlement of Love Canal

With the passage of Superfund, public and legislative attention turned to other matters, but the cleanup of Love Canal went quietly forward. By July 1989, a total of 1,030 families had left the area. Residents in all but two of the original 239 homes and all but seventy-two of the second 564 homes chose to move, as did most of the renters in the nearby housing project. Contractors razed the 99th Street Elementary School and the neat rows of houses adjacent to the six-block-long canal and then targeted their remediation efforts at containing the rubble in the forty-acre Love Canal landfill. Beyond the landfill, cleanup of the Emergency Declaration Area included decontaminating the area's storm sewers; dredging 3,000 feet of creek bed contaminated from rainwater runoff; returning to the landfill 11,000 cubic yards of contaminated soil at the neighboring 93rd Street Middle School that was transferred there in the 1960s; and excavating lesser amounts of soil from three contaminated "hotspots" created when former landowners stole fill from the canal before the problem was detected.[67]

Despite the massive restoration, Love Canal remained deserted well into the 1990s. As of December 1991, only about twenty-five families had moved into the neighborhood after the federal government declared the area safe for resettlement. According to journalist Leslie Gruson:

> Their refurbished homes sparkle[d] with new paint like oases in a sprawling desert of abandoned and decaying houses. Despite efforts to rejuvenate the area, it still [felt] and [looked] like a ghost town, or perhaps more accurately, a ghost suburb. The streets [were] silent, devoid of children. To prevent vandalism, most of the 200 still-abandoned houses [had] single burning porch lights, silent beacons of better times.[68]

All that remained visible of the dump itself was a pasture, isolated by miles of gleaming cyclone fence covered with Day-Glo yellow, diamond-shaped warning signs reading: "Danger—Hazardous Waste Area—Keep Out." Stretching at exact intervals like distance markers on a driving range were brilliant orange pipes used to vent and monitor the landfill.[69]

CONCLUSIONS

Although it has been cleaned up, Love Canal remains a symbol of public fears about hazardous waste. Ironically, most experts believe those fears are greatly exaggerated. They lay blame for the public's misapprehension of the risks squarely at the feet of the media, which played a critical role in the cycle of activism and political response at Love Canal: through their coverage of scientific studies and residents' ailments, journalists raised local citizens' awareness of and concern about the threats posed by buried chemicals. Once local citizens mobilized, the media's extensive and sympathetic coverage of their complaints, and its framing of the story as a classic David and Goliath tale, attracted the sympathy of the public.

Concerned about the potential liability, as well as costs likely to spiral, local and state officials resisted responding to residents' complaints for as long as possible. They hoped instead to address the problem quietly in anticipation that the furor would die down. Then, once media coverage had raised the visibility of Love Canal, government officials expected that scientific analysis would clarify the dimensions of the problem and suggest an appropriate remedy. Instead, scientific studies—most of which were conducted hastily—only heightened tensions between residents and officials without pinpointing health effects. Ultimately, politicians at both the state and national levels felt compelled to respond—not because the scientific evidence confirmed the problem at Love Canal but because the media had created a strong sense of urgency among residents and the national public.

In hindsight, Governor Carey, Representative LaFalce, and other elected officials have acknowledged that while the initial Love Canal evacuation was necessary, the second was probably an overreaction to citizen activism—and particularly the "hostage-taking" event—rather than a product of careful evaluation. In the intervening years, some followup studies have confirmed the initial findings of adverse health effects at Love Canal, but reputable evaluators have been highly critical of their methodology. Other followup studies have shown few effects that can be decisively attributed to chemicals: in late 1982, the EPA and the U.S. Public Health Service released the results of a major assessment, which found that the Love Canal neighborhood was no less safe for residents than any other neighborhood in Niagara Falls. Less than a year later, the federal Centers for Disease Control reported that they too had found Love Canal residents no more likely to suffer chromosomal damage than residents living elsewhere in Niagara Falls.[70] Another followup study released by the DOH in August 2001 failed to find elevated cancer rates among Love Canal residents.[71]

In fact, it is notoriously difficult to prove the existence of residential cancer clusters like the one suspected at Love Canal. Among hundreds of exhaustive, published investigations of such clusters in the United States, not one has convincingly identified an environmental—as opposed to an occupational or medical—cause.[72] Michael Brown, one of the original journalists covering Love Canal for the *Niagara Gazette*, concludes that "perhaps science is simply not up to the task of proving a toxic cause and effect." He points out that "because residents move in and out, because families suffer multiple ailments . . . , because the effects of chemicals when they interact with one another are all but unknown, and because the survey populations are quite limited, attempts to prove a statistically significant effect may be doomed to failure."[73] Although the existence of neighborhood cancer clusters is suspect, however, public horror of them is real. As physician Atul Gawande points out, "Human beings evidently have a deep-seated tendency to see meaning in ordinary variations that are bound to appear in small samples."[74]

The difficulty of documenting environmental and health effects of chronic exposure to toxic chemicals has rendered common law liability an ineffectual tool for addressing such problems. As the book *A Civil Action* makes vividly clear, individual citizens who believe they have been harmed by the activities of large, multinational corporations are at a severe disadvantage because legal liability in such cases is difficult to prove.[75] To prevail in a toxic tort case, plaintiffs must demonstrate not only that the alleged polluter was responsible for the harmful substance but also that the substance caused the injuries suffered, both of which can be enormously difficult to prove. The defendants have virtually unlimited resources with which to demolish the building blocks of such arguments. To avert this problem, Superfund shifts the burden of proof to polluters by establishing strict liability for hazardous waste dump sites. The Superfund mechanism also creates incentives for companies to behave in a precautionary way, since complying with current disposal rules does not constitute a defense against liability in the future. Critics charge that, in practice, Superfund throws money at sites that pose negligible risks and constitutes little more than a subsidy for lawyers and hazardous waste cleanup firms.[76] However, Superfund remains a widely popular program—not only because it addresses widely held fears but because it dispenses money to congressional districts—and even the most ardent congressional reformers are cautious about attacking it.

QUESTIONS TO CONSIDER

- Why did a local story about a toxic waste dump become a national crisis?
- Did the government react appropriately to the events at Love Canal? Why or why not?
- How did the events at Love Canal affect the design and passage of Superfund, the most expensive environmental program in the history of the United States or any other nation?
- What have we learned about the dangers posed by abandoned hazardous waste and about the efficacy of the Superfund law for dealing with such sites?

Notes

1. Verlyn Klinkenborg, "Back to Love Canal: Recycled Homes, Rebuilt Dreams," *Harpers Magazine,* March 1991, 72.
2. For instance, extrapolating from animal tests is difficult because species vary in their responses to chemicals; animals in the lab are often exposed to substances through different routes than are humans in the environment; and testers expose animals to massive doses of a substance. Epidemiological studies involve human subjects and larger samples, but it is notoriously difficult to isolate the effects of a single chemical. Moreover, such studies rely on statistical methods that may fail to detect the kinds of increases in lifetime cancer risks that regulators are concerned about. Finally, cellular analyses do not always reveal a substance's hazardous properties, nor do they quantify the low-dose risk of chemical carcinogens. For a detailed explanation of the shortcomings of these methods, see John D. Graham, Laura C. Green, and Marc J. Roberts, *In Search of Safety: Chemicals and Cancer Risk* (Cambridge: Harvard University Press, 1988).
3. Mark E. Rushefsky, *Making Cancer Policy* (Albany: State University of New York Press, 1986).
4. Dorothy Nelkin, *Controversy,* 3d ed. (Newbury Park, Calif.: Sage Publications, 1984), 16.
5. Graham et al., *In Search of Safety.*
6. William Glaberson, "Coping in the Age of 'Nimby,'" *New York Times,* June 19, 1988, Sec. 3, 1.
7. Charles Piller, *The Fail-Safe Society: Community Defiance and the End of American Technological Optimism* (New York: Basic Books, 1991).
8. Susan Hunter and Kevin M. Leyden, "Beyond NIMBY: Explaining Opposition to Hazardous Waste Facilities," *Policy Studies Journal* 23 (winter 1995): 601–619.
9. Paul Slovic, "Perceptions of Risk: Reflections on the Psychometric Paradigm," in *Social Theories of Risk,* ed. Sheldon Krimsky and Dominic Golding (Westport, Conn.: Praeger, 1992), 117–152; Gregory E. McAvoy, "Partisan Probing and Democratic Decisionmaking: Rethinking the Nimby Syndrome," *Policy Studies Journal* 26 (summer 1998): 274–293.
10. Quoted in Daniel Goleman, "Assessing Risk: Why Fear May Outweigh Harm," *New York Times,* February 1, 1994, C1.
11. Martin Linsky, "Shrinking the Policy Process: The Press and the 1980 Love Canal Relocation," in *Impact: How the Press Affects Federal Policymaking,* ed. Martin Linsky (New York: Norton, 1986), 218–253.
12. David L. Protess et al., "The Impact of Investigative Reporting on Public Opinion and Policy Making," in *Media Power in Politics,* 3d ed., ed. Doris A. Graber (Washington, D.C.: CQ Press, 1994), 346–359.

13. David Pritchard, "The News Media and Public Policy Agendas," in *Public Opinion, the Press, and Public Policy*, ed. J. David Kennamer (Westport, Conn.: Praeger, 1992), 103–112.

14. Paul Peterson, *City Limits* (Chicago: University of Chicago Press, 1981); Kee Warner and Harvey Molotch, *Building Rules: How Local Controls Shape Community Environments and Economies* (Boulder, Colo.: Westview Press, 2000).

15. Matthew Crenson, *The Un-Politics of Air Pollution: A Study of Non-Decisionmaking in the Cities* (Baltimore: Johns Hopkins University Press, 1971).

16. The main components of the buried wastes were benzene hexachloride (a byproduct of the pesticide lindane), chlorobenzene, dodecyl mercaptan, sulfides, benzyl chloride, and benzoyl chloride. See Allan Mazur, *A Hazardous Inquiry: The Rashomon Effect at Love Canal* (Cambridge: Harvard University Press, 1998).

17. Adeline Levine, *Love Canal: Science, Politics, and Public Policy* (Lexington, Mass.: Lexington Books, 1982).

18. Michael Brown, *Laying Waste: The Poisoning of America by Toxic Chemicals* (New York: Washington Square Press, 1981).

19. Levine, *Love Canal,* 11.

20. Linsky, "Shrinking the Policy Process."

21. Andrew Danzo, "The Big Sleazy: Love Canal Ten Years Later," *Washington Monthly,* September 1988, 11–17.

22. Steven R. Weisman, "Hooker Company Knew About Toxic Peril in 1958," *New York Times,* April 11, 1979, B1.

23. Levine, *Love Canal.*

24. Donald McNeil, "Upstate Waste Site May Endanger Lives," *New York Times,* August 2, 1978, A1.

25. Mirex was used in the South to control ants and as a flame retardant and plasticizer before its use was restricted by the Food and Drug Administration.

26. PCBs, which are used to insulate electronic components, are known to kill even microscopic plants and animals.

27. Quoted in Levine, *Love Canal,* 19.

28. Mazur, *A Hazardous Inquiry.*

29. Brown, *Laying Waste.*

30. Lois Marie Gibbs, *Love Canal: My Story* (Albany: State University of New York Press, 1982), 15–16.

31. Quoted in Donald McNeil, "Upstate Waste Site: Carey Seeks U.S. Aid," *New York Times,* August 4, 1978, B14.

32. McNeil, "Upstate Waste Site May Endanger Lives."

33. Brown, *Laying Waste.*

34. Mazur, *A Hazardous Inquiry.*

35. Brown, *Laying Waste*; McNeil, "Upstate Waste Site May Endanger Lives."

36. Donald McNeil, "Health Chief Calls Waste Site a Peril," *New York Times,* August 3, 1978, A1.

37. Quoted in ibid.

38. Donald McNeil, "First Families Leaving Upstate Contamination Site," *New York Times,* August 5, 1978, 1.

39. Under an emergency declaration, the government can pay only for temporary relocation to save lives, protect public health, and protect property. A disaster declaration, by contrast, is intended to help a community recover after such events as floods or earthquakes in which it is necessary to rebuild houses, schools, highways, and sewer systems.

40. Gibbs, *Love Canal,* 81.

41. Donald McNeil, "3 Chemical Sites Near Love Canal Possible Hazard," *New York Times,* December 27, 1978, B1.

42. Gibbs, *Love Canal.*

43. Ibid., 59.
44. Levine, *Love Canal*, 24.
45. "Love Canal Families Unwilling to Go Home Facing Motel Eviction," *New York Times*, November 8, 1979, B4.
46. Human beings have forty-six chromosomes in every cell. As new cells grow and reproduce by division, newly formed chromosomes and their genes are normally exact, complete replications of the originals. Ordinarily, environmental changes such as variations in temperature or barometric pressure, diet, or muscular activity have no effect on the process; moreover, a low level of mutation occurs spontaneously and is difficult to attribute to any specific cause. However, contact with radiation, chemicals, and other environmental hazards may cause abnormal changes in the structure of chromosomes. In some such cases, chromosome material may be missing; more rarely, additional material is detected.
47. Josh Barbanel, "Homeowners at Love Canal Hold 2 Officials Until F.B.I. Intervenes," *New York Times*, May 20, 1980, A1; Josh Barbanel, "Peaceful Vigil Resumed at Love Canal," *New York Times*, May 21, 1980, B1.
48. Dr. Paigen gave the following explanation: toxic chemicals, two of which—chloroform and trichloroethylene—have traditionally been used as operating room anaesthetics, can act on the nervous system in two ways. They can attack the nerve fibers themselves or the fattier myeline sheath that encases the nerve fibers. "Chemicals which are soluble in fat, as the Love Canal chemicals tend to be, tend to concentrate in fatty tissues such as the nervous sheath," she said. Dr. Paigen said the damage showed up in two of the peripheral nervous systems tested. "These are the sensory nerves which control touch and feelings," she said. But she added that the findings probably meant that those who showed peripheral nervous system damage had also suffered some damage to the central nervous system. Quoted in Dudley L. Clendinen, "New Study Finds Residents Suffer Nerve Problems," *New York Times*, May 21, 1980, B7.
49. Quoted in Irving Molotsky, "President Orders Emergency Help for Love Canal," *New York Times*, May 22, 1980, A1.
50. Quoted in Josh Barbanel, "Many at Love Canal Insist on U.S. Aid Before Moving," *New York Times*, May 27, 1980, B3.
51. Quoted in John Noble Wilford, "Panel Disputes Chromosome Findings at Love Canal," *New York Times*, June 14, 1980, 26.
52. Ibid.
53. Quoted in Irving Molotsky, "Love Canal Medical Study Backed," *New York Times*, June 16, 1980, B4. Although Dr. Killian had once supervised Dr. Picciano, he dismissed suggestions he might be biased, pointing out that he had no role in the Biogenics study and had participated in the evaluation of it at the request of the EPA.
54. Robin Herman, "Report Cites Miscarriage Rate at Love Canal in 60's," *New York Times*, June 24, 1980, D16.
55. Quoted in Georgia Dullea, "Love Canal Families Are Left With a Legacy of Pain and Anger," *New York Times*, May 16, 1980, A18.
56. Ibid.
57. Quoted in Dudley L. Clendinen, "Love Canal is Extra Tough on Children," *New York Times*, June 9, 1980, B1.
58. Quoted in Richard J. Meislin, "Carey Panel Discounts 2 Studies of Love Canal Health Problems," *New York Times*, October 11, 1980, 25.
59. Josh Barbanel, "Love Canal Skeptic Favors Relocation," *New York Times*, October 12, 1980, 39.
60. Daniel Mazmanian and David Morell, *Beyond Superfailure: America's Toxics Policy for the 1990s* (Boulder, Colo.: Westview Press, 1992), 6.
61. John A. Hird, *Superfund: The Political Economy of Environmental Risk* (Baltimore: Johns Hopkins University Press, 1994).

62. Congress actually deleted the strict, joint, and several liability provision from the law immediately before its passage, but the court subsequently reinstated the requirement through its interpretation of the statute. See Mazmanian and Morell, *Beyond Superfailure.*
63. As political scientist John Hird points out, "That the prospect of an incoming conservative Republican administration did not doom the Superfund effort entirely in 1980 is a testimony to the political appeal for both Republicans and Democrats of a hazardous waste cleanup program seen as vital by their constituents." See Hird, *Superfund,* 186.
64. Lawrence Mosher, "Environment," *National Journal,* 12 December 30, 1980, 2130.
65. Walter A. Rosenbaum, *Environmental Politics and Policy,* 5th ed. (Washington, D.C.: CQ Press, 2001).
66. U.S. General Accounting Office, *Superfund: Progress Made by EPA and Other Federal Agencies to Resolve Program Management Issues,* RCED-99-111.
67. Andrew Hoffman, "An Uneasy Rebirth at Love Canal," *Environment,* March 1995, 5–9, 25–30.
68. Leslie Gruson, "Home to Some Is Still Love Canal to Others," *New York Times,* December 9, 1991, B1.
69. Ibid.
70. Walter A. Rosenbaum, *Environmental Politics and Policy,* 4th ed. (Washington, D.C.: CQ Press, 1998).
71. New York State Department of Health, "Love Canal Follow-Up Health Study," August 2001, http://www.health.state.ny.us/nysdoh/lcanal/cancinci.htm.
72. Atul Gawande, "The Cancer-Cluster Myth," *New Yorker,* February 8, 1999, 34–37.
73. Michael Brown, "A Toxic Ghost Town," *Atlantic Monthly,* July 1989, 23–28.
74. Gawande, "The Cancer-Cluster Myth."
75. Jonathan Harr, *A Civil Action* (New York: Vintage, 1995).
76. See, for example, Marc K. Landy and Mary Hague, "The Coalition for Waste: Private Interests and Superfund," in *Environmental Politics: Public Costs, Private Rewards,* ed. Michael S. Greve and Fred L. Smith (New York: Praeger, 1992), 67–87.

Recommended Reading

Gibbs, Lois Marie. *Love Canal: My Story.* Albany: State University of New York Press, 1982.
Hird, John A. *Superfund: The Political Economy of Environmental Risk.* Baltimore: Johns Hopkins University Press, 1994.
Levine, Adeline. *Love Canal: Science, Politics, and Public Policy.* Lexington, Mass.: Lexington Books, 1982.
Mazur, Allan. *A Hazardous Inquiry: The Rashomon Effect at Love Canal.* Cambridge: Harvard University Press, 1998.

Web Sites

http://www.epa.gov/superfund (EPA Superfund site)
http://www.epa.gov/history/topics/lovecanal (EPA Love Canal site)
http://www.health.state.ny.us/nysdoh/lcanal/lcanal.htm (New York State Department of Health site)
http://ublib.buffalo.edu/libraries/projects/lovecanal (University of Buffalo site)

CHAPTER 4

Government Secrets at Rocky Flats

In March 1992, the federal government fined Rockwell International $18.5 million for horrific crimes against the environment: letting toxic chemicals and radioactive plutonium wastes poison the soil and groundwater around Colorado's Rocky Flats nuclear weapons plant. Yet according to the grand jurors who heard the case, the penalty was far too lenient. Furthermore, said the jurors, the Department of Energy (DOE) never fully acknowledged its responsibility for allowing the facility and its surroundings to become contaminated. In short, the government and its contractors conducted substandard maintenance, concealed health statistics, and violated numerous environmental laws. The result was severe contamination of the environment around the plant and a breach of public trust that fueled the anger of citizens demanding cleanup of the facility. Currently, that cleanup is well under way, and the DOE plans to turn the site into a wildlife refuge by 2010—at a cost of $6 billion.

This case shares some features with the story of Love Canal. As in New York, local and state officials in Colorado were reluctant to sanction a major polluter, fearing the economic ramifications of doing so. Although initially complacent about the plant, residents eventually became alarmed by media coverage of scientific reports suggesting contamination and potential threats to their health and property values. Critical media coverage combined with citizen activism, in turn, prompted elected officials both locally and nationally to look more closely at the plant's activities.

Beyond these similarities, however, the Rocky Flats case has some unique attributes, the most important of which is that the government was the polluter in this case. Rocky Flats is just one part of a massive weapons complex built by the federal government during the cold war. The facilities in this complex operated according to a particular logic, in which weapons production was defined as an urgent concern and all other considerations were secondary. With secrecy fostering an exclusive, symbiotic relationship between government agencies and their private contractors, plant managers took minimal precautions to protect workers and the environment. Members of Congress, theoretically guardians of the public interest, provided little oversight of the weapons production system because the military and its backers had formulated a potent framing of the issue: the risk to national security of opening up nuclear weapons plants to scrutiny far outweighed the risk to the environment or workers' health posed by activities within the plants. As one commentator describes it: "For decades, the nuclear weapons enterprise functioned as a culture apart from society, holding absolute power made possible by secrecy. The weapons complex was run by a tiny elite, unconstrained by any democratic process."[1]

But such closed "subsystems," even when backed by powerful allies, are vulnerable to exposure, for while governmental transgressions can be suppressed for a long time, whistleblowers inevitably come forward. When they do, challengers wielding alternative definitions of the problem capitalize on new information to support their claims. If they can attract media attention, challengers often can get the problem onto the government's agenda. Over time, the feedback between negative media coverage and critical public reaction (or politicians' fear of one) can prompt a major policy response: whereas enthusiasm leads to the creation of new governmental institutions and subsystems, waves of criticism lead to their breakup—and often to the creation of a new subsystem with different goals.[2]

Redirecting the nuclear weapons complex will not be simple, however. Repairing the environmental damage done by governmental polluters will involve confronting two quandaries that face all toxic waste cleanup efforts: where does the waste go, and when is a site clean enough? Local NIMBY (not-in-my-backyard) groups make transporting and disposing of hazardous waste a political rather than a technical enterprise because they limit the range of disposal options available. The result is that toxic wastes remain on sites never designed to accommodate long-term storage. Furthermore, once a polluted area is designated a Superfund site, the law creates incentives for citizens to insist on "Cadillac cleanups."[3] Such demands, say detractors, raise the cost of cleanup and ignore the reality that resources are limited and that excessive spending at one site means neglect at others.

In the case of the Rocky Flats nuclear weapons facility, all of these elements come together in a story that reveals the fundamental conflict between defense and environmental policymaking.

BACKGROUND

As the following description makes clear, the Rocky Flats nuclear weapons plant is no ordinary industrial complex:

> Rolling ranch land dotted by clumps of pine trees line the road to Rocky Flats. In contrast to the scenic foothills of the Rocky Mountains that rise just over the next ridge, the plant is a nondescript mass of mostly windowless, aging industrial buildings, known by numbers, not names. Just inside the main gate, a huge safety-first billboard is followed by one that reads "National Security: Our Responsibility"—a deadly serious message. Rocky Flats is one of the nation's most closely guarded facilities. Coiled barbed wire tops each of two wire-mesh fences that surround the plutonium-processing buildings, about half the plant's area. Four guard towers, reminiscent of a high-security prison, loom overhead. Paramilitary security guards patrol the periphery in armored vehicles with mounted automatic weapons. The 250-member security force includes a SWAT team and is equipped with antiaircraft guns.[4]

Access to Rocky Flats is highly restricted, and until recently there were activities shrouded in secrecy. As a result, accidents and leaks at the plant—many of which date back to its very beginning—went virtually unreported and their consequences undocumented.

Choosing a Site

The Rocky Flats facility is a legacy of the full-scale nuclear weapons production program launched by President Harry Truman at the start of the cold war in the early 1950s. In 1951, the Atomic Energy Commission (AEC) initiated Project Apple, with the goal of finding a place to manufacture the plutonium triggers to detonate a new generation of atom bombs. The AEC hoped to have a plant built and operating by the end of the year, and it hired a consulting firm—the Austin Company of Cleveland, Ohio—to locate an appropriate site.

Project Apple principals decided that the ideal site would be no fewer than five and no more than twenty-five miles from a city of at least 25,000 in order to attract top-quality scientists and researchers. (This was a striking decision, considering that under the wartime Manhattan Project, Lieutenant General Leslie Groves required that plutonium processing facilities be located *at least twenty miles away from* any city of more than 10,000 people, for safety reasons.[5]) Within two months, the Austin Company had narrowed the search to Denver, Colorado, "the one location that [could] combine nationally known recreational facilities and the services of a large metropolitan center."[6] The consultants identified seven possible sites, although they quickly eliminated five whose prevailing wind patterns were unfavorable. They ultimately settled on Rocky Flats, a mesa at the foot of the Rocky Mountains about fifteen miles northwest of Denver. At the time, the land between the city and the proposed site was covered with sagebrush.

In making this decision, the AEC did not consider environmental or public health concerns, the site's underlying geological structure, or its suitability for radioactive waste disposal.[7] Nor, ironically, did the site-selection team study wind patterns. According to team member Francis Langell of Dow Chemical, the company that originally managed the plant, "There was no real discussion of wind patterns. It wasn't a serious consideration."[8] Instead, the team simply assumed that most wind currents came from the south as they did at Stapleton Airport, twenty-seven miles from the foot of the Rockies. In fact, the winds at Rocky Flats rush down the mountain canyons and usually blow east or southeast—toward Denver.

Ignorant of possible hazards posed by a nuclear weapons manufacturing plant, and reflecting the generally incautious attitude of most Americans toward nuclear technology at the time, area residents welcomed the $45 million "A-plant," which promised employment and revenue for the modest city of 567,000. "There's Good News Today," reported the *Denver Post* on March 23, 1951.[9] Groundbreaking for the first permanent buildings began in July 1951;

by the following year the plant was on line, employing 200 workers in twenty buildings. By 1954, the plant was fully operational, and by the 1960s the number of workers had grown to 3,000.

Rocky Flats Operations

Decision making about Rocky Flats operations was restricted to a select few. The government hired contractors to manage workers there, as it did in all its weapons manufacturing facilities. For the first fourteen years, Dow Chemical Company ran the operations under contract to the AEC. In 1975, Rockwell International replaced Dow. During Rockwell's tenure, the Energy Research and Development Administration (ERDA) superseded the AEC, and shortly thereafter the Energy Department replaced the ERDA as the responsible agency. In Congress, an unusual arrangement facilitated an extraordinarily closed system of nuclear weapons policymaking: the Joint Committee on Atomic Energy, comprising nine members from each chamber, had exclusive jurisdiction over "all bills, resolutions, and other matters in the Senate and the House of Representatives relating primarily to the [Atomic Energy] Commission or to the development, use, and control of atomic energy."[10]

Within the Rocky Flats plant itself, the need for secrecy shaped operations. The plant had two primary functions, both highly classified. First, workers shaped plutonium into first-stage fission bombs, the softball-sized pits that trigger the second-stage fusion reaction in hydrogen bombs. In addition, workers recovered and recycled plutonium from retired warheads and manufacturing residues using acids or high-voltage electrical currents to strip the metal from other materials.[11] Among the toxic substances emitted during these processes were: americium and plutonium (both radioactive carcinogens), beryllium (a probable inhalation carcinogen), carbon tetrachloride (a probable inhalation carcinogen), chloroform (a probable carcinogen), methylene chloride (a probable inhalation carcinogen), tetrachloroethylene, and trichloroethylene. Reflecting the secrecy surrounding the plant's mission, security "was so tight that only a handful of people had clearances to get into more than one building, and most employees had no idea what went on in areas of the plant other than their own. Plant employees were bussed from the front gate to their own buildings, since no personal vehicles were allowed on site."[12] The engineers who designed the plant were forbidden to discuss their work with anyone; Jim Stone, the mechanical engineer who designed the notorious plutonium processing Building 771, never even saw the site or knew its orientation.[13]

Early Accidents, Leaks, and Coverups

Secrecy surrounded not only Rocky Flats' day-to-day operations but also its poor safety record. The plant experienced numerous fires during its first two decades, the biggest of which broke out late in the evening of September 11,

1957, when the plutonium inside a glove box in Building 771 ignited.[14] Those boxes had been manufactured with flammable materials, and since many had not been changed in four years, they contained large quantities of plutonium. In turn, the high-efficiency particulate aerosol (HEPA) filters designed to prevent plutonium from escaping the building caught fire, spewing plutonium dust and smoke into the atmosphere. After failing to put out the blaze with carbon dioxide, firefighters resorted to dousing it with water (which they had been reluctant to use, fearing a plutonium criticality chain reaction); in the meantime, however, they turned on the ventilation fans, spreading the flames throughout the building.[15]

Because the fire melted stack radiation monitors, plant managers had no idea how much plutonium escaped, and they could not monitor emissions until seven days later. Even then, however, the monitors detected levels of radioactive elements 16,000 times greater than the standards of the time.[16] Nevertheless, officials took no emergency action to protect the public, nor did they warn local residents, cities, or health agencies. There was little media coverage and therefore little public reaction: a front-page story in the *Denver Post* reported on the fire but provided little explanation; a story buried in the back pages of the *Rocky Mountain News* quoted AEC officials who said that "no spread of radioactive contamination of any consequence" had occurred; and the *Boulder Daily Camera* did not even report it.[17] Despite contamination of the building and the absence of filters to keep plutonium out of the environment, Rocky Flats resumed limited production two days after the fire in order to meet a deadline.

Twelve years later, on May 11, 1969, another major fire occurred. This blaze began when plutonium kept in an open can within a glove box ignited spontaneously and burned for four hours, causing $45 million in damage ($200 million in 2000 dollars). A government report said that "the fire was out of the top of the [foundry] with flames about 18 inches high. One of the two firemen heard two loud reports (like rifle shots) and saw two fireballs (about basketball size) go to the ceiling."[18] Firemen used so much water to douse the fire (again, carbon dioxide had no effect) that it flowed downhill through a 267-foot tunnel and into Building 771, the most dangerous building in the complex.[19] While critics estimated that the fire sent at least 2,200 pounds of plutonium into the atmosphere—enough for 220 warheads—plant officials insisted that little or none had been released.[20] This time, Denver and Boulder papers reported the fire. The AEC provided little concrete information about its origins or consequences, however, even though, according to its classified report on the fire, only the "heroic efforts of the firefighters" prevented a "major release of plutonium to the environment."[21]

In addition to these large fires, Rocky Flats experienced hundreds of smaller ones, as well as numerous other problems, the most notable of which stemmed from the practice of burning uranium-laden oil in open pits. Workers also buried more than 5,000 thirty- and fifty-gallon steel barrels containing plutonium-laden waste oil on a hillside behind the plant.[22] Dow company managers did not remove the barrels until 1967, even though they knew of the leaks as early as 1959. The site was not capped until 1969, and in the interim, an estimated 5,000 gallons of plutonium-contaminated oil leaked into the soil and was scattered during windstorms.[23]

THE CASE

Because there was so little press coverage and such tight control of information during the 1950s and 1960s, the public remained largely ignorant of the accidents and negligent practices at Rocky Flats. The 1969 fire galvanized a group of Boulder-area scientists, however, and in the early 1970s they conducted a series of studies that prompted a gradually intensifying cycle of negative media attention to and public criticism of the plant. Activists took advantage of each new development to promote their view that the facility constituted an unacceptable public health threat. By the mid-1980s, the cold war justification for concealment at Rocky Flats and other military installations had faded, replaced by an insistence on openness and accountability that extended even to nuclear weapons facilities. While the original framing of the problem—in which contamination was a minor side effect of national security—had allowed devastating levels of air, water, and soil pollution, the new definition prompted a hazardous waste cleanup on an unprecedented scale.

Scientists Sound the Alarm

In the early 1970s, scientific reports of contamination at Rocky Flats opened a window of opportunity for advocates of closing the facility and dismantling the nation's nuclear arsenal. In 1969, a group of nuclear chemists, known as the Colorado Committee for Environmental Education, at the National Center for Atmospheric Research in Boulder had begun conducting soil tests around Rocky Flats. In 1970, they reported that plutonium contamination two miles east of the plant was up to 250 times higher than the levels attributable to fallout from nuclear tests worldwide.[24] They found that eight miles east of the plant, in Westminster—which had become one of Denver's largest suburbs—the levels were ten times the normal level.[25] The media latched onto these studies, running stories increasingly skeptical of the AEC and its assurances of plant safety.[26]

Then, in 1973, the Boulder scientists learned that the plant had accidentally released between 500 and 2,000 curies of tritium into the Great Western Reservoir 1.5 miles to its east.[27] Alerted by their concern, in 1974 the Jefferson County one and a half Commission asked Carl Johnson, the county's Health Department director, to investigate the soil of a proposed housing development two and a half miles east of the plant. Johnson found that some of the area's soil exceeded the Colorado plutonium contamination standards by a factor of seven.[28]

Landowners who had hoped to develop property nearby were alarmed by Johnson's findings and filed lawsuits against Dow, Rockwell, and the DOE in

1975. They demanded $23 million in damages, claiming that fallout from the plant had rendered their land valueless. The lawsuits in turn prompted local and federal officials to reexamine development in the area, and in the mid-1970s, the federal government established a 6,166-acre environmental and security buffer zone around the plant's 384-acre core. In 1978, the U.S. Department of Housing and Urban Development (HUD) temporarily stopped processing subdivisions, mortgage insurance, and other housing assistance within a seven-and-a-half-mile radius of Rocky Flats. Finally, in 1979, after repeated requests from the EPA, HUD began to require that realtors issue warnings about plutonium contamination to all homebuyers purchasing federal mortgage insurance within a ten-mile radius of the plant.[29]

During this time, on his own initiative, Johnson had begun conducting the first major epidemiological study of the health effects of Rocky Flats on its neighbors. In the first of two controversial reports issued in the late 1970s, he concluded that Denver's overall cancer rates were higher than expected and higher still in neighborhoods near Rocky Flats. The pattern, he said, was consistent with soil contamination, which he measured at up to 380 times background levels at off-site locations. In the second study, Johnson found that infant mortality and adult cancer rates rose as one moved closer to the plant. Leukemia deaths among Jefferson County children, which were below the national average before Rocky Flats opened, he said, were above the national average shortly after the plant began operating and twice the national average after the 1957 fire.[30]

Plant managers and even some scientists who opposed Rocky Flats criticized Johnson's statistical methodology, and in 1981, the county fired him. Advocates focusing on Rocky Flats as part of their nuclear disarmament campaign nevertheless seized on Johnson's findings in their efforts to raise public concern and redefine nuclear weapons production there as a public health threat. The Rocky Flats Action Group, formed in 1974, conducted a public education campaign about the plant and advocated converting it to peaceful uses. The high point of their organizing efforts came in 1982, when more than 20,000 protesters rallied at the state capitol; a year later, an estimated 15,000 linked arms and tried to encircle the plant.

Public attention to such activities was short-lived, however; in fact, many residents were hostile to these "outside agitators." In general—as in the Love Canal case—local officials and many residents were reluctant to look too closely at the plant's operations because it was a mainstay of the local economy. With an annual budget of half a billion dollars, the plant represented 1 percent of the state's manufacturing economy and generated about 6,000 direct and thousands more indirect jobs.[31]

Then, as media coverage of Johnson's studies waned, the window of opportunity for shutting Rocky Flats closed. In 1982 HUD retracted its order to warn prospective homebuyers on the grounds that the state had begun to distribute information on emergency procedures for homes within four miles of the plant. Soon afterward, the state—protecting its own economic development interests—also stopped giving out information. The government's definition of the plant as a crucial component of national security and the local economy held sway.

Health Threats Draw Renewed Attention to Rocky Flats

In the mid-1980s, however, a second window of opportunity for Rocky Flats opponents opened when a series of pollution problems came to light. In particular, highly publicized scares about plutonium contamination of drinking water in 1985 and 1986 galvanized the plant's neighbors. The AEC had built the facility directly on top of a creek that feeds the Great Western Reservoir; the plant also abutted a creek that flows to Standley Lake, another reservoir two miles away. After scientists first raised concerns in the 1970s, engineers built a series of holding ponds to catch runoff from the plant so it could be tested for radioactivity or toxic chemicals. That system did not prevent the eventual release of millions of gallons of polluted water, however, and in 1987, Rockwell International finally admitted that groundwater around Rocky Flats was contaminated.[32] The DOE proceeded to release some details about how several areas of the plant were dangerously contaminated with plutonium, uranium, and deadly solvents. The EPA identified 166 separate hazardous waste dumps on the reservation, contending that one of them—Hillside 881— was the most polluted site in America and posed a clear danger to the area's drinking water.

As public concern rose, the DOE's once impermeable façade seemed to be eroding. Congress had abolished the Joint Committee on Atomic Energy in 1977 and transferred responsibility for nuclear weapons oversight to the Armed Services Committees in each chamber, thereby creating opportunities for congressional critics of the nuclear weapons complex to become more involved in policymaking. Still, the DOE steadfastly maintained its autonomy and need for secrecy. In 1985, Dow, Rockwell, and the DOE agreed to settle with the landowners out of court for nearly $10 million. The defendants devised a plan to minimize adverse publicity: as part of the settlement, the landowners agreed not to call any witnesses and to allow the defense's expert witnesses to testify unchallenged. In return, the plant agreed to reduce radioactivity to the 1973 Colorado standard for plutonium in soil. Remarkably, another provision of the settlement called for Jefferson County to purchase 800 acres of the contaminated property for $2 million (half its appraised value) and create a park.[33]

The Incinerator Prompts Citizen Mobilization

If the worrisome reports about drinking water constituted the fuse, then the incinerator proposal was the spark that ignited local citizen activism. Residents were already becoming wary of the plant when, in January 1987, officials announced plans to incinerate thousands of tons of mixed radioactive and chemical wastes in a fluidized-bed incinerator.[34] If the state approved it, the plant would begin a ten-day trial incineration, the first burning of mixed radioactive and hazardous wastes in the country. Then, if state health officials determined the process was environmentally and technologically sound, plant managers intended to undertake full-scale incineration in the summer of 1987.

Plant officials argued that burning the waste was necessary because there was no federally sanctioned disposal site for their mounting stockpiles of mixed wastes. "We have some 18,000 gallons of liquid wastes that are, in the main, machinery solvents resulting from activities involving depleted uranium metals," said Rockwell spokesman Gene Towne. "But by law, we cannot transport a hazardous liquid waste containing radioactive material."[35] Plant engineers planned to seal the inert ash generated by the incinerator in concrete and ship it to a planned disposal site in Nevada. Towne emphasized that "maximum safeguards" had been taken, saying "there [would] be no health effects from this particular technology" and "the chances of anything getting out [were] minute."[36]

Despite Rockwell's assurances, many residents were alarmed and unwilling to put their faith in government experts' risk assessments. Richard E. Dryden, a thirty-five-year-old printer who lived with his family within view of the weapons facility, said, "Our reaction has gone from curiosity to concern to more recently panic." His wife, Charlene, said of Rockwell's safety promises, "I do not buy it. No way! They're testing us. We're the guinea pigs. Nobody knows what plutonium is going to do in the long term. My boys may not have healthy children some day."[37] Residents like the Drydens were particularly affronted by the incinerator proposal because they were already grappling with a Highway Department plan to build a new beltway, construction of which would churn tons of dust into the air. High winds, which routinely close Highway 93 on the plant's western edge, would disperse the dust widely.

The incinerator proposal, following on the heels of the drinking water scares and the highway plan, finally catalyzed local opposition to Rocky Flats. A group of Denver area citizens, led by veteran peace activist Jan Pilcher and homemaker Joan Seeman, established Citizens Against Rocky Flats Contamination (CARFC) early in 1987. Pilcher had been a member of the Rocky Flats Action Group in the 1970s and was well versed in lobbying, orchestrating public demonstrations, and arranging educational events. Reflecting the difference in risk standards employed by experts and laypeople, CARFC raised questions about the health and environmental effects of the incinerator, which had not been studied, and demanded that experts provide a worst case scenario. (Organizers were well aware that the incinerator was only one of a multitude of potential health threats posed by the weapons plant, and perhaps not even the gravest one, but they also knew that few technologies motivate opposition as readily as toxic waste incineration.[38])

At a public meeting called by Colorado Rep. David Skaggs, irate neighbors shouted down Rocky Flats officials. The momentum generated at the meeting prompted residents to form additional, smaller groups and keep the pressure on local politicians. Incinerator opponents inundated the Colorado Department of Health with 1,500 letters, and CARFC gathered more than 18,000 signatures on a petition to stop the facility. Municipal officials and small business owners spoke out against the test burn, and Governor Roy Romer found himself besieged by mail from angry constituents.[39]

CARFC buttressed its credibility in opposing the incinerator with evidence gathered by the Boulder scientists. The scientists claimed that the incinerator posed a major risk of explosion and that Rocky Flats managers had no means of monitoring or controlling emissions of vapors such as uranium hexafluoride. They concluded: "The equipment, the plan, the monitoring, and the documentation are so flawed and deficient, so threatening to public safety that the application is beyond expectation of remedy."[40] Colorado politicians, all of whom had initially favored the incinerator, demanded health studies before consenting to the test burn.

Rocky Flats management finally agreed to postpone the burn until July, but in the interim, a scientific panel convened by Representative Skaggs ascertained that the plant had already used the incinerator nine times since 1978 to burn twenty-four tons of unidentified—possibly radioactive—waste.[41] CARFC and the Sierra Club filed suit to prevent the test burn, arguing that it violated environmental laws, and Rocky Flats was forced to delay the test indefinitely to prepare an environmental impact assessment. Finally, amid unrelenting public opposition fueled by press reports of a small fire at the incinerator, the project ground to a halt.

Ironically, even as public concern about Rocky Flats was growing, local officials continued to annex nearby land for development. With planned and actual acquisitions of adjacent land by surrounding cities and towns, the brush land between Rocky Flats and Denver in 1951 was fast becoming a populous stream of office buildings, businesses, and homes.[42] One consequence of this development was that in 1988, the U.S. General Accounting Office (GAO) ranked groundwater contamination at Rocky Flats the most serious environmental threat at any of the country's nuclear weapons facilities.[43]

Whither the Waste?

No sooner had they stopped the incinerator project than yet another issue confronted residents of the rapidly growing Denver suburbs. Throughout the 1980s, the nuclear industry—both its electric power and weapons divisions—faced the prospect of being buried in its radioactive byproducts. Each year, Rocky Flats alone was generating about 16,000 tons of poisonous trash, including 75,000 cubic feet of transuranic radioactive clothing, glass, solvents, oils, and metals contaminated with plutonium or americium. Since opening, Rocky Flats had shipped its refuse to the DOE's Idaho National Engineering Plant for "temporary storage," with its ultimate destination the government's Waste Isolation Pilot Plant (WIPP), a giant hole in a salt bed 2,150 feet beneath southeastern New Mexico. The plan was for WIPP to start receiving clothing and tools contaminated by radiation from Rocky Flats and nine other atomic plants in December 1988. But safety concerns and legal problems forced the government to postpone the opening date to the 1990s at the earliest.

The delay in opening WIPP triggered a posturing contest between Governor Romer and Idaho's governor, Cecil Andrus, both of whom hoped to get credit for being responsive to agitated constituents. Rocky Flats was producing less than its usual quota of trash because federal inspectors had shut down most of the facility in October 1988, after two unprotected employees and a DOE safety inspector had stumbled into an unmarked room where workers were cleaning and repairing plutonium-contaminated equipment, and all three had inhaled radioactive particles. Despite the closure, enough of the plant remained operational to generate nearly a boxcar of hazardous wastes each week. In late 1988, when it became clear that WIPP would not open on schedule, Governor Andrus put his foot down and sent one of the boxcars back to Colorado. There it sat, outside the plant beside six more boxcars and a yard full of drums and crates, all packed with toxic waste.[44]

This arrangement was untenable, however, as Rocky Flats would be in violation of the federal Resource Conservation and Recovery Act (RCRA) if it stored more than 1,600 cubic yards of hazardous waste on site.[45] By May 1989, Rocky Flats was approaching the 1,600-cubic-yard limit, at which point Governor Romer could have ordered the plant to shut down. Instead, the governor tried to stave off the nuclear waste crisis by convening a meeting in Salt Lake City with Idaho's governor Andrus, New Mexico's governor Garrey Carruthers, and top DOE officials. The group agreed on a tentative compromise: to press Congress to pass a land-swap bill essential to opening WIPP while the DOE searched for an interim storage site and provided financial aid to the states.[46] The group was unable to resolve the short-term waste disposal problem, however.

In September 1989, White House chief of staff John Sununu appealed personally to the governors of the seven western states to accept Rocky Flats' waste on a temporary, emergency basis so that the U.S. government could maintain its bomb production. With the collapse of communism, however, politicians found themselves unable to persuade their constituents to sacrifice on behalf of national security, and—fearing electoral repercussions—all seven governors refused. In desperation, the DOE prevailed upon Governor Romer to store railcars filled with Rocky Flats waste at a U.S. Army training site in southern Colorado near the small town of Trinidad, one of the state's poorest municipalities with a population of only 9,000. A private company offered to administer the wastes at the new site, offering jobs, a new telephone system, hospital expansion, and other benefits as sweeteners to the town. Trinidadians were not impressed: "About 500 angry Trinidadians attended a meeting to discuss the plan. They shouted down company representatives with cries of 'Get out of town! . . . Store it in your backyard!'"[47] Finally, the DOE acquired a super-compactor to reduce waste volume at Rocky Flats, thereby forestalling the waste crisis until some future date.

The EPA/FBI Investigation

Topping off Rocky Flats' woes, years of secrecy and arrogance by plant managers and their overseers were coming home to roost. In 1987, former Rocky Flats engineer Jim Stone—frustrated with plant managers' unresponsiveness to his complaints about safety violations and inaction at the state level—tipped off the FBI about suspected violations of environmental laws at the site. This whisteblowing triggered a two-year investigation called Operation Desert Glow. On June 6, 1989, the investigation culminated in a raid in which more than seventy FBI and EPA agents spent three weeks searching the facility. Agents seized over a million pages of internal documents and claimed to have found evidence to corroborate charges of improperly handled wastes and illegal use of outdated equipment.[48] The raid opened yet another window of opportunity—this time a national one, since the entire nuclear weapons complex had come under fire while the investigation was under way.

Within a month, environmental officials had uncovered another mystery at the trouble-prone facility: traces of radioactive strontium and cesium that a nuclear chain reaction could produce—even though there was no nuclear reactor at the site.[49] The EPA demanded a study to determine how the mysterious isotopes got to Rocky Flats. Then, one month after the FBI raid, DOE officials found ten radiation safety problems during a one-week inspection, including one involving leaking boxes of radioactive waste. "The radiological protection program at Rocky Flats continues to be inadequate," wrote one inspector.[50]

The DOE responded by trying to salvage its image. In the summer of 1989, while continuing to insist that the plant was operating safely, newly appointed energy secretary James Watkins announced that he would end nearly fifty years of secrecy. To boost the agency's declining credibility with Congress and the public, Watkins declared that the DOE would allow state environmental officials to inspect its plants. If they uncovered any violations, Watkins said, the agency would fire operators. The DOE also announced its intention to have state safety teams conduct aerial surveillance. Signaling a substantial shift in federal priorities, Watkins assured the press that protecting health and the environment was as important as weapons output, and he announced plans to reward contractors for running safe plants.[51] To placate Governor Romer, who was threatening to close down Rocky Flats permanently, Watkins pledged $1.8 million to tighten environmental monitoring and $700,000 for the first year of a study of health effects on the area residents.[52] Shortly thereafter, to emphasize its openness, the DOE began to make available to independent researchers its storehouse of health information on workers in the bomb-making plants from the 1940s through 1990.

Redefining the Problem

Although they defused some of the political momentum behind reform, Watkins' efforts were insufficient to stem the tide of negative publicity. A rapid-fire series of revelations about mismanagement and contamination, combined with charges of a conspiracy between the DOE and Rockwell, enabled critics to redefine nuclear weapons production at the facility. No longer was Rocky Flats vital to national security; instead, it was a site at which a venal contractor, backed by a corrupt federal agency, was imposing deadly hazards on its unwitting neighbors. Substantiating this definition of the problem, a federal affidavit—based on the FBI investigation and brought before a grand jury in August 1989—alleged that Rockwell and the DOE had broken environmental laws, including RCRA and the Clean Water Act, in treating, storing, and disposing of both radioactive and toxic waste. It also charged that employees had falsified information to conceal the contamination. Finally, the FBI and EPA alleged that not only had the DOE failed to police Rockwell as it should have, but it had actually encouraged and then helped to cover up the contractor's mistakes.

During grand jury deliberations, the DOE continued to try to reopen Rocky Flats, despite the fact that in September the EPA had added the site to its Superfund National Priorities List (NPL). Impeding DOE efforts, however, was a series of damaging reports about plutonium contamination at the site. In theory, the banks of filters sitting in metal frames were protecting the public from plutonium. But that, according to Dr. John Gofman, a former associate director of Lawrence Livermore Laboratory in California and a specialist on the health effects of low-level radiation, was "not a happy thought for the residents of Colorado."[53] Joe Goldfield, one of the chemical engineers who had helped to develop the filters, was similarly pessimistic: "People have the idea that all dangerous radioactive materials are protected from the public by steel and concrete walls. At Rocky Flats, the protection is fragile paper filters subject to cracking, fires, and being blown out in an explosion."[54] The condition of those filters' frames was also questionable, according to Goldfield and former plant workers.

In October 1989, independent scientists reported finding several kilograms of plutonium in the plant's ventilation ducts, well beyond the point at which the HEPA filters were supposed to stop such releases. In November 1989, the DOE finally closed the plant to conduct a $1 billion safety overhaul. Three months later, the plant's new manager, EG&G of Wellesley, Massachusetts,[55] released a stunning piece of news: there were sixty-two pounds of plutonium scattered along miles of ventilation ducts at the plant, enough to make seven nuclear bombs.[56] In at least one building, filters whose frames had been replaced "did not seal properly, due to surface deterioration of the framework as a result of age."[57] Furthermore, later in the summer EG&G announced that it would remove only thirteen pounds of the plutonium before the plant reopened. Robert Nelson, the DOE plant manager, did not specify how much plutonium ultimately would be removed, saying only that "there will always be some amount of plutonium in the ducts."[58] Another DOE spokesman said that "in all of the plutonium buildings, there are multiple stages of filters. . . . We will have no duct with more than 400 grams of plutonium in it. This is the quantity of plutonium that cannot go critical in any configuration."[59] Given the plant's history of fires, his words did not reassure people living in the area. Making matters worse, in May 1990, Germak Fletcher Associates, a consulting firm, released a study that cited serious management problems at the plant since EG&G had taken over in January.

That summer, the Senate Armed Services Committee—which for years had backed Rocky Flats—changed its tune in response to the negative publicity and began to question whether the DOE had completed enough of the safety improvements it had projected when it shut down the plant in 1989. The Defense and Energy Departments continued to pressure Rocky Flats managers to reopen the plant, contending that the Pentagon's next generation of nuclear weapons, including advanced cruise missiles and the powerful 475-kiloton warhead for Trident II submarines, could not be manufactured as long as it was closed. Defending the rush to restart weapons production, Energy Secretary Watkins said in an interview with the *New York Times* that "national security requires a prompt reopening of the plant but the reasons cannot be publicly discussed because they are classified."[60] Colorado's Sen. Tim Wirth responded that the recent nuclear reduction treaty made weapons production *less* urgent, not more so. A Congressional Research Service report found that preventing Rocky Flats from manufacturing pits for another two years would have only "modest consequences for national security."[61]

Further tarnishing the DOE's image were allegations of incompetence and corruption in the ongoing safety overhaul at Rocky Flats. A May 1991 department audit found that although federal law requires that projects costing more than $1.2 million be paid for with specific congressional appropriations, contractors were stringing together the general plant project money to pay for construction projects that cost well over $1.2 million. Some of the most egregious examples occurred at Rocky Flats, where EG&G had financed a $37.4 million project to improve the security of plutonium by allocating the cost of the project among at least thirty general plant construction accounts. Secretary Watkins rationalized the practice as a way of avoiding the delays plant managers feared might result from congressional review.[62]

In October 1990, EG&G had replaced its plant manager amid revelations about management failures and employees' charges that managers were risking unsafe conditions in their frenzy to restart the plant.[63] In July 1991, the plant failed a readiness review after inspections that cost $1.5 million. In September, an internal Energy Department report heavily criticized the work done to improve safety when an investigative team found numerous problems in the criticality safety program, which is meant to ensure that plutonium bomb fuel is never accidentally assembled in a critical mass that can set off a chain reaction. Investigators also found flaws in worker safety protection.[64]

Exacerbating negative perceptions of the plant, in October 1991, two former Rocky Flats technicians filed a civil suit against the facility in which they described plant management as bumbling and heavy handed. In the suit, filed in Boulder County District Court, Jaqueline Brever and Karen Pitts claimed that they were threatened, harassed, and forced out of their jobs because managers and coworkers feared they would supply evidence to federal agents that the incinerator had been running when plant officials vowed it was shut down. The technicians quoted the manager of plutonium operations telling a staff meeting a few days after the FBI raid that "whistle blowers will be dealt with severely and completely."[65]

Redefining the Problem Prompts Policy Change

The FBI investigation, combined with the exposés of the late 1980s and early 1990s, clearly favored Rocky Flats critics' definition of nuclear weapons production. Ultimately, that reframing of the problem prompted a massive policy shift. In his January 1992 State of the Union Address, President George Bush announced the cessation of production at Rocky Flats. Shortly thereafter, Secretary Watkins formally transformed Rocky Flats' mission to decontamination and decommissioning. In March 1992, the grand jury delivered an explosive report in which it proposed to indict three DOE officials and five Rockwell employees. U.S. attorney general Michael Norton refused to sign the indictments, however, rendering them invalid, and instead announced that Rockwell had agreed to plead guilty to ten violations of environmental laws (five felonies and five misdemeanors) and pay a fine of $18.5 million. In exchange, the Justice Department promised not to indict any Rockwell employees.

The grand jury was furious with this plea agreement. Apparently, the prosecution had outlined for the jurors the charges to which Rockwell eventually pleaded guilty—charges that they considered too lenient. At the time, Norton told them it would be "inadvisable" for them to prepare a report. Nevertheless, the twenty-two members of the panel, inflamed by what they had heard in the courtroom, continued to meet, preparing their own indictment under the leadership of a Denver lawyer on the panel as well as a forty-two-page draft report. They even went so far as petitioning Congress for an investigation and writing to President-elect Bill Clinton to ask for a special prosecutor.[66] When the plea bargain was announced in September, someone leaked the grand jury report to the press, and—in a breach of the secrecy surrounding grand jury proceedings—a Denver weekly newspaper, *Westword*, published a long account of the two-and-a-half-year investigation. In it, the grand jury depicted the DOE as incompetent and, at times, duplicitous, alleging that:

> For forty years, federal, Colorado, and local regulators and elected officials have been unable to make the Department of Energy and the plant's corporate operators obey the law. Indeed, the plant has been and continues to be operated by government and corporate employees who have placed themselves above the law and who have hidden their illegal conduct behind the cloak of "national security." Government and corporate employees have breached the public's trust by engaging in a continuous campaign of distraction, deception, and dishonesty. Little has changed at Rocky Flats since

the FBI raid. Employees of the DEO and of EG&G continue to violate many federal environmental laws.[67]

Additional evidence of mismanagement surfaced as national investigative reporters took up the issue. In December 1992, a *U.S. News & World Report* article noted that the DOE had created five ponds at Rocky Flats in which to store low-level radioactive and hazardous wastes. The idea was that contaminated liquid would evaporate into the air. In 1985, DOE officials ordered Rockwell to clean up the sludge residue in the ponds. Rockwell's approach—mixing the sludge with concrete and then disposing of the hardened blocks—had failed miserably. As a result, DOE's projected cleanup cost of $27 million had escalated to $131 million and was anticipated to reach $169 million; moreover, the agency did not expect the ponds to be cleaned up before 2009. In addition, the article pointed out, between 1990 and 1991, EG&G awarded at least eleven "no bid" contracts to its own subsidiaries. Those contracts increased from an estimated $2.8 million to $10 million, and work on seven of the eleven contracts was completed behind schedule.[68]

By the end of 1992, between the grand jury report and the ongoing media revelations, environmental problems in the nuclear weapons complex had become sufficiently public that Congress felt compelled to act. Largely in response to the scandals at Rocky Flats, Congress passed the Federal Facilities Compliance Act holding federal facilities to the same environmental standards as private companies. Moreover, in December, the House Science, Space, and Technology Committee held hearings on the Rockwell plea bargain. The committee's final report, issued in January 1993, charged that the Justice Department had given Rockwell too sweet a deal. The most benign interpretation, according to the report, was that the Justice Department simply regarded environmental crimes as unimportant; at worst, Justice may have gone out of its way to downplay the DOE's failure to oversee Rockwell's activities.[69] Kenneth Fimberg, the government's lead prosecutor, defended the plea agreement saying that the fine against Rockwell was roughly five times as high as the previous record for a hazardous waste case and, in his opinion, taking the case to trial would have been extremely risky.[70] Prosecutors also felt that fairness prevented them from indicting individuals who had simply followed bad public policy.[71]

Cleaning Up Rocky Flats

Although off to a slow start, cleanup activities at Rocky Flats and throughout the nuclear weapons complex accelerated in the mid-1990s. In 1994, the DOE renamed the Rocky Flats plant the Rocky Flats Environmental Technology Site (RFETS) to reflect its new objective of environmental restoration, waste management, decommissioning, decontamination, and economic development. In 1995, the DOE chose Kaiser-Hill as the new site contractor, and the following year the DOE, the EPA, and the Colorado Department of Public Health and Environment (CDPHE) signed a new Rocky Flats Cleanup

Agreement to replace the original signed in 1991.[72] Under the agreement, the CDPHE is overseeing cleanup in the former weapons production area, and the EPA is responsible for cleaning up the buffer zone. Early plans for the closure of Rocky Flats called for cleanup to be done and the DOE to withdraw by 2065 at an estimated cost of nearly $37 billion. After designating it an Accelerated Closure site in 1997, the DOE drew up a new closure strategy that set 2006 as the target cleanup date, with a price tag of $7.5 billion (in 2000 dollars).

Deciding on the appropriate level of cleanup is a major impediment to reaching the goal of closure by 2006, however, particularly given citizens' wariness of government experts. The agreement requires the plant to be cleaned up to a level that safely supports future uses, such as open space or light industry. It also requires that surface water flowing on and off site be made safe for any and all uses. Citizen groups raised objections to the soil cleanup standards established in 1996, arguing that the remaining amount of plutonium exceeded levels for similar projects around the world. To allay citizens' concerns, the DOE announced in 1997 that it would fund a citizen-directed scientific assessment of the soil standards and, in January 1998, formed an oversight panel including representatives of local government, public interest groups, and academic institutions, along with local citizens. The panel then hired an independent contractor to recommend final soil cleanup levels. Rocky Flats officials also gathered a team of specialists to conduct separate studies of the way actinides (plutonium, americium, and uranium) move in soil and water, to determine how safe it is to leave such contaminants in the environment. A citizen committee, the Rocky Flats Citizens Advisory Board (RFCAB), is overseeing the actinide studies.

Furthermore, because some contamination will remain, Rocky Flats will need to be monitored in perpetuity. The Rocky Flats Coalition of Local Governments and the RFCAB are collaborating to decide on long-term stewardship issues. The original plan was to leave the buffer zone as open space, complete with hiking and biking trails, and to use the industrial core for open space or industrial redevelopment. In 1999 and again in 2001, Colorado Sen. Wayne Allard and Rep. Mark Udall sponsored a bill to turn the site into a wildlife refuge, a move the RFCAB endorsed. About 250 species of wildlife use the high plains grassland, streams, and ponds that surround the site; observers have documented the presence of twenty species of sparrows, nineteen species of ducks, and thirteen species of neotropical warblers on the site.

Some environmentalists, as well as abutting towns, were concerned that refuge designation would allow the DOE to embrace lower cleanup standards and thus refused to support the bill.[73] To address this fear, its authors inserted language requiring the DOE to clean up the site to the levels established by the "regulators, the public, and interested state and federal agencies based on science, law and agreements reached with the public."[74] In other words, the bill specifically prohibits the use of the wildlife refuge designation to avoid strict cleanup standards. On the other hand, such standards mean both uncertainty and high costs: the cost of DOE's entire cleanup effort has mounted continuously since it began in the early 1990s. In 1999, officials estimated the cost at $168 billion; by 2000, the estimate had reached $212 billion, and DOE anticipated the cost could exceed $300 billion.[75]

OUTCOMES

Although serious cleanup efforts are under way, critics are dubious that Kaiser-Hill can close Rocky Flats by 2006. The GAO cites as a primary obstacle the difficulty of getting the necessary permits and the number of containers needed to transport and dispose of waste: the site accumulated as much as twenty-one tons of nuclear materials—fourteen tons of plutonium and seven tons of enriched uranium—during its forty years of operation; in addition, there are hundreds of thousands of fifty-five-gallon drums of low-level radioactive waste, low-level mixed waste, transuranic waste, and hazardous wastes.[76] There was enough radioactive waste on the site to fill a nineteen-story building the size of a football field.[77] The site closure plan calls for shipping it all off site.

By spring 2001, eighty-one structures of the original 802-building complex had been reduced to concrete slabs.[78] Kaiser-Hill had also installed three of four planned groundwater treatment systems, each of which can intercept a contaminated plume of groundwater before it can surface and funnels it through treatment cells that remove or reduce the contaminants.[79] Contractors had drained 4,060 gallons of volatile plutonium solutions from leaking pipes and tanks and unearthed another thirty tons of depleted uranium from outdoor trenches.[80] Thousands of pounds of plutonium pits had been shipped to the Pantex facility near Amarillo, Texas, and Kaiser-Hill expected the task of shipping plutonium-contaminated metals and powders to be completed by 2002.

Hundreds of thousands of cubic meters of radioactive and mixed wastes remained to be transported off site, however, and workers had only recently embarked on the job of detoxifying the area. Among the tasks to be completed were:

- finding the approximately 1,100 pounds of plutonium that "somehow became lost" in ductwork, drums, and gloveboxes;
- cleaning thirteen "infinity rooms," in which radioactivity levels were so high that instruments went off the scale when measurements were attempted; and
- trucking out three loads of radioactive waste a day.[81]

In addition, Kaiser-Hill had yet to characterize much of the contaminated soil, delaying remediation plans, which cannot be made until the extent of contamination is determined. The Rocky Flats Cleanup Agreement set an interim "soil action level" of 651 picocuries of plutonium per gram of soil, but decision makers were considering other, more stringent levels (115 picocuries or less).[82] A report commissioned by the DOE and released in February 2000 recommended a much lower level of thirty-five picocuries of plutonium per gram of soil and suggested that levels as low as ten picocuries per gram may be necessary to ensure compliance with surface water standards. The soil cleanup level established could have a dramatic impact on the scope and cost of cleanup.

Further raising the costs are snags that have hampered the cleanup. In December 2000, plant officials disclosed that ten workers cleaning Building 771, the site's most contaminated building, had tested positive for exposure to radiation. More worrisome still, officials were unable to find the source of the radiation, and an earlier inspection had revealed that at least one radiation monitor in the building had malfunctioned.[83] In January 2001, the DOE revealed that Rocky Flats had fourteen criticality incidents in 1999 and five in 2000. Kaiser-Hill, which had been fined $700,000 for safety violations since 1996, acknowledged there were 138 worker-injury cases in 1999 and ninety-one in 2000.[84]

CONCLUSIONS

While the Rocky Flats case is unique in some respects, secrecy and disregard for environmental laws have been endemic throughout the defense establishment. The Pentagon's vast enterprise produces well over a ton of toxic wastes every minute, a yearly output that some contend is greater than that of the top five U.S. chemical companies combined. To make matters worse, the military branch of the federal government has for decades operated almost entirely unfettered by environmental laws. The armed forces have contaminated virtually every one of their installations in the United States and, undoubtedly, hundreds more overseas. At the majority of the military's contaminated facilities, huge quantities of toxic wastes dumped into the ground have seeped beyond their fences and into local groundwater. As journalist Seth Shulman noted in the early 1990s, "The military routinely [sanctioned] practices that [had] long been illegal for private firms operating in this country . . . even in the face of hard evidence that pollutants [had] contaminated the drinking water of nearby residents, the Pentagon . . . tried to keep the dumping secret and thereby knowingly threatened the health of millions of U.S. citizens."[85]

Secrecy bred arrogance and carelessness among government officials: as Douglas Pasternak of *U.S. News & World Report* makes clear, the DOE bears much of the responsibility for the contractor violations at Rocky Flats. Because of personnel or budget constraints, DOE officials were sometimes incapable of assessing contractor performance, so they allowed companies to assess their own work. The DOE almost never challenged these evaluations; in fact, the agency used them to help determine the amount of contractors' fees and bonuses. At Rocky Flats, despite numerous problems, Rockwell filed a positive assessment of its management. That assessment was rewritten, with only modest changes, at the DOE's Rocky Flats office and typed on DOE letterhead. The department then passed the report on to the agency's Albuquerque field office, which sent it unchanged to Washington for approval.[86] Nor was Rocky Flats the only culprit: a December 1988 DOE report listed 155 instances of environmental contamination at weapons plants and laboratories, many of which resulted from disposing of nonradioactive toxic waste using techniques that had been banned in private industry for more than a decade.[87]

Just as secrecy spawned recklessness, exposure enabled critics to redefine weapons production at Rocky Flats. New information disclosed by whistle-blowers, government investigators, and journalists supported an alternative portrayal of the plant as an imminent threat to the health of surrounding residents—which in turn prompted a public outcry. Over time, the feedback that developed among public outrage, media coverage, and congressional investigations created incentives first for Colorado politicians and eventually the president and Congress to support a massive nuclear weapons cleanup program.

The redefinition of weapons production at Rocky Flats was the product of a pragmatic alliance between mainstream environmental groups and local NIMBY activists. Working with NIMBY groups poses a dilemma for some environmentalists, however: they embody the participatory ideal that environmentalists cherish, yet they can thwart serious attempts to solve problems. One adverse consequence of NIMBYism is that toxic waste has been accumulating at sites that are ill-prepared to manage it in the long term. Unlike sites specifically chosen for hazardous waste disposal, such locations have not been scrutinized for their hydrological and geological fitness. Nor have the containers in which substances are housed been designed for long-term storage.

Finally, a major obstacle to the cleanup at Rocky Flats and other military installations is lack of agreement on how clean is clean enough. The EPA, in conjunction with the DOE, is establishing separate cleanup standards at each federal installation. Many observers suggest that cleanup levels ought to be tied to future land uses, pointing out that "it makes little sense to impose the same cleanup standards on a future airport or industrial site as on a future playground."[88] On the other hand, most acknowledge that future land uses are speculative. Moreover, it is difficult to ascertain the level of risk posed by a contaminated site, so even if participants agreed on the likely future use of the land, they would almost certainly still argue over what constitutes a safe level of cleanup. Such debates, which often pit citizens against experts, pose a potent challenge to democratic decision-making procedures. At Rocky Flats, managers are making conspicuous efforts to link citizens and experts in cleanup decisions in hopes of averting gridlock.

QUESTIONS TO CONSIDER

- What explains the careless management of Rocky Flats and other nuclear weapons plants?
- What safeguards do we have for ensuring that the government is not a major source of pollution?

- How can citizen groups, with their newfound influence, bring balance to decisions about appropriate cleanup plans for nuclear weapons production facilities, rather than simply cause gridlock?

Notes

1. Charles Piller, *The Fail-Safe Society: Community Defiance and the End of American Technological Optimism* (New York: Basic Books, 1991), 75.
2. Frank R. Baumgartner and Bryan D. Jones, *Agendas and Instability in American Politics* (Chicago: University of Chicago Press, 1993).
3. See, for example, Marc Landy and Mary Hague, "The Coalition for Waste: Private Interests and Superfund," in *Environmental Politics: Public Costs, Private Rewards,* ed. Michael S. Greve and Fred L. Smith (New York: Praeger, 1992), 67–87.
4. Piller, *The Fail-Safe Society,* 39.
5. Bryan Abas, "Rocky Flats: A Big Mistake From Day One," *Bulletin of Atomic Scientists* 45 (December 1989): 19–24.
6. Ibid., 20.
7. Len Ackland, *Making a Real Killing: Rocky Flats and the Nuclear West* (Albuquerque: University of New Mexico Press, 1999).
8. Quoted in Abas, "Rocky Flats, 20."
9. Mark Miller, "Trouble at Rocky Flats," *Newsweek,* August 14, 1989, 19.
10. The 1946 Atomic Energy Act, quoted in Ackland, *Making a Real Killing,* 33–34.
11. ChemRisk, "Reconstruction of Historical Rocky Flats Operations & Identification of Release Points" (Report produced for the Colorado Department of Public Health, August 1992).
12. Ibid., 51.
13. Ackland, *Making a Real Killing.*
14. Glove boxes are enclosed, lead-lined containers that are filled with inert gases designed to prevent the spontaneous combustion that occurs when plutonium comes into contact with moist air. Glove boxes are sealed with protective rubber gloves. Workers put their hands in the gloves and reach through portholes to handle radioactive materials inside the boxes.
15. Colorado Department of Public Health and Environment, "Summary of Findings: Historical Public Exposure Studies on Rocky Flats," August 1999.
16. Abas, "Rocky Flats." Dow's official investigation report, which was classified until 1993, stated that 18.3 pounds of plutonium were unaccounted for after the fire, but health physicists have estimated the actual plutonium release at between 1.8 ounces and 1.1 pounds. See Ackland, *Making a Real Killing.*
17. Ackland, *Making a Real Killing*; Piller, *The Fail-Safe Society.*
18. Quoted in Mark Obmascik, "Price of Peace," *Denver Post,* June 25, 2000, A1.
19. Ibid.
20. Piller, *The Fail-Safe Society*; Colorado Department of Public Health, "Summary of Findings."
21. Quoted in Ackland, *Making a Real Killing,* 158.
22. Michael Janofsky, "Workers Cleaning Nuclear Arms Site for Wildlife Preserve Test Positive for Radiation," *New York Times,* December 8, 2000, A19.
23. Colorado Department of Public Health, "Summary of Findings."
24. The radioactivity released in atmospheric tests is dispersed in the upper atmosphere, whereas Rocky Flats' releases stay much closer to the surface. See Abas, "Rocky Flats."
25. Abas, "Rocky Flats."
26. Ackland, *Making a Real Killing.*
27. Tritium is the sole radioactive isotope of the element hydrogen.
28. Abas, "Rocky Flats."

29. Piller, *The Fail-Safe Society*.
30. Carl Johnson, "Cancer Incidence in an Area Contaminated with Radionuclides Near a Nuclear Installation," *Ambio*, August 1981, 176–182; Carl Johnson et al., "Cancer Incidence and Mortality, 1957–1981, in the Denver Standard Metropolitan Area Downwind From the Rocky Flats Nuclear Plant," paper presented at the epidemiological section of the American Public Health Association (November 11, 1983).
31. Ackland, *Making a Real Killing*.
32. James Baker, "A New Scare at Rocky Flats," *Newsweek*, June 26, 1989, 60.
33. Abas, "Rocky Flats."
34. Such devices use 1,000-degree Fahrenheit smokeless, flameless chemical reactions to incinerate waste.
35. Quoted in Thomas J. Knudson, "Families Fear Test on Nuclear Waste," *New York Times*, April 23, 1987, A16.
36. Ibid.
37. Ibid.
38. Piller, *The Fail-Safe Society*.
39. Ibid.
40. Quoted in Piller, *The Fail-Safe Society*, 52.
41. Ibid.
42. Abas, "Rocky Flats."
43. U.S. General Accounting Office, "Nuclear Health and Safety: Summary of Major Problems at DOE's Rocky Flats Plant," RCED-89-53-BR (October 1988).
44. George J. Church, "Playing Atomic NIMBY," *Time*, December 26, 1988, 29.
45. Until 1984, the DOE managed the mixed hazardous and radioactive wastes generated by its facilities independent of any outside supervision. That year, however, a court ruling subjected DOE facilities to the federal Resource Conservation and Recovery Act (RCRA), which establishes a "cradle to grave" tracking system for such wastes and requires firms that handle hazardous waste to obtain a waste disposal permit from the EPA or an authorized state agency. The state of Colorado established the 1,600-cubic-yard limit on on-site mixed and hazardous wastes. After initially resisting state control, in 1986, the DOE submitted to state jurisdiction over its hazardous and mixed wastes because it feared having to reveal "patently illegal" waste management practices at the plant. See Piller, *The Fail-Safe Society*. Colorado Health Department officials cited Rocky Flats in 1988 for nine violations of hazardous waste disposal laws, but a year later they had not determined the amount of the fine—it could have been as much as $25,000 for each violation—let alone collected any money. See Abas, "Rocky Flats."
46. Church, "Playing Atomic NIMBY."
47. Piller, *The Fail-Safe Society*, 74.
48. Miller, "Trouble at Rocky Flats."
49. "Nuclear Mystery," *Time*, June 26, 1989, 31.
50. Quoted in Abas, "Rocky Flats, 24."
51. Vicky Cahan, "Energy Czar—and Environmental Activist?" *Business Week*, July 24, 1989, 54.
52. Thomas Graf, "Safety Pact Reached Reached on Rocky Flats," *Denver Post*, June 17, 1989, 1.
53. Quoted in Minard Hamilton, "Papered Over," *Mother Jones*, November–December 1990, 29.
54. Ibid.
55. In September 1989, the DOE and Rockwell had agreed to terminate Rockwell's management contract.
56. Hamilton, "Papered Over,"
57. Ibid, 29.
58. Quoted in ibid., 29.
59. Ibid.

60. Quoted in Matthew L. Wald, "As U.S. Struggles to Restart Colorado Bomb Plant, Critics Question Its Need," *New York Times*, July 25, 1991, A18.

61. R. Jeffrey Smith, "Ultimate Recycling: Nuclear Warheads," *Science*, May 24, 1991, 1056.

62. Keith Schneider, "New Irregularities Found at A-Weapons Plants," *New York Times*, May 24, 1991, A13.

63. "Manager of Troubled Arms Plant is Removed," *New York Times*, October 21, 1990, 25.

64. Matthew L. Wald, "New Setbacks for Nuclear Arms Complex," *New York Times*, September 10, 1991, A17.

65. Quoted in Matthew L. Wald, "Plutonium Plant Accused in Civil Suit," *New York Times*, October 26, 1991, A6.

66. "The Rocky Flats Cover-up, Continued," *Harper's Magazine*, December 1992, 19–23.

67. Quoted in ibid., 19. In response to the report's publication, Judge Sherman Finesilver ordered the FBI to investigate whether jurors had violated federal grand jury secrecy laws, but that investigation eventually was dropped.

68. Douglas Pasternak, "A $200 Billion Scandal," *U.S. News & World Report*, December 14, 1992, 34–47.

69. Michael Lemonick, "Sometimes It Takes a Cowboy," *Time*, January 25, 1993, 58.

70. Ibid.

71. Matthew L. Wald, "Nuclear Fingerprints All Over, But Try to Find the Hands," *New York Times*, June 7, 1992, E4.

72. In 1991, the DOE, the EPA, and the CDPHE signed the Rocky Flats Interagency Agreement identifying 178 contaminated areas at the site and establishing a comprehensive plan for environmental restoration.

73. Theo Stein, "Flats Touted as Wildlife Refuge," *Denver Post*, February 22, 2001, B1; Kevin Flynn, "Arvada Backs Flats as Refuge," *Denver Rocky Mountain News*, August 29, 2000, 18A.

74. Representative Mark Udall, "Introduction of Rocky Flats National Wildlife Refuge Act," U.S. Congress, House, *Congressional Record* 107th Cong., 1st sess., March 1, 2001.

75. Associated Press, "Cost of Rocky Flats Cleanup $400 Million Higher Than Expected" (April 21, 2000); Walter A. Rosenbaum, *Environmental Politics and Policy*, 5th ed. (Washington, D.C.: CQ Press, 2001).

76. Rocky Flats Coalition of Local Governments, et al., "Rocky Flats Closure" (April 2000).

77. U.S. General Accounting Office, *Nuclear Cleanup: Progress Made at Rocky Flats, but Closure by 2000 is Unlikely, and Costs May Increase*, GAO-01-284.

78. Ibid. Those eighty-one structures comprised 196,000 square feet, or 5 percent of the total square footage. At the end of 2000, 721 structures comprising 3.4 million square feet remained to be demolished.

79. Ibid.

80. Obmascik, "Price of Peace."

81. Ibid.

82. A soil action level is the level that, when exceeded, triggers an evaluation, remedial and/or management action. See GAO, *Nuclear Cleanup*.

83. Janofsky, "Workers Cleaning Nuclear Arms Site."

84. Stacie Oulton, "Flats Cleanup Violations Cited," *Denver Post*, January 9, 2001, B4.

85. Seth Shulman, *The Threat at Home* (Boston: Little, Brown, 1992), xiii.

86. Pasternak, "A $200 Billion Scandal."

87. See Pat Towell, "Need for a Massive Cleanup May Slow Weapon-Building," *Congressional Quarterly*, January 20, 1990, 178–183.

88. John A. Hird, *Superfund: The Political Economy of Environmental Risk* (Baltimore: Johns Hopkins University Press, 1994), 111.

Recommended Reading

Ackland, Len. *Making a Real Killing: Rocky Flats and the Nuclear West.* Albuquerque: University of New Mexico Press, 1999.
Shulman, Seth. *The Threat at Home.* Boston: Little, Brown, 1992.

Web Sites

http://www.em.doe.gov/index4.html (DOE site)
http://www.rfcab.org (Rocky Flats Citizen Advisory Board site)
http://www.rfets.gov (Rocky Flats Environmental Technology site)

CHAPTER 5

Oil Versus Wilderness in the Arctic National Wildlife Refuge

The controversy over drilling for oil on the Coastal Plain of Alaska's Arctic National Wildlife Refuge (ANWR) has raged for more than fifteen years, beginning shortly after the passage of the Alaska National Interest Lands Conservation Act (ANILCA) in 1980. The conflict pits those who want to explore for oil and gas in the remote refuge against those who want to see the area off-limits to all development. An unusual statutory provision in ANILCA requires congressional approval for oil exploration, so this battle has been waged almost entirely in Congress. Over the years, it has featured fierce public relations campaigns by each side, as well as a variety of legislative maneuvers. Most recently, the refuge seized the spotlight as the major environmental issue debated in the 2000 presidential campaign and the centerpiece of newly elected President George W. Bush's national energy policy.

The ANWR (pronounced "anwar") dispute has all the hallmarks of the longstanding divide between proponents of natural resource extraction and advocates of wilderness preservation. Such controversies are particularly intractable because the two sides are separated by fundamental and irreconcilable value differences. In contrast to controversies over human health, which involve relatively consensual values, decision making about ANWR confronts ecological values, about which differences are wide and often unbridgeable. For wilderness advocates, compromise is unthinkable: any development in a pristine area constitutes a complete loss, a total violation of the spiritual and aesthetic qualities of the place. For development proponents, such an attitude reflects a lack of concern about human economic needs. The chasm between the two sides also arises from their differing views about what constitutes "security"[1]: environmentalists believe that security lies in fulfilling a long-term obligation to preserve wild places, whereas cornucopians believe that security depends on spurring economic growth and creating jobs.

The tactics employed by both sides reflects their strategic focus on the legislative arena, where the battle over ANWR will be decided. Ordinarily, development interests pursue their policy goals out of the limelight, in the administrative arena if possible. Even in Congress, in the absence of public attention, an influential industry combined with local interests in economic development can usually have its way. In this case, however, wilderness advocates have managed to expand the scope of the conflict, using symbols and metaphors to transform a local battle into a national fight, thereby changing dramatically the dynamics of the legislative process. Forced to respond, development advocates have adopted symbols and metaphors of their own to appeal to such widely held values as economic growth, national security, and local control. In support of their definitions of the problem, both sides interpret technical and scientific information in ways consistent with their own values. And both sides latch onto focusing events to shape public perceptions and open windows of opportunity for policy change.

Nor are advocates the only ones engaged in problem definition: decision makers, too, frame information in ways consistent with their values. Experts within administrative agencies choose among plausible assumptions in formulating the official models and projections on which policy decisions are based. The crafting of official reports often reveals tension between an agency's professionals and its political appointees, however. The former are primarily driven by professional norms and standards, while the latter share the ideology of the White House. Not surprisingly, the two are sometimes incompatible.

This case also features an unusual twist on typical natural resource policymaking: wilderness advocates in the ANWR debate are advantaged by the fact that not drilling is the status quo, and it is always much easier to *block* policy change than it is to *bring about* policy change. This advantage is enhanced by the legislative complexity of energy policymaking: at least two committees in each chamber, and as many as seven in the House, claim jurisdiction over energy decisions. Ordinarily, a single committee has jurisdiction over a bill; however, since the 1970s, multiple referral—or referral of a bill to more than one committee—has become increasingly common, particularly in the House. Multiple referral, which can be simultaneous or sequential, complicates the legislative process because a bill must clear all of the committees of reference before it can go to the floor.[2] Legislating a national energy policy is also daunting because so many organizations mobilize in response to the myriad provisions that threaten to impose costs or promise to deliver benefits. The involvement of multiple interests brings controversy and the possibility of antagonizing one or more of them, something legislators prefer to avoid.

Finally, the ANWR decision involves two stakeholders with independent claims. The Canadian government has voiced its desire to be included in decision making about the refuge because area wildlife migrates across national borders. Two Native American tribes, who have prior (and, in this case, competing) claims on the region's land and resources, also demand a voice in the decision making. Native Americans and Canadians have sided with one coalition or the other in this controversy; like scientific and economic evidence, their claims serve primarily as weapons wielded by both sides in their efforts to prevail.

By exploring the relationship between problem definition and legislative policymaking, this chapter shows why the ANWR debate has been so persistently difficult to resolve and what the prospects are for the future.

BACKGROUND

The ANWR debate is the most recent manifestation of a century-old conflict over Alaska's resource-based economy and the state's relationship to the federal government. The battle over the trans-Alaska pipeline, in particular, set the stage for the passage of the Alaska National Interest Lands Conservation Act (ANILCA) in 1980, which, in turn, created the legal and institutional context for the protracted conflict over ANWR. Shortly after ANILCA's passage, two distinct coalitions formed: one to advocate wilderness designation for the newly established refuge, the other to promote oil and gas development in the region.

A History of Resource Exploitation in Alaska

From the time the United States acquired the Alaska territory from Russia in 1867, American adventurers seeking to make their fortunes have exploited the area's natural resources. The first terrestrial resource to attract attention was gold. Discovery of the Klondike gold fields in 1896, at a time when the territory's white population was little more than 10,000, precipitated an influx of prospectors and others hoping to profit from the boom. Development there from the late 1800s to mid-1900s conformed to the boom-and-bust cycle typical of natural resource–based economies. Prior to the declaration of Alaskan statehood in the late 1950s, the federal government set aside millions of acres of land to conserve natural resources—including coal, oil, gas, and timber—in order to exploit them in the national interest.

Environmentalists had long expressed concern about saving Alaska's natural beauty as well; as early as the 1930s, Bob Marshall began pleading for the preservation of Alaskan wilderness.[3] While the U.S. Navy was searching for oil and gas, the National Park Service began to investigate Alaska's recreational potential, and in 1954—after surveying the Eastern Brooks Range—it recommended that the federal government preserve the northeastern corner of Alaska for its wildlife, wilderness, recreational, scientific, and cultural values. Fearing inroads by environmentalists, Alaska boosters such as Robert Atwood—editor and publisher of the *Anchorage Daily Times*—and Walter Hickel—millionaire real estate developer, contractor, and hotelier—advocated statehood to support greater economic development. In 1957, a pro-statehood pamphlet declared: "If Alaska becomes a state, other people, like ourselves, will be induced to settle here without entangling federal red tape and enjoy an opportunity to develop this great land."[4]

On January 3, 1959, after more than a decade of debate, Congress made Alaska a state, and for the next twenty years, the state and its native tribes jockeyed to select lands for acquisition. In 1966, Interior Secretary Stewart Udall froze applications for title to Alaska's unappropriated land until Congress could settle outstanding native claims. The same year, however, Walter Hickel was elected governor. With Hickel's swearing-in began a long period of development in the state, best symbolized by the rush to develop the Prudhoe Bay oil field that began with Atlantic Richfield's strike in the winter of 1967–1968.[5]

The Trans-Alaska Pipeline Controversy

In 1969, President Richard Nixon appointed Walter Hickel secretary of the interior, a position from which he was well placed to act as a policy entrepreneur for his pet project: the trans-Alaska pipeline. On February 10, 1969, the "big three" companies that had been developing oil reserves on the North Slope area of ANWR came together into a loose consortium, calling themselves the Trans-Alaska Pipeline System (TAPS), and announced plans to build a 798-mile-long pipeline from the oil fields at Prudhoe Bay to the port of Valdez. This announcement coincided with a surge in national environmental consciousness, however, making a clash over the project inevitable. At first, opponents were able to delay the project by citing technical impediments, administrative and legal requirements, and native claims.[6] The history of the oil industry's destructive practices in the Arctic also generated public skepticism about TAPS. During 1970, resistance crystallized, and national environmental groups filed three lawsuits to try to stop the pipeline, citing the Mineral Leasing Act and the National Environmental Policy Act (NEPA).[7] Nevertheless, in January 1971, an Interior Department staff report recommended building the pipeline even though it would cause unavoidable environmental damage.

By this time, President Nixon had replaced Hickel with Rogers Morton, who was dubious about the pipeline and wanted more information. Interior Department hearings held in February 1971 "became a showcase of unyielding positions" in which environmentalists warned that the pipeline would destroy pristine wilderness, while oil interests claimed that Alaskan oil was economically essential and that environmental risks were minimal.[8] Activists subsequently formed the Alaska Public Interest Coalition (APIC) to coordinate and intensify the public campaign against the pipeline.[9] Complicating matters for APIC, however, was the December 1971 passage of the Alaska Native Claims Settlement Act (ANCSA), which had been strongly supported by oil and gas interests. ANCSA transferred to native Alaskans ownership of 44 million acres and proffered a settlement of nearly $1 billion—half of which was to be paid from oil production royalties—thereby giving native Alaskans a powerful financial incentive to support oil development. At the same time, the act prohibited the state of Alaska or its native tribes from selecting lands within a proposed oil pipeline corridor to be part of the 44 million acres, thereby ensuring that neither the state nor a native tribe could use its property rights to block the project.

In 1972, the Interior Department released its final environmental impact statement (EIS) on the pipeline.[10] Environmentalists immediately challenged the EIS in court, arguing that it was based on unreliable data and failed to consider transportation alternatives. Public sentiment remained strongly against the pipeline until the summer of 1973, when forecasts of an energy crisis opened a window of opportunity for development advocates. The oil industry capitalized on the specter of an oil shortage to generate approval for the pipeline, and in July the Senate narrowly passed the Gravel Amendment,

which declared that the Interior Department's EIS fulfilled all the requirements of NEPA, thus releasing the project from further legal delay.[11] Just
before the end of its 1973 session, Congress passed the Trans-Alaska Pipeline
Authorization Act (361–14 in the House and 80–5 in the Senate), and on
November 16, President Nixon signed it into law.[12]

The Alaska National Interest Lands Conservation Act (ANILCA)

Although development interests prevailed in the pipeline controversy,
environmentalists in the 1960s and 1970s succeeded in staking some claims to
Alaska as well. On December 9, 1960, Interior Secretary Fred Seaton set aside
8.9 million acres as the Arctic National Wildlife Range. Then, acting under Section 17d(2) of ANCSA, which authorized the secretary to set aside "national
interest" lands to be considered for national park, wilderness, wildlife refuge,
or national forest status, Seaton added 3.7 million acres to the existing Arctic
National Wildlife Range. In the late 1970s, environmentalists began to campaign for federal protection for the lands Seaton had set aside. Their campaign
ended in 1980, when Congress enacted ANILCA, which placed 104 million
acres of public domain land under federal protection.[13] The act reclassified the
original 8.9-million-acre Arctic National Wildlife Range as the Arctic National
Wildlife Refuge, adding to the refuge all lands, waters, interests, and submerged lands under federal ownership at the time Alaska became a state.
ANILCA also added to the original refuge 9.1 million acres of adjoining public lands, extending west to the pipeline and south to the Yukon Flats National
Wildlife Refuge.

ANILCA made significant compromises, however, such as excluding from
federal protection areas with significant development potential. The provision
of particular consequence was Section 1002, which instructed the Interior
Department to study the mineral and wildlife resources of the refuge's 1.5 million-acre Coastal Plain to determine its suitability for oil and gas exploration
and development. Although the House of Representatives had favored
wilderness designation for this area, often called the "ecological heart" of the
refuge, the Senate had resisted in the absence of a thorough assessment of its
oil and gas potential. Section 1002 prohibited leasing, development, and production of oil and gas in the refuge unless authorized by Congress.[14]

At first glance, oil and gas production might appear to be anathema in a
refuge: the statutory purpose of the refuge system, established in 1966, is "to
provide, preserve, restore, and manage a national network of lands and waters
sufficient in size, diversity, and location to meet society's needs for areas
where the widest possible spectrum of benefits associated with wildlife and
wildlands is enhanced and made available."[15] More specifically, ANILCA says
that ANWR is to be managed:

(i) to conserve fish and wildlife populations and habitats in their natural
diversity including, but not limited to, the Porcupine caribou herd (including

the participation in coordinated ecological studies and management of this herd and the Western Arctic caribou herd), polar bears, grizzly bears, muskox, Dall sheep, wolves, wolverines, snow geese, peregrine falcons, and other migratory birds and Arctic char and grayling; (ii) to fulfill the international treaty obligations of the United States with respect to fish and wildlife and their habitats; (iii) to provide, in a manner consistent with purposes set forth in subparagraphs (i) and (ii), the opportunity for continued subsistence uses by local residents; and (iv) to ensure, to the maximum extent practicable and in a manner consistent with the purposes set forth in subparagraph (i), water quality and necessary water quantity within the refuge.

On the other hand, a key provision of Section 4(d) of the act that establishes the refuge system authorizes the use of a refuge for any purpose, including mineral leasing, as long as that use is "compatible with the major purpose for which the area was established." In fact, private companies hold mining as well as oil and gas leases on many of the nation's wildlife refuges, and oil and gas exploration and development take place in twenty-nine of them.[16] While there is little documentation of the environmental impact of resource development in wildlife refuges, in a 1991–1992 survey a substantial number of managers in the U.S. Fish and Wildlife Service, which administers the refuge system, describe oil and gas operations in their refuges as incompatible with wildlife protection.[17] But with funding of only $2 per acre, compared to $13 per acre for the Park Service and $7 per acre for the Forest Service, the Fish and Wildlife Service has limited resources with which to resist such incursions.[18]

THE CASE

The Arctic National Wildlife Refuge is the most northerly unit, and the second largest, in the National Wildlife Refuge System. It encompasses about 19.6 million acres of land in northeast Alaska—an area almost as large as New England. It is bordered to the west by the trans-Alaska pipeline corridor, to the south by the Venetie-Arctic Village lands and Yukon Flats National Wildlife Refuge, to the east by Canada, and to the north by the Beaufort Sea. Fairbanks, the nearest city, is about 180 miles south of the refuge boundary by air. Two villages, Kaktovik on Barter Island and Arctic Village on the south slope of the Brooks Range, are immediately adjacent to the refuge.

The refuge encompasses a full range of boreal forest, mountain, and northern slope landscapes and habitats. It contains the four tallest peaks and the most glaciers in the Brooks Range. The refuge's northern edge descends to the Beaufort Sea and a series of barrier island and lagoons, while the valley slopes are dotted with lakes, sloughs, and wetlands. In the southeastern portion, the Porcupine River area, groves of stunted black spruce grade into tall, dense spruce forests. As well as containing portions of the key calving ground for the 130,000-member Porcupine caribou herd and critical habitat for the endangered peregrine falcon, ANWR is home to snow geese, tundra swans, wolves, wolverines, arctic foxes, lynx, marten, and moose. The rivers, lakes, and lagoons contain arctic grayling, lake trout, whitefish, northern pike, turbot, arctic cod, and several varieties of salmon. The waters offshore harbor summering bowhead whales, and the coastal lagoons provide year-round habitat for polar bears and ringed and bearded seals.

Although a quintessential wilderness little visited by humans, ANWR is an unusual poster child for the preservationist cause: it is not among the most aesthetically spectacular of America's wild places. Yet advocates of preservation have created a powerful image of the refuge as the nation's last remaining true wilderness, whose very existence is a symbol of the American frontier. Their opponents have also crafted a compelling case, however, in which oil development in the Coastal Plain of the refuge will enhance Americans' economic and military security at a marginal risk to an unappealing landscape.

The ANWR Coalitions

Spearheading the movement to preserve ANWR's Coastal Plain is the Alaska Coalition, a consortium of seventy-five Alaskan, national, and international environmental groups. Among the most influential members are the Sierra Club, the Wilderness Society, the Natural Resources Defense Council, the National Wildlife Federation, the Audubon Society, and the Trustees for Alaska. Backing the environmentalists are the Gwich'in Eskimos, a subgroup of the Athabascan tribe that for thousands of years has relied on the Porcupine caribou herd for its survival. The government of Canada, another player on this side, also opposes opening the refuge to development because the Porcupine caribou and other wildlife regularly migrate across the Canadian border.

The primary force behind the campaign to open up the ANWR to development is the oil industry, which has always been a formidable presence in U.S. politics. The industry is particularly influential in Alaska because the state's economy is dependent on oil; the state government derives about 85 percent of its revenues from oil royalties[19]; and instead of paying income tax, Alaskans receive an approximately $1,000 annual dividend from oil revenues. Taking no chances, the industry also contributes heavily to the campaigns of the state's elected officials. Supporting the oil companies as well are the Inupiat Eskimos, who live in Kaktovik and are represented by the Arctic Slope Regional Corporation (ASRC). Not only have oil revenues brought prosperity to the small community of Inupiat living within the refuge, but in an effort to build native support for development, Congress authorized the ASRC to acquire 92,160 acres of subsurface mineral interests underlying the Inupiat's claim, should Congress ever open the refuge to oil and gas development. In 1987, the ASRC formed the Coalition for American Energy Security (CAES), which subsequently grew to include motorized recreation, agriculture, labor, maritime, transportation, and other interests and quickly became the primary lobbying arm on behalf of ANWR development.

Battling to Define the Problem, 1986–1992

From the outset, the parties in this debate defined the problem in contrasting ways, describing scientific and economic risks and uncertainties in ways that were consistent with their values. Proponents of drilling argued that the nation needs to develop its domestic oil reserves to preserve national security and boost the economy, and they asserted that the supply available in ANWR was significant enough to justifiy the minimal risk of environmental harm. In contrast, opponents of development pointed out that the amount of oil that ANWR is likely to hold would satisfy just a tiny fraction of total domestic demand and therefore would only marginally reduce the nation's dependence on foreign oil. Moreover, they said, development would certainly create air and water pollution; generate toxic wastes; disturb wildlife habitat; and, most importantly, destroy the wilderness character of the landscape. By the late 1980s, when the conflict was in full swing, both sides had developed elaborate arguments about the national interest in ANWR and had marshalled and interpreted scientific and economic evidence to support their claims and rebut those of their opponents.

The Potential Benefits of Oil and Gas Development. The U.S. Department of Interior has developed the authoritative models predicting the amount of oil that lies under the refuge's Coastal Plain. The first of these, the 1987 *Arctic National Wildlife Refuge, Alaska, Coastal Plain Report*, known as the "1002 Report," concluded that there was a 19 percent chance of finding economically recoverable oil reserves.[20] The report judged it possible to recover between 600 million and 9.2 billion barrels of oil, with a mean of 3.2 billion barrels. If that average were correct, the Coastal Plain would be the third largest oil field in U.S. history. According to the report's mean case scenario, ANWR would produce 147,000 barrels per day by the year 2000, peak at 659,000 barrels per day in 2005, fall over the next decade to 400,000 barrels per day, and continue to decline for the remaining thirty- to fifty-year life of the field. At its peak, ANWR's production would equal 4 percent of U.S. consumption, 8 percent of domestic production, and about 9 percent of imports, while increasing GNP by $74.9 billion and reducing the annual trade deficit by approximately $6 billion.[21]

Wielding these official estimates, proponents of development advanced the argument that developing the Coastal Plain would enhance national security. They cited the country's growing dependence on imported oil, noting that of the 17.3 million barrels per day consumed in 1990, oil imports averaged 7.6 million barrels per day, with 2.1 million of those coming from the politically unstable Middle East. In 1990, the Energy Department predicted that, without changes in the nation's energy policy, imports would account for 65 percent of the nation's oil supply by 2010. Using evocative language, drilling advocates stressed America's vulnerability to reliance on foreign oil: "Remember that two million barrels of oil a day coming down that pipeline from Alaska's

Prudhoe Bay played a major role in breaking OPEC's grip. And recall how that grip felt, with its lines at the gasoline pumps and aggravated inflation."[22] Alaska Republican Sen. Ted Stevens warned that "without the Arctic Wildlife Range resources, this nation faces the threat of a precarious future in which OPEC nations would be able to hold another and perhaps more serious oil embargo over our heads."[23]

Environmentalists used the same information but framed it differently to argue that the amount of recoverable oil that *might* lie within the refuge was unlikely to enhance the nation's energy security, noting that it would most likely amount to "less than 200 days worth of oil at current consumption rates" and "less than 3 percent of our daily demand."[24] Environmentalists also contended that the nation's need for additional oil supplies was more apparent than real. They pointed out that the rise in U.S. petroleum imports in the late 1980s was accompanied by a decline in conservation—which was not surprising since the price of oil was low and federal incentives to conserve had atrophied. Environmentalists had official data to support their claims as well: the Congressional Research Service estimated that energy conservation R&D expenditures in real dollars fell from $322 million in 1981 to $129 in 1989. Funding for renewable energy R&D also dropped dramatically, from $708 million in 1981 to $110 million in 1990, before rising to $157 million in 1991.[25] Reflecting the low oil prices and lack of conservation incentives, automotive fuel efficiency fell in the late 1980s for the first time since 1973. Daniel Lashof, senior scientist for the Union of Concerned Scientists, concluded: "There is simply no way we can produce our way to energy security. [Oil from ANWR] cannot significantly affect world prices or world markets for oil. The only way we can insulate our economy from price shocks is by improving our efficiency and reducing our total consumption of oil."[26]

Drilling advocates had a subsidiary argument about the benefits of drilling in the refuge, however: they claimed that opening ANWR to development would ease the federal deficit and create jobs. In 1990, the pro-development CAES suggested that if DOI's high-end estimates of the refuge's oil potential were correct, GNP could rise by $50.4 billion by 2005 and reduce the trade deficit by billions of dollars. Citing a 1990 study by Wharton Econometrics Forecasting Associates, the CAES contended that developing a 9.2-billion-barrel oil field (the high-end estimate, on which they again chose to focus) would create 735,000 jobs by 2005. Literature produced by the CAES reinforced its claims: at the height of the controversy, the organization was distributing a glossy, eight-page monthly newsletter with articles entitled "Leasing ANWR Could Ease Budget Woes" and "Rising Oil Prices Push Up U.S. Trade Deficit," as well as a postcard-sized map of the United States showing the dollar amounts generated in each state by existing oil development in the North Slope area.

Environmentalists responded to the deficit argument in turn, pointing out that non-DOI analysts using different oil price projections and revised tax and financial assumptions had generated very different total expected present values of developing ANWR. In 1990, those values ranged from $0.32 billion to $1.39 billion, compared to DOI's $2.98 billion.[27] Furthermore, they pointed out, GNP figures disguise the allocation of oil revenues, most of which go to oil companies. To highlight the self-interested motives of the pro-drilling coalition, environmentalists noted that the oil industry reaped more than $41 billion in profit from North Slope oil development and transportation between 1969 and 1987, according to a study done for the Alaska Department of Revenue.[28]

Anti-drilling advocates added that developing photovoltaics, wind, and other alternative energy sources would yield new jobs as well. Such jobs, they contended, would also have the advantage of being local and stable, not subject to the boom-and-bust cycles that have ravaged Texas, Oklahoma, and Alaska. Finally, environmentalists reiterated that conservation measures could have a much bigger impact on domestic oil consumption, and thus on the trade deficit, than increased domestic oil production. For instance, they said, an increase in fuel economy standards to 40 mpg for new cars and 30 mpg for light trucks could save more than 20 billion barrels of oil by 2020—more than six times the total amount the government believed lay under ANWR's Coastal Plain.

The Environmental Costs of Oil and Gas Development. Not only did environmentalists contest estimates of the economic and security value of ANWR reserves, but they also raised the specter of certain and catastrophic ecological impacts of oil development in the refuge. Most importantly, they emphasized, ANWR's Coastal Plain provides insect relief and is the calving grounds for the Porcupine caribou herd, the second largest caribou herd in Alaska and the seventh largest in the world. They pointed out that most biologists believe the cumulative disturbance resulting from North Slope oil field activity has prevented many Central Arctic herd caribou from feeding optimally, resulting in reduced summer weight gain, decreased pregnancy rates, and increased mortality. Biologists forecast similar effects on the Porcupine caribou herd in the event of Coastal Plain development.

Anti-drilling advocates also highlighted biologists' concern about the effect on the approximately 2,000 polar bears that roam the stretch from northwestern Alaska to the Northwestern Territories in Canada. Studies show that pregnant polar bears consistently use the Coastal Plain and the refuge lands to the east as sites for onshore denning during the winter. Although only a relatively small number of female bears use the 1002 area for dens, the area is nonetheless important: researchers found that the productivity of land dens in the Beaufort Sea polar bear population from 1981 to 1989 was significantly higher than that of dens on the offshore ice pack. Furthermore, biologists believe that the Beaufort Sea polar bear population can sustain little, if any, additional mortality of females; the number of animals dying annually is already equal to the number born each year.[29]

Supporting environmentalists' position was the Interior Department's own 1002 Report, which warned of poor long-term prospects for wildlife in a developed Coastal Plain based on wildlife studies at Prudhoe Bay:

> Post-development studies indicate an absence of calving near the coast of Prudhoe Bay during 1976–85, possibly due to avoidance of the area by caribou. Despite apparent changes in distribution, the populations of both caribou herds have been increasing. At some point, however, incremental loss and modification of suitable calving habitat could be expected to result in population declines. Similarly, at some time, cumulative habitat loss within the region potentially could result in changes in habitat distribution or population reductions of other species including muskoxen, wolves, wolverines, polar bears, snow geese, and arctic grayling.[30]

Also providing official support for the environmentalists' position was a paper sent by the Canadian government in February 1987, pointing out that "The migratory wildlife populations that range between Canada and the United States are a special category of resource . . . not owned exclusively by either country . . . . Each country, therefore, has obligations to conserve these stocks and their habitats so that the value of the wildlife to the other country is not unacceptably reduced."

The oil industry rejected environmentalists' assertion that oil development would disturb wildlife, emphasizing the uncertainty surrounding scientific estimates of likely wildlife impacts. A BP Exploration publication portrayed environmentalists as unscientific and misanthropic, saying "Claims of serious adverse effects on fish and wildlife populations are simply not supported by scientific data and may in fact represent an objection to the presence of humans in a wild area."[31] The industry got a boost when Interior Secretary Donald Hodel wrote an editorial in the *New York Times* saying "we do not have to choose between an adequate supply of energy on the one hand and a secure environment on the other. We can have both."[32]

The two sides also disputed the size of the footprint that would be made by oil development on the Coastal Plain. The CAES pointed out that oil operations on the Coastal Plain would occupy only nineteen square miles, an area roughly the size of Washington, D.C.'s Dulles Airport. Environmentalists responded that while the Prudhoe Bay complex covers a mere 9,000 acres, that acreage is spread out over 800 square miles. The Office of Technology Assessment concurred, saying:

> although the industry argues—correctly—that the actual coverage of the surface is likely to be less than one percent of the coastal plain, the physical coverage would be spread out like a spiderweb, and some further physical effects, like infiltration of road dust and changes in drainage patterns, will spread out from the land actually covered.[33]

Environmentalists added that the oil industry had a poor record at both estimating likely environmental impacts and repairing damage, citing a Fish and Wildlife Service report comparing the actual and predicted impacts of the trans-Alaska pipeline and the Prudhoe Bay oil fields. The report concluded that the actual area of gravel fill and extraction was 60 percent greater than expected; gravel requirements surpassed predictions by 400 percent; and road miles exceeded the planned number by 30 percent.[34]

Finally, environmentalists noted that although it does support a host of wildlife, ANWR's Coastal Plain is a fragile arctic ecosystem and is more vulnerable than temperate ecosystems to damage from industrial activity. To support this claim, they pointed out that ANWR is an arctic desert, receiving an average of only seven inches of moisture a year, while the subsoil, permafrost, remains frozen year round, and only the top few inches to three feet of soil thaw in the summer. The combination of low temperatures, a short growing season, and restricted nutrients limit the area's biological productivity. Because plants grow slowly, any physical disturbance—even driving vehicles across the terrain in winter—can scar the land for decades, and regrowth can take centuries.[35] In addition, like other arctic areas, ANWR contains large concentrations of animal populations but relatively low diversity. Mammal populations, in particular, gather in large numbers, thereby heightening their vulnerability to catastrophe. Arctic plants are more sensitive to pollutants than are species that grow in warmer climates. Toxic substances persist for longer periods of time in cold environments than in more temperate climates. And the severe weather and complex ice dynamics of the arctic complicate both environmental protection and accident cleanup.[36]

In addition to wielding different causal stories and numbers in the debate, the two sides adopted contrasting symbols. Environmentalists characterized the refuge as the last great American wilderness, a vast expanse of untrammeled landscape that provides a home for increasingly rare arctic wildlife. They likened opening the refuge to "destroy[ing] America's Serengeti" for a few weeks' supply of oil.[37] In contrast, proponents of development described the area as a barren, marshy wilderness in the summer and a frozen desert the rest of the year. "ANWR's Coastal Plain is no Yellowstone," according to a *Wall Street Journal* editorial. The rhetoric reveals the polarization between opposing camps' values: there is no possibility of compromise; opening the refuge to any development represents a defeat to advocates of preservation.

The Political Contest, 1986–1992

These competing arguments had a profound impact on legislative politics. By nationalizing the issue, environmentalists enabled legislators to claim credit with their environmentalist constituents for protecting the refuge. Development interests responded by trying to persuade uncommitted legislators that developing the refuge would provide their constituents with jobs, cheap oil, and international security. Both sides tried to capitalize on focusing events to gain the upper hand. Protection advocates were advantaged because not drilling is the status quo, and it is easier to block a policy change in Congress than to enact one. Further weakening the prospects for oil development, ANWR falls under the jurisdiction of multiple committees in Congress, which also makes obstructing policy change easier. Finally, the sheer complexity of national energy policy makes it contentious and therefore unattractive to most legislators, who want to avoid provoking opposition.

ANWR Gets on the Congressional Agenda. In late 1986, Trustees for Alaska and other environmental groups learned that the Interior Department planned to circulate for public review the EIS it had prepared for oil leasing in ANWR at the same time it submitted the statement to Congress. Reflecting the Reagan administration's position, William Horn, assistant interior secretary for fish and wildlife, justified releasing the draft report to the public and Congress simultaneously on the grounds that the refuge might contain "a supergiant oil field that does not exist anywhere else in the United States."[38] The environmentally oriented Alaska Coalition promptly filed a lawsuit against the department, arguing successfully that the National Environmental Policy Act (NEPA) requires public participation in the preparation of an EIS prior to its release to Congress. Compelled by the court, the Fish and Wildlife Service held public hearings in January 1987.

On June 1, 1987, after finally incorporating public comments and responses, Secretary Hodel submitted a final report on the oil and gas potential of the Coastal Plain, the projected impacts of development, and a recommendation that Congress authorize oil and gas leasing in the 1002 area. In the opening paragraph of the report, Hodel stated that "the 1002 area is the nation's best single opportunity to increase significantly domestic production over the next 40 years."[39] On the second page, Hodel embraced a national security argument in support of his conclusions, saying production from the area would "reduce U.S. vulnerability to disruptions in the world market and could contribute to our energy security."[40] Finally, after projecting only minimal impacts on caribou and muskoxen, the report assured readers that oil development and wildlife could coexist.

Immediately, both the Natural Resources Defense Council and the Steering Committee for the Gwich'in filed lawsuits against the DOI, alleging that the report failed to properly evaluate potential environmental damage. The Gwich'in suit also claimed that the Interior Department had overestimated the revenues to be gained from drilling by using unrealistically inflated assumptions about oil prices. The plaintiffs requested that a new report to Congress and a new EIS be prepared addressing the survival of Gwich'in culture and based on realistic revenue projections.

Congressional Action, 1987–1989. Concurrently with the legal battles over the adequacy of the 1002 EIS, Congress began debating the merits of developing the refuge. In 1987, sponsors introduced seven bills concerning ANWR, five of which would have opened up the 1.5 million-acre Coastal Plain to oil and gas exploration, development, and production. In the House, two committees—

Merchant Marine and Fisheries, and Insular and Interior Affairs—held extensive but inconclusive hearings.

In the Senate, Republican William Roth of Delaware introduced S 1804, an ANWR wilderness bill, while fellow Republican Frank Murkowski of Alaska introduced S 1217, a bill to open up the refuge. Both the Senate Energy and Natural Resources and the Senate Environment and Public Works committees held extensive hearings but failed to report bills to the floor. S 1217 was stopped at least in part because of a series of scandals that broke in 1987. First, in July, the press revealed that the DOI had begun dividing the Coastal Plain among Alaskan native corporations for leasing to oil companies without congressional approval.[41] Shortly thereafter, environmentalists discovered that the DOI had excluded the conclusion of one of its own biologists that oil development would result in a 20 to 40 percent decline in the Porcupine caribou population.[42] What the DOI claimed was an editing error environmentalists attributed to political censorship. Either way, the controversy was sufficient to derail the bill's progress.

The following year, Don Young's House Subcommittee on Fisheries and Wildlife Conservation and the Environment approved (28–13) a pro-leasing bill (HR 3601). The subcommittee considered but did not adopt several environmentally oriented amendments. Instead, the bill attempted to soften the impact of drilling by requiring oil and gas development to impose "no significant adverse effect" on the environment; establishing a three-mile-wide coastal "insect relief zone" for caribou; and allowing only "essential facilities" within 1.5 to three miles of the coast. The House took no further action on the bill, however, because Udall's Interior Committee—the majority of whom did not support leasing—claimed equal jurisdiction over the matter and refused to report out a bill.[43] The Senate also debated both wilderness and oil leasing in ANWR in 1988. As in the House, multiple jurisdiction over the bill enabled advocates of protection to thwart supporters of drilling.[44]

With the inauguration of George H.W. Bush as president in 1989, environmentalists hoped their prospects might improve. In January, the Alaska Coalition sent a petition signed by 100 environmental groups and local civic associations to the new president and his recently designated interior secretary, Manuel Lujan Jr. (a former member of Congress who had introduced legislation to open the refuge) requesting that they protect the refuge from development.[45] The letter affected the administration's language but not its position: in February, President Bush called for "cautious development" of ANWR. Backed by the approval of the Bush administration, the Senate Energy and Natural Resources Committee reported S 684 favorably on March 16, 1989 by a vote of 12–7.[46]

The House Merchant Marine and Interior committees also had been holding ANWR hearings, and a week after the Senate committee's report, Democrat Walter Jones of North Carolina introduced a companion bill (HR 1600) to open up the refuge.[47] House deliberations were interrupted in March, however, by what was for environmentalists a serendipitous focusing event: the

Exxon Valdez oil spill, which inundated Alaska's Prince William Sound with nearly 11 million gallons of oil. Environmentalists capitalized on the devastating impact of the spill and of subsequent news coverage of oil-soaked wildlife. Jones reluctantly conceded the issue, citing hysteria: "We hoped before the oil spill to come out with a bill in July," he said, "but due to the emotional crisis this spill has created, we think it is best to put it on the back burner for the time being until the emotionalism has subsided."[48] Even the pro-development Bush White House acknowledged that "it will be some time before [ANWR legislation] is considered."[49] Within Alaska, where support for drilling had run high, the oil industry was chastened: Alaska governor Steve Cowper expected the spill to "cause a permanent change in the political chemistry in Alaska."[50]

At least in the short run, the Valdez spill helped environmentalists derail industry's arguments that reserves could be developed without threatening environmental harm. Chairman and chief executive of ARCO Lodwrick Cook confessed that "ARCO and the [oil] industry have lost a certain amount of credibility because of this spill, and we're going to have to work toward recapturing that."[51] On the advice of Interior Secretary Lujan, the oil industry launched a major public relations campaign.[52] It was confident that approval of an oil-spill preparedness bill, combined with the passage of time, would defuse public ire over the Valdez fiasco. In fact, within a year, visible signs of damage to Prince William Sound had disappeared, and supporters of oil exploration in ANWR prepared to revisit the issue.

Congressional Action, 1990–1992. In the summer of 1990, international events opened a window of opportunity for drilling advocates. The threat of war in the Persian Gulf following the invasion of Kuwait by Iraqi forces sparked renewed debate over dependence on foreign oil and bolstered support for drilling in ANWR. Louisiana's Billy Tauzin expressed his contempt for environmental values when he said: "It's amazing to me how we could put caribou above human lives—our sons and daughters."[53] Although the Bush administration insisted that the subsequent U.S. invasion (in January 1991) did not constitute a "war for oil," proponents of domestic oil and gas development seized on the event to revive drilling proposals. By September, the oil industry and its backers in the Bush administration were again pressing Congress to open the Coastal Plain to drilling. As one House aide remarked, "The Middle East crisis wiped the Exxon Valdez off the ANWR map as quickly as the Exxon Valdez wiped ANWR off the legislative map."[54]

Pressing its advantage, in April 1991 the Bush administration's development-friendly Interior Department released a revised estimate of the probability of finding oil in ANWR from 19 percent to 46 percent—a level almost unheard of in the industry—and raised its estimate of peak production to 870,000 barrels per day by the year 2000. Based on 1989 data, which included more accurate geological studies and test wells drilled on the periphery of the refuge, the DOI's U.S. Geological Survey (USGS) now estimated that the

Coastal Plain most likely contained between 697 million and 11.7 billion barrels of oil.[55]

In hopes of exploiting the administration's support, in the 102nd Congress pro-drilling senators Bennett Johnston, R-La., and Malcolm Wallop, R-Wyo., introduced S 1120, the Bush administration's "National Energy Security Act of 1991," Title IX of which permitted development of ANWR's Coastal Plain. In an effort to win over several Democratic senators who had denounced the plan because it was not accompanied by higher automotive fuel economy standards, Johnston's bill included a provision directing the Secretary of Transportation to raise Corporate Average Fuel Economy (CAFE) standards substantially (though the provision did not specify how much). In a further effort to appease pro-environment legislators, Johnston proposed that federal proceeds from ANWR oil be used to fund energy conservation and research. Although Johnston touted the bill as a compromise, its purpose was clear from the preamble: "to reduce the Nation's dependence on imported oil, to provide for the energy security of the Nation, and for other purposes."[56]

Again, however, anti-drilling advocates were able to use unforeseen developments to bolster their depiction of the oil industry as greedy profiteers. In January 1991, the *New York Times* reported that in the last quarter of 1990, oil industry profits jumped dramatically as oil prices skyrocketed in anticipation of war. Net income for Exxon, the world's largest oil company, soared more than threefold, while Mobil's profits climbed 45.6 percent, Texaco's 35 percent, and Amoco's 68.6 percent. "In fact," journalist Thomas Hayes reported, "each of these quarterly earnings might have been much larger, but each of the top five lowered their reported profit with bookkeeping tactics that oil giants often employ legally to pare taxes in periods when profits—and public resentment—are high."[57] Moreover, instead of an oil shortage, the world was experiencing a glut, as Saudi Arabia increased its output and demand slumped.

Although these developments diluted pro-dilling arguments, the Senate Energy Committee was persuaded by the Interior Department's revised estimates of the probability of finding oil in the refuge and the promise of jobs in the deepening recession, and in late May 1991 the committee approved S 1120 by a vote of 17–3. The sheer comprehensiveness of the energy bill undermined its prospects, however, for its myriad provisions prompted the mobilization of a host of interests. Energy consumer groups joined environmentalists, fearing that measures to restructure the utility industry would raise electricity rates. The auto industry, which opposed the CAFE standards, as well as small utilities disadvantaged by some provisions in the bill, also sided with the opposition faction. The pro-drilling coalition gained the support of large electric utilities that stood to benefit from the bill's provisions, as well as the nuclear power industry lobby. Coalitions on both sides waged an all-out war for public opinion and the votes of uncommitted members of Congress.

Further hampering the bill's chances of passing, in October 1991, the Senate Environment and Public Works Committee approved legislation that would prohibit oil and gas drilling in ANWR, and six Democratic senators pledged to filibuster[58] Johnston's bill if it came up for a vote on the floor.[59] On November 1, Johnston called for a vote on cloture, which would have ended the filibuster, but failed by ten votes to get the necessary three-fifths majority. The bill's complexity had simply created too much highly charged opposition for senators to risk the political fallout that accompanies a controversial decision. The Senate did pass a national energy bill in 1992, by a vote of 94–4, but it was stripped of both ANWR and automobile fuel efficiency provisions.

The House also considered bills authorizing oil and gas leasing in the refuge in 1991 and 1992. In 1991, the House postponed consideration of an ANWR drilling bill after allegations surfaced that Alyeska, operator of TAPS, had coercively silenced its critics. Mo Udall reintroduced his ANWR wilderness bill, but it did not make it to the floor for a vote. On May 2, 1992, the House passed (381–37) an energy bill similar to S 1120, but without provisions on ANWR or fuel efficiency standards.

ANWR Proposals on the Quiet, 1993–1999

The election of Bill Clinton to the presidency in 1993 temporarily punctured the hopes of drilling advocates, as the newly installed administration made its staunch opposition to oil development in the refuge clear. Based on more conservative geologic and economic assumptions than those made by its predecessor, in June 1995 the Clinton administration's Interior Department reduced its estimate of economically recoverable oil in the refuge to between 148 million and 5.15 billion barrels. The department's 1995 *Coastal Plain Resource Assessment* also affirmed that "there would be major environmental impacts from oil and gas development on the coastal plain" and documented even greater dependence of the Porcupine caribou herd on the 1002 area than had earlier reports.[60]

Nevertheless, in 1995, after two years of relative quiescence, congressional sponsors resumed their efforts to open up the refuge, hoping that the ascension of the Republican-controlled 104th Congress had opened a new window of opportunity for a pro-drilling policy. A chief difference between 1995 and preceding years was that two ardent proponents of drilling had acquired positions of power on the very committees that previously had obstructed efforts to open the refuge: Frank Murkowski of Alaska had become chairman of the Senate Environment and Natural Resources Committee, and Don Young, also of Alaska, had assumed control of the House Resources Committee.[61] Both chairmen promptly announced their intention to attach ANWR drilling provisions to the omnibus budget reconciliation bill in the fall.[62] Such a strategy was promising because small riders attached to major bills tend to attract less public notice than individual pieces of legislation and, perhaps more importantly, the reconciliation bill cannot be filibustered. Moreover, the president was less likely to veto omnibus legislation than a less significant bill.

By the middle of the legislative session, ANWR defender Sen. Joseph Lieberman, D-Conn., was expressing his concern that a majority in both houses favored opening the refuge. Sure enough, the fiscal 1996 budget resolution (H Con Res 67), approved by the House and adopted by the Senate in May, assumed $1.3 billion in revenue from ANWR oil leases. Furthermore, the day before passing the resolution, the Senate voted 56–44 to kill an amendment that would have prohibited exploration in the Coastal Plain. Emphasizing the Coastal Plain's role as "the biological heart of the refuge" and ANWR's status as "one of the last remaining wildernesses" in the United States and the world, Clinton's interior secretary, Bruce Babbitt, voiced the administration's resistance to the congressional proposal.[63] Citing the ANWR provision as one of the chief reasons, President Clinton vetoed the 1996 budget bill, and ultimately the provision's sponsors backed down and removed that provision.

Undaunted, drilling advocates continued their campaign to open the refuge. In 1997, the *Washington Post* reported that Arctic Power—a group formed in 1992 to promote drilling in the refuge—had contracted with a Washington, D.C.–based lobbying group to target Democratic Sens. John Breaux and Mary Landrieu of Louisiana with information about the economic ties between Alaska and their state. In support of their national security argument, drilling advocates touted a Department of Energy finding that while domestic oil production had been declining, the percentage of U.S. oil that is imported rose from 27 percent in 1985 to nearly 50 percent in 1997. In 1998, revised USGS estimates bolstered drilling advocates' claims: based on new geological information, technological advances, and changes in the economics of North Slope drilling, the agency predicted a 95 percent chance of recovering more than 3.5 billion barrels of oil from the refuge and a 5 percent chance of finding more than 11.6 billion barrels. At a price of $20 per barrel, the mean estimate of the amount of economically recoverable oil was 3.2 billion barrels.[64] A fact sheet from the House Resources Committee embraced the new figures and said: "The fact is, ANWR will help balance the budget, create jobs, increase domestic production, reduce oil import dependence and the trade deficit."

Despite concerted efforts by congressional proponents, however, the Clinton administration's unwavering opposition stymied efforts to open the refuge for the remainder of the decade. While sponsors introduced bills in the 105th Congress (1997–1998), Congress did not debate the issue. In the 106th Congress (1999–2000), sponsors again introduced both wilderness designation and energy development bills. In addition, assumptions about revenues from ANWR were originally included in the FY2001 budget resolution as reported by the Senate Budget Committee, but the House-Senate conference committee rejected the language, and it was excluded from the final budget passed in April 2000.

The 2000 Presidential Campaign and President Bush's Energy Policy

In the summer of 2000, the debate over ANWR's fate again seized the national spotlight when presidential candidate George W. Bush expressed his support for oil development there. The issue subsequently became a main point of contention between Bush and the Democratic candidate, Vice President Al Gore: while Gore adopted the rhetoric of environmentalists about the superior benefits of conservation and the importance of preserving wilderness, Bush cited the nation's need for energy independence and the slowing economy's vulnerability to higher energy prices. When Bush won the election, drilling advocates again felt certain a window of opportunity had opened.

Hoping to boost support for drilling, a spokesman for ARCO—which would be a key beneficiary of permission to drill in the refuge—testified at a House Resource Committee hearing that the company had learned a lot about environmentally friendly oil development over the years. "We can explore without leaving footprints," he said, "and the footprint required for new development is a tenth of what it once was."[65] BP Amoco, another leading player in Alaskan oil, contended that technological advances enable it to extract oil with minimal environmental impact: thanks to cutting-edge technology for steering drill bits, the newest wells occupy a much smaller footprint than older wells; pipelines are built higher, to let caribou pass beneath them, and feature more elbows, which reduce the amount of oil spilled in an accident; and often, rather than constructing roads, companies simply airlift workers to the site.[66]

To buttress its credibility, BP spent much of the 1990s trying to transform its image from black to green; it acknowledged the threat of climate change and embraced alternative fuels. (Taking no chances, the company also donated tens of thousands of dollars to the pro-development lobbying group Arctic Power, as well as to Republican politicians, including George W. Bush.[67]) The company's British CEO wrote in a memo to employees that BP's values "may be manifested in different ways, but they have much in common: a respect for the individual and the diversity of mankind, a responsibility to protect the natural environment."[68] Environmentalists remained skeptical, however: the World Wildlife Fund's Francis Grant-Suttie said that "on the PR level they have been successful at differentiating themselves from others, but by virtue of what they're doing on the coastal plain, you can see it's sheer rhetoric."[69]

Hoping that the recent spike in oil prices would improve his prospects, newly elected President Bush assigned members of his administration to lay the groundwork for yet another push in Congress. Drilling advocates were confident, and opponents worried, that a sympathetic president and his allies in Congress would be able to capitalize on concerns about high energy prices and California's energy deregulation fiasco to win passage of a drilling bill.[70] In early January 2001, the National Academy of Sciences' National Research Council convened a sixteen-member panel at the request of Congress to study the effects of oil development on Prudhoe Bay, but most observers expected Congress to vote on ANWR before the panel submitted its report. Affirming these expectations, during his first month in office Bush said: "I campaigned hard on the notion of having environmentally sensitive exploration at ANWR, and I think we can do so."[71] Claiming that the nation faced an energy crisis, at the end of January President Bush created a task force headed by Vice President

Dick Cheney to devise ways to reduce America's "reliance upon foreign oil" and to "encourage the development of pipelines and power-generating capacity in the country."

OUTCOMES

As of the autumn of 2001, ANWR remained closed to oil exploration but had not been legally designated as wilderness. In February, Sen. John Kerry, D-Mass.—in a clear bid to establish his own presidential credentials—vowed to filibuster any proposal to open the refuge. Still, less than two weeks later Sen. Frank Murkowski, R-Alaska, introduced a 300-page energy bill that would do just that, and Senate majority leader Trent Lott announced his support for the bill, saying "American dependence on foreign oil threatens our national security and our freedom."[72] As the spring wore on, Vice President Cheney continued to emphasize the administration's commitment to increasing the nation's oil supply.

The Bush administration's actions set in motion yet another ferocious lobbying campaign featuring Arctic Power, which hired the lobbying firm of Patton Boggs, as well as the public relations firm Qorvis and media consultant Alex Castellanos, to compose a series of radio and television ads. In late March, Arctic Power announced the formation of a new coalition: the Energy Stewardship Alliance. At the same time, the Audubon Society launched its own ad campaign, and Audubon and Defenders of Wildlife began mobilizing citizens to send emails and faxes to Congress.

The arguments employed by both sides had changed little over the years. Proponents of drilling emphasized economic security and reducing dependence on foreign sources. They targeted environmental restrictions, in particular, as hindrances to energy independence. Development opponents pointed out that Americans continue to use more than twice as much energy per capita as the Swiss, Germans, and Japanese, all of whom enjoy comparable standards of living.[73] They argued that conservation, not exploration, is the solution to our energy woes. In a recent *New York Times* editorial, Thomas Friedman cited the NRDC's estimate that by increasing the average fuel efficiency of new cars, SUVs, and light trucks from 24 to 39 mpg in a decade we could save 51 billion barrels of oil, more than fifteen times the likely yield from ANWR.[74] Likening ANWR to a cathedral, Friedman compared drilling to online trading in church on a Palm Pilot, saying, "It violates the very ethic of the place."

In a blow to the Bush administration's plans, the House Budget Committee released a budget for 2002 that did not include anticipated oil revenue from drilling in the refuge, saying that it would provoke too much controversy. The chairman of the Senate Budget Committee indicated he was likely to follow suit. By the end of March, although continuing to emphasize increasing the supply of fossil fuels rather than conserving and developing alternative fuels, the administration seemed to be backing away from ANWR drilling proposals.[75]

By the summer of 2001, although Vice President Cheney took to the road to promote an energy plan focused on developing domestic supplies, the context of the issue had once again changed: oil prices were falling, supplies had stabilized, and the sense of crisis—so critical to passing major legislation—had vanished. Moreover, while the administration's energy plan passed in the House in August 2001, its prospects in the Democratic-controlled Senate were dim.

CONCLUSIONS

This case reveals in stark terms the polarization between advocates of natural resource development and proponents of wilderness. Advocates of drilling in ANWR see little value in preserving a place that few people will visit; for them, preserving the refuge is tantamount to placing the welfare of animals above that of human beings. In contrast, those who value wilderness take satisfaction in simply knowing that it exists; as one biologist says: "There are a lot of people who will never get to the refuge, but I get some peace of mind knowing that there is an area of naturalness on such a scale."[76] Wilderness advocates are adamant in their opposition to any kind of development in ANWR; compromise is defeat. Tim Mahoney, chairman of the Alaska Coalition, says: "To say that we can have oil and caribou is akin to saying that we can dam the Grand Canyon and still have rocks."[77] Assurances that oil companies now have the technological capability to minimize the environmental impact of drilling makes little impression on wilderness advocates. As Deborah Williams, executive director of the Alaska Conservation Foundation, concludes: "The one thing you can't get away from is that in the end, even with all this technology, you've got a massive industrial complex."[78]

Given the chasm separating the two sides, it is clear that the massive amounts of information generated and rhetoric employed during the more than fifteen years of debate over the ANWR are not aimed at changing the minds of the opposition. Instead, advocates direct evidence and arguments at the public and uncommitted members of Congress, with the goal of shaping legislators' perceptions of public opinion on the issue and the likely electoral consequences of their vote. Drilling advocates have tried to capitalize on focusing events—particularly the Gulf War in the 1980s and rising energy prices in the 1990s—to cast the issue of ANWR drilling as a source of economic and national security, just as they used the energy crisis of 1973 to get approval for the Alaskan pipeline. They have tried to take advantage of windows of opportunity, such as the turnover in congressional leadership in the mid-1990s and the election of George W. Bush in 2000.

To date, however, environmentalists have fended off development interests' efforts. In part, this is a tribute to their success in generating national support by using the refuge's "charismatic megafauna"—particularly caribou and polar bears—to reinforce the symbolism of the last remaining wilderness. In addition, while the refuge is not permanently protected under the status quo, it will take a policy change to open the area to development. This has given environmentalists an advantage in the legislative arena, where they have used multiple jurisdiction (in the House), filibusters (in the Senate), and the threat of a presidential veto to thwart ANWR exploration bills. Finally, preventing change is easier than promoting it in the area of energy policy, where the complexity of legislation prompts diverse interests to mobilize. Interest group activity on both sides in turn have stymied congressional decision making, as legislators fear the electoral repercussions of taking positions on highly controversial issues.

How long environmentalists can prevail is another matter. They acknowledge that with the inauguration of President Bush, the momentum is on the side of the oil industry. So far, public disapproval of Bush's environmental policy proposals has prompted him to moderate his position on energy issues, but he may simply be awaiting a favorable focusing event. At the same time, wilderness designation for the refuge is unlikely, and even a legal wilderness designation would not ensure the area's protection. Such designations are subject to congressional reversals, and for environmentalists, once the refuge is opened, it will be lost forever.

QUESTIONS TO CONSIDER

- Why has the conflict over the Arctic National Wildlife Refuge been so intractable?
- How have opponents of drilling in the refuge managed to fend off the powerful oil industry?
- What do you think are the prospects for ANWR drilling in the future? Why?
- Are there any mechanisms with which to protect the refuge permanently?

Notes

1. As political scientist Deborah Stone observes, apparently universal values such as "security" mean different things to different people. See Deborah Stone, *Policy Paradox: The Art of Political Decision Making* (New York: Norton, 1997).
2. For more detail on the impact of multiple referral on the legislative process, see Garry Young and Joseph Cooper, "Multiple Referral and the Transformation of House Decision Making," in *Congress Reconsidered*, 5th ed., ed. Lawrence C. Dodd and Bruce J. Oppenheimer (Washington, D.C.: CQ Press, 1993), 211–234.
3. Roderick Nash, *Wilderness and the American Mind*, 3d ed. (New Haven: Yale University Press, 1982).
4. Quoted in Peter A. Coates, *The Trans-Alaska Pipeline Controversy: Technology, Conservation, and the Frontier* (Bethlehem: Lehigh University Press, 1991), 84.
5. John Strohmeyer, *Extreme Conditions: Big Oil and the Transformation of Alaska* (New York: Simon and Schuster, 1993).
6. The pipeline required permits from the state of Alaska and the Department of Interior.
7. The first suit charged that TAPS was asking excessive rights of way under the Mineral Leasing Act of 1920. A second suit joined one filed by native villagers that did not want the pipeline to cross their property. Finally, a third suit claimed that the

Department of Interior had not submitted an environmental impact statement (EIS), as required by the National Environmental Policy Act (NEPA). See Strohmeyer, *Extreme Conditions.*

8. Strohmeyer, *Extreme Conditions,* 83.

9. APIC comprised a diverse set of interests, including the Sierra Club, the Wilderness Society, the National Wildlife Federation, the National Rifle Association, Zero Population Growth, Common Cause, the United Auto Workers, and others.

10. NEPA requires federal agencies to prepare an EIS for any major project.

11. Coates, *The Trans-Alaska Pipeline Controversy.* Congress had already amended the Mineral Leasing Act of 1920 to make environmentalists' other legal challenge to the pipeline moot.

12. Strohmeyer, *Extreme Conditions.*

13. Public domain land is federally owned land that has not been designated for a specific purpose and is still eligible for withdrawal under federal land laws.

14. This is an unusual provision; ordinarily, the Fish and Wildlife Service can allow oil development in a wildlife refuge without congressional approval.

15. U.S. Department of Interior, *Arctic National Wildlife Refuge, Alaska, Final Comprehensive Conservation Plan, Environmental Impact Statement, Wilderness Review, Wild River Plans* (Washington, D.C.: U.S. Government Printing Office, 1988), 12.

16. Douglas Jehl, "Wildlife and Derricks Coexist but the Question Is the Cost," *New York Times,* February 20, 2001, A1.

17. Ibid.

18. Ted Williams, "Seeking Refuge," *Audubon,* May–June 1996, 34–45, 90–94.

19. As part of its statehood deal, Alaska got title to 90 percent of the revenues from oil development within its borders.

20. Estimates of the recoverable amount of oil vary depending on the price of oil and the costs of extraction. Projections of the former depend on a host of variables; the latter depend on technological developments, geography, and environmental regulations.

21. U.S. Department of Interior (DOI), *Arctic National Wildlife Refuge, Alaska, Coastal Plain Resource Assessment: Report and Recommendation to the Congress of the United States and Final Legislative Environmental Impact Statement* (Washington, D.C.: U.S. Fish and Wildlife Service, 1987).

22. Peter Nulty, "A Compromise the Caribou Will Like," *Fortune,* May 24, 1987, 9.

23. Quoted in Philip Shabecoff, "U.S. Proposing Drilling for Oil in Arctic Refuge," *New York Times,* November 25, 1986, A1.

24. Lisa Speer et al., *Tracking Arctic Oil* (Washington, D.C.: Natural Resources Defense Council, 1991), 30.

25. "National Energy Policy," *Congressional Digest,* May 1991, 130–160.

26. Quoted in "National Energy Policy," 153.

27. Speer et al., *Tracking Arctic Oil.*

28. Ibid.

29. U.S. House of Representatives, Committee on Merchant Marine and Fisheries, "ANWR Briefing Book," April 1991.

30. U.S. DOI, *Arctic National Wildlife Refuge,* 163–164.

31. BP Exploration (Alaska) Inc., *Major Environmental Issues,* 3d ed. (Anchorage: BP Exploration, 1991).

32. Donald P. Hodel, "The Need to Seek Oil in Alaska's Arctic Refuge," *New York Times,* June 14, 1987, Sec. IV, 25.

33. U.S. Office of Technology Assessment, *Oil Production in the Arctic National Wildlife Refuge: The Technology and the Alaskan Context* (Washington, D.C.: Office of Technology Assessment, 1987), OTA-E-394.

34. U.S. Fish and Wildlife Service, *Comparison of Actual and Predicted Impacts of the Trans-Alaska Pipeline Systems and Prudhoe Bay Oilfields on the North Slope of Alaska* (Fairbanks: U.S. Fish and Wildlife Service, 1988).

35. Gail Osherenko and Oran Young, *The Age of the Arctic: Hot Conflicts and Cold Realities* (New York: Cambridge University Press, 1989).
36. Ibid.
37. Shabecoff, "U.S. Proposing Drilling."
38. Quoted in Shabecoff, "U.S. Proposing Drilling."
39. U.S. DOI, *Arctic National Wildlife Refuge*, 1.
40. Ibid.
41. Joseph A. Davis, "Alaskan Wildlife Refuge Becomes a Battleground," *Congressional Quarterly Weekly Report*, August 22, 1987, 1939–1943.
42. Ibid.
43. Joseph A. Davis, "ANWR Bill Clears One Hurdle but Real Test is Yet to Come," *Congressional Quarterly Weekly Report*, May 7, 1988, 1206.
44. Joseph A. Davis, "Prognosis is Poor for Arctic Oil Drilling Bill," *Congressional Quarterly Weekly Report*, May 21, 1988, 1387.
45. Philip Shabecoff, "Bush Is Asked to Ban Oil Drilling," *New York Times*, January 25, 1989, A16.
46. Joseph A. Davis, "Arctic-Drilling Plan Clears Committee," *Congressional Quarterly Weekly Report*, March 18, 1989, 578.
47. The House considered three other bills to open the refuge and one to designate the area as wilderness in 1989.
48. Quoted in Philip Shabecoff, "Reaction to Alaska's Spill Derails Bill to Allow Oil Drilling in Refuge," *New York Times*, April 12, 1989, A17.
49. Ibid.
50. Quoted in Richard Mauer, "Oil's Political Power in Alaska May Ebb With Spill at Valdez," *New York Times*, May 14, 1989, A1.
51. Quoted in Richard W. Stevenson, "Why Exxon's Woes Worry ARCO," *New York Times*, May 14, 1989, Sec. 3, 1.
52. Philip Shabecoff, "Oil Industry Gets Warning on Its Image," *New York Times*, April 4, 1989, B8.
53. Quoted in Phil Kuntz, "ANWR May be Latest Hostage of Middle East Oil Crisis," *Congressional Quarterly Weekly Report*, September 8, 1990, 2827–2828.
54. Ibid.
55. For comparison, experts estimated that the Prudhoe Bay oil field—North America's largest—contains about 14 billion barrels of recoverable oil.
56. Holly Idelson, "Senate Panel Moves Energy Bill Without Mileage Standards," *Congressional Quarterly Weekly Report*, May 25, 1991, 1369–1370.
57. Thomas Hayes, "Oil's Inconvenient Bonanza," *New York Times*, January 27, 1991, A4.
58. A filibuster is a tactic that is only available in the Senate and involves employing "every parliamentary maneuver and dilatory motion to delay, modify, or defeat legislation." Walter Oleszek, *Congressional Procedures and the Policy Process*, 4th ed. (Washington, D.C.: CQ Press, 1996), 249.
59. Christine Lawrence, "Environmental Panel Sets Up Floor Fight Over ANWR," *Congressional Quarterly Weekly Report*, October 19, 1991, 3023.
60. U.S. Department of Interior, *Arctic National Wildlife Refuge, Alaska, Coastal Plain Resource Assessment: Report and Recommendation to the Congress of the United States* (Washington, D.C.: U.S. Government Printing Office, 1995).
61. Republicans renamed the House Interior Committee the House Resources Committee.
62. The budget reconciliation bill reconciles tax and spending policies with deficit reduction goals.
63. Allan Freedman, "Supporters of Drilling See an Opening," *Congressional Quarterly Weekly Report*, August 12, 1995, 2440–2441.
64. U.S. Geological Survey, News release (April 17, 1998).
65. Quoted in Andrew Revkin, "Hunting for Oil: New Precision, Less Pollution," *New York Times*, January 30, 2000, D1.

66. Neela Banerjee, "Can BP's Black Gold Ever Flow Green?" *New York Times,* November 12, 2000, Sec. 3, 1; Revkin, "Hunting for Oil."
67. In the year 2000, BP contributed $50,000 to Arctic Power, $34,421 to candidate Bush (compared to $4,250 to candidate Gore), and $613,870 to the Republican Party. See Banerjee, "Can BP's Black Gold Ever Flow Green?"
68. Quoted in Banerjee, "Can BP's Black Gold Ever Flow Green?"
69. Ibid.
70. Andrew Revkin, "Clashing Opinions at a Meeting on Alaska Drilling," *New York Times,* January 10, 2001, A1.
71. Quoted in Joseph Kahn and David E. Sanger, "President Offers Plan to Promote Oil Exploration," *New York Times,* January 30, 2001, A1.
72. Lizette Alvarez, "Energy Bill Likely to Set Off Fierce Policy Fight," *New York Times,* February 26, 2001, A1.
73. Michael Zimmerman and Carolyn Watkins, "The U.S. Needs a Federal Energy Policy," *Christian Science Monitor,* December 2, 1987, 13.
74. Thomas Friedman, "Drilling in the Cathedral," *New York Times,* March 2, 2001, A23.
75. Katherine Q. Seelye, "Facing Obstacles on Drilling for Arctic Oil, Bush Says He'll Look Elsewhere," *New York Times,* March 30, 2001, A13.
76. Quoted in Banerjee, "Can BP's Black Gold Flow Green?"
77. Quoted in Davis, "Alaskan Wildlife Refuge Becomes a Battleground."
78. Quoted in Revkin, "Clashing Opinions at Meeting."

Recommended Reading

Speer, Lisa, et al. *Tracking Arctic Oil.* Washington, D.C.: Natural Resources Defense Council, 1991.
Strohmeyer, John. *Extreme Conditions: Big Oil and the Transformation of Alaska.* New York: Simon and Schuster, 1993.

Web Sites

http://www.r7.fws.gov/nwr/arctic (FWS site)
http://agdc.usgs.gov/data/projects/anwr/webhtml (USGS site)
http://www.arcticprotection.org (Arctic Protection Network site)
http://www.anwr.org (Pro-development web site)
http://www.dog.dnr.state.ak.us/oil/products/maps/maps.htm (State of Alaska site, with oil development maps)

CHAPTER 6

Federal Grazing Policy
Some Things Never Change

When President Clinton took office in January 1993, he declared his intention to raise fees for grazing livestock, end below-cost timber sales, and charge royalties for mining on the nation's public lands. Within six months, however, the president had retreated from that position. This was just the latest in a century-long series of failed attempts to curtail the prerogatives of resource users on federal lands. For the last 150 years, ranchers with permits to graze sheep and livestock have been transforming public rangelands—which comprise a diverse array of ecosystems—into desert. Yet the nation's two largest land managers, the Forest Service and the Bureau of Land Management, have been reluctant to implement policies to restore the western range, and any efforts to do so have been deflected by ranchers' congressional supporters.

Federal grazing policy exemplifies the extent to which history—specifically past policies—constrains current policy debates and decisions. The legacies of past policies influence the present in several ways. First, the ideas embedded in an agency's authorizing statutes, along with their subsequent interpretations by the courts, shape the agency's view of its mandate; an agency is likely to resist adopting practices contrary to its founding mission.[1] Second, congressional reactions to their decisions create a sense of what is appropriate and legitimate behavior among agency employees; thus, congressional oversight shapes the agency's organizational culture and standard operating procedures. And third, as sociologist Theda Skocpol observes, past policies "affect the social identities, goals, and capabilities of interest groups that subsequently struggle or ally in politics."[2] Groups organized around a particular policy can severely constrain an agency's choices among alternatives.[3] In addition, over time, policies deferential toward user groups create a sense among beneficiaries that they have vested property rights in the resource and must be compensated if those claims are terminated.[4]

Key among these historical factors has been the ability of a minority of members of Congress to exert a virtual monopoly on legislative and administrative decision making. Members of Congress concerned about local economic interests try to protect them by gaining positions on committees and subcommittees with jurisdiction over the issues most relevant to those interests[5]—in this case the authorizing appropriations subcommittees that control public lands. From that vantage point, lawmakers can stave off policy changes perceived as damaging to development interests in a variety of ways: committees set the legislative agenda because they have gatekeeping power; they originate bills and then get a second crack at them after the conference committee does its work; and they exercise considerable control over agencies under their jurisdiction through informal oversight and carefully structured administrative procedures.[6] Finally, Congress affects an agency's policy implementation by determining whether it has sufficient resources—both in terms of budget and capable staff—for the task. In fact, political scientist Herbert Kaufman finds that appropriations subcommittees, particularly in the House, are among the most zealous superintendents of every bureau.[7]

Some political scientists argue that the constraints and incentives created by Congress "stack the deck" in agency decision making in favor of constituencies important to its congressional overseers.[8] In truth, the extent to which a single interest can dominate policymaking on an issue varies, depending on the intensity of congressional interest and the number of committees with jurisdiction.[9] Internally simple, autonomous, and unified Congress-agency "subsystems"— like the grazing policy subsystem—are notoriously difficult for reformers to infiltrate.

To break a minority's grip on policy in such a subsystem, challengers must raise public concern sufficiently to give congressional leaders outside the subsystem incentives to expend their political capital. They must also make a case compelling enough to persuade uncommitted legislators to get on the bandwagon. This typically involves redefining a problem to highlight an aspect the public heretofore had not considered, such as an activity's environmental costs, and thereby shifting public (and hence election-conscious legislators') attention to the issue.[10] Reframing an issue is not simple, however, especially when supporters of the status quo wield potent symbols of their own. Reformers need a compelling political story, complete with villains and victims and the threatened loss of something the public values.

This chapter explores how reformers have sought change in federal grazing policy on numerous occasions and why they have met with limited success. Unlike most of the other cases in this book, therefore, this one is largely a story of policy inertia rather than policy change.

BACKGROUND

"There is perhaps no darker chapter nor greater tragedy in the history of land occupancy and use in the United States than the story of the western range," lamented Earl H. Clapp in 1936 in *The Western Range*.[11] Although the public domain[12] rangeland was in deplorable condition when federal managers assumed control in the early 1900s, policies to regulate its use in the first two-thirds of the twentieth century did little to restore it. Both the Forest Service and the Bureau of Land Management (BLM) established grazing lease and permit systems during this period, but federal land managers faced enormous resistance when they tried to restrict grazing. Legal scholar Charles Wilkinson describes the essence of range policy as "a series of attempts to resuscitate the range from the condition it reached in the late 1800s . . . [that] proceeded in the face of ranchers who continue to assert their 'right' to graze herds without regulation."[13] Because the grazing policy subsystem was so tightly controlled, the history of federal grazing policy is one in which ranchers' congressional allies thwarted efforts to restore the range.

Introducing Grazing in the West

The introduction of cattle onto the western range began during the century following the Revolutionary War, as the federal government sought to dispose of its vast landholdings west of the Mississippi. Although large portions of the West were too dry for homesteaders to cultivate, the vast, grassy rangelands were a gold mine for cattle- and sheep-raisers. Because homesteading laws forbade any single claimant to acquire more than 160 acres—an area considered uneconomical for stockraising in the arid West[14]—ranchers devised creative methods to gain access to larger expanses of prairie and grasslands. One commonly used approach was to find and claim a 160-acre plot with access to water and timber (perhaps supplementing this acreage with dummy claims bought from other homesteaders or family members); build a base ranch there with a residence, hay pastures, corrals, and barns; and then establish informal control over a much larger area by illegally fencing the surrounding public domain. In the spring, summer, and fall, ranchers would turn their stock loose to graze on tens of thousands of acres of public lands (see Map 6-1).[15]

By the 1870s and 1880s, stockmen had spread across the West. Between 1865 and 1885, the cattle population skyrocketed from an estimated three to four million, mostly in Texas, to about 26 million, along with 20 million sheep. Unregulated use of the western range by livestock was destroying it, however: grazing depleted or degraded over 700 million acres of grassland during this early period, and massive cattle die-offs occurred periodically in the late 1800s and early 1900s. Although stockmen blamed these disasters on severe weather, the cattle were clearly vulnerable to natural fluctuations because overgrazing had so debased the range.[16]

The Origins of Grazing Regulation

Federal regulation of grazing began in 1906, when Forest Service Director Gifford Pinchot announced his intention to require stockmen whose cattle or sheep grazed on national forests to obtain a permit and pay a fee. The proposed charge was $0.05 per animal unit month (AUM—one unit is one horse or cow, or five sheep or goats). Although this charge was less than one third of the forage's market value, stockmen rebelled, insisting that the agency could not tax them through administrative fiat.[17] Eventually the stockmen acquiesced to Forest Service regulation, however, recognizing that restricting access would protect their own interests in the range. Permittees soon began to exploit their "permit value" by adding it to the sale price of their ranches.[18]

Map 6-1 The Western Range

Source: Debra L. Donahue, *The Western Range Revisited: Removing Livestock from Public Lands to Conserve Native Biodiversity* (Norman: University of Oklahoma Press, 1999), p. 8. Reprinted with permission © Linda M. Marston.

Not surprisingly, the combination of low fees and lax congressional homesteading policies increased the demand for national forest range. At the same time, the onset of World War I prompted the Forest Service to issue temporary grazing permits and allow stock numbers far greater than the carrying capacity of the range. As a result, between 1908 and 1920, stockraising on the national forests rose from 14 million AUMs to an all-time high of 20 million AUMs.[19] In 1919, when the House Appropriations Committee began insisting on more substantial grazing fee increases, mostly in hopes of raising revenue to offset war debts, Sen. Robert Stanfield of Oregon—a rancher and permittee himself—orchestrated a full-scale challenge. He held hearings on the fee system and the general administration of rangelands and traveled throughout the West to stir up ranchers' complaints.

Stanfield's "stage managed senatorial attack on Forest Service policy" led forestry experts and conservationists to retaliate.[20] Representatives of the Society of American Foresters and the American Forestry Association toured the country and wrote editorials and press releases criticizing the livestock industry. The eastern press also struck back: the *New York Times* charged that western senators were resisting the "march of civilization" and called for their attacks to be checked; the *Saturday Evening Post* ran an article by Chief Forester William Greeley condemning the demand by stockmen to secure special privileges for a few users.[21] Despite the spirited defense by conservationists, however, the Forest Service ultimately retreated from its proposal.

While Forest Service permittees were resisting efforts to raise grazing fees, those who ran their livestock on the remaining public domain continued to fend off attempts to regulate *those* lands as well. By the mid-1930s, however, a series of droughts—exacerbated by a precipitous fall in livestock prices during the Depression—had brought about a crisis in the industry, and some leading ranchers began to believe that a government leasing program on the public domain could stabilize the industry. They opposed a program administered by the Forest Service, though, worrying that it would charge them the economic value of the forage and reduce the number of cattle permitted on the land. To placate the stockmen, President Franklin D. Roosevelt's interior secretary, Harold Ickes, promised ranchers favorable conditions if the public domain remained under his department's jurisdiction.[22]

In 1934—with the support of the large public domain ranchers—Congress passed the Taylor Grazing Act (named after sponsor and Forest Service critic Edward Taylor of Colorado), which created the Division of Grazing in the Department of Interior and established a system of grazing permits for public domain land akin to the one administered by the Forest Service. To avoid the vitriolic criticism ranchers had leveled at the Forest Service over the years, the new division set grazing fees at $0.05 per AUM, even though by this time Forest Service fees were three times that amount. And to avoid the perception that the grazing division was a distant bureaucratic organization centered in Washington, Secretary Ickes established a decentralized administration that drew its chief officers not—as the Forest Service did—from a pool of trained professionals but from men with "practical experience" who had been residents of public lands states for at least a year. Finally, the Taylor Grazing Act and its early amendments required that the secretary define regulations for grazing districts "in cooperation with local associations of stockmen." The grazing advisory boards thus created quickly became the dominant force in administering the system, particularly because the division was chronically underfunded and understaffed.[23]

Grazing Policy Controversies, 1940–the late 1960s

By the time the Taylor Act was passed, the public domain grasslands of the West were already severely depleted. When federal land managers tried to regulate grazing, however, ranchers' congressional allies intervened. In 1944, when Director Clarence Forsling proposed tripling the grazing fee from $0.05 to $0.15 per AUM, the congressional response was "immediate and harsh."[24] Sen. Pat McCarran of Nevada, head of the Senate Public Lands Committee, held a series of inflammatory hearings in the West, and shortly thereafter Congress essentially dismantled the division, which had been renamed the Grazing Service.[25] In 1946, President Truman combined the remnants of the service with the General Land Office to form the Bureau of Land Management. The BLM began its life with no statutory mission, yet with responsibility for administering 3,500 laws enacted over the previous century. It had only eighty-six people to oversee more than 150 million acres of land, and its initial budget crisis was so acute that the grazing advisory boards paid part of some administrators' salaries.[26]

The Forest Service also ran afoul of the stock industry in the mid-1940s. In 1945, when Forest Service grazing permits were due for a decennial review, the agency planned to reduce the number of livestock on the range, shorten the grazing season, and exclude stock altogether in some areas in an effort to rejuvenate the land.[27] Rep. Frank Barrett of Wyoming felt such a move warranted a punitive response and gained authorization to investigate grazing policies. Emulating McCarran and Stanfield before him, Barrett's committee traveled throughout the West soliciting criticism of the Forest Service.

Conservationists again were outraged at what they called "the great land grab." Bernard DeVoto, a noted western historian, used his *Harper's Magazine* column to protest, writing in one essay that:

> A few groups of western interests, so small numerically as to constitute a minute fraction of the West, are hellbent on destroying the West. They are stronger than they otherwise would be because they are skillfully manipulating in their support sentiments that have always been powerful in the West—the home rule which means basically that we want federal help without federal regulation, the "individualism" that has always made the small Western operator a handy tool of the big one, and the wild myth that stockgrowers constitute an aristocracy in which all Westerners somehow share.[28]

The *Atlantic Monthly* rushed to defend the land management agencies with an article by Arthur Carhart, claiming the Barrett hearings were "rigged" and designed to "throw fear into the U.S. Forest Service," as evidenced by the "transparent manipulations of the meetings, the bias displayed by the chairman . . . the very odor of the meetings."[29] Articles critical of the livestock industry also appeared in *The Nation, Colliers, Reader's Digest,* and hundreds of daily newspapers.

But again, although conservationists managed to stir up the eastern establishment sufficiently to block rancher-friendly legislation, the incendiary hearings caused the land management agencies to retreat from their reform efforts. To improve relations with the stockmen, for example, the Forest Service agreed to cut fees in return for range improvements and to hold hearings on reducing cattle numbers at the request of the affected rancher. As scholars Samuel Dana and Sally Fairfax note,

> The events of 1945–1950 . . . amply demonstrated that congressional supporters of the reactionary cattle operators were quite prepared to destroy an agency that did not meet their peculiar set of goals—through budget cuts, legislative enactment, and simple harassment. Obviously, the ability of a McCarran or a Barrett to hold "hearings" year after year and to tie up the time of BLM and Forest Service officials testifying, gathering data, and defending themselves is a tremendous weapon that members of Congress used to bring recalcitrant officials into line.[30]

In the 1950s, under the Eisenhower administration, the Forest Service became even more deferential to ranchers, providing its permittees fencing, stock driveways, rodent control, poisonous and noxious plant control, revegetation of grass and shrubs, water development, corrals and loading facilities, and brush control. In the opinion of Forest Service critic William Voigt, "No changes in Forest Service policy with respect to grazing have been more critical than those which had shifted so much of the burden of rehabilitating the damaged forest ranges from individual permittees to the taxpayer at large."[31] In addition, Forest Service and BLM grazing fees, although they rose occasionally during this period, fell even further below the real market value of the forage.

Little changed in the 1960s. In 1961, newly inaugurated President John F. Kennedy raised the stakes when he delivered a message on natural resources that elevated the issue of public lands user fees, but the only concrete result was more studies. Then, touting an interdepartmental report showing that fees were well below their economic value, in 1969, President Lyndon Johnson's Bureau of the Budget announced what would have been the most progressive grazing policy shift in history: both the BLM and the Forest Service were to raise their fees to a market-value $1.23 per AUM and thenceforward index fees to the rates on private lands. The agencies were to phase in the increase over a ten-year period. Although grazing fees did rise during the following years, however, the stockmen—with the help of their congressional allies—were once again able to stave off a substantial portion of the planned increase.[32]

THE CASE

With the advent of the environmental era in the late 1960s and early 1970s came a spate of new environmental laws that affected public lands management, most notably the National Environmental Policy Act (NEPA), the Clean Air and Water Acts, and the Endangered Species Act. At the same time, conservation biologists and range ecologists were beginning to provide the scientific basis for a challenge to the existing range management regime. Encouraged by these developments, environmentalists hoped to use their newfound political clout to challenge ranchers' dominance over federal grazing policy. Each push for reform met forceful opposition from ranchers and their congressional allies, however; and unable to redefine the grazing issue in a way that captured public attention, environmentalists made only marginal gains.

The Reformers' Argument

The environmentalists' case was (and remains) that livestock overgrazing was destroying the western range and that federal land management practices were exacerbating rather than ameliorating this trend. At a minimum, environmentalists' argued, ranchers' prerogatives ought to be severely curtailed and the range restored to ecological health.

The Condition of the Range. Environmentalists charged that when ranchers graze extremely large numbers of livestock, there can be serious, long-term, and sometimes permanent damage to the range. They pointed out that overgrazing, the primary cause of desertification worldwide, had left a lasting imprint on over two-thirds of the land in eleven western states. According to Texas Tech soil scientist Harold Dregne, by the mid-1970s, 98 percent of the arid lands in the western United States—some 464 million acres of rangeland, both privately and publicly owned—had undergone some degree of desertification.[33] The scientific understanding of the ecological effects of grazing was limited, and there was controversy, in particular, over the impact of livestock grazing on rangeland plants. Nonetheless, most conservation biologists agreed that past overgrazing had eroded soil, destroyed watersheds, and extinguished native grasses and other vegetation on which wildlife feed.[34]

There were several reasons for this. First, cattle eat the most palatable and digestible plants first. Such selective grazing, combined with the limited tolerance of some plant species for grazing, can prompt shifts in the composition of plant communities.[35] Second, cows are heavy consumers of water which is in short supply west of the 98th Meridian. Beyond that line, precipitation drops below twenty inches a year, the lower limit for many nonirrigated crops, and even more importantly, it falls irregularly, leading to frequent droughts. Third, herds of cattle compact the soil, making rainwater run off, which causes erosion, gullying, and channel cutting.

Environmentalists pointed out that cattle are particularly destructive to the West's precious riparian zones, the lush, vegetated areas surrounding rivers and streams. The ecological importance of such zones is enormous because they sustain a much greater quantity of species than the adjoining land. Riparian areas provide food, water, shade, and cover for fish and wildlife; they also benefit humans by removing sediment from the water table, acting as sponges holding water and stabilizing both streamflow and the water table, and dissipating flood waters. Cattle degrade riparian zones by eating tree seedlings, particularly the cottonwoods, aspen, and willow on which such species as bald eagles and great blue herons rely. Cattle trampling on and grazing streamside vegetation also cause streambanks to slough off, channels to widen, and streams to become shallower, which in turn makes the fish smaller and scarcer. Because most of the original riparian areas in the West were homesteaded early on, the ones that remained were even more crucial.[36]

Finally, environmentalists contend that in addition to grazing itself, livestock management practices have serious ecological consequences. Fences limit the movement of wildlife; water development reduces the supply of water for wildlife and depletes aquifers; predator control has extirpated species such as wolves, mountain lions, and bears from their historic ranges; and vegetation controls—such as herbicide spraying and plowing and seeding—have reduced plant species diversity.

During the 1980s, after numerous attempts to assess rangeland conditions, federal managers, oversight agencies, professional and advocacy organizations, and academic scientists had concluded that more than half of both private and public rangeland was in fair or poor condition.[37] Moreover, many range managers pointed out that the important consideration was not what percent of the allotment was in good shape, but which portion. Barry Reiswig, manager of the Sheldon Wildlife Refuge in Nevada and Oregon, said: "You'll hear lots of [range conservationists], even people on my staff, crowing about how 99 percent of the range is in good or excellent condition, but they ignore the fact that the one percent that is trashed—the riparian zones—is really the only part important for most wildlife species."[38] Data collected by the U.S. General Accounting Office (GAO) confirmed that most of the West's riparian areas were in poor condition; a 1990 EPA report concurred saying: "Extensive field observations in the late 1980s suggest riparian areas throughout much of the West are in the worst condition in history."[39]

The Failure of Range Management. Environmentalists also contend that federal grazing policy has failed to restore, and in some cases has further depleted, a range already badly damaged by early ranching practices. According to their critics, the BLM and Forest Service allow too many cattle to graze with too few restrictions on the roughly 31,000 allotments these agencies administer. Critics cited a 1988 GAO finding that, on about 18 percent of the BLM's allotments and 21 percent of Forest Service allotments, the authorized grazing levels exceeded the carrying capacity of the land.[40] Moreover, critics believe that by undercharging ranchers for grazing, federal land managers encourage overgrazing, a claim supported by numerous studies that find federal grazing fees are well below rates charged on comparable private lands.

Environmentalists also challenge a third aspect of grazing policy, range improvement, which is a euphemism for developing water supplies, fencing, seeding, and making other investments—all with the goal of enhancing the forage supply rather than restoring the range to ecological health. Critics note that although ranchers generally condone such improvements, they often oppose riparian restoration projects—the ones most important to environmentalists—because they involve prohibiting access to stream banks.[41] Finally, several GAO reports have supported environmentalists' complaints that federal land managers do not enforce trespass rules.[42] Trespass includes stocking more cattle than authorized; running livestock on an allotment before the opening date, after closing, or during the wrong season; or grazing livestock on public land without a permit.

In an effort to undermine the cowboy symbolism of their opponents, reformers charge that current grazing fees, overstocking, and lax enforcement constitute a subsidy to wealthy hobby ranchers, not the rugged individuals that the word "rancher" connotes. While some of the approximately 23,000 western BLM and Forest Service permittees are small ranchers, they say, the main beneficiaries are large ranchers with historical ties to the public lands. As evidence, they cite GAO studies saying that 3 percent of livestock operators in the West use 38 percent of the federal grazing land, while less than 10 percent of federal forage goes to small-time ranchers (those with less than 100 head of cattle). Only 15 percent of BLM permittees have herds of 500 or more animals, but they account for 58 percent of BLM's AUMs.[43] Similarly, stockmen with over 500 animals comprise only 12 percent of Forest Service permittees but account for 41 percent of the agency's AUMs.[44] To make their argument more concrete, reformers name the wealthy individuals, partnerships, and corporations that work many of the largest allotments. Rock Springs Grazing Association of Wyoming, for example, controls 100,000 acres; J. R. Simplot, said to be the wealthiest man in Idaho, ranches 964,000 acres; the Metropolitan Life Insurance Company has permits for 800,000 acres; and the Zenchiku Corporation of Japan controls 40,000 acres. Union Oil and Getty Oil, as well as the Mormon Church, are also large permit holders.[45]

While some environmentalists would like to see grazing abolished entirely from BLM and Forest Service land, many have more modest goals. First and foremost, they demand that public lands ranchers pay grazing fees equivalent to the market value of the forage, noting that current fees cover only 37 percent of BLM and 30 percent of Forest Service program administration costs.[46] Second, they insist that federal land managers reduce the number of cattle to a level the land can comfortably support. Third, they want more opportunities for public participation, particularly by environmentalists, in rangeland management decisions.

Ranchers' Resistance to Reform

Public lands ranchers did not take environmentalists' assaults lying down. They respond that public and private fees are not comparable because it costs more to run cattle on public lands. Those who ranch on public lands, they argue, must provide such capital improvements as fencing and water that owners supply on private lands. Moreover, they point out, the value of their lease or permit was long ago capitalized into the cost of the associated ranch; thus, a cut in cattle numbers would unfairly devalue their ranches. Permittees portray themselves as an important part of the livestock industry, although the public lands supply only about 2 percent of the forage consumed by beef cattle.[47] They further contend that because many of them are marginal, family operations, an increase in grazing fees could put them out of business and destabilize the communities in which they operate. Ranchers' most formidable rhetorical weapons are not reasoned arguments, however, but the potent symbols they wield: cowboys, rugged individualism, and freedom from control by a distant and oppressive federal government.

In any case, permittees' influence derives less from their public arguments than from their historic ties to members of Congress who sit on the public lands authorizing committees and appropriations subcommittees. Legislators from the Rocky Mountain states in particular have secured positions on the House and Senate Interior (now Resources and Energy and Nature Resources) committees, from which they can fend off efforts at grazing policy reform. As a result, in spite of their small numbers and their minority status in the livestock industry as a whole, public lands ranchers have held onto their privileged status. As journalist George Wuerthner marvels, "There are more members of the Wyoming Wildlife Federation than there are ranchers in the entire state of Wyoming, but it is ranchers, not conservationists, who set the agenda on public lands."[48]

Permittees' influence is enhanced by their association with the academic community in western land grant colleges and universities. As one commentator observes: "This community specializes in rangeland management and has, with few exceptions, been solidly allied with ranching interests which, in turn, have the political power to determine higher education budgets and sometimes serve as regents of various schools."[49] The permittees' clout also lies in part with their allies in banking and real estate. Charles Wilkinson explains:

> Ranches are usually valued for loan purposes based on AUMs, and the appraised value will drop if the AUMs drop. A decrease in AUMs thus will reduce a rancher's ability to raise capital and will weaken the security on existing loans. . . . As Charles Callison, longtime observer of range policy, has told me: "It's one thing when western congressmen hear from the ranchers. But they really leap into action when the bankers start getting on the telephone."[50]

Finally, many prominent stockmen affect policy directly by holding elected or appointed office: former President Ronald Reagan's BLM director, Robert Burford, is a millionaire BLM rancher; Wyoming's former senators Clifford Hansen and Alan Simpson, as well as New Mexico Rep. Joe Skeen are cattlemen; former senator Paul Laxalt is a sheep rancher; and Reps. Robert Smith of Oregon and Jim Kolbe of Arizona come from ranching families.

The Federal Land Policy Management Act, 1971–1976

Undaunted by ranchers' impressive political resources, in the early 1970s, advocates of grazing policy reform hoped to capitalize on the window of

opportunity opened by Earth Day and began to press Congress for new legislation. The most obvious route by which to alter grazing policy was through
the organic act that BLM had been prodding Congress to pass for a decade.[51]
Between 1971 and 1974, the Senate approved several bills granting BLM statutory authority, but proposals foundered in the House, primarily on the issue
of grazing fees.

Finally, in the 94th Congress (1975–1976), the Senate approved a bare-bones
authorization bill sponsored by Henry Jackson, D-Wash., and supported by
the Ford administration. The House managed to settle on a bill as well, though
its version was clearly pro-rancher, gutting BLM law enforcement authority
and increasing local control over BLM and Forest Service planning.[52] It also
contained four controversial grazing provisions, all beneficial to ranchers.
First, it established a statutory grazing fee formula based on beef prices and
private forage costs, with a floor of $2.00 per AUM. Second, it improved ranch-
ers' tenure by granting ten-year permits as the rule, rather than the exception.
Third, it required BLM to compensate ranchers for private improvements of
the land if it canceled their permits. And fourth, it resurrected and prescribed
the composition of local grazing advisory boards, which Congress had
replaced with multiple-use advisory boards one year earlier.[53] The Interior
Committee narrowly approved the bill, 20–16; and the full House—deferring
to the committee—also approved it, 169–155.

Because the House and Senate versions were substantially different, it was
unclear whether the conference committee could reconcile them, but at the last
minute the conferees reached a compromise. House negotiators offered to
implement the rancher-friendly fee formula for two years but in the meantime
conduct a study of the issue, a deal Senate conferees refused. House members
then offered to drop the grazing fee formula altogether but freeze current fees,
an option also unpalatable to Senate conferees. Finally, the Senate conferees
made a counteroffer that the House conferees accepted: a one-year freeze on
grazing fees, accompanied by a one-year study of the fee issue conducted
jointly by the Agriculture and Interior departments.[54] Once the study was
completed, Congress could take up the issue again. The conference bill passed
the House on September 30 and the Senate on October 1, just hours before the
94th Congress adjourned. Grazing interests objected to the deletion of their
preferred grazing fee formula and encouraged the president to pocket veto the
bill, but President Ford signed the Federal Land Policy and Management Act
(FLPMA) into law on October 21, 1976. Although disappointed about the grazing fee provision, overall, livestock interests were satisfied with the legislative
outcome.

The Carter Administration, 1977–1980

The following year, the expiration of the grazing fee freeze and the election
of a pro-environmental president opened another window of opportunity for

reformers, and a flurry of legislative activity ensued. In the autumn of 1977, President Jimmy Carter's Agriculture and Interior departments released their congressionally mandated study of grazing fees and proposed raising fees to a uniform $1.89 per AUM for the 1978 season. The fees would rise thereafter no more than 12 percent per year until they reached a market value of $2.38 per AUM. Livestock groups, opposed in principle to a market-value system, called the proposal "unfair and unrealistic." Worried about the Carter administration's propensity for reform, ranchers opted for their favorite tactic: deferral. They urged the administration to let Congress decide. The administration responded by freezing fees at the 1977 level, while ranchers pressured Congress to adopt a one-year moratorium on increases.[55]

By the fall of 1978, Congress had produced yet another grazing bill, the Public Rangelands Improvement Act (PRIA), which had two major provisions: range improvement funding and a statutory grazing fee formula. Not surprisingly, the former had near-universal support, but the latter was highly controversial. Environmentalists, as well as both the BLM and the Forest Service, supported a market value–based fee similar to the one that had technically been in place since 1969 (although fee increases had rarely taken effect in practice); livestock interests agitated for a fee with built-in profits (based on forage costs and beef prices). After bitter debates in the House and Senate, both chambers passed the PRIA with the rancher-approved formula and a provision prohibiting annual fee increases or decreases of over 25 percent of the previous year's fee. Its language reflects the committees' rationale: "To prevent economic disruption and harm to the western livestock industry, it is in the public interest to charge a fee for livestock grazing permits and leases on the public lands which is based on a formula reflecting annual changes in the cost of production."[56] President Carter signed the bill on October 25, 1978.

Although constrained by the PRIA, Carter's BLM did embark on a program of intensive, conservation-oriented range management in which Director Frank Gregg encouraged agency staff to conduct range inventories and cut grazing permit allocations if they found forage supplies insufficient to support assigned levels. The reduction program was short-lived, however. Public lands ranchers sounded the alarm about what they regarded as the agency's heavy-handed tactics, and rancher ally Idaho Sen. James McClure succeeded in attaching an amendment to the 1980 appropriations bill that mandated a two-year phase-in for any stock reduction of more than 10 percent.[57]

Though thwarted by Senator McClure, the BLM initiative fueled ranchers' antagonism toward federal land managers, and they instigated the Sagebrush Rebellion, a disjointed attempt to transfer ownership of federal lands to western states. While the rebels did not accomplish the transfer (nor is it clear the majority even wanted to),[58] they did succeed in drawing attention to their plight. Their cause was sufficiently visible that, in the 1980 presidential campaign, Republican candidate Ronald Reagan declared himself a sagebrush rebel.

The Reagan Administration, 1981–1988

In the early 1980s, federal grazing fees fell to $1.37 as a consequence of sluggish beef prices. In the meantime, reformers and livestock interests mustered their forces for a confrontation at the upcoming window of opportunity when the PRIA expired in 1985. Although the battle lines were drawn in Congress, the position of the White House had shifted considerably. In contrast to his predecessor, newly elected President Reagan made no secret of his sympathy for public lands ranchers.[59] Upon taking office, he appointed livestock industry supporters to key positions in the Interior Department: Secretary James Watt was a lawyer with the Mountain States Legal Foundation, which litigates on behalf of ranchers and other resource extraction interests, and BLM director Robert Burford was a Colorado rancher "who had jousted repeatedly with the BLM, most often over his own grazing violations" and argued there was a tremendous capacity for increasing beef production on America's rangeland.[60]

The administration drew on all its resources to alter BLM's range management agenda, changing the mix of professionals (including laying off ecologists), the budget, and the structure of the agency. In addition, Director Burford used informal rulemaking processes to increase ranchers' security. The centerpiece of Burford's grazing program was the Cooperative Management Agreement (CMA) program. In theory, the agency provided exemplary ranchers with CMAs, which allowed them to manage their allotments virtually unimpeded. In 1985, however, a federal district court declared that the CMA approach illegally circumvented BLM's statutory obligation to care for overgrazed public rangeland.[61] Although forbidden to formally transfer authority for the public range to ranchers, the Interior Department managed to accomplish the same result through neglect: under pressure from Reagan's political appointees, BLM range managers were compelled to abandon the stock reductions begun by the Carter administration.

Environmentalists could only hope to make inroads into grazing policy when the grazing fee issue returned to the congressional agenda in 1985. By that time, environmental groups, fiscal conservatives in the administration, and some BLM and Forest Service officials had formed a loose coalition to press for higher grazing fees. Reformers launched an all-out campaign in the media, labeling public lands ranchers as "welfare cowboys" and deploring low grazing fees as a subsidy in an era of high deficits and fiscal austerity. Hoping to shame public officials and reduce the influence of livestock interests, journalists investigated stories about BLM or Forest Service officials who had been fired or transferred for trying to implement environmental reforms.[62]

Buttressing the reformers' case were the results of yet another grazing fee analysis. In March 1985, the BLM and Forest Service completed a four-year study in which twenty-two professional appraisers collected data for every county in the West that had rangeland. The researchers discovered that fees on private lands averaged $6.87 per AUM, nearly five times higher than fees for comparable public land, and that the fees charged by other federal agencies averaged $6.53 per AUM.[63] The study presented for congressional consideration five alternative fee formulas, all involving a fee hike.

Congress failed to come up with grazing legislation that would satisfy both environmentalists and ranchers, however, and since the authorization for the PRIA formula expired at the end of 1985, authority to set the fee reverted to the Reagan administration. Although environmentalists directed their best efforts at influencing President Reagan, they never had a chance. On December 13, 1985, Sen. Paul Laxalt, R-Nev.—a close friend of the president's and a sheep rancher himself—delivered a letter from a group of mainly western, Republican senators urging the president to freeze the grazing fee. Eventually, twenty-eight senators and forty representatives joined the lobbying effort.

In late January 1986, the Office of Management and Budget (OMB) pulled out of the alliance with environmentalists. OMB Director James Miller wrote to President Reagan that he was backing off in recognition of the political sensitivity of the issue, but he did recommend freezing fees for no more than one year in order to pressure Congress to act.[64] To the dismay of environmentalists, President Reagan ignored Miller's advice and issued Executive Order 12,548 extending the PRIA fee formula indefinitely (see Table 6-1). The executive order effectively hamstrung BLM and Forest Service efforts to rehabilitate the range because the cost of administering the grazing program substantially exceeded revenues from grazing fees under the PRIA system, and the enormity of the federal deficit precluded any additional funding for either agency.

The Bush Administration, 1989–1992

In 1988, advocates of higher grazing fees began to prepare a run at the 101st Congress, hopeful that changes in the composition of the House Interior Committee—which had been a major obstacle to reform—would improve their prospects. In the 1970s, reform-minded California Democrat Phillip Burton had taken over the committee chairmanship and begun recruiting environmentally oriented members. For a brief period, ranching allies were in the minority; by 1991, only nine of the committee's twenty-six Democrats hailed from the West, and three of those were from urban areas of Los Angeles, Oakland, and Salt Lake City. Despite such changes, however, livestock interests' allies continued to fend off pro-environmental reforms.

In 1990, the House adopted (251–155) an amendment to the Interior Appropriations bill that would have increased the grazing fee sharply. The provision was dropped in conference with the Senate, however, where pro-ranching western senators narrowly prevailed on the issue in return for rescinding their opposition to oil exploration in the Outer Continental Shelf. The same year, Sen. Bruce Vento, D-Minn., tried to attach his BLM authorization bill (containing a grazing fee increase) to the budget reconciliation bill in an effort to circumvent western senators. The bill did not promise enough deficit reduction to satisfy the Budget Committee, however, and was dropped.[65]

Table 6-1

Annual Grazing Fees for the Bureau of Land Management and the Forest Service, 1940–1999

Year	BLM Fee ($ per AUM)	Forest Service Fee ($ per AUM)
1940	$0.05[a]	$0.15
1945	0.05	0.25
1950	0.10	0.42
1955	0.15	0.37
1960	0.22	0.51
1965	0.30	0.46
1970	0.44	0.60
1975	1.00	1.11
1976	1.51	1.60
1977	1.51	1.60
1978	1.51	1.60
1979	1.89	1.93
1980	2.36	2.41
1981	2.31	2.31
1982	1.86	1.86
1983	1.40	1.40
1984	1.37	1.37
1985	1.35[b]	1.35[b]
1986	1.35	1.35
1987	1.35	1.35
1988	1.54	1.54
1989	1.86	1.86
1990	1.40	1.81
1991	1.97	1.97
1992	1.92	1.92
1993	1.86	1.86
1994	1.95	1.98
1995	1.61	1.61
1996	1.35	1.35
1997	1.35	1.35
1998	1.35	1.35
1999	1.35	1.35

Source: U.S. Forest Service and Bureau of Land Management.

[a]The BLM began charging fees in 1936, and from 1936 to 1946 the fee was 5 cents per AUM.

[b]The Public Rangeland Improvement Act of 1978 set a minimum fee of $1.35 per AUM.

In 1991, opposition from westerners on the House Interior Committee forced Rep. George "Buddy" Darden, D-Ga., to drop an amendment to a BLM reauthorization bill dramatically increasing grazing fees. Darden, as well as Rep. Mike Synar, D-Okla., also introduced separate bills to the Interior Committee to increase grazing fees. Meeting resistance from that committee, the two took their case to the Appropriations Committee, and on June 6, the House Appropriations Subcommittee on Interior voted to raise grazing fees by 33 percent. New information bolstered the efforts of fee-increase advocates: in late June the GAO released a report highly critical of the current fee formula, concluding the formula kept grazing fees low by double counting ranchers' expenses. Under the formula, when ranchers' expenses went up, the fee went down, so the fee was 15 percent lower in 1991 than it had been in 1975. In contrast, private grazing land lease rates had risen 17 percent in the same period.[66]

On July 23, the House voted overwhelmingly to add a grazing fee amendment to the BLM reauthorization bill despite Interior Committee opposition. The House also approved Darden's amendment to boost grazing fees through the 1992 Interior Appropriations bill by a 329–44 vote. These votes signaled changes in the proportion of pro-environmental western representatives in the chamber, which reflected the shifting demographics of the West: as the region urbanized, environmentalists, recreation advocates, and tourism interests were gaining political representation. Again, however, western senators—who continued to speak primarily for the traditional economic interests—managed to deflect attempts to raise grazing fees, and the BLM reauthorization bill simply disappeared in the Senate without a hearing. The negotiation over the appropriations bill was more convoluted, but the end result was the same.[67]

The Early Clinton Years, 1993–1994

With the election of Bill Clinton to the presidency and Al Gore to the vice presidency, environmentalists perceived another window of opportunity for federal grazing policy reform. President Clinton confirmed their expectations when, immediately upon taking office, he announced his plan to cut subsidies for grazing, as well as timber, mining, and water on the public lands. Bruce Babbitt, Clinton's secretary of interior, also adopted a markedly different tone from that of his recent predecessors and was well received by park rangers, biologists, and other land managers who had suffered through years of political pressure to favor industrial uses of the land. He got a standing ovation from a roomful of federal employees when he proclaimed: "I see us as the department of the environment. . . . We are about the perpetual American love affair with the land and the parks."[68] Clinton delighted environmentalists with his appointment of Jim Baca as head of the BLM. Baca had been New Mexico's land commissioner and was a former board member of the Wilderness Society.

Some members of Congress found Clinton's position refreshing as well. George Miller, head of the House Interior Committee, claimed that most westerners embraced the changes that Clinton was proposing. According to Miller, "Reagan and Bush were just holding back the future. They were the last gasp of an outdated philosophy."[69] Others were not so optimistic about prospects for reform, especially when resource users banded together into what they called the Wise Use Movement, an amalgamation whose objective was to promote unfettered access to public lands (see chapter 10). These interests continued to have fiercely protective and influential congressional sponsors, particularly in the Senate.

It was pro-ranching western senators that Clinton was especially wary of alienating; he would need their support to pass his legislative agenda. On March 16, capitalizing on the president's frail majority, seven western senators led by Democrat Max Baucus of Montana met with Clinton to discuss trading their support for his economic program for his dropping public land management reform. Two weeks later, the president backed off his initial proposal to raise fees for commercial uses of public resources.

Undaunted, in August 1993, Interior Secretary Babbitt proposed to add to the appropriations bill a provision that more than doubled grazing fees on federal lands and imposed tough environmental standards on ranchers. In response, Sen. Pete Domenici, R-N.M., and Sen. Harry Reid, D-Nev., proposed an amendment placing a one-year moratorium on Babbitt's ability to spend any money to implement his grazing policy. Because of the issue's low salience outside the West, the Senate deferred to Domenici and Reid, 59–40.[70]

The House instructed its negotiators on the bill to reject the Senate moratorium, however. In response, Senator Reid—hoping to put the grazing policy issue to bed—worked out a compromise with Babbitt and key House Democrats to resolve the differences between the two chambers by increasing grazing fees (though only to $3.45, far short of the $4.28 Babbitt wanted) but imposing fewer land management requirements. Babbitt agreed, and the House and Senate conferees approved Reid's amendment.

In late October, the full House approved Senator Reid's grazing compromise, but the Senate was unable to muster the sixty votes necessary to head off a filibuster by Senator Domenici, who viewed the bill as too pro-environment. Republicans achieved near-perfect unity in support of Domenici's filibuster, and five western and northern plains Democrats joined them. After failing three times to invoke cloture (54–44 on the final try), Reid agreed to drop the grazing compromise, Domenici stopped stalling the bill, and on November 9 the Senate and House sent the revised version without grazing fee language to President Clinton.[71] Again, ranching interests had fended off reform.

Following this series of highly publicized congressional debacles, Babbitt vowed to raise grazing fees administratively. But President Clinton continued to be hampered by a precarious congressional coalition and was loathe to antagonize even a few key western Democrats. In fact, Babbitt was compelled to oust BLM Director Baca in an effort to placate western governors and senators who had complained about his aggressive approach to rangeland management. Even Babbitt himself began pursuing a more conciliatory approach, unveiling a proposal whose main attribute was local flexibility. Though the proposal would have doubled grazing fees over three years, Babbitt sought to defuse opposition with a two-tier fee structure that charged small ranchers less and offered a 30 percent discount to ranchers who improved the land.

Notwithstanding the grazing fee increase, environmentalists criticized the administration sharply for backpedaling. "This appears to be a complete reversal from the proposal we saw in August [of 1993]. It's headed away from reform," said Nancy Green, a specialist on federal lands issues at the Wilderness Society.[72] Babbitt defended his position, saying it reflected his view that "those closest to the land, those who live on the land, are in the best position to care for it."[73] But no one expected a system of local advisory councils dominated by ranchers to result in any serious scaling back of grazing privileges. Confirming environmentalists' worst fears, by December 1994, Babbitt had retracted the grazing fee increase altogether and delayed the effective date of many of the proposed environmental regulations.

The Republican Congress Retaliates, 1995–2000

A window of opportunity opened for ranchers to expand their privileges when the Republicans assumed control of Congress in 1995. In the early spring, Senator Domenici introduced the Public Rangeland Management Act (S 852), a bill designed to preempt Secretary Babbitt's proposed rule changes. The bill raised grazing fees by a nominal amount, thereby heading off the substantial increase sought by Babbitt and the majority of members of Congress, and enhanced permittees' autonomy on and control over federal grazing allotments. Most importantly, the bill excluded from land management decisions anyone but ranchers and adjacent property owners by creating 150 advisory boards consisting solely of ranchers.

In July, the Senate Energy and Natural Resources Committee approved the bill over the objections of the BLM, whose acting director, Mike Dombeck, fumed: "This bill takes the public out of public lands. It returns land management to an era of single use at taxpayers' expense."[74] Because it propped up cattle operations that might otherwise have left the public lands, fiscal conservatives deplored the measure as well. Karl Hess, a senior fellow at the Cato Institute, said it would "create and sustain a land-use monopoly that is anathema to American values and harmful to the West."[75] Domenici's proposal stalled when it became clear it could not garner the sixty votes necessary to break an anticipated filibuster supported by Democrats and moderate Republicans.

After adding several amendments, a House subcommittee approved a bill (HR 1713) that barred the secretary of interior from setting national rangeland standards; gave ranchers proportional title to improvements, such as fencing, landscaping, and ponds; and lengthened the term of a grazing lease from ten to fifteen years. Like Domenici's failed effort, however, HR 1713 never reached the floor. Sponsors of both bills then tried to insert a modest fee increase provision into the budget reconciliation bill, again in hopes of averting Babbitt's much more substantial one, but that rider was dropped before the bill went to the president. In a final attempt at an end-run around Babbitt's rules, the Senate attached a provision to the Interior Appropriations bill to postpone implementation until November 21, but President Clinton vetoed the bill.

In the meantime, in August 1995, Babbitt finally issued new grazing rules. The regulations set federal standards for all rangelands and allowed the federal government to claim title to all land improvements and water developments made by ranchers on public lands. They established regional "resource advisory councils," with guaranteed spots for environmentalists, to help the BLM devise grazing guidelines for each state and write comprehensive plans for preserving rangeland ecosystems. The rules also limited ranchers' rights to appeal BLM decisions to reduce the number of animals on an allotment. Not surprisingly, environmentalists applauded the regulations, while ranchers were enraged.

In 1996, ranchers' Senate allies managed to pass a bill (S 1459) aimed at overturning Babbitt's grazing rules. The House Resources and Energy and Natural Resources (formerly House and Senate Interior) Committee approved a similar bill, but it met resistance in the full House from a coalition of environmentalists and fiscal conservatives and faced a certain presidential veto. The bill died at the end of the session. Frustrated westerners in the House also attempted to insert pro-grazing provisions into the omnibus parks bill by holding hostage funding for New Jersey's Sterling Forest, a priority for many easterners. Finally, in September, western representatives abandoned that effort as well, recognizing, according to James Hansen, R-Utah, that pressing forward would carry an unacceptable political price.[76]

Although their legislative efforts stumbled, ranchers got a boost from the courts. Scheduled to go into effect in March 1996, Babbitt's rules had been held in abeyance until legal challenges by five livestock groups were resolved. In June, U.S. District Judge Clarence Brimmer rejected several of the reforms on the grounds that they would "wreak havoc" on the ranching industry and exceed the BLM's legislative authority. Brimmer ruled that the provision to weaken ranchers' rights to renew federal grazing permits was illegal because the Taylor Grazing Act specified "grazing preference" to ensure that ranchers and their creditors had some certainty about their tenure. Judge Brimmer also rejected the rules giving the government title to future range improvements and allowing conservationists to acquire grazing permits.[77] The judge did uphold the agency's right to check on permittees' compliance with regulations and to suspend or cancel a permit if the lessee is convicted of violating environmental laws.[78]

Finding their efforts to impose across-the-board reforms stymied by the courts, the Forest Service and BLM began targeting individual sites on which to implement rangeland improvement measures. In an uncharacteristically bold move, BLM officials proposed in July 1997 to reduce grazing by one-third across 1.3 million acres in Owyhee County, Idaho, and to restrict off-road vehicles to marked trails. Some locals were aghast at the plan and vowed to resist it; revealing the depth of the county's antipathy toward federal regulators, Owyhee Sheriff Gary Amman warned that federal agents "risk[ed] being thrown in jail if they venture[d] into the county."[79] Ranchers and their supporters began employing a variety of tactics to thwart land managers, including intimidation and violence (see chapter 10). Nor were such tactics limited to ranchers: radical environmentalists began cutting fences and otherwise sabotaging ranching operations.[80]

In October 1997, the House passed a "grazing reform" measure (HR 2493) that raised grazing fees by 15 percent, again in hopes of deflecting attempts to raise fees more substantially; lengthened ranchers' lease terms; and eased restrictions on ranching permits. This was a major victory for ranching advocates, as the House had been a "major burial ground for grazing bills" in the 104th Congress.[81] The Senate Resources and Energy and Natural Resources Committee (formerly House and Senate Interior) marked up and reported HR 2493 without amendment on July 29th, 1998, but the bill did not reach the Senate floor. Grazing reform has since been on the back burner.

OUTCOMES

Livestock grazing on public lands has been relatively stable for the last thirty years, with annual grazing levels between eight and nine million AUMs on national forest land and around ten million AUMs on BLM land.[82] The agencies are moving away from the "excellent/good/fair/poor" system of evaluating rangeland because it is too simplistic and controversial; instead, they have begun focusing on "ecosystem function" relative to management objectives. The Department of Interior's *Rangeland Reform '94: Draft Environmental Impact Statement* remains the BLM's most comprehensive evaluation of rangeland conditions. Based on the ecosystem function criterion, *Rangeland Reform '94* describes the condition of vegetation on BLM lands as: 67 percent of the land it had evaluated was static or had reached management objectives; 20 percent moving toward management objectives; 13 percent moving away from management objectives; and 14 percent was undetermined.[83] Using the same classification scheme, a Forest Service assessment in 2000 found that during the mid- to late 1990s, nearly 50 percent of the allotments it had evaluated met its management objectives; nearly 40 percent were moving toward those objectives; and 13 percent were failing.[84]

While both BLM and Forest Service rangelands seem to be stable or improving, however, both agencies lack the funding and the personnel to evaluate their allotments systematically or to repair past damage. The BLM's *Rangeland Reform '94* notes that "there is still much progress to be made. Rangeland ecosystems are still not functioning properly in many areas of the West. Riparian areas are widely depleted and some upland areas produce far below their potential. Soils are becoming less fertile."[85] The report also concludes that public land riparian areas "have continued to decline and are considered to be in their worst condition in history."[86] Moreover, the Forest Service's *RPA Assessment 2000* points out there continues to be "little information available to identify integrative indicators for assessing changes in ecological processes at a broad scale."[87]

Frustrated with the pace and contentiousness of attempts to promote rangeland conservation and discouraged by the polarization between ranchers and environmentalists, some groups have begun cautiously experimenting with voluntary, collaborative approaches. One of the earliest and most famous of these, the Malpai Borderlands Group, was initiated in the mid-1990s. The group is a nonprofit organization comprising nine members, eight of whom are ranchers, dedicated to restoring and maintaining "the natural processes that create and protect a healthy, unfragmented landscape to support a diverse, flourishing community of human, plant, and animal life in our Borderlands region."[88] A pivotal member of the group is a representative of the Nature Conservancy, which in 1990 bought the nearby Gray Ranch as part of its Last Great Places campaign. The group has assembled scientists, as well as federal and state land managers, to help it stake out what it calls "the radical center." Among other land management mechanisms, the Malpai Borderlands Group employs controlled burns to rejuvenate the range. It also created the concept of grass banking, a means by which ranchers can trade a promise to protect their land from suburban development in exchange for the right to graze their livestock on grass-rich land during dry years.

The notions of controlled burns, grass banking, and collaborative management more generally have since spread throughout the West, and other organizations—including the Six-Six Group, the Northern Lights Institute, and the Quivira Coalition—are springing up to promote them more widely. In the fall of 2000, the Conservation Fund, the Northern New Mexico Stockmen's Association, the U.S. Forest Service, the Cooperative Extension Service of New Mexico State University, the Quivira Coalition, and the Malpai Borderlands Group sponsored a conference to introduce the grassbank concept to ranchers and community organizers from seven states. Some groups on both sides of the issue remain suspicious of collaborative problem solving, however. Caren Cowan, executive director of the New Mexico Cattle Growers' Association, did not attend the conference, saying: "We don't oppose grass banks as a tool per se, but we don't want anyone to tell us how to run our business."[89] Similarly, hard-line environmental groups, such as the Forest Guardians of Santa Fe and the Southwest Center for Biodiversity, did not attend the conference and continue to oppose livestock grazing on public lands altogether.

CONCLUSIONS

The nearly 100-year history of federal grazing policymaking has been a tug-of-war between conservationists and ranchers. The overall pattern that emerged over the first sixty-five years of grazing management was one in which western members of Congress were able to stave off most reforms and rescind or ameliorate those initiatives that did pass. In the absence of wide-spread public concern about and scrutiny of federal grazing policy, which might prompt legislators from outside the West to expend their political capital on the issue, western members found myriad ways to insulate their ranching constituents from short-term economic harm: in the statutes that govern BLM and Forest Service grazing policy they mandated a rancher-friendly approach to planning and management, empowering rancher-dominated advisory boards and keeping grazing fees low. When land managers got out of line, ranchers' congressional allies on agency oversight committees used intimidation to promote greater deference to ranchers—holding hearings to embarrass agency officials; delaying by moratoria, studies, and reports; and wielding budgetary threats. In a more subtle exercise of control, congressional supporters of the livestock industry contacted agencies' Washington staff and urged them to discipline or even transfer aggressive range managers.

The repeated use of such tactics over time established the context in which environmentalists launched modern grazing policy reform efforts. By the 1970s, ranchers' congressional allies had achieved firm control over the public lands authorizing committees and appropriations subcommittees in both chambers. They had cowed BLM and Forest Service range managers with their punitive responses to efforts at environmentally friendly range management, their unwillingness to raise grazing fees, and their minimal budgetary allocations. Thus, when environmentalists challenged the permissive grazing policy regime, they encountered a dispirited federal bureaucracy and a well-guarded congressional fortress. Unable to provoke widespread public outrage about the deterioration of the western range, and lacking opportune focusing events that might attract public attention, environmentalists consistently found themselves foiled.

The tenacity with which western members of Congress continue to protect their constituents reflects both their convictions and the intense electoral pressure they face. The rationale offered by western senators for their ardent defense of grazing privileges is best described by Wyoming Sen. Malcolm Wallop, himself a rancher, who says: "The public lands were reserved for the expansion of the economy. The variety of uses on public lands provides for economic stability."[90] Others are more circumspect: pro-environment Arizona Rep. Mo Udall abandoned his proposal to raise grazing fees in the early 1980s saying "I haven't seen the light, but I have felt the heat."[91] Apparently, Udall judged ranchers' electoral clout accurately; the National Cattlemen's Association lobbied heavily against Rep. Mike Synar and Rep. Buddy Darden after they tried to raise grazing fees, and both lost their seats in 1994.

Of course, the political power of ranchers is not immutable. Over the years, reformers have infiltrated the House and Senate public lands oversight committees, traditionally the bastions of those interested in protecting public lands users. Demographic changes in the Rocky Mountain West have reduced the consequences of opposing ranching interests for representatives in some districts. As the region urbanizes, constituents' demands for outdoor recreation and for environmental quality have intensified.[92] Moreover, as the timber and mining industries decline in the face of worldwide competition and mechanization, the recreation industry has begun to supersede extractive industries in jobs and revenues generated. Unless environmentalists can muster sufficient clout in the public lands states to counteract the resources users, however, the institutions of Congress will provide myriad opportunities to stymie reform. This is, perhaps, why the most promising recent developments in rangeland management have come not as a result of traditional congressional, or even administrative, reforms but rather have grown out of the voluntary, collaborative ventures that have begun to spring up in the Rocky Mountain West.[93]

QUESTIONS TO CONSIDER

- Why do federal land management agencies, ostensibly the stewards of public resources, allow ranchers to graze cattle at levels that exceed the carrying capacity of the land?
- Why, despite their successes in other policy areas, have environmentalists made so little headway in reforming federal grazing policy?
- What sorts of approaches seem most likely to bring about changes in grazing on the western range, and why?

Notes

1. Judith Goldstein, "Ideas, Institutions, and American Trade Policy," *International Organization* 42 (winter 1988): 179–217; Christopher M. Klyza, *Who Controls Public Lands? Mining, Forestry, and Grazing Policies, 1870–1990* (Charlotte: University of North Carolina Press, 1996).
2. Theda Skocpol, *Protecting Soldiers and Mothers: The Political Origins of Social Policy in the United States* (Cambridge: Harvard University Press, Belknap Press, 1992), 58.
3. Francis Rourke points out that agencies try hard to cultivate client groups because the ability to command strong political support is an important source of agency power. Francis E. Rourke, *Bureaucracy, Politics, and Public Policy*, 3d ed. (Boston: Little, Brown, 1976).
4. Charles F. Wilkinson, *Crossing the Next Meridian: Land, Water, and the Future of the West* (Washington, D.C.: Island Press, 1992).
5. Richard F. Fenno, Jr., *Congressmen in Committees* (Boston: Little Brown, 1973); Kenneth A. Shepsle, *The Giant Jigsaw Puzzle: Democratic Committee Assignments in the Modern House* (Chicago: University of Chicago Press, 1978).
6. Kenneth A. Shepsle and Barry R. Weingast, "The Institutional Foundations of Committee Power," *American Political Science Review* 81 (March 1987): 85–104; Randall L. Calvert, Matthew D. McCubbins, and Barry R. Weingast, "A Theory of Political Control and Agency Discretion," *American Journal of Political Science* 33 (August 1989): 588–611.
7. Herbert Kaufman, *The Administrative Behavior of Federal Bureau Chiefs* (Washington, D.C.: Brookings Institution, 1981).
8. See, for example, Matthew D. McCubbins, Roger G. Noll, and Barry R. Weingast, "Administrative Procedures as Instruments of Political Control," *Journal of Law, Economics, and Organization* 3 (1987): 243–277.
9. Keith Hamm, "The Role of 'Subgovernments' in U.S. State Policy Making: An Exploratory Analysis," *Legislative Studies Quarterly* 11 (August 1986): 321–351;

James Q. Wilson, *Bureaucracy* (New York: Basic Books, 1989). Wilson points out that the extent to which Congress can constrain a bureaucracy also depends on the type of task the agency performs and the level of support in its political environment.

10. Bryan D. Jones, *Reconceiving Decision-Making in Democratic Politics: Attention, Choice, and Public Policy* (Chicago: University of Chicago Press, 1994).

11. Quoted in Debra L. Donahue, *The Western Range Revisited: Removing Livestock to Conserve Native Biodiversity* (Norman: Oklahoma University Press, 1999), 2.

12. The term "public domain" refers to land that the federal government had neither disposed of nor set aside in federally managed reserves.

13. Wilkinson, *Crossing the Next Meridian*, 90.

14. Congress established the 160-acre limit with the Land Ordinance of 1785, which divided western land into 6 x 6–mile townships, subdivided into one-mile squares containing four 160-acre plots. The goal was to create a system of small freeholders that would ultimately become a prosperous republican society. According to historian Richard White, "It was an ideal more suited to the East than to the West and more appropriate for the American past than the American future." Richard White, *"It's Your Misfortune and None of My Own": A New History of the American West* (Norman: University of Oklahoma Press, 1991), 142.

15. Wilkinson, *Crossing the Next Meridian*.

16. Ibid.

17. William D. Rowley, *U.S. Forest Service Grazing and Rangelands: A History* (College Station: Texas University Press, 1985).

18. Ibid.

19. William Voigt, Jr., *Public Grazing Lands: Use and Misuse by Industry and Government* (New Brunswick: Rutgers University Press, 1976).

20. Samuel T. Dana and Sally K. Fairfax, *Forest and Range Policy,* 2d ed. (New York: McGraw-Hill, 1980), 137.

21. Rowley, *U.S. Forest Service Grazing.*

22. At the time, the Interior Department was responsible for disposing of the public domain but did not have any regulatory authority over unclaimed lands. Like any good bureau chief, Ickes wanted to retain control of his "turf" and thus sought ways to avoid turning over public domain land to the Agriculture Department's Forest Service. Getting the support of ranchers, through rancher-friendly policies, was key to retaining Interior Department control.

23. Phillip Foss, *Politics and Grass* (Seattle: University of Washington Press, 1960).

24. E. Louise Peffer, *The Closing of the Public Domain* (Stanford: Stanford University Press, 1951), 264.

25. Easterners, disgruntled with the extent to which grazing fees subsidized ranchers (fee receipts were one-fifth of program expenditures) unwittingly collaborated with western, anti–Grazing Service interests to slash the agency's budget. See William L. Graf, *Wilderness Preservation and the Sagebrush Rebellions* (Savage, Md. Rowman and Littlefield, 1990).

26. Dana and Fairfax, *Forest and Range Policy.*

27. Ibid.

28. Bernard DeVoto, *The Easy Chair* (Boston: Houghton Mifflin, 1955), 254–255.

29. Quoted in Paul W. Gates and Robert W. Swenson, *History of Public Land Law Development* (Washington, D.C.: U.S. Government Printing Office, 1968), 629.

30. Dana and Fairfax, *Forest and Range Policy*, 186.

31. Voigt, *Public Grazing Lands*, 132.

32. Klyza, *Who Controls Public Lands?*

33. Harold E. Dregne, "Desertification of Arid Lands," *Economic Geography* 3 (1977): 322–331.

34. Reed F. Noss and Allen Y. Cooperrider, *Saving Nature's Legacy: Protecting and Restoring Biodiversity* (Washington, D.C.: Island Press, 1994).

35. Ibid.
36. George Wuerthner, "How the West Was Eaten," *Wilderness* (spring 1991): 28–37.
37. U.S. General Accounting Office, *Rangeland Management: Comparison of Rangeland Condition Reports,* GAO/RCED-91-191 (July 1991). One prominent dissenter, Thadis Box, pointed out that two issues confound our understanding of range conditions. First, he claimed that data on range conditions were old or nonexistent. Second, he argued that range conditions must be evaluated with respect to some management objective. If the goal was to provide better forage for cattle, the trend for rangelands had, on average, been upwards over a number of decades and that the range was in the best condition of the twentieth century. See Thadis Box, "Rangelands," in *Natural Resources for the 21st Century* (Washington, D.C.: American Forestry Association, 1990), 113–118.
38. Quoted in Wuerthner, "How the West Was Eaten," 32–34.
39. U.S. General Accounting Office, *Public Rangelands: Some Riparian Areas Restored but Widespread Improvement Will be Slow,* GAD/RCED-88-105 (June 1988); EPA Report cited in Wuerthner, "How the West was Eaten."
40. GAO, *Rangeland Management: More Emphasis Needed on Declining and Overstocked Grazing Allotments,* GAO/RCED-88-80 (June 1988).
41. GAO, *Public Rangelands: Some Riparian Areas Restored.*
42. U.S. General Accounting Office, *Rangeland Management: BLM Efforts to Prevent Unauthorized Livestock Grazing Need Strengthening,* GAO/RCED-91-17 (December 1990); GAO, *Rangeland Management: Interior's Monitoring Has Fallen Short of Agency Requirements,* GAO/RCED-92-51 (February 1992).
43. GAO, *Rangeland Management: More Emphasis Needed.*
44. U.S. General Accounting Office, *Rangeland Management: Profile of the Forest Service's Grazing Allotments and Permittees,* GAO/RCED-93-141FS (April 1993).
45. William Kittredge, "Home on the Range," *New Republic,* December 13, 1993, 13–16.
46. U.S. Congress, House, Committee on Government Operations, *Federal Grazing Program: All Is Not Well on the Range* (Washington, D.C.: U.S. Government Printing Office, 1986).
47. Private lands in the East, which are far more productive per acre, support 81 percent of the livestock industry, and private lands in the West sustain the remaining 17 percent. The small western livestock industry is quite dependent on public grazing privileges, however; about one-third of western cattle graze on public land at least part of the year.
48. Wuerthner, "How the West Was Eaten," 36.
49. Philip L. Fradkin, "The Eating of the West," *Audubon,* January 1979, 120.
50. Wilkinson, *Crossing the Next Meridian,* 108.
51. An organic act articulates an agency's mission. Recall that the BLM was created as part of an executive reorganization, so it did not have an overarching, congressionally defined purpose.
52. Irving Senzel, "Genesis of a Law, Part 2," *American Forests,* February 1978, 32–39.
53. Klyza, *Who Controls Public Lands?*
54. Ibid.
55. Ibid.
56. PL 95-514; 92 Stat. 1803; 43 USC Section 1901 *et seq.*
57. Wilkinson, *Crossing the Next Meridian.*
58. Robert H. Nelson, "Why the Sagebrush Revolt Burned Out," *Regulation,* May–June 1984, 27–43.
59. The Reagan administration had two goals for the public lands. First, it wanted to make the nation's resources more accessible to those who wished to exploit them. Second, it hoped to reduce government intervention in the economy. See Robert F. Durant, *The Administrative Presidency Revisited: Public Lands, the BLM, and the Reagan Revolution* (Albany: State University of New York Press, 1992).

60. Durant, *The Administrative Presidency Revisited,* 59.
61. Wilkinson, *Crossing the Next Meridian.*
62. For example, the *New York Times, High Country News,* and *People* magazine all covered Forest Service district ranger Don Oman's story. When Oman, a twenty-six-year veteran of the Forest Service, tried to regulate grazing in the Sawtooth Forest in southern Idaho, ranchers threatened to kill him if he was not transferred. Instead of accepting a transfer, Oman filed a whistleblower's complaint with the Inspector General's office of the Agriculture Department. See Timothy Egan, "Trouble on the Range as Cattlemen Try to Throw Off Forest Boss's Reins," *New York Times,* April 19, 1990, Sec. 1, 1.
63. Klyza, *Who Controls Public Lands?*
64. Ibid.
65. "BLM Reauthorization Died in Senate," *1991 CQ Almanac* (Washington, D.C.: CQ Press, 1992), 216.
66. U.S. General Accounting Office, GAO, *Rangeland Management: Current Formula Keeps Grazing Fees Low,* GAO/RCED-91-185BR (June 1991).
67. Phillip A. Davis, "After Sound, Fury on Interior, Bill Signifies Nothing New," *Congressional Quarterly Weekly Report,* November 2, 1991, 3196.
68. Quoted in Timothy Egan, "Sweeping Reversal of U.S. Land Policy Sought by Clinton," *New York Times,* July 21, 1995, A1.
69. Ibid.
70. Catalina Camia, "Administration Aims to Increase Grazing Fees, Tighten Rules," *Congressional Quarterly Weekly Report,* August 14, 1993, 2223.
71. Catalina Camia, "The Filibuster Ends; Bill Clears; Babbitt Can Still Raise Fees," *Congressional Quarterly Weekly Report,* November 13, 1993, 3112–3113.
72. Quoted in Associated Press, "Local Control of Rangeland Touted by U.S.," *Boston Globe,* February 15, 1994, 7.
73. Ibid.
74. Quoted in Timothy Egan, "Grazing Bill to Give Ranchers Vast Control of Public Lands," *New York Times,* July 21, 1995, A1.
75. Karl Hess, Jr., "Grazing at the Public Trough," *Wall Street Journal,* July 12, 1995, A14.
76. "Grazing Rules Bill Fizzles in House," *1996 CQ Almanac* (Washington, D.C.: CQ Press, 1997), Sec. 4, 14–16.
77. Pamela Baldwin, *Federal Grazing Regulations: Public Lands Council v. Babbitt* (Washington, D.C.: Congressional Research Service, 2000).
78. Ranchers' judicial victory was short-lived, however. In September 1998, the 10th Circuit Court of Appeals rejected key parts of the Brimmer ruling: it restored to the BLM the authority to reduce the number of cattle allowed by permits and retain title of range improvements on public lands. The court concurred with Brimmer's rejection of conservation-use permits, however. See Baldwin, *Federal Grazing Regulations.*
79. Quoted in *Greenwire,* July 13, 1997.
80. James Brooke, "It's Cowboys vs. Radical Environmentalists in New Wild West," *New York Times,* September 20, 1998, A31.
81. "House Backs Grazing Fee Increase," *1997 CQ Almanac* (Washington, D.C.: CQ Press, 1998), Sec. 3, 32.
82. U.S. Forest Service, *2000 RPA Assessment of Forest and Range Lands* (Washington, D.C.: U.S. Department of Agriculture, 2001).
83. Donahue, *The Western Range Revisited.*
84. John E. Mitchell, *Rangeland Resource Trends in the United States,* Report no. RMRS-GTR-68 (Fort Collins, Ohio: U.S.D.A. Forest Service, Rocky Mountain Research Station, 2000).
85. Quoted in Donahue, *The Western Range Revisited,* 58–59.
86. Ibid., 59.
87. U.S. Forest Service, *2000 RPA Assessment,* 50.

88. Jake Page, "Ranchers Form a 'Radical Center' to Protect Wide-Open Spaces," *Smithsonian,* June 1997, 50–60.
89. Quoted in Sandra Blakeslee, "On Remote Mesa, Ranchers and Environmentalists Seek Middle Ground," *New York Times,* December 26, 2000, F4.
90. Quoted in Phillip A. Davis, "Cry for Preservation, Recreation Changing Public Land Policy," *Congressional Quarterly Weekly Report,* August 3, 1991, 2151.
91. Ibid.
92. The 2000 census showed that the West is now nearly as urban as the Northeast, with more than three-quarters of its residents living in cities.
93. For testimonials about collaborative environmental problem solving in the West, see Phil Brick et al., *Across the Great Divide: Explorations in Collaborative Conservation and the American West* (Washington, D.C.: Island Press, 2001).

Recommended Reading

Dana, Samuel T., and Sally K. Fairfax. *Forest and Range Policy,* 2d ed. New York: McGraw-Hill, 1980.
Donahue, Debra L. *The Western Range Revisited.* Norman: University of Oklahoma, 1999.
Noss, Reed F., and Allen Y. Cooperrider. *Saving Nature's Legacy: Protecting and Restoring Biodiversity.* Washington, D.C.: Island Press, 1994.
Wilkinson, Charles F. *Crossing the Next Meridian: Land, Water, and the Future of the West.* Washington, D.C.: Island Press, 1992.

Web Sites

http://www.blm.gov/nhp/index.htm (BLM site)
http://www.fs.fed.us (Forest Service site)
http://www.grazingactivist.org (Public Lands Grazing Activist site)

CHAPTER 7

Jobs vs. the Environment

Saving the Northern Spotted Owl

In the late 1980s, the federal government became embroiled in one of the most notorious environmental controversies in the nation's history. At issue was the government's obligation to protect the northern spotted owl, a creature that makes its home almost exclusively in the old-growth forests of the Pacific Northwest. The debate transcended disagreement over the fate of any particular species, however; it was yet another eruption of the long-standing confrontation between fundamentally different philosophies about the relationship between humans and nature. It pitted those determined to preserve the vestiges of the nation's old-growth forest against those who feared losing their way of life and the region's historical economic base.

This case vividly illustrates the evolving role of science and environmental values in natural resource management agencies' decision making. Each federal bureau with jurisdiction over environmental issues has a distinctive orientation that arises out of its founding principles and subsequent development. Congress created many of these agencies, including the U.S. Forest Service and the Bureau of Land Management (BLM), to pursue the dual objectives of conserving natural resources for future generations and maintaining the stability of the industries and communities that depend on using those resources. Such missions predisposed the agencies to treat resources as commodities and pay little attention to their aesthetic or ecosystem values. As the grazing policy case in chapter 6 shows, pressure from members of Congress sympathetic to industries that use and extract resources reinforced this orientation, as did the fact that for many years they dealt almost exclusively with ranching and timber interests on these issues.

Beginning in the 1970s, however, the Forest Service and the BLM began incorporating environmental values and environmental science into their decision making. This happened in part because new laws required both agencies to hire more environmental scientists; to collect biological data on species, water quality, and other ecosystem amenities; and to take factors such as fish, wildlife, and watershed health into account in planning. In addition, the agencies' new generation of employees was more diverse and grew up in an era when environmentalism was part of mainstream American culture.[1] The infusion of scientific and environmentally oriented personnel, combined with directives to take factors besides resource extraction into account in decision making, contributed to a gradual shift over the 1980s in these agencies' organizational cultures.[2] Agency employees, particularly scientists, began to make more ecologically sound assumptions when generating information on which decisions are based.

Enhancing the influence of environmentally oriented employees on agency decision making has been the increasing number, growing vigilance, and expanding clout of environmental groups concerned about preserving ecosystems. While the grazing policy case exemplifies the extent to which members of Congress can constrain agencies on behalf of commodity interests, the spotted owl case shows how environmentalists can challenge the dominance of extractive interests. To succeed, advocates transformed scientific claims about the spotted owl and old-growth forests into political symbols and compelling causal stories. Frustrated with the slow pace of BLM and Forest Service responses to the plight of the spotted owl, environmentalists resorted to a tactic that has become a staple of the environmental movement: litigation.

Lawsuits can slow the pace of decision making and prompt the collection of information. Moreover, judicial involvement changes the dynamics of environmental controversies in part by raising the level of scrutiny to which agency decision making is exposed. During the 1970s, the courts became more activist in reviewing regulations, justifying their behavior on the grounds that congressional delegation of vast authority to agencies made them more susceptible to "capture" by particular interests and that judicial intervention was necessary to ensure fairness.[3] While scholars and judges have debated the merits of reviewing the substance or merely the procedures of agency decision making, both approaches have the same goal: getting agencies to "elaborate the basis for their decisions and to make explicit their value choices in managing risks."[4] That, in turn, has elevated environmentally oriented scientists who can provide solutions to the challenges posed by new statutory requirements.

In addition to forcing agencies to justify their decisions, lawsuits raise an issue's visibility, which generally favors previously excluded groups. Forced into the limelight, economic interests retaliate against environmentalists' advocacy with arguments about the reliance of the region's economy on extractive jobs, the importance of low-cost resources for the nation's well-being, and the tradeoff between economic growth and environmental protection. Organizations generate predictions of the economic impacts of imposing environmental restrictions on resource extraction, forecasts that depended heavily on the assumptions used. And, as previous cases have made clear, neither side in this controversy is persuaded by the other; rather, the purpose of both sides' efforts is to win over the uncommitted public and persuade elected officials that the issue is salient.

BACKGROUND

In the eighteenth, nineteenth, and early twentieth centuries, timber companies, railroads, and homesteaders cleared most of the nation's primeval forest as they moved westward. But for many years, the enormity and impenetrability of the nearly 20 million acres of the Pacific Northwest's old-growth forest daunted explorers. In the late 1800s, the federal government gave most of the West's grandest old-growth forest—the biggest trees on the flattest, most fertile soil—to timber companies and railroads to facilitate westward expansion and economic development. (In all, states and the federal government gave railroads about 223 million acres of land. The idea was that the railroads would enhance the value of the surrounding, government-owned land, and purchasers would pay more for it.) The government also transferred some forestland to the states and to Native Americans.

At the same time, Congress began to set aside some western land in forest reserves, in recognition of the timber industry's cut-and-run practices in the Midwest. In 1905, Congress established the Forest Service within the Department of Agriculture to administer the national forests.[5] Forest Service chief Gifford Pinchot established the agency's founding principle: "The continued prosperity of the agricultural, lumbering, mining, and livestock interests is directly dependent upon a permanent and accessible supply of water, wood, and forage, as well as upon the present and future use of these resources under businesslike regulations, enforced with promptness, effectiveness, and common sense."[6]

Although the national forests were open to logging, not until the lumber requirements of World War I pushed a railroad out to the farming village of Forks, Washington, did logging in the Pacific Northwest begin in earnest. Then, after World War II, demand for northwest timber skyrocketed. By the mid-1980s, when the spotted owl controversy was coming to a head, private companies had virtually denuded the region's privately owned old growth. (In the early 1980s, the upheaval in New York's financial markets had spurred a spate of corporate takeovers, and timber companies with uncut assets became prime takeover targets for raiders who then clearcut their holdings to pay off debts). State land management agencies, responding to state policies to manage their forests for maximum dollar benefits, logged most of the state-owned old growth during the 1980s as well.

As a result of these logging practices, when the spotted owl controversy erupted, nearly 90 percent of the remaining old-growth forest was on federal lands. These federally managed lands fall under a variety of designations and receive varying degrees of protection. The law prohibits logging in national parks and monuments, which are managed by the National Park Service. Congress also has designated roadless portions of the land managed by the U.S. Forest Service and the BLM as wilderness. The protected old growth in both the parks and wilderness areas tends to be on rocky, high-altitude lands, however; nearly all of the remaining, low-elevation old growth is on Forest Service and BLM lands that are eligible for logging.[7]

By the mid-1980s, it was becoming apparent to many observers that the old-growth forests on Forest Service and BLM land were going the way of those on private and state lands. A host of federal laws passed in the 1960s and 1970s required those agencies to incorporate recreation, watershed, and wildlife concerns into their land management, but logging remained the dominant use of federal forestland in the region. In part this is because the timber industry had become inextricably bound up with the region's economy: in 1985, the industry accounted for almost 4 percent of the workforce in western Oregon and 20 percent of the area's total manufacturing sector employment.[8] In 1988, the Forest Service estimated that 44 percent of Oregon's economy and 28 percent of Washington's were directly or indirectly dependent on national forest timber.[9] Many small communities and some entire counties relied almost entirely on the industry for their livelihoods. In 1990, a journalist described the integral role of logging in the economy of Douglas County, Oregon, saying: "Oregon produces more lumber than any state, and Douglas County boasts that it is the timber capital of the world. . . . There one can tune in to KTBR, feel the roads tremble beneath logging trucks, and watch children use Lego sets to haul sticks out of imaginary forests."[10]

The enormous old-growth trees have a particular niche within the logging economy of the Pacific Northwest. Timber companies use huge, scissors-like machines called "fellerbunchers" to log second-growth forests (which have been harvested and replanted and thus contain smaller trees), whereas harvesting old-growth stands is labor intensive, relying on highly skilled cutters. Many of the region's small, independent mills use old-growth logs to make specialty products. And old-growth timber is highly profitable; it provides long stretches of clear-grained lumber and therefore can sell for triple what similar second-growth timber is worth. In about seventy towns in the two states, the local sawmill is the largest single private taxpayer and employer.[11] In addition to providing jobs in the private sector, logging on federal lands generates revenues for local governments. The federal government returns 25 percent of revenues derived from timber sales on federal lands to the county in which the forest is located. These revenues are earmarked primarily for schools and roads. Ten Oregon counties earn between 25 and 66 percent of their total income from federal timber sales.[12]

Federal law requires the Forest Service and the BLM to harvest trees at a sustainable pace—that is, by the time the last tree of the virgin forest is cut, the first tree of the regrown forest should be big enough to harvest.[13] During the 1980s, however, under pressure from Reagan administration appointees, the agencies accelerated the rate at which timber companies were allowed to cut, and logging substantially exceeded new growth. Congress, hoping to preserve community stability, forced the Forest Service to cut even more than the agency itself considered sustainable.[14] As the rate of cut increased during the 1980s, environmentalists became alarmed that not only were federal land managers ignoring the principles of sustainable yield, but that all the trees over 200 years old would be gone in less than thirty years.

THE CASE

While conflict over the spotted owl raged during a fifteen-year period from the mid-1980s through the 1990s, the issue actually arose a decade earlier when agency scientists first sounded the alarm. In 1968, a twenty-two-year-old Oregon State University student named Eric Forsman and his adviser, Howard Wight, had begun to study the biology and ecology of the owl, and they quickly became concerned about Forest Service harvesting practices. By the early 1970s, Forsman was pestering anyone who might be able to help him protect spotted owl habitat: the Corvallis Oregon City Council; the Audubon Society; the Forest Service; and the BLM. Although federal land management agencies were gradually becoming more receptive to scientists' ecological concerns, their long-standing timber bias circumscribed their willingness to act protectively. Eventually, environmentalists, impatient with the pace of policy change, took the agencies to court to force their hand.

Land Managers Try to Solve the Problem Quietly

Reacting to Forsman's inquiries and spurred by the imminent passage of a federal endangered species protection law, the Director of the Oregon State Game Commission established the Oregon Endangered Species Task Force (OESTF). At its first meeting, on June 29, 1973, the OESTF formally acknowledged the importance of the old-growth forest for wildlife and its disappearance from Oregon. The group also arrived at a minimum habitat recommendation of 300 acres per nest for northern spotted owls—an estimate based on Forsman's best guess, since no one knew much about either the non-game animals on Forest Service land or the extent of the old-growth forest.[15]

Neither the Forest Service—which holds about 68 percent of the owl's habitat in northern California, Oregon, and Washington (see Map 7.1)—nor the BLM was particularly interested in the OESTF's recommendations; agency managers feared the precedent that setting aside areas for individual species might establish. Thus, when the task force sent plans around, the agencies responded that there was insufficient scientific data on which to base a management decision with such potentially devastating economic consequences. In December 1973, Congress passed the Endangered Species Act (ESA), however, and the Fish and Wildlife Service (FWS) included the spotted owl on a list of potentially endangered species. In October 1977, the OESTF recommended that land managers protect 400 pairs of owls (290 on Forest Service land, ninety on BLM land, and twenty on state and private land) and requested that 300 acres of contiguous old growth be set aside for each pair of owls. Hoping to avert a decision to list the owl under the ESA, which would severely curtail their management options, both the Forest Service and the BLM reluctantly agreed to follow the OESTF's recommendations.

Local environmentalists were dissatisfied with the degree of owl protection in the agencies' plans, however. Led by the Oregon Wilderness Coalition (OWC), they filed an administrative appeal with the Forest Service in February 1980 on the grounds that its plan was implemented without preparing an environmental impact statement (EIS) as required by the National Environmental Policy Act (NEPA).[16] The regional forester, whose decision was

Map 7-1 Spotted Owl Habitat

Source: U.S. Forest Service.

supported by the chief forester, rejected the appeal on the grounds that this was not a major federal action but simply an affirmative step to protect the owls until a formal management plan was complete. The Forest Service declared its intent to conduct a "proper biological analysis," as required by the National Forest Management Act (NFMA), in preparing the regional plan.[17] The appellants decided not to try their luck in court but instead to await the biological analysis in the Region 6 (Pacific Northwest) Plan.

Shortly thereafter, in spring 1981, the BLM also became embroiled in a controversy over its owl management plan for the Coos Bay district.[18] When environmentalists appealed the plan, the timber industry retaliated with a local media campaign portraying spotted owl protection as a threat to industry and the region's economy. Under the leadership of Reagan appointees, the BLM was disposed to side with timber, but local agency officials were acutely aware that environmentalists could escalate their demands by petitioning to list the spotted owl as an endangered species. Facing intense pressure from the Oregon Department of Fish and Wildlife, in 1983 the BLM engineered a compromise in which it agreed to manage the land to maintain habitat sufficient for ninety pairs of spotted owls and revisit the issue within five years.[19]

The Emerging Science of Owls and Old-Growth Forests

Even as Forest Service and BLM managers were wrangling with environmental and timber interests over their owl protection guidelines, agency scientists were requesting more acreage for the owl. In developing the Region 6 Guide, the Forest Service had designated the spotted owl as the indicator species for the old-growth ecosystem, and government biologists were grappling with its viability.[20] Additional research had clarified the owl's habits; for instance, radio telemetry data—gathered by fitting radio transmitters into tiny backpacks strapped on the owls—suggested that it needed a much greater habitat area than Forsman had suspected. By 1981, scientists were suggesting that the agencies expand their owl reserves from 300 to 1,000 acres.

In addition to studying the owl, government biologists were learning more about the ecological value of the old-growth forest and biological diversity in general. Forest Service ecologist Jerry Franklin was among the first to draw attention to the potential value of old growth. In 1981, he released the first comprehensive ecological study of the Pacific forest. His research defined a "classic old growth" forest as one that is more than 250 years old, with enormous trees, big downed logs, and standing snags (dead trees). Some trees in these forests have survived 1,000 years or more and reached heights of 300 feet and diameters of six feet. In late-succession forests, there is also a healthy understory, a mixed and layered canopy, and light-filled gaps, as well as an abundance of ferns, moss, lichens, and other epiphytic plants.[21]

Franklin found that old growth, once thought to be a biological desert since it lacked big game, was actually with life. He discovered that the system was rich with symbiotic links: lichen and moss on the trees are not parasites, but metabolize nitrogen from the air and feed the trees that support them. Some tree voles eat truffles buried in the forest humus, excreting the undigested spores throughout the forest. The truffles are fungus colonies that, in turn, enable the roots of trees to extract nutrients from the soil. Woodpeckers rely on standing dead trees because the wood of young trees is too hard and gums their beaks with sap. Fallen dead wood houses a multitude of amphibians. And the wider spacing of trees in old-growth stands provides flying room for predators and sunlight for a second layer of young trees.[22] Finally, he suggested that in addition to storing carbon and thereby serving as a hedge against global warming, old growth plays an integral role in regulating water levels and quality, cleaning the air, enhancing the productivity of fisheries, and enriching and stabilizing the soil.[23] Scientists were uncertain about how much old-growth forest was needed to sustain the intricate ecosystem of the Pacific Northwest, however; in fact they were not even sure how much viable old growth existed.[24]

The Forest Service Region 6 Guide

Notwithstanding these scientific advances, between 1981 and 1984, the Forest Service produced a Final Region 6 Guide—a document that

> clearly looked like it had not fully incorporated information generated in the previous four years, and . . . was walking a line between what was seen as biologically legitimate and what was seen as politically and economically correct. . . . The level of owl protection at the forest level remained fairly minimal and dependent on the benevolence of the individual forest managers.[25]

Environmental groups filed another administrative appeal in the fall of 1984, challenging both the methodology and management measures of the Region 6 Guide. While the forestry chief again supported the regional forester's rejection of the appeal, this time the deputy assistant secretary of agriculture overruled him and required the region to prepare a supplemental environmental impact statement (SEIS) on spotted owl management in the summer of 1985.

The Forest Service conducted its assessment relatively quickly, since its plans were already behind schedule. After intense negotiations among factions within the agency, in July 1986, the service released its two-volume draft SEIS. Within months, the Forest Service had received 41,000 comments on the report, only 344 of which supported its owl recommendations.[26] Environmentalists, aware that they needed powerful scientific ammunition not just rhetoric to press their case, had recruited eminent Stanford population biologist Paul Ehrlich and population geneticist Russell Lande of the University of Chicago to create alternative owl viability models. The Forest Service tried to revise the plan modestly, hoping to satisfy both environmentalists and timber interests, but the final SEIS—released in April 1988—did little to quell rumblings on either side.

The Pressure Mounts to List the Owl as Endangered

Although many within the agencies were beginning to see the value of the old-growth forest and the spotted owl, to environmentalists and concerned scientists the rate of actual policy change seemed glacial. As scientific knowledge advanced, it became increasingly clear that federal managers' actions fell far short of what was needed to protect the owl and its habitat. In fact, forest managers—under pressure from the White House and members of Congress—more than doubled the federal timber harvest between 1982 and 1988 from less than three to more than five billion board feet. While mainstream, national environmental groups, such as Audubon and the Sierra Club, were concerned about the rapid demise of the old-growth forests, however, they were reluctant to confront directly the biggest industry in the Pacific Northwest. They felt that there was little public support in the region for the cause, and they did not want to provoke a backlash against the ESA or the environmental movement more generally. Andy Stahl of the Sierra Club Legal Defense Fund (SCLDF) even made a special trip to northern California to dissuade a pair of earnest environmentalists from petitioning the FWS to list the owl as endangered.[27]

In October 1986, however, an obscure environmental organization based in Cambridge, Massachusetts, called GreenWorld requested that the FWS list the northern spotted owl. After finding further action might be warranted, the FWS Region 1 (Pacific Northwest) director assigned three biologists to prepare a status report. But less than a year after the process began—under pressure from the Reagan administration and against the advice of its own biologists—the Region 1 director signed the FWS finding that, although declining in number, the spotted owl was not endangered. Mainstream environmentalists—who had finally joined the fray after GreenWorld submitted its petition—were livid at what they charged was a political rather than a science-based decision. In May 1988, the SCLDF sued the Interior Department and FWS on the grounds that the agency had ignored scientific evidence clearly showing the owl to be endangered in the Olympic Peninsula and Oregon Coast Range. Six months later, Judge Thomas Zilly of the U.S. District Court for the Western District of Washington found that the FWS had acted in an "arbitrary and capricious" manner by failing to demonstrate a rational connection between the evidence presented and its decision. The court gave the FWS until May 1, 1989, to provide additional evidence.

Affirming Judge Zilly's ruling and further arming environmentalists, in February 1989, a review of the listing process by the U.S. General Accounting Office (GAO) found that "Fish and Wildlife Service management substantively changed the body of scientific evidence. . . . The revisions had the effect of changing the report from one that emphasized the dangers facing the owl to one that could more easily support denying the listing petition."[28] The GAO found that two of the three scientists had concluded the owl was already endangered, but FWS management had ignored them. Administrators also had deleted a section warning that Forest Service logging would lead to the owl's eventual extinction and had excised a twenty-nine-page scientific appendix supporting this conclusion, replacing it with a new report prepared by a forest industry consultant. Finally, although the decision-making process was largely undocumented, the Region 1 director admitted that his decision was based in part on a belief that top FWS and Interior Department officials would not accept a decision to list the owl as endangered. According to the

GAO, "These problems raise serious questions about whether FWS maintained its scientific objectivity during the spotted owl petition process."[29]

Interest Group Confrontations: Lawsuits and PR Campaigns

While the FWS struggled with the listing question and federal land managers tried to navigate a middle course in planning, environmental activists pressed ahead on other fronts. They had already persuaded both Washington and Oregon to designate the owl as a state-listed endangered species, and they were gumming up the timber sales process by appealing hundreds of individual sales.[30] Now they began pursuing injunctions against logging on the federal lands inhabited by the owl, claiming that neither the Forest Service nor the BLM had satisfied its obligations under NEPA, NFMA, the O&C Lands Act, the Migratory Bird and Treaty Act, and other laws.[31] In late 1987, the SCLDF represented Portland Audubon and other environmental groups in a lawsuit challenging the BLM's logging of spotted owl habitat in Oregon (*Portland Audubon Society v. Lujan*). In 1988, a Portland judge, Helen Frye, issued a temporary injunction that halved timber harvesting on BLM lands in Oregon. The Seattle chapter of the National Audubon Society, the Oregon Natural Resources Council (ONRC), and more than a dozen other plaintiffs also filed suit challenging the adequacy of the Forest Service's plans to safeguard the owl (*Seattle Audubon Society v. Robertson*). The plaintiffs convinced Federal District Judge William Dwyer to enjoin the Forest Service from conducting timber sales scheduled for 1989. These temporary injunctions had dramatic effects: they halted 165 timber sales throughout the Pacific Northwest, slashing the amount of timber available for harvesting on federal lands in 1989 from 5.4 billion board feet to 2.4 billion board feet.

Environmentalists recognized that, in the long run, they needed more than legal support for their position, however. Furthermore, they knew the battle could not simply be waged in Oregon and Washington, where timber was a pillar of the economy. Ultimately, they would have to create a vocal, national constituency for the old-growth forest by persuading millions of Americans that, even if they did not live in the Pacific Northwest, they needed to protect the old-growth forest because it was a national treasure. The environmentalists' national PR campaign was manifold: they coined the term "ancient forest" to describe the area; sponsored hikes, tours, and flyovers to capitalize on the shocking visual impacts of clearcutting; wrote articles for national magazines from the *New Yorker* to *National Geographic*; and toured the country with a giant redwood in tow to dramatize the plight of the Northwest's trees.

While mainstream environmental groups pursued conventional means, more radical groups engaged in guerrilla tactics. Earth First! members, for instance, camped out on plywood platforms in trees scheduled to be cut down. They sat on boxes of company dynamite to prevent blasting, spiked trees, set their feet in cement-filled ditches, chained themselves to timber equipment, and buried themselves in rocks to stop bulldozers from moving up logging roads. Their approach did not always engender sympathy for their cause, but it made mainstream environmentalists appear reasonable by comparison.

Although the timber industry would have preferred to resolve the conflict locally, where its influence was greatest, it did not react passively to environmental activism. Timber workers quickly organized themselves into coalitions, such as the 72,000-member Oregon Lands Coalition. Like the environmentalists, these groups recognized the power of rhetoric and display. On July 1, 1989, the First Annual American Loggers Solidarity Rally came to Forks, Washington, the self-proclaimed timber capital of the world. A reporter for *Audubon* magazine describes the scene, as hundreds of logging trucks rolled into town honking their horns:

> Yellow balloons and flags and legends. "No timber, no revenue, no schools, no jobs." Over a picture of a mechanical crane: "These birds need habitats, too." On the side of a truck: "Enough is enough!" In the hands of a child: "Don't take my daddy's job." On a sandwich board: "Our Ancient Trees are Terminally Ill."[32]

Speaker after speaker at the rally derided environmentalists as frivolous and selfish.

Political organization was less straightforward for the timber industry than for loggers, however, because the timber industry consists of at least two components with different economic needs and political agendas. Six large timber companies led by Weyerhauser have already logged the old growth on the more than seven million acres they own in the Northwest, so their future in the region lies in harvesting managed stands of smaller trees. Thus, although some leading timber companies had a stake in ensuring access to the old-growth forests, the companies most affected were the small sawmills that are entirely dependent on federal timber for their log supply.

Ultimately, big timber, fearing their lands would be scrutinized next, joined the smaller operators in working aggressively behind the scenes to counteract environmentalists' pressure. They made substantial campaign contributions to candidates supporting their position and worked through their lobbying organizations, the American Forest Resource Alliance (AFRA) and the National Forest Products Association (NFPA), to assemble evidence supporting their argument that the government should not protect the owl until scientists were certain the bird was endangered. To mobilize popular sentiment, industry groups submitted editorials and took out advertisements in local newspapers. Since environmentalists had nationalized the issue, logging supporters also worked to transform the issue into a concern of carpenters, builders, and consumers nationwide. They activated allies in industries that relied on cheap wood, such as the National Homebuilders Association, which ran a full-page ad in newspapers blaming the spotted owl for "soaring lumber prices."

The Region's Elected Officials Get Involved

With the BLM and Forest Service paralyzed by court-ordered injunctions and interest groups up in arms, politicians from California, Oregon, and Washington began to seek legislative solutions to the impasse. Members of Congress wanted to appease voters interested in timber, but they were loathe to propose modifying existing environmental laws, recognizing that such actions would attract negative publicity and therefore garner little support from members outside the region. So in the summer of 1989, as the controversy was heating up, Oregon's senator Mark Hatfield and governor Neil Goldschmidt convened a meeting of timber industry representatives, environmentalists, and federal officials. After some acrimonious debate, Hatfield offered a one-year compromise plan that protected some areas of the forest while allowing old-growth harvesting to continue in others. More importantly, the plan prohibited anyone from seeking injunctions to prevent logging. Although the timber industry was satisfied, environmentalists objected. Nonetheless, Hatfield and Sen. Brock Adams of Washington discreetly introduced the "compromise" as a rider to the Department of Interior appropriations bill, and President Bush signed it into law in October.[33]

The Hatfield-Adams amendment forced Judge Dwyer in Seattle to rescind his temporary injunction and allow timber sales to proceed. It also compelled Judge Frye in Portland to dismiss the pending case against the BLM. During the subsequent nine months, while the Sierra Club Legal Defense Fund appealed those rulings to the Ninth Circuit Court of Appeals, more than 600 timber sales went forward, leaving only sixteen fiscal year 1990 sales that could be challenged. Thus, Congress found a short-term solution while avoiding the generic problem of reconciling habitat protection with timber harvesting—a strategy legislators hoped would placate timber advocates without unduly arousing environmentalists.

The Thomas Committee Report

The Hatfield-Adams amendment was clearly inadequate for the long run, however, especially because in June 1989 the FWS reversed itself and announced its intention to designate the northern spotted owl as threatened, thereby compelling the federal government to protect the bird and its habitat. Recognizing the need for a high-profile, credible owl protection plan, in October 1989, the secretaries of agriculture and interior named a federal Interagency Scientific Committee to formulate a strategy to save the owl (the Hatfield-Adams amendment had mandated the formation of this committee). To enhance the group's legitimacy, the agency heads chose veteran Forest Service biologist Jack Ward Thomas as its chair; thereafter, the group was known as the Thomas Committee. Thomas selected for his core team the five foremost spotted owl experts in the world, including Eric Forsman and Barry Noon, an expert on mathematical modeling of bird populations.

After six months of study, the Thomas Committee recommended a system of habitat conservation areas (HCAs) on federal lands that constituted a radical departure from previous conservation management. The plan prohibited logging in HCAs and allowed cutover lands within HCAs to return to old-growth status. The plan preserved 7.7 million acres of habitat, of which 3.1 million acres was timberland designated for harvest. The remainder was land already in national parks or wilderness areas or otherwise too remote, steep, high, or scenic for logging.[34]

Although the plan incorporated up-to-date conservation biology, Thomas was a pragmatist and therefore tried to steer clear of the explosive issue of old-growth preservation; he made it clear that in its deliberations the committee did not consider "how much old growth shall be preserved, where, and in what form."[35] In fact, 41 percent of the land within the HCAs consisted of recent clearcuts, non-forested lands and deciduous areas, and private lands (most of which had been logged). The committee also acknowledged that its plan constituted a minimum—not an optimal—strategy to prevent the owl's extinction; it would still result in a 40 to 50 percent reduction in the owl population over the next century. After a panel of scientists convened by the Bush administration conceded they could not challenge the report's merits, the Forest Service announced its intention "not to be inconsistent" with the report's recommendations and halted tree sales in the area.[36]

The Argument Shifts to Economic Costs

With an authoritative scientific document like the Thomas Committee report on the table, the only recourse open to opponents was to demonstrate that implementation costs would be astronomical. Thereafter, timber industry groups hastened to project the potential impact of the plan on timber-harvest levels and employment in the region. On July 9, 1990, the American Forest Resource Alliance sponsored a gathering at the National Press Club in Washington, D.C., at which a panel of statisticians contended that over the next decade the Thomas Plan would cost the region 102,757 jobs. In contrast, the Wilderness Society, the U.S. Forest Service, and the Scientific Panel on Late-Successional Forest Ecosystems (known as the Group of Four, or G4) assembled by some congressional staff all estimated the region would lose between 30,000 and 35,000 jobs as a result of technological change, federal forest plans, and Thomas Committee recommendations combined. The Bush administration quoted a Forest Service projection of 28,000 jobs lost for all three spotted owl states, while some members of Congress cited a figure of only 13,000.

Two factors account for most of the differences between these job loss estimates. First, each group independently estimated the extent of the timber-harvest reductions that forest protection measures would cause. Some analysts assumed that mid-1980s harvest levels would continue in the absence of environmental restrictions, while others recognized that such levels were unsustainable even in the absence of regulations. Second, groups used different estimates to translate changes in the harvest level into changes in employment. For example, most analysts agreed that for every billion board feet of timber harvested, an estimated 9,000 jobs were created in direct woods work, milling, and production. But there was far less consensus on how many indirect jobs, such as work in restaurants and stores, resulted. Some put the ratio at 1:1, while others put it at 4:1 or 5:1. As a result, the estimates of job impact for each billion-board-foot change ranged from 18,000 to 50,000.[37]

Furthermore, the American Forest Resource Alliance concluded that ESA restrictions would result in significant timber-harvest reductions on private lands, eliminating more than 62,000 additional jobs. In contrast, the Forest Service, the G4, and the Wilderness Society predicted an *increase* in private timber-harvest levels, as well as a reduction in log exports, in response to public lands harvest declines and rising timber prices. Finally, groups that opposed spotted owl protection predicted a smaller number of jobs lost to technological change (8,000) than did groups supporting owl protection (12,000).

Regardless of which projections they believed, many commentators foresaw economic and social catastrophe for the region if the government undertook preservation measures. A reporter for *Time* magazine speculated that

> Real estate prices would tumble, and states and counties that depend on shares of the revenue from timber sales on federal land could see those funds plummet. Oregon would be the hardest hit, losing hundreds of millions of dollars in revenue, wages and salaries, say state officials. By decade's end the plan could cost the U.S. Treasury $229 million in lost timber money each year.[38]

A joint Forest Service–BLM study predicted the unraveling of the very fabric holding some communities together, claiming that "in severe cases of community dysfunction, increased rates of domestic disputes, divorce, acts of violence, delinquency, vandalism, suicide, alcoholism and other social problems are to be expected."[39]

Congress Takes Up the Issue

By 1990, the spotted owl was front-page news across the country, and in the legislative session that followed, some ambitious members of Congress crafted legislation to protect the old-growth forest in hopes of capitalizing on national concern. The House Interior Subcommittee on National Parks and Public Lands and the House Agriculture Subcommittee on Forests, Family Farms, and Energy each debated forest protection bills in 1990. Neither pleased environmentalists, who argued the timber levels were too high, or timber lobbyists, who argued they were too low. Unable to move a bill out of committee, it appeared likely that Congress would once again pass a one-year bill specifying timber levels and limiting judicial review.

On September 19, 1990, plans to attach another rider to the appropriations bill were scrapped, however, when the Ninth Circuit Court of Appeals in San

Francisco sided with the SCLDF and found the judicial review provision in the Hatfield-Adams amendment to be unconstitutional. Judge Harry Pregerson wrote for a unanimous panel that the amendment "does not establish new law, but directs the court to reach a specific result and make certain factual findings under existing law in connection with two cases pending in federal court," which contravenes the principle of separation of powers.[40] It was the first time in 120 years that an act of Congress had been overturned on such grounds, and the unexpected ruling—coming only twelve days before the previous year's timber harvest bill was to expire—left Congress in a bind. Should it waive environmental laws for a year and risk provoking a public furor? Or should it approve a package that would conform to environmental laws but antagonize timber interests?

On September 21, 1990, the Bush administration unveiled a plan to do the former. An administration study group, which included the secretaries of agriculture and interior, as well as representatives of the Environmental Protection Agency (EPA) and the Office of Management and Budget (OMB), called for a 20 percent reduction in the 1991 timber harvest. The group recommended that Congress approve a timber-sale program of 3.2 billion board feet in Forest Service Region 6 but permit no timber sales from the HCAs designated by the Thomas Committee. It also proposed to exempt timber sales in the Pacific Northwest from the two major laws (NFMA and NEPA) governing Forest Service behavior, and requested that Congress convene an Endangered Species Committee, or God Squad, to conduct a full review of federal timber sales and land management plans.[41] In yet another sign of polarization among parties, the administration plan inflamed both environmentalists and timber interests.

Congress had only ten days from receipt of the plan to pass a timber program for the next fiscal year. Congressional leaders chose instead to rely on the advice of federal scientists and devise their own proposal to allow harvesting of about three billion board feet annually, 25 to 30 percent below the 1990 level. By the end of the session, however, the congressional proposal's sponsors had failed to gain majority support, and yet another year passed with no resolution to the controversy. During the winter and spring of 1991, Congress considered another slew of proposals, but opponents managed to tie them up in committees, and logging in owl country remained at a virtual standstill.

The Crisis Escalates

At this point, two events outside of Congress increased the urgency of the spotted owl issue. First, on April 26, 1991, the FWS announced plans to designate as critical habitat and thus ban logging on 11.6 million acres of forest in the Pacific Northwest to ensure the owl's survival.[42] Three million of those acres were on private land and included not only old growth but land where old growth might be grown in the future to link up habitat areas. Furthermore, unlike the Thomas Committee's plan, the FWS's set-aside did not even include the nearly four million acres already reserved in parks and wilderness areas.

The federal government had not proposed anything so sweeping in its entire history. Although the FWS later reduced its figure to a little less than seven million acres—under pressure from the timber industry and the BLM to exclude private, state, and Native American lands—the protected area remained considerable.

Second, in May 1991, environmentalists won their battle in Judge Dwyer's court to block all new Forest Service timber sales in the old-growth forest until the service could present an acceptable plan to protect the spotted owl habitat. In October 1991, still unable to engineer a long-term solution, Congress acceded to Interior Secretary Manuel Lujan's request to convene the God Squad, composed of seven cabinet-level officials, to review forty-four BLM timber sales in spotted owl habitat in Oregon. On May 14, 1992, the God Squad voted to allow logging on thirteen of the forty-four disputed tracts. The BLM was unable to implement the committee's decision, however, because Judge Frye issued an injunction against the BLM until the agency submitted a credible plan to protect the owl. Compounding the problem for policymakers, in July, Judge Dwyer made his injunction against the Forest Service permanent. He ordered the service to draft plans protecting not only the owl but a number of other species dependent on the ancient forest. Basing his ruling more on NFMA than on the controversial ESA, Dwyer left the environmentalists in a temporarily impregnable legal position from which they had little incentive to compromise. In the ancient forests of the Pacific Northwest, harvests had dropped as much as 90 percent.

The rulings both opened a window of opportunity and seriously constrained the federal government's options: in order to lift the injunctions, the Forest Service and the BLM had to revise their spotted owl protection plans to satisfy the criteria of NFMA and NEPA, or Congress had to pass new legislation to override existing land management laws. The Bush administration did not offer salvation; in mid-May, Secretary Lujan had released the (FWS's) official owl recovery plan, as mandated by the ESA. That plan sought to revive the owl's population to levels high enough that it could be removed from the list of threatened species; it set aside 5.4 million acres of natural forest land and 2.1 million acres of wilderness and national parks. Lujan estimated this plan would cost up to 32,000 jobs, a level he called unacceptable. The secretary simultaneously had released his own "preservation plan," prepared by an ad hoc committee, which emphasized saving regional timber jobs: it set aside 2.8 million acres of timberland and 1.5 million acres of parks and wilderness, and protected an area that could support only 1,340 pairs of owls, a level most biologists regarded as unsustainable.

Neither the official plan nor Lujan's alternative received much support in Congress. Environmentalist legislators pointed out that neither approach would protect the owl or the old-growth forest, while industry supporters complained that both plans would cost too many jobs. In the meantime, for the third successive year, subcommittees of the House Interior and Agriculture committees were working on ancient forest protection bills. None of those bills emerged from their respective committees, however, and Congress failed yet again to pass a comprehensive forest management plan.

The Clinton Plan

The spotted owl controversy had become sufficiently visible to be a campaign issue in the 1992 presidential race, and the election of President Bill Clinton widened the window of opportunity for environmentalists hoping to gain permanent protection for the old-growth forests. In April 1993, as they had promised on the campaign trail, President Clinton and Vice President Al Gore held a summit in Portland, Oregon, with four cabinet members, as well as scientists, environmentalists, timber workers, and industry officials. The administration hoped to bypass Congress and resolve the spotted owl problem by submitting a forest plan that would serve as the EIS required by Judge Dwyer.

In the meantime, environmentalists got an unexpected boost in early May, when the Society of American Foresters urged a dramatic departure from the century-old practices of the U.S. timber industry. In an uncharacteristically pointed report, the society said that cutting trees at the rate of regrowth would not protect the forests over time; instead, the society recommended an "ecosystem approach" to forestry that would base logging decisions on protection of wildlife, water quality, and overall ecological health. Frances Hunt, a forester for the National Wildlife Federation said of the report, "If you read between the lines, what it is saying is what the profession was taught, and what it helped teach, has turned out to be wrong and we are going to have to make amends for past mistakes."[43]

On July 1, President Clinton unveiled his long-awaited Northwest Forest Plan. Of the variety of forest management options considered, the one endorsed—Option 9—allowed annual timber harvests of 1.2 billion board feet from old-growth forests on federal lands, down from a high of more than five billion board feet per year in 1987 and 1988, and less than the approximately three billion board feet per year of the early 1980s. Option 9 also reflected the latest ecological thinking: it set up reserve areas for the owl in which logging was limited to some salvage of dead or dying trees and some thinning of new trees, but only if it posed no threat to the species. It established ten "adaptive management" areas of 78,000 to 380,000 acres each for ecological experiments. And it tried to protect entire watersheds in an attempt to head off controversies over endangered salmon and other fish species.

In addition to its owl protection measures, the Northwest Forest Plan provided $1.2 billion over five years to assist workers and families in Oregon, Washington, and northern California. It also supported retraining or related logging activities such as cleaning up logging roads and streams. The White House estimated that 6,000 jobs would be lost immediately under its plan, but anticipated that employing displaced timber workers to repair streams and roads would create more than 15,000 new jobs over five years. Most elements of the plan could be implemented administratively, without congressional approval. Thus the plan shifted the status quo: if Congress wanted to raise timber harvest levels from those designated in the plan, it would have to change existing environmental laws.

Critics on both sides immediately lambasted the plan. Then, in December, about four dozen scientists released a report providing strong evidence that the spotted owl population was declining and the trend was accelerating. A particular concern, the scientists said, was that the survival rate of adult females had declined 1 percent per year between 1985 and 1993, a time when capturing and banding of individual owls provided reliable data.[44] Biologists said that new data "suggest that the Northwest's old-growth forest ecosystems may already be approaching the extinction threshold for the northern spotted owl," and they cast serious doubt on whether the population could survive any additional habitat loss. Moreover, they argued that "political compromise and scientific uncertainty should not be used to justify overexploitation for short-term economic and political gain at the cost of future sustainability."[45]

Scientists' reservations and the timber industry outcry notwithstanding, in early March 1994, the administration affirmed Option 9 as the final blueprint for timber cutting in the Pacific Northwest and announced its intention to present the plan to Judge Dwyer. For the plan to pass muster, the judge had to find it scientifically sound, so the question before the court was whether the plan represented a scientific consensus or a politically expedient compromise. In December 1994, Judge Dwyer approved Option 9. Although either side could appeal, his seventy-page opinion addressed every substantive objection raised by environmentalists and the timber industry and thus left little room for legal challenge. In approving the plan, however, Judge Dwyer made his reservations plain: "The question is not whether the court would write the same plan," he said, "but whether the agencies have acted within the bounds of the law."[46] He also said that any more logging sales than the plan contemplated would probably violate environmental laws and admonished the government to monitor owl populations carefully in the future. Finally clear of legal hurdles, the Northwest Forest Plan took effect in early 1995.

The Timber Salvage Rider

Protection advocates' triumph was not only limited but short-lived because a window of opportunity opened for timber industry allies when Republicans assumed control of Congress in 1995. Idaho Sen. Larry Craig introduced a bill to accelerate logging in areas where trees had been damaged by fire or insects but still retained some commercial value. The bill eliminated citizens' rights of administrative and judicial appeal and suspended provisions of the ESA and NEPA[47]; it also promoted logging in roadless areas and opened up sections of the forest that had been closed because of spotted owl restrictions.[48] Rep. Charles Taylor of North Carolina, a tree farmer and staunch property rights advocate, hastily assembled a similar bill in the House. Taylor's bill directed the Forest Service to triple its current salvage timber volume over a two-year period, requiring the sale of an unprecedented 6.2 billion board feet of "salvage" timber over two years—an amount approximately double the 1994 yield from the entire national forest system.[49] In tacit recognition that no such quantities of salvage existed, the bill authorized the Forest Service to sell not just dead or dying trees but any "associated" green trees.

The premise of these initiatives was that there was a forest health crisis that needed to be addressed. At hearings on the bill, however, many scientists disputed the existence of such a crisis and challenged the appropriateness of thinning and salvage logging as a remedy for forest ills in any case.[50] Professional organizations such as the American Fisheries Society, the Society for Conservation Biology, the Wildlife Society, and the Ecological Society of America all protested the salvage program as it was rushed through Congress as a rider to the 1995 Emergency Supplemental Rescissions Act. According to journalist Kathie Durbin, however, congressional Republicans used the specter of wildfires to alarm constituents who were largely ignorant of forest ecology; thus, even skeptical members were concerned about jeopardizing the seats of western Democrats by voting against the rider.[51]

After years of efforts to protect the spotted owl and old-growth forest, federal land managers were stunned by the potential impact of the timber salvage rider.[52] On March 11, 1995, Lydon Werner, head of the BLM timber sale program for western Oregon, wrote a memo to BLM state director Elaine Zielinski saying that the BLM "would suffer a severe setback in the implementation of the Northwest Forest Plan [if the rider passed]. We support the need to improve forest health and expedite the salvage of diseased, infested, or dead and dying timber; however we are opposed to this amendment. . . . We believe [the sales] should occur in compliance with existing laws and management plans."[53] Even agency officials who supported salvage logging were dubious about the scale of the program envisioned by Congress: "Physically, there's no way we could get it done," said Walt Rogers of the Lowman Ranger District in Idaho.[54]

Responding to a deluge of mail from forest activists and a spate of editorials opposing the timber salvage provision, President Clinton vetoed the Budget Rescissions Act on June 7, citing as one reason the anti-environmental riders. In a series of backroom negotiations orchestrated by Senator Hatfield, however, Clinton reached an agreement with Congress on a budget-cutting bill that included the timber salvage rider. Despite the vehement opposition of top advisers, including Vice President Gore, Clinton finally signed the measure on July 27. In doing so, he assured environmental activists that his administration would adhere to environmentally sound practices when implementing the rider.

The bills' congressional sponsors had no intention of allowing that to happen. The day that Clinton signed the Rescissions Act, a group of three senators and three representatives sent a letter to Agriculture Secretary Dan Glickman and Interior Secretary Bruce Babbitt reminding them that the rider applied to all unawarded timber sales in western Oregon and western Washington, regardless of their status as endangered species habitat. When President Clinton sent a directive to his department heads to begin implementing the rider in an "environmentally sound manner," Senate authors of the rider went on the attack, berating administration representatives in a hearing and threatening to cut off the agencies' funding. In a series of rulings issued throughout the fall of 1995, U.S. District Judge Michael Hogan affirmed the congressional sponsors' interpretation of the law, dismissing challenges to timber sales released under the rider.

Although they received relatively little attention in the national press, the sales initiated under the timber salvage rider stimulated tremendous concern in the Pacific Northwest, where environmental activists were up in arms about what they dubbed "logging without laws."[55] Events in the Pacific Northwest in February 1996 made the environmentalists' case even more credible within the region, as flooding caused devastating mudslides in heavily logged parts of Idaho, Montana, Oregon, and Washington. The floods ripped out logging roads, triggered massive landslides, and dumped soil, debris, and giant conifers into streams. During a tour of the Pacific Northwest, after being greeted in Seattle by more than 1,000 demonstrators protesting the timber salvage rider, Clinton called the rider "a mistake" and advocated its repeal.[56]

Manifesting the change in its orientation, the Forest Service resisted congressional efforts to promote logging, and in July 1996, U.S. agriculture secretary Dan Glickman acknowledged that the Forest Service had suffered a severe loss of credibility over the timber salvage rider. He announced strict new guidelines that restricted logging in roadless areas and cutting of healthy trees as part of its "forest health" treatments. The agency subsequently withdrew some of its largest and most controversial roadless area sales, restrictions that were expected to reduce 1996 timber sale levels by 12 percent in Oregon and Washington alone. In June 1997, Forest Service Chief Mike Dombeck announced that the agency was shifting its focus: "We are in the midst of a profound change—a change of values and priorities. . . . Our challenge is to make watershed health, ecosystem health, the health of the land—whatever you wish to call it—our driving force."[57] In January 1998, after the timber salvage rider had expired, Dombeck announced an eighteen-month moratorium on logging in roadless areas in the national forests, explaining that the Forest Service was changing its emphasis from timber extraction to stewardship. (Furious, congressional Republicans threatened to reduce the Forest Service to a "custodial role" if it did not manage the national forests primarily for logging.) Unperturbed, in 1999 the Clinton administration announced its intention to ban road building on 43 million acres of undeveloped national forest, and on November 13—shortly before leaving office—Clinton approved a rule banning virtually all commercial logging from 54 million national forest acres.[58]

At the same time, congressional allies of the timber industry showed no signs of giving up; between 1996 and 2000, they introduced myriad "fire salvage" and "forest health" bills. Scalded by the timber salvage rider experience, Democrats and moderate Republicans resisted, suspecting these bills were thinly veiled efforts to increase logging on the national forests. Timber industry supporters were delighted, however, when newly elected President George W. Bush declared in spring 2001 that he would not enforce the Clinton administration ban on logging in roadless portions of the national forest system but instead would let communities decide the fate of their own roadless areas.

OUTCOMES

The combined impact of the spotted owl injunctions and the timber salvage rider on the ecological health of the Pacific Northwest forest ecosystem remains unclear. After environmentalists filed suit against the Bush administration for failing to protect the spotted owl, timber harvests on federal lands in Washington and Oregon dropped by more than 50 percent, from over five billion board feet in 1987, 1988, and 1989 to under three billion board feet in 1992 (see Table 7-1).[59] Shortly thereafter, the timber harvest dwindled to almost zero. After the passage of the timber salvage rider in July 1995, the Forest Service began ramping up timber sales east of the Cascades, in the Rockies, the Great Lakes, and the Southeastern Coastal Plain. Initially, the response from the timber industry was anemic: the Forest Service did not get a single purchase bid in the first three months after the law was signed. But timber companies responded enthusiastically to the opening up of old-growth stands west of the Cascades. There, logging proceeded on several previously closed stands, over the objections of government and university scientists as well as environmental protestors. Between 1995 and 1997, between 770 and 870 million board feet of national forest timber were harvested in the Pacific Northwest annually.

On June 14, 1996, however, the Ninth Circuit Court of Appeals overturned the decision by Judge Hogan, ruling that in the absence of clear direction from Congress, the Forest Service and BLM must use scientific criteria to determine where ESA-listed marbled murrelets were nesting. The ruling saved several thousands of acres of coastal old growth, as well as four hotly contested sales on the Umpqua and Siskiyou National Forests.[60] By the summer, there were signs that damaging timber sales were slowing down, although congressional advocates continued to push for more liberal fire salvage policies. The prognosis for the owl and the old-growth forest it inhabits was improving but still tenuous. Tom Tuchmann, the Clinton administration's choice to direct the implementation of its Northwest Forest Plan, insisted that the timber sales associated with the timber salvage rider would have a minimal ecological impact in the long run. "What we're talking about is less than 600 million board feet of the last of the old sales," he said. "It's less than one percent of all late-successional and old-growth habitat."[61] Notwithstanding Tuchman's optimism, however, scientists reported in 2000 that the owl population was declining at a rate of 3.9 percent annually, not the 1 percent forecast in the Northwest Forest Plan.[62]

While the ecological impacts of the spotted owl restrictions and subsequent timber salvage rider remain uncertain, the economic impacts are somewhat clearer. When the courts ordered restrictions on logging, Oregon mill owner Michael Burrill said, "They just created Appalachia in the Northwest."[63] Many commentators envisioned the timber communities of Oregon and Washington turning into ghost towns, and at first it seemed as though the bleak forecasts were coming true. In 1990, a *U.S. News & World Report* article on the town of

Table 7-1

Amount of Timber Offered for Sale, Sold, and Harvested by the Forest Service in the Pacific Northwest, Fiscal Years 1981–1997, in millions of board feet

Year	Timber Offered	Timber Sold	Timber Harvested
1981	5488	5481	3126
1982	4857	4642	2525
1983	4746	4916	3868
1984	4926	4962	4539
1985	5367	4753	4761
1986	5271	5060	4965
1987	5271	5273	5597
1988	5056	4919	5408
1989	4413	2811	5231
1990	5048	3997	3878
1991	1094	2106	3167
1992	684	638	2130
1993	630	634	1661
1994	436	317	1127
1995	776	307	877
1996	908	830	775
1997	951	776	767

Source: U.S. Forest Service.

Mill City reported that those loggers who found jobs often had to travel across state to keep them; their wives were taking jobs for the first time; and there were increases in teenage pregnancy, spouse abuse, the number of suicide calls to hotlines, and the number of runaway children.[64] Between 1989 and 1996, the region lost 21,000 jobs in the forest products industry.[65]

But because the spotted owl injunctions hit at about the same time as the national recession, many observers found it difficult to separate the effects of the two.[66] Moreover, many analysts believed that two major structural changes in the industry that had begun more than a decade before the spotted owl controversy erupted were largely responsible for job losses in the region. First, throughout the 1980s, the timber industry was shifting its operations from the Pacific Northwest to the Southeast: during the 1980s, the seven largest forest-products companies reduced their mill capacity by about 35 percent in the Pacific Northwest, while raising it by 121 percent in the South.[67] Second, automation reduced the number of timber jobs in the Northwest. As a result of mechanization, timber employment in Oregon and Washington fell by about 27,000 jobs between 1979 and 1989, even though the harvest was roughly the same in both years.[68] Third, exports of logs overseas, particularly to Japan and

China, cost the region local mill jobs.[69] Finally, during the 1980s and early 1990s, urban and suburban development encroached on an average of 75,000 acres of timberland each year in Washington and Oregon.[70]

In any case, subsequent changes in the Pacific Northwest suggested that it was a region in transition away from a timber-based economy toward a more diversified one. Between 1988 and 1994, the total number of jobs in the Pacific Northwest grew by 940,000 and earnings rose 24 percent, according to a 1995 study endorsed by dozens of Northwest economists.[71] In October 1995, three years into a drastic curtailment of logging, Oregon posted its lowest unemployment rate in over a generation, just over 5 percent. The state gained nearly 20,000 jobs in high technology, with companies like Sony opening up factories and Hewlett Packard expanding in the state. By early 1996, for the first time in history, high technology surpassed timber as the leading source of jobs in Oregon. Even some of the most timber-dependent counties in southern Oregon reported rising property values and a net increase in jobs. In fact, only two of the thirty-eight counties in the spotted owl region experienced a decline in total employment between 1990 and 1996.[72]

Even more startling, as the number of logging jobs fell, the average wage in Oregon rose. In 1988, the peak year for timber cutting, per capita personal income in Oregon was 92 percent of the national average, whereas in 1999, it was over 94 percent of the national average.[73] Conditions continued to improve as the 1990s wore on, with even places like the remote Coos Bay, once the world's largest wood-products shipping port, cashing in on the high-tech boom.[74] Moreover, the state attained this without sacrificing its role as the nation's timber basket, producing five billion board feet a year. Even though numerous timber mills closed because they could no longer get the big trees, operations like Springfield Forest Products had retooled and were hiring.[75]

The economic picture is not entirely rosy, however; the transition from a resource-based to a service-based economy has taken its toll. In isolated pockets, such as Burns and Hoquiam in Washington, rural poverty has intensified. Inflation in some rural counties was in the double digits through the 1990s. Moreover, while the service economy has produced a cleaner industrial base, it also has a dark side: the gap between rich and poor has widened. The wealthy are buying luxury homes as well as SUVs—which now make up more than half the new vehicles sold in the Northwest and are likely to outnumber cars by 2005—trends that threaten to undermine the environmental gains associated with reduced natural resource extraction.[76]

CONCLUSIONS

The spotted owl challenge was a litmus test for federal land managers trying to adjust to environmentalism. With its spectacular old-growth forests, combined with a historic economic dependence on timber, the region was a powder keg waiting to be ignited, and the spotted owl provided the spark. For over a decade, the Forest Service and BLM, the two agencies primarily responsible for managing the owl's habitat, wrestled quietly with protecting it while maintaining timber harvest levels. Although agency scientists accumulated compelling evidence suggesting that the owl and its dwindling old growth were in trouble, the agencies' long-standing commitments to timber harvesting, as well as political pressure from the region's elected officials, made a dramatic departure from the status quo unlikely. Agency scientists found themselves isolated, as political appointees tried to steer policy in directions decided by political expediency rather than science.

Frustrated with the slow pace of change in agency priorities, environmentalists filed lawsuits in hopes of changing the political dynamics of the issue. Court rulings in Washington and Oregon changed the status quo radically, from extensive logging to no logging of old-growth forests. The litigation elevated ecology and conservation biology relative to timber harvesting and raised the status of agency scientists who had been overruled in the 1970s and early 1980s but now offered the only way through the impasse at which the agencies found themselves. Court-ordered injunctions also helped environmentalists raise the national visibility of preserving old-growth forests, a phenomenon that was manifested in the candidates' attention to the issue during the 1992 presidential campaign, as well as in a burgeoning number of congressional proposals to protect the region's forests.

The national campaign that ensued highlights the political potency of environment versus economy rhetoric. Whenever environmental regulations are proposed, advocates of natural resource development publicize projections of massive job losses and dire economic repercussions, and the spotted owl controversy was no exception. Wielding studies conducted at the region's universities, as well as by government agencies and timber industry interest groups, opponents of spotted owl protection measures crafted a powerful case about the human costs of such interventions. Environmentalists responded with their own studies suggesting that owl protection measures were not the primary culprit behind lumber price increases or job losses in the region's timber industry. Over time, the relationship between environment and economy has proven to be more complex than either side portrayed it. Nevertheless, according to Bill Morisette, mayor of Springfield, Oregon, "Owls versus jobs was just plain false. What we've got here is quality of life. And as long as we don't screw that up, we'll always be able to attract people and businesses."[77]

QUESTIONS TO CONSIDER

- Why did the northern spotted owl come to national prominence as a symbol of the conflict between preservation and development?
- How have the Forest Service and the BLM handled the challenges posed by demands that they take environmental, and not just extractive, considerations into account when managing the nation's land and natural resources?
- What strategies should environmentalists consider in trying to redirect the nation's land management agencies?

Notes

1. Greg Brown and Charles C. Harris, "The Implications of Work Force Diversification in the U.S. Forest Service," *Administration & Society* 25 (May 1993): 85–113.
2. Ibid.; Paul A. Sabatier, John Loomis, and Catherine McCarthy, "Hierarchical Controls, Professional Norms, Local Constituencies, and Budget Maximization: An Analysis of U.S. Forest Service Planning Decisions," *American Journal of Political Science* 39 (February 1995): 204–242; Ben Twight and Fremont Leyden, "Measuring Forest Service Bias," *Journal of Forestry* 97 (1989): 35–41.
3. Agency capture refers to the situation in which agencies are responsive to a particular interest rather than considering the public interest in decision making.
4. David M. O'Brien, *What Process Is Due?* (New York: Russell Sage Foundation, 1987), 159.
5. Congress actually passed the Forest Service's Organic Act in 1897, but did not transfer the national forests from the Interior Department to the Agriculture Department until 1905.
6. The Pinchot Letter, quoted in Charles F. Wilkerson, *Crossing the Next Meridian: Land, Water, and the Future of the American West* (Washington, D.C.: Island Press, 1992), 128.
7. Forest Service Region 6 comprises twelve national forests: the Olympic, Mt. Baker–Squonalmie, and Gifford Pinchot National Forests in western Washington; the Mt. Hood, Willamette, Umpqua, Rogue River, Suislaw, and Siskiyou National Forests in western Oregon; and the Klamath, Six Rivers, and Shasta-Trinity National Forests in northern California. The BLM oversees forestland in six management districts. In Oregon and California, the BLM manages land reclaimed by the federal government during the Depression from the O&C Railroad. These lands are exempt by statute (the O&C Lands Act of 1937) from much of the restrictive legislation governing the national forests and are heavily logged.
8. Jeffrey T. Olson, "Pacific Northwest Lumber and Wood Products: An Industry in Transition," in *National Forests Policies for the Future*, vol. 4 (Washington, D.C.: The Wilderness Society, 1988).
9. U.S. Department of Agriculture–Forest Service, *Final Supplement to the Environmental Impact Statement for an Amendment to the Pacific Northwest Regional Guide, Volume 1, Spotted Owl Guidelines* (Portland: Pacific Northwest Regional Office, 1988).
10. Ted Gup, "Owl vs. Man," *Time*, June 25, 1990, 60.
11. Roger Parloff, "Liti-slation," *American Lawyer,* January–February 1992, 82.
12. Ibid.
13. A sustainable-yield harvest is one that can be regenerated in perpetuity. Sustainable yield is not a static concept, however; as scientists learn more about the factors that affect forest health, they revise their ideas about what harvest levels are sustainable.
14. Research by the *Portland Oregonian* showed that, in 1986, Congress ordered the Forest Service to sell 700 million board feet more than the agency proposed; in 1987, it ordered an extra billion board feet; in 1988, the increase was 300 million; and in 1989, it was 200 million. (A board foot is an amount of wood fiber equivalent to a one-inch thick, one-foot wide, one-foot long board. A billion board feet of lumber provides enough wood for about 133,000 homes.) See William Dietrich, *The Final Forest: The Battle for the Last Great Trees of the Pacific Northwest* (New York: Penguin, 1992).
15. Steven L. Yaffee, *The Wisdom of the Spotted Owl: Policy Lessons for a New Century* (Washington, D.C.: Island Press, 1994).
16. An administrative appeal is the first stage in the formal process by which a citizen can force an agency to reexamine and explicitly justify a decision.
17. The NFMA, passed in 1976, requires the Forest Service to draw up multiple-use plans that balance logging with non-commodity values, such as wilderness, wildlife, and recreation, for each forest in the national forest system.

18. BLM timber management plans are revised every ten years. The plans due in the early 1980s had to conform to the Sikes Act, the Federal Land Policy and Management Act, and the Endangered Species Act. See Yaffee, *The Wisdom of the Spotted Owl*.

19. Yaffee, *The Wisdom of the Spotted Owl*.

20. NFMA regulations require the Forest Service to identify indicator species, whose health reflects the condition of the entire forest ecosystem, and to determine the viability of those species' populations.

21. An epiphytic plan is one that grows on other plants. See Jerry F. Franklin et al., "Ecological Characteristics of Old-Growth Douglas-Fir Forests," General Technical Report PNW-118 (Portland: Pacific Northwest Forest and Range Experiment Station, 1981).

22. Ibid. Scientists are uncertain about the extent to which various species depend exclusively on old-growth tracts. Research has yielded ambiguous information, mostly because wildlife biologists have compared young and old "natural" forests but have not systematically compared the robustness of species in natural and managed stands. Recent research suggests that for many species it is not the age of the stand but its structural components that are critical.

23. Ibid.

24. Yaffee, *The Wisdom of the Spotted Owl*.

25. Steven L. Yaffee, "Lessons About Leadership From the History of the Spotted Owl Controversy," *Natural Resources Journal* 35 (spring 1995): 392.

26. Yaffee, *The Wisdom of the Spotted Owl*.

27. Dietrich, *The Final Forest*.

28. U.S. General Accounting Office, *Endangered Species: Spotted Owl Petition Evaluation Beset by Problems*, GAO/RCED-89-79 (February 1989).

29. Ibid.

30. David Seideman, "Terrorist in a White Collar," *Time*, July 7, 1990, 60.

31. Courts issue injunctions on timber sales if a plaintiff proves that "irreparable harm" will occur and if there is a "substantial likelihood" that the plaintiff will prevail at trial.

32. John G. Mitchell, "War in the Woods II," *Audubon*, January 1990, 95.

33. A rider is an amendment that is not germane to the law. Sponsors of such amendments use them to avoid public scrutiny.

34. Kathie Durbin, "From Owls to Eternity," *E Magazine*, March–April 1992, 30–37, 64–65.

35. Quoted in ibid.

36. Dietrich, *The Final Forest*.

37. Neil Samson, "Updating the Old-Growth Wars," *American Forests*, November–December 1990, 17–20.

38. Gup, "Owl vs. Man," 57.

39. Quoted in ibid., 58.

40. Quoted in Parloff, "Liti-slation," 82.

41. The ESA provides for the creation of a cabinet-level Endangered Species Committee (informally known as the God Squad), to grant exemptions from the act's provisions for economic reasons. Congress can pass legislation to convene the God Squad only if an agency can prove to the Interior secretary that it has exhausted all other alternatives. (Otherwise, the law requires the federal government to come up with a plan based on science.) In the seventeen years prior to the spotted owl controversy, Congress had convened the God Squad only twice.

42. The ESA requires the designation of critical habitat for any species listed as threatened or endangered.

43. Quoted in Scott Sonner, "In Switch, Foresters Push Ecosystem Policy," *Boston Globe*, May 2, 1993, 2.

44. John H. Cushman, Jr., "Owl Issue Tests Reliance on Consensus in Environmentalism," *New York Times*, March 6, 1994, 28.

45. Quoted in ibid.

46. Quoted in John H. Cushman, Jr., "Judge Approves Plan for Logging in Forests Where Rare Owls Live," *New York Times*, December 22, 1994, 1.

47. More precisely, the bill required the Forest Service to consider the environmental impacts of the sale program but specified in advance that the sales satisfied the requirements of various environmental laws.

48. U.S. Congress, Senate, *Hearing Before the Subcommittee on Forests and Public Land Management of the Committee on Energy and Natural Resources*, 104th Congress, March 1, 1995 (Washington, D.C.: U.S. Government Printing Office, 1995).

49. Tom Kenworthy and Dan Morgan, "Panel Would Allow Massive Logging on Federal Land," *Washington Post*, March 3, 1995, A1.

50. Most scientists concurred that many western forests were in trouble, particularly the dry, low- to medium-elevation forests once dominated by fire-dependent species like ponderosa pine and western larch. A history of fire suppression, combined with timber harvesting practices, had dramatically altered such forests. While in some forests thinning and salvage logging may have been appropriate, however, scientists maintained that there was no "one size fits all" prescription. See Tom Kenworthy, "Forests' Benefits Hidden in Tree Debate," *Washington Post*, April 18, 1995, A1.

51. Kathie Durbin, *Tree Huggers: Victory, Defeat, and Renewal in the Ancient Forest Campaign* (Seattle: The Mountaineers, 1996).

52. The Forest Service had undertaken a comprehensive environmental study of the ten national forests in the area, and pending completion of that study recommended interim protection for the remaining patches of old-growth trees. The agency's scientific panel wanted a comprehensive study of the effectiveness of thinning and salvage before undertaking such a program. See Kenworthy, "Forests' Benefits Hidden."

53. Quoted in Durbin, *Tree Huggers*, 255.

54. Quoted in Kenworthy, "Forests' Benefits Hidden."

55. Brad Knickerbocker, "The Summer of Discontent for Greens, Monks in the West," *Christian Science Monitor*, July 24, 1995, 3.

56. Durbin, *Tree Huggers*.

57. Quoted in *Greenwire*, June 25, 1997.

58. Between the draft and the final rule, the administration added roadless areas of the Tongass National Forest in Alaska to the ban. See Hel Bernton, "Forest Chief Asks Reduced Logging," *Oregonian*, March 30, 1999, online; Douglas Jehl, "Expanded Logging Ban is Proposed for National Forests," *New York Times*, November 14, 2000, A12.

59. Ed Niemi, Ed Whitelaw, and Andrew Johnston, *The Sky did NOT Fall: The Pacific Northwest's Response to Logging Reductions* (Eugene: ECONorthwest, 1999).

60. Durbin, *Tree Huggers*.

61. Quoted in ibid., 263. Only about half of the total national forest harvest in the Pacific Northwest between 1995 and 1997 came from the western forests covered by the Northwest Forest Plan.

62. Associated Press, "Owl Disappears," July 10, 2000, ABCNews.com.

63. Quoted in Timothy Egan, "Oregon Foiling Forecasters, Thrives as It Protects Owl," *New York Times*, October 11, 1995, A1.

64. Betsy Carpenter, "The Light in the Forest," *U.S. News and World Report*, April 5, 1993, 40.

65. Niemi et al., *The Sky Did NOT Fall*.

66. Thousands of jobs did disappear during the recession, but the continued harvest of trees sold two or three years before delayed the full impact of owl protection. More-

over, many loggers migrated to work in Alaska and Rocky Mountain forests. Niemi and his coauthors estimate that about 9,300 workers in Washington and Oregon lost their jobs between 1990 and 1994 as a consequence of spotted owl restrictions. See Niemi et al., *The Sky Did NOT Fall.*

67. "Log On," *Economist,* November 5, 1992, 26.
68. Niemi et al., *The Sky Did NOT Fall.* Moreover, because industry had forced the timber workers' unions to take a pay cut during the 1980s, in 1989 timber workers received paychecks that were less than two-thirds of those they had received a decade earlier.
69. Recognizing the severe impact of raw log exports, the federal government banned such exports from federal and state lands in the West, but timber companies circumvented the ban by substituting logs from private land for export and cutting national forest timber for domestic sale. See Michael Satchell, "The Endangered Logger," *U.S. News and World Report,* June 25, 1990, 27–29.
70. Dietrich, *The Final Forest.*
71. Thomas M. Power, ed., "Economic Well-Being and Environmental Protection in the Pacific Northwest: A Consensus Report by Pacific Northwest Economists," (Economics Department, University of Montana, December 1995). Another study found 27 percent and 15 percent increases respectively in the region's total employment and per capita income. See Niemi et al., *The Sky Did NOT Fall.*
72. Niemi et al., *The Sky Did NOT Fall.*
73. State of Oregon, Bureau of Economic Analysis, "Oregon Per Capita Personal Income" (May 2001), http://www.olmis.org/pubs/single/pepi.pdf.
74. Sam Howe Verhovek, "Paul Bunyan Settling into His New Cubicle," *New York Times,* August 21, 2000, A1.
75. Egan, "Oregon Foiling Forecasters."
76. Alan Thein Durning, "New Environment Hurt by Raging Consumerism," *Seattle Post-Intelligencer,* July 13, 1999, A9.
77. Quoted in Egan, "Oregon Foiling Forecasters."

Recommended Reading

Dietrich, William. *The Final Forest: The Battle for the Last Great Trees of the Pacific Northwest.* New York: Penguin, 1992.

Durbin, Kathie. *Tree Huggers: Victory, Defeat, and Renewal in the Ancient Forest Campaign.* Seattle: The Mountaineers, 1996.

Yaffee, Steven L. *The Wisdom of the Spotted Owl: Policy Lessons for a New Century.* Washington, D.C.: Island Press, 1994.

Web Sites

http://www.fs.fed.us/r6/welcome.htm (Forest Service, Pacific Northwest Region site)
http://www.fs.fed.us./pnw (Forest Service Pacific Northwest Research Station site)
http://www.or.blm.gov/forest plan/nwfptitl.htm (BLM's Northwest Forest Plan-Related Documents site)

CHAPTER 8

The New England Fisheries Crisis

In early 1993, many New Englanders were startled to learn that there was a crisis in the region's cod, flounder, and haddock fisheries. Apparently the groundfish[1] were on the verge of collapse, and federal regulators intended to shut down for an indefinite period Georges Bank—a 6,600-square-mile area more than 100 miles offshore that was once the most prolific fishing grounds in the world. The fishermen were in an uproar, and many charged that the federal management regime instituted in 1976, not overfishing, was the culprit. Regulators held firm, however, pointing out that government scientists had been warning of the groundfish's demise for well over a decade. Since then, fishery rules have been tightened even further, and some groundfish species have recovered modestly, but a long-term solution remains elusive.

The New England fisheries case illuminates the complexity of managing common property resources, the special challenges of which were captured in a model popularized by Garrett Hardin in a 1968 *Science* magazine article entitled "The Tragedy of the Commons." According to Hardin's model, when a resource is open to everyone, those who use it will inevitably overexploit it: "the logic of the commons remorselessly generates tragedy."[2] The tragedy of the commons applies to fisheries in the following way: as more fishers enter a fishery, each one eventually experiences declining yields for the same unit of effort. As the margin of profit shrinks, each rational fisher redoubles his or her efforts, recognizing that if he or she cuts back for the good of the resource, someone else will catch the fish. In doing what is individually rational, however, fishers produce a result that is collectively disastrous.

From Hardin's perspective, the only way to avert this outcome is for an authoritarian state to strictly regulate use of the resource or to convert the commons into private property. In the latter regime, owners of the resource theoretically have a stake in conserving it because they now have the sole rights to the "economic rents" it generates. As political scientist Elinor Ostrom points out, however, "neither the state nor the market [has been] uniformly successful in enabling individuals to sustain long-term, productive use of natural resource systems."[3] Furthermore, Ostrom cites numerous examples of creative institutional arrangements devised by communities to solve the problems of managing common property resources. In doing so, Ostrom draws our attention to the myriad factors that can complicate or simplify common property resource management—from a community's culture, history, and tradition to the political system in which decisions are made—making clear that no single solution will apply.

This case also illustrates the challenges posed by management schemes in which regulated interests play a major role in devising and implementing government policy. Federal law mandates that regional fishery councils, made up of members who understand the resource, formulate the rules under which fisheries operate. In theory, such an approach enables regulators to take into account the perspectives of the regulated sector, and thereby to make rules that are both fair and enforceable. Alternatively, if they are not involved in decision making, regulated interests often perceive rules as arbitrary and coercive and resist complying with them. As is true of every policy—from provisions in the tax code to anti-theft measures—regulators cannot simply institute and enforce a set of rules; they rely on voluntary cooperation of those who must abide by them. On the other hand, if regulated interests dominate the rulemaking process, it is likely to generate policies that benefit those interests rather than the public.

Finally, this case increases our understanding of the pivotal role of litigation in bringing about major environmental policy shifts. As both the grazing policy and spotted owl cases (in chapters 6 and 7) reveal, once a single interest has become entrenched in a subsystem, it is difficult to dislodge. Attempts to alter policy from both outside and within an agency encounter resistance from its clientele, congressional overseers, and even its own personnel who have become accustomed to a particular routine. However, a successful legal challenge can shift the internal balance of power, empowering those who previously were isolated—in this case, agency scientists. By requiring an agency to move in a particular direction, the courts can also narrow the range of options it considers.

The story of the Northeast fisheries crisis illustrates dramatically the impact of "clientelism" on natural resource management, as well as how advocates can use lawsuits to open up a subsystem and redirect a recalcitrant agency.

BACKGROUND

The history of New England is inextricably tied to the fish found off its shores. In the year 1500, explorer John Cabot described the Grand Banks area off Northeast Canada as so "swarming with fish [that they] could be taken not only with a net but in baskets let down with a stone."[4] From Canada to New Jersey, the waters teemed with cod, supporting a stable fishing industry for 450 years. Groundfish—not just cod but also yellowtail flounder, haddock, American plaice, and pollock—were the backbone of the entire region's fishing trade. In fact, the "sacred cod," a commemorative wooden plaque, still hangs in the Massachusetts State House symbolizing the state's first industry and the source of its early wealth. For many years, the ports of Gloucester and New Bedford were among the nation's most prosperous.

At the turn of the twentieth century, however, major technological innovations began to destabilize the New England groundfish populations. In particular, steam-powered trawlers that drag nets across the ocean floor introduced concern about bottom-dwelling animals and plants. By 1930, the groundfish-ing fleet was sufficiently large that it had prompted a crash in the Georges Bank haddock fishery. Still, fishing in New England was primarily a small-scale affair, and after fishers shifted their effort northward, the haddock stocks recov-ered. The same pattern repeated itself for other species: because of the modest harvests overall, there was no persistent recruitment overfishing, so depleted stocks could rebound when fishers moved on to other species.[5]

In the mid-1950s, however, huge factory ships from Europe and the Soviet Union began to roam the North Atlantic just beyond U.S. coastal waters. Some of those boats exceeded 300 feet in length, could bring in as much as 500 tons of fish in a single haul, and could process and deep-freeze 250 tons a day. They operated around the clock in all but the worst weather and stayed at sea for a year or more.[6] Called "factory-equipped freezer stern trawlers," or factory trawlers for short, the fleet was "a kind of roving industrial complex."[7] As fish-eries expert William Warner describes the scene, the ships "paced out in long diagonal lines, plowing the best fishing grounds like disk harrows in a field."[8] Between 1960 and 1965, total groundfish landings increased from 200,000 to 760,000 metric tons.[9]

For many years after the first factory trawler invasion, Canadian and Amer-ican fishery officials clung to the hope that the fleets of both countries could withstand the assault. Some hoped that the International Commission for Northwest Atlantic Fisheries (ICNAF) might reverse the tide of overfishing in 1970, when it instituted a management system allocating quotas by country, with the sum of each species equal to the total recommended catch. Those quo-tas ended groundfish harvesting on Georges Bank by all but American and Canadian fishers, but enormous damage had already been done: between 1963 and 1974, groundfish populations declined almost 70 percent, and by 1974 many species had fallen to the lowest levels ever recorded.[10] Haddock was at an all-time low throughout its Northwest Atlantic range; the species was so rare, in fact, that biologists feared the end of a commercially viable fishery, if not extinction. Even the bountiful cod was showing signs of decline, as were the redfish, yellowtail flounder, and many other prime market fish.

The year 1974 marked the turning point. In that year alone, 1,076 fishing vessels swarmed across the Atlantic to fish North American waters. Their catch of 2.176 million metric tons was ten times the New England catch and triple the Canadian Atlantic catch.[11] Although the total was huge, however, the catch per vessel was down, and the fish were running smaller than before, despite the fact that the foreign vessels were fishing longer hours with improved methods over a larger range for a greater part of the year. In fact, the foreign catch had been better for five of the preceding six years—slowly declining from a peak of 2.4 million metric tons in 1968—with fleets of equal or lesser size.[12]

In 1976, alarmed by the foreign fleets and the precarious status of fish stocks, the federal government passed the Magnuson Fisheries Conservation and Management Act, named after its sponsor, Washington Sen. Warren Magnuson (who was primarily concerned with the health of his region's fishing industry). The act had two goals: to rejuvenate the American fishing fleet and to restore and conserve fish stocks. It unilaterally asserted U.S. jurisdiction over fisheries within an Exclusive Economic Zone that extended 200 miles from the coast and authorized the National Marine Fisheries Service (NMFS), a line office of the U.S. Department of Commerce's National Oceanographic and Atmospheric Administration (NOAA), to administer the nation's resources between three and 200 miles off the coast.[13] The Magnuson Act also established eight regional councils to work with the five regional NMFS offices to develop management plans for the offshore fisheries.

The act directed that regional councils comprise federal and state officials, as well as "individuals who, by reason of their occupation or other experience, scientific expertise, or training are knowledgeable regarding the conservation and management of the commercial and recreational harvest."[14] While the act vests final authority for rulemaking with the secretary of commerce, Congress clearly intended the councils to play the dominant role. According to the legislative history of the act:

> The regional councils are, in concept, intended to be similar to a legislative branch of government. . . . The councils are afforded a reasonable measure of independence and authority and are designed to maintain a close relationship with those at the most local level interested in and affected by fisheries management.[15]

THE CASE

The Magnuson Act allows the Department of Commerce to reject or accept a council's fishery management plan (FMP) but not to change it, an arrangement that from the beginning encouraged acceptance of lax plans. The NMFS was reluctant to try to impose its own plan over council objections, as the rules would be nearly impossible to enforce without fishers' compliance. Exacerbating the NMFS's weak position was the tendency of members of Congress to intervene on behalf of fishing interests whenever the council did impose strict rules. Finally, although the region's fishing industry was not unified, it managed to dominate policy because it encountered little opposition; aside from New England Fisheries Science Center (NEFSC) scientists, few voices spoke out on behalf of fishery conservation and precautionary management. Most environmental groups were not paying attention to fisheries—they were far more interested in marine mammals and ocean pollution—nor were they alerting the public to the impending groundfish collapse.

Scientists' Assessments of New England's Groundfish

Like rangeland and forestry science, both of which historically were dominated by concerns about resource extraction rather than ecosystem health, fisheries science has been governed by the short-term need to determine management objectives. In practice, this has meant developing expedient indicators that managers can use, primary among which are fish stock assessments. A stock assessment includes estimates of the abundance of a particular fish stock (in weight or number of fish) and the rate at which the fish are being removed as a result of harvesting and other causes (mortality). A stock assessment also includes one or more reference estimates of the harvesting rate or abundance at which the stock can maintain itself in the long term. Finally, a stock assessment typically contains one- to five-year projections for the stock under different management scenarios.

Because they can't actually count the fish, scientists use a variety of data to estimate the abundance of each stock and its population trends. The two most important data sources are reports on the commercial fish landing—including the number of fish caught, their size, and the ratio of fish caught to the time spent fishing (catch per unit of effort)—and NMFS resource surveys. Landing data tell only part of the story since many fish caught are discarded because they are too small to sell, exceed the catch limit, or belong to a species whose catch is prohibited. These discards, known as bycatch, comprise a large portion of fishing mortality worldwide.[16] Unlike fishing boats, which search for the largest aggregations of fish, research trawlers conduct stratified random sample surveys of a wide range of locations. Such "fishery-independent" surveys are especially important for schooling species because fishers can maintain high catch rates on them by selectively targeting areas where the fish congregate. The New England groundfish survey, which began in 1963, is the nation's oldest and most reliable and provides the longest time-series data.[17] Although they acknowledged that their projections were uncertain and their understanding of groundfish biology and life history incomplete, in the mid-1970s NEFSC scientists began issuing strong warnings—based on stock assessment—about the need to cut back fishing of the region's groundfish.

Based on the results of its groundfish survey and landing data, when the Magnuson Act took effect at the end of 1976, scientists advised the New England Fishery Management Council—which has primary responsibility for crafting the region's groundfish FMP—to set 1977 Gulf of Maine and Georges Bank commercial cod catches at approximately half the levels reached between 1970 and 1974. Scientists feared that fishing beyond the recommended level would lead to a precipitous decline. They also noted a pronounced decline in haddock since 1967 and found yellowtail flounder stocks "severely depressed." They recommended strict catch limits to enable the groundfish stocks to recover.

Establishing a "Cooperative" Management Regime

The council was reluctant to follow scientists' advice, however. In theory, the cooperative management regime mandated by the Magnuson Act would ensure that managers took both the best available science and the needs and expertise of fishers into account when developing conservation measures. The councils soon became a focal point for controversy, however, because in practice members know a lot more about catching and marketing fish than about marine biology or natural resource stewardship. The New England Council, in particular, was dominated by current or former commercial fishermen, who were understandably reluctant to impose stringent controls on their peers.[18] One former council member explains: "As members of the community, it's difficult for them to divorce themselves from the consequences of their actions."[19]

In response to scientists' warnings about decimated stocks, the newly appointed council did put some restrictions in place. Modeling its approach on the ICNAF regulatory regime, the council imposed catch quotas, prohibited fishing in spawning areas, required large-holed mesh (to allow young fish to escape), enacted minimum fish size requirements, and limited the amount of yellowtail flounder that could be caught per trip. In its first year of operation, however, fishers often exceeded total catch quotas, so the NMFS frequently had to close the fishery unexpectedly. As a result, "the trip limits were perceived as unfair; many fish were mislabeled and handled illegally; and the closures were extremely unpopular."[20] In addition, public council meetings were unfocused and chaotic; council members vacillated and were reluctant to make difficult choices, which tarnished their image as decision makers. An editorial in a 1978 issue of the *National Fisherman* magazine revealed some fishers' antipathy toward managers:

> Years ago, the fish business was pretty simple. There was the fish, fishermen, the buyers and sellers of fish, and people who ate fish. Everything seemed t'go along fairly well. There were just enough fishermen to catch just the amount of fish that fish eaters would eat. Everybody made their fair share of money.
>
> Then along came the first fishcrat. . . . He made a pitch to his brother bureaucrat f'some funds. There want no trouble in getting the dough cause everybody knows that bureaucrats control all the purse strings.
>
> Well, the first fishcrat was so successful, he hired a bureau, the first fishcrat bureau. They went all over hell telling people things they didn't want t'know, how not t'do something right n'talkin' in a strange language nobody could understand, especially dumb fishermen.[21]

Making matters worse for the council, many fishermen simply did not believe NMFS scientists' assessments that many of the groundfish species were in trouble. The divergence between scientists and fishers was more than simply fishers in denial about the status of the resource; fishers had a host of complaints about stock assessments, some of which were well founded. They criticized the NEFSC for using ancient gear that did not detect or catch fish as effectively as modern gear. (NEFSC scientists explained that they had standardized the survey in myriad ways—from using the same boats and gear to survey methods—to ensure a consistent time-series of comparable data.) Fishers also regarded fishery science as inaccessible because it relied heavily on complex mathematical models that few but the most specialized scientists could understand. Finally, fishers pointed out that fishery science was weakest in an area that was crucial for fishery management: understanding fish behavior, life history, and interaction with other species. This, they noted, was where their own anecdotal knowledge—which scientists historically have dismissed—was likely to be most valuable.

The fishers' perspective, in other words, was cornucopian. Seeming to justify that perspective, high groundfish landings in the early part of 1977 belied scientists' pessimism. According to one observer,

> codfish landings throughout New England were nearly twice what they [had been] the previous spring (13.4 million pounds compared to 7.3 million pounds). . . . Piers in Gloucester and New Bedford were groaning under the load of spring landings and there was much concern that the processing houses for frozen fish were going to be grossly inadequate. Processors were running their facilities seven days a week in June and adding extra shifts, and still they could not keep up with the boats.[22]

The surge in landings was probably the fruit of ICNAF's quota system; nevertheless, the credibility gap between scientists and fishers began to widen.

Although unified by their distrust of scientists and contempt for fishery managers, New England's fishers were deeply split in other respects, and this complicated fishery management even further. The fishers were divided by gear type, vessel size, vessel ownership, fishing style, and port of origin. Large trawlers accused small boats of taking advantage of loopholes in the laws and lax enforcement of fishery regulations to fish out of season or use illegal nets. Small boat owners blamed trawlers with their advanced sonar tracking system for cleaning out the ocean. Gillnetters pointed out that, unlike trawlers, they did not catch juvenile fish and did not tear up the ocean bottom. Longliners said their gear did not affect the bottom either, and was even more selective. Both derided draggers for pounding the bottom with their heavy doors. The bottom otter trawl,[23] other gear types pointed out, had the greatest bycatch problem because unwanted fish were damaged in the net, brought up too quickly, or not thrown back soon enough. Draggers, on the other hand, complained about ghost-net fishing, lost lines, and hooks "souring" the bottom. The Maine Yankees disparaged the New Bedford Portuguese and the Gloucester Sicilians, who in turn criticized each other.[24] Unable to reconcile the myriad divisions, the council simply tried to devise rules that would be perceived as "democratic"—that is, affecting everyone equally.

Devising a Multispecies Groundfish Fishery Management Plan

After the first year of council operations, differences between scientists and fishermen, uncertainty about the exact administrative procedures needed to ensure timely implementation of plans, apparent misunderstandings between the council and the NMFS, the vagueness of the concepts on which the plans were supposed to be based, and the inexperience of many council members as fishery managers all lowered morale and undermined the process.[25] In spring 1978, in hopes of moving away from the short-term, reactionary policymaking it had engaged in thus far, the council set to work on a more comprehensive, long-term fishery management plan.

Ironically, nearly four years after it began, the council submitted a 1982 Interim Groundfish FMP for Commerce Department approval that substantially *weakened* controls on fishing. Encouraged by apparent improvement in the stocks and under heavy pressure from fish processors, the council had abandoned trip limits and quotas; instead, the plan allowed open fishing and required only "age-at-entry" controls in the form of minimum fish sizes and minimum mesh sizes. In a nod to conservation, the plan retained some spawning area closures (March to May) and instituted voluntary catch reporting as a data collection device.

After sustained pressure from several (though not all) fishing groups, the Commerce Department agreed to forgo the usual four- to six-month comment period and implement the Interim Plan immediately under emergency regulations, a procedure normally reserved for a resource in jeopardy. The decision came after the commerce secretary and federal fisheries officials met in Washington with fish dealers who spoke of the "disaster" that had befallen their businesses in the past two years. According to the processors, the quotas had prevented the boats from bringing in enough fish to meet operating costs or consumer demand.

During the years following implementation of the Interim Plan, federal scientists continued to urge the New England panel to institute more restrictive measures. Early on, it became apparent that age-at-entry controls were insufficient to protect fish stocks. Many fishers were not complying with minimum mesh size requirements, so juvenile fish were virtually unprotected. In response to loan guarantees and generous depreciation and operating cost allowances added to the federal tax code, fishers had begun investing in new boats and high-tech equipment.[26] Because entry to the fishery was unlimited, the number of otter trawlers doubled between 1976 and 1984, even as the size and efficiency of the boats increased substantially.[27] The result was that, by 1980, the New England fleet was catching 100,000 metric tons of cod, haddock, and yellowtail flounder—double the 1976 level—off Georges Bank, the Gulf of Maine, and Cape Cod. The industry was taking 50 to 100 percent more than the already weakened groundfish stocks could sustain, but although NEFSC cruises started to show stocks dropping, catches (and thus fishers' optimism) remained high until 1983, at which point they started to decline.[28]

The Northeast Multispecies FMP

Despite its apparent failure to curb fishing, the council proposed formalizing the open fishing regime in 1985 as the Northeast Multispecies FMP. Initially the NMFS gave only conditional approval to the plan because agency officials, heeding their own scientists' advice, were concerned that the lack of direct controls on fishing mortality would lead to overfishing. In 1987, however, after fishers got the New England congressional delegation to weigh in heavily on the side of indirect controls, NMFS approved the plan, requesting only modest adjustments to remedy its deficiencies.[29]

Not surprisingly, the new FMP did little to improve the prospects for New England's groundfish: stock assessments continued to show increases in mortality rates and corresponding decreases in stock sizes. This situation was not unique to New England, and NMFS officials were becoming increasingly frustrated with the regional councils' impotence. In 1989, in response to the critical 1986 NOAA *Fishery Management Study,* NOAA scientists revised a crucial section of the Magnuson Act regulations: the Section 602 Guidelines for National Standards to assist in the development of FMPs. The original guidelines had not defined the term "overfishing," which appears in the Magnuson Act only once: "Conservation and management measures shall prevent overfishing while achieving, on a continuing basis, the optimum yield from each fishery for the U.S. fishing industry."[30] In contrast, the 1989 guidelines mandated that each FMP define overfishing, a significant advance for fishery conservation.[31] The rationale for the change was clear: it was impossible to prevent overfishing if there was no standard against which to measure it and therefore no way of saying for certain that it was occurring. The second key revision to the guidelines read: "If data indicate that an overfished condition exists, a program must be established for rebuilding the stock over a period of time specified by the Council and acceptable to the Secretary."[32]

The 602 Guidelines revisions had an enormous, albeit not immediate, impact on New England. When the guidelines were revised, the New England Groundfish FMP—like most others—did not define overfishing; in fact, the plan did not even specify an optimal yield.[33] The council had eliminated optimal yield figures because they were too controversial and instead had begun defining optimal yield as "the amount of fish actually harvested by U.S. fishermen in accordance with the measures listed below." In other words, if the measures in the plan were insufficient (and the evidence strongly suggested they were), there was nothing in the plan to prevent overfishing.

The 1985 FMP had retained this definition of overfishing but added one new element. It incorporated biological targets for stocks covered by the plan: the total catch should not exceed 20 percent of the maximum spawning potential (MSP) for most stocks. Although the 20-percent-of-MSP targets were intended to ensure sufficient reproductive potential for long-term replenishment of stocks, the plan's management measures were inadequate to achieve those goals. Seeking to comply with changes in the 602 Guidelines, the New England Council proposed that the overfishing definitions for groundfish be the 20-percent-of-MSP targets already included in the 1985 FMP. The council simultaneously acknowledged that it was not meeting those targets—in effect, admitting that overfishing was occurring. Under such circumstances, the revised guidelines required the council to develop a recovery plan for the overfished stocks, but since they did not specify a deadline, the council reacted slowly.

Among the many reasons for the council's tardiness, the most important was that representatives of the fishing industry remained dubious about the need for new fishing controls. Those council members who did perceive such a need anticipated strong resistance. Then, when the council finally proposed restrictive measures, the Massachusetts congressional delegation—at the behest of fishermen—preempted the council process by introducing legislation setting out measures and a time frame for restructuring the fishery.[34] The consequence was that "nineteen months after admitting that groundfish stocks were overfished, the council had not seriously begun to tackle the effort reduction that it had decided was necessary to end overfishing. Moreover, the NMFS showed no signs of stepping in with a Secretarial plan."[35]

The Conservation Law Foundation Lawsuit

In early 1991, NMFS scientists reported that New England fishers were catching less than half as many groundfish as a decade earlier. The Massachusetts Offshore Groundfish Task Force estimated that lost landings were costing the region $350 million annually, with 14,000 jobs lost.[36] According to NEFSC scientists, spawning stocks were now less than one-twentieth what they had been when the Magnuson Act was passed. But despite scientists' dire prognoses, council members remained reluctant to act, arguing that the series of halfway measures they had passed in the 1980s would, given time, enable stocks to rebound.

In June 1991, frustrated with the council's inertia and hoping to force it to act, the Conservation Law Foundation (CLF) filed a lawsuit against the secretary of commerce. CLF, a nonprofit organization headquartered in Boston, had been tracking the scientific reports on New England fisheries for years, but had lacked a legal hook until the 602 Guidelines revisions. The legal theory underpinning the CLF complaint was that the Magnuson Act imposed a mandatory duty on the secretary of commerce to ensure that all FMPs met the national (602) standards. In August 1991, the CLF and the NMFS settled the case by signing a consent decree that compelled the New England Council to develop a stock rebuilding plan. If it had not done so by a specified deadline, the secretary was required to devise a plan. In compliance with the settlement, the council began to develop Amendment 5 to the New England Groundfish FMP.[37]

The lawsuit had an important, if not immediately obvious, impact. Previously, fishing interests, despite their lack of cohesiveness, had managed to dominate fishery policy largely because neither environmentalists nor the general public was attentive to the issue of overfishing. By forcing the agency's hand, however, the lawsuit empowered conservation-oriented managers on the council and within NMFS; they could now argue that they had no choice but to impose stringent regulations. The NMFS was quick to use its new clout. On June 3, 1993, after receiving yet another report from its scientists that groundfish were severely depleted, the NMFS issued an emergency order closing the eastern portion of Georges Bank to fishing for a month just two days after the area had opened for the season.[38]

Amendment 5

Hoping to eliminate the need for more emergency closures, on June 30, 1993, the beleaguered New England Council finally approved Amendment 5 to the Northeast Multispecies FMP. Its goal was to reduce the groundfish catch to 50 percent of pre-1994 levels in seven years. To accomplish this, the plan included a variety of measures, including a moratorium on groundfishing permits. It also greatly limited the number of days fishers could catch groundfish: as of June, they were allowed to be out year round, with the exception of periodic closures, but the number of days allowed was to go down each year until, by 1998, large boats (draggers) could fish only 110 days each year. The plan also limited fishers to 2,500 pounds of haddock each trip and increased the mesh size of nets in most areas to 5.5-inch diamonds or six-inch squares to allow young fish to escape. In addition, it required vessel owners and operators to possess valid fishing permits and to keep elaborate fishing logs detailing the species caught and bycatch.

As the council awaited Commerce Department approval of the plan, the bad news on New England groundfish stocks continued to roll in. During a two-day meeting in early December, NMFS northeast regional director Richard Roe sought to ban haddock fishing indefinitely off the East Coast in response to reports of drastic declines in landings—from 40,000 metric tons per year in the early 1970s to only eighty metric tons in 1993. Still, the council resisted; it endorsed emergency measures to preserve the dwindling stocks but stopped short of endorsing a complete ban. Instead, by a 10–4 vote, the council recommended that NMFS impose a 500- to 1,000-pound limit on haddock catches by commercial fishing boats and close the portion of Georges Bank where haddock spawn.

As the crisis deepened, the council found itself with less and less wiggle room, however. Responding to warnings from its own scientists, at the beginning of Christmas week, Canada imposed sharp restrictions on haddock and other bottom feeders in nearly all of its Atlantic region. Following suit, on Thursday of that week, the NMFS ordered that New England boats be allowed no more than 500 pounds of haddock per trip and that haddock spawning grounds be closed in January, a month earlier than usual. Then, in late February 1994, federal regulators announced their intention to shut down even more valuable fishing grounds: in addition to Georges Bank, they planned to close a large swath of the Great South Channel and portions of Stellwagen Bank and Jeffreys Ledge.

Finally, on March 1, the provisions of Amendment 5 were scheduled to take effect. Fishers found this series of apparently arbitrary regulations, culminating in the imposition of Amendment 5 rules, infuriating; they believed that government bureaucrats had gotten out of hand. They contended that the days-at-sea limits would impose exorbitant costs on fishers: most fishing boat owners are independents who have high fixed costs—as much as $100,000 per month in loan payments—even if they never leave port. To attract public sympathy for their plight, an armada of more than 100 fishing vessels from New Bedford, Gloucester, Provincetown, Chatham, and elsewhere in the region jammed Boston Harbor.

Scientists Issue Another Warning

Making matters more uncomfortable for regulators, Amendment 5 began to look obsolete even before it took effect. In August 1994—only months after the council adopted it—NEFSC scientists released more bad news. In an advisory report, they warned that even reducing fishing by 50 percent over the next five to seven years, as Amendment 5 promised to do, probably would not be enough to save the groundfish. Of the yellowtail flounder, once the backbone of southern New England fishing ports, the report said: "The stock has collapsed! Fishing mortality on this stock should be reduced to levels approaching zero."[39] According to the report, of every 100 yellowtail flounder alive at the beginning of the year, only eight survived the year. Under this pressure, the breeding population had declined to record lows (see Figure 8-1).

The report was also skeptical about the potential for recovery of the Georges Bank cod. In 1993, cod mortality in the fishing ground hit a record high, while the number of mature adults dropped to a record low (see Figure 8-2). Fishermen had hoped that the relatively large cod harvests of 1989 and 1990 meant that this fish were weathering the crisis relatively well, but NEFSC researchers believed those years to be an aberration. Scientists noted that two years previously the Canadians had closed their cod fishery off the Newfoundland coast expecting a quick recovery, but the cod population had dropped another 25 percent in the first year of the closure. By 1994, the Canadians were estimating that a recovery was not likely until the late 1990s. And Georges Bank was in worse shape than the Canadian fisheries because fishers had depleted the area to an all-time low, taking more than 70 percent of the groundfish swimming there each year. As a result, the Georges Bank catch had plummeted to its lowest level since the 1970s. Moreover, the cod's recovery was jeopardized because cod predators, such as the spiny dogfish, were becoming an ever larger proportion of the fish.

Alan Peterson of the Northeast Fisheries Science Center at Woods Hole estimated that it would take ten to twelve years before the Georges Bank cod stock would be healthy enough that regulators could afford to increase the harvest. Even a twelve-year comeback was no sure thing, he said, because the cod's fate was complicated by natural cycles such as colder-than-average ocean temperatures or increased salinity, which could reduce the survival of young cod. Peterson urged the New England Council to go even further than Amendment 5 and shut down almost all fishing. It could then selectively reopen fisheries

Figure 8-1 Yellowtail Flounder, Georges Bank, East of Massachusetts

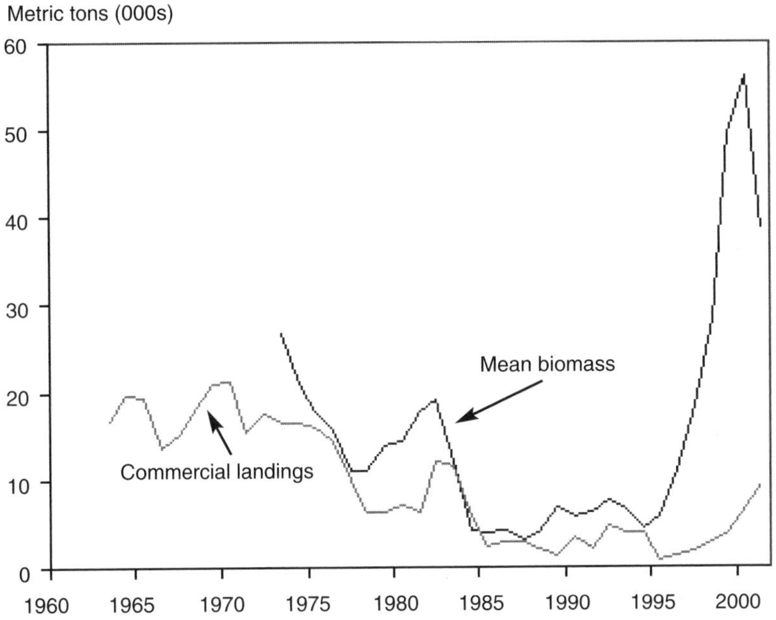

Metric tons (000s)

Source: S. X. Cadrin, J. D. Neilson, S. Gavaris, and P. Perley, *A Report of the Transboundary Resource Assessment Committee Meeting No. 3,* Northeast Fisheries Science Center. Reference Document 00-10, 2000; Report of the Multispecies Monitoring Committee, 2001, http://www.nefsc.org/index.htm.

that were still healthy and where nets did not accidentally catch cod or other vanishing species.

Fish Stocks Crash

On October 14, 1994, fearing that if it didn't bite the bullet the NMFS would decide for it, the groundfish committee of the New England Council recommended that drastic new measures, including expanded closures of offshore fishing areas and annual catch limits for many species, be considered. It had been less than six months since most of the Amendment 5 rules had taken effect, and fishers complained bitterly that the council had not waited long enough to assess their impact. Nevertheless, nearly two weeks later the council voted as an emergency measure to close indefinitely vast areas of the Gulf of Maine, including Georges Bank, and to close immediately 4,500 square miles of fishing grounds for spawning. To prevent trawlers displaced by the ban from overfishing elsewhere, the council proposed a quota system limiting catches closer to shore.

Then, on December 12, 1994, the Department of Commerce officially closed the entire 6,600-square-mile area of Georges Bank and announced its intention

Figure 8-2 Atlantic Cod, Georges Bank and South

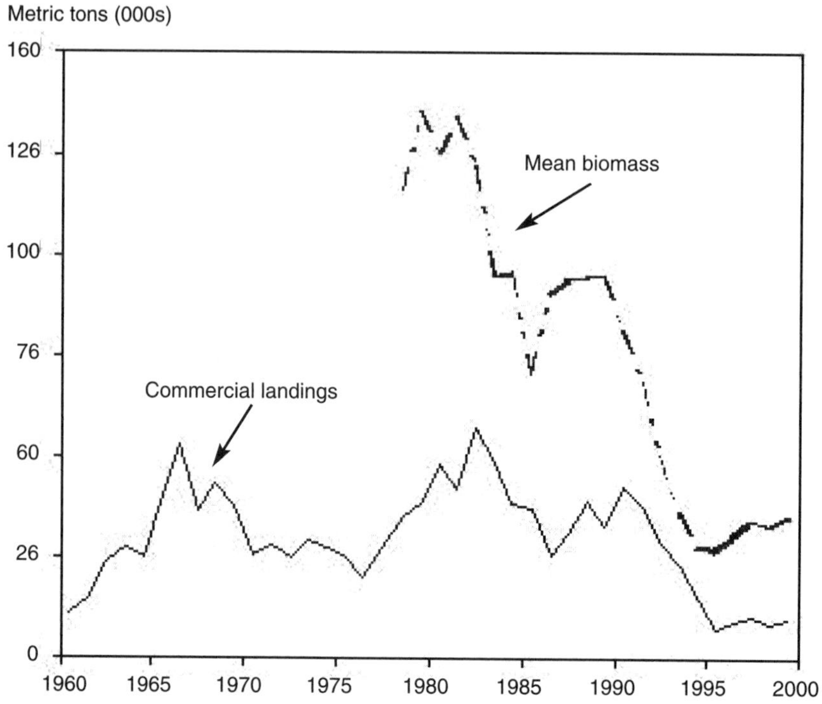

Metric tons (000s)

Source: L. O'Brien, and N. J. Munroe, *Assessment of the Georges Bank Cod Stock for 2001*, Northeast Fisheries Science Center. Reference Document 01-10, 2001; Report of the Multispecies Monitoring Committee, 2001, http://www.nefsc.org/index.htm.

to lift the ban no earlier than March 1995. Many fishers were, predictably, incensed. In their complaints a familiar refrain echoed: the scientists don't really understand the condition of the fishery; they don't know where to look for the fish. "One scientist says one thing and another scientist says something else," scoffed Gloucester fisherman Jay Spurling. "They're not even out on the water; they don't see the things we see. . . . I think they're making a huge mistake."[40] Other fishers lamented the end of the only way of life they had ever known: "I've been a fisherman for 25 years," said Vito Seniti, also of Gloucester. "My father was a fisherman, and his father, and his father before. What am I gonna do now, deliver pizzas?"[41] Fishers' desperation notwithstanding, in January 1995, regulators extended the ninety-day closure indefinitely to give themselves time to come up with a real plan.

Bailing Out the Fishers

While the council wrangled over regulations, the formidable Massachusetts congressional delegation began seeking federal money to ameliorate the hardship, concentrated primarily around the ports of Boston, Gloucester, and New Bedford. Sen. John Kerry and Rep. Gerry Studds proposed legislation to create the New England Fisheries Reinvestment Program to disburse grants throughout the region. At the urging of New England's members of Congress, the commerce secretary, Ron Brown, declared the Northeast fishery to be in an economic emergency and granted $30 million in aid to fishers and their families.

Even more important, after a year of lobbying, in March 1995, the Commerce Department initiated a $2 million Fishing Capacity Reduction Program—or boat buyout—to compensate fishers who retired their fishing vessels and groundfish permits and thereby reduced excess capacity in the fleet. Rather than embarking on a full-scale buyout, which could cost as much as $100 million, the department hoped to learn from the pilot program how to design an appropriate program. In August, the department announced it would expand the buyout by $25 million but shrewdly made the money contingent on the New England Council showing progress on a groundfish stock rebuilding program, a potent incentive that Commerce hoped would entice fishermen to support new regulations.

Amendment 7 and Contrasting Problem Definitions

The buyout proposal came not a moment too soon. In mid-1995, the NMFS received more alarming reports from NEFSC scientists: the measures taken under Amendment 5 and proposed since were insufficient to ensure stock recovery; in fact, things were getting worse. So the agency began to pressure the New England Council to come up with yet another amendment to its FMP—one that would cut back fishing of groundfish by 80 rather than 50 percent. Fishers' reaction ranged from disbelief to fury as meetings on the new Amendment 7 got under way in fall 1995.[42] The fishers had been blaming each other—different gear types, different ports—for the depletion of the fish, but the new proposals gave them a common foe: government regulators. As the council debated the terms of Amendment 7, the fishers continued to plead that changes to Amendment 5 were premature and that it was too early to tell whether the new rules had been effective.

Underlying these debates were the contrasting ways that environmentalists and fishers defined the problem: whereas environmental organizations emphasized the ecological risks and espoused a precautionary approach, many fishers demanded proof that Amendment 5 was not working and that the stocks had, in fact, collapsed. They tried to persuade the council that the risk lay in imposing strict new rules that would cause certain economic pain in the face of scientific uncertainty. As Maggie Raymond, spokeswoman for the Associated Fisheries of Maine, put it, if the plan takes effect "and then you realize you've gone too far, then it's too late. You've already put everybody out of business."[43]

Again the New England congressional delegation weighed in on behalf of the beleaguered fishers. Maine Sens. Olympia Snowe and William Cohen and

Rep. James Longley Jr. submitted letters of opposition to Amendment 7. Rep. Longley wrote: "Make some modifications if you must, but do not destroy Maine's groundfishing industry solely to accomplish faster recovery rates."[44] Snowe encouraged the council to resist pressure from the NMFS to move more quickly.[45] The Massachusetts delegation also weighed in. Sen. Ted Kennedy, as well as Reps. Barney Frank, Peter Torkildsen, and Joe Kennedy, urged the NMFS to postpone further fishing restrictions until the socioeconomic impacts of the changes on fishing communities had been assessed.

The council was clearly in a bind. Empowered by the CLF lawsuit and backed by a coalition of environmental groups, NMFS regional director Andy Rosenberg was firm in his insistence that the council make conserving the fish its primary concern. NEFSC scientists were becoming increasingly certain that the groundfish decline was continuing unabated, despite measures instituted the previous year. Even some fishers doubted the wisdom of phased-in conservation rules: John Williamson, a fisher from Kennebunkport, Maine, pointed out that the council's year-and-a-half-long deliberation constituted a sufficient phase-in for the plan.[46] Others agreed that fishers needed to take responsibility for the health of the fishery and stop resisting conservation measures. With the NMFS threatening to withhold the money for the boat buyout unless it reduced fishing effort dramatically and the congressional delegation undermining its attempts to do so, the council spent meeting after meeting trying to arrive at an amendment that everyone could live with.

After rejecting the option of banning groundfishing altogether, the council began working with a mix of three alternatives: closing large fishing territories; reducing days at sea; and carving the fishery into regions, each with its own quotas. Complicating the decision were concerns that the rules affected all fishers equally, regardless of gear type or boat size. Finally, in late January 1996, the council agreed on Amendment 7 by a vote of 11–3 and sent its proposal to the commerce secretary for review. Bowing to congressional pressure, the proposal gradually phased in days-at-sea limits for cod, haddock, and yellowtail flounder and instituted "rolling" closures of 9,000 square miles of fishing grounds.[47] Under the plan, a typical boat was allowed 139 days at sea in 1996 and 88 in 1997, a considerable reduction from the 250–300 days previously allowed.[48] The plan also limited the total allowable catch (TAC) for cod to 2,770 metric tons in 1996, about one-third of the 1993 catch, and reduced it further in 1997.[49] Despite the accommodations made to the fishing industry, many fishers remained opposed, and congressional representatives notified Secretary Brown of their concerns about economic harm. Nevertheless, the Commerce Department approved Amendment 7, and it went into effect in July 1996.

Six months later, at the December 11–12 New England Council meeting, the Multispecies Monitoring Committee (MMC) delivered its first assessment of Amendment 7.[50] The good news was that overfishing had been halted for all stocks except Gulf of Maine cod, and all were showing increases for the first time in years. The MMC remained cautious, however, noting that most stocks still needed to double or triple in size before they would reach minimum acceptable levels and that the measures contained in Amendment 7 would not be enough to accomplish this goal. It recommended a 62 percent cut in fishing for yellowtail and a 57 percent reduction in cod harvests on Georges Bank. The council voted to begin drawing up further rules and to consider such drastic proposals as reducing the number of days at sea for cod fishing to as few as fourteen for the 1997 season.[51]

Reauthorizing the Magnuson-Stevens Act

While the New England Council was wrestling with Amendment 7, events in New England as well as problems in the Gulf Coast and Pacific Northwest fisheries put pressure on Congress as it began its reauthorization of the Magnuson Act in 1996. (The act had expired on September 30, 1993, but Congress had failed so far to reauthorize it.) Critics of the law identified several failings they wanted to see Congress address, but above all they contended it was vague in its fishery conservation mandate. In particular, although the 1989 revisions required each FMP to contain an objective and measurable definition of overfishing and a recovery plan in the event that overfishing occurred, some critics wanted to see those guidelines delineated in the statute itself. Nor did the act specify the period of time within which councils were to address overfishing once it had been identified. Moreover, the concept of optimum yield, defined as a fishery's maximum sustainable yield "modified by any relevant economic, social, or ecological factor" was clearly open to a wide variety of interpretations.

In 1996, Congress finally passed the Sustainable Fisheries Act (SFA), an amendment to the Magnuson Act that addressed that law's three biggest deficiencies: overfishing, bycatch, and habitat degradation. The SFA mandated that each fishery management plan include a definition of overfishing for the fishery, a rebuilding plan for overfished stocks, a timetable of less than ten years for reaching recovery, conservation and management measures to avoid bycatch, and a description of essential habitats and management measures to protect them. The law gave the councils two years to amend their existing plans and prepare new ones where necessary.

The Focus Shifts to Gulf of Maine Cod

Although NEFSC reports in late 1997 confirmed that several groundfish species had begun to recover, they also made it clear that the region faced a crisis in the Gulf of Maine cod fishery. The new SFA requirements, combined with continuing evidence of a precipitous decline in stocks, severely restricted the council's options. In early January 1998, following yet another round of scientific reports documenting the cod's decline, the council announced that rules aimed at reducing the total cod catch by 63 percent would take effect in May 1998. Throughout the spring, NMFS announced in rapid succession the implementation of Framework Adjustments 24 and 25 to the groundfish FMP.[52] In April, Framework Adjustment 24 limited Gulf of Maine cod landings to 1,000 pounds per day and total days at sea to fourteen. A month later,

Framework Adjustment 25 reduced the cod landing limit to 700 pounds per day and instituted a four-step rolling closure of inshore fisheries. The measure stipulated that the NMFS might reduce the limit to 400 pounds per day once 50 percent of the total allowable catch (TAC) of 1,783 metric tons was reached. By June, that limit was reached, and the NMFS reduced the cod landing limit to 400 pounds. By late summer, the council had no choice but to consider closing the Gulf of Maine fishery entirely.

In December 1998, the council heard yet another bleak scientific presentation by the Multispecies Monitoring Committee documenting serious overfishing of Gulf of Maine cod, which were at a record low notwithstanding strict fishing rules. Because the SFA requires that the cod population not drop below 7,500 metric tons, and scientists believed it was already down to around 8,300, the committee concluded by recommending an 80 percent catch reduction—to a total of 792 metric tons—in 1999.[53] "You want to get these (catches) as close to zero as possible," asserted MMC chair Steven Correia.[54] Accomplishing such a goal without creating new problems would be no mean feat, however. Extremely low catch limits exacerbate the problem of bycatch, as fishers are forced to throw away any fish above the limit. Furthermore, both days-at-sea limits and ocean closures prompt fishers to shift their efforts to alternative species or new fishing grounds; partly as a result of pressure from displaced groundfishers, shrimp, herring, and lobster fisheries were facing crises of their own.

In response to the MMC's recommendations, the council announced an emergency three-month closure, to begin in February 1999, of the cod fishery off the Massachusetts coast. The council's action, targeting the area where cod were concentrated, set off yet another round of protests. While Maine fishers cheered, Massachusetts and New Hampshire fishers were outraged. In January 1999, when the council took up proposals to address the Gulf of Maine cod problem more permanently, it faced an industry split by two major divides: Maine fishers insisted that Massachusetts and New Hampshire fishers needed to share the burden of rescuing the cod; and small boat owners, which are limited to inshore fisheries, demanded regulations that did not discriminate between them and large boats (the latter have more flexibility to pursue fish offshore). As the fishers lined up behind competing plans, their congressional representatives echoed their concerns, further highlighting the tension among states.[55]

The council had three proposals before it, all aimed at meeting the goals for cod established by the MMC: a plan to expand the existing regulatory regime of days at sea and daily catch limits, combined with rolling closures; a plan to ban groundfishing all spring and summer in waters within forty miles of the coast between Cape Cod and south of Portland; and a plan to divide the gulf into inshore and offshore fisheries and require every boat to limit itself to one or the other.[56] After a long and rancorous debate, the council rejected all three. Journalist David Dobbs says that, by the final meeting, "no one trusted anyone. All the council members looked exhausted or scared or depressed or angry . . . and most of the audience appeared on the verge of rage or despair."[57] After the lunch break, security guards barely averted a violent confrontation between audience members and the council. At 1:00 A.M., the council finally came up with Framework Adjustment 27, which expanded the previous year's rolling closures and cut the daily catch limits, while authorizing the administrator to cut the daily trip limits to as low as five pounds if landings exceeded half the TAC of 800 metric tons.[58]

Under pressure from Massachusetts and New Hampshire members and over the objections of members from Maine, the council opened inshore cod grounds off Portsmouth, New Hampshire, and Gloucester, Massachusetts. Thus, it was hardly surprising when less than a month after the measures went into effect, fishers hit the 400 metric ton trigger point, and the NMFS reduced the daily catch limit on cod to thirty pounds. Fishers were dumbfounded. "Fishermen all over the Gulf were catching cod no matter what they did to avoid them," Dobbs reports, describing one fisher who—despite his efforts to catch flounder without ensnaring cod—found that all he could do was catch the two in even proportions.[59] Fishers found the waste horrific and complained bitterly to the NMFS that its scientific assessments were inaccurate. The agency held firm, however, continuing to defend its view by saying that the cod populations had not increased overall but had contracted into their core areas, so that when those areas reopened the fishers were right on top of them.[60]

The events of the summer of 1999 thus exacerbated, rather than ameliorated, the antagonism between fishers and scientists. In light of the season's abundant cod catches, fishers and some scientists were intrigued by a theory put forth by fisher and marine scientist Ted Ames suggesting that what managers regard as single stocks may, in fact, be several genetically distinct subpopulations with distinct spawning and migration habits.[61] According to this theory, different cod stocks return to breed in the place where they were born, so if that area is wiped out, the stock is unable to reestablish itself. The multiple-stock theory is consistent with the failure of the inshore cod fishery to rebound even after strict fishing limits were put in place. The implications of such a theory for management could be profound: if stocks follow different patterns of spawning and migration, fishery management regulations ought to be tailored more precisely to the requirements of individual stocks.[62] The NMFS continued to resist jettisoning its two-stock division, however, largely for pragmatic reasons.[63]

OUTCOMES

Fishery scientists and managers are cautiously optimistic about the prognosis for New England's groundfish. The *28th Northeast Regional Stock Assessment Workshop*, issued in January 1999, found that Gulf of Maine stocks of white hake, American plaice, and yellowtail flounder remained seriously depleted. As a result, total and spawning biomass continued to decline, reducing the probability of a recovery. Georges Bank and Southern New England winter flounder looked a bit better: fishing mortality had declined, and there was some evidence that the number of spawning-sized adults had increased. Nevertheless, scientists contended that both stocks needed further protection from overharvesting to recovery fully.[64] NOAA's 2000 report on the northeast fisheries reiterated that although there had been modest improvements in some stocks, the overall situation remained dire: of twenty-three stocks, seventeen (75 percent) were low abundance. At the same time, sixteen (70 percent) were overexploited, and six (26 percent) were fully exploited.[65]

As the New England Council was preparing to make final groundfishing rules for 2001, the NMFS reported that the measures imposed to reduce the harvest of Gulf of Maine cod finally may have achieved the rates scientists thought necessary to reverse the stock's decline. The NMFS found that the total cod landings approached the target of 1,364 metric tons, compared to landings in 1996, 1997, and 1998 that had been double the target.[66] In apparent confirmation of scientists' conservatism, a study published in the *Canadian Journal of Fisheries and Aquatic Sciences* in February 2001 by NEFSC scientists presented strong evidence of a link between spawning stock abundance and the subsequent numbers of groundfish. Based on that relationship, the scientists set odds on the recovery of various groundfish stock that ranged from as good as 22:1 for Georges Bank Yellowtail flounder to as poor as 1:2 for Gulf of Maine cod.[67]

Seeming to confirm scientists' tentative optimism about some stocks, in May 2000, the Portland Fish Exchange reported that the volume of groundfish traded on the exchange had increased for the first time in seven years. The exchange ended its fiscal year on March 31 with 19.1 million pounds landed and sold, up from 18 million pounds the year before.[68] After posting a 33 percent increase in fish landings in 2000, the exchange predicted a near-record volume again in 2001. While such signs are positive, fishery managers remain concerned about the long term because the fleet still has a much greater capacity to catch fish than the waters can sustain. As of 2000, more than 3,600 New England boats had permits to catch groundfish—about 10 percent fewer than in 1996 because of the buyout—but not all were actively fishing. Managers worried that even the slight rebound in fish stocks would prompt fishers with permits to resume fishing, which could undermine recovery efforts. To address this concern, in 2000, Congress authorized a $10 million program to purchase latent groundfishing permits.

Moreover, while managers were positive about the effectiveness of the council's plan, environmentalists were not. Reviewing the progress of NMFS in implementing the SFA in September 1999, the Marine Fish Conservation Network—a watchdog organization comprising nearly ninety environmental groups—issued a highly critical report of the NMFS's implementation of the SFA. The network alleged that the NMFS was accepting plans that were insufficiently precautionary to ensure the fisheries' health, pointing out that:

> there have been practically no new measures to reduce bycatch or bycatch mortality. Essential fish habitat has been designated but not protected. Only preliminary progress has been made in ending overfishing and rebuilding fish stocks. Many of these failures are the result of councils making incremental improvements where substantial changes are required.[69]

The report particularly disparaged the New England Council, which it said was continuing to allow overfishing of Gulf of Maine cod and other ground-fish and had failed to address bycatch and essential habitat concerns.

Reflecting the impatience of environmental groups, in late May 2000, the Ocean Law Project filed a lawsuit against the Department of Commerce on behalf of the Conservation Law Foundation, the Natural Resources Defense Council, the Center for Marine Conservation, and the National Audubon Society. The lawsuit, which concerns the groundfish FMP submitted by the New England Council and approved by the Commerce Department in April 2000, asks the court to force the NMFS to adopt a plan that sets bycatch rules and establishes a more stringent definition of overfishing.[70] Council officials admit that the plan they submitted does not meet the standards set out by SFA but note that, anticipating a time-consuming public review process, they wanted to get something in place by the deadline.[71]

CONCLUSIONS

Since 1976, New England fishery managers have spun their wheels trying to institute effective schemes to save the groundfish while simultaneously pre-serving the character of the New England fishery. For two decades, cooperative management—as mandated by the Magnuson Act—translated into trying to devise conservation measures that did not antagonize anyone. For the most part, the resulting policy consisted of reactionary measures prompted by crises; until recently, those measures did little more than slow the demise of the fish-ers at the expense of the fish. Moreover, the shift to a more restrictive fishing regime was not the result of a recognition by the council or fishers that scien-tists were right. In fact, in the early 1990s, exploitation rates of cod and yellow-tail flounder were 55 and 65 percent of biomass, respectively, even though sci-entists recommended exploitation levels of 13 and 22 percent.[72] Rather, the CLF lawsuit empowered NMFS officials to force the council's hand.

Many commentators believe that even the more stringent measures of the late 1990s will fail to save the groundfish in the long run unless managers ruth-lessly impose a regulatory regime on fishers or create private property rights in the fishery. Their pessimism stems from their adherence to the model of behavior embodied in the tragedy of the commons model. Certainly the behavior of New England fishers over the last two and a half decades is con-sistent with that model: individual fishers reacted to whatever measures fish-ery managers put in place by expanding their effort in other ways. They pur-sued short-term economic gains at the expense of the long-term health of the fishery, and few seemed prepared to sacrifice their catch without assurances that others would do the same.

Some analysts have questioned the assumptions that underlie the tragedy of the commons model, however, arguing that people are not always as self-serving, individualistic, and short-sighted as the model posits.[73] They point to communities that have successfully managed their common property resources, such as the Maine lobster fishers, who have maintained a system of self-regulation for more than a century.[74] While this and other examples suggest that the tragedy of the commons is not inevitable, they have limited applicability. Elinor Ostrom argues that successful co-management is more likely to succeed where common property resources have been managed by a settled, homogeneous population under long-enduring institutions, so that the populations believe they or their children will reap the benefits of conservation and are thus more likely to adhere to agreements.[75] After examining unsuccessful experiments with co-management, such as the Canadian effort to establish a cooperative regime in the Bay of Fundy, anthropologist James McGoodwin concludes that co-management can generate new problems or heighten old ones: members' organizations may become embroiled in internal disputes or run into trouble if they have insufficient autonomy; unless they receive sufficient technical assistance, they may not be competent to carry out the responsibilities delegated to them.[76]

All of these caveats resonate: the fishermen of New England are not ideal candidates for co-management because they do not trust each other, do not communicate regularly, and have little experience forming binding agreements with one another. They value above all their independence and their egalitarian view that "anyone should be able to go out and fish."[77] And they remain uneasy with the scientists who provide the information on which management decisions are based.[78] Thus, workable solutions in New England are likely to depend heavily on controlling access to the fishery rather than on cooperative schemes.

The most popular approach to controlling access to fisheries involves distributing individual transferable quotas (ITQs) to individual fishers or fishing enterprises. Under an ITQ system, the owner of a quota share has exclusive rights to a particular fishery, to take a certain proportion or amount of fish in the fishery, and—in most instances—to sell or lease that right to others.[79] ITQs are currently the most widely discussed solutions for overcrowded fisheries, but implementing an ITQ system can have broad and controversial social consequences; for example, such systems can concentrate the benefits of a fishery in the hands of a privileged few. Consolidation of the industry is not inevitable under an ITQ system, however; in Alaska's fishery, quotas for small boat owners are allocated in blocks, and no single owner can have more than five blocks.[80]

The Australian lobster fishing regime is one example of a successful ITQ system. Beginning in the 1960s, the Australian government set a limit on the total number of lobster traps and then assigned licenses to working fishers. From then on, any newcomer had to buy a license from someone already working in the fishery, much the way the New York taxi medallion system works. Australian lobster fishers now work 187 days a year (compared to as many as 240 days per year for Rhode Island lobstermen), tending sixty traps apiece (versus as many as 800 by a typical lobsterman in Rhode Island). Proponents of the Australian system point out that it has not only rejuvenated the stocks and enhanced the lives of the fishers (who make significantly more than their American counterparts); it has also eased tension between fishers and scientists, who are now working collaboratively to keep the fishery healthy.[81]

Currently, there is a congressionally mandated ban on ITQs—adopted under pressure from fishermen who feared losing open access to the nation's fisheries. The National Academy of Sciences has endorsed ITQs, however, and Congress is considering lifting the ban. While New England fishers would almost certainly resist the imposition of such a system, it is likely to be the first solution on the table when the next window of opportunity for policy change opens.

QUESTIONS TO CONSIDER

- Why did the government wait, despite repeated warnings from scientists, until cod, haddock, and flounder stocks were decimated before acting to save the fishery?
- What kind of regulation will prevent this problem from recurring in the future? Do we have the political will to undertake conservation measures?
- Why are those whose livelihoods depend on fish the most outspoken in their opposition to such programs?

Notes

1. Groundfish, or demersals, dwell at or near the bottom of the sea. The New England groundfish include members of the cod family (cod, haddock, hakes, pollock), flounders, dogfish sharks, and skates.
2. Garrett Hardin, "The Tragedy of the Commons," *Science* 162 (December 13, 1968): 1243–1248.
3. Elinor Ostrom, *Governing the Commons: The Evolution of Institutions for Collective Action* (New York: Cambridge University Press, 1990), 1.
4. Quoted in Carl Safina, "Where Have All the Fishes Gone?," *Issues in Science and Technology* (spring 1994): 38.
5. Recruitment overfishing occurs when fishers reduce too many spawning adults and thereby affect the population's ability to reproduce. See Steven A. Murawski et al., "New England Groundfish," in National Marine Fisheries Service, *Our Living Oceans: Report on the Status of U.S. Living Marine Resources, 1999*, NOAA Technical Memo. NMFS-F/SPO-41 (December, 1999).
6. William Warner, *Distant Water: The Fate of the North Atlantic Fishermen* (Boston: Little, Brown, 1983).
7. Rodman D. Griffin, "Marine Mammals vs. Fish," *CQ Researcher*, August 28, 1992, 744.
8. Warner, *Distant Water,* viii.
9. A metric ton is equal to 1,000 kilograms, or approximately 2,200 pounds. See Murawski et al., "New England Groundfish."
10. National Marine Fisheries Service, *Our Living Oceans: Report on the Status of U.S. Living Marine Resources, 1993*, NOAA Technical Memo NMFS-F/SPO-15 (December, 1993).
11. Warner, *Distant Water.*
12. Ibid.
13. The coastal fisheries (zero to three miles off the coast) are managed by states and by interstate compacts.
14. PL 94-265, 90 Stat. 331; 16 USC sections 1801–1882.
15. Quoted in H. John Heinz III Center for Science, Economics, and the Environment, *Fishing Grounds: Defining a New Era for American Fisheries Management* (Washington, D.C.: Island Press, 2000), 87.

16. The United Nations Food and Agriculture Organization estimates that 84 million metric tons of marine fish are landed worldwide each year, and another 27 million metric tons of marine fish are killed as bycatch. See United Nations Food and Agriculture Organization, *The State of the World Fisheries and Aquaculture, 1996* (Rome: Food and Agriculture Organization, 1996); D. L. Alverson et al., "A Global Assessment of Fisheries Bycatch and Discard," *FAO Fisheries Technical Paper 339* (Rome: Food and Agriculture Organization, 1994).

17. National Research Council, *Review of Northeast Fishery Stock Assessments* (Washington, D.C.: National Academy Press, 1998).

18. Currently, the council has eighteen voting members: the regional administrator of the NMFS; the principal state officials with marine fishery responsibility from Maine, New Hampshire, Massachusetts, Rhode Island, and Connecticut; and twelve members nominated by the governor and appointed by the secretary of commerce. The council also has four nonvoting members: one each from the U.S. Coast Guard, the U.S. Fish and Wildlife Service, the U.S. Department of State, and the Atlantic States Marine Fisheries Commission.

19. Quoted in Heinz Center, *Fishing Grounds,* 88.

20. Eleanor M. Dorsey, "The 602 Guidelines on Overfishing: A Perspective from New England," in *Conserving America's Fisheries,* ed. R. H. Stroud (Savannah, Ga.: National Coalition for Marine Conservation, 1994), 181–188.

21. "Cap'n Sane says," *National Fisherman,* May 1978.

22. Quoted in David E. Pierce, *Development and Evolution of Fishery Management Plans for Cod, Haddock, and Yellowtail Flounder* (Boston: Massachusetts Division of Marine Fisheries, 1982), 13.

23. An otter trawl is a funnel-shaped net that is dragged on the bottom of the sea.

24. Madeleine Hall-Arber, "'They' Are the Problem: Assessing Fisheries Management in New England," *Nor'Easter* (fall–winter 1993): 16–21.

25. Sonja V. Fordham, *New England Groundfish: From Glory to Grief* (Washington, D.C.: Center for Marine Conservation, 1996).

26. The standard investment tax credit was available to anyone, but was especially appealing to capital-intensive industries like fishing. The fishery-specific Capital Construction Fund program allowed fishing boat owners to set aside and invest pretax dollars for later use in upgrading or buying fishing boats. The Fishery Vessel Obligation Guarantee Program (FOG) provided government-guaranteed boat-building loans at lower interest rates and longer payback periods than traditional five-year loans. These and other incentives—such as fuel tax relief, gear replacement funds, and market expansion programs—attracted fishers into the industry and encouraged existing boat owners to expand and upgrade their boats. See David Dobbs, *The Great Gulf* (Washington, D.C.: Island Press, 2000); Heinz Center, *Fishing Grounds.*

27. Murawski et al., "New England Groundfish."

28. Dobbs, *The Great Gulf.*

29. Dorsey, "The 602 Guidelines."

30. PL 94-265, 90 Stat. 331.

31. Dorsey, "The 602 Guidelines."

32. Ibid.

33. In theory, optimal yield is the level of catch that will allow the stocks to sustain themselves, modified by any relevant economic, social, or ecological factor.

34. Heinz Center, *Fishing Grounds.*

35. Dorsey, "The 602 Guidelines, 185."

36. Massachusetts Offshore Groundfish Task Force, *New England Groundfish in Crisis—Again,* Publication No. 16, 551-42-200-1-91-CR (December 1990).

37. Previous amendments had involved non-groundfish species.

38. In prior years, the NMFS had closed Area 2 of Georges Bank between February 1 and May 31 to protect spawning groundfish. The emergency order extended the

closure and enlarged the covered area. See John Laidler, "U.S. Emergency Order Shuts Part of Georges Bank to Fishing," *Boston Globe,* June 4, 1983, 31.

39. Northeast Fisheries Science Center (NEFSC), *Report of the 18th Northeast Regional Stock Assessment Workshop: Stock Assessment Review Committee Consensus Summary of Assessments* (1994), NEFSC Ref. Doc. 94-22.

40. Quoted in Sam Walker, "Georges Bank Closes, Ending an Era," *Christian Science Monitor,* December 12, 1994, 1.

41. Ibid.

42. Amendment 6 pertained to the scallop fishery.

43. Quoted in Edie Lau, "Panel Backs Cutting Days for Fishing," *Portland Press Herald,* October 26, 1995, 1B.

44. Linc Bedrosian, "Portland: Amendment 7 is Sheer Lunacy," *National Fisherman,* December 1995, 17.

45. Edie Lau, "Council to Phase in Restraints," *Portland Press Herald,* December 15, 1995, 1A.

46. Ibid.

47. Rolling closures are area closures that are instituted one after the other, as stocks migrate.

48. Andrew Garber, "Lawsuit Put on Fast Track," *Portland Press Herald,* August 9, 1996, 2B.

49. The actual 1996 cod catch was 6,957 metric tons. See Andrew Garber, "Report Calls for Deeper Cuts in Catches to Save Groundfish," *Portland Press Herald,* December 7, 1996, 1A.

50. The monitoring committee includes scientists, managers, and a fisherman.

51. Garber, "Report Calls for Deeper Cuts in Catches to Save Groundfish"; "New England Fisheries News" (Boston: Conservation Law Foundation, December 1996).

52. A framework adjustment can be implemented more quickly than a full-blown plan amendment.

53. Keep in mind that if the population were healthy, it could support an annual catch of 10,900 metric tons. See John Richardson, "Fisheries Imbalance Infuriates Senators," *Portland Press Herald,* June 27, 1999, 1B.

54. Quoted in John Richardson, "Panel to Vote on Drastic Cod Limits," Portland Press *Herald,* December 10, 1998, 4B.

55. John Richardson, "Fishery Closure Also Lifts Hopes," *Portland Press Herald,* December 12, 1998, 1B.

56. Dobbs, *The Great Gulf.*

57. Ibid., 153.

58. "Closure and Trip Limits Are Part of Framework 27," *NMFS Northeast Region News,* April 30, 1999.

59. Dobbs, *The Great Gulf,* 161.

60. Ibid.

61. John Richardson, "Forum Questions Migration Theory for Groundfish," *Portland Press Herald,* October 29, 1997, 8B.

62. David Dobbs notes that fishers distinguish between resident and school cod and inshore-spawning versus offshore spawning stocks. See Dobbs, *The Great Gulf.*

63. NMFS managers point out that thus far its predictions based on a two-stock divison have been accurate; moreover, they worry about disrupting the long-running data set that is based on that distinction.

64. "Scientific Analyses Confirm Need to Improve Protection of Five Stocks from Overharvesting," *Northeast Fisheries Science Center News,* January 27, 1999; http://www.nefsc.nmfs.gov/press_release/news99.02.html.

65. NOAA, *Status of Fishery Resources Off the Northeastern United States* (Washington, D.C.: U.S. Department of Commerce, 2000).

66. "Gulf of Maine Cod Near Landings Target for First Time," *NMFS Northeast Region News,* January 18, 2000.

67. The scientific team tested six fish population models emphasizing different variables, such as environmental factors or the size of spawning stock, to see which generated results that were most consistent with the actual performance of eleven groundfish stocks over nearly four decades. The spawning stock biomass models most accurately predicted the behavior of eight of the eleven stocks. See "Study Offers Support for Fishery Management," *NMFS Northeast Fisheries Science Center News,* April 16, 2001.

68. John Richardson, "Groundfish Landings Increase for First Time in Seven Years," *Portland Press Herald,* May 9, 2000, 1A.

69. Marine Fish Conservation Network, *Lost at Sea* (Washington, D.C.: Marine Fish Conservation Network, 1999), 10.

70. The law allows the Commerce Department to approve or disapprove all or part of a plan, but it does not permit the secretary to change any part of a plan unilaterally.

71. Associated Press, "Hard Line on Fishing is Pushed in Lawsuit," *Portland Press Herald,* May 23, 2000, 2B.

72. National Research Council, *Sustaining Marine Fisheries* (Washington, D.C.: National Academy Press, 1999).

73. James R. McGoodwin, *Crisis in the World's Fisheries* (Stanford: Stanford University Press, 1990).

74. James M. Acheson, "Where Have All the Exploiters Gone?" in *Common Property Resources: Ecology and Community-Based Sustainable Development,* ed. Fikret Berkes (London: Bellhaven Press, 1989), 199–217.

75. Ostrom, *Governing the Commons.*

76. McGoodwin, *Crisis in the World's Fisheries.*

77. Hall-Arber, "'They' Are the Problem."

78. Chitrita Banerji, "Between the Devil and the Deep Blue Sea," *Conservation Matters* (summer 1995): 4–10; Hall-Arber, "'They' Are the Problem."

79. Heinz Center, *Fishing Grounds.*

80. Peter Weber, *Net Loss: Fish, Jobs, and the Marine Environment* (Washington, D.C.: Worldwatch Institute, 1994).

81. John Tierney, "A Tale of Two Fisheries," *New York Times Magazine,* August 27, 2000, 38–43.

Recommended Reading

Dobbs, David. *The Great Gulf.* Washington, D.C.: Island Press, 2000.

Fordham, Sonja V. *New England Groundfish: From Glory to Grief.* Washington, D.C.: Center for Marine Conservation, April 1996.

H. John Heinz III Center for Science, Economics, and the Environment. *Fishing Grounds: Defining a New Era for American Fisheries Management.* Washington, D.C.: Island Press, 2000.

National Academy of Sciences. *Sustaining Marine Fisheries.* Washington, D.C.: National Academy Press, 1999.

Web Sites

http://www.nefmc.org (New England Fishery Management Council site)

http://www.heinzctr.org/PROGRAMS/fisheries/program_overview.htm (Heinz Center for Science, Policy, and the Environment site)

http://www.nmfs.noaa.gov (NMFS site)

http://www.nefsc.nmfs.gov (NEFSC site)

CHAPTER 9

Climate Change

The Challenges of Formulating International Environmental Policies

The possibility that human activity is changing the earth's climate achieved notoriety in the United States in 1988, when NASA scientist James Hansen, testifying before Congress, expressed "ninety-nine percent confidence" that "the greenhouse effect has been detected, and it is changing our climate now."[1] Alerted by the concern of Hansen and other scientists, the United Nations established the Intergovernmental Panel on Climate Change (IPCC), comprising 2,000 leading experts from around the world, to assess the extent and likely impacts of climate change. Beginning in 1990, the IPCC has reported with increasing certainty that human-made emissions of greenhouse gases are causing rapid and potentially damaging changes in the global climate. The IPCC is the most distinguished international group of scientists ever assembled to address a policy question; yet the United States has demonstrated little political will to address the problem.

The climate change case vividly confirms that science does not change policy directly, but rather that political factors shape the relationship between science and policy. Like the New England fisheries (described in chapter 8), the global climate is a commons, so formulating policies—even in the face of scientific consensus—is hampered by collective action problems. That is, because both responsibility for and the impacts of climate change are diffuse, individual nations have an incentive to free ride on the improvements made by other nations. Such obstacles are likely to be even more formidable in the international arena than they are within or across regions in the United States because no international institutions can enforce binding decisions on sovereign nations. Instead, nations must cooperate to address the problem, a prospect that some political scientists find improbable.

Traditionally, American scholars who study international relations have portrayed nations as unitary actors with a single interest: survival. According to this perspective, nations do not cooperate with one another unless it is in their self-interest to do so. For realists, a nation's interest is self-evident: each wants to maintain its security and power relative to other countries. In this view, "the potential for international cooperation is limited, and international laws and institutions are likely to be fragile and impermanent."[2] Extending this view, neorealists contend that international cooperation may arise if a single state with a preponderance of power (a "hegemon") is willing to use its resources to transform international relations.[3] Liberal theorists (and neoliberal institutionalists), in contrast, contend that nations are interdependent and that their common interests lead them to work together. More recently, a third school of thought has emerged that builds on the notion of interdependence and emphasizes the concept of international regimes, comprising "principles, norms, rules, and decision making procedures around which participants' expectations converge in a given issue area."[4]

International environment scholars adopting this third perspective have turned their attention to how and why such regimes develop and persist. In particular, they argue that a nation's self-interest is *not* a given but must be discovered. Political scientist Helen Milner offers a key insight into this process, noting that "cooperation among nations is affected less by fears of other countries' relative gains or cheating than it is by the domestic distributional consequences of cooperative endeavors. Cooperative agreements create winners and losers domestically; therefore they generate supporters and opponents. The internal struggle between these groups shapes the possibility and nature of international cooperative agreements."[5]

The ability to define or frame a problem domestically, then, is likely to be a key determinant of a nation's position on international environmental agreements. As the preceding cases in this book have made clear, environmentalists have had great success defining problems in ways that enabled them to challenge policies favoring development interests. Enhancing their credibility have been highly reputable knowledge brokers—experts who translate scientific explanations into political stories—as well as an avalanche of scientific consensus panel reports. But business interests have not been passive; they have responded by forming interest groups and funding experts and think tanks. As political scientists Darrell West and Burdett Loomis point out, well-heeled interests have become adept at generating information and embedding it in narratives of their own.[6] With their virtually unlimited resources, business coalitions can pay top lobbyists to craft such stories and disseminate them among legislators, their staffs, and other opinion leaders. They can also inundate the public with their messages via TV, radio, direct mail, telemarketing, and billboards.

A nation's position on an international environmental agreement also depends on whether its domestic supporters can build a majority coalition around a particular solution. Throughout the climate change negotiations, the United States has resisted greenhouse gas emissions targets and insisted that policies to reduce those emissions be flexible and rely heavily on market-based approaches. In theory, marked-based mechanisms can prompt greater innovation while reducing emissions much more cheaply than one-size-fits-all mandates. More importantly for U.S. negotiators, market-based tools generate support among companies likely to profit from new opportunities and defuse opposition among conservative policy experts. Such approaches pose a moral dilemma for some members of the international community, however, because they allow wealthy polluters to pay others to clean up rather than engaging in such efforts themselves.

This case explores the political challenges of tackling what political scientist Robert Putnam has called the two-level game, in which policymakers try simultaneously to "maximize their own ability to satisfy domestic pressures while minimizing the adverse consequences of foreign developments."[7]

BACKGROUND

Modern scientific interest in climate change originated in the 1950s, but more than a century earlier, scientists had recognized the "greenhouse effect" of atmospheric gases. In 1827, French scientist Jean-Baptiste Fourier found that atmospheric gases help keep the climate warm by trapping thermal radiation in a fashion he likened to the role of glass in a greenhouse. In 1860, a British scientist, John Tyndall, measured the absorption of infrared radiation by carbon dioxide (CO_2) and water vapor. In 1896, Swedish scientist Svante Arrhenius estimated that doubling CO_2 concentrations would raise the average global temperature by 5 to 6 degrees Celsius. American geologist T. C. Chamberlin warned independently that the fossil fuel combustion that accompanied industrialization could lead to an out-of-control greenhouse effect. In 1938, British meteorologist G. D. Callendar calculated the actual warming due to CO_2 from burning fossil fuels using data gathered from 200 weather stations around the world. Callendar's report was met with skepticism, however; the prevailing scientific view during the first half of the twentieth century was that climate remains constant, experiencing only short-term fluctuations.[8]

It was not until the late 1950s that scientists revisited the possibility that greenhouse gases might accumulate in the atmosphere and eventually cause global warming. In 1957, Roger Revelle and Hans Suess of the Scripps Institute of Oceanography published a paper to that effect after they discovered that the oceans had not absorbed as much CO_2 as previously assumed. Revelle and Suess coined an expression that subsequently became a catchphrase of climate change policy advocates, claiming that human beings were carrying out a unique, "large scale geophysical experiment."[9] Prompted by these concerns, in 1957, Revelle's graduate student, Charles David Keeling, instituted routine measurements of CO_2 at the observatory in Mauna Loa, Hawaii. By the early 1960s, instruments at the observatory were detecting steady increases in CO_2 concentrations (see Figure 9-1). In 1963, the Conservation Foundation issued a report entitled *Implications of the Rising Carbon Dioxide Content of the Atmosphere*, one of the first to speculate on the possible consequences of this trend. Shortly thereafter, a group of White House science advisers led by Roger Revelle concluded that a projected 25 percent increase in atmospheric CO_2 concentrations could cause marked changes in the earth's climate, with possibly deleterious consequences for humans.[10]

By the 1970s, scientific interest was clearly turning toward the impact of humans on the global environment.[11] Scientists studying climate debated whether changes in CO_2 concentrations were likely to produce global warming or global cooling, but over time scientific opinion converged on the warming

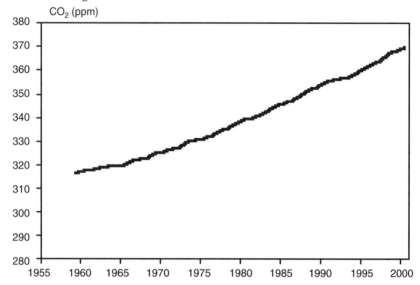

Figure 9-1 Mauna Loa Annual Mean Carbon Dioxide

Source: Scripps Institution of Oceanography; National Oceanic and Atmospheric Administration.

Note: Atmospheric concentrations of CO_2 are expressed in parts per million (ppm) and reported in the 1999 SIO manometric mole fraction scale. Missing values are denoted by –99.99. In years where one monthly value is missing annual values were calculated by substituting a fit value (4-harmonics with gain factor and spline) for that month and then averaging the twelve monthly values.

hypothesis. The National Academy of Sciences (NAS) launched a series of efforts to assess the scientific understanding of CO_2 and climate, all of which called for more research but also warned about the potentially severe impacts of changes in the global climate. A 1979 NAS report advised that a "wait-and-see policy may mean waiting until it is too late" to avoid significant climatic changes.[12] In 1979, the World Meteorological Organization (WMO), which in 1974 had begun to examine the evidence, convened a major international conference on the topic in Geneva.[13] The final statement of the First World Climate Conference introduced the importance of factors besides greenhouse gas emissions and adopted a decidedly precautionary tone: "We can say with some confidence that the burning of fossil fuels, deforestation, and changes of land use have increased the amount of carbon dioxide in the atmosphere . . . and it appears plausible that [CO_2 increases] can contribute to a gradual warming of the lower atmosphere, especially at high latitudes."[14]

Scientists' basic concern was that the planet was experiencing a runaway greenhouse effect. They knew that the earth's atmosphere helps keep the planet warm in part by trapping thermal radiation, a feature known as the greenhouse effect. This process begins when the earth absorbs radiation from the sun in the form of visible light; that energy is then redistributed by the

Figure 9-2 The Global Carbon Cycle

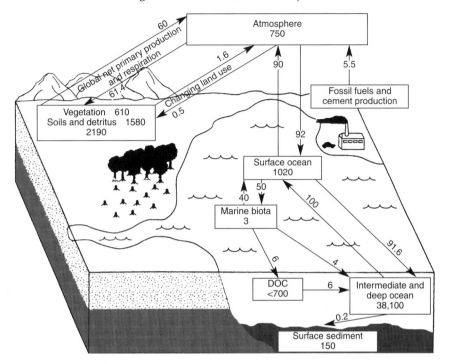

Source: IPCC, ed. J. T. Houghton, et al., *Climate Change 1994* (New York: Cambridge, 1995).

Note: The numbers in boxes indicate the size of GtC of each reservoir. On each arrow is indicated the magnitude of the flux in GtC/yr (DOC = dissolved organic carbon).

atmosphere and the ocean and re-radiated to space at a longer (infrared) wavelength. Most of that thermal radiation in turn is absorbed by greenhouse gases in the atmosphere, particularly water vapor, CO_2, methane, chlorofluorocarbons (CFCs), and ozone. The absorbed energy is then re-radiated both downwards and upwards. The result is that the earth's surface loses less heat to space than it would in the absence of greenhouse gases and therefore stays warmer than it would otherwise (see Figure 9-2).[15]

By the early 1980s, scientists were becoming even more vocal. In 1980, delegates to another international climate conference, in Villach, Austria, issued warnings about global warming, and in 1983, the U.S. Environmental Protection Agency (EPA) released a report suggesting that global temperature increases could strain environmental, economic, and political systems.[16] In 1985, scientists from twenty-nine countries again met in Villach, where they "agreed that human activity was causing increases in atmospheric concentrations of greenhouse gases, which, in turn, would raise global mean surface temperatures."[17] Participants estimated that a doubling of atmospheric concentrations of CO_2 could lead to an increase in the global mean surface temperature of 1.5 to 4.5 degrees Celsius, and they encouraged policymakers to begin considering responses.[18] More scientific consensus that humans were altering the global climate emerged from two subsequent climate workshops in 1987, one in Villach and the other in Bellagio, Italy.

THE CASE

Despite their increasingly urgent tone, the periodic scientific bulletins of the 1970s and 1980s generated little social or political response. Instead, a series of weather episodes—combined with the activism of scientific knowledge brokers—focused public attention on the scientific case for climate change. That attention in turn generated political support for United Nations–sponsored efforts to comprehend climate change and its implications. The improving scientific understanding did not translate into policy, however; instead, it mobilized powerful interests opposed to international climate change policy. Those interests have used their resources to emphasize scientific uncertainty and economic consequences and thereby undermine support for climate change policies in the United States. In the hopes of defusing domestic opposition, U.S. negotiators have promoted market-based policy solutions.

International Concern Leads to an Intergovernmental Panel

The knowledge broker widely credited with galvanizing politicians in the U.S. is NASA's James Hansen, who on June 23, 1988, testified at a hearing before the Senate Energy and Natural Resources Committee that human-induced global warming was imminent and that the phenomenon was sufficiently well understood that policymakers should act to address it. Hansen's testimony was highly publicized, in part because the summer of 1988 was one of the hottest and driest on record in North America. Hurricanes and other freak weather events around the world further enhanced the public's receptivity to the idea that the climate was changing. Although scientists were tentative in attributing the heat to global warming, the severe weather provided an obvious hook for the media.

Between June 27 and 30, more than 300 scientists, government officials, environmentalists, and industry representatives from forty-eight countries assembled at a conference in Toronto on the global security implications of climate change. Adopting a tone of alarm, the Toronto Conference Statement said that "humanity is conducting an unintended, uncontrolled, globally pervasive experiment whose ultimate consequence could be second only to global nuclear war."[19] The statement recommended that governments begin negotiating a global convention as a framework to protect the atmosphere[20]; agree to reduce global emissions of CO_2 to 20 percent below 1988 levels by 2005; and create a "World Atmosphere Fund" from taxes on fossil fuel consumption in industrial countries.[21] Shortly after the Toronto Conference, several world leaders—including Britain's Prime Minister Margaret Thatcher, a former skeptic—made statements about the need for a response to climate change.

As the scientific convergence grew, the United Nations Environment Programme (UNEP) and the WMO jointly sponsored the creation of the Intergovernmental Panel on Climate Change (IPCC) to provide policymakers with a scientific foundation for international negotiations. The IPCC met for the first time in November 1988, elected Swedish scientist Bert Bolin as its chair, and formulated a threefold mandate: to review the existing scientific literature on climate change and report on the scientific consensus (Working Group I); to assess the environmental and socioeconomic impacts of climate change (Working Group II); and to formulate response strategies (Working Group III). Shortly thereafter, Working Group I of the IPCC began its work in Geneva under the direction of John Houghton, a well-respected British climatologist.

The Bush Administration Demurs

Reflecting the heightened international attention, in 1989, the UNEP Governing Council and the UN General Assembly adopted resolutions calling on governments to prepare a framework convention on climate change, as well as protocols containing concrete commitments based on scientific knowledge and taking into account the needs of developing countries.[22] In July 1989, the statement of the Group of Seven major industrial democracies' annual summit called for "the early conclusion of an international convention to protect and conserve the global climate."[23] Rather than leading the charge, however, the Bush administration refused to propose or support climate policies, emphasizing instead the scientific uncertainties.

To justify his position, President Bush relied heavily on a paper issued by the conservative George C. Marshall Institute, entitled "Scientific Perspectives on the Greenhouse Problem," that downplayed the scientific consensus on climate change and concluded that it would be premature to impose policies to reduce greenhouse gas emissions. The president continued to tout the theme of scientific uncertainty in his April 1990 opening speech to a seventeen-nation White House Conference on Science and Economics Research Related to Global Climate Change, in which he said that before acting "what we need are facts."[24] In lieu of policy proposals, Bush called for further research and a 60 percent increase in spending on research.

Hoping to pressure the administration, forty-nine Nobel Prize winners and 700 members of the NAS issued a public appeal, saying "there is broad agreement within the scientific community that amplification of the Earth's natural greenhouse effect by the buildup of various gases introduced by human activity has the potential to produce dramatic changes in climate. . . . Only by taking action now can we insure that future generations will not be put at risk." The scientists' petition did not have much impact on Bush, however, nor did the May 1990 presentation by the IPCC of its interim findings. Drawing on the work of 170 scientists from twenty-five countries, the IPCC report said that:

- Emissions resulting from human activities are substantially increasing the atmospheric concentrations of the greenhouse gases: CO_2, methane, CFCs, and nitrous oxides (NO_x). For example, worldwide human-made emissions of CO_2, the main greenhouse gas, increased from less than 100 million tons per year before the industrial revolution to six billion tons per year in 1990. As a result, atmospheric concentrations of CO_2 rose from 280 ppmv to more than 350 ppmv and are continuing to climb.
- The evidence from the modeling studies, observations, and sensitivity analyses indicate that the sensitivity of the global mean surface temperature to doubling CO_2 is unlikely to lie outside the 1.5 to 4.5 degrees Celsius range.
- There are many uncertainties in scientists' predictions, particularly with regard to the timing, magnitude, and regional patterns of climate change.
- Global mean surface air temperature has increased by 0.3 to 0.6 degrees Celsius over the last 100 years.
- The size of this warming is broadly consistent with predictions of climate models, but it is also of the same magnitude as natural climate variability. Thus, the observed increase could be largely due to this natural variability; alternatively, natural variability combined with other human factors could have offset a still larger human-induced greenhouse warming.
- The unequivocal detection of the enhanced greenhouse effect from observations is not likely for a decade or more.[25]

The IPCC calculated that an immediate 60 percent reduction in CO_2 emissions would be needed to halt the buildup of CO_2 in the atmosphere.

The IPCC's Working Group II tried to forecast the consequences of climate change, again acknowledging that its predictions were highly uncertain and based on a number of simplifying assumptions. Along with an increase in severe weather events and a higher incidence of infectious diseases, among the most serious potential consequences of a rapid increase in global temperatures projected by the IPCC was a rise in global sea level of between four and twelve inches in the next fifty years. Even at the low end of such a rise, coastal areas everywhere would be more vulnerable to flooding, and some regions would be partially submerged.

The tentative tone of the initial IPCC report notwithstanding, many European leaders responded with alacrity; between May and December 1990, fourteen of the Organization for Economic Cooperation and Development's (OECD) twenty-four member countries initiated policies to stabilize or reduce emissions of greenhouse gases.[26] In contrast, the United States continued to equivocate: in August, the American delegation clashed with other nations attending a meeting in Sweden to finalize the policymakers' summary of the IPCC report, insisting on amendments emphasizing scientific uncertainty.[27] President Bush continued to downplay the scientific consensus, and the American delegation again prevented the establishment of any timetables or targets for the stabilization of greenhouse gas emissions.[28] Their primary concern was to ensure that any actions taken would not curtail economic growth. Despite U.S. resistance, however, the final conference statement reported a clear scientific consensus had emerged on global warming expected during the twenty-first century. It added that if the increase of greenhouse gas concentrations was not stemmed, the predicted climate change would place stress on natural and social systems unprecedented in the past 10,000 years.

The UN pressed ahead as well, establishing the Intergovernmental Negotiating Committee (INC) to generate a convention in advance of the United Nations Conference on Environment and Development (UNCED) scheduled for June 1992. The INC met at five two-week sessions between February 1991 and May 1992, during which the negotiators agreed on a process modeled after the one that produced the much acclaimed 1987 Montreal Protocol on Substances that Deplete the Ozone Layer: they would first establish a framework convention on the basic issues and then, at a later date, negotiate a protocol specifying the more concrete obligations of each country.[29] During this period, President Bush made it clear that he would not attend the Earth Summit in Rio de Janeiro if negotiators produced a climate convention containing specific timetables or goals.

The January 1992 release of the Supplementary Report to the IPCC Scientific Assessment precipitated yet another round of publicity for the scientific consensus on climate change. Between 1990 and 1992, scientists had begun to incorporate the cooling effects of stratospheric ozone depletion and aerosols (airborne sulfur dioxide particles) into their models, resulting in a much greater consistency between those models and observed temperatures. The supplement reaffirmed the conclusions of the 1990 report and added several new findings refining their understanding of global warming; key among these was that the anomalously high global temperatures of the 1980s continued into 1990 and 1991, the warmest years on record.

Media coverage of the scientific consensus on climate change kept the international community on track. In May 1992, at UNCED in Rio, 154 governments signed the Framework Convention on Climate Change (FCCC), the primary goal of which is the "stabilization of greenhouse gas concentrations in the atmosphere at a level that would prevent dangerous anthropogenic (human) interference with the climate system."[30] The FCCC divides signatories into Annex I (developed) and Annex II (transitional and developing) nations, in recognition that the former are responsible for the bulk of the world's greenhouse gases, and creates an obligation for Annex I nations to reduce their emissions to 1990 levels. The FCCC specifies that policies devised under the convention should achieve equity through "common but differentiated responsibilities" and pay special attention to disproportionately burdened developing nations, such as small island states. Most notably, the FCCC states that policies should be consistent with the "precautionary principle," which involves acting prudently in the absence of scientific certainty. The Bush administration signed the agreement reluctantly, with the understanding that it intended to encourage, but not mandate, emissions reductions.[31] In October 1992, the U.S. Senate ratified the FCCC.

The Clinton Administration: Hopes for U.S. Leadership Bloom and Fade

With the inauguration of President Bill Clinton, advocates of climate change policies were hopeful that the United States would take a more proactive role in negotiations. Bolstering expectations, Clinton announced his support for the FCCC and for CO_2 emissions reductions. After failing to get a national energy tax through Congress, however, the president quickly retreated: the 1993 White House Climate Change Action plan included about fifty voluntary federal programs aimed at promoting energy conservation but did not address greenhouse gas emissions directly. The administration projected the plan would reduce emissions by about 109 million tons per year by 2000—enough to return them to their 1990 levels of 1.58 billion tons.

By the time governments gathered for the First Conference of the Parties (COP 1)[32] in Berlin in spring 1995, however, it was clear the Clinton administration's plan was failing to stem the tide of U.S. CO_2 emissions, which were in fact almost 5 percent above 1990 levels. (This was partly because any gains achieved under the plan were offset by the declining average fuel efficiency of American cars, thanks largely to the boom in sport utility vehicles.[33]) In fact, only Germany and the United Kingdom were on target to reduce their emissions to 1990 levels by 2000.[34] Two additional factors lent urgency to the talks. First, in 1994, IPCC Chairman Bert Bolin (an international knowledge broker) had suggested that even if all Annex I governments met their commitments, it would not be sufficient to achieve the FCCC objective of preventing dangerous human interference with the climate system.[35] Second, in the spring and fall of 1994, negotiators had met five times to lay the groundwork for the upcoming COP, and each time the group was split by divisions between developed and developing nations.

Negotiators at COP 1 thus were faced with two questions: whether Annex I countries should adopt binding emissions reductions and whether emissions reductions obligations should be extended to Annex II countries. The parties ultimately agreed on the Berlin Mandate, which specified that any legal instrument that resulted from formal negotiations scheduled to take place in Kyoto, Japan, would impose emissions reductions only on Annex I countries; the 134 developing nations, including China, India, and Mexico, would be exempt. They did not, however, resolve the issue of binding emissions reductions. The United States pressed for a "joint implementation" mechanism that would allow industrialized countries to earn credit if they financed emissions reductions in developing countries where, presumably, they could be made more cheaply. The parties ultimately agreed to a modest version of such a mechanism but, more importantly, committed themselves to a schedule for adopting a protocol at COP 3, to be held in Kyoto in December 1997.

In August 1995, the Ad Hoc Group on the Berlin Mandate (AGBM) began meeting to establish the emissions targets for industrialized nations. In December 1995, in the midst of the AGBM meetings, the IPCC produced its Second Assessment Report. Having dramatically improved its climate models, the IPCC was willing to make projections with much greater confidence, and it concluded that "the balance of the evidence suggests that there is a discernible human influence on global climate."[36] On the other hand, scientists downgraded their estimates of the magnitude of global warming: the IPCC projected that the mean global temperature would increase between 1 and 3.5 degrees Celsius (2–6 degrees Fahrenheit) by 2100, and most believed it would be in the lower half of that range. It forecast, however, that global mean sea level would rise between six inches and three feet, and that changes in spatial and temporal precipitation patterns would occur.[37] Finally, the IPCC concluded that a 60–80 percent reduction in CO_2 emissions would be necessary just to stabilize concentrations of greenhouse gases.

Defining the Climate Change Problem in the United States

The 1995 IPCC report set the stage in the United States for a monumental battle to define the climate change problem in advance of the impending Kyoto meeting. Scientists had put the problem on the public agenda, and environmentalists eagerly adopted the scientific story, defining global warming as an imminent crisis. Their most powerful weapon was the vocal support of prominent scientists and highly visible consensus panels. However, powerful opponents, spearheaded by the oil and coal industries, responded with a well-financed lobbying campaign in a four-pronged attack: they argued that models of climate change are highly uncertain; that a warmer earth would not be so bad, particularly for the United States; that imposing policies to avert climate change would cripple the American economy; and that imposing emissions limits on industrialized nations without holding developing countries to similar targets would unfairly disadvantage the United States. Both sides launched all-out public relations campaigns, recognizing that whoever succeeded in defining the problem was likely to dictate the solution.

Environmentalists Use Scientists' Warnings. Among the earliest and most powerful proponents of policies to address climate change were members of the scientific community that studied the global climate. Throughout the 1980s, scientific consensus reports were accompanied by recommendations that the international community formulate policies *before* the effects became irreversible. Proponents of acting immediately portrayed such action as an "insurance policy against the potentially devastating and irreversible impacts of global warming."[38]

Environmentalists enthusiastically seized on scientific warnings to advance their overarching goal of limiting human impact on the natural environment. As early as 1984, the Environmental Defense Fund's Michael Oppenheimer wrote an op-ed piece for the *New York Times* featuring the evocative language that environmentalists are so adept at employing:

> With unusual unanimity, scientists testified at a recent Senate hearing that using the atmosphere as a garbage dump is about to catch up with us on a global scale. . . . Carbon dioxide emissions from fossil fuels combustion and other "greenhouse" gases are throwing a blanket over the Earth. . . . The sea level will rise as land ice melts and the oceans expand. Beaches will erode while wetlands will largely disappear. . . . Imagine life in a sweltering, smoggy New York without Long Island's beaches and you have glimpsed the world left to future generations.[39]

For environmentalists, climate change conveniently linked a host of concerns, from deforestation to air pollution, and implicated industrial nations' demand for growth and luxury.

The national media initially furthered environmentalists' cause by publicizing James Hansen's 1988 testimony before the Senate Committee on Energy and Natural Resources.[40] More importantly, the media linked scientists' climate change predictions to the heat, droughts, and freak weather events of 1988, thereby generating public alarm. The media also gave warming concerns a boost every time it covered the IPCC bulletins outlining the worldwide scientific consensus on the contours of the problem. By the late 1990s, the media were reporting on individual scientific studies as well, keeping a spotlight trained on the issue.

Opponents Challenge the Scientific Consensus. Opponents of climate change policies termed Hansen's testimony and the subsequent media coverage hysterical. To support these views, they cited a handful of outspoken scientific skeptics who challenged the IPCC estimates of both the likelihood and the consequences of climate change. Among the most prominent of these skeptics were Pat Michaels, assistant professor of climatology at the University of Virginia; S. Fred Singer, professor of climatology at the University of Virginia; Robert Balling, a geographer at the University of Arizona; and Richard Lindzen, an atmospheric physicist at MIT.

The skeptics pointed out that scientists had only a rudimentary understanding of the feedbacks in the climate system. For instance, they noted that early climate models contained only crude estimates of the effects of the ocean, yet ocean circulation is coupled with atmospheric circulation in a complex and critical way.[41] Furthermore, skeptics highlighted the potential impact of aerosols (small particles) and clouds on climate change and argued that the magnitude of observed warming to date was modest compared to the large, natural variability of the system and that scientists' predictions were based on theories and general circulation models (GCMs) that are difficult to confirm.[42]

In addition to emphasizing scientific uncertainty, some skeptics accused environmentalists of using science to achieve political ends—scaremongering to promote radical solutions to a problem for whose existence there was little evidence.[43] They charged that environmentalists' messages were invariably apocalyptic; that the media published such stories to sell newspapers and television time; and that the resulting publicity, in turn, abetted environmental groups' fundraising efforts.[44] Warnings about climate change, according to the skeptics, were part of a larger, coordinated effort to "establish international controls over industrial processes and business operations."[45]

Finally, climate change skeptics went directly after the IPCC and its members. In 1994, Frederick Seitz attacked the authors of the IPCC scientific summaries, contending that they had distorted the views of scientists and created the impression of a consensus where none existed. (Defenders of the process of writing the summary responded that it was cautious and consensual; that participants agreed to the summaries at plenary meetings; and that none had expressed subsequent dissatisfaction with the final product.[46]) In May 1996, opponents launched personal attacks on two eminent scientists, Benjamin Santer, a climate modeler at the Lawrence Livermore Laboratory, and Tom Wigley, a senior scientist at the National Center for Atmospheric Research. Seitz accused Santer of deleting references to scientific uncertainty from the 1995 IPCC report. Both the *Wall Street Journal* and the *New York Times* published this allegation, although neither paper confirmed its veracity with any of the participants in the process. (In fact, not one IPCC scientist confirmed the charges against Santer, and forty-two signed a letter to the *Wall Street Journal* in his defense.[47])

Although few in number, skeptics took advantage of the media's adherence to the journalistic norm of presenting "both sides" of an issue, regardless of the relative merits of each side's argument. Further magnifying their impact, opponents invested heavily in disseminating skeptics' views—financing the publication and distribution of books, magazines, pamphlets, and press releases to undermine the credibility of climate change theories among the public. In addition to funding a quarterly publication entitled *World Climate Review,* Western Fuels—a coal industry lobbying organization—spent $250,000 on a video entitled *The Greening of Planet Earth,* which argued that global warming will be beneficial for the human race and for the United States in particular. Economist Thomas Gale Moore, the predominant exponent of this theme, pointed out that service industries can prosper as equally in a warm climate (with air conditioning) as a cold one (with central heating). In fact, Moore argued, higher temperatures combined with more CO_2 in the atmosphere enhance plant and crop growth, thereby providing more food for our burgeoning global population.[48]

In the early 1990s, a group of utility and coal companies created the Information Council on the Environment (ICE) to promote arguments skeptical of climate change theory. The ICE ultimately disbanded when environmentalists exposed it to the media, but its goal of creating public confusion about climate change had already been accomplished. More enduring was the Global Climate Coalition (GCC), which spun off from the National Association of Manufacturers in 1989. The GCC had fifty-four industry members, primarily from the coal, oil, and automobile industries, and spent heavily on its anti–climate change campaign.[49]

Opponents Shift Focus to Costs. In addition to defining climate science as highly uncertain and ambiguous, opponents of climate change policies highlighted the costs of adopting policies to limit greenhouse gas emissions. According to them, policies to curb emissions of greenhouse gases would have exorbitant costs and would lead to "worldwide recession, rising unemployment, civil disturbances, and increased tension between nations as accusations of cheating and violations of international treaties inflamed passions."[50] Taking precautionary action, wrote one journalist in *Forbes,* could "spell the end of the American dream for us and the world."[51]

In the GCC's $13 million advertising campaign in advance of the Kyoto meeting in 1997,

> television viewers were warned that strict reductions in greenhouse gases would have catastrophic economic consequences, endangering the lifestyle of every American. Gasoline would shoot up by fifty cents or more a gallon; heating and electricity bills would soar, while higher energy costs would raise the price of almost everything Americans buy. The livelihoods of thousands of coal miners, auto-workers, and others employed in energy-related fields were on the line.[52]

Those hoping to prevent the imposition of CO_2 emissions limits seized on a 1990 study by the Bush administration's Council of Economic Advisors that estimated the cost of cutting carbon emissions by 20 percent by the year 2100 at between $800 billion and $3.6 trillion. The report concluded that until there was a solid scientific understanding of climate change, "there is no justification for imposing major costs on the economy in order to slow the growth of greenhouse gas emissions."[53] Opponents claimed that even a no-regrets policy, in which nations adopt such practices as conserving energy and increasing reliance on energy-efficient vehicles and public transit, would be nothing more than a "first, expensive, and ineffectual step down the road to programs that will cripple one of the most vital foundations of modern civilization—our energy supplies."[54]

The environmental Alliance to Save Energy responded with an analysis showing that U.S. carbon emissions could be cut by 25 percent by 2005 and 70 percent by 2030 at a net savings of $2.3 trillion over forty years.[55] The 1991 NAS report, *Policy Implications of Global Warming,* concurred, arguing that the United States could reduce its greenhouse gas emissions between 10 and 40 percent of 1990 levels at low cost, or even net savings, if the proper policies were implemented. A 1992 study by William Cline, of the Institute for International Economics, suggested that "social cost-benefit ratios are favorable for an aggressive program of international abatement."[56] Cline pointed out that opponents of climate change policies failed to take into account the possibility of cost-effective energy efficiency measures and technological innovation.

But the opponents of climate change policies dismissed efforts to rebut their arguments; well-organized and -funded, they were adept at disseminating their perspective. At the Rio Earth Summit in 1992, the executive director of the GCC maintained that some of the proposals under consideration could cost the United States $95 billion and 550,000 jobs.[57] The Coalition for Vehicle Choice, financed by the U.S. auto industry and related groups, spent years trying to convince small business, labor, and local civic groups throughout the United States that the treaty would be "bad for America." In October 1997, immediately prior to the Kyoto meeting, the group ran an ad to that effect in the *Washington Post* with the endorsement of 1,300 groups.[58]

Opponents Raise the Equity Issue. Finally, in the mid-1990s, opponents began framing the approach embodied in the Kyoto Protocol as inequitable—making the protocol, and not climate change, the problem. They insisted it would be unfair for developing countries to escape commitments to greenhouse gas emissions reductions, since in the future they were likely to be the major emitters while the industrialized nations' share of emissions would decline dramatically. They pointed out that several large developing countries—including China, India, South Korea, and Mexico—were already producing 44 percent of global fossil fuel emissions and were likely to surpass the emissions levels of the developed countries between 2020 and 2030. In addition, said critics, developing countries were responsible for much of the deforestation and other land-use practices that had eliminated carbon sinks.[59]

The developing nations and many environmentalists responded that the United States, with only 4 percent of the world's population, generated one-quarter of the world's greenhouse gas emissions and that industrialized nations were responsible for 70 percent of the human-made greenhouse gases currently in the atmosphere. Moreover, they noted that developing nations were likely to suffer the most serious consequences of climate change but were least well positioned, financially or technologically, to mitigate, adapt to, or recover from those impacts. Dr. Mark Mwandosya of Tanzania, chairman of the developing country caucus at Kyoto, pointed out: "Very many of us are struggling to attain a decent standard of living for our peoples, and yet we are constantly told that we must share in the effort to reduce emissions so that industrialized countries can continue to enjoy the benefits of their wasteful lifestyle."[60]

The Kyoto Protocol

As the Kyoto meeting drew near, the battle to shape the U.S. position intensified. In hopes of creating support for U.S. leadership, in June 1997, more than 2,500 American scientists endorsed the *Scientists' Statement on Global Climatic Disruption*. The statement claimed that:

> further accumulation of greenhouse gases commits the earth irreversibly to further global climatic change and consequent ecological, economic, and social disruption. The risks associated with such changes justify preventive

action through reductions in emissions of greenhouse gases. It is time for the United States, as the largest emitter of greenhouse gases, to . . . demonstrate leadership in a global effort.[61]

After receiving the statement, President Clinton—addressing a Special Session of the UN General Assembly—said that "the science [of climate change] is clear and compelling," and he promised to bring to the Kyoto conference "a strong American commitment to realistic and binding limits that will significantly reduce our emissions of greenhouse gases."[62] The following month, Clinton launched an effort to convince the public that climate change was real by holding a conference of experts and a series of well-publicized regional panels.[63]

The administration's international credibility was dubious, however, given that in 1996 U.S. emissions of greenhouse gases grew 3.4 percent, and by 1997, U.S. greenhouse gas emissions were about 7.4 percent greater than they had been in 1990.[64] At this rate of growth, U.S. emissions of greenhouse gases promised to be 13 percent above 1990 levels by 2000.[65] Further hampering the administration's ability to negotiate was the passage by the U.S. Senate, on June 12, 1997, of a nonbinding resolution (the Byrd-Hagel Amendment) that it would not give its advice and consent to any agreement that did not require developing countries to reduce their emissions or that would result in "serious harm to the economy of the United States." Concerned about building domestic support for the treaty, Clinton began emphasizing the importance of cooperation by China and other developing nations. At the seventh AGBM meeting in Bonn in October, U.S. negotiators pressed the other parties to commit both developing and industrialized nations to emissions reductions.

After meeting resistance in Bonn, the United States again raised the issue at the eighth and final AGBM session, which coincided with the third COP in Kyoto. Nearly 6,000 UN delegates from more than 160 countries attended the ten-day conference that opened on December 1, 1997. In addition, 3,600 representatives of environmental and industry groups and nearly 3,500 reporters poured into Kyoto. Leading the sixty-member U.S. delegation, Undersecretary of State Stuart Eizenstadt began by taking a hard line, saying, "We want an agreement, but we are not going [to Kyoto] for an agreement at any cost."[66] Undaunted, both the German and British ministers proposed substantial reductions in greenhouse gas emissions from their 1990 levels by 2010: Germany proposed a 15 percent cut; the United Kingdom, a 20 percent cut. Meanwhile, the latest computer models were projecting that greenhouse gas emissions would have to be lowered by 70 percent to negate global warming.[67]

By the fourth day of the Kyoto meeting, a *New York Times* editorial declared that a "near miracle" would be required to salvage an agreement. The thorniest issue remained the degree to which developing countries would be required to impose emissions controls. Led by the Chinese delegation, the developing countries adamantly resisted U.S. pressure, so in a last-ditch effort to facilitate international agreement without provoking a domestic backlash, President

Clinton dispatched Vice President Al Gore to give the American delegates more flexibility. On Monday, December 8, Gore told members of the conference that President Clinton would allow the U.S. delegation to offer emissions reductions beyond those originally proposed (1990 levels between 2008 and 2012) in return for opening the door in Kyoto to language requiring emissions reductions by developing countries. COP Chairman Raul Estrada proposed a compromise that would allow developing countries to reduce emissions voluntarily and gave Annex I nations the option of accepting differentiated emissions reductions commitments for 2008–2012. In the negotiations that followed, the Chinese led a bloc of developing nations (the G77) who vigorously opposed the compromise, however, and the resulting protocol, which emerged just as the meeting was closing, embodied the United States' worst case scenario: it went beyond the original target for U.S. reductions but provided no mechanism for making developing countries reduce their emissions.[68]

Under the Kyoto Protocol, the European Union must reduce emissions of six greenhouse gases by 8 percent below 1990 levels, the U.S. by 7 percent, and Japan by 6 percent. Twenty-one other industrialized nations have a 5.2-percent target. Annex I nations have five options for meeting their emissions reductions obligations: they can put in place policies to lower national emissions; they can enhance carbon sinks, such as forests; they can take advantage of emissions-trading opportunities once such a trading system is developed; they can engage in joint implementation, which allows Annex I parties to earn credit for projects that lower emissions in other Annex I countries; or they can get credit for employing "Clean Development Mechanisms" (CDMs), through which developed countries transfer energy-efficiency technology to developing countries. Developing countries are allowed to "opt in" to emissions controls but are not bound by mandatory emissions reductions, and delegates did not back a U.S. proposal that industrial nations be allowed to trade "emissions quotas" but instead agreed to consider such mechanisms in 1998.

Opponents of climate change policies were appalled by the agreement; in a press conference before leaving Kyoto, Sen. Chuck Hagel (coauthor of the Byrd-Hagel Amendment) vowed that there was "no way, if the president signs this, that the vote in the United States Senate will even be close. We will kill this bill."[69]

Selling the Kyoto Protocol Back Home

Recognizing that he lacked Senate support, President Clinton decided not to submit the protocol for ratification but instead proposed a five-year, $6.3 billion package of tax breaks and research spending in pursuit of the protocol's emissions reductions goals—measures that most experts regarded as too modest to have much impact on America's $500 billion fossil fuel–based economy.[70] By executive order, Clinton also directed the federal government, the world's largest energy consumer, to reduce petroleum use in federally owned cars to 20 percent below 1990 levels by 2005 and reduce greenhouse gases from federal buildings by 30 percent by 2010.[71] At the same time, the administration continued its campaign to persuade the public that the science underpinning the protocol was valid.

Even as the Clinton administration struggled to generate public support for climate change policies, opponents geared up for the Senate battle. Recognizing the political potency of the scientific consensus generated by the IPCC, by early spring 1998, a high-powered group including the American Petroleum Institute, Chevron, and Exxon had already planned a multimillion-dollar campaign to undermine that consensus. Aimed primarily at the public, the plan was to recruit a cadre of skeptical scientists and train them to convey their views persuasively to science writers, editors, columnists, and newspaper correspondents.[72] Some tactics adopted by opponents raised eyebrows: Frederick Seitz, director of the conservative Marshall Institute and former member of the National Academy of Sciences, circulated among thousands of scientists a petition against climate change policies, accompanied by a letter on stationery designed to resemble NAS letterhead. The Academy quickly disavowed the letter, which claimed to report on a scientific study concluding that CO_2 emissions did not pose a climatic threat.[73]

In response to industry's anti–climate change campaign, in May 1998, the Pew Charitable Trusts established the Pew Center for Global Climate Change, funded by a $5 million annual grant from the foundation and administered by Eileen Claussen, former deputy assistant secretary of state for environmental affairs. The center's objective was to bolster the credibility of climate change science. Getting on the bandwagon, American Electric Power, U.S. Generating Company, Maytag, Whirlpool, 3M, Toyota, Sunoco, United Technologies, Boeing, and Lockheed Martin endorsed the Center's goals: in an ad published in the *New York Times*, they publicly accepted the views of most scientists that enough was known about the environmental impact of climate change to take steps to address the consequences, and they promised to seek new ways to reduce their own emissions of greenhouse gases.[74] By the fall of 1998, twenty major U.S. companies, including three electric power companies and two oil companies, had joined the Pew Center. In October, the international oil companies Royal Dutch/Shell and British Petroleum also committed themselves to substantial voluntary reductions in their emissions.

Proponents of climate change policies also began publicizing a set of Clinton administration reports that downplayed the costs of cutting CO_2 emissions. A report issued in the late 1990s by the Department of Energy buttressed environmentalists' position that the United States could reduce its fuel use by making fairly simple and inexpensive changes that would have little impact on the economy.[75] A 1997 report by the Interlaboratory Working Group, a consortium of U.S. national labs, also concluded that large, low-cost energy savings were possible in the United States.[76] Finally, a 1998 report from Clinton's Council of Economic Advisors reiterated the NAS claim that if policies were designed correctly, the effects on energy prices and the costs to the United States of meeting the Kyoto Protocol emissions targets could be extremely modest.[77] In response to these reports, the industry-sponsored Edison Power Research Institute commissioned its own series of economic studies suggesting that agriculture, forestry, and outdoor recreation "are all projected to benefit from a slightly warmer, wetter, CO_2-enriched world."[78]

While factions in the United States debated the potential costs of implementing the Kyoto Protocol, it was increasingly unclear to scientists whether—even if its obligations were fulfilled—the treaty would slow global warming. In an analysis published in *Science* in January 1998, former IPCC chair Bert Bolin predicted that the CO_2 level in the atmosphere would climb to 382 ppmv (from 370 ppmv) by 2010 even if countries strictly obeyed their Kyoto commitments. Bolin noted that the Kyoto reductions would be "an important first step" but would be "far from what is required to reach the goal of stabilizing the concentration of CO_2 in the atmosphere."[79]

The Hague, 2000

This was the context in which talks to resolve outstanding issues from Kyoto resumed at the fourth COP in Buenos Aires, Argentina, which began in early November 1998. Hoping to facilitate consensus there, the Clinton administration had worked assiduously to forge bilateral agreements with developing countries on voluntarily limiting their CO_2 emissions. By the time negotiations got under way, however, only Argentina had agreed to join Annex I voluntarily and thereby accept emissions reductions obligations. (Thereafter, Kazakhstan and Bolivia announced their willingness to do the same.) On November 12, 1998, the United States finally signed the Kyoto Protocol, adding its name to the collection of more than 150 signatories (only one of which, Romania, had actually ratified the treaty). Little of substance was accomplished at the meeting, however.

Among the main issues that remained unresolved at the close of COP 4 were the role of developing nations and the status of international emissions trading. In a promising development on the former, the G77 was no longer monolithic: China and India were leading the faction opposed to emissions limits on developing countries, but African and Latin American countries were increasingly interested in making emissions reductions in exchange for aid. The second point was stickier: U.S. negotiators were tenacious about emissions trading because they thought it might defuse domestic opposition, but Europeans and many third world nations objected that the United States was trying to buy its way out of reducing its own emissions.[80]

As officials around the globe wrestled to find solutions everyone could agree on, the scientific evidence continued to pour in. In March 1999, a study published in the journal *Nature* concluded that the growing season in the northern temperate zone, from the sub-Arctic to the Mediterranean region, had lengthened by about eleven days since 1970. The authors attributed the shift to a rise in daily temperatures caused by the general warming of the climate. Their findings were consistent with a series of studies reported in 1996 and 1997 that detected early spring and a longer growing season in the northern hemisphere.[81] Moreover, the effects of climate change were becoming increasingly visible and dramatic: in December 1999, scientists reported that 1999 had joined 1998 as one of the two warmest years on record. The following summer, eyewitness reports of open water from melting ice at the North Pole made headlines. A scientist at the Applied Physics Laboratory at the University of Washington confirmed that polar ice thickness had decreased from 10.2 feet in the 1960s and 1970s to 5.9 feet in the 1990s. Nor was the decrease an isolated phenomenon; it was widespread in the central Arctic Ocean and most pronounced in the eastern Arctic. Such findings confirmed climate model predictions that the Arctic would be among the first regions to respond to a global warming trend.[82]

Although the influx of scientific reports lent urgency to the climate change talks, the sixth Conference of the Parties (COP 6) in the Hague in November 2000 foundered once again. The Hague conference was supposed to be the final meeting to set policies for greenhouse gas emissions reductions, and efforts to translate vague commitments to specific policies promised to be contentious. Prior to the meeting, the Clinton administration again made its precautionary framing clear; testifying before the Senate Foreign Relations and Energy and Natural Resources Committee in September 2000, the undersecretary for global affairs, Frank Loy, argued that:

> As policymakers, we must base our decisions on the best scientific evidence available. But we would fail in our duty to safeguard the health and well-being of our citizens and the environment they cherish if we waited to act until the details of the climate system have been fully understood. The science tells us that this would be a recipe for disaster, for we will only fully confirm the predictions of climate science when we experience them, at which point it will be too late. Instead, we should ask, "Are the risks great enough to justify taking action?" When it comes to the challenge of climate change, the answer is an emphatic "yes."[83]

At the same time, to placate its critics, the administration continued to embrace the language of economic growth, efficiency, cost-effectiveness, and the primacy of markets. U.S. negotiators left for the Hague determined to obtain unlimited use of emissions-trading mechanisms and credit for land-use practices included in the agreement.

Although negotiators were initially hopeful, after eleven days of draining bargaining among the 170 countries attending, U.S. insistence that it be permitted to meet its greenhouse gas reduction obligations using forest and agricultural land management, rather than CO_2 emissions reductions, proved to be an insurmountable hurdle. Critics were dubious about relying on forests to curb CO_2, pointing out that research suggested the role of forests and soils in sequestering CO_2 was not straightforward.[84] Through the final night and into the early morning, environmental groups helped the European delegation analyze a variety of formulas for calculating carbon equivalents attributable to forest protection. At 3:00 A.M., a small cadre of British, American, and European diplomats shook hands on a deal; the following day, however, the complex formula turned out to be unacceptable to many in the European Union. Jurgen Tritin, the German environment minister, explained that his country's opposition to forest credits was deeply rooted and derived from a sense that the United States and its collaborators were trying to get something for nothing.[85]

Observers were struck by the irony that while previous talks had stumbled because of irreconcilable differences between developing and developed nations, or between environmentalists and industry, the Hague negotiations fell apart primarily because of a schism within the environmental movement itself. While mainstream American environmental groups, as well as many climate change scientists, supported the pragmatic U.S. solutions of emissions trading and forest conservation credits, hard liners, such as Greenpeace, backed the German position. "We're better off with no deal than a bad deal," crowed Bill Hare of Greenpeace moments after the negotiations ended.[86] The hard-line groups equated compromise with corruption and abdication to business interests but, ironically, found themselves allied with business in opposition to any treaty. For other environmentalists, though, the failure to reach agreement at the Hague was particularly worrisome in light of the upcoming U.S. election. Dr. Michael Oppenheimer, senior scientist at Environmental Defense, warned that if George W. Bush became president, it would only become more difficult for American and European negotiators to find common ground.

OUTCOMES

Shortly after another round of talks in Ottawa collapsed in January 2000, a new report issued by the IPCC suggested that earlier climate change estimates may have been conservative and that the global climate could warm by as much as 10.5 degrees Fahrenheit by the end of the twenty-first century. The IPCC confirmed that temperatures rose one degree Fahrenheit in the twentieth century, blamed at least part of the increase on fossil fuel combustion, and warned that it represents the most rapid change in ten millennia.[87] At a separate scientific meeting in San Francisco in February, scientists attributed the recently documented melting of equatorial glaciers in Africa and Peru to global warming.[88] Other observational evidence that the climate was already warming was pouring in. Scientists documented thawing permafrost, delayed freezing, earlier break-up dates of river and lake ice, and longer growing seasons at mid- to high latitudes.[89] And a study reported in *Nature* suggested yet another concern: droughts caused by global warming could prompt northern soils to release CO_2 into the air, speeding up changes in the climate.[90]

In February 2001, the IPCC released a report entitled "Climate Change 2001: Impacts, Adaptations, and Vulnerability" that summarized the work of 700 scientists. The 1,000-page report concluded ominously that "projected climate changes during the 21st century have the potential to lead to future

large-scale and possible irreversible changes in Earth systems," with "continental and global consequences." Among those consequences may be more
"freak" weather conditions, such as cyclones, floods, and droughts; massive
displacement of population in the most-affected areas; greater risk of diseases
like malaria; and extinction of entire species, as their habitat is eliminated.
Over time, said the report, global warming is also likely to cause large reductions in the Greenland and West Antarctic ice sheets and a substantial slowing
of the circulation of warm water in the North Atlantic. Finally, the report also
warned that changes in rainfall patterns due to climate change, combined with
patterns of population growth, would likely lead to enormous pressure on
water supplies.[91]

Despite mounting concern among scientific experts, the election of President George W. Bush and Vice President Dick Cheney—both former oilmen—
dimmed hopes for U.S. leadership on a climate change agreement. The newly
elected president took office saying that more research on climate change was
needed before any policies were undertaken and, in March 2001, the president
vowed not to seek CO_2 emissions reductions. He outlined his view in a letter
to four prominent Republican senators who had been critical of his campaign
promise to support CO_2 emissions trading. "At a time when California has
already experienced energy shortages, and other Western states are worried
about price and availability of energy this summer," Bush said, "we must be
very careful not to take actions that could harm consumers. This is especially
true, given the incomplete state of scientific knowledge of the causes of and
solutions to, global climate change and the lack of commercially available
technologies for removing and storing carbon dioxide."[92] Although justified
as a response to an "energy crisis," Bush supporters attributed his change of
heart to a last-minute lobbying campaign by congressional Republicans and
top industry leaders.[93]

As if to put an exclamation point on its position, the administration's 2002
budget proposal cut spending on energy efficiency programs by 15 percent.[94]
In addition, Bush's energy plan, released in May 2001, emphasized loosening
environmental regulations and developing new fossil fuel supplies.[95] After
meeting with the president in early April and failing to change his mind, European leaders announced their intention to move forward with the Kyoto
process even without American leadership. Admonishing the president, the
European Union's environmental commissioner Margot Wallstrom said that
"other countries are reacting very strongly against the U.S."[96]

The Bush administration's position, while pleasing to some industrialists
and their congressional supporters, perplexed other members of his own
party, many of whom have solid environmental records.[97] Furthermore, public opinion polls revealed substantial public support for action on global
warming. Confirming the results of many previous surveys, a July 2001 *New
York Times*/CBS News Poll found that 72 percent of the public believed it was
necessary to take immediate steps to counter global warming; more than half
said the United States should abide by the Kyoto accord.[98] And a January 2001

Gallup poll found that 40 percent of Americans worried about global warming "a great deal," up five points since 1989 and much higher than the level of concern reported (27 percent) in 1997.[99]

Recognizing his political vulnerability, Bush commissioned an expert panel that could provide cover for yet another flip-flop on the issue. Not surprisingly, the panel—which comprised eleven leading atmospheric scientists including Richard Lindzen, an outspoken climate change skeptic—"reaffirmed the mainstream scientific view that the earth's atmosphere is getting warmer and that human activity is largely responsible."[100] Although the president subsequently conceded the scientific point, he continued to inflame Europeans by opposing the Kyoto Protocol and emissions limits as a mechanism for addressing the problem.

Bush's resistance notwithstanding, in November 2001, negotiators representing 178 countries hammered out the details of the Kyoto Protocol, and many large industrial countries said they were likely to ratify the agreement.[101] Although it was only a first step, environmentalists were pleased: "The parties have reached complete agreement on what's an infraction, how you decide a case, and what are the penalties," said David Doniger of the Natural Resources Defense Council. "That's as good as it gets in international relations."[102]

CONCLUSIONS

Domestic opposition has hampered efforts to build the support that American leaders need to pursue climate change policies. Opposing greenhouse gas reductions is a potent coalition of fossil fuel and fuel-dependent industries that have both deep pockets and strong, longstanding ties to elected officials. This coalition has lobbied intensely to ensure that members of Congress are aware of their position. They have also undertaken a costly public relations battle in which they wield a potent threat: economic collapse. As they define the problem, the certain economic costs of acting vastly outweigh the highly uncertain and potentially negligible risks of inaction. The extensive efforts by opponents of climate change policies to undermine the credibility of mainstream scientists reinforce the importance of problem definition in American politics—not only in bringing about policy change but in preventing it.

Daniel Sarewitz and Roger Pielke suggest that environmentalists have erred in focusing on greenhouse gas emissions. They argue that such a focus is politically divisive, pitting developing countries against industrialized nations and fossil fuel industries against environmentalists. They recommend instead emphasizing society's vulnerability to weather, arguing that:

> as an organizing principle for political action, vulnerability to weather and climate offers everything that global warming does not: a clear, uncontroversial story rooted in concrete human experience, observable in the present, definable in terms of unambiguous and widely shared human values, such as the fundamental rights to a secure shelter, safe community, and a sustainable environment.[103]

Rather than adopt a new problem definition, some proponents of climate change policies have tried to disrupt alliances among economic interests in the United States by pushing for market-based mechanisms, such as emissions trading schemes, to reduce greenhouse gas emissions worldwide. Such an approach recognizes that within the United States, where low energy prices and unlimited energy use have come to be seen as rights, climate change solutions that do not require major disruptions in energy supply or prices are more likely to be favorably received.[104] Moreover, many American environmental groups are increasingly disposed to work cooperatively with industry rather than impose top-down regulations. In mid-October 2000, Environmental Defense and a handful of the world's largest corporations—including Shell, DuPont, Alcan, Pechiney, and Ontario Power Generation—formed the Partnership for Climate Action to "champion market-based mechanisms as a means of achieving early and credible action on reducing greenhouse gas emissions that is efficient and cost-effective."[105] Gaining international acceptance for such policies is a challenge, however; in some European countries, such as Germany and France, environmentalists have substantial political clout and are less inclined to let industry dictate policies. Still, to the surprise of many observers, in the fall of 2001, the European Union agreed to trading mechanisms for greenhouse gases to gain the support of Japan, Canada, and Russia.

QUESTIONS TO CONSIDER

- Why has the United States resisted efforts to forge international agreements on CO_2 emissions reduction policies, and why is the European Union's position so different?
- What are the prospects for international agreement on policies to prevent or mitigate the damage from climate change, and why?
- Should Americans be concerned about the pace at which the U.S. government is responding to this issue?

Notes

1. Statement of Dr. James Hansen, Director, NASA Goddard Institute for Space Studies, Greenhouse Effect and Global Climate Change, Hearing Before the Committee on Energy and Natural Resources, United States Senate, 100th Congress, First Session on the Greenhouse Effect and Global Climate Change, Part 2 (June 23, 1988).
2. Norman J. Vig, "Introduction," in *The Global Environment: Institutions, Law, and Policy,* ed. Norman J. Vig and Regina S. Axelrod (Washington, D.C.: CQ Press, 1999), 3.
3. Ian H. Rowlands, "Classical Theories of International Relations," in *International Relations and Global Climate Change* (Cambridge: MIT Press, 2001), 43–65.
4. Stephen Krasner, quoted in Vig, "Introduction," 4.
5. Helen Milner, *Interests, Institutions, and Information: Domestic Politics and International Relations* (Princeton: Princeton University Press, 1997), 9–10.
6. Darrell M. West and Burdett A. Loomis, *The Sound of Money: How Political Interests Get What They Want* (New York: Norton, 1999).
7. Robert D. Putnam, "Diplomacy and Domestic Politics: The Logic of Two-Level Games," *International Organization* 42 (3): 434.

8. Ian Rowlands, *The Politics of Global Atmospheric Change* (New York: Manchester University Press, 1995); Matthew Paterson, *Global Warming and Climate Politics* (New York: Routledge, 1996).
9. Roger Revelle and Hans E. Suess, "Carbon Dioxide Exchange Between Atmosphere and Ocean and the Question of an Increase of Atmospheric CO_2 During the Past Decade," *Tellus* 9 (1957): 18–27.
10. President's Science Advisory Committee, *Restoring the Quality of Our Environment: Report of the Environmental Pollution Panel* (Washington, D.C.: The White House, 1965), 126–127.
11. See, for example, William W. Kellogg, "Global Influences of Mankind on the Climate," in *Climatic Change*, ed. John Gribbin (New York: Cambridge University Press, 1978), 207–227.
12. National Academy of Sciences, *Carbon Dioxide and Climate: A Scientific Assessment* (Washington, D.C.: National Academy of Sciences, 1979).
13. Enduring cooperation among meteorologists began with the First International Meteorological Conference in 1853. Twenty years later, the International Meteorological Organization (IMO) was established. After World War II, the IMO turned into the World Meteorological Organization (WMO), and the latter began operating in 1951. See Paterson, *Global Warming.*
14. Quoted in William W. Kellogg, "Predictions of a Global Cooling," *Nature* (August 16, 1979): 615.
15. John Houghton, *Global Warming: The Complete Briefing*, 2d ed. (New York: Cambridge University Press, 1997).
16. Stephen Seidel and Dale Keyes, *Can We Delay a Greenhouse Warming? The Effectiveness and Feasibility of Options to Slow a Build-Up of Carbon Dioxide in the Atmosphere* (Washington, D.C.: U.S. Environmental Protection Agency, September 1983).
17. Rowlands, *The Politics of Global Atmospheric Change*, 72.
18. World Meteorological Organization, *Report of the International Conference on the Assessment of the Role of Carbon Dioxide and of Other Greenhouse Gases in Climate Variations and Associated Impacts, Villach, Austria, 9–15 October*, WMO Publication no. 661 (Geneva: World Meteorological Association, 1986).
19. Quoted in Michael Molitor, "The United Nations Climate Change Agreements," in *The Global Environment*, ed. Vig and Axelrod, 221.
20. A framework convention is a broad but formal agreement; a protocol contains more concrete commitments. Both must be signed and ratified by participating nations.
21. Molitor, "The United Nations Climate Change Agreements."
22. Paraphrasing United Nations General Assembly Resolution 44/207 (1989).
23. Quoted in Paterson, *Global Warming*, 37.
24. Quoted in Michael Weisskopf, "Bush Says More Data On Warming Needed," *Washington Post*, April 18, 1990, A1.
25. IPCC Working Group I, *Climate Change: The IPCC Scientific Assessment*, ed. J. T. Houghton, G. J. Jenkins, and J. J. Ephraums (New York: Cambridge University Press, 1990).
26. Rowlands, *The Politics of Atmospheric Change*, 79.
27. John Hunt, "U.S. Stand on Global Warming Attacked," *Financial Times*, August 30, 1990, 4.
28. Rowlands, *The Politics of Atmospheric Change*, 80.
29. Molitor, "The United Nations Climate Change Agreements."
30. For the complete text of the FCCC, http://www.unfccc.de.
31. C. Boyden Gray and David B. Rivkin, Jr., "A 'No Regrets' Environmental Policy," *Foreign Policy* 83 (summer 1991): 47–65.
32. The COP comprises representatives of each signatory nation.
33. Steven Greenhouse, "Officials Say U.S. is Unlikely to Meet Clean-Air Goal for 2000," *New York Times*, March 30, 1995, A6.

34. Molitor, "The United Nations Climate Change Agreement."
35. Bert Bolin, "Report to the Ninth Session of the INC/FCCC" (Geneva: IPCC, February 7, 1994), 2.
36. IPCC Working Group I, *Climate Change 1995: The Science of Climate Change*, ed. J. T. Houghton et al. (New York: Cambridge University Press, 1996), 4.
37. Ibid.
38. Stuart Eizenstadt, Under Secretary of State for Economic, Business, and Agricultural Affairs, Statement before the Senate Foreign Relations Committee, February 11, 1998.
39. Quoted in Daniel Sarewitz and Roger A. Pielke, Jr., "Breaking the Global-Warming Gridlock," *Atlantic Monthly*, July 2000, 57.
40. Stephen H. Schneider, *Global Warming: Are We Entering the Greenhouse Century?* (San Francisco: Sierra Club Books, 1989).
41. Houghton, *Global Warming*.
42. To estimate the influence of greenhouse gases in changing climate, researchers run models for a few (simulated) decades and compare the statistics of the models' output to measures of the climate. Although observations of both past and present climate confirm many of the predictions of the prevailing models of climate change, at least some of the data used to validate the models are themselves model outputs. Moreover, the assumptions and data used to construct GCMs heavily influence their predictions, and those elements are themselves selected by scientists who already know what they expect to find. See Steve Rayner, "Predictions and Other Approaches to Climate Change Policy," in *Prediction: Science, Decision Making and the Future of Nature*, ed. Daniel Sarewitz, Roger A. Pielke, Jr., and Radford Byerly, Jr. (Washington, D.C.: Island Press, 2000), 269–296.
43. Michael L. Parsons, *The Truth Behind the Myth* (New York: Plenum Press, 1995).
44. Patrick J. Michaels, *Sound and Fury: The Science and Politics of Global Warming* (Washington, D.C.: Cato Institute, 1992).
45. S. Fred Singer, "Benefits of Global Warming," *Society* 29 (March–April 1993): 33.
46. Ross Gelbspan, *The Heat Is On: The High Stakes Battle over Earth's Threatened Climate* (New York: Addison-Wesley, 1997).
47. William K. Stevens, "At Hot Center of the Debate on Global Warming," *New York Times*, August 6, 1996, C1.
48. Thomas Gale Moore, "Why Global Warming Would Be Good for You," *Public Interest* (winter 1995): 83–99.
49. Gelbspan, *The Heat Is On*.
50. Thomas Gale Moore, *Climate of Fear: Why We Shouldn't Worry About Global Warming* (Washington, D.C.: Cato Institute), 1–2.
51. Warren T. Brookes, "The Global Warming Panic," *Forbes*, December 25, 1989, 98.
52. Gale E. Christianson, *Greenhouse: The 200-Year Story of Global Warming* (New York: Penguin Books, 1999), 258.
53. U.S. Council of Economic Advisors, *Economic Report of the President* (Washington, D.C.: U.S. Government Printing Office, February 1990), 214.
54. Moore, *Climate of Fear*, 2.
55. Rowlands, *The Politics of Atmospheric Change*, 139.
56. William R. Cline, *Global Warming: The Economic Stakes* (Washington, D.C.: Institute for International Economics, 1992), 1–2.
57. Rowlands, *The Politics of Atmospheric Change*, 137.
58. John J. Fialka, "Clinton's Efforts to Curb Global Warming Draws Some Business Support, but It May Be Too Late," *Wall Street Journal*, October 22, 1997, A24.
59. Frank Loy, Undersecretary for Global Affairs, Statement before the Committee on Foreign Relations and the Committee on Energy and Natural Resources, United States Senate (September 28, 2000).

60. Quoted in William K. Stevens, "Greenhouse Gas Issue: Haggling Over Fairness," *New York Times*, November 30, 1997, 6.
61. Quoted in Molitor, "The United Nations Climate Change Agreements," 219–220.
62. Quoted in ibid., 220.
63. Willett Kempton, "How the Public Views Climate Change," *Environment* 39 (November 1997): 12–22.
64. John H. Cushman, Jr., "U.S. Says Its Greenhouse Gas Emissions Are at Highest Rate in Years," *New York Times*, October 21, 1997, A22.
65. John H. Cushman, Jr., "Why the U.S. Fell Short of Ambitious Goals for Reducing Greenhouse Gases," *New York Times*, October 20, 1997, A15.
66. Quoted in Christianson, *Greenhouse*, 255.
67. Ibid., 256.
68. Molitor, "The United Nations Climate Change Agreements."
69. Quoted in James Bennet, "Warm Globe, Hot Politics," *New York Times*, December 11, 1997, A1. The protocol takes effect once it is ratified by at least fifty-five nations; the terms become binding on an individual country after its government ratifies the treaty.
70. Joby Warrick, "Reassessing Kyoto Agreement, Scientists See Little Environmental Advantage," *Washington Post*, February 13, 1998, A14.
71. Frank Loy, "Remarks at the International Climate Change Partnership Earth Technology Forum" (Washington, D.C., October 30, 2000).
72. John H. Cushman, Jr., "Industrial Group Plans to Battle Climate Treaty," *New York Times*, April 26, 1998, A1.
73. William K. Stevens, "Science Academy Disputes Attacks on Global Warming," *New York Times*, April 22, 1998, A20.
74. John H. Cushman, Jr., "New Policy Center Seeks to Steer the Debate on Climate Change," *New York Times*, May 8, 1998, A13.
75. Andrew Revkin, "The Tree Trap," *New York Times*, November 26, 2000, 16.
76. Interlaboratory Working Group, *Scenarios of U.S. Carbon Reductions: Potential Impacts of Energy Technologies by 2010 and Beyond* (Berkeley and Oak Ridge: Lawrence Berkeley National Laboratory and Oak Ridge National Laboratory, September 1997), Rept. No. LBNL-40533 and ORNL-444.
77. Council of Economic Advisors, *The Kyoto Protocol and the President's Policies to Address Climate Change: Administration Economic Analysis* (Washington, D.C.: Executive Office of the President, July 1998).
78. Robert Mendelsohn et al., "Introduction," in *The Impact of Climate Change on the United States Economy*, ed. Robert Mendelsohn and James E. Neumann (New York: Cambridge University Press, 1999), 15.
79. Bert Bolin, "The Kyoto Negotiations on Climate Change: A Science Perspective," *Science*, January 16, 1998, 330–331.
80. John H. Cushman, Jr., "Big Problem, Big Problems: Getting to Work on Global Warming," *New York Times*, December 8, 1998, G4.
81. William K. Stevens, "March May Soon Be Coming in Like a Lamb," *New York Times*, March 2, 1999, A1.
82. John Noble Wilford, "Open Water at the Pole Is Not so Surprising, Experts Say," *New York Times*, August 29, 2000, C1.
83. Loy, Statement.
84. By employing prudent land use practices, the United States argued, parties can "sequester" CO_2—that is, they can store it in wood and soils, thereby preventing its release into the atmosphere. Critics were dubious about heavy reliance on forests to curb CO_2, however, pointing out that while forests currently do offset about one-quarter of the world's industrial CO_2 emissions, research at the Hadley Center in the United Kingdom indicated that many of the recently planted forests would, by the middle of the twenty-first century, begin releasing carbon back into the

atmosphere. Moreover, they noted, during the same period, warming was likely to increase the amount of carbon released by soils, particularly in the peatland forests of the northern latitudes.

85. Andrew Revkin, "Treaty Talks Fail to Find Consensus in Global Warming," *New York Times*, November 26, 2001.

86. Quoted in Andrew C. Revkin, "Odd Culprits in Collapse of Climate Talks," *New York Times*, November 28, 2000, C1.

87. "Climate Panel Reaffirms Major Warming Threat," *New York Times*, January 23, 2001, D8.

88. Kilimanjaro has lost 82 percent of the icecap it had in 1912. In the Alps, scientists estimate 90 percent of the ice volume of a century ago will be gone by 2025. See Eric Pianin, "U.N. Report Forecasts Crises Brought On by Global Warming," *Washington Post*, February 20, 2001, A6.

89. Ibid.

90. James Glanz, "Droughts Might Speed Climate Change," *New York Times*, January 11, 2001, A16.

91. "Paradise Lost? Global Warming Seen as Threat," *Houston Chronicle*, February 20, 2001, A1.

92. Quoted in Douglas Jehl and Andrew C. Revkin, "Bush, in Reversal, Won't Seek Cuts in Emissions of Carbon Dioxide," *New York Times*, March 14, 2001, A1.

93. Douglas Jehl, "Bush Ties Policy Shift to an 'Energy Crisis,'" *New York Times*, March 15, 2001, A10.

94. Joseph Kahn, "Energy Efficiency Programs Are Set for Bush Budget Cut," *New York Times*, April 5, 2001, A16.

95. Douglas Jehl, "A New Focus on Supply," *New York Times*, May 18, 2001, A1.

96. Douglas Jehl, "U.S. Rebuffs European Plea Not to Abandon Climate Pact," *New York Times*, April 4, 2001, A14.

97. Robin Toner, "Environmental Reversals Leave Moderate Republicans Hoping for Greener Times," *New York Times*, April 4, 2001, A14.

98. Edmund L. Andrews, "Frustrated Europeans Set Out to Battle U.S. on Climate," *New York Times*, July 16, 2001, A3.

99. Darren K. Carlson, "Scientists Deliver Serious Warning About Effects of Global Warming," Gallup Poll Releases (January 23, 2001).

100. Katharine Q. Seelye and Andrew C. Revkin, "Panel Tells Bush Global Warming is Getting Worse," *New York Times*, June 7, 2001, A1.

101. To gain legal force, the treaty must be ratified by at least fifty-five countries, including a group responsible for at least 55 percent of the greenhouse gas emissions from industrial countries in 1990.

102. Quoted in Andrew C. Revkin, "Deal Breaks Impasse on Global Warming Treaty," *New York Times*, November 11, 2001, Sec. 1, 1.

103. Sarewitz and Pielke, "Breaking the Global-Warming Gridlock," 64.

104. The United States releases about twice as much CO_2 per capita as other advanced countries. The main reason for the disparity is not a more robust economy (we do not have anywhere near twice the per capita GDP); rather, we have much lower fuel taxes. See Paul Krugman, "Sins of Emission," *New York Times*, November 29, 2000, A31.

105. "Global Corporations and Environmental Defense Partner to Reduce Greenhouse Gas Emissions," Environmental Defense Press Release (October 17, 2000).

Recommended Reading

Gelbspan, Ross. *The Heat Is On: The High Stakes Battle over Earth's Threatened Climate.* New York: Addison-Wesley, 1997.

Houghton, John. *Global Warming: The Complete Briefing,* 2d ed. New York: Cambridge University Press, 1997.
Michaels, Patrick J. *Sound and Fury: The Science and Politics of Global Warming.* Washington, D.C.: Cato Institute, 1992.
Paterson, Matthew. *Global Warming and Climate Politics.* New York: Routledge, 1996.
Victor, David G. *The Collapse of the Kyoto Protocol and the Struggle to Slow Global Warming.* Princeton: Princeton University Press, 2001.

Web Sites

http://www.iisd.ca/climate/index.html (UNFCCC site)
http://www.ipcc.ch/ (IPCC site)
http://www.epa.gov/globalwarming/ (EPA site)

CHAPTER 10

Backlash

Wise Use, Property Rights, and the Anti-Environmental Movement

In 1995, a reaction against environmentalism that had been growing in scale and intensity since the late 1980s found expression in Congress with the ascension of the Republican party. Anti-environmentalists had been waging an increasingly sophisticated battle against environmental regulations across the country, and their efforts culminated in several legislative proposals: bills to compensate property owners whenever government regulations reduced the value of their property; a revamped Clean Water Act that dramatically curtailed wetlands protection; and a revised Endangered Species Act (ESA) that virtually dismantled endangered species protection. Congress ultimately did not pass any of the major anti-environmental bills proposed in the mid-1990s, in part because environmentalists mobilized rapidly to raise public awareness and resist these legislative incursions. Although it retreated, however, the anti-environmental movement did not disappear; its persistence has left members of Congress, agency personnel, and environmental activists circumspect and prompted them to consider new strategies in order to prevail in the long run.

The anti-environmental backlash of the 1990s was not unprecedented; the West has a long history of anti-environmental, anti-government activism. The most recent backlash was more effective than its predecessors, however, in part because it was led by politically sophisticated policy entrepreneurs. When a talented entrepreneur adopts an issue, he or she can significantly increase the probability that Congress will consider and approve a policy innovation.[1] To have an impact, a policy entrepreneur must invest resources—time, energy, and skill—in softening up policymakers and the public and then linking solutions to problems when a window of opportunity opens.[2] A savvy entrepreneur knows how to identify problems, network in policy circles, shape the terms of debate, and build coalitions.[3] Among the entrepreneur's challenges is the need to craft messages and policy goals that are sufficiently idealistic to appeal to the true believers but not so extreme that they repel potential supporters.[4]

To succeed in bringing about policy change, entrepreneurs must create a situation in which a majority of legislators believe they can get credit from—or at least avoid punishment by—voters for their position. They must believe, in other words, that the issue is salient to voters. One indication of an issue's salience is the extent of grassroots mobilization: it is difficult for politicians to ignore an organized contingent of the electorate because such mobilization reflects intense concern. On the other hand, politicians find it hard to reconcile the intense preferences of a narrow group of loyal party activists and the more centrist views of the general electorate on salient issues.[5] Another resource politicians use to assess their vulnerability on an issue is polling data. The information generated by polls can be misleading, however. Polling results often contain internal contradictions; for example, a single poll may show overwhelming support for environmental preserves, such as wilderness areas and wild and scenic rivers, while simultaneously revealing a ferocious fear of government in all its forms.[6] In addition, polls are notoriously poor at detecting the amount of immediate, personal interest people have in an issue. With occasional exceptions, the environment ranks low as Gallup's "most important problem" (MIP); in fact, it was mentioned by only 1 percent of those surveyed in January 1995.[7] But because salience measures, such as the MIP question, are headline-sensitive, they are untrustworthy guides to how the public will respond to proposed policy changes.[8]

Politicians can try to placate vociferous constituents while avoiding the salience trap by concealing their choices, thereby making it difficult for voters to trace responsibility for a policy.[9] Alternatively, legislators can reduce the visibility of policies by attaching them as riders to larger bills, or legislative leaders can use their control over the calendar to move a bill quickly and avoid giving the opposition time to mobilize.

By the same logic, though, opponents can thwart such maneuvers by raising their visibility. Defenders of the status quo also can take advantage of institutional differences between the House, which is often more responsive to short-term changes in public sentiment, and the Senate, which tends to react more cautiously. (State-level representation makes the Senate slower to adjust to demographic shifts, and Senate procedures make it easier for a minority to block change.) Finally, the president can play a critical role in blocking policy change by using the formidable veto. A two-thirds majority in both chambers is required to override a presidential veto; thus, the mere threat of a veto is often enough to discourage members of Congress from pursuing a policy. At a minimum, a veto threat is likely to limit how far Congress is willing to diverge from the president's preferred policy.[10] Even if no new laws are passed, however, a backlash can have potent political effects: it can chasten advocates, administrators, and even legislators into retreating from their ambitious reform agendas, adopting new, more conciliatory approaches, and considering alternative policy tools.

This chapter on the anti-environmental backlash of the 1990s illuminates the difficulties politicians face in determining an issue's salience and explores the tactics—particularly the rhetorical devices—advocates have used to both advance and resist policy reversals.

BACKGROUND

After a brief honeymoon in the late 1960s and early 1970s, environmentalism began to encounter resistance. By the late 1970s and early 1980s, several local organizations had formed to repel changes in national forest logging regulations, federal wilderness designations, and restrictions on landowners living in or near national parks.[11] Among the first of these organized efforts was the Sagebrush Rebellion of the late 1970s (see chapter 6). That movement, which consisted primarily of ranchers disgruntled with Carter administration efforts to rehabilitate the western range, fizzled with the election of President Ronald Reagan, who was sympathetic to its aims and whose administration itself was anti-government and anti-environmental. But in the late 1980s and the 1990s, a reinvigorated environmental movement breathed new life into anti-environmentalism and prompted the rise of the Wise Use and property rights movements.

The Anti-Environmental Reagan Administration

The Reagan administration temporarily defused the emerging anti-environmental backlash by holding new environmental legislation at bay and by undertaking a series of administrative reforms to reduce the burden of existing regulations on industry and private property owners. Immediately after his inauguration, President Reagan—who had campaigned on an anti-government platform—created the Task Force on Regulatory Relief to review environmental regulations. Shortly thereafter, he issued Executive Order 12291, which required all executive agencies to conduct (and the Office of Management and Budget to oversee) a benefit-cost analysis on any proposed regulations and to refrain from promulgating those regulations unless the benefits outweighed the cost. Reagan also issued the little noticed but symbolically important Executive Order 12630, which required a "Takings Impact Analysis" of most government regulations, in order to discourage the enactment of government rules affecting private property.

Among the most effective of President Reagan's efforts to blunt the teeth of environmental regulations was the installation of development advocates James Watt and Anne Gorsuch (later Burford), respectively, as secretary of interior and EPA administrator. These senior officials proceeded to reorganize their agencies and reinterpret environmental laws to make them more consistent with the president's anti-regulatory agenda.[12] Gorsuch, a former Colorado legislator and a corporate attorney who specialized in challenging federal regulations, virtually halted enforcement of CERCLA (the Superfund Act). Her activities eventually provoked a congressional inquiry, and in 1984, she (and twenty other appointees) resigned in hopes of sparing the president further embarrassment. James Watt was the former president of the Mountain States Legal Foundation, which sues the government on behalf of private landowners and public lands resource users. Watt favored rapid development and disposal of public lands and justified his approach to Congress by saying that he saw no point in preserving lands because he did "not know how many future generations we can count on before the Lord returns."[13] Reagan's outspoken appointees provoked a backlash of their own, however: environmental groups saw an explosion in membership and sharp increases in donations.[14] National polls taken throughout the 1980s indicated that Reagan had greatly overestimated the level of public support for trimming environmental regulations.[15]

The Wise Use Movement

The resurgence of environmentalism in turn gave new impetus to anti-environmental activism. Beginning in the late 1980s, shortly after the election of President George Bush, anti-environmental policy entrepreneurs united two main branches of the movement, the Wise Use and the property rights movements. Anti-environmentalism gained widespread recognition after a 1988 conference in Reno, Nevada, where veteran political activists Ron Arnold and Alan Gottlieb brought together under a single banner a disparate array of groups whose common objective was to remove environmental restrictions from public lands. Dubbing the amalgamation the Wise Use movement, Arnold and Gottlieb prepared an agenda that included developing oil and gas reserves in the Arctic National Wildlife Refuge; eliminating restrictions on wetlands development; opening all public lands, including national parks and wilderness areas, to mineral and energy production; redesignating 70 of the 90 million acres of the National Wilderness Preservation System for motorized trail travel, limited commercial development, and commodity use; instituting civil penalties against anyone who legally challenged economic action or development on federal lands; and recognizing private rights to mining claims, water, grazing permits, and timber contracts on federal lands.[16]

A small number of umbrella organizations, most headquartered in the West, began to coordinate Wise Use activities. Among those organizations were the Blue Ribbon Coalition, which represented some 500,000 off-road vehicle users; Gottlieb and Arnold's Center for the Defense of Free Enterprise (CFDFE), whose overarching goal was to promote and defend an unfettered capitalist economy; the Western States Public Lands Coalition (WSPLC); and its subsidiary, People for the West! (PFW!), formed by mining companies in 1989 to improve their industry's public image.[17] Some of these organizations were industry fronts; the Marine Preservation Association, for example, which defined marine preservation as the promotion of petroleum and energy company interests, had fifteen oil company members.[18] Others, such as PFW!, were financed almost entirely by the industries that benefitted from their activities: in 1992, 96 percent of PFW!'s $1.7 million budget came from corporate donors, led by NERCO minerals, Cyprus Minerals, Chevron, and Heclo Mining; and PFW!'s chairman, Bob Quick, was the national director of state legislative affairs for the Asarco Mining Company.[19]

The Wise Use movement boasted a citizen following as well, however; although critics downplayed its grassroots membership, Arnold claimed that Wise Use mailing lists reached more than three million people, of which one million actively participated in meetings and wrote letters to legislators.[20] Among the state and local groups that comprised the Wise Use movement's base were the California Desert Coalition, formed in 1986 to oppose the California Desert Protection Act; the Shasta Alliance for Resources and Environment, which was concerned with northern California resource management policies; and the Oregon Lands Coalition, whose members—including agricultural, ranching, and timber interests—counted among their primary goals limiting federal protection for endangered species. A 1993 study commissioned by the Wilderness Society reported that these groups

> are apparently genuine grassroots. That is, they [comprise] local individuals addressing local concerns who joined with other individuals, groups, and funders as a matter of common concern. It is true that special interests have in many cases fostered local wise use groups . . . but it is foolish to lay this movement solely at the doorstep of Exxon, Georgia Pacific, or Kawasaki. Real people have perceived a real threat. The national wise use movement is attempting to give these grassroots groups coherence; it did not give them life.[21]

Don Judge, an executive secretary for the AFL/CIO who battled the Wise Use movement in Montana, pointed out that while big business interests were exploiting the suffering of local people to further their own aims, they found a receptive audience: "You cannot destroy entire communities without getting a backlash," said Judge, "and whenever there's a backlash of emotion, there's always somebody with a lot of money that manipulates that emotion to their benefit."[22]

The Wise Use movement also subsumed officials from the county supremacy movement, which arose in 1989 when Catron County, New Mexico, passed an ordinance asserting its authority to veto federal environmental protection regulations, defining federal grazing permits as private property rights, and authorizing the county sheriff to arrest federal or state officials trying to enforce federal statutes. More than thirty-five counties subsequently passed similar statutes. The main impetus for the county movement was the perception that eastern elites were trying to impose their policy preferences on westerners, who have an entirely different culture. The rallying cry of the county supremacy movement was that easterners were waging a "war on the West." Two clearinghouses were established in 1989 to coordinate the activities of the county movement: the Utah-based National Federal Lands Conference and the Coalition of Arizona/New Mexico Counties for Stable Economic Growth, based in Catron County.

The Property Rights Movement

A second component of the anti-environmental coalition was the property rights movement, the bulk of whose membership lay east of the Mississippi. Chuck Cushman, head of the American Land Rights Association, was a prime mover and, like Arnold and Gottlieb, was a skillful policy entrepreneur. Portraying himself as leading a holy crusade against environmentalists, Cushman used his organizational skills and shrewd political mind to unify the disparate grievances of landowners. Cushman's own organization, the National Inhold-ers Association, defended the rights of those who own land within the bound-aries of national parks. He forged alliances with other major property rights groups, such as the Washington, D.C.–based Defenders of Property Rights, which wanted to "bring about a sea change in property rights law through strategically filed lawsuits and groundbreaking property rights legislation."[23]

The property rights movement's fundamental tenet was that property rights are paramount, and property owners ought to be compensated when government regulation devalues their property. Advocates based this claim on the Fifth Amendment to the Constitution, which guarantees compensation for property taken by eminent domain. One of the most outspoken proponents of private property rights, Nancie Marzulla, president of Defenders of Property Rights, testified before the Senate Judiciary Committee in 1995 that "Today, environmental regulations destroy property rights on an unprecedented scale. Regulations designed to protect coastal zones, wetlands, and endangered species habitats, among others, leave many owners stripped of all but bare title to their property."[24] Marzulla contended that the focus on property rights emerged out of the Wise Use movement as individuals began to feel the impact of burgeoning federal and state environmental regulations on their day-to-day lives.[25] Galvanized by wetlands policy revisions, endangered species protection efforts, public park and greenway expansions, scenic river corridors, land-use planning, zoning laws, and growth management plans, the property rights movement gained steam in the early 1990s.[26]

THE CASE

In 1991, 400 Wise Use and property rights groups joined forces to form the Alliance for America, an umbrella organization whose agenda was to disman-tle environmental regulations affecting both private and public lands. While the movement was only loosely coherent, it boasted an impressive mailing list and network of organizations that it could mobilize in response to perceived threats. Unifying these groups were their members' cornucopian values of human supremacy over nature, individual freedom and economic growth, and technology as the solution to environmental problems. A small number of sophisticated policy entrepreneurs devised the movement's two-pronged strategy, which entailed crafting dual messages—one to appeal to hard-core activists and the other to attract mainstream support—and challeng-ing environmentalism in the legislative, administrative, and judicial arenas simultaneously.

Using Ideas to Mobilize Support

Anti-environmental policy entrepreneurs mobilized followers with power-ful ideas expressed in skillfully-crafted rhetoric. Most observers credit Ron Arnold with sparking the Wise Use movement in 1979 with a series of articles in *Logging Management Magazine* in which he called for an activist movement to defeat the environmental movement. Arnold appropriated the phrase "wise use" from conservationist Gifford Pinchot because it was both headline-friendly and "rich with symbolism."[27] Adopting the stock-in-trade of their adversaries, anti-environmental groups quickly became expert at mounting grassroots campaigns. In 1988, Arnold advised resource companies to stop defending themselves and let citizens get out in front "because citizen groups have credibility and industries don't."[28] To enhance their populist image, Wise Use groups began holding rallies, sponsoring petition drives, and launching T-shirt and bumper sticker campaigns.[29] The broader Alliance for America initiated an annual "Fly in for Freedom," which brought local Wise Use and property rights activists to Washington, D.C., for meetings with members of Congress.

Arnold, Gottlieb, Cushman, and others attracted supporters by defining environmental regulations rather than environmental damage as the problem, using potent symbols and metaphors. In doing so, they were careful to craft separate messages for hard-core true believers and average citizens. Speaking to activists, anti-environmental leaders used incendiary rhetoric to depict a conspiracy among elitist environmentalists, government officials, and the media to take away citizens' rights. For example, Arnold said: "We are sick to death of environmentalism and so we will destroy it. We will not allow our right to own property and use nature's resources for the benefit of mankind to be stripped from us by a bunch of eco-fascists."[30]

In their public campaigns, however, anti-environmental leaders adopted a more moderate tone, framing environmental regulations as choosing the environment over jobs in order to tap into working people's economic anxieties. For example, promotional literature for People for the West! read: "Don't allow Congress to lock us out of all 730 million acres of public lands. . . . People will lose jobs, rural communities will become ghost towns, education for our children will suffer, and state and local governments will forfeit critical income for policy, fire protection, roads, and social services."[31]

To mobilize followers, anti-environmental leaders tapped into powerful American values of community autonomy, wielding the rhetoric of individual rights, liberty, and government tyranny. Pamela Neal, executive director of the Public Lands Council, which represented 31,000 cattle and sheep ranchers, argued: "It was free enterprise and private property rights that created America and made this nation great. Instead of protecting that independence, the government is making us servants of an environmental movement that I can only liken to socialism."[32] Arnold described environmentalists as "part of an elite, part of the Harvard Yard crowd in three-piece suits and expensive shoes that is destroying the middle class."[33] In contrast, according to Arnold, the Wise Use movement represented ordinary citizens: "The environmental movement is the establishment now, and we're the rebels coming to tear them down. Now they're Goliath and we're David, and we intend to put the stone in their head."[34] Painting environmentalists as extremists, Chuck Cushman characterized preservationism as "a new pagan religion" whose members "worship trees and animals and sacrifice people."[35] In contrast, Wise Use and property rights advocates portrayed themselves as moderates, seeking a balance between human activities and the preservation of nature.

Among the most effective public relations tools were anecdotes that capitalized on anti-government sentiment, depicting the government as the villain and private property owners, ranchers, loggers, and miners as innocent victims. Some of the most effective were the following:

- In 1986, Gaston Roberge, a retired businessman from Scarborough, Maine, was on the verge of selling his 2.8-acre lot in Old Orchard Beach to a developer for $440,000. When federal officials heard about the deal, however, they declared the Roberge property a wetland under the Clean Water Act and therefore required a special permit before it could be developed. After the buyer changed his mind about the purchase, Roberge launched an expensive legal battle that resulted, nearly ten years later, in a $338,000 settlement with the Justice Department.[36]
- One snowy September night, Montana rancher John Shuler thought he saw a grizzly bear outside his house. Grabbing his rifle, he raced outside to find three bears devouring his sheep herd. When he fired a warning shot in the air, a fourth bear emerged and turned to attack him. In fear for his life, Shuler shot and killed the bear, thereby taking an endangered species, a crime for which the Environmental Protection Agency fined him $4,000.[37]
- Taiwanese immigrant Taung Min-lin bought a 723-acre parcel of California scrub land in 1990, intending to farm it. As it turned out, his land was home to three endangered species: the Tipton kangaroo rat, the blunt-nosed leopard lizard, and the San Joaquin kit fox. In February 1994, state and federal agents raided Lin's farm, carted off his tractor, and filed criminal charges against him for violating the Endangered Species Act.[38]
- In 1990, the government fined Paul Tudor Jones II $1 million, required him to make a $1 million contribution to an environmental group, and sentenced him to eighteen months probation after he filled wetlands on his Maryland property as part of an effort to create a private wildlife refuge. Jones's project manager, marine engineer William Ellen, refused to settle his case and was charged with five felony counts of knowingly filling wetlands and sentenced to six months in prison.[39]

Anti-environmentalists did not rely on anecdotes alone, however. Bolstering their credibility was a host of conservative think tanks that underwrote public relations campaigns and helped to build an intellectual foundation for the movement. These organizations generated studies, op-eds, and briefing papers in support of two lines of argument: there is no scientific certainty on which to base environmental regulations, and environmental regulations harm the economy and impinge on individual liberty. The Heritage Foundation led the charge against natural resource management agencies and environmental legislation, holding an annual conference at which directors of business-sponsored "public interest" law firms assembled and strategized. In

1990, coinciding with the twentieth anniversary of Earth Day, the foundation issued a report on "ecoterrorism"; it singled out the environmental movement as "the greatest single threat to the American economy."[40]

The Cato Institute, another Washington, D.C.–based libertarian think tank, promoted "free-market environmentalism," while downplaying the dangers associated with environmental problems. A 1993 Cato publication entitled *Apocalypse Not* argued that "much of the modern environmental movement is a broad-based assault on reason and a concomitant assault on freedom."[41] The Science and Environmental Policy Project, founded in 1990 by the Reverend Sun Myung Moon–funded Washington Institute for Values in Public Policy and subsequently allied with Virginia's George Mason University, also held conferences and seminars aimed at discrediting arguments that ozone depletion, global warming, acid rain, pesticide exposure, and toxic waste exposure pose real or potential threats to human health.[42]

Legal Theory and Litigation

In addition to its public relations campaign, anti-environmentalists developed a sophisticated legal capacity in hopes of emulating the successes of the environmental movement. The Center for the Defense of Free Enterprise disseminated anti-environmental literature and maintained its own legal defense fund.[43] The Pacific Legal Foundation was the first business-sponsored "public interest" law firm; by the mid-1990s, there were twenty-three of them.[44] The Mountain States Legal Foundation, made famous by its president, former Interior Secretary James Watt, filed legal actions all over the West contesting federal regulatory actions. The Competitive Enterprise Institute, the Federalist Society, the Washington Legal Foundation, and others also litigated pro bono on behalf of businesses opposing environmental laws and regulations.

The county supremacy movement made legal theory the centerpiece of its resistance to federal environmental regulations. The movement asserted the autonomy of counties by passing ordinances that defied federal hegemony over land within county borders, instead granting county officials decision-making power over those lands. Their authors based the legitimacy of such ordinances on three legal theories. First, they contended that the Constitution gives the federal government authority only over lands it legally owns—that is, land within Washington, D.C., defense facilities, and other "needful buildings." Second, they argued that the federal government retained land in new territories only with the understanding that it would eventually divest itself of this land and return it to the states. Finally, county commissioners pointed out that the National Environmental Policy Act (NEPA) requires the federal government to cooperate with state and local governments to "preserve important historic, cultural, and other aspects of our natural heritage." County supremacy advocates defined their culture as one that favored resource extraction.[45]

Although it was eager to test these legal theories in court, the county supremacy movement was not particularly successful. In January 1994, a state court judge ruled a Boundary County, Idaho, ordinance illegal, saying it violated the supremacy clause of the U.S. Constitution.[46] U.S. District Court Judge Lloyd George made a similar ruling in 1996, when he overturned a Nye County, Nevada, ordinance and affirmed the right of the federal government to own and administer public lands in the state.[47]

Like the county supremacists, property rights advocates relied heavily on legal theory and litigation to advance their policy goals. Their primary legal claim was that regulatory actions that reduced the value of property constituted takings, as defined by the Fifth Amendment to the Constitution.[48] That claim gained credibility with the publication in 1985 of a book entitled *Takings: Private Property and the Power of Eminent Domain,* by the University of Chicago's libertarian law professor, Richard Epstein. Epstein argues that under the Fifth Amendment the government must pay property owners whenever environmental regulations, health and safety rules, or zoning laws limit the value of their property.[49]

The courts were more hospitable to property rights claims than to county supremacy arguments. Although the idea of regulatory takings dates back to the nineteenth century, the Supreme Court accepted few regulatory takings cases after the 1930s. In the 1980s, however, the court began to reconsider property rights claims, which were arising in greater numbers in response to the spate of new federal environmental laws. In 1987, a California Case (*Nollan v. California Coastal Commission*) sparked a trend in jurisprudence that was closely watched by property rights advocates and environmentalists alike. The plaintiffs in this case lived on the coast and wanted to replace their 504-square-foot bungalow with a new house nearly twice as large as the original. The Coastal Commission agreed to grant them a permit if they would allow public access to the beach in front of their property. The Nollans contended that there was no relationship between that requirement (known as an exaction) and their request, and the Supreme Court agreed. Court watchers regarded this as the first major land-use case in the modern era in which a property owner prevailed against the government on a takings issue.[50]

Between 1992 and 1995, property rights advocates were successful in two more important Supreme Court cases. First, the Court backed a claim by South Carolina beachfront property owner and developer David Lucas (*Lucas v. South Carolina Coastal Commission*). In 1986, Lucas bought two lots on a barrier island off South Carolina for $1 million. Two years later, the state passed the Beachfront Management Act, which prohibited development in areas vulnerable to erosion. In 1992, the Court held that since Lucas had suffered a total loss of property value as a result of a law passed after he purchased the land, he should receive financial compensation. More generally, the Court ruled that compensation is required when legislation deprives an owner of "all economically beneficial or productive use" of his property.[51]

Second, in 1994, in a case brought by Oregonians in Action (*Dolan v. City of Tigard*), a property rights group partly financed by timber companies, the Court ruled 5–4 in favor of a plumbing supply store owner. The city refused to grant Dolan a permit to expand her store unless she turned over 10 percent of her property for a public bicycle path. In this case, the Court said that zoning officials may impose exactions only if they are related to the proposed development or are "roughly proportional" to any harms the development may cause. Again, this case indicated a willingness on the part of the Court to overturn state and local regulations it found unduly burdensome for landowners.

Notwithstanding these highly publicized victories, however, there was no strong judicial shift in favor of takings claims, and legal scholars continued to puzzle over their significance. As many commentators noted, the cases cited above were exceptional and involved extreme circumstances. Nevertheless, plaintiffs continued to file lawsuits claiming takings under a variety of circumstances.[52] At a minimum, they hoped that landowners' increasing propensity to challenge land-use regulations, combined with the court's apparent willingness to hear such cases, would deter state lawmakers from enacting such rules or at least force them to conduct more explicit benefit-cost calculations before doing so.[53]

Another legal tactic anti-environmentalists began using is what two University of Denver professors labeled SLAPPs—Strategic Lawsuits Against Public Participation. Such lawsuits, employed primarily by developers and corporations, were powerful deterrents because they could bankrupt those who attempted to use administrative or legal procedures to obstruct development. For example, in West Virginia, the DLM Coal Corporation filed a multimillion-dollar libel action against Rick Webb and his nonprofit environmental group after they requested an EPA hearing on pollution of rivers by mine runoff and published an editorial in their newsletter criticizing strip mining. In Squaw Valley, California, a developer filed a $75 million suit against stunt skier Rick Sylvester for speaking out and writing letters to the editor against a planned development. And in Louisville, Colorado, a developer sued local activist Betty Johnson for unlimited damages after she organized a petition drive for a growth moratorium.[54] The goal of such suits was not necessarily to win and collect damages but rather to intimidate potential critics and stifle dissent; although 83 percent were dismissed before reaching trial, they cost defendants tens of thousands of dollars, as well as tremendous amounts of time and energy.[55]

Harassment and Intimidation

Finally, in addition to its lobbying, legal activism, and political campaigns, the anti-environmental movement had a more sinister side: federal officials were threatened, terrorized, and occasionally physically harmed when they tried to enforce environmental laws. In the summer of 1994, Nye County (Nevada) Commissioner Dick Carver used a bulldozer to open a closed Forest Service logging road while an armed crowd cheered him on. "All it would have taken was for [the forest ranger] to draw a weapon," Carver later bragged, "and 50 people with sidearms would have drilled him."[56] In Catron

County, Nancy and Clyde Brown wrote an open letter to the U.S. Fish and Wildlife Service threatening: "I think bureaucrats better back off before someone gets seriously hurt. Who among you would want to loose [*sic*] your life for a bird . . . or a microscopic minnow?"[57] And shortly after the Fish and Wildlife Service reintroduced wolves into Yellowstone National Park, one of the radio-collared animals was found shot to death next to a partially eaten calf on the ranch of seventy-four-year-old rancher Eugene Hussey. When Fish and Wildlife agents returned to investigate, Sheriff Brett Barsalon forced them to retreat, telling them to leave Hussey alone and threatening to "go to Plan B" if they did not. (A veterinary medical examiner found that the calf was already dead at the time the wolf scavenged its carcass and had probably been moved to the site—presumably to lure the wolf.)

In *War Against the Greens*, journalist David Helvarg relays a host of incidents in which environmental activists were victims of terror tactics. After Ellen Gray, director of the Pilcuk Audubon Society in Everett, Washington, finished testifying at a County Council hearing in favor of a land-use ordinance to protect local streams and wetlands, a man stood up in front of her with a noose and said: "This is for you." In Eureka Springs, Arkansas, Greenpeace USA's director of toxics research Pat Costner returned home to find her house burned to the ground. Arson investigators found abundant evidence that the fire had been set. In 1992, there were several attacks on Diane Wilson, a shrimper protesting expansion of a Taiwanese-owned plastics plant near her home in Seadrift, Texas. Assailants shot at her mother-in-law, who lived on her property, as well as at her dog (which was hit). Her boat was sabotaged and almost sank. According to Helvarg, the late 1980s and early 1990s saw

> a startling increase in intimidation, vandalism, and violence directed at grassroots environmental activists. Observers of this trend have documented hundreds of acts of violence, ranging from vandalism, assaults, arsons, and shootings to torture, rape, and possibly murder, much of it occurring in rural and low-income communities. Simple acts of intimidation—phone harassment, anonymous letters, and verbal threats of violence—may number in the thousands.[58]

Jacqueline Vaughn Switzer, who offers a balanced assessment of the anti-environmental movement in her 1997 book *Green Backlash*, suggests that environmentalists exaggerate the extent of anti-environmental militancy. Even if it attracted few adherents, however, the radical fringe served a purpose: it drew attention to the cause while rendering mainstream anti-environmental activists moderate by comparison.

The Legislative Response to Anti-Environmentalism

Events in Congress in the early 1990s reflected the success of anti-environmentalists at defining environmental *regulations,* rather than environmental harms, as the problem. Riding the coattails of Bill Clinton and Al Gore, the

Democrat-controlled 103rd Congress initiated an ambitious environmental agenda, but the session turned out to be a bust for environmentalists. Only one major environmental bill—the California Desert Protection Act—passed during this period, while Republicans and conservative Democrats foiled efforts to reauthorize Superfund, the Clean Water Act, and other major environmental laws. Anti-environmental forces also derailed a bill to elevate the EPA to a cabinet-level department in early 1994.

Having stymied environmentalists in the 103rd Congress, anti-environmentalists perceived a window of opportunity to advance their own agenda after the 1994 elections, which resulted in Republican majorities in both the House and Senate.[59] As part of their campaign, Republican leaders had devised the "Contract With America" which, although it did not mention environmental regulations explicitly, included three provisions that curbed the federal government's ability to impose such rules: cutting unfunded mandates to states and localities, requiring federal agencies to conduct benefit-cost analyses and risk assessments before promulgating regulations, and reimbursing property owners for reductions in their property values that result from regulations.

After the Republican victory, House Commerce Committee Chairman Thomas L. Bliley, Jr., summarized the party's position: "The American people sent us a message in November, loud and clear: Tame this regulatory beast. Our constituents want us to break the Federal stranglehold on our economy and get them out of the decisions that are best left to the individual."[60] Majority Whip Tom DeLay of Texas announced the goal of GOP regulatory reform was to "make sure that American small business and the American taxpayer don't become the next endangered species."[61] When asked by a reporter if there was any government regulation he would retain, DeLay—who compared the EPA to the Gestapo—responded: "I can't think of one."[62]

The House leadership then selected virulently anti-environmental Alaskan Don Young to chair the Resources (formerly Natural Resources) Committee. "I'm the one in charge now," Young gloated. Environmentalists "are going to have to compromise. . . . If not, I'm just going to ram it down their throats."[63] Young, who in December 1994 described environmentalists as a "self-centered bunch, the waffle-stomping, Harvard-graduating, intellectual bunch of idiots," proceeded to stock his committee with conservative Republican freshmen.[64] Although Republican leaders in the Senate promoted pro-environmental John Chafee of Rhode Island to the chairmanship of the Environment and Public Works Committee, they loaded his committee with anti-environmental members as well.[65]

Pursuing Policy Change Through the Budget. The primary vehicle for congressional efforts to roll back environmental protection was the budget. By attaching anti-environmental riders to the fiscal 1996 omnibus spending bill, sponsors hoped to sidestep debate and avoid galvanizing environmentalists. Among the myriad anti-environmental measures added to the spending bill in 1995 were provisions to:

- impose a moratorium on new listings under the Endangered Species Act;
- transfer responsibility for the newly created Mojave National Preserve from the preservation-oriented National Park Service to the more commodity-oriented Bureau of Land Management;
- institute a ninety-day moratorium on proposed grazing regulations that the cattle and sheep industries oppose;
- curtail the ecological assessment of the Columbia River Basin;
- dismantle Energy Department conservation programs;
- increase the harvest from the Tongass National Forest in Alaska; and
- open up the Arctic National Wildlife Refuge to oil drilling.

Environmentalists responded by launching a campaign to mobilize their movement's grassroots, stimulating emails, phone calls, and letters to members of Congress in opposition to the riders. Their efforts paid off: fifty-one Republicans joined a majority of Democrats in approving (212–206) an amendment deleting the anti-environmental riders.[66] In a subsequent vote, the Republican leadership managed to persuade enough members to reinstate the riders, but in mid-November of 1995, President Clinton vetoed the omnibus budget act, citing the anti-environmental riders as the main obstacle. The ensuing week-long shutdown of the federal government focused public attention on the riders—precisely what their sponsors had hoped to avoid—and empowered opponents of the measures. While stopgap spending bills reopened the government, Clinton held firm, and Congress ultimately was compelled to drop most of the anti-environmental provisions in order to get a budget passed.

Protecting Private Property Rights. In addition to attaching riders to the budget, anti-environmentalists in the 104th Congress pursued another, slightly more visible line of attack. In March 1995, the House passed the Private Property Rights Act, which entitled property owners to receive compensation for any "measurable" reduction in the value of their property resulting from environmental restrictions on otherwise lawful use of it.[67] To receive compensation, a property owner would submit a written request within ninety days of notice of a final government action restricting property use. Within 180 days, the agency would have to offer the owner the fair market value of the property minus the fair market value of the property if the government action were implemented. A property owner could reject the agency's offer and request binding arbitration.[68] One sign of the property rights movement's effectiveness at raising the salience of their concerns was that more than a third of House Democrats joined Republicans in passing the measure, even as most acknowledged that it would halt many regulations at their inception.

Property rights legislation fared less well in the Senate, however. An effort to attach property rights riders to the spending bill stalled. Majority Leader Bob Dole, R-Kan., got thirty-one cosponsors for a companion to the House bill but failed on three back-to-back cloture votes to bring his measure (S 343) to a vote.[69] And although the Judiciary Committee approved a bill (S 605) similar to Dole's, it too was quashed by the threat of a filibuster.

Anti-environmentalists promoted property rights measures in state legislatures as well. All fifty states considered measures in the early 1990s, and by the end of 1995, eighteen legislatures had passed laws requiring regulators to consider the effects of new regulation on property owners. Most of these laws required state governments to conduct a takings impact assessment before proposing regulatory action, but some also included compensation provisions.[70] While state legislatures were eager to pass takings laws, however, voters seemed less enthusiastic. In 1995, the Washington State legislature approved a takings initiative financed by the timber and building industries.[71] But the passage of this initiative prompted a pro-environmental backlash, in which 10,000 volunteers rounded up more than twice the number of signatures necessary to delay enactment of the initiative by putting it on the ballot as a referendum.[72] Washington voters proceeded to reject the referendum by a three-fifths majority, even though takings-bill supporters outspent the opposition two to one.[73] A year earlier, relatively conservative Arizona voters had rejected by the same margin a measure that would have required state or local officials to consider whether any new regulation violated private property rights.

Voters' resistance to property rights legislation was almost certainly the result of a campaign by an unlikely alliance of environmentalists, some commercial interests, civil rights groups, children's groups, and organizations representing cities, states, and churches. The coalition developed a coherent set of arguments against property rights legislation, alerting voters to the possibility that the takings impact assessment process and compensation requirements would severely limit government's ability to regulate in the public interest. The coalition also pointed out that implementing compensation rules would create a bureaucratic and legal morass and would cost governments millions of dollars annually.[74] Citing a University of Washington study, the coalition noted that economic impact assessments alone could cost local governments between $305 and $986 million a year, and thus could eat up as much as 10–50 percent of the budget of such large jurisdictions as Seattle's King County.[75]

Dismantling Wetlands Protection. Aside from writing bills to guarantee private property rights, House Republicans also tried to revise the Clean Water Act to drastically reduce protection for the nation's wetlands.[76] Federal wetlands regulation had been controversial since the 1970s, when Section 404 of the Clean Water Act of 1972 authorized the EPA and the Army Corps of Engineers to regulate the discharge of dredged or fill materials into "navigable waters." Because wetlands regulations were a particular object of anti-environmentalists' wrath, congressional leaders in the 104th Congress wasted no time in crafting bills to dismantle them. In spring 1995, House Transportation and Infrastructure Committee chairman Bud Shuster, R-Penn., introduced a radical set of revisions to the Clean Water Act (HR 961), including provisions to restrict federal wetlands protection and compensate landowners whose property values declined more than 20 percent as a result of federal regulations. Shuster's bill required federal agencies to delineate the nation's wetlands and categorize them as Type A, B, or C, in declining order of "ecological importance." It limited land-use activities only on Type A wetlands and allowed no more than 20 percent of any county to be designated Type A.[77] In April, the House Transportation Committee approved HR 961 by 42–16.

The House bill set off a firestorm among scientists and environmentalists, who were furious because regulated industries such as International Paper, as well as industry groups like the Chemical Manufacturers Association, had helped draft the legislation.[78] Robert Perciasepe, a top water quality official from the EPA, called the bill "a program of counterfeit wetlands protection," saying that it "propose[d] scientifically unsound methods of identifying wetlands that the Association of State Wetlands Managers estimates would eliminate some 60 to 80 percent of the nation's wetlands from regulatory protection, including large parts of the Everglades and the Great Dismal Swamp."[79]

One day before the House opened debate on the bill, the National Academy of Sciences (NAS) released a congressionally mandated 268-page report, authored by seventeen prominent wetlands experts, laying out the scientific consensus on wetlands delineation. The report made it clear that the approach outlined in the House bill, with its insistence on narrow, quantitative definitions, was unscientific for a host of reasons. For example, the House bill required that a wetland be saturated for twenty-one consecutive days in the growing season, even though the NAS report contended that a wetland may experience periodic saturation for shorter periods, in the root zone of plants rather than at the surface, and not necessarily in the months between the spring thaw and the autumn frost. Moreover, the report noted, a uniform definition of wetlands cannot take into account the wetness of a wetland relative to its surrounding landscape. Areas that would be considered only marginal wetlands in the Northeast, for example, may constitute critical riparian areas in the arid West.[80]

When the chairman of the NAS committee, William M. Lewis, Jr., called the House bill's requirements "arbitrary," Rep. Jimmy Hayes, D-La.—the author of the wetlands provisions—responded that the academy was meddling in politics by releasing its report the day before debate on the bill was scheduled to begin. Hayes pointed out that whether or not to protect wetlands was at heart a *political* decision to be made by Congress, not one that could be dictated by science.[81] To those, such as Maryland Republican Wayne Gilchrest, who argued that wetlands deserved special protection, Hayes responded that the property rights of individuals were more important than protecting ecologically worthless wetlands.[82]

As expected, on May 16, the House passed the Clean Water Act rewrite by 240 to 185. Echoing the rhetoric of property rights advocacy groups, Jimmy Hayes called the decision a "vote on the distinction between the rights of individuals and the arrogance of power and government."[83] With forty-five conservative Democrats voting for the bill and thirty-four moderate Republicans voting against it, however, the volume of crossover voting troubled supporters of the legislation.[84] The revolt against the Republican leadership spurred by Sherwood Boehlert, R-N.Y., attracted widespread media coverage, making the Senate reluctant to act. In the end, the Senate refused to adopt a similar measure, and President Clinton vowed to veto any such bill.

Endangered Species Act Reform. Like wetlands regulations, endangered species protection became a favorite object of anti-environmentalists' derision in the late 1980s and early 1990s, particularly after the spotted owl debacle (see chapter 7). It was not surprising, then, that the 104th Congress chose the Endangered Species Act (ESA) as its third major target. When it passed the ESA virtually unanimously in 1973, Congress did not anticipate its impact; most supporters viewed it as a way to protect such national icons as the bald eagle, the grey whale, and the grizzly bear. In fact, early on, the ESA did provide a means to support "charismatic megafauna": more than two-thirds of the species on the list in 1973 were birds and mammals. By the mid-1990s, however, the number of listed species had jumped from 114 to 1,516; moreover, nearly two-thirds of listed species were plants, and there were almost as many protected invertebrates as birds and mammals combined.[85] Opponents of the act multiplied, as it became a formidable tool—"the pit bull of environmental laws"—in the hands of environmentalists.[86]

By the time the act came up for reauthorization in 1992, demands for major reform had begun to escalate. In an effort to deflect criticism of the ESA and head off more permanent legislative revisions, the Clinton administration began proposing administrative changes to increase the law's flexibility.[87] Among the administration's proposals were rules exempting small landowners from regulations and requiring independent scientific peer review of all listing decisions. The administration also adopted a series of innovative practices in hopes of salvaging the act. For instance, it began allowing developers to pay a fee for destroying habitat and then using the money raised to purchase other tracts of habitat or buy permanent conservation easements from private landowners.[88] And it espoused cooperative regional conservation plans, such as the one built around the endangered California gnatcatcher in San Diego (see chapter 12).

ESA reform sponsors Richard Pombo, R-Calif., in the House and Dirk Kempthorne, R-Idaho, in the Senate were unmoved by the Clinton administration's gestures, however. Early in the legislative session, House Resources Committee Chairman Don Young, R-Alaska, named revamping the ESA his top legislative priority, and he was certain he had the votes to bring a tough bill to the House floor. He boldly predicted that the House would finish its work on the ESA by August. To ensure the plan's success, Young created an endangered species task force chaired by Richard Pombo, a conservative rancher and vocal property rights advocate. In doing so, he undercut New Jersey Republican Jim Saxton, the moderately pro-environmental chairman of the Resources Subcommittee on Fisheries, Wildlife and Oceans, which normally has jurisdiction over endangered species.[89]

In mid-March, Pombo began holding hearings in which anti-ESA speakers told their stories and presented their recommendations for revising the ESA. As in the wetlands debate, anti-ESA proponents' arguments relied heavily on rhetoric and anecdote. Environmentalists countered by distributing "fact sheets" purporting to tell the true stories behind the anecdotes. They posted emergency alerts on websites and sent email bulletins to their members asking them to contact their senators and representatives to oppose ESA rewrites. Scientists spoke out on behalf of the act. They pointed out that many American plants and animals were in dire need of its protection, noting that more than 950 domestic species of plants and animals and more than 560 foreign species were listed as endangered or imminently threatened with endangerment; that thousands of others were candidates for listing; and that nearly two-thirds of all mammals were either listed or candidates for listing, along with 14 percent of birds, 12 percent of plants, and 10 percent of fish. While acknowledging its flaws, Dennis D. Murphy, president of the Society for Conservation Biology, argued that the ESA was "the most effective tool in the tool kit for preserving this country's biological diversity."[90]

Scientists' pleas notwithstanding, in April 1995, Sen. Slade Gorton, R-Wash., unveiled his own version of the ESA, which—to environmentalists' dismay— was written largely by lawyers representing the industries most affected by the law. The Gorton bill did away with most of the strict requirements to save plants and animals that biologists said were headed for extinction. In their place, it allowed a political appointee—typically the secretary of interior—to decide whether and how to save a species. Gorton's bill also abolished the government's principal method of enforcing the ESA on private property: fines or imprisonment for those who destroy the habitat of an endangered species. Gorton trumpeted that his proposal didn't "undo everything that's been done [under the ESA]. But I suspect it would end up having that effect."[91]

Neither Gorton's bill nor Senate ESA bills introduced by Dirk Kempthorne, R-Idaho, or Harry Reid, D-Nev., made much progress, however. A House ESA revision (HR 2275) proposed in September 1995 by Young and Pombo failed to move beyond approval by the House Resources Committee. While Pombo's hearings had garnered publicity, they had also galvanized environmental activists and delayed any legislative action until the fall, by which time the anti-environmentalists had lost momentum. Further complicating matters, activists on the right began criticizing the Young-Pombo bill for not going far enough. The so-called Grassroots ESA Coalition, an alliance of property rights and Wise Use groups, preferred repealing the act altogether and replacing it with a voluntary wildlife management scheme. As Rob Gordon, executive director of the free-market conservation group National Wilderness Institute, remarked: "There are some fundamentally different worldviews on the Endangered Species Act within the [Republican] party. That makes it real difficult to horse trade."[92]

While they were unable to accomplish their goal of substantially revising the ESA, congressional Republicans were able to achieve some significant victories. Backed by constituents who feared the identification of more species requiring protection, Congress withdrew funding for the National Biological Service. Congress also imposed a moratorium on new endangered species listings and critical habitat designations until December 31, 1996, or until the act was reauthorized, whichever came first.

OUTCOMES

Anti-environmentalists scored some victories in 1995, but environmentalists responded adroitly to legislative attacks by galvanizing their grassroots base and spurring legislative defenders to action. Perceiving Republicans' anti-environmental stance as a liability in the 1996 elections, congressional Democrats lambasted their colleagues in the press. By summer 1995, the Republican party's unanimity had dissolved, as moderate Republicans like New Jersey's Jim Saxton, New York's Sherwood Boehlert, and Rhode Island's John Chafee began to challenge the party's anti-environmental initiatives. In late 1995, House Speaker Newt Gingrich granted that the party's conservative wing had mishandled the environmental issue all spring and summer.[93] John McCain, R-Ariz., warned that "polls indicate that the environment is the voters' number one concern about continued Republican leadership of Congress" because Republicans were viewed as "too eager to swing the meat axe of repeal when the scalpel of reform is what's needed."[94]

By the end of 1995, moderate Republicans had persuaded fellow party members to back off, and in early 1996, Congress authorized the president to lift the moratorium on listing endangered species, which he did in late April. In March 1996, Gingrich appointed a task force on the environment—chaired by adversaries Sherwood Boehlert and Richard Pombo—in hopes of reconciling the ideological and regional differences that had riven the party. In late April, the Senate finally cleared by 88–11 the fiscal 1997 omnibus appropriations bill (HR 3019) after Republicans were forced to retreat on almost all their anti-environmental riders. By mid-May 1996, supporters of property rights legislation in Congress were also on the defensive. Republican staff members announced that they were canceling plans to bring Sen. Bob Dole's bill to the Senate floor because it could not muster even the majority of votes needed to save face, never mind the sixty needed to break an anticipated filibuster.[95] Also in mid-May, the task force released a one-page "vision statement and principles," which it billed as a blueprint for the party's new environmental agenda.[96] In September 1996, a chastened Congress proceeded to approve a fiscal 1997 appropriations bill that contained relatively few anti-environmental riders. Many of those originally included were dropped after the administration expressed its opposition.[97]

In late 1996, recognizing the potency of environmentalists in his electoral coalition and hoping to establish a legacy, President Clinton launched an environmental counteroffensive. In the midst of the presidential campaign, Clinton established a 1.7-million-acre national monument in the red rock country of southern Utah using authority granted under the Antiquities Act of 1906. Then, in November, the EPA proposed strict new standards for airborne particulates and ground-level ozone. In December, the Army Corps of Engineers decided to phase out over two years Reagan-era regulations enabling fast-track approval for property owners to drain wetlands smaller than ten acres. Finally, on December 13, the administration terminated the two-year-old and much reviled timber salvage program (see chapter 7) two weeks before it was due to expire.[98] Republicans' objections to the president's actions were muted. As Rep. Henry Bonilla, R-Texas, pointed out, "We can't just charge ahead in the way we did in the last few years. In the [public relations] battle, we have been defeated."[99]

The anti-environmental movement was down but not out, however. In 1999, Jeff Rauch, executive director of Public Employees for Environmental Responsibility, noted that "Though the flamboyant challenges to the federal government of the mid-1990s abated after the shock of the Oklahoma City bombing in 1995, the number of reported death threats, discoveries of pipe bombs, arsons of buildings, and other incidents against the Forest Service and . . . the Bureau of Land Management keeps rising."[100] Using greater savvy in drawing up their bills, and abandoning their confrontational tone, opponents of strict environmental protection regulations forged ahead in the 105th and 106th Congresses (1997–2000). In September 1998, a coalition of prominent environmental groups tried to draw public attention to the anti-environmental activity quietly taking place in Congress by taking out a full-page ad in the *New York Times* labeling the 105th Congress the "worst ever" with respect to the environment. The ad lambasted Congress for being on the verge of passing nearly seventy anti-environmental riders, more than twice as many as the 104th Congress had attached to appropriations bills. President Clinton continued to use his veto power to hold off the most damaging of these for the remainder of his term, but with the advent of the more conservative Bush administration in 2001, anti-environmentalists' legislative fortunes may rebound.[101]

CONCLUSIONS

The anti-environmental movement that emerged in the late 1980s and gathered steam through the early 1990s was "a desperate effort to defend the hegemony of the cultural and economic values of the agricultural and extractive industries of the rural West."[102] It employed a wide array of tactics to enhance its impact on policymaking at the state and national levels. Its leaders brought together an explosive coalition of westerners advocating unrestricted access to federal lands and easterners concerned with private property rights, integrating them under the banner of individual freedom. Though heavily backed by industry, anti-environmental leaders galvanized ordinary citizens by reframing environmental policies as means by which elitist environmentalists impose their values and preferences on ordinary Americans. They publicized politically compelling stories of heroes, victims, and villains and drew on longstanding American values of community autonomy and antipathy toward the federal government. Even more remarkably, anti-environmentalists appropriated the staple tactics of the environmental movement, from grassroots organizing to nationalizing policy conflict to filing lawsuits. On occasion, the anti-environmental movement has taken the monkey-wrenching of the environmental left to a new level, using violence and intimidation against environmental researchers and activists, as well as federal officials trying to implement environmental regulations.

Anti-environmentalists were sufficiently visible by the mid-1990s to galvanize congressional Republicans to pursue electoral credit by proposing anti-environmental legislation. Because they thought they were responding to a potent national sentiment, anti-environmental members of Congress were taken aback by the strength of the public reaction to their initiatives. It appears that many Republicans in the 1990s fell into the "salience trap," assuming that because most people did not mention the environment as the nation's most important problem in polls that the environmental consensus had dissolved. In fact, throughout the early 1990s, an annual survey conducted by Roper Starch Worldwide Inc. and Times Mirror Magazines consistently showed that more than three-quarters of Americans viewed themselves as active environmentalists or sympathetic to the environmentalist cause.[103] A majority of Americans also expressed their willingness to sacrifice economic growth for environmental protection.[104] A 1995 *Time*/CNN poll found that 63 percent of those questioned opposed any reduction in protection for endangered species; 59 percent opposed the expansion of logging, mining, or ranching on public lands; and fully two-thirds were against opening the Arctic National Wildlife Refuge to oil and gas exploration.[105] In the summer of 1995, Republican pollster Frank Lutz, one of the architects of the Contract With America, conceded that: "The public may not like or admire regulations, may not think more are necessary, but it puts environmental protection as a higher priority than cutting regulations."[106]

Latent public opinion alone would not have been sufficient to prevent change, however; environmentalists had to respond to the anti-environmental backlash by mobilizing supporters, suggesting that public opinion needs to be activated and brought to the attention of politicians to have an impact. Enhancing their influence, environmentalists formed alliances with a variety of groups, from the League of Cities to the United Mine Workers of America, to defeat anti-environmental legislation. Just as anti-environmentalists have tried to associate environmentalism with communism, environmentalists linked their foes with the religious right and militant militia groups in the West. They publicized violent incidents and demonized Wise Use leaders in hopes of diluting the movement's appeal to moderate conservatives. They also exposed anti-environmentalists' tactics of attaching riders to spending bills and hustling legislation through Congress with minimal debate, charges that a largely sympathetic press corps repeated willingly.

Throughout the 1990s, threats of a Senate filibuster or a presidential veto held off the most serious anti-environmentalist attacks, but as William

Cronon, an environmental historian at the University of Wisconsin, admonishes environmentalists:

> We fool ourselves if we imagine that these new anti-environmental threats or their underlying cultural causes will simply go away. We need to figure out why certain kinds of anti-environmental arguments—about property rights, about excessive government regulation, about state interference with private liberty—are resonating with the public today more than 15 years ago. That means we have to look carefully at what our enemies are saying to find out what's right about it.[107]

Many environmentalists have, in fact, reassessed the traditional approaches to environmental protection in the 1990s in response to the backlash those regulations engendered. The remaining cases in this volume explore the ways that new approaches to addressing environmental problems are changing environmental politics.

QUESTIONS TO CONSIDER

- What are the roots of the anti-environmental backlash?
- Are the concerns of Wise Use and property rights advocates justified, and why?
- Should the anti-environmental backlash prompt environmentalists to reexamine their goals and strategies? If so, what sorts of approaches should environmentalists adopt?

Notes

1. Michael Mintrom and Sandra Vergari, "Advocacy Coalitions, Policy Entrepreneurs, and Policy Change," *Policy Studies Journal* 24 (1996): 420–434.
2. John Kingdon, *Agendas, Alternatives, and Public Policies,* 2d ed. (New York: Harper-Collins College, 1995); Carol S. Weissert, "Policy Entrepreneurs, Policy Opportunists, and Legislative Effectiveness," *American Politics Quarterly* 19 (April 1991): 262–274.
3. Michael Mintrom, "Policy Entrepreneurs and the Diffusion of Innovation," *American Journal of Political Science* 41 (July 1997): 738–770.
4. Jane Mansbridge, *Why We Lost the ERA* (Chicago: University of Chicago Press, 1986).
5. Lawrence R. Jacobs and Robert Y. Shapiro, *Politicians Don't Pander: Political Manipulation and the Loss of Democratic Responsiveness* (Chicago: University of Chicago Press, 2000).
6. Timothy Egan, "The 1994 Campaign: Western States," *New York Times,* November 4, 1994, A29.
7. Everett Carll Ladd and Karlyn H. Bowman, *Attitudes Toward the Environment: Twenty-Five Years After Earth Day* (Washington, D.C.: AEI Press, 1995).
8. Robert Cameron Mitchell, "Public Opinion and the Green Lobby: Poised for the 1990s?" in *Environmental Policy in the 1990s,* ed. Norman J. Vig and Michael E. Kraft (Washington, D.C.: CQ Press, 1990), 81–99.
9. R. Douglas Arnold, *The Logic of Congressional Action* (New Haven: Yale University Press, 1990).

10. Keith Krehbiel, *Pivotal Politics: A Theory of U.S. Lawmaking* (Chicago: University of Chicago Press, 1998).
11. Jacqueline Vaughn Switzer, *Green Backlash: The History and Politics of Environmental Opposition in the United States* (Boulder, Colo.: Lynne Rienner, 1997).
12. Norman J. Vig, "Presidential Leadership: From the Reagan to the Bush Administration," in *Environmental Policy in the 1990s*, ed. Vig and Kraft, 33–58.
13. Quoted in Philip Shabecoff, *A Fierce Green Fire* (New York: Farrar, Straus, and Giroux, 1993), 208.
14. Mitchell, "Public Opinion and the Green Lobby."
15. Ibid.
16. Alan Gottlieb, ed., *The Wise Use Agenda* (Bellevue, Wash.: Free Enterprise Press, 1989).
17. Margaret Kriz, "Land Mine," *National Journal*, October 23, 1993, 2531–2534.
18. Sandra Davis, "Fighting Over Public Lands," in *Western Public Lands and Environmental Politics*, ed. Charles Davis (Boulder, Colo.: Westview Press, 1997), 11–31.
19. Samantha Sanchez, "How the West Is Won," *American Prospect*, March–April 1996, 37–42.
20. Kate O'Callaghan, "Whose Agenda for America," *Audubon*, September–October 1992, 80–91.
21. Macwilliams Cosgrove Snider, *The Wise Use Movement: Strategic Analysis and the Fifty State Review* (Washington, D.C.: Environmental Working Group, March 1993), 27.
22. Quoted in O'Callaghan, "Whose Agenda," 84.
23. Nancie G. Marzulla, "The Property Rights Movement: How It Began and Where It Is Headed," in *Land Rights: The 1990s Property Rights Rebellion*, ed. Bruce Yandle (Lanham, Md.: Rowman and Littlefield, 1995), 22.
24. Quoted in Kenneth Jost, "Property Rights," *CQ Researcher*, June 16, 1995, 516.
25. Marzulla, "The Property Rights Movement."
26. Ibid.
27. Thomas A. Lewis, "Cloaked in a Wise Disguise," in *Let the People Judge: Wise Use and the Private Property Rights Movement*, ed. John Echeverria and Raymond Booth Eby (Washington, D.C.: Island Press, 1995), 13–20.
28. Quoted in Sanchez, "How the West Is Won."
29. Ibid.
30. Quoted in Marla Williams, "Save the People!" *Boston Globe*, January 13, 1992.
31. Quoted in O'Callaghan, "Whose Agenda," 84.
32. Quoted in Williams, "Save the People!"
33. Ibid.
34. Quoted in Switzer, *Green Backlash*, 197.
35. Quoted in O'Callaghan, "Whose Agenda," 84.
36. Keith Schneider, "Fighting to Keep U.S. Rules from Devaluing Land," *New York Times*, January 9, 1995, A1.
37. Ann Reilly Dowd, "Environmentalists Are on the Run," *Fortune*, September 9, 1994, 91–92, 96–100.
38. Jost, "Property Rights."
39. Karol J. Ceplo, "Land Rights Conflicts in the Regulation of Wetlands," in *Land Rights*, ed. Yandle, 103–149.
40. Quoted in David Helvarg, *The War Against the Greens* (San Francisco: Sierra Club Books, 1997), 20.
41. Ben Bolch and Harold Lyons, *Apocalypse Not: Science, Economics, and Environmentalism* (Washington, D.C.: Cato Institute, 1993).
42. Helvarg, *War Against the Greens*.
43. Phil Brick, "Determined Opposition: The Wise Use Movement Challenges Environmentalism," *Environment*, October 1995, 17–20, 36–41.

44. Some experts have questioned whether such firms rightly qualify for nonprofit status as "public interest" charities. One law professor who examined 132 cases brought by the Pacific Legal Foundation found that seventy of them were invalid by the terms of the IRS requirements and another sixteen were questionable. See Helvarg, *The War Against the Greens.*

45. Switzer, *Green Backlash.*

46. Mark Dowie, "The Wayward West," *Outside,* November 1995, 59–67, 152–154.

47. Timothy Egan, "Court Puts Down Rebellion Over Control of Federal Land," *New York Times,* March 16, 1996, 1.

48. The Fifth Amendment reads: "No person shall . . . be deprived of life, liberty, or property, without due process of law; nor shall private property be taken for public use without just compensation."

49. Richard Epstein, *Takings: Private Property and the Power of Eminent Domain* (Cambridge: Harvard University Press, 1985).

50. Karen Curran, "Judge's Decision to Have Impact on Property Owners," *Boston Globe,* March 12, 1995, A1.

51. Joseph L. Sax, "Property Rights and the Economy of Nature: Understanding Lucas v. South Carolina Coastal Commission," *Stanford Law Review* 45 (May 1993), 1433–1455; see also James J. Rinehart and Jeffrey J. Pompe, "The Lucas Case and the Conflict Over Property Rights," in *Land Rights,* ed. Yandle, 67–105.

52. Although it is a less visible forum, plaintiffs also pursued claims in the U.S. Court of Federal Claims. See Switzer, *Green Backlash.*

53. Rinehart and Pompe, "The Lucas Case."

54. Helvarg, *War Against the Greens.*

55. Ibid.

56. Quoted in Dowie, "The Wayward West, 64."

57. Ibid. See also Richard Lacayo, "This Land is Whose Land?" *Time,* October 23, 1995, 68–71.

58. Helvarg, *War Against the Greens,* 13.

59. Nearly half of the seventy-three new members of the House received a zero rating for 1995 from the League of Conservation Voters.

60. Quoted in Bob Benenson, "GOP Sets the 104th Congress on a New Regulatory Course," *Congressional Quarterly Weekly Report,* June 17, 1995, 1693–1701.

61. Quoted in Scott Allen, "'Contract' Reframes Issue of Environment's Worth," *Boston Globe,* February 6, 1995, 25.

62. Quoted in Allan Freedman, "Accomplishments, Missteps Mark Congress' Record," *Congressional Quarterly Weekly Report,* October 12, 1996, 2918–2922.

63. Quoted in Margaret Kriz, "Out of the Wilderness," *National Journal,* April 8, 1995, 864.

64. Ibid.

65. They staffed the committee with eight members whose League of Conservation scores were less than 25 percent and League of Private Property Rights scores were over 80 percent. See ibid.

66. Freedman, "Accomplishments, Missteps."

67. The law defined property as land, any interest in land, and any proprietary water right.

68. Allan Freedman, "Property Rights Bill Advances but Faces Uncertainty," *Congressional Quarterly Weekly Report,* December 23, 1995, 3884–3885.

69. Allan Freedman, "GOP Trying to Find Balance After Early Stumbles," *Congressional Quarterly Weekly Report,* January 20, 1996, 151–153.

70. Neal R. Pierce, "Takings—The Comings and Goings," *Congressional Quarterly Weekly Report,* January 6, 1996, 37.

71. Because the initiative was not originated by the state government, the Washington measure could not be amended by the legislature or vetoed by the governor. The

only recourse for opponents was to gather 90,000 signatures within ninety days of legislative approval.

72. Louis Jacobson, "Land-Rights Battle with Fresh Twists," *National Journal*, October 14, 1995, 2537–2540.

73. Switzer, *Green Backlash*.

74. Timothy Egan, "Unlikely Alliances Attack Property Rights Measures," *New York Times*, May 15, 1995, A1.

75. Jacobson, "Land-Rights Battle."

76. The term "wetlands" encompasses a variety of shallow water, periodically flooded, and high-ground water environments. Wetlands perform a host of ecological functions: they store flood waters by absorbing overflow waters during excessively wet periods and gradually releasing water as a river or stream recedes; they filter sediments and pollutants out of the water supply; and they replenish groundwater systems and provide critical habitat for fish and wildlife, including nearly half of all federally listed threatened and endangered species. By the early 1990s the nation had lost more than half of its original wetland endowment, with only about 95 million acres of wetlands remaining in the lower forty-eight states, and was continuing to lose about 250,000–300,000 acres of wetlands each year, or about thirty acres an hour, to development and cultivation. See Dianne Dumanoski, "Heavy Toll Seen if 'Drier' Wetlands Are Developed," *Boston Globe*, December 10, 1991, 11; Jon Kusler, "Wetlands Delineation: An Issue of Science or Politics?" *Environment*, March 1992, 7–11, 29–37; Douglas A. Thompson and Thomas G. Yocom, "Losing Ground," *Technology Review*, August/September 1993, 20–29.

77. Bob Benenson, "Clean Water Law Revisions Mark Arrival of New Era," *Congressional Quarterly Weekly Report*, April 8, 1995, 1018–1019.

78. John H. Cushman, Jr., "Industry Helped Draft Clean Water Law," *New York Times*, March 22, 1995, A1.

79. Quoted in John H. Cushman, Jr., "House Panel Backs Easing of U.S. Water Standards," *New York Times*, March 30, 1995, A21.

80. John H. Cushman, Jr., "House and Science Panels Clash on Wetlands," *New York Times*, April 7, 1995, A30.

81. Ibid.

82. John H. Cushman, Jr., "Scientists Reject Criteria for Wetlands Bill," *New York Times*, May 10, 1995, 1.

83. Quoted in John H. Cushman, Jr., "Crossover Votes on U.S. Pollution Bill Clouds Future of Environmental Issues," *New York Times*, May 15, 1995, A12.

84. Ibid.

85. Margaret Kriz, "Caught in the Act," *National Journal*, December 16, 1995, 3090–3094.

86. Donald Barry of the World Wildlife Fund, quoted in Timothy Egan, "Strongest U.S. Environmental Law May Become Endangered Species," *New York Times*, May 26, 1992, A1.

87. John H. Cushman, Jr., "Babbitt Seeks to Ease Rules in Bid to Rescue Imperiled Species," *New York Times*, March 7, 1995, C4.

88. William K. Stevens, "Future of Endangered Species Act in Doubt as Law Is Debated," *New York Times*, May 16, 1995, C1.

89. Kriz, "Caught in the Act."

90. Quoted in Stevens, "Future of Endangered Species Act."

91. Quoted in Timothy Egan, "Industries Affected by Endangered Species Act Help a Senator Rewrite its Provisions," *New York Times*, April 13, 1995, A20.

92. Quoted in Kriz, "Caught in the Act."

93. David S. Cloud and Jackie Koszczuk, "GOP's All-or-Nothing Approach Hangs on a Balanced Budget," *Congressional Quarterly*, December 9, 1995, 3709–3715.

94. John McCain, "Nature Is Not a Liberal Plot," *New York Times*, November 22, 1996, A31.

95. Margaret Kriz, "Taking Issue," *National Journal*, June 1, 1996, 1200–1204.
96. Ibid.
97. Freedman, "Accomplishments, Missteps."
98. Allan Freedman, "GOP Cautious on Easing Rules Despite Clinton's Forays," *Congressional Quarterly Weekly Report*, January 18, 1997, 168–170.
99. Quoted in Freedman, "GOP Cautious," 170.
100. Jeff Rauch, "Nature's Guardians Still Face Disrespect," *New York Times*, December 22, 1999, A30.
101. Katharine Q. Seelye, "Bush Team is Reversing Environmental Policies," *New York Times*, November 18, 2001, A1.
102. Ralph Maughan and Douglas Nilson, "What's Old and What's New About the Wise Use Movement" (Idaho State Department of Political Science, April 23, 1993); http://www.nwcitizen.com/publicgood/reports/maughan.htm.
103. Benenson, "GOP Sets the 104th Congress on a New Regulatory Course"; Ladd and Bowman, *Attitudes Toward the Environment.*
104. Benenson, "GOP Sets the 104th Congress on a New Regulatory Course"; The Gallup Poll, April 22, 1995. Ladd and Bowman challenge the results of questions asking respondents to choose between economic growth and environmental protection. They point out that many Americans don't believe there is a tradeoff between growth and the environment. They also note that people are also reluctant to support environmental protection in their own community if it means that jobs will be lost as a result. See Ladd and Bowman, *Attitudes Toward the Environment*, 23–27.
105. Benenson, "GOP Sets the 104th Congress on a New Regulatory Course."
106. Quoted in Margaret Kriz, "Drawing a Green Line in the Sand," *National Journal*, August 12, 1995, 2076.
107. Quoted in Kriz, "Taking Issue."

Recommended Reading

Echeverria, John, and Raymond Booth Eby, eds. *Let the People Judge: Wise Use and the Private Property Rights Movement.* Washington, D.C.: Island Press, 1995,
Helvarg, David. *The War Against the Greens.* San Francisco: Sierra Club Books, 1997.
Switzer, Jacqueline Vaughn. *Green Backlash: The History and Politics of Environmental Opposition in the United States.* Boulder, Colo.: Lynne Rienner, 1997.
Yandle, Bruce, ed. *Land Rights: The 1990s Property Rights Rebellion.* Lanham, Md.: Rowman and Littlefield, 1995.

Web Sites

http://www.ewg.org/ (Environmental Working Group site)
http://www.cato.org/ (Cato Institute site)
http://www.heritage.org/ (Heritage Foundation site)

CHAPTER 11

Market-Based Solutions

Acid Rain and the Clean Air Act Amendments of 1990

The Clean Air Act of 1970 was the federal government's first serious step toward reducing the nation's air pollution (see chapter 2). In 1977, Congress amended the Clean Air Act and scheduled it for reauthorization in 1981. President Ronald Reagan opposed any action on the bill, however, and Congress was deeply divided on the issue of acid rain.[1] As a result, the act languished in Congress throughout the 1980s. Finally, after a decade of stalemate, Congress and the Bush administration agreed on a clean air plan that included as its signature provision an innovative allowance trading approach to reducing emissions that cause acid rain. The regulations required by the Clean Air Act Amendments of 1990 took effect in 1995 and aimed by the year 2000 to cut emissions of sulfur dioxide in half.

This case elucidates several important aspects of legislative policymaking. First, it illustrates the importance of regional concerns in Congress. The desire to protect local or regional economic interests has commonly been the force behind resistance to making environmental policy more protective. The regional emphasis of Congress is particularly pronounced in this case because acid rain is a transboundary problem: those who bear the environmental burden of its effects are in a different region than those who cause it. As previous cases have made clear, members of Congress use every weapon at their disposal to resist the imposition of direct, visible economic costs on their constituents. The organization and procedures of Congress provide many potential roadblocks: authorizing subcommittees can delete legislative provisions during markup; committee chairmen can prevent a bill from reaching the floor, as can a majority of committee members; and legislative leaders, such as the Speaker of the House or the Senate Majority Leader, can refuse to schedule a vote on a bill. Even if a bill does reach the floor, its opponents may attach enough hostile amendments to cripple it, or, in the Senate, a minority can filibuster it.

Because it is relatively easy to block policy change, leadership is essential to the passage of major new laws. The president sets the legislative agenda and thus plays a pivotal role in initiating policy change and mobilizing legislative supporters. The president can deploy his political resources—which range from political favors to his popularity and prestige—to assemble a legislative coalition. Executive-legislative branch rivalry is intense, however, so even when the same party controls the White House and Congress, skilled leaders in both the House and Senate are also necessary to shepherd a policy through the cumbersome legislative process. Like the president, congressional leaders have a variety of resources at their disposal—from the authority to set the agenda to the ability to distribute rewards for cooperation. At least as important, though, are their personal negotiating skills and the relationships and reputations they have built with fellow members of Congress.

In the legislative contest, science can play a critical, if indirect, role. While opponents of new regulation emphasize scientific uncertainty and call for more research in hopes of delaying change, proponents of new policies rely on scientific evidence to buttress their claims of environmental harm and the need for prompt government action. If environmentalists have succeeded in persuading the public that a problem is serious and warrants remediation, a legislative leader is more likely not only to adopt the issue but also to be able to recruit allies. The more widely accepted a causal story for a salient problem, the less credible opposing positions become.[2] Moreover, such stories provide rank-and-file members with handy explanations for their positions that they can give constituents.[3]

Advocates can also facilitate policy change by furnishing leaders with a novel solution that helps to break a logjam. By providing a new way to address a problem, policy entrepreneurs can change the political landscape, broadening supportive coalitions or breaking up opposing ones. The allowance trading mechanism proposed for acid rain was particularly effective because it appealed to conservatives who believe such market-based approaches are superior to conventional approaches in two respects. First, market-based policy instruments allow polluters who can clean up cheaply to do more and those for whom cleanup is costly to do less, which in theory reduces overall pollution to the desired level at a minimum total cost. Second, market-based tools create incentives for firms to create and adopt new technologies and to continue to reduce pollution beyond the target level because they continue to save money by doing so.[4]

Finally, this case illustrates the way international pressure can change legislative dynamics. Because pollutants emitted in the United States precipitate in Canada, the Canadian government, as well as Canadian scientists and environmentalists, pushed to get acid rain onto the U.S. policy agenda and then actively tried to influence policy. According to one observer, the issue "overshadowed almost all other elements of the bilateral relationship" between the United States and Canada.[5] Moreover, although they had little direct effect on the legislative process, the Canadians provided a steady stream of reliable information to and publicity for the pro-regulation side, which in turn, helped to shape public and elite views about the need for controls.

BACKGROUND

Scientists began documenting the effects of acid rain more than 100 years ago. Robert Angus Smith, a nineteenth-century English chemist was the first to detect the occurrence of acid precipitation. He conducted extensive tests of its properties, but his research was largely ignored. Not until the late 1960s did Swedish soil scientist Svante Oden rekindle scientific interest in acid rain. Integrating knowledge from the scientific disciplines of limnology, agricultural science, and atmospheric chemistry, Oden developed a coherent analysis of the behavior of acid deposition over time and across regions.[6] Oden's research laid the groundwork for conclusions unveiled at the 1972 United Nations Conference on the Human Environment in Stockholm. At the conference, a group of Swedish scientists presented a case study demonstrating that acid precipitation attributable to sulfur dioxide (SO_2) emissions from human-made sources—primarily industrial processes and utilities—was having adverse ecological and human health effects. These findings prompted further research efforts in other countries to identify the causes of acid deposition and to document its direct and indirect environmental impacts.

Acid Rain Gets on the U.S. Agenda

Scientific concern about acid rain was a primary factor in getting the problem on the U.S. political agenda. In 1975, the U.S. Forest Service sponsored an international symposium on acid rain, and shortly thereafter Professor Ellis Cowling, a Canadian expert, testified at a congressional hearing on the need for more funding to study the phenomenon. In 1977, President Jimmy Carter's Council on Environmental Quality suggested that the United States needed a comprehensive national program to address the acid rain problem. This argument gained momentum in the executive branch, and in 1978 Carter began to take steps toward that goal. Calling acid precipitation "a global environmental problem of the greatest importance," the president asked Congress to expand funding for research and to investigate possible control measures under the Clean Air Act. He also established the Bilateral Research Consultation Group on the Long-Range Transport of Air Pollution to conduct a joint investigation with Canada.

Fueling environmentalists' interest in acid rain policy, a series of reports in 1978, 1979, and 1980 by the International Joint Commission (IJC), which had been created to address U.S.-Canada water quality issues in the Great Lakes, suggested that if not controlled, acid rain could render 50,000 lakes in the United States and Canada lifeless by 1995, destroy the productivity of vast areas of forest, and contaminate the drinking water supplies of millions of people.[7] Then, the Bilateral Research Consultation Group issued two reports, in October 1979 and November 1980, which together comprised the first comprehensive statement of scientific knowledge about acid rain and its likely effects in eastern North America. One of the group's key findings was that at least half of Canada's acid deposition originated in the United States, whereas only 15 percent of the United States' acid rain came from Canada.[8]

The Carter Administration Responds

The concern among environmentalists and high-level Canadian officials generated by these reports created pressure on the United States to address acid rain. In 1980, President Carter signed the U.S.-Canada memorandum of intent to negotiate an agreement on transboundary air pollution. He also approved the Acid Precipitation Act of 1980, which established the Interagency Task Force on Acid Precipitation and charged it with planning and implementing the National Acid Precipitation Assessment Program (NAPAP), a comprehensive research program to clarify the causes and effects of acid rain.

Impatient for a more substantial policy response, Canadian and U.S. advocates of acid rain controls appealed directly to the EPA to regulate acid rain-causing emissions under the Clean Air Act. Although Carter's EPA administrator Douglas Costle conceded that government intervention was warranted, he also expressed concern about the political risks, noting that, "in an election year, it is best to keep your head down rather than embark on a new environmental regulation program."[9] In the administration's final days, Costle acknowledged that U.S. emissions were contributing significantly to acid rain over sensitive areas of Canada and laid the groundwork for the next EPA administrator to invoke CAA Section 115, under which the EPA can require states to reduce the impact of air pollution on foreign countries.

THE CASE

In the early 1980s, the topic of acid rain moved from the relative obscurity of scientific inquiry into the political spotlight. During the Carter administration, despite the president's commitment to research, few Americans considered acid rain a policy problem. Yet three years later a Harris poll found that nearly two-thirds of those questioned were aware of acid rain and favored strict controls on SO_2 emissions.[10] By this time, acid rain had also become a serious foreign policy issue between the United States and Canada, and environmentalists had begun pressuring members of Congress to introduce controls as part of the Clean Air Act reauthorization. Both the president and powerful members of Congress opposed such measures, however, and for nearly a decade used their political resources to thwart such efforts.

The Emerging Scientific Consensus on Acid Rain

By the early 1980s, scientists in Sweden, Norway, Canada, and the United States had developed a substantial body of evidence to support a theory of the causes of acid rain. They knew that the precursors to acid rain, SO_2 and nitrogen oxides (NO_x), were released by a variety of natural mechanisms, such as volcanic eruptions, lightning, forest fires, microbial activity in soils, and biogenic processes, but that industrial activity that relies on burning fossil fuels was spewing these substances into the air in quantities that dwarfed nature's output. They also knew that in 1980, the United States emitted about 27 million tons of SO_2 and 21 million tons of NO_x; that the thirty-one states east of the Mississippi River emitted about 80 percent of that SO_2 (22 million tons) and two-thirds of the NO_x (14 million tons); that nearly three-quarters of the SO_2 emitted east of the Mississippi came from power plants; and that forty

enormous coal-fired plants clustered in the Midwest and the Ohio and Tennessee Valleys—a single one of which emitted about 200,000 tons of SO_2 a
year—were responsible for almost half of the region's SO_2 emissions.[11]

Furthermore, scientists were beginning to recognize that because these
enormous plants had smokestacks as high as the tallest skyscraper, the SO_2
they emitted was traveling hundreds or even thousands of miles downwind,
turning to acid and falling to earth along the way. Thus, they suspected, more
than 50 percent of the acid sulfate in the Adirondacks of New York came from
midwestern sources; about 20 percent came from the large metal smelters in
Ontario, Canada; and less than 10 percent originated in the Northeast.
Although the sources of NO_x were more diverse than those of SO_2, scientists
estimated that more than half of all NO_x emissions also came from the smokestacks of power plants and industrial sources and that automobiles, as well as
other forms of transportation, were the second major source of NO_x.

Scientists were increasingly confident in their comprehension of the consequences of acid rain as well, particularly for aquatic systems. They knew that
healthy lakes normally had a pH of around 5.6 or above; that when a lake's pH
dropped to 5.0, its biological processes began to suffer; and that at pH 4.5 or
below, a lake was generally incapable of supporting much life. Because precipitation in the eastern United States averaged pH 4.3, lakes and streams in
that region whose soils lacked alkaline buffering had become highly acidic.[12]
Lakes at high altitudes appeared to be particularly sensitive to acid rain
because, surrounded only by rocky outcroppings, they tended to be poorly
buffered. Furthermore, researchers discovered that when water ran off snow
or ice or during snowmelt, high-altitude lakes received a large pulse of acid
capable of killing fish and other aquatic life outright.[13]

Scientific understanding of the impacts of acidification on terrestrial ecosystems, particularly evergreen forests, was more uncertain, and they had only a
sketchy understanding of the complex interaction between acid rain and other
pollutants. Since the 1960s, scientists had observed a massive decline in many
forests in parts of Europe and the eastern United States, particularly in high-
elevation coniferous forests. For example, in sites above 850 meters in New
York's Adirondacks, the Green Mountains of Vermont, and the White Mountains of New Hampshire, more than half of the red spruce had died. At lower
elevations, researchers had documented injury to both hardwoods and soft-
woods. This loss of forest vitality could not be attributed to insects, disease, or
direct poisoning, since it was occurring in stands of different ages with different histories of disturbance or disease; pollution was the only known common
factor affecting all of them. In spite of the dimensions of forest decline, however, scientists had been unable to establish a firm causal link between acid rain
and forest damage (although all the hypotheses to explain failing tree health in
the United States and Europe implicated acid rain—if not as a lethal agent then
as a major stress). Laboratory and field studies showed that acid deposition
could damage leaves, roots, and microorganisms that form beneficial, symbiotic associations with roots; impair reproduction and survival of seedlings;

leach nutrients such as calcium and magnesium from soils; dissolve metals such as aluminum in the soil at levels potentially toxic to plants; and decrease a plant's resistance to other forms of stress, including pollution, climate, insects, and pathogens.[14]

Scientists had also learned that acid rain had adverse effects on soil and that although the forests in the Northeast and Canada grew on naturally acidic soils, acid rain could still damage these soils. The explanation for this was that most of the important ions in soil were positively charged—hydrogen (acidity); calcium and magnesium (nutrients); and aluminum, lead, mercury, and cadmium (heavy metals)—and were thus bound to the negatively charged surface of large, immobile soil particles. But acid deposition depleted the ability of soil particles to bind positively charged ions and thus unlocked the acidity, nutrients, and toxic metals.[15] Even in lakes that had not begun to acidify, the concentration of calcium and magnesium in the water was increasing with time, suggesting that these nutrients were being leached from surrounding soils.

In addition to its ecological impacts, scientists suspected that acid rain damaged human health, directly or indirectly. They had determined that once acid rain dissolved mercury, lead, cadmium, and other toxic metals in the environment, it transported them into drinking water supplies and thereby into the food chain. In addition, some reports suggested that downwind derivatives of SO_2, known as acid aerosols, posed respiratory health threats to children and asthmatics in the eastern United States. Finally, studies showed that particles of acid sulfate scattered light and reduced visibility, creating a haze that was most pronounced in summer but was present in all seasons. In the eastern United States, visibility was about twenty-five to forty miles absent pollution; it declined to as little as one mile during pollution episodes.

Resistance to Acid Rain Controls in the Reagan Administration

The emerging scientific consensus notwithstanding, upon taking office in 1981, President Reagan made his opposition to acid rain controls clear. Neither he nor the members of his administration believed the benefits of mitigating acid rain outweighed the costs of regulating generators of SO_2 and NO_x. David Stockman, head of the Office of Management and Budget (OMB) during Reagan's first term, expressed the administration's cornucopian view when he queried: "How much are the fish worth in those 170 lakes that account for four percent of the lake area of New York? And does it make sense to spend billions of dollars controlling emissions from sources in Ohio and elsewhere if you're talking about a very marginal volume of dollar value, either in recreation or commercial terms?"[16] But administration officials were rarely so forthright about their values; instead, they staunchly continued to contest the science and cite "scientific uncertainty" as a rationale for delay in formulating a policy to reduce SO_2 and NO_x emissions.

In June 1981, the National Academy of Sciences (NAS) released a comprehensive study of the effects of acid rain and other consequences of fossil fuel combustion. The report's authors concluded that "continued emissions of sulfur and nitrogen oxides at current or accelerated rates, in the face of clear evidence of serious hazards to human health and to the biosphere, will be extremely risky from a long-term economic standpoint as well as from the standpoint of biosphere protection."[17] The NAS called for a 50 percent reduction in the acidity of rain falling in the Northeast. The Reagan administration, while not actually disputing the Academy's scientific findings, labeled the report as "lacking in objectivity." In October 1981, the EPA issued a press release reiterating the administration's position that "scientific uncertainties in the causes and effects of acid rain demand that we proceed cautiously and avoid premature action."[18]

In 1982, the EPA released its own "Critical Assessment" of acid rain, a long-awaited, 1200-page document that was the combined effort of fifty-four scientists from universities and research institutes around the country. The report's findings clearly indicated a link between human-made emissions in the Midwest and dead and dying lakes and forests, materials damage, and human health effects in the eastern and southeastern United States and southeastern Canada. But high-level, politically sensitive EPA administrators downplayed the report, refusing to draw inferences from it or employ the models proposed in it.

In February 1983, the United States and Canada released the results of the bilateral study initiated by President Carter in 1980. The two countries had hoped to reach a consensus, but they deadlocked over a key section of the report dealing with the effects and significance of acid rain. In an unusual move that reflected high-level opposition to acid rain controls in the United States, the two nations issued separately worded conclusions:

The Canadians concluded the reducing acid rain "would reduce further damage" to sensitive lakes and streams. The U.S. version omitted the word "damage" and substituted "chemical and biological alterations." The Canadians concluded that "loss of genetic stock would not be reversible." The U.S. version omitted the sentence altogether. The Canadians proposed reducing the amount of acid sulfate deposited by precipitation to less than 20 kilograms of acid sulfate per hectare per year—roughly a 50 percent reduction—in order to protect "all but the most sensitive aquatic ecosystems in Canada." The United States declined to recommend any reductions.[19]

The Reagan White House decided not to have the U.S.-Canada report peer reviewed by the NAS as originally planned and instead hand-picked a scientific panel to review it. To the administration's dismay, however, its own panel strongly recommended action, saying "it is in the nature of the acid deposition problem that actions have to be taken despite the incomplete knowledge. . . . If we take the conservative point of view that we must wait until the scientific knowledge is definitive, the accumulated deposition and damaged environment may reach the point of irreversibility."[20] Although the panel delivered its interim conclusions to the White House well in advance of the House Health and Environment Subcommittee hearings on acid rain, the administration did not circulate them. Instead, administration officials testified before the subcommittee that no action should be taken until further study was done.

It appeared that administration obstruction might end when William Ruckelshaus, a respected environmentalist and the original head of the EPA, assumed leadership of the beleaguered agency in 1983. But although Ruckelshaus described acid rain as one of the "cosmic issues" confronting the nation and named it a priority, it quickly became apparent that the White House had no intention of pursuing acid rain regulation. Moreover, by August 1984, the White House still had not released the report prepared by its panel, leading some members of Congress to question whether the administration had suppressed it. Gene Likens, director of the Institute of Ecosystem Studies of the New York Botanical Gardens and a member of the panel, expressed his irritation in an interview with the *New York Times:*

> I have been concerned for some time that the Administration is saying that more research is needed because of uncertainty about acid rain. I think that is an excuse that is not correct. You can go on exploring scientific uncertainty forever. We must do something about acid rain now. Clearly in this case, it was an economic consideration that was most important to the Reagan Administration because of the cost of fixing the problem.[21]

When a spokesman for the White House attributed the delay to panel chairman William Nierenberg, director of the Scripps Institute of Oceanography, he retorted: "Let me say that somebody in the White House ought to print the damn thing. I'm sick and tired of it. What we said was, as practicing scientists, you can't wait for all the scientific evidence."[22]

The administration not only refused to release the scientific reports but went so far as to alter key passages of an EPA report entitled "Environmental Progress and Challenges: An EPA Perspective," moderating statements about the urgency of environmental problems. The OMB deleted a sentence referring to the findings of a recent NAS report on the adverse effects of acid rain and replaced a sentence on EPA's intent to establish an acid rain control program with one that simply called for further study of the problem.[23]

Congressional Divisions in the Reagan Years

While the White House dawdled, a coalition of environmental lobbyists urged legislators to pass comprehensive Clean Air Act revisions, including provisions to reduce acid rain. Richard Ayres, cofounder of the Natural Resources Defense Council (NRDC), was the leading policy entrepreneur for the Clean Air Coalition, an umbrella organization of environmental and other lobbies trying to link SO_2 and NO_x control policies to the acid rain problem. The coalition counted among its allies the Canadian Coalition on Acid Rain (CCAR), the first registered Canadian lobby in the United States to work for a nongovernmental, nonbusiness citizens' organization and a vocal participant in the U.S. policy debate.[24] At the same time, however, a unified coalition of utilities, industrial polluters, the eastern and midwestern high-sulfur coal industry, the United Mine Workers (UMW), and public officials from eastern and midwestern coal-producing states made its opposition to acid rain controls known to Congress.

Members of the House and Senate split over three central issues, all of which involved the regional allocation of costs and benefits. First, how much and how quickly should polluters have to reduce SO_2 emissions?[25] Proposals generally called for reductions of between eight and twelve million tons of SO_2 emissions from 1980 levels, the bulk of which would have to be made by the midwestern states that burned large quantities of high-sulfur coal.[26] Second, what means should polluters be able to use to reduce SO_2 emissions? Allowing utilities to switch from high-sulfur to low-sulfur coal would be the most cost-effective solution for some, but members from high-sulfur coal–producing states such as Kentucky, West Virginia, Pennsylvania, and Illinois feared major job losses if fuel switching became widespread. On the other hand, requiring all generators to install scrubbers was unacceptable to western states already using low-sulfur coal. The third and most contentious issue was who would pay for the proposed reduction in SO_2 emissions. One financing model employed the "polluter pays" principle; the second included subsidies for the regions bearing the greatest share of the cleanup costs. While midwestern representatives opposed "polluter pays," western and southern states disliked cost-sharing because they neither caused nor suffered from the effects of acid rain.

Congressional leaders sympathetic to opponents of regulation capitalized on a membership sharply divided along regional lines to foil efforts at acid rain legislation. The Senate Energy Committee—led by senators from coal-mining states, such as Wendell Ford, D-Ky., and Richard Lugar, R-Ind.—opposed acid rain controls. In contrast, in the relatively liberal Senate Environment and Public Works Committee, which comprised members from eastern states affected by acid rain, Republican Robert Stafford of Vermont and Democrat George Mitchell of Maine both introduced bills to curtail emissions of acid rain precursors with a variety of financing provisions, and the Environment Committee repeatedly endorsed these proposals.[27] But in each session Majority Leader Robert Byrd, of high-sulfur coal–producing West Virginia, was able to block consideration of the bills on the Senate floor.

Similar regional divisions stymied efforts in the House. The Energy and Commerce Committee annually debated but failed to approve bills to distribute the costs of emissions reductions across electricity users nationally. On several occasions, the committee's powerful chairman, John Dingell, D-Mich., made deft use of his parliamentary power to scuttle clean air legislation because he feared it would include more stringent automobile emissions standards. In 1984, the Energy Committee's Health and Environment Subcommittee Chairman Henry Waxman, a liberal California Democrat, teamed up with Gerry Sikorski of Minnesota and 125 others to sponsor a major acid rain bill. The Waxman-Sikorski measure established a goal of a ten-million-ton reduction in SO_2 and a four-million-ton reduction in NO_x and distributed the cost nationally by creating a fund financed by a one mill (one-tenth of a cent) federal tax per kilowatt hour of electricity used. But insurmountable political divisions among the constituencies of the Health and Environment Subcommittee killed the measure; environmentalists, supported by recreation interests from New England and New York and the Canadian government, demanded more stringent restrictions than the bill provided, while coal miners and utilities refused to support any action at all.

Prospects for Controls Improve in the Bush Administration

During the Reagan years, interests that opposed reauthorization of the Clean Air Act were able to rest assured that they had friends in high places, both in Congress and the White House. As the Reagan administration drew to a close, however, several factors combined to open a window of opportunity for proponents of acid rain controls. First, in 1987, the House got a rare chance to vote on clean air legislation: Rep. Dingell—who had been bottling up Clean Air Act revisions in committee—sponsored legislation to extend clean air deadlines into 1989 in hopes of taking the urgency out of producing a new clean air bill before the 1988 elections.[28] But the Dingell amendment lost, 162–247. Instead, the House backed a pro-environmental amendment pushing the deadlines only to August 1988, thereby keeping the heat on Congress to write a new clean air law. Waxman and others interpreted the vote to mean that they had the support to pass clean air legislation if only they could get it out of committee and onto the floor.[29] In the Senate, the prospects for clean air legislation improved as well when Robert Byrd stepped down as majority leader and was succeeded by George Mitchell of Maine, a determined advocate of acid rain controls.

Perhaps most importantly, presidential candidate George Bush made reauthorizing the Clean Air Act a centerpiece of his campaign for the presidency. Bush and his advisers hoped to capitalize on a pro-environmental backlash against the Reagan years: memberships in environmental groups had exploded during the 1980s, and public opinion polls revealed that a large majority of Americans considered themselves environmentalists.[30] Furthermore, acid rain control was especially important to Canadian prime minister Brian Mulroney, a confidante of Bush.[31] Reflecting these influences, in a speech in Detroit, candidate Bush repudiated the Reagan administration approach, saying "the time for study alone has passed." He went on to offer a detailed plan "to cut millions of tons of sulfur dioxide emissions by the year 2000."[32] Although his position on many issues ultimately would disappoint environmentalists, Bush did follow through on his campaign promise to offer revisions to the Clean Air Act. Soon after taking office, he assembled a team of advisers to craft a White House version of what would become the Clean Air Act Amendments of 1990.

An Innovative Allowance Trading Plan. The Bush team spent most of its time working on the acid rain details of the Clean Air Act reauthorization, and

these provisions proved to be the most innovative part of the president's proposal. The group selected a system of allowance trading combined with a
nationwide cap on total SO_2 emissions designed by Dan Dudek of the Environmental Defense Fund (EDF). This market-based mechanism, which environmental policy entrepreneurs had been softening up in the policy community for more than a decade, aimed to reduce SO_2 emissions by ten million tons
by the year 2000. Utilities could meet their emissions allowance using any of a
variety of methods, or they could purchase allowances from other plants and
maintain the same level of emissions. The plan was founded on a simple premise: the federal government should not dictate levels of pollution control
required of individual companies as it had in the more conventional regulations of the 1970 Clean Air Act. Rather, it should set a limit total emissions and
distribute tradable allowances to all polluters, thereby creating incentives for
individual companies to reduce their own pollution at lowest cost.

Politically, the allowance-trading system had several advantages over more
conventional approaches. It satisfied Bush's preference for market-based regulatory solutions. Moreover, because it was designed by EDF and had been
floating around the environmental community for some time, the White
House thought the emissions trading scheme unlikely to arouse the ire of environmentalists. The plan generated a potent coalition of supporters that
included the clean coal–burning western states (whose utilities would not be
forced to install scrubbers or subsidize acid rain controls), eastern and western
producers of low-sulfur coal (for which demand was likely to accelerate),
Republican advocates of less governmental interference in the market (for
whom a trading system satisfied both efficiency and individual liberty concerns), and the northeastern states affected by acid deposition. Within this
alliance, of course, different groups had concerns about the details of the plan.
In particular, representatives of western states worried that their utilities,
which were already relatively clean, would not be able to obtain allowances
that could facilitate economic growth in their states and that most of the
allowances would be concentrated in the Midwest.

Those who stood to lose the most under the White House plan and conse-
quently mobilized to oppose it were the UMW, with its strong presence in
high-sulfur coal mines, and the midwestern utilities that traditionally relied
on high-sulfur coal. The UMW argued that the bill would force major coal purchasers to shift to low-sulfur coal, jeopardizing thousands of coal-mining jobs.
Midwesterners contended that the Bush plan was skewed against them: nine
states responsible for 51 percent of the nation's SO_2 emissions were going to
have to accomplish 90 percent of the reduction and bear 73 to 80 percent of the
cost—in the form of higher electricity bills—in the first phase of the plan.

The Bush Plan in the Senate. Thus, when Bush presented his plan to Congress, the battle lines were already drawn. In the Senate, Majority Leader
Mitchell realized that most of the resistance to clean air legislation would come
from outside the Environment and Public Works Committee, since the

regional balance of the committee clearly favored supporters of acid rain controls: of its sixteen members, five were from New England, two were from New York and New Jersey, and four others were from the Rocky Mountain states that produce low-sulfur coal. Furthermore, Sen. Max Baucus of Montana had assumed the chairmanship of the Environmental Protection Subcommittee upon Mitchell's ascension to majority leader, and he had consistently supported clean air legislation—in part because Montana produces and uses low-sulfur coal, which many utilities would adopt under a market-based system. The ranking minority member of the subcommittee, John Chafee of Rhode Island, also had a strong environmental record; moreover, his state had low per capita SO_2 emissions and thus had little to lose from stringent acid rain controls. So the committee was able to mark up and approve (15–1) the president's clean air bill with relative ease. The controversy arose later, in the full Senate.

It took ten full weeks from its introduction on January 23, 1990, for the Senate to pass the Clean Air Act Amendments. During that time, the chamber worked continuously on the bill, virtually to the exclusion of all other business. The lengthy process was unusual in at least one respect: there was no extended talk and procedural delay on the Senate floor; rather, Senator Mitchell presided over most of the debate behind closed doors in his suite. Commented Sen. Tom Daschle of South Dakota, "In my [12] years in Congress, I have never seen a member dedicate the attention and devotion to an issue as George Mitchell has done on clean air. He has used every ounce of his energy to cajole senators and come up with imaginative solutions."[33] As majority leader, Mitchell was both a persistent advocate of clean air legislation and a pragmatist: he wanted a clean air bill, and he knew that he would have to strike deals to get one. As a result, he often antagonized environmentalists, who hoped for greater regulatory stringency and less compromise than Mitchell was willing to tolerate. For instance, despite objections from some major environmental groups, Mitchell and Baucus embraced the emissions trading system devised by the Bush team in exchange for White House acceptance of changes in other parts of the bill.

Although there was clear momentum in the Senate in favor of reaching agreement on the clean air bill, the Appalachian and midwestern senators, led by Senator Byrd, were not ready to give up their fight to diffuse the region's acid rain cleanup costs. With extensive help from his aide, Rusty Mathews, Byrd crafted a formula that won the approval of coal-state senators: he proposed to give midwestern power plants bonus emissions credits to encourage them to adopt scrubbers rather than low-sulfur coal. An informal head count revealed that the Senate would not support Byrd's plan, however, and he was forced to scramble to salvage something from the acid rain debate. Mathews came up with another alternative: giving the heaviest polluters extra credits in Phase I to help them buy their way out of the cleanup effort. Eventually, Byrd and his cosponsor, Sen. Christopher Bond, R-Mo., were able to persuade Mitchell and others to accept the modification known as the Byrd-Bond amendment in exchange for their support on the acid rain provisions of the bill. Finally, on April 3, the Senate passed its version of the Clean Air Act Amendments by a vote of 89–11.

Acid Rain Controls in the House. The decade-long rivalry between Henry Waxman of California and John Dingell of Michigan continued to dominate the clean air debate in the House Energy and Commerce Committee. Dingell had chaired the full committee since 1979, and Waxman had chaired the Health and Environment Subcommittee since 1981. To augment his influence and counteract Waxman, Dingell had worked assiduously with House Speaker Jim Wright of Texas to recruit sympathetic members to Energy and Commerce. By 1990, one-third of the committee's members were from the industrial heartland—the Midwest had nine seats and the Appalachian coal states another seven—and only two were from New England. Nevertheless, when the Bush administration presented its proposal, Dingell took the advice of some important allies in the House (most notably Majority Whip Tony Coelho) as well as his wife, Debbie (a General Motors executive), that delay and defensive tactics would no longer succeed, and he would have to get on the bandwagon if he wanted to avoid blame for inaction. According to one Democratic aide, "Dingell always knew that he could delay action for a time, but that then he would have to fight for the best deal he could get."[34]

Dingell had assigned Waxman's Environment Subcommittee responsibility for marking up most of the clean air package but had strategically referred the two most controversial titles of the bill—acid rain and alternative fuels—to the Subcommittee on Energy and Power chaired by Philip Sharp of Indiana. Sharp had long opposed acid rain legislation in hopes of protecting Indiana's dirty, old utilities. In November 1989, Sharp told reporters he hoped to dramatize his concerns about the administration's proposal by stalling the acid rain provisions in his subcommittee. Two of Sharp's midwestern allies on the committee, Edward Madigan, R-Ill., and Terry Bruce, D-Ill., publicly criticized Chairman Dingell for failing to deliver on a promise to help solve their cost-sharing problems. In an effort to patch things up, Dingell unveiled a plan to enroll support among the "cleans"—predominantly western states—for a cost-sharing program that would relieve some of the burden on the midwestern "dirties."[35]

The decade-long recalcitrance of the utility lobby and its supporters in the House had not earned them many friends, however, and the midwestern contingent was unable to persuade members from other states to accept their cost-sharing proposals. The utilities also had increased their vulnerability to tough controls by stubbornly insisting throughout the 1980s that there was no acid rain problem and refusing to provide members of Congress and their aides with information on their operations. Making matters worse for the utilities, the Bush plan had fractured the anti-regulation coalition: midwestern representatives were split between those concerned about the utilities (who wanted flexibility in reducing their emissions) and those who wanted to protect high-sulfur coal miners (who preferred a scrubber mandate). The utilities themselves were deeply divided depending on their energy source and the extent to which they had already engaged in pollution control. In particular, the heavily polluting utilities and those that had already begun to clean up—such as those in New York, Wisconsin, and Minnesota—could not resolve their differences.

To facilitate negotiations among members of this fractious group, nearly all of the committee meetings were conducted behind closed doors and often at night. By freeing them of the speechmaking and position-taking associated with public hearings on controversial legislation, Dingell (like Mitchell in the Senate) hoped to spare rank-and-file lawmakers the constant pressure to serve constituent demands.[36] The "dirties" and "cleans" finally agreed on a compromise in which midwestern utilities got more time to reduce emissions, greater flexibility on emissions credits, and funds to speed development of technology to reduce coal emissions. Members from the "clean" states extracted some concessions as well, obtaining for their utilities greater flexibility under the trading system, and they got all the permits the midwesterners initially had been reluctant to give them. The Energy and Commerce Committee completed its drafting of the clean air legislation on April 15, and the full House passed the bill on May 23 by a vote of 401–21.

Reconciling the House and Senate Bills. Following Senate and House passage of their separate versions of the clean air bill, all that remained was to reconcile the differences in conference committee. The House conferees controlled most aspects of the conference committee bill, but the Senate prevailed on the acid rain provisions.[37] (Its version of those provisions was more coherent and closer to the original Bush administration plan.) Despite their failures in the House and Senate chambers, however, midwestern representatives still hoped to extract some relief from the conference committee. Phil Sharp and his colleagues worked during the final days to salvage aid to their region, requesting additional allowances to ease the pain for coal-fired utilities that would be hardest hit by the new rules. The midwesterners among the House conferees settled on a proposal to give some additional credits to Illinois, Indiana, and Ohio utilities each year until 1999. After 2000, ten midwestern states would get a small number of extra allowances each year.[38]

When they presented the plan to a group of key House and Senate conferees, however, the reaction was unenthusiastic. Rep. Dennis Eckart of Ohio then took the plan to Senator Mitchell, who agreed to support it in exchange for a few concessions. In the end, said Eckart, Senator Mitchell broke the impasse by convincing the conference members to pacify the Midwest. In the process, the midwesterners lost on some other demands, including a provision in the House bill that would have protected high-sulfur coal mining jobs by requiring utilities to install pollution control devices rather than switching to low-sulfur coal.[39]

In general, despite the extra allowances granted to some midwestern utilities, the acid rain provisions represented a big loss for the Midwest and the old, dirty generating units. The final bill, according to one veteran Washington lobbyist, "proved the axiom that divided industries do badly on Capitol Hill."[40]

House conferees did manage to extract from the Bush administration a concession on displaced worker assistance, even though the president had threatened to veto the bill if it included unemployment benefits to workers who lost jobs as a result of the law. Once the conferees had resolved or agreed to abandon the remaining issues, the final package had to pass the House and Senate. Reflecting the momentum behind the law and the skills of the legislative leaders who had shepherded it through the legislative process, the six days of debate that followed were perfunctory. The House passed the clean air conference report 401–25 on October 26, and the Senate passed it 89–10 the following day. President Bush signed the Clean Air Act Amendments into law on November 15, 1990.

Implementing the Acid Rain Provisions of the 1990 CAAA

Title IV of the 1990 Clean Air Act Amendments (CAAA) required a nationwide reduction in SO_2 emissions by ten million tons—roughly 40 percent from 1980 levels—by the year 2000. To facilitate this, it established a two-phase SO_2 allowance trading system under which the EPA issues each utility a certain number of allowances, each of which permits its holder to emit one ton of SO_2 in a particular year or any subsequent year.[41] A utility that generates more emissions than it receives allowances for may reduce its emissions through pollution control efforts or may purchase allowances from another utility. A utility that reduces its emissions below the number of allowances it holds may trade, bank, or sell its excess allowances. (Anyone can hold allowances, including utilities, brokers, environmental groups, and private citizens.) Title IV also mandated a two-million-ton reduction in NO_x emissions by 2000. To achieve this reduction, the law required the EPA to establish emissions limitations for two types of utility boilers by mid-1992 and for all other types by 1997. Finally, Title IV required all regulated utilities to install equipment to monitor SO_2 and NO_x emissions continuously to ensure compliance.

EPA Rulemaking under Title IV. For opponents of acid rain regulations, the implementation of Title IV was the last remaining opportunity to subvert the goal of reducing SO_2 and NO_x emissions. Less than a year and a half after signing the much-heralded Clean Air Act Amendments, President Bush instituted the Council on Competitiveness headed by Vice President Dan Quayle. The council was driven, in Quayle's words, by "the desire to minimize regulations and to make regulations as unburdensome as possible while meeting the requirements of the statutes."[42] Bush wanted to retreat from the most onerous commitments of the act because, with a reelection campaign imminent, he needed to accommodate his allies in the Republican party and in the business community. Efforts to derail the program were largely unsuccessful, however. On January 15, 1991, the EPA issued a report delineating the dozens of deadlines the agency would have to meet to comply with the new law. By summer 1991, the agency had resolved most of the major SO_2 rulemaking issues; the following December it published its proposed rules for notice and comment; and by early 1993, it had promulgated its final SO_2 regulations.[43]

Vigorous and supportive congressional oversight helped to ensure that the regulatory process stayed on track. Because committee Democrats wanted to take credit for the act as the 1992 presidential and congressional races neared, high-ranking members of the authorizing committees monitored Clean Air Act implementation zealously. In April 1992, Waxman wrote an angry *New York Times* editorial chiding the Bush administration for failing to issue the regulations necessary to carry out the act. Even Dingell was Waxman's ally in this effort; although he generally was not a fan of agency discretion, Dingell made sure the EPA had the wherewithal to write rules under the CAAA. One manifestation of this support was the agency's ability to increase its FY1992 acid rain staff from fifteen to sixty-three.

In addition to congressional oversight, the statute itself contained clear guidelines and strict penalties for noncompliance and for failure by the agency to put SO_2 regulations in place, a feature that reflected Congress's determination to make the act self-enforcing. Henry Waxman explained that "the specificity in the 1990 Amendments reflects the concern that without detailed directives, industry intervention might frustrate efforts to put pollution control steps in place. . . . History shows that even where EPA seeks to take strong action, the White House will often intervene at industry's behest to block regulatory action."[44] A comparison between the statutory provisions for NO_x and SO_2 reveals the importance of statutory design for effective implementation. Although the EPA required utility boilers to meet new NO_x emissions requirements, there was no emissions cap, so overall emissions continued to rise. Moreover, the NO_x provisions did not contain a hammer: NO_x limitations did not apply unless rules were actually promulgated, so there was considerable incentive for delay and obstruction by regulated sources. In fact, the NO_x rule was delayed by a court challenge and thus was not finalized until early 1995. (NO_x reductions began in 1996 and were increased in 2000.) According to one EPA analyst, "Poor statutory construction [for NO_x regulation] has cost the environment in terms of delayed protection, has cost the industry in terms of burner reconfiguration expenditures, and has cost the public, who ultimately pays the capital, administrative, and litigation expenses."[45]

The Emissions Trading System. Between 1991 and 1992, the EPA issued all 182 Phase I permits for SO_2; certified the continuous monitoring systems that utilities had installed and tested; and developed an emissions tracking system to process emissions data for all sources. The SO_2 trading system's first phase required 263 units in 110 coal-fired utility plants (operated by sixty utilities) in twenty-one eastern and midwestern states to reduce their SO_2 emissions by a total of approximately 3.5 million tons per year beginning in 1995. The EPA allocated allowances to utilities each year based on a legislative formula.[46] The agency provided some units with bonus allowances, the subject of so much congressional haggling: for example, high-polluting power plants in Illinois,

Indiana, and Ohio got additional allowances during each year of Phase I that they could sell to help generate revenues to offset cleanup costs. To appease clean states, the EPA also allowed plants to receive extra allowances if they were part of a utility system that had reduced its coal use by at least 20 percent between 1980 and 1985 and relied on coal for less than half of the total electricity it generated. Additional provisions gave clean states bonus allowances to facilitate economic growth.

Phase II, which began in 2000, tightened emissions limits on the large plants regulated in Phase I and set restrictions on smaller, cleaner coal-, gas-, and oil-fired plants. Approximately 2,500 units in 1,000 utility plants were brought under the regulatory umbrella in Phase II, during which the EPA issued 8.95 million allowances for one ton of SO_2 emissions each to utilities annually. To avoid penalizing them for improvements made in the 1980s, Title IV permitted the cleanest plants to increase their emissions between 1990 and 2000 by roughly 20 percent. Thereafter, they were not allowed to exceed their 2000 emission levels. The EPA did not allocate allowances to utilities that began operating after 1995; instead, it required them to buy into the system by purchasing allowances. This ensured that overall emissions reductions were not eroded over time.

Once it set up the system, the EPA's ongoing role in allowance trading became simply to receive and record allowance transfers and to ensure at the end of each year that a utility's emissions did not exceed the number of allowances held. Each generator has up to thirty days after the end of the year to deliver to the EPA valid allowances equal to its emissions during the year. At that time, the EPA cancels the allowances needed to cover emissions. If a generator fails to produce the necessary allowances, the EPA can require it to pay a $2,000-per-ton excess emissions fee and then offset the excess emissions in the following year. Since the excess emissions fee is substantially higher than the cost of complying with the law by buying allowances, the market is likely to enforce much of the emissions reductions.

The EPA also maintains a reserve of 300,000 special allowances that it can allocate to utilities that develop qualifying renewable energy projects or institute conservation measures. The agency is establishing the reserve by reducing Phase II allowances by 30,000 annually between 2000 and 2009. In addition, the EPA is considering other mechanisms to promote the use of conservation and renewable energy. Furthermore, the EPA maintains a reserve of allowances for auctions and sales by withholding 2.8 percent of the total allowances each year. Auctions and sales are open to anyone and are conducted by sealed bid.

OUTCOMES

On March 29, 1993, the Chicago Board of Trade held its first of three SO_2 allowance auctions. The auction reaped $21 million and attracted more participants than most observers had expected.[47] The EPA managed to sell the allowances it was offering at prices ranging from $130 to $450 per allowance, with an average price of $250. Over the next four years, allowance prices declined even further, from $180 to $159 to $132 and finally to $68 in 1996; by mid-1997, allowance prices had settled in the $90–$100 range, and hovered around $140 by 2000.[48]

The Economic Impacts of the Allowance Trading System

The low allowance prices suggested that utilities were investing more heavily in compliance than projected and expected to have more allowances than they needed in 1995. On the other hand, some observers worried that such low prices might cause utilities that had planned to install pollution control devices to reconsider because it might prove cheaper simply to buy more allowances. Indeed, one utility that bid in the auction, the Illinois Power Company, stopped construction on a $350 million scrubber and began making private deals to stockpile permits that it intended to use between 1995 and 2000.[49]

Nevertheless, a 1996 Resources for the Future report suggested that utilities had cut pollution even though most were not trading allowances.[50] (The study found that the bulk of EPA-cited trades were record-keeping changes in which utilities consolidated ownership.) But even without trades, study author Dallas Burtraw noted that by allowing utilities to choose how to achieve compliance, the acid rain control program had created a dynamic marketplace in which pollution control alternatives compete directly with one another. The result was both price cuts and innovation among marketers, coal rail transporters, and scrubber manufacturers. Although the price of scrubbers had dropped, for more than half of all utilities fuel switching and blending with low-sulfur coal was the compliance option of choice. As a result, from 1990 to 1994, production of low- and medium-sulfur fuels expanded by 28 percent, while high-sulfur fuel production fell by 18 percent.[51] But the most important factor accounting for lower compliance costs, according to Burtraw, was the nearly 50 percent reduction in transportation costs for moving low-sulfur coal from the Powder River Basin to the East.[52]

The Ecological Impacts of Title IV

Early assessments of Title IV revealed some impressive and unexpected accomplishments. According to the EPA, emissions from Phase I utilities were 5.4 million tons in 1996, or 35 percent below that year's emissions cap of 8.3 million tons.[53] Overall, SO_2 emissions declined 17 percent, from 23.7 million tons in 1990 to 19.6 million tons in 1998.[54] Moreover, the U.S. Geological Survey (USGS) found that in 1995 sixty-two sites in the mid-Atlantic and Ohio River Valley regions experienced, on average, a 13.8 percent decline in sulfur compounds and an 8 percent drop in hydrogen ions. The authors attributed this "greater than anticipated" decline to the implementation of Phase I of the CAAA.[55]

Neither this nor subsequent assessments of the act have been entirely sanguine, however. Between 1996 and 2001, it became increasingly clear that the reductions mandated in Title IV would not be sufficient to stem the ecological damage done by acid rain. A report released in April 1996, based on more than three decades of data from New Hampshire's Hubbard Brook Forest, suggested that the forest had not bounced back as quickly as expected.[56] "Our view and that of soil scientists had been that soils were so well buffered that acid rain didn't affect them in any serious way," said ecologist Gene Likens, commenting on the report.[57] Even though the acid had abated, however, its effects lingered. Vegetation in the Hubbard Brook Experimental Forest had nearly stopped growing since 1987, and the pH of many streams in the Northeast remained below normal. Researchers speculated, and subsequent evidence confirmed, that years of acid deposition had depleted the soil's supply of alkaline chemicals and that the soil was recovering slowly.[58] A second likely cause of the slow recovery of Hubbard Brook was that, because NO_x emissions did not decline, nitrates continued to acidify the rain falling in the Northeast.

The Hubbard Brook findings were consistent with the observations of plant pathologist Walter Shortle of the U.S. Forest Service. In fall 1995, Shortle's group had reported in the journal *Nature* that because acid rain was no longer sufficiently neutralized by calcium and magnesium, it was releasing aluminum ions from minerals into the soil, where they are toxic to plants.[59] Another study, conducted in the Calhoun Experimental Forest in South Carolina, confirmed that acid rain dissolved forest nutrients much faster than was previously believed.[60] And in October 1999, the USGS concurred that while sulfur levels in rain and streams continued to decline, the alkalinity of stream water had not recovered.[61] Taken together, these findings suggested that the SO_2 reductions mandated by the Clean Air Act were insufficient for some ecosystems to recover.

New Research Spurs Calls for More Controls

In the late 1990s, in response to these findings, pressure began mounting for strict NO_x emissions controls. In November 1997, the EPA called for new state air pollution plans to cut the NO_x emissions of utilities and other large sources in the states east of the Mississippi by 85 percent. In 1998, over the protests of midwestern governors and power plant executives, the EPA ordered twenty-two states in the East and Midwest to reduce emissions of NO_x by an average of 28 percent, mainly during the summer.[62] In 1999, New York Sen. Daniel Patrick Moynihan proposed new legislation to cut SO_2 by 50 percent more than required by the 1990 amendments and reduce NO_x by 70 percent by 2005, while establishing an NO_x trading scheme similar to that created for SO_2. The bill attracted minimal support in Congress, however, where some members thought the government had done enough to address the issue.[63]

Bolstering Moynihan's case was a 1999 NAPAP report summarizing recent research on acid rain. The report pointed out that while the 1990 CAAA made significant improvements, acid precipitation was more complex and intractable than was thought when that law was passed. The authors noted that high elevation forests in the Colorado Front Range, West Virginia's Allegheny Mountains, the Great Smoky Mountains of Tennessee, and the San Gabriel

Mountains of Southern California were saturated or near saturated with nitrogen; the Chesapeake Bay was suffering from excess nitrogen, some of which was from air pollution; high-elevation lakes and streams in the Sierra Nevadas, the Cascades, and the Rocky Mountains appeared to be on the verge of chronically high acidity; and waterways in the Adirondacks were becoming more acidic, even as sulfur deposits declined.[64] The report concluded that if deposits of sulfur and nitrogen were not reduced, these sensitive forests, lakes, and soils would continue to deteriorate. According to Jack Cosby, a University of Virginia environmental scientist, "It's been the near consensus of scientists that the Clean Air Act amendments haven't gone far enough."[65]

A second report, issued by the U.S. General Accounting Office (GAO) in March 2000, confirmed that while sulfur levels had declined substantially in the vast majority of the Adirondack's waterways, nitrogen levels continued to rise in nearly half of them.[66] The report suggested that nitrogen levels were rising because the Adirondack's older forests were taking up less nitrogen than newer forests, allowing the remainder to seep into lakes and streams, and because the buffering capacity of Adirondack soils had been depleted by prolonged exposure to acid rain. A study published in the March 2001 issue of *Bioscience* confirmed that although acid rain had decreased 38 percent since controls were implemented, lakes, streams, and forests in the Northeast continued to suffer.[67] New York officials and environmental groups seized on these reports as further ammunition for their case that Congress needed to tighten acid rain controls.[68] Officials representing midwestern utilities remained adamant that further controls were unnecessary, however, pointing out that it was too early to evaluate the impacts of existing NO_x reductions, which took effect in 1996 and were tightened in 2000. While most supported policies to reduce acid rain, even scientists were dubious about proposals that focused only on utility emissions, pointing out that much of the nitrogen in the atmosphere came from motor vehicle emissions.[69]

While Congress wrestled with the issue, proponents pursued controls on another front with greater success. In September 1999, New York attorney general Elliot Spitzer announced his intention to sue seventeen southern and midwestern power plants, as well as several utilities in New York state, to force them to reduce their acid rain–causing emissions. Spitzer employed a novel argument under the Clean Air Act: that power companies had expanded and upgraded their old plants sufficiently to be considered new plants for regulatory purposes.[70] In November, Connecticut attorney general Richard Blumenthal said he would follow Spitzer's lead and sue sixteen coal-fired power plants.[71] The EPA, also following Spitzer's example, filed lawsuits or administrative enforcement actions against more than 100 companies across the country. By the end of 2000, the strategy appeared to be bearing fruit: in November 2000, the Virginia Electric Power Company agreed to a landmark $1.2 billion settlement in which it must cut SO_2 and NO_x emissions from its eight coal-burning plants by 70 percent, or 252,000 tons per year, within twelve years.[72] A month later, the Cinergy Corporation of Cincinnati reached a settlement with the EPA in which it agreed to spend $1.4 billion over twelve years to cut SO_2 from its ten coal-burning plants in Kentucky.[73]

CONCLUSIONS

The acid rain case provides a vivid example of the interaction between science and politics in environmental policymaking. Critics of the 1990 Clean Air Act Amendments point out that Congress had virtually completed work on the bill before the multimillion dollar National Acid Precipitation Assessment Program report, commissioned by President Carter ten years earlier, had even been released. Of course, NAPAP had already released drafts of the report, and its major findings were already well established. More importantly, though, just as opponents of acid rain controls justified their position on the grounds of scientific uncertainty, proponents of acid rain controls had used the scientific consensus throughout the 1980s to build a compelling political story that raised the issue's salience. By generating support among voters, advocates created incentives for leaders to appropriate the issue; hoping to capitalize on widespread public concern in the United States and Canada, presidential candidate Bush promised to address the acid rain problem.

Advocates of acid rain controls then seized on the political window of opportunity opened by the election of President Bush and the ascension of George Mitchell to majority leader in the Senate to link a market-based solution to the acid rain problem. Such an approach changed the political dynamics of the issue because it was palatable to many conservatives. The emissions trading scheme also broke up the formidable coalition of utilities that had been monolithic in their opposition to regulations.

The CAAA ultimately passed by overwhelming majorities in both chambers, making manifest both the power of well-placed opponents to maintain the status quo against a popular alternative and the importance of legislative leaders in facilitating a successful policy challenge. President Bush's imprimatur on the new bill contrasted sharply with the Reagan administration's obstruction and was critical for attracting Republican support. Congressional leaders, particularly George Mitchell but also John Dingell, brokered deals within the emissions trading system that were crucial to building a majority coalition. Their willingness to hold meetings behind closed doors, away from the scrutiny of lobbyists, was particularly decisive.

As it turned out, although there have been some disputes over implementing the emissions trading program, overall it has accomplished its objectives. It has brought about greater reductions in SO_2 emissions at lower costs than expected. Ironically, however, subsequent scientific research suggests that further emissions controls, particularly for NO_x, will be needed to address the acid rain problem. In the absence of a legislative window of opportunity, proponents of tighter controls have pursued their goals in court; though they have been successful so far, the Bush administration is unlikely to lend its support to such an approach.

QUESTIONS TO CONSIDER

- How did the SO_2 emissions trading policy, a significant departure from the status quo, become law?
- What role has science played in the development of U.S. acid rain policy?
- Why has the emissions trading program been more effective—economically and ecologically—than a uniform emission limiting approach might have been?
- What are the drawbacks of the emissions trading approach?

Notes

1. Acid rain is the common term that describes all forms of acid precipitation as well as dry deposition of acid materials. It occurs when sulfur and nitrogen combine with oxygen in the atmosphere to produce sulfur dioxide (SO_2) and nitrogen oxides (NO_x). Within hours or days, these pollutants spontaneously oxidize in the air to form sulfate and acid nitrate, commonly known as sulfuric and nitric acids. These acids usually remain in the atmosphere for weeks and may travel hundreds of miles before settling on or near the earth in rain, snow, mist, hail, or in dry form. While all types of precipitation are somewhat acidic—"pure" rainfall has a pH of about 5.6—in industrial regions, the pH of rain is often around 4.0 and can drop as low as 2.6. Scientists measure the relative acidity of a solution on a logarithmic potential hydrogen (pH) scale. A neutral substance has a pH value of 7.0. An acidic substance has a pH of less than 7.0, whereas an alkalinic one has a pH of greater than 7.0. Furthermore, because the pH scale is logarithmic, a full pH unit drop represents a tenfold increase in acidity. See Larry Canter, *Acid Rain and Dry Deposition* (Chelsea, Mich.: Lewis Publishers, 1996).
2. Judith A. Layzer, "Sense and Credibility: The Role of Science in Environmental Policymaking." Unpublished Ph.D. dissertation, MIT, 1997.
3. John W. Kingdon, *Congressmen's Voting Decisions,* 3d ed. (Ann Arbor: University of Michigan Press, 1989).
4. Robert N. Stavins, "Market-Based Environmental Policies," in *Public Policies for Environmental Protection,* 2d ed., ed. Paul R. Portney and Robert N. Stavins (Washington, D.C.: Resources for the Future, 2000), 31–76.
5. Alan Schwartz, quoted in Leslie R. Alm, *Crossing Borders, Crossing Boundaries: The Role of Scientists in the U.S. Acid Rain Debate* (New York: Praeger, 2000), 8.
6. At the same time, Ontario government researchers were documenting lake acidification and fish loss in a wide area surrounding Sudbury and attributing those effects to SO_2 emissions from the Sudbury smelters. This work was suppressed by the Ontario government, however. See Don Munton, "Dispelling the Myths of the Acid Rain Story," *Environment* 40 (July–August 1998): 4–7, 27–34.
7. Andrew Morriss, "Supporting Structures for Resolving Environmental Disputes Among Friendly Neighbors," in *Acid Rain and Friendly Neighbors,* rev. ed., ed. Jurgen Schmandt, Judith Clarkson, and Hilliard Roderick (Durham: Duke University Press, 1988), 217–252.
8. Marshall E. Wilcher, "The Acid Rain Debate in North America: 'Where You Stand Depends on Where You Sit,'" *The Environmentalist* 6 (1986): 289–298.
9. Quoted in Philip Shabecoff, "Northeast and Coal Area are at Odds Over Acid Rain," *New York Times,* April 19, 1980, A22.
10. James L. Regens and Robert W. Rycroft, *The Acid Rain Controversy* (Pittsburgh: University of Pittsburgh Press, 1990).
11. Roy Gould, *Going Sour: The Science and Politics of Acid Rain* (Boston: Birkhauser, 1985).

12. Only 5–10 percent of the water in a lake comes from rain that has fallen directly on the lake; most of the water is runoff from the surrounding watershed and has thus been neutralized by the alkaline soil.

13. Acidity can kill fish in several ways: by interfering with their salt balance, by causing reproductive abnormalities, by leaching aluminum into the lake at levels toxic to fish gills, or by killing the organisms on which they feed.

14. Gould, *Going Sour*; Office of Technology Assessment, *Acid Rain and Transported Air Pollutants: Implications for Public Policy* (Washington, D.C.: Office of Technology Assessment, 1984); U.S. General Accounting Office, *An Analysis of Issues Concerning Acid Rain*, GAO/RCED-85-13 (December 1984).

15. Gould, *Going Sour*.

16. Quoted in Regens and Rycroft, *The Acid Rain Controversy*, 85.

17. National Research Council, *Atmosphere-Biosphere Interactions: Toward a Better Understanding of the Ecological Consequences of Fossil Fuel Combustion* (Washington, D.C.: National Academy Press, 1981).

18. Quoted in Gould, *Going Sour*, 30.

19. Ibid., 32.

20. Quoted in ibid., 33.

21. Quoted in Michael Kranish, "Acid Rain Report Said Suppressed," *New York Times*, August 18, 1984, 1.

22. Quoted in ibid.

23. Philip Shabecoff, "Toward a Clean and Budgeted Environment," *New York Times*, October 2, 1984, A28.

24. Alm, *Crossing Borders, Crossing Boundaries*.

25. Congress focused on SO_2 emissions because scientists believed SO_2 was the primary culprit in acid rain (accounting for more than two-thirds of the acidity) and because it was the simplest—both technically and politically—to address.

26. The heaviest sulfur-emitting states in the proposed acid rain control region were Ohio, Pennsylvania, Indiana, Illinois, Missouri, Wisconsin, Kentucky, Florida, West Virginia, and Tennessee. These states accounted for two-thirds of the SO_2 emissions emitted by the thirty-one states east of the Mississippi. See Steven L. Rhodes, "Superfunding Acid Rain Controls: Who Will Bear the Costs?" *Environment*, (July–August), 1984, 25–31.

27. Two of the more prominent proposals were reported out of the Environment Committee in 1982 and 1984 (S 3041). Both required a ten-million-ton reduction in SO_2 emissions in the thirty-one-state region east of the Mississippi. Both allowed fuel switching. In 1985, Senator Stafford introduced the Acid Rain Control Act, which divorced the issue from the Clean Air Act revisions and contained provisions similar to those in S 3041.

28. Karl Hager, "The 'White House' Effect Opens a Long-Locked Political Door," *Congressional Quarterly Weekly Report*, January 20, 1990, 139–144.

29. Richard Cohen, *Washington at Work: Back Rooms and Clean Air*, 2d ed. (Boston: Allyn and Bacon, 1995).

30. For example, Cambridge Reports found the percent of people who said the amount of government regulation and involvement in environmental protection was "too little" increased from 35 percent in 1982 to 53 percent in 1988. A series of polls conducted by the *New York Times*/CBS News asked a national sample of Americans whether they agreed with the following statement: "Protecting the environment is so important that requirements and standards cannot be too high, and continuing environmental improvements must be made regardless of cost." In 1981, 45 percent said they agreed with this statement. By the end of Reagan's first term, this proportion had increased to 58 percent and in 1988, shortly before he left office, had climbed to 65 percent. Between 1980 and 1989, membership in the major, national environmental groups grew from 4 percent (Audubon) to 67 percent (Wilderness

Society) annually; the Sierra Club tripled in size over the course of the decade. See Robert Cameron Mitchell, "Public Opinion and the Green Lobby," in *Environmental Policy in the 1990s,* ed. Norman J. Vig and Michael E. Kraft (Washington, D.C.: CQ Press, 1990), 81–99.

31. Marc K. Landy, Marc J. Roberts, and Stephen R. Thomas, *The Environmental Protection Agency: Asking the Wrong Questions,* exp. ed. (New York: Oxford University Press, 1994).
32. Quoted in Norman J. Vig, "Presidential Leadership and the Environment: From Reagan and Bush to Clinton," in *Environmental Policy in the 1990s,* 2d ed., ed. Norman J. Vig and Michael E. Kraft (Washington, D.C.: CQ Press, 1994), 80–81.
33. Quoted in Cohen, *Washington at Work,* 96.
34. Ibid., 82.
35. The clean states wanted assurances that they would get credit for earlier emissions reductions and would be allowed to expand their utility capacity if needed without busting tight emissions caps. They also did not want to foot the bill for other states' cleanup.
36. Cohen, *Washington at Work.*
37. Alyson Pytte, "Clean Air Conferees Agree on Industrial Emissions," *Congressional Quarterly Weekly Report,* October 20, 1990, 3496–3498.
38. In Phase I, Illinois, Indiana, and Ohio utilities each got 200,000 extra allowances per year; in Phase II, ten midwestern states got 50,000 extra allowances each year.
39. Alyson Pytte, "A Decade's Acrimony Lifted in Glow of Clean Air," *Congressional Quarterly Weekly Report,* October 27, 1990, 3587–3592.
40. Quoted in Cohen, *Washington at Work,* 128.
41. These allowances are like checking account deposits; they exist only as records in the EPA's computer-based tracking system, which contains accounts for all affected generating units and for any other parties that want to hold allowances.
42. Quoted in Cohen, *Washington at Work,* 211.
43. Brian McLean, "Lessons Learned Implementing Title IV of the Clean Air Act," 95-RA120.04 (Washington, D.C.: U.S. Environmental Protection Agency, 1995).
44. Quoted in Landy et al., *The Environmental Protection Agency,* 290.
45. McLean, "Lessons Learned," 9.
46. For example, in Phase I, an individual unit's allocation was based on the following formula: the product of a 2.5-pound SO_2 per million BTU emission rate multiplied by the unit's average fuel consumption for 1985–1987.
47. Barnaby J. Feder, "Sold: $21 Million of Air Pollution," *New York Times,* March 30, 1993, B1.
48. Munton, "Dispelling the Myths"; Raymond Hernandez, "Albany Battles Acid Rain Fed by Other States," *New York Times,* May 2, 2000, A1.
49. Feder, "Sold."
50. Dallas Burtraw, "Trading Emissions to Clean the Air: Exchanges Few but Savings Many," *Resources,* (winter 1996), 3–6.
51. Munton, "Dispelling the Myths."
52. Burtraw, "Trading Emissions."
53. U.S. General Accounting Office, *Air Pollution: Overview and Issues on Emissions Allowance Trading Programs,* GAO/T-RCED-97-183 (July 1997).
54. U.S. General Accounting Office, *Acid Rain: Emissions Trends and Effects in the Eastern United States,* GAO/RCED-00-47 (March 2000).
55. James A. Lynch, Van C. Bowersox, and Jeffrey W. Grimm, "Trends in Precipitation Chemistry in the United States, 1983–1994: An Analysis of the Effects in 1995 of Phase I of the Clean Air Act Amendments of 1990, Title IV," USGS Report 96-0346 (Washington, D.C.: U.S. Geological Service, 1996).
56. G. E. Likens, C. T. Driscoll, and D. C. Buso, "Long-Term Effects of Acid Rain: Response and Recovery of a Forest Ecosystem," *Science,* April 12, 1996, 244–246.

57. Quoted in Jocelyn Kaiser, "Acid Rain's Dirty Business: Stealing Minerals from Soil," *Science,* April 12, 1996, 198.

58. William K. Stevens, "The Forest That Stopped Growing: Trail Is Traced to Acid Rain," *New York Times,* April 16, 1996, C4. A series of studies by Lars Hedin and six colleagues, published in 1994 in the journal *Nature,* found that reductions in the release of alkaline particles offset the cuts in sulfates by 28 to 100 percent. See William K. Stevens, "Acid Rain Efforts Found to Undercut Themselves," *New York Times,* January 27, 1994, A14.

59. Gregory B. Lawrence, Mark B. David, and Walter C. Shortle, "A New Mechanism for Calcium Loss in Forest-Floor Soils," *Nature* 378 (November 9, 1995): 162–165.

60. Daniel Markewitz et al., "Three Decades of Observed Soil Acidification in the Calhoun Experimental Forest: Has Acid Rain Made a Difference?" *Soil Science Society of America Journal* 62 (October 1998): 1428–1439.

61. "Good News–Bad News Story for Recovery of Streams from Acid Rain in Northeastern U.S." USGS News Release (October 4, 1999).

62. John R. Cushman, Jr., "U.S. Orders Cleaner Air in 22 States," *New York Times,* September 25, 1998, A14.

63. James Dao, "Study Sees Acid Rain Threat in Adirondacks and Beyond," *New York Times,* April 5, 1999, A19.

64. Ibid.

65. Quoted in ibid.

66. GAO, *Acid Rain: Emissions Trends.*

67. Kirk Johnson, "Harmful Effects of Acid Rain Are Far-Flung, Study Says," *New York Times,* March 26, 2001, B1.

68. James Dao, "Acid Rain Law Found to Fail in Adirondacks," *New York Times,* March 27, 2000, A1.

69. Ibid. Because stationery sources reduced their NO_x emissions in the 1980s, by 1998, on- and off-road vehicles and engines accounted for 53 percent of NO_x emissions.

70. Because the 1970 CAA grandfathers old plants but imposes strict emissions standards on new plants, many utilities began making significant expansions and upgrades but characterized them as routine maintenance.

71. Dao, "Acid Rain Law Found to Fail."

72. Richard Perez-Pena, "Plants in South to Cut Emissions That Produce Smog in Northeast," *New York Times,* November 16, 2000.

73. Randal C. Archibold, "Tentative Deal on Acid Rain Is Reached," *New York Times,* December 22, 2000, A2.

Recommended Reading

Alm, Leslie. *Crossing Borders, Crossing Boundaries: The Role of Scientists in the U.S. Acid Rain Debate.* New York: Praeger, 2000.

Cohen, Richard. *Washington at Work: Back Rooms and Clean Air,* 2d ed. Boston: Allyn and Bacon, 1995.

Gould, Ray. *Going Sour: The Science and Politics of Acid Rain* (Boston: Birkhauser, 1985).

Regens, James L., and Robert W. Rycroft. *The Acid Rain Controversy.* Pittsburgh: University of Pittsburgh Press, 1990.

Web Sites

http://bqs.usgs.gov/acidrain/index.htm (U.S. Geological Survey site)

http://www.epa.gov/rgytgrnj/programs/artd/air/acidrain/acidrain.htm (EPA's, acid rain site)

http://nadp.sws.uiuc.edu/ (National Atmospheric Deposition Program site)

http://www.rff.org/Default.htm (Resources for the Future site)

CHAPTER 1 2

Ecosystem-Based Solutions

Restoring the Florida Everglades

The Everglades is a freshwater marsh encompassing the area from Lake Okeechobee south to the tip of Florida.[1] It is one of the flattest and most extensive wetland ecosystems in the world. In its natural form, the Everglades is a slow-moving river between forty and seventy miles wide and only a few feet deep. It is bordered to the east by the Atlantic Coastal Ridge, now a highway, and to the west by the Big Cypress Swamp. Once a thriving habitat for wading birds, alligators, and a host of other species, the Everglades has been in decline since the 1940s, when the government began work on a vast hydrologic project designed to make the area more hospitable to settlers and farmers. Although signs of the ecosystem's decline were evident for decades, it was not until 1988, when the U.S. attorney general for South Florida filed a lawsuit against the state for failing to enforce its own water quality laws, that serious political attention turned to the issue. By 2001, the Everglades restoration was well under way and beginning to show small signs of success.

Like the spotted owl and New England fisheries cases, the Everglades case highlights the role of litigation in bringing about more protective environmental policy within an administrative system that evolved to promote economic development. Lawsuits can increase the likelihood that policy will become more protective in several ways. First, while the same value judgments are at stake in the judicial arena as in other political arenas, a lawsuit can force decision makers to make their values explicit. Such exposure favors advocates of protective policies, since development-oriented policies—which directly benefit private interests—tend to be more difficult to justify publicly. In addition, by requiring agencies to document the rationale for their decisions, lawsuits spawn technical information on which advocates can build a case for more protective policy. Finally, lawsuits can raise the visibility of an environmental problem by attracting media coverage, thereby providing advocates an opportunity to redefine and raise its salience. As we know from previous cases, if environmentalists succeed in drawing national attention to a problem, they have a better chance of overwhelming local economic development interests, particularly in the legislative arena. In particular, if they can generate widespread concern, aspiring political leaders are more likely to seek recognition by attending to the problem. And leadership is critical to overcoming resistance to policy change and ending stalemate.

A second theme of this case is the way that the changing scientific understanding of ecosystem functioning has affected politics and policy solutions.

Popular ecological notions of balance, carrying capacity, and the stability of natural systems underpinned environmentalist thinking and the environmental policies of the 1970s.[2] More up-to-date environmental thinking recognizes the complexity of population and ecosystem dynamics and the consequent need to expect surprises. It now appears, says ecologist Daniel Botkin, that "change is intrinsic and natural at many scales of time and space in the biosphere."[3] While holism may be ecologically sensible, however, it is incompatible with the fragmented jurisdictions of governmental agencies and inconsistent with the kinds of piecemeal, incremental solutions to which the U.S. political system is best suited.[4] Moreover, the experimental, adaptive management solutions environmental scientists increasingly recommend are anathema to many elected officials who are reluctant to dispense authority to administrative agencies without imposing strict accountability measures. Such solutions even trouble some environmentalists, who worry that administrative flexibility creates opportunities for development interests to regain control of policy once public attention has shifted.

A related theme of the case is the complexity of policymaking that involves a multiplicity of federal and state agencies and the importance of coordination and cooperation among them for successful policy implementation. The Everglades restoration effort adopts a cutting-edge, collaborative approach designed to coordinate the decisions of agencies with a stake in the Everglades ecosystem. However, such cooperative efforts are likely to encounter myriad obstacles. Among the most daunting impediments is each agency's desire to protect its turf and autonomy.[5] In addition, federal-state tensions are likely to erupt over which goals should be paramount and the means for pursuing them.

BACKGROUND

The Everglades originally covered 9,000 square miles, originating at headwaters in a series of lakes and streams south of Orlando and extending more than 100 miles to Florida Bay. Two hundred years ago, the lakes of the Everglades headwaters overflowed during the spring and summer rains. Streams and sloughs carried the water to Lake Okeechobee, which swelled over its banks. Thence, a slow-moving sheet of water would migrate across a gently sloping sawgrass plain.[6] Eventually, the water reached the twenty-mile-wide depression of the Shark River Slough, which is the entrance to the modern Everglades National Park.[7] Finally, the water drained into the mangrove forests and salt marshes of Florida Bay. Historically, an average of four million acre-feet of water a year flowed southward in a vast sheet, and one or two million acre-feet reached the Bay and the Gulf of Mexico. This hydrologic regime—combined with the region's frequent droughts, fires, and hurricanes—produced a mosaic of plant communities, which in turn sustained a variety of endemic wildlife.[8]

The Central and South Florida Project

Efforts to "reclaim" the Everglades for development date back more than 150 years.[9] In the 1840s, Florida's first state legislature called the Everglades "wholly valueless" and asked the U.S. Congress for help to drain it.[10] After a century-long series of failed attempts at reclamation, the federal government embarked on a successful water control project. After a succession of dry spells between 1931 and 1945, including one of the worst droughts in Florida's history, two fierce hurricanes hit the Everglades in 1947, dropping 100 inches of rain and inundating 90 percent of southeastern Florida. These events were the catalyst for congressional approval of the Central and South Florida (C&SF) Flood Control Project, a billion-dollar hydrologic project proposed by the Army Corps of Engineers. The governor approved the plan in February 1948, and the following year the legislature formed the Central and Southern Florida Flood Control District to act as the federal government's local partner on flood control. Ironically, even as it launched the nation's most ambitious hydrologic development project, Congress was simultaneously designating the Everglades National Park, comprising the southwestern section of the Everglades.[11] In addition, earlier in the decade, Marjory Stoneman Douglas had published her much-admired paean to the ecosystem entitled *The Everglades: River of Grass*, in which she warned against tampering with the Everglades.[12]

Nevertheless, beginning in 1950 and continuing over the next twenty years, the Corps dug, widened, or deepened 978 miles of canals; built 990 miles of levees; installed 212 tide gates, floodgates, and other control structures; and built 30 pumping stations to drain water from potential farmland (see Map 12.1).[13] The Corps began by establishing a perimeter levee through the eastern portion, blocking the sheetflow so that lands east of the levee would be protected from flooding.[14] The levee, which was about 100 miles long, became the westward limit of agricultural, residential, and other land development for the lower east coast from West Palm to Homestead; it severed 16 percent of the Everglades from its interior.[15]

Except for a couple of isolated tracts, the thousand-square-mile area south of Lake Okeechobee and north of the Everglades National Park was cleared for farmland, most of which was eventually devoted to sugar cane. The Everglades Agricultural Area (EAA), as this swath is known, encompassed about 27 percent of the historic Everglades. The Corps designated for water conservation the acreage between the EAA and the park, bounded by the eastern perimeter levee and an incomplete western levee at the edge of the Big Cypress Swamp. It then divided that reservation into three wetland impoundments called Water Conservation Areas (WCAs), which encompassed nearly one-third of the historic Everglades. The northernmost of these, WCA1, eventually became the Arthur R. Marshall Loxahatchee National Wildlife Refuge, managed by the U.S. Fish and Wildlife Service (FWS). Federal engineers built levees to separate the WCAs and interconnecting canals and water structures, managed by the Corps, to regulate their water supply.

Map 12-1 Central and South Florida Flood Control System

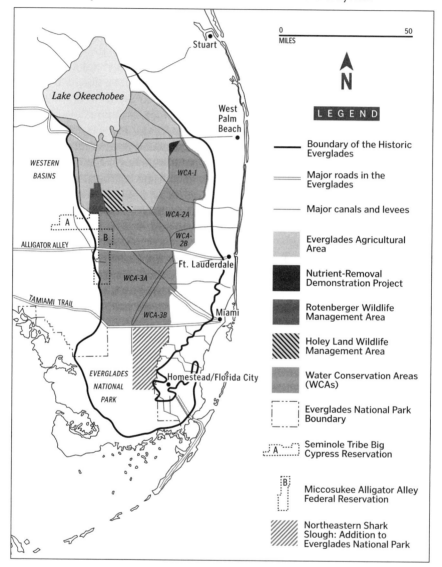

Source: Thomas E. Lodge, *The Everglades Handbook: Understanding the Ecosystem* (Boca Raton, Fla.: CRC Press, 1998). Reprinted with permission.

Note: The Miccosukee Indians have interests in lands bordering the Tamiami Trail in much of WCA-3a.

In another triumph for development interests, cattle ranchers and landowners succeeded in getting the C&SF Project to include plans to channelize the meandering, hundred-mile-long Kissimmee River. Over the objections of the FWS and the Florida Game and Fresh Fish Commission, both of which argued that the project would seriously disturb the region's ecology, that endeavor got under way in the early 1960s.[16] When the Corps sliced a fifty-mile-long channel (C-38) down the middle of the river, it destroyed 80 percent of the surrounding marshes and 90 percent of the duck population. Water levels in the aquifer dropped, and the amount of nutrients flowing into Lake Okeechobee jumped, resulting in severe eutrophication.[17]

In 1963, the Corps dug drainage canal C-111 along the park's eastern boundary and completed L-29, a levee and canal along the north boundary of Everglades National Park that delineated the southern edge of WCA3. The early 1960s were a time of drought in South Florida, and the new levee choked off what little water was arriving from the north. Compounding the pressures on the ecosystem were two major new highways, Alligator Alley and the Tamiami Trail, that spanned the width of South Florida and obstructed the southward flow of water. In addition, developers dug 183 miles of canals outside the Big Cypress Preserve, which borders the park to the west, to facilitate construction of an enormous real estate boondoggle. The canals lowered the water table by more than two feet and discharged 1.6 billion gallons of fresh water annually into the Ten Thousand Islands estuary.[18]

By the late 1960s, Everglades National Park had been deprived of its water supply and appeared doomed. Frantic park officials begged for more water to no avail; the Corps and the district refused, arguing that water had to go first to people, not animals. Following the drought of 1970–1971, the worst in forty years, reports from the park claimed that 90 percent of the wading birds had disappeared and that alligators and panthers, as well as other plant and animal species, were critically endangered. The environmental stresses on South Florida were becoming apparent in other ways as well: as periodic muck fires raged, soil subsided at more than an inch a year, and salt water intruded into freshwater supplies.

Environmentalists Mobilize

At this point, environmentalists—backed by a small group of the state's prominent scientists—began mobilizing to resist a series of development proposals. Environmentalists' first major triumph occurred in 1969, when they convinced President Nixon to call a halt to the Cross-Florida Barge Canal project. The same year, they scored another stunning victory with the defeat of the Big Cypress jetport proposal.[19] These engagements marked the beginning of the dissolution of the exclusive, development-controlled South Florida water "subgovernment"—a relatively impermeable network of government agencies, congressional committees, and private interests oriented toward development.[20] As a result of these two major controversies, Florida's environmentalists gained political stature, and in 1970 they successfully petitioned the U.S. Congress for a law requiring the Corps to release a minimum of 315,000 acre-feet of water annually into the parched Everglades National Park.[21]

Buoyed by these successes, environmentalists began to lobby the state of Florida for a comprehensive new land and water management policy. A groundswell of public support for environmental protection bolstered their efforts; Floridians, according to pollster Patrick Caldwell, were becoming much more interested in "quality of life" and issues such as growth, overpopulation, pollution, and water shortages had become highly salient.[22] Also encouraging were a series of changes in the state government, including a legislative overhaul, the election of a conservationist governor, and the passage of a new constitution.[23]

In response to the state's budding environmentalism, in 1972 the legislature enacted a series of land and water management reforms. Among the most critical for the Everglades was the Water Resources Act of 1972, which transformed the Central and South Florida Flood Control District into the South Florida Water Management District (SFWMD) and vested in it responsibility for water supply and quality. In addition, the Florida Environmental Land and Water Management Act (ELMS) ensured "a water management system [to] reverse the deterioration of water quality and provide optimum utilization of [the state's] limited water resources" and allowed the governor to designate "areas of critical state concern."[24] Three years later, in 1975, the Florida legislature consolidated control over water quantity and quality, as well as drinking water standards, in the Department of Environmental Regulation; it also required the new agency to supervise the state's five water management districts and the preparation of state water plans.

THE CASE

While the state's new laws promised to enhance its technical capacity to incorporate environmental values into water management, development interests remained firmly entrenched in the day-to-day operations of the C&SF Project's elaborate water distribution system. As a result, the Everglades continued to show unmistakable signs of distress. Recognizing this, in the early 1980s environmentalists seized on the window of opportunity opened by a series of environmental disasters to challenge Everglades policy. Unable to raise the issue's salience sufficiently to prompt legislative change, environmentalists turned to another venue, the courts, where they had greater success.

The Save Our Everglades Campaign

A succession of environmental crises opened a window of opportunity for protective Everglades policies in the 1980s. In the late 1970s, large algae blooms appeared on the already troubled Lake Okeechobee. Scientists attributed the problem to nitrogen and phosphorous flowing from dairy farms along the Kissimmee River and the backpumping of nutrients from the EAA to the south of the lake. To clean up the lake, the SFWMD required the EAA to stop pumping its water into it. Instead, the EAA began diverting the waste-water through the Everglades National Park by way of the Water Conservation Areas, despite park and refuge scientists' warnings that this would cause ecological problems in the park. Scientists at the Loxahatchee National Wildlife Refuge were hardly surprised, therefore, when in 1981 they noticed an excess of phosphorous in the system and a corresponding change in the mix of plants: cattails were crowding out the sawgrass.[25] Then, in 1980–1981, a yearlong drought dried out much of the Everglades muck, prompting fires that burned out of control and sent clouds of noxious smoke billowing over Miami, Fort Lauderdale, and the Palm Beaches. An underground wedge of salt water moved inland, tainting some freshwater supplies and threatening others.[26]

Capping the series of disasters, in 1983, torrential rains struck the state, and the Corps opened the floodgates into the park, deluging it with three and a half times the minimum amount of water set by Congress in 1970. During what is usually the dry season, five billion gallons flowed into the park daily.[27] The influx devastated wading bird nesting and inundated alligator habitat. At the same time, commercial and recreational fishermen began to complain about the degradation of the Florida Bay, where fish populations were plum-meting. The area had once been one of the world's most productive fish hatcheries, with its mixture of salt and fresh water and vast mangrove forests; by the early 1980s, however, murky patches of algae were blooming on its surface.

Prompted by scientific concern about South Florida's ecological future, a coalition of sixty environmental groups, commissions, and local municipalities mobilized to launch a political campaign to transform the water management priorities of South Florida from fostering economic development to repairing the Everglades ecosystem. With participation estimated at 250,000, it was the largest coalition ever to gather around a single environmental issue in the state.[28] Included in the coalition were the Florida Wildlife Federation, Friends of the Everglades, the Florida Audubon Society, the Coalition to Repair the Everglades, Defenders of the Environment, and the Everglades Protection Association. Acting as a policy entrepreneur was Governor Bob Graham, who in 1983 announced his "Save Our Everglades" initiative. In an effort to redefine the Everglades problem to emphasize ecology rather than urban water supply, Graham linked human survival with the ecosystem's health, saying that the region faced "an awesome truth. Our presence here is as tenuous as that of the fragile Everglades. The complicated ecosystems that support delicate swamp lilies and great blue herons are the source of our water."[29] After declaring his intent to save the Everglades, Graham dispatched staff around the state to settle environmental disputes, began lobbying for protective legislation, instituted reforms in several key agencies, and—perhaps most importantly—appointed five new, environmentally oriented board members and a new executive director to the SFWMD.[30]

Notwithstanding the strong backing of Governor Graham, however, environmentalists had difficulty raising the salience of the Everglades' ecological problems. Observers attributed the public's inattention to the elusiveness of the landscape's splendor. Bruce Babbitt described the challenges of generating passion about a swamp, saying "there aren't any glaciers in the Everglades, there aren't any grizzly bears, there aren't any 500-foot waterfalls. We've been a little slow in expanding our image of parks to include equally important but more subtle kinds of ecosystems."[31] Patti Webster, an environmental activist, agreed that "getting people interested in saving the manatee isn't a problem, but getting them to love a swamp is a real challenge."[32] Even those who lobbied on behalf of the park pointed out that it could be a brutal place. As one park ranger noted, "the temperature gets up to 95 degrees with 100 percent humidity [in the summer], and there are thunder and lightning storms like I've never imagined, and every day the mosquitoes are so thick you can't breathe. It's miserable."[33]

The National Park Service, which was environmentalists' prime ally in recruiting public and political support, was incapable of generating the scientific information and expertise that might have helped to document and dramatize the Everglades' problems. From its inception in 1916, the Park Service had struggled with its schizophrenic mission "to conserve the scenery and the natural and historic objects and the wildlife therein *and* to provide for the enjoyment of same in such manner and by such means as will leave them unimpaired for the enjoyment of future generations [emphasis mine]."[34] The service's ongoing preoccupation with attracting visitors detracted from its ability to manage the parks with ecological sensitivity and to develop scientific capabilities, and for decades the agency ignored pleas from outsiders to improve the scientific basis for park management.[35]

In 1976, marking a striking departure from Park Service tradition, a prominent Florida Republican named Nathaniel Reed convinced Congress to establish the South Florida Research Center (SFRC) within the Everglades National Park. The center's scientists began studying historic water records, installing a network of water gauges, monitoring rainfall, and systematically examining the parks' wildlife and vegetation. By the early 1980s, their studies were yielding sobering results. For instance, upon completion of his ten-year study of the effects of water levels on alligators, park scientist James Kushlan reported that insufficient water was not the problem; instead, high water was flooding alligator and woodstork nesting sites and threatening those species. His conclusion was unpopular with park management, however; in fact, according to Kushlan, "The Superintendent told me he did not even want to read my study. If he read it he would have to design a management plan to satisfy it, and manipulation of water levels was a lot more risky than doing nothing."[36] The superintendent suppressed the study, and shortly thereafter the chief of the SFRC issued an order prohibiting all center scientists from publishing the results of their work. Frustrated with those restrictions, Kushlan and several of his colleagues left the service for university positions. By the mid-1980s, all but one of the scientists at the SFRC had been replaced by nonprofessional technicians. Richard Briceland, who was chief scientist in the mid-1980s during the heyday of the Save Our Everglades campaign, was actually a mechanical engineer.

Resisting the Everglades Rescue. The Save Our Everglades initiative not only lacked broad public support and powerful institutional allies; it also faced formidable opposition in the sugar industry, which wielded tremendous political clout in both the state legislature and the U.S. Congress. Beginning in the eighteenth century, Congress had provided the sugar industry with generous subsidies and highly restrictive import quotas.[37] Throughout this period, the Florida legislature was also deferential to sugar despite its exploitative labor practices and environmental abuses, in part because of the legislature's traditional rural bias and its recognition of the economic potency of the industry, but also because sugar executives provided their allies with generous campaign contributions.[38]

The sugar industry also maintained strong ties to the SFWMD, which by the 1980s was a wealthy, powerful, and highly professionalized entity with broad policymaking authority. Although the district's initial purpose was flood control, the Florida Water Resources Act of 1972 made Everglades protection part of its mandate.[39] In the early 1980s, with its broader mission and under the influence of environmentally oriented board members appointed by Governor Graham, the district began to acquire a more progressive reputation. Overall, however, the SFWMD continued to be preoccupied with short-term economic development needs over long-run ecological considerations; top management still consisted of development-oriented engineers; and standard operating procedures were based on the requirements of economic growth in the region.

Finally, the sugar industry was a key client of the Army Corps of Engineers, the federal agency that—in partnership with the SFWMD—was responsible for managing South Florida's water supply. From its inception in 1802, the Corps had been a versatile agency but one primarily oriented toward economic development; since 1850, the Corps' main responsibility had been to build, maintain, and operate flood control and other water development projects to facilitate farming and real estate development. In 1936, Congress established a national flood control policy and gave the Corps even greater authority over this area. Finally, in 1937 and 1941, Congress removed certain local participation and approval requirements from the Corps' authorizing statute, "paving the way for the Corps to become the engineer consultants and contractors of the U.S. Congress."[40]

Although the Corps was the nation's premier development organization, it did begin to incorporate environmental protection into its standard operating procedures after the passage of the National Environmental Policy Act in 1970. By the late 1970s, the agency was consulting advisory boards composed of planning and environmental professionals and a range of interest groups. In addition, all the agency's offices had a distinct unit whose primary purpose was to provide environmental input into planning. Notwithstanding its movement toward greater consideration of environmental costs, however, in the mid-1980s, the Corps was still regularly denying the SFWMD the permits it needed to undertake Everglades restoration and was widely seen as impeding such efforts.[41]

The Governmental Response. The Save Our Everglades campaign was ineffectual when pitted against the well-heeled team of the SFWMD and the Corps, combined with a Florida legislature that was reluctant to antagonize wealthy development interests. Nevertheless, Governor Graham continued to promote environmental initiatives and, as a result, did accomplish some noteworthy policy changes. At Graham's behest, the state continued to fine-tune its planning and growth management apparatus, although it did so without directly confronting the sugar industry on the Everglades issue. Most importantly, in 1987, the legislature approved the Surface Water Improvement and Management (SWIM) Act, requiring the water districts to develop plans to prevent and reverse degradation of the state's waters. The SWIM Act also set targets for the amount of phosphorous entering Lake Okeechobee and established a technical advisory council to study the effects of phosphorous on the WCAs and other areas south of the lake. Finally, the act specified that water management districts "shall not divert water to . . . the Everglades National Park in such a way that state water quality standards are violated [or] that nutrients in such waters adversely affect indigenous vegetation communities or wildlife."[42]

Although the district expressed its commitment to devise and implement a SWIM plan, the prospects for bringing about major changes in the Everglades regime in the administrative arena appeared bleak. Newly elected governor Bob Martinez had appointed five new SFWMD board members, including several with close ties to the sugar industry and vegetable growers.[43] In any case, SWIM plans by themselves do not mandate particular actions, and neither the state nor the district was taking serious steps to change the hydrologic regime. As one highly respected former SFWMD board member put it, the district was "drifting" on the issue of water quality in 1988 and was not giving it adequate attention.[44]

Mounting Evidence of Ecosystem Decline

By the late 1980s, scientists had formulated a clear picture of how land use and water management practices in South Florida had damaged the Everglades ecosystem. They understood that the extensive network of canals, levees, and pumps had dramatically altered the balance among the four key hydrologic variables that govern the region's ecological health: the timing of water releases, the distribution of the water flow, the amount of water released, and the water quality. As a result of the changes to the system, at least twenty-six species of plants and animals were threatened or endangered. Among the species in trouble were the Florida panther, the West Indian manatee, the southern bald eagle, the Cape Sable sparrow, the brown pelican, the indigo snake, and several varieties of sea turtle. Endemic plants, tropical trees, and rare orchids were disappearing as well.

In particular, there had been an alarming decline in the population of wading birds: by the late 1980s, the historic giant rookeries of the southern Everglades were gone, and although new rookeries had appeared in the Water Conservation Areas north of the park, they were smaller and appeared unstable. Biologist John Ogden noted that by the late 1980s, the number of nesting wood storks, an indicator species, had dropped 80 percent since the 1960s.[45] The birds' decline was closely related to changes in the hydroperiod—that is, the timing and quantity of water flowing into the Everglades. Historically, the birds timed their nesting around slow-moving dry fronts. They started nesting in November or December and raised their young during the dry season, when the receding water along the wetlands' edge left behind shallow pools of water filled with prey. Changes in the area's hydrology had disrupted the normal cycle, however, leaving deeper pools that dried out more slowly and creating abrupt shifts between wet and dry periods, so in many years the nesting season was virtually nonexistent.[46]

Another of the Everglades' keystone species, the American alligator, had also suffered from the alterations in the hydroperiod, although the effects of those changes initially were masked because the animal population rebounded after the federal Endangered Species Act eliminated poaching.[47] Having survived since the age of the dinosaurs, alligators were adaptable and willing to use human-made canals for breeding. Nevertheless, alligators suffered when too much water flooded their nests early in the wet season. As the alligators dwindled, wading birds could no longer rely on the alligator holes and trails that once enhanced their habitat by providing a home for prey, some of which would survive to repopulate the adjacent marshes during the rainy season.[48]

Finally, scientists were piecing together the causes of some other disturbing trends in the region, particularly in Florida Bay. The bay, located between the Everglades National Park and the Florida Keys, is a large, shallow, coastal lagoon that contains numerous islands fringed with mangroves and mud shoals. Signs of decline appeared in Florida Bay in the 1970s and accelerated in the 1980s. About fifteen square miles of seagrass died in the western half of the bay between 1987 and 1990, and about ninety square miles were damaged. The coral reef in the Florida Bay—the only such reef in the continental United States—was also in an alarming state of deterioration. And scientists were witnessing spectacular declines in the populations of wading seabirds, sponges, and mangrove trees. Fish and shellfish had virtually disappeared; in fact, in 1985, park officials banned commercial fishing in the bay.

The Lawsuit

Activated by scientists' concern and frustrated with the intransigence of the SFWMD and the Corps, environmentalists began to explore legal avenues through which to change governmental priorities. They were having difficulty finding a legal toehold when the newly appointed acting U.S. attorney for South Florida, Dexter Lehtinen, called them into his office to ask which environmental problem his office ought to tackle next. Environmentalists responded that the decline of the Everglades was the single most important issue facing the state.[49] Lehtinen proposed suing the state in federal court for failing to enforce its own water quality laws by allowing the EAA to pump water into the Loxahatchee National Wildlife Refuge without obtaining a permit from the district and thereby inflicting a nuisance on the refuge and the park.[50] Recognizing that Lehtinen was better positioned to mount a legal challenge than they were, environmentalists dropped their own legal exploration and, at Lehtinen's invitation, joined the Justice Department's suit.[51]

The lawsuit further polarized environmental and development interests, and for three years the parties were at an impasse. While a resolution appeared elusive, the environmental coalition took advantage of the publicity surrounding the lawsuit to promote its cause. They used the scientific evidence relating phosphorous levels to the Everglades' decline as a basis for a compelling causal story: they pointed out that the EAA lay directly in the path of the region's historic sheetflow and thereby severed the connection between Lake Okeechobee and the park, and that sugar cane fields—which occupied the bulk of the EAA—were responsible for most of the phosphorous flowing into the Everglades.[52] It was not difficult to portray the sugar executives as greedy and dishonest: they were making enormous profits while reaping millions annually in government subsidies,[53] and they were notorious for their exploitative labor practices and close connections to the political establishment. While sugar was the main character in the political story, however, environmentalists had far wider ambitions than simply extracting money from polluters. According to Assistant Attorney General Richard Stewart, "Agricultural pollution was . . . only the opening wedge in a much larger issue. It was really a question of changing the culture of the district, the state, and the industry."[54]

Of course, once environmentalists went public with their attack on sugar, the industry retaliated in kind, in hopes of minimizing the groundswell of public support for restoration and defusing antipathy toward "big sugar." They began by asserting that the cattails in the refuge and the park were neither as extensive nor as voracious as environmentalists contended, and they cited alternative explanations for the presence of cattails, emphasizing such natural factors as fire, hydroperiod changes, and sediments from Lake Okeechobee. Once it became clear that phosphorous was a prime culprit behind the Everglades' deterioration, the sugar industry began marshalling scientific evidence to refute environmentalists' position that they bore primary responsibility for the high phosphorous levels. To enhance their credibility, the EAA hired Curtis Richardson, a Duke University wetlands expert, and the Florida Sugar Cane League retained a respected Florida scientist who had worked for the phosphate industry and held a position on the board of the Florida Wildlife Federation.[55] These experts pointed out that growing sugar cane required relatively little fertilizer and that cane did not have to be replanted annually, so it caused less erosion than other crops. They added that sugar was not the only source of phosphorous and was a relatively benign one at that.[56]

Settling the Lawsuit. Environmental activists' efforts were beginning to bear fruit: even before the lawsuit, the U.S. Congress—which had been apathetic about Florida's environmental problems throughout much of the 1980s—had taken its first big step toward Everglades restoration by passing the Everglades National Park Protection and Expansion Act, which authorized the purchase of over 107,000 acres east of the park. The goal of the acquisition was to enable the park to regain 55 percent of the natural water flow to the Shark River Slough, a flow that had been reduced 90 percent by the Corps.[57] In 1990, Congress appropriated additional money for the park to develop a plan for restoring a more natural flow of water through the Everglades. Everglades restoration had also become Florida's premier environmental issue. Reflecting its growing salience, gubernatorial challenger Lawton Chiles made the lawsuit a central issue in his campaign, ridiculing Martinez' passivity and pointing out that millions of dollars were being wasted on legal fees. Chiles subsequently won the election, partly on the strength of his campaign pledge to settle the Everglades lawsuit.

The combination of Governor Chiles' leadership and environmentalists' ongoing efforts to popularize the issue advanced the cause of Everglades restoration toward a tipping point. On his first day in office, Chiles delivered a speech at the annual meeting of the Everglades Coalition and told the gathering that as commander-in-chief of the state's environmental programs he would settle the Everglades lawsuit within six months.[58] Although his initial effort—a summit involving environmentalists, state and district officials, and the sugar industry—was a flop, Chiles proceeded to operate on other fronts. One of the governor's main emissaries was Carol Browner, a former aide who became his secretary of the Department of Environmental Regulation and took the lead in negotiations with the Justice Department. Chiles also appointed to the SFWMD board five environmentally oriented members.

As part of the effort to settle the lawsuit, industry and government scientists met to try to establish the scientific parameters of the dispute. Once they sat down together, the scientists were able to agree fairly easily on the level of phosphorous that would be harmful to the Everglades: approximately ten parts per billion (ppb). The scientists also converged on the idea that building a large, artificial wetland to filter the water draining from the EAA would solve the problem. The more challenging (and politically loaded) question was: how large a wetland would be necessary to bring EAA waters down to an acceptable standard?[59]

While scientists were resolving the technical questions, environmentalists turned sugar's continuing intransigence to their advantage in building their case in public and the legislature. They added economic arguments to their arsenal of scientific justifications for Everglades restoration, enlisting hotel and dive shop owners in the Keys, as well as sport and commercial fishermen from Florida Bay. They continued to pursue urban interests, as well, recognizing that they would be key to the campaign's long-term success: there were more than five million people living along the state's Gold Coast, and urban interests were displacing farmers as the most important economic political force. Area residents relied for clean water on the Biscayne Aquifer, which—as environmentalists pointed out—depended on a healthy, functioning Everglades. Environmentalists' effort to appropriate the economic high ground was captured by Tom Martin, director of the National Audubon Society's Everglades campaign, when he said: "It's become clear that the economic health of South Florida is tied to its environmental health. South Florida's economy is based on growth. . . . Saving the Everglades isn't just for the birds. It's jobs."[60]

Recognizing the Everglades' increasing popularity, members of the Florida legislature got on the restoration bandwagon. In addition to appropriating matching funds to buy land for conversion to wetlands, in the spring of 1991, the legislature unanimously passed a critical piece of legislation: the Marjory Stoneman Douglas Act, which rendered moot several of the issues in the lawsuit. The act specified numerical standards for the quality of water passing through the EAA pumps, required the SFWMD to apply to the Department of Environmental Regulation for permits for those pumps, and directed the district to make farmers get permits for water draining off their lands. The act also required the district to prepare a SWIM plan "to bring facilities into compliance with applicable water quality standards and restore the Everglades hydroperiod."[61] Finally, the law authorized the SFWMD to condemn land and build artificial wetlands, thereby facilitating the restoration.

Shortly thereafter, the governor broke the legal impasse that had stymied negotiators for three years by stipulating in court that the water flowing into the Everglades was polluted. Over a two-month period following Chiles' concession, the scientific task force agreed that at least 34,700 acres of artificial wetlands (at an estimated cost of $400 million to build) would be necessary to purify water flowing into the park.[62] On July 8, six months after Chiles took office, the parties to the lawsuit submitted a thirty-page settlement to District Court Judge William Hoeveler, who approved it nine months later, after rejecting a slew of appeals by the sugar companies. Under the 1992 Consent Decree, the state of Florida agreed to implement a water quality restoration plan by building artificial filtration marshes, imposing best management practices (BMPs)[63] on farms, and requiring agricultural runoff to meet an interim phosphorous limit of 50 ppb and a long-term limit of 10 ppb. For environmentalists, the Consent Decree was only a first step, however, because the quality of the water flowing into the Everglades was only part of the problem. Disruption of the hydroperiod remained to be addressed. (Although both the Consent Decree and the Marjory Stoneman Douglas Act referred to restoring the Everglades hydroperiod, neither provided specifics on how this would be done.)

More importantly, although the court, the federal government, the state, and the district were amenable to the Consent Decree, the sugar industry—

which had not been a formal party to either the lawsuit or the settlement—was not. The industry was willing to implement the BMPs set forth by the district, but it resisted the more expensive remedy of building artificial wetlands. In spring 1992, the industry launched a PR campaign to denigrate the settlement as unreasonable and unfair. When sugar executives made it clear that they were prepared to spend millions on court battles, Florida officials and the Justice Department felt compelled to embark on another round of negotiations in the spring of 1992.

Another Round of Negotiations. This time around, any interested parties—including both sugar and environmentalists—were invited to join the talks. Like the discussions leading up to the original settlement, the second round of negotiations involved a technical group, whose job was to devise a plan to address the water quality and hydroperiod problems in the Everglades. Like its predecessor, the technical group reached agreement on the range of acceptable phosphorous levels fairly easily and by early 1993 had also come up with a plan to create artificial wetlands and simultaneously improve the hydroperiod. The technical group's proposal, known as the Mediated Technical Plan, subsequently became the basis for the debate over who would pay for the restoration.

Throughout the negotiations, the sugar industry continued to challenge the growing scientific consensus in hopes of deflecting public ire and avoiding financial responsibility; while privately exploring alternatives to artificial wetlands for reducing the flow of phosphorous off its lands, publicly the industry continued to maintain that phosphorous was not a serious problem and that, in any case, sugar was not the culprit behind elevated phosphorous levels.[64] As late as July 1993, a Flo-Sun spokesman said that "it's not true that cattails are caused by phosphorous—it's because of flooding."[65] U.S. Sugar President J. Nelson Fairbanks continued to adhere to the theory that phosphorous was already in the water when it entered the cane fields from Lake Okeechobee or that it seeped up from underground. Sugar industry executives also resorted to economic and equity arguments: U.S. Sugar's vice president, Robert Buker, commented that "the deal that was struck will bankrupt South Florida."[66] U.S. Sugar President Fairbanks suggested that since the Corps built the C&SF system, it should have to fix it.

The sugar industry was increasingly isolated in its stance, however; recognizing that momentum for restoration was building, both the SFWMD and the Corps had gotten on the bandwagon. After the 1991 settlement, the district had begun developing a "natural systems" model to quantify the actual water level and flow in the primeval Everglades. By the early 1990s, the Corps, once perceived as the primary obstacle, was taking the lead on Everglades restoration. Even its harshest critics were impressed with the Corps' alacrity, though many attributed its chameleon-like shift to its ability to spot and take advantage of lucrative, budget-enhancing opportunities rather than to a genuine philosophical transformation.

Federal Leadership Propels the Restoration Forward

In 1993, a series of personnel changes opened another political window of opportunity for Everglades restoration—this time at the federal level. The newly installed Clinton administration dramatically changed the climate for environmental protection in Washington: Clinton appointed Carol Browner, a key player in Governor Chiles' administration, as EPA administrator. Although she recused herself from the Everglades dispute, Browner encouraged Clinton's pro-environment interior secretary, Bruce Babbitt, to be a policy entrepreneur on the issue.[67] In addition to these executive-branch changes, several congressional shifts had major consequences for the Everglades as well: Democrat George Miller of California took over the chairmanship of the House Interior Committee, and two new members of Congress from South Florida—both advocates of Everglades research and restoration—obtained positions on the House Appropriations Committee.

Shortly after he was appointed, Interior Secretary Babbitt—hoping to make resolution of the Everglades a national model of ecosystem-level environmental problem solving—invited his top assistants, as well as key state officials and executives from Flo-Sun and U.S. Sugar, to come to Washington, D.C., and settle their differences. In July 1993, a jubilant Babbitt held a press conference to proclaim that the parties had reached a tentative agreement to split the costs of implementing the Mediated Technical Plan (devised as part of the second round of settlement negotiations): the agricultural community would pay 50 percent (between $233 and $322 million over twenty years); the federal government would pay 8 percent; and the state of Florida would pitch in the remaining 42 percent.[68] The basic agreement, known as the "Statement of Principles," involved a combination of BMPs and nearly 40,000 acres of Stormwater Treatment Areas (STAs), or artificial wetlands. The sugar executives agreed to withdraw their lawsuits so that the details of the plan could be worked out.

While some environmentalists were cautiously optimistic about the deal Babbitt had brokered, others were outraged. For many environmentalists, the principle was clear: the sugar industry had polluted the Everglades and it—not the taxpayers—ought to pay to clean it up. Audubon's Joe Browder denounced Babbitt for compromising on the Everglades. Others questioned whether the plan entailed a real, long-term obligation on the part of the sugar industry because the new settlement was, in many respects, less ambitious than the 1991 settlement: it called for only as many acres of wetlands as necessary to reduce the concentration of phosphorous in the water entering the park to 50 ppb, whereas the 1991 litigation settlement had included a second-phase target of 10 ppb.[69] Within months of announcing the agreement, opposition from environmental groups had crystallized: nineteen national and state-level organizations wrote to Secretary Babbitt asking that 70,000–120,000 acres of EAA land be set aside for wetlands and requesting additional treatment for any water brought into the Everglades to restore the hydroperiod if it was below water quality standards.

Laying the Groundwork for a Restoration Plan. Challenges to the Statement of Principles notwithstanding, the restoration effort moved forward. To facilitate interagency coordination among the myriad federal entities whose cooperation would be required, as well as to build the scientific capability and credibility that would be necessary for this unprecedented enterprise, Secretary Babbitt established the South Florida Ecosystem Restoration Task Force, comprising assistant secretaries from six federal agencies and representing ten bureaus.[70] The task force charter, signed in September 1993, set forth the goal of establishing an ecosystem-based science program. To accomplish this, the task force created the South Florida Management and Coordination Working Group, headed by Everglades National Park Superintendent Dick Ring. Ring, in turn, created three subgroups to coordinate the research agenda for South Florida. The Science Subgroup reached out to state and university scientists and facilitated scientific cooperation and consensus.[71]

In parallel, the Corps' C&SF Project Comprehensive Review Study, or Restudy, authorized by Congress as part of the 1992 Water Resources Development Act, also adopted a multi-agency, cooperative approach to planning the restoration effort in recognition of the "public, political, and media interest in the restoration of the South Florida ecosystem."[72] Congress hoped that by involving all the stakeholders, the Corps' planning effort could gain widespread support, which would reduce the likelihood that any individual agency would subsequently undermine the project.[73] A collaborative approach was also intended to enhance the production and flow of information; taking advantage of many sources of expertise in the system, the Restudy team included civil engineers, hydraulic engineers, cost engineers, biologists, ecologists, resource managers, community planners, economists, GIS (geographic information system) specialists, and real estate experts.

While the reconnaissance phase of the Corps-led Restudy got under way, the Interior Department's Science Subgroup was already at work on the scientific underpinning of a restoration plan. In late November, the subgroup released a draft report that stunned opponents of Everglades restoration. The report, which reflected the team's holistic, ecosystem-scale thinking, outlined many of the tenets that scientists believed should ground the restoration effort, foremost among which was that "hydrologic restoration is a necessary starting point for ecological restoration."[74] To that end, the report proposed permanently flooding 195,000 of the 450,000 acres under cultivation in the EAA.[75] The remainder of the EAA, the report suggested, should be under water 60 percent of the time. The timing of the report's release, just days before the final meeting of the sugar industry, farmers, and federal and state officials to sign an agreement on the restoration, was a public relations disaster. Within weeks, the sugar industry had withdrawn its support for the fragile political agreement.[76]

The sugar industry proceeded to file thirty-six lawsuits challenging the state's plans to implement the technical plan, and a trial was scheduled for April 25, 1994. Preempting the trial, however, on April 15 the Florida legislature passed another major statute to increase the protectiveness of Everglades policy: the Everglades Forever Act. The new law put an end to the sugar industry's legal maneuvering by stating as fact the need for Everglades cleanup and hydroperiod remediation, asserting the suitability of the cleanup program as a remedy for these problems, and condoning the Statement of Principles (negotiated by Babbitt) as a basis for remediation. It went even further than the Statement of Principles by incorporating suggestions from the environmental community to improve on the Mediated Technical Plan. The Everglades Forever Act enabled restoration to begin in earnest by requiring the state to administer a $700 million Everglades cleanup that comprised a water treatment system, extensive research and monitoring, and a regulatory program.[77] Most importantly, the act simply mandated a substantial financial contribution from agriculture, thereby aborting what promised to be a series of time-consuming administrative and judicial proceedings instigated by the sugar industry.

Although the Everglades Forever Act eliminated some potential legal hurdles, proponents of restoration were aware that for the project to survive in the long run, it needed both public support and reliable funding. To enhance public acceptance of the restoration, in 1994 Governor Chiles appointed a forty-seven-member citizens' Commission for a Sustainable South Florida. In addition to the governor's council, the Corps and SFWMD held workshops to gather public comments on the Restudy. They held three rounds of large public meetings in 1993 and 1994, with up to 700 people at each, and made plans for smaller, focus group sessions to discuss specific issues in subsequent years. The results of three Everglades-related ballot initiatives in 1996 affirmed the growing public commitment to Everglades cleanup and restoration but also the ability of the sugar industry to sway the public on the particulars. Voters endorsed two of the proposed constitutional amendments: the first required those who polluted the Everglades to pay for its cleanup; the second established a trust fund for Everglades cleanup money. The third amendment would have imposed a penny-a-pound tax on sugar to finance the $700 million cleanup. The sugar industry targeted this, the most concrete of the three proposals; it spent $23 million on TV ads to convince voters to oppose the tax and won with the support of 54 percent of the electorate.[78]

After the election, financing of the Everglades cleanup remained uncertain, particularly after the Florida State Supreme Court said that the polluters-pay amendment could not be implemented unless the legislature passed a law requiring it. Prospects for the restoration project improved, however, when the federal government proffered some financing. Because Florida was the nation's fourth most populous state and thus a pivotal source of electoral college votes, it had become the focus of both Democratic and Republican presidential campaigns. Given its burgeoning popularity within the state and nationally, the restoration project became an obvious source of political credit claiming as the 1996 presidential race heated up.[79] Between 1994 and 1996, Congress came up with nearly $5 million annually to buy land for buffer areas around the park; moreover, at the instigation of Republican presidential candidate Bob Dole, the

Senate Agriculture Committee inserted into the 1996 omnibus farm bill $200 million for the Everglades.[80] Not to be outdone during the election year, Vice President Al Gore—on behalf of President Clinton—officially endorsed the restoration project in February of 1996 and proposed going well beyond the terms of the 1994 Everglades Forever Act by spending $500 million over the next several years on top of the $100 million the federal government had already committed to the Interior Department's Everglades Restoration Fund.[81]

In addition to providing budgetary support, in October 1996, Congress affirmed its backing for the planning portion of the restoration with Section 528 of the Water Resources Development Act of 1996. Entitled "Everglades and South Florida Ecosystem Restoration," the provision directed the Restudy to provide "a proposed comprehensive plan for the purpose of restoring, preserving, and protecting the South Florida ecosystem."[82] The law required the Corps to develop the plan in cooperation with the SFWMD and in consultation with the South Florida Ecosystem Restoration Task Force, and to submit it to Congress by July 1, 1999. The act allowed the Corps to begin implementing restoration projects as deemed necessary by the Corps, the state of Florida, and the Task Force, and it authorized appropriations of $75 million from 1997 to 1999 to carry out such projects. Once sold on the restoration, a bipartisan Congress endorsed it again the following year, appropriating $269 million for fiscal year 1998 and $221 million for fiscal year 1999. Funding over the long haul remained tenuous, however.

The Restoration Plan. In October 1998, the Corps unveiled a draft of its $7.8 billion plan, the Comprehensive Everglades Restoration Plan, devised as part of the C&SF Restudy. Far more extensive than the cleanup plans envisioned by the plaintiffs in the original lawsuit or subsequently devised under the Everglades Forever Act, the Restudy plan covered 18,000 square miles from the northern edge of the Kissimmee River drainage near Orlando to Florida Bay along the Keys, and its fundamental goal was to "get the water right." To do this, the plan proposed to remove more than 500 miles of human-made impediments to reestablish natural water flows and create about 30,000 acres of wetlands—in addition to the more than 40,000 acres of wetlands already under development—to treat urban and agricultural runoff before discharging it into the Everglades. To address the competing needs of water development and flood control, the Corps intended to create reservoirs and underground aquifers and to reuse wastewater, all of which would allow it to retain in the system over 90 percent of the 1.7 million acre-feet of water per year that used to be pumped into the ocean.

Although the plan was announced with great fanfare, opponents of restoration were hardly vanquished. Dubious business and agricultural leaders pointed out that the technology needed to accomplish the plan's objectives was untested. Opponents also generated dire predictions of the economic impact of the project: the Florida Citizens for a Sound Economy estimated that residents would lose 2,879 jobs and $120 per household per year in taxes and water fees.[83] (In contrast, the Corps estimated that its plan would create between 3,900 and 6,800 jobs.) Nor had the sugar industry been quiescent while the Restudy developed its plan.[84] It had been working behind the scenes and, as the public turned its attention elsewhere, allies of the sugar industry slipped two bills through the Florida state legislature in spring 1998. The first bill gave the legislature direct oversight over the Corps; the second made it more expensive for the federal government to acquire land for the restoration. Environmentalists breathed a sigh of relief when Governor Chiles vetoed both bills, calling them "a poison pill" that would jeopardize the state-federal partnership.[85]

In addition to trying to subvert the restoration, the sugar industry, as well as dairy and other farmers, continued to make every effort to shape the plan. While environmental groups (and the Science Subgroup) supported a plan to take more land out of the EAA, sugar executives successfully lobbied the Corps to seek alternative approaches. So instead of building a large reservoir on sugar lands, the Corps plan relied on expensive, underground storage systems for water around the lake and created a reservoir north of the lake. What land the sugar industry did relinquish under the plan was not actually lost but rather swapped with the federal government for land bought from a willing seller. In short, according to critics, the sugar companies not only survived the battle over Everglades restoration; they guaranteed their future water supply.[86]

Even as opponents of the restoration tried to gut the plan, environmentalists assailed it from the other side. Park officials criticized the proposal for meeting the demands of urban water users without giving the park and Biscayne Bay the water they need to survive. In their December 1998 report, Park Service scientists said that "the consensus opinion of the Everglades National Park staff is that there is insufficient evidence to substantiate the claim that [the plan] will result in recovery of a healthy, sustainable ecosystem. Rather, we find substantial, credible evidence to the contrary."[87] In response to the criticisms of park officials, the Corps began looking into capturing billions of gallons of urban runoff and diverting it to wells, reservoirs, and filter marshes. Using this and other sources, scientists thought they could get another 112 billion gallons per year for the park and Bay. There were objections to this remedy, however: urban runoff is polluted, and drainage changes would likely exacerbate problems with the timing of water delivery to the park.

In addition, breaking with the Everglades Coalition, which endorsed the comprehensive plan, the Sierra Club objected to the plan's emphasis on engineering, rather than natural, solutions and asked that it be reviewed by an independent panel of nationally known scientists. A group of leading ecologists agreed with the Sierra Club and Park Service's positions and in late January 1999 sent a letter to Secretary Babbitt saying the Corps' plan had deep, systemic failings.[88] Ecologist Stuart Pimm pointed out that "there is very little restoration, and most of it doesn't come for the next 25 years."[89] Pimm also voiced concern about the scheme's reliance on a hydrologic model that he said was unrealistic. He argued the approach embodied in the plan was basically flawed because it retained the fragmentation and compartmentalization of the Everglades as well as "the notion that the entire system can be managed in perpetuity" by humans.[90] To deflect criticism, the South Florida Ecosystem Restoration Task Force decided unanimously in February 1999 (and the SFWMD agreed) to submit the restoration plan for review to an independent panel assembled by the National Academy of Sciences.

After months of public comment and tinkering, in April 1999, the Corps released the Final Integrated Feasibility Report and Programmatic Environmental Impact Statement for the Comprehensive Restoration Plan. In response to public comments on the draft document, and in an effort to appease environmentalists, the revised plan proposed to complete many key environmental projects in less than a decade, more than doubling the pace of the draft restoration plan. Under the new, accelerated schedule, forty-four of sixty-eight projects would be finished by 2010. By that time, water would flow in a broad sheet through state-owned marshes from southern Palm Beach County to the Everglades National Park. The Corps would fill a major canal and remove parts of a levee in that marsh and raise ten miles of the Tamiami Trail to let water pass. About 130,000 acres of reservoirs would be completed, and urban and agricultural runoff would be cleansed by 28,000 new acres of STAs.[91] While some environmentalists were pleased with the Corps' responsiveness, others continued to identify fundamental problems with the plan.

Approving and Implementing the Restoration Plan. The effort to fund and implement the restoration plan not only galvanized environmentalists and sugar executives, it also laid bare tensions between the federal government and the state of Florida, as well as among the variety of agencies whose cooperation was needed. On July 1, 1999, the administration presented its ten-volume, 4,000-page restoration plan to Congress, which planned to hold hearings on the report before incorporating it into the 2000 Water Resources Development Act. The influence of environmentalists and their allies in the federal government was evident in the final plan, which included more water for the park, an expanded role for the Interior Department in South Florida water management decisions, and a pledge to make ecosystem restoration, not urban water supply, the plan's top priority. The White House voiced enthusiastic support for the plan and proposed to spend $312 million for the Everglades, a 35 percent increase over funds already designated for the project.

Getting approval from the Republican Congress was another story, however. Both the House and the Senate recommended large cuts in funding from the $150 million requested by the Interior Department for restoration work in 2000 to $90 million (Senate) and $114 million (House). In June of 1999, the House Appropriations Committee approved $114 million but said it would not release $42 million for land purchases until it had a binding agreement with details of where, when, and how water would flow and how clean it would be because members wanted to ensure that federal priorities—water would be for the Everglades, not development—prevailed. Members of appropriations committees in both chambers cited a General Accounting Office (GAO) report released that April, which found that interagency feuds had raised costs as much as $80 million and delayed for more than two years restoration projects that were then under way.[92]

Exacerbating congressional skepticism, in May 1999 Florida's newly elected Republican governor, Jeb Bush, approved a sugar industry-supported bill, similar to those that had been vetoed by Governor Chiles, requiring the Department of Environmental Regulation to review any restoration work before Congress authorized money for it and resurrecting a state condemnation law that could drive up the purchase price of some land by one-third or more. In the same session, a bill authorizing $100 million per year in state bond money died, and the legislature failed to appropriate any funds for restoration. The primary consequence of these efforts was to make Congress, and the appropriations committees in particular, even warier of Florida's commitment to ecosystem restoration. Ultimately, on October 22, 1999, Congress passed an appropriations bill with only $10 million for Everglades restoration, conditional on a binding agreement involving all parties to provide specific volume, timing, location, and duration of water flows to guarantee an "adequate and appropriate" water supply to South Florida's natural areas, including all national parks, preserves, and wildlife refuges, "to ensure a restored ecosystem."[93] The House Appropriations Committee also requested an annual report on how federal funds were spent and a detailed plan of how restoration would be done. Congressional efforts to give ecosystem goals precedence over agricultural and municipal interests delighted environmentalists but infuriated Governor Bush.

With Florida a key state in the presidential race, the Everglades restoration again became an object of credit claiming for both candidates as the campaign heated up in early 2000. Competing for environmental votes both nationally and in Florida, Vice President Gore introduced an Everglades bill that gave restoring the ecosystem clear precedence over municipal and agricultural users; split power between the Corps and Interior; relegated the governor to an advisory role; and restrained the Corps' propensity for construction by requiring congressional scrutiny of all new building projects. In addition, the administration plan required an independent scientific panel to oversee Corps activity.[94] Nor was the salience of Everglades restoration, both nationally and in Florida, lost on George W. Bush's campaign. In recognition of this, Governor Bush's approach to Everglades restoration shifted abruptly during the 2000 presidential race, and in July 2000, he shepherded through the legislature the Everglades Restoration Investment Act, a bill to spend $2 billion over ten years on the restoration project.

OUTCOMES

Given the confluence of positive forces surrounding the Everglades restoration in the 1990s, it is hardly surprising that only a few years after some of the initial projects were launched they were already bearing fruit. By the mid-1990s, the state and federal governments between them had acquired more than 325,000 acres of parks, preserves, and wildlife refuges. In January 1999, the sugar industry, federal government, and state officials agreed to a multi-million dollar land purchase and swap that provided more than 62,000 acres toward the Everglades restoration. Efforts to improve water quality and restore the hydroperiod also seemed to be promising. As early as 1992, by following BMPs recommended by the SFWMD, the EAA had already achieved reductions of as much as 35 to 40 percent in the concentration of phosphorous coming off its fields.[95] In 1996, one year after the cleanup officially got under way, the SFWMD reported that farmers had achieved a 68 percent reduction in the amount of phosphorous they discharged. In addition, the SFWMD reported that its experimental pollution-control project, in which phosphorous-laden water is diverted to marshes filled with phosphorous-absorbing plants, was operating better than expected. The Corps reported that using iterative testing it had already improved conditions within the Shark River Slough substantially by restoring a more natural hydrologic regime.

On December 11, 2000, President Clinton signed the Water Resources Development Act of 2000, which approved the Comprehensive Everglades Restoration Plan and authorized $1.4 billion for ten specific restoration projects that will constitute the framework for future efforts.[96] Threats to the long-term viability of the restoration project remain, however. The gravest of these is the pressure for development that will accompany South Florida's booming population, which is expected to double to 12 million by 2050. Massive population growth could exacerbate political pressures to divert water from the ecosystem to water users, a concern for scientists and environmentalists who are already worried that the plan is biased in favor of development and will not succeed in restoring the Everglades. Curbing growth requires a political will that few state governments have demonstrated; the resulting urban sprawl has become a priority for American environmentalists who recognize that fragile ecosystems, such as the Everglades, depend on their vigilance.

CONCLUSIONS

Like the New England fisheries and spotted owl cases, the Everglades case demonstrates how environmentalists have used litigation to change the political dynamics of an environmental issue. For years, the ecological decline of the Everglades was apparent, yet agricultural interests—and particularly the sugar industry—were sufficiently ensconced within state and federal policymaking institutions to resist efforts to revive the ecosystem. At the state level, sugar executives had strong, longstanding ties with members of the legislature, a relationship whose effects had been magnified by the historic malapportionment of state legislators to rural areas. The sugar industry had also fared well in the U.S. Congress, discreetly obtaining subsidies that enabled it to remain more than competitive with Caribbean sugar. And sugar was a force within the state and federal agencies responsible for allocating water in South Florida; their historic ties had developed into a symbiotic relationship in which sugar interests had an assured water supply at the expense of the environment.

In its lawsuit against the state of Florida, the federal Department of Justice argued that the state had failed to enforce its own water pollution laws in South Florida. The legal hook, while novel, was less important than the way the lawsuit transformed the politics of Everglades restoration. Above all, the litigation simultaneously created myriad opportunities for press coverage and fractured the alliance among the Corps, the SFWMD, and the sugar industry. From environmentalists' perspective, the lawsuit served a third, critical function: through the technical agreement, it assembled the disparate science into a coherent consensus, which in turn provided a firm foundation for a compelling political story in which the villainous sugar industry had heedlessly destroyed one of the nation's most precious wetlands, the Everglades.

With its newfound popularity, the Everglades became a focus of the governor's race in Florida, and candidate Chiles was able to use it to his advantage. Having promised to settle the suit in his campaign, Chiles was obligated to resolve the issue, and his imprimatur further enhanced public support for the restoration. The growing national salience of the issue subsequently made it the object of competition for credit between candidates in both the 1996 and 2000 presidential campaigns, as well as both parties in Congress. Political competition, in turn, spawned federal funding.

The Everglades controversy ultimately resulted in a restoration plan that was more ambitious than anything the initial plaintiffs could have imagined. Once the federal government had assembled a team of scientists to craft a solution, the possibility of getting a genuinely comprehensive plan increased dramatically. By coordinating the activities of all the agencies that would be affected by a comprehensive plan, the Corps reduced the likelihood that any agency would defect or subvert the plan during implementation. Efforts at collaboration did not eliminate interagency feuding or ensure that the project would experience smooth sailing once approved, however. Obstacles to interagency cooperation remain substantial; aside from the sheer logistical complexity, each agency has its own mission and jealously guards its turf.

There has not only been a considerable amount of disharmony among the agencies that are to implement the restoration but also between the federal and state governments, which are funding and administering the plan jointly. Federal-state tension over the restoration in part reflects the differences in federal and state politics. Whereas federal officials can get credit for responding to environmental concerns, at the state level, the pressure to serve agricultural, commercial, and municipal interests is enormous. Throughout the process of formulating a restoration plan, sugar interests made it clear that they would do whatever was necessary to stymie it if their demands were not met. They have the resources to intimidate state politicians; aside from holding up the plan in court, they can wait out environmental interests—which rely heavily on public attention—and then go back to the legislature, where they wield credible threats of the state's economic demise.

Congressional resistance to funding the restoration project in the late 1990s also reflects the tension between the requirements of the evolving science of ecosystem restoration and the demands of accountability. The overriding problem is that the approach described by the Corps—recapturing billions of gallons of water that currently flow into the Atlantic and storing it in reservoirs or pumping it 1,000 feet underground, and pumping it out as needed—is purposefully broad and flexible. Administrators want to be able to adjust the system in response to new information. Whereas traditionally Congress authorizes Corps projects only after seeing a precise blueprint, the restoration plan is nothing more than a roadmap with details to be worked out and adaptations to be made as the project proceeds. Congress is reluctant to grant the Corps that kind of latitude, however, worrying that the project's ecological goals will be subverted in favor of development interests. While environmentalists applaud congressional insistence that ecological goals be paramount, the accountability Congress demands may undermine the novel ecological management principles of experimentation and adaptation on which the plan is based.

QUESTIONS TO CONSIDER

- How will environmentalists maintain public support for the Everglades restoration over its projected twenty-year lifetime?
- Will scientists be able to devise a plan that actually restores the ecological health of the region? If so, will government have the political will to take the necessary steps to implement that plan? What will the political obstacles be?

Notes

1. A marsh is a wetland dominated by low, herbaceous (nonwoody) vegetation, whereas in a swamp the dominant plants are trees.
2. Dan Tarlock, "Environmental Law: Ethics or Science?" *Duke Environmental Law and Policy Forum* 7 (fall 1996): 193–223.
3. Daniel B. Botkin, *Discordant Harmonies: A New Ecology for the Twenty-First Century* (New York: Oxford University Press, 1990), 9.
4. Craig Thomas, *Bureaucratic Landscapes: Interagency Cooperation and the Protection of Biodiversity* (Cambridge: MIT Press, forthcoming).
5. Ibid.
6. The limestone plate decreases in elevation by only 5.3 meters over its entire 100-mile span. See C. S. Holling, Lance H. Gunderson, and Carl J. Walters, "The Structure and Dynamics of the Everglades System: Guidelines for Ecosystem Restoration," in *Everglades: The Ecosystem and Its Restoration,* ed. Steven M. Davis and John C. Ogden (Delray Beach, Fla.: St. Lucie Press, 1994), 741–767.
7. Everglades National Park is at the southern tip of the Everglades, which now covers only 6,000 square miles.
8. David McCally, *The Everglades: An Environmental History* (Gainesville: University Press of Florida, 1999).
9. Ironically, "reclaiming" a wetland means filling it or otherwise drying it out to make it habitable for humans.
10. Alan Mairson, "The Everglades: Dying for Help," *National Geographic,* April 1994, 2–35.

11. Congress had actually authorized the park in 1934, but some of the land (850,000 acres donated by the state of Florida) was not forthcoming until the mid-1940s. The park, which comprised less than one-quarter of the historic freshwater Everglades, was dedicated in 1947.

12. One admirer writes that Douglas "tied the [Everglades'] many physiographic provinces together and made the strange aquatic kingdom understandable to millions who might otherwise have been blind to its subtle beauty, aquatic complexity, and unique natural history." See Steven Yates, "Marjory Stoneman Douglas and the Glades Crusade," *Audubon*, March 1983, 113–127.

13. "Development of the C&SF Project," http://restudy.org/history.htm.

14. Sheetflow is the gradual flow of shallow water, moving as slowly as twenty feet per day, from Lake Okeechobee to the southern tip of Florida.

15. Thomas E. Lodge, *The Everglades Handbook* (Delray Beach, Fla.: St. Lucie Press, 1994).

16. Ranchers and landowners persuaded Sen. Spessard Holland to include the Kissimmee flood control works in the Corps' 1948 Comprehensive Plan, and Congress approved this phase of the project in the Flood Control Act of 1954. Nothing was done, however, until a series of floods prompted renewed calls for action. The Corps then proposed a $31-million project to channelize the Kissimmee River and build control structures to regulate its flow. The project was completed in 1971. See Nelson Manfred Blake, *Land Into Water—Water Into Land* (Tallahassee: University Presses of Florida, 1980).

17. Eutrophication occurs when water becomes rich in mineral and organic nutrients, causing plant life, especially algae, to proliferate, thereby reducing the dissolved oxygen content of the water and killing native organisms.

18. Lodge, *Everglades Handbook*.

19. Blake, *Land Into Water*.

20. Robert S. Gilmour and John McAulay, "Environmental Preservation and Politics: The Significance of 'Everglades Jetport,'" *Political Science Quarterly* 90 (winter 1975–1976): 719–738.

21. Reflecting the Everglades' national appeal, Sen. Gaylord Nelson, D-Wisc., and Sen. Edmund Muskie, D-Maine, sponsored the measure over the opposition of Florida's Sen. Spessard Holland. The bill required the C&SF Project to deliver to the park 315,000 acre-feet of water or 16.5 percent of total water deliveries, whichever was less.

22. Blake, *Land Into Water*.

23. In 1967, the Florida legislature had begun redistricting to increase the legislature's representativeness in accordance with the 1962 Supreme Court ruling that legislative malapportionment was unconstitutional. The impact of the legislative overhaul was magnified by the election in 1966 of environmentally oriented Governor Claude Kirk and then Reuben Askew. Enhancing the impact of these electoral changes, the state adopted a progressive new constitution in 1968.

24. Florida Environmental Land and Water Management Act, F. S. 380–021.

25. Where cattails are thick, no wildlife can penetrate, and no sunlight reaches the aquatic vegetation.

26. Jeffrey Kahn, "Restoring the Everglades," *Sierra*, September–October 1986, 40–43.

27. Kevin Hansen, "South Florida's Water Dilemma: A Trickle of Hope for the Everglades," *Environment*, June 1984, 14–20, 40–42.

28. Rose Mary Mechem, "In Florida, the Grass is No Longer Greener," *National Wildlife*, October–November 1982, 51–55.

29. Quoted in Kahn, "Restoring the Everglades," 41–42.

30. The district has a nine-member, unpaid board, with members serving for four-year terms.

31. Quoted in Mairson, "Everglades," 7.

32. Ibid.

33. Ibid., 10.

34. Quoted in Jeanne Nienaber Clarke and Daniel C. McCool, *Staking Out the Terrain,* 2d ed. (Albany: State University of New York Press, 1996), 70.

35. Alston Chase, *Playing God in Yellowstone* (New York: Harcourt Brace, 1987).

36. Quoted in ibid., 252.

37. In the 1700s, sugar was regarded the way oil is now: as a key to national security. Once supportive policies were established, they were difficult to dislodge in the absence of a major public challenge. The Agriculture and Food Act of 1981 restricted sugar imports and provided domestic producers loans of 18 cents per pound of raw sugar.

38. In 1981, sugar accounted for $600 million of the EAA's $700 million revenues. See Hansen, "South Florida's Water Dilemma." Sugar companies are regularly among the top contributors to Florida's state and federal politicians. See, for example, the Center for Responsive Politics', "The 1990 Farm Bill," http://www. opensecrets.org/pubs/cashingin_sugar/sugar05.html.

39. It's also worth noting that the SFWMD's predecessor, the Central & South Florida Flood Control District, spearheaded the campaign to stop the South Florida jetport in 1969.

40. Clarke and McCool, *Staking Out the Terrain,* 21.

41. For example, in 1983, after two years of drought and a season of torrential rains, the Corps released billions of gallons of water into the park, wreaking havoc among the nesting birds. When the park's research director, Gary Hendrix, notified the SFWMD that wildlife populations had sunk so low that only swift emergency action to restore the park's wet and dry seasons would give them a fighting chance at recovery, the district encouraged park officials to come up with a plan for distributing water more equally throughout the park during floods. The district endorsed the plan, but the Corps was reluctant to implement it without congressional approval and would only agree to a more conservative approach. In 1985, after Congress authorized a two-phase, five-year experimental water release program, the district began to experiment with using existing technologies to try and mimic the area's natural water flow patterns. While the revised flow was an improvement, it was insufficient to remedy the park's problems.

42. Surface Water Improvement and Management Act, F.S. 373-4595 (2)(a)(1).

43. Dewitt John, *Civic Environmentalism: Alternatives to Regulation in States and Communities* (Washington, D.C.: CQ Press, 1994).

44. Ibid.

45. Norman Boucher, "Smart as Gods," *Wilderness,* winter 1991, 11–21.

46. Lodge, *Everglades Handbook.*

47. The alligator poaching industry flourished in the 1960s, as the state of Florida curtailed legal alligator hunting. Poaching only began to decline after the 1973 placement of the alligator on the federal endangered species list because the law imposed stiff penalties for poaching.

48. Frank J. Mazzoti and Laura Brandt, "Ecology of the American Alligator in a Seasonally Fluctuating Environment," in *Everglades,* ed. Davis and Ogden, 485–505.

49. John, *Civic Environmentalism.*

50. The central legal issue was whether the state needed permits for the pumps at the southern edge of the EAA and, if so, what were the proper standards for phosphorous in the water passing through those pumps. The Justice Department initially chose to litigate the suit in federal court on the grounds that the nuisance created by the state's failure to regulate victimized two federal entities: the Everglades National Park and the Loxahatchee Wildlife Refuge.

51. The environmental groups that signed on as plaintiffs in the suit included the Wilderness Society, the Florida Wildlife Federation, the Florida and National Audubon Societies, the Sierra Club Legal Defense Fund, and the Environmental Defense Fund. See John, *Civic Environmentalism.*

52. In 1991, sugar cane occupied 457,000 acres of the EAA, more than seven times the acreage occupied by all other agricultural commodities. The number of acres in the EAA devoted to sugar cane had doubled since the 1970s.

53. The Wilderness Society commissioned a study to estimate the value of those public subsidies and used the results to further galvanize public sentiment against the industry.

54. Quoted in John, *Civic Environmentalism*, 155.

55. John, *Civic Environmentalism*, 155.

56. Industry consultants pointed out that water from cane fields is relatively low in phosphorous. Water from cane fields contains about 75–120 ppb of phosphorous; by comparison, they pointed out, a sample of effluent from a municipal sewage treatment plant contained 100 ppb of phosphorous; a sample of drinking water from Tallahassee contained 80 ppb of phosphorous; and rain over the Everglades occasionally contained as much as 60–70 ppb of phosphorous. Park scientists retorted that the normal level of phosphorous in the park is only 7–14 ppb. See ibid.

57. Mairson, "The Everglades." The surprise was that approximately 60 percent of the swampland targeted for acquisition was owned by 10,000 individuals, most of them absentee landlords, who had purchased the property through the mail.

58. John, *Civic Environmentalism*.

59. Efforts to reach agreement on this question were hampered by lawyers' refusals to release critical information to the group. See ibid.

60. Quoted in Margaret Kriz, "Mending the Marsh," *National Journal*, March 12, 1994, 593.

61. Marjory Stoneman Douglas, Everglades Protection Act, F. S. 373-4592 (3) (a) (1).

62. United States v. SFWMD, et al., Case No. 88-1886-civ-Hoeveler, *Settlement Agreement*, Appendix B.

63. For dairy farms, BMPs include installing drains to carry away water from where cows stand and drop manure. For sugar cane farms, BMPs include letting storm water stand in fields rather than draining it off, so that the soil does not dry out and oxidize, leaving high concentrations of phosphorous to be swept up in a pulse during the next heavy rainfall. Another BMP for sugar cane and other farms is to fertilize more precisely, applying chemicals to the roots of crops rather than spreading them in swaths across entire fields.

64. In January 1992, executives from the Sugar Cane Cooperative acknowledged privately that the real issue was not whether phosphorous was a problem but how much the sugar industry would have to pay to clean it up. See John, *Civic Environmentalism*.

65. Quoted in Ben Barber, "Trouble in Florida's 'River of Grass,'" *Christian Science Monitor*, July 9, 1993, 3.

66. Quoted in William Booth, "Everglades Accord Indicative of EPA Designee's Approach," *Washington Post*, January 11, 1993, A4.

67. John, *Civic Environmentalism*.

68. The present value of the plan was $465 million; the estimated value over the life of the project was $700 million.

69. John, *Civic Environmentalism*.

70. Participants included representatives of the Department of Interior (the National Park Service, Fish and Wildlife Service and U.S. Geological Survey), the Commerce Department (the National Marine Fisheries Service), the Army Corps of Engineers, the EPA, the Department of Agriculture, and the Department of Justice.

71. George Frampton, Testimony Before the U.S. House of Representatives Subcommittee on National Parks, Forests, and Public Lands of the Committee on Natural Resources, June 23, 1994 (Washington, D.C.: U.S. Government Printing Office, 1994).

72. U.S. Army Corps of Engineers, *Final Feasibility Report and Programmatic Environmental Impact Statement* (April 1999), 1; http://restudy.org/.

73. In addition to the federal agencies involved in the task force, the Restudy included representatives of the state of Florida, the SFWMD, county and local governments, and the Miccosukee and Seminole tribes.

74. The Science Subgroup of the South Florida Management and Coordination Working Group, *Federal Objectives for the South Florida Restoration* (November 1993), 1.

75. Bill Gifford, "The Government's Too-Sweet Deal," *Washington Post,* January 9, 1994, C3.

76. Tom Kenworthy, "Administration, Sugar Industry Talks on Everglades Restoration Deadlock," *Washington Post,* December 17, 1993, A17.

77. However, the Everglades Forever Act also pushed the target date for achieving 10 ppb of phosphorous from 2002, as the 1991 settlement had required, to 2006. See the Everglades Forever Act, F. S. 373-4592 (1994).

78. Paul Roberts, "The Sweet Hereafter," *Harper's Magazine,* November 1999; David Olinger, "Everglades Fight Enters Next Round," *St. Petersburg Times,* November 1996, 4B.

79. Republican pollster Frank Luntz found that 68 percent of Florida voters would be less likely to vote for a congressional candidate who either accepted donations from the sugar industry or opposed a tax on the sugar industry that would raise funds to restore the Everglades. See Courtney LaFountain and Christopher Douglas, "Save the Everglades—and $3 Billion," *Journal of Commerce and Commercial,* March 13, 1996.

80. John R. Cushman, Jr., "Panel Agrees on Overhaul of Farm Aid," *New York Times,* March 22, 1996, A1.

81. John R. Cushman, Jr., "Clinton Backing Vast Effort to Restore Florida Swamps," *New York Times,* February 18, 1996, A1.

82. Water Resources Development Act of 1996, P.L. 104-303 sect. 528 (b)(l)(A)(i).

83. Robert P. King, "Business Group Rips Everglades Restoration Plan's Costs," *Palm Beach Post,* November 10, 1998, B1.

84. An analysis by the Center for Responsive Politics showed that in the three election cycles between 1994 and 1998, the Fanjul family donated $575,000 to campaigns for federal offices, and their sugar companies contributed at least $843,000 to the Democratic and Republican national committees. Over the same period, the U.S. Sugar Corp. donated $584,000 to national committees, while employees gave $276,000 to federal candidates. See James C. McKinley, Jr., "Sugar Industry's Pivotal Role in Everglades Efforts," *New York Times,* April 16, 1999, A1.

85. Jan Hollingsworth, "Environmentalists Fear Law Will Sap Everglades Plan," *Tampa Tribune,* May 7, 1999, 1.

86. McKinley, "Sugar Industry's Pivotal Role."

87. Quoted in Tony Reichhardt, "Everglades Plan Flawed, Claim Ecologists," *Nature,* February 11, 1999, 462.

88. Ibid. The signatories were Stuart Pimm of the University of Tennessee, Paul Ehrlich of Stanford, E. O. Wilson of Harvard, Gary Meffe of the University of Florida, Peter Raven of the Missouri Botanical Garden, and Gordon Orians of the University of Washington.

89. Quoted in William K. Stevens, "Everglades Restoration Plan Does Too Little, Experts Say," *New York Times,* February 22, 1999, A1.

90. Ibid.

91. Cyril T. Zaneski, "Army Corps Plans to Double Pace of Everglades Restoration," *Miami Herald,* March 29, 1999, A1.

92. U.S. General Accounting Office, "South Florida Ecosystem Restoration: An Overall Strategic Plan and a Decision-Making Process Are Needed to Keep the Effort on Track," GAO/RCED-99-121 (April 22, 1999).

93. Craig Pittman, "Glades Funding Restriction Irks State Officials," *St. Petersburg Times,* October 23, 1999, 5B.

94. Cyril Zaneski, "Senators Plan Jumpstart for $7.8 Billion Everglades Restoration," *Congress Daily/A.M.,* June 27, 2000.

95. William Booth, "Sweet Progress in Everglades," *Washington Post,* September 4, 1996, A1.

96. Those projects include key storage reservoirs, impoundments, and stormwater treatment areas. See U.S. Army Corps of Engineers, "Everglades Plan Approved, $14 Billion in Projects Authorized Now" (News Release No. 00-91, December 11, 2000).

Recommended Reading

Davis, Steven M., and John C. Ogden, eds. *Everglades: The Ecosystem and Its Restoration.* Delray Beach, Fla.: St. Lucie Press, 1994, 741–767.

Lodge, Thomas E. *The Everglades Handbook.* Delray Beach, Fla.: St. Lucie Press, 1994.

McCally, David. *The Everglades: An Environmental History.* Gainesville: University Press of Florida, 1999.

Web Sites

http://everglades.fiu.edu/library/index.html (Florida International University site)

http://serc.fiu.edu/ (Florida International University's Southeast Environmental Research Center site)

http://www.sfwmd.gov/koe_section/2_everglades.html (SFWMD site)

CHAPTER 13

Local Collaboration and Compromise

Using Habitat Conservation Plans to Save Southern California's Endangered Landscape

In the early 1990s, five southern California counties embarked on an experiment that represented a last-ditch effort to save the region's remaining natural habitat without halting development altogether. This unprecedented undertaking—perhaps the largest, most complete conservation planning exercise ever attempted[1]—involved devising regional landscape maps and then negotiating among developers, landowners, and local, state, and federal government officials to agree on a long-term plan for managing growth while preserving swaths of undisturbed natural areas. And it attempted all of this "smack in the middle of some of the most expensive, desirable, and booming real estate in America."[2] President Clinton's interior secretary, Bruce Babbitt, touted the San Diego program as marking "the beginning of a new chapter in American conservation history."[3] Even as many are heralding such local, collaborative efforts, however, critics are challenging their effectiveness.

The decision to experiment with collaborative, ecosystem-level planning in California was a response to frustration with conventional mechanisms for endangered species protection. For both environmentalists and developers, such approaches have serious shortcomings. Environmentalists and conservation biologists recognize that the Endangered Species Act (ESA), with its focus on individual species, is a poor tool for protecting entire ecosystems and is often invoked only once a species and its habitat are in such poor condition that they may not recover. Moreover, the Fish and Wildlife Service (FWS) has neither the clout nor the funding to enforce the ESA on private land, where many endangered species reside. Developers resent the ESA because it creates uncertainty in planning and can impose costly delays on projects. Many on both sides dislike the contentious, litigious politics that has accompanied implementation of the ESA.

Thus, advocates, experts, and government officials have converged on local, collaborative approaches to environmental problem solving in which "citizen leaders from government and business . . . mobilize their deep concern for a place close to home and turn that concern into creative and far-reaching cooperative ventures."[4] In theory, such approaches have two advantages over more conventional environmental policymaking. First, if communities are allowed to make meaningful decisions, and all stakeholders are involved in the process from the outset, collaborative decision making should yield agreement and induce voluntary compliance—and hence more durable solutions than those reached through a top-down, adversarial process. According to their enthusiasts, "programs are more likely to be implemented successfully if they are supported and owned by affected groups."[5] Second, if communities have sufficient technical information and the capacity to absorb that information, they will craft solutions that are environmentally superior to the one-size-fits-all prescriptions generated by conventional regulatory processes.[6] In short, proponents believe that by changing the process by which decisions are made, local, collaborative approaches can change the kinds of solutions that are possible and enhance the likelihood of their long-term durability.

Although it has been widely endorsed, the concept of local, collaborative environmental problem-solving has also prompted vigorous debate. Critics have queried whether such approaches actually foster meaningful citizen participation and whether civic environmentalism places an excessive burden on citizens, who are disadvantaged relative to development interests.[7] Other critics fear that arrangements granting equal status to citizens and scientists weaken the influence of science on policy and wonder whether collaboration yields genuine environmental protection.[8] In short, it remains to be seen whether local, collaborative environmental problem-solving actually yields the expected procedural and substantive benefits in practice.

It is important to assess not only the process of formulating a plan, but also the extent to which implementation of a program or plan, once crafted, advances or hinders the achievement of policy goals. As noted in the Everglades case, scientists increasingly emphasize the need for experimentation and adaptation; policies to protect ecosystems must be sufficiently flexible, they argue, to accommodate surprises and incorporate new information and scientific learning.[9] On the other hand, such flexibility leaves plans and programs vulnerable at the implementation stage: as political scientists Aaron Wildavsky and Jeffrey Pressman observe, implementation in our federal system is inherently hazardous because most programs must clear myriad decision points, any one of which can delay or even halt program activity altogether.[10] Even when there is broad agreement on a program's goals, the more entities—from federal and state agencies to local governmental officials—that have to sign on for a program to work, the less likely it is that the program will achieve its stated goals. Thus, the relative success of a collaborative process can only be assessed over time, as it is implemented by stakeholders.

This case examines both the creation and implementation of the San Diego Multiple Species Conservation Plan and, in doing so, illuminates the promise and pitfalls of collaborative, ecosystem-level policymaking.

BACKGROUND

A mosaic of coastal sage scrub (CSS), a distinctive mix of sage and other low-growing, drought-tolerant shrubs that is found nowhere else in the United States, once spread across 2.5 million acres from Ventura County to San Diego. Between 1940 and 1995, however, southern California's population quintupled to 17.5 million, growing at a rate twice that of Bangladesh.[11] The seemingly endless demand for southern California real estate that accompanied this boom produced skyrocketing land values, with lots ranging from $200,000 to $3 million per acre.[12] As a result of the burgeoning agricultural, commercial, and residential development, the FWS estimated that by 1991, the region had lost more than 85 percent of its original CSS habitat, leaving only between 343,000 and 444,000 acres.[13] The remaining patches, many of which had been degraded by human activities and fire, were highly fragmented across five southern California counties—Los Angeles, Orange, Riverside, San Bernardino, and San Diego—though most of them (125,000–150,000 acres) were in San Diego.

Similar devastation had occurred in the region's chaparral, grassland, and riparian habitats.[14] The rapid disappearance of habitat in turn had driven hundreds of the region's small mammals, birds, and plants to the brink of extinction; with more than 200 species considered imperiled, there were more endangered and threatened plants and animals in San Diego County than in any other place in the lower forty-eight states.[15] The situation was exacerbated by the fact that 80 percent of CSS was privately owned,[16] and endangered species tend to fare poorly on private land relative to federally owned land.[17]

Protecting Endangered Species on Private Land

The main vehicle for protecting species and habitats on both public and private lands is the federal ESA, which requires the FWS—or, for marine species, the National Marine Fisheries Service—to identify and publish lists of species that are in imminent danger of going extinct (endangered) or likely to become endangered in the foreseeable future (threatened). Anyone can petition the FWS to list a species. Once a petition is submitted, the agency must decide whether a listing is warranted based solely on the available scientific evidence. After deciding to list a species the agency is supposed to designate critical habitat and develop a recovery plan.[18] Section 7 of the ESA, the provision of the act that historically has been most controversial, prohibits the destruction or adverse modification of critical habitat by actions carried out, funded, or authorized by a federal agency (see chapter 7).

More recently, however, Section 9 of the ESA has come under attack. Section 9 prohibits the "take" by any party, public or private, of species listed as endangered. The act defines "take" as "harass, harm, pursue, hunt, shoot, wound, kill, trap, capture, or collect, or attempt to engage in any such conduct," and the FWS has interpreted this phrase as empowering the federal government to prosecute landowners who destroy a species or its habitat. In the more than twenty-five-year lifespan of the ESA, however, the federal government has been reluctant to take action against private property owners. The Department of Justice rarely prosecutes people for killing a species and even more infrequently penalizes those who destroy its habitat.[19] Since 1990, when the FWS listed the northern spotted owl as a threatened species, the

Department of Justice has not prosecuted a single company for destruction of spotted owl habitat; the FWS has lost the few civil actions it has filed. The Interior Department has only twice gone to court to block logging activities that threatened spotted owls.[20]

The FWS is not dilatory; rather, it is vastly understaffed and underbudgeted for the chore of implementing the ESA. It has 210 enforcement agents nationwide, with 175 in the field, and they are enforcing several other laws in addition to the ESA.[21] It is also difficult to get a conviction for damaging habitat. In the absence of a "corpse," prosecutors must show that habitat destruction inevitably would have killed or injured a species or created a significant likelihood of injury. Thus, according to the director of law enforcement for the FWS's West Coast region: "If I say I want someone prosecuted for shooting a bald eagle, no problem. But if I want a person prosecuted for cutting near a bald eagle nest, the U.S. attorney is much less inclined to take the case. That's true even though the permanent harm that is done from harvesting too close to a bald eagle nest is far greater than the harm done by shooting a single eagle."[22]

Moreover, members of Congress put immense pressure on the FWS to ignore ESA violations on private land, thereby undermining the agency's enforcement capability. Even those who support the act worry that legal action against property owners will agitate opponents of the ESA and galvanize their sympathetic congressional representatives. These concerns are justified: in the late 1980s and early 1990s, the backlash against the ESA mounted, and efforts to dilute or repeal the act gained momentum in Congress (see chapter 10). In Southern California, frustration with the ESA ran high following restrictions to protect the Stephens Kangaroo Rat in Riverside County in the late 1980s. T-shirts emblazoned with a picture of a rat being smashed by a mallet and the words "Kangaroo Rat Whackers Association" proliferated; farmers applied rodenticide to their fields and refused to leave them fallow, all to prevent the rats from taking up residence on their property.[23]

A Policy Innovation: Habitat Conservation Plans

Finding itself stymied in its efforts to protect species on private land, the FWS was intrigued by the concept of habitat conservation plans that emerged in the early 1980s. The agency actually approved a prototype HCP in 1980 in the absence of any statutory authorization. It had used the novel approach to resolve a conflict over developing the habitat of three rare species of butterfly—particularly the federally listed Mission Blue and Callippe Silverspot butterflies—on the San Bruno Mountain in San Francisco.[24] After lengthy negotiations, a consortium comprising the primary landowner and developer, environmental groups, and local, state, and federal officials came up with a management plan that allowed some destruction of butterflies but also reserved large swaths of the mountain as protected habitat.[25] The plan also provided for the establishment and funding of long-term habitat management and restoration. The FWS was not certain that it had the legal authority to authorize such deals, however, and was therefore reluctant to make HCPs common practice, so in 1982, the real estate lawyers who had brokered the San Bruno deal acted as policy entrepreneurs and persuaded Congress to amend the ESA to provide for HCPs.

The 1982 amendments included Section 10(a), under which a landowner can negotiate a deal with the FWS that allows him to destroy some portion of a listed species' habitat as long as he has prepared a satisfactory HCP that explains how he will "mitigate" the loss. More precisely, the amendments require HCPs to specify the impact that would result from a take, the steps that would be taken to minimize and mitigate such impacts, the funding that would be available to implement those steps, the alternative action considered by the applicant and reasons such alternatives were rejected, and other measures the Secretary of Interior may require as "necessary and appropriate" for purposes of the plan. The FWS may grant a Section 10(a) incidental take permit only if the take will be incidental to an otherwise lawful activity; the applicant will minimize and mitigate the impacts of the taking; and the taking will "not appreciably reduce the likelihood of survival and recovery of species in the wild."

Although the 1982 amendments did not mandate a specific process for devising HCPs, a common approach soon emerged. First, the federal government appoints a steering committee comprising representatives of major stakeholders: the environmental community; landowners; developers; and local, state, and federal resource management agencies. The committee then hires consultants to prepare background biological and land-use studies. The plans themselves usually create habitat preserves using a variety of mechanisms, including fee-simple acquisitions or dedication by the landowner in exchange for development rights elsewhere. In addition, HCPs generally include provisions for habitat management, ecological restoration, and ongoing research and monitoring. They may also involve predator and exotic species controls and well as land-use regulations. Finally, HCPs may offer financial incentives to landowners who preserve habitat, including tradable credits that the landowner can sell to someone else who must mitigate for development in another location, or they may set up a system in which developers pay a set per-acre price to the city or county, which then uses the money to buy conservation land. Controversy surrounding HCPs most often arises over the amount of habitat to preserve, the boundaries and configuration of the proposed reserves, the means of financing plans, and which entities will oversee the administration of the plan.[26]

THE CASE

In the early 1990s, within the national context of ineffectual enforcement of the ESA on private land, an incipient backlash against endangered species protection, and the recent emergence of HCPs, Southern California faced an impending collision between environmentalists and developers over a small songbird called the coastal California gnatcatcher. A policy expert had inadvertently laid the foundation for this "train wreck" by providing credible scientific evidence that environmentalists could use to make claims—both in agencies and in the courts—under the ESA. Perceiving the potential costs associated with an ESA listing of the gnatcatcher, development interests mobilized. Instead of pursuing adversarial politics in venues where they had fared poorly under the act in the past, however, a developer acted as a policy entrepreneur, promoting local, collaborative ecosystem-scale planning, a new solution that had been floating around the environmental policy community for some time. Proponents of the collaborative planning approach hoped it would redefine the problem as species *and* jobs rather than species *versus* jobs.[27] They hoped that redefinition, in turn, would facilitate a new kind of politics—one in which developers and environmentalists worked cooperatively rather than competitively.

The Coastal California Gnatcatcher

The story began, unremarkably, in 1979, when UCLA biology graduate student Jonathan Atwood was casting around for a dissertation topic that would enable him to do his research locally. Atwood took on the task of sorting out the various species of *Polioptila*, a genus of small songbirds native to the Southwest whose classification scheme was imprecise.[28] In the course of his research, Atwood found that, contrary to what ornithologists previously believed, the black-tailed gnatcatcher and the California gnatcatcher could not mate with one another and therefore were distinct subspecies. Atwood found that the coastal California gnatcatcher (*Polioptilac. californica*) made its home exclusively among the low-elevation (below 300 meters) coastal sage scrub and used chaparral, grasslands, and riparian areas for dispersal and foraging.[29] As its habitat had become increasingly fragmented, the gnatcatcher became more vulnerable to parasitism and nest predation and thus extinction. In 1989, the American Ornithologists Union concurred with Atwood's findings and officially designated the coastal California gnatcatcher as a distinct subspecies. The implications of this designation were profound: if the coastal California gnatcatcher was a subspecies that relied for its survival on coastal sage scrub, then it was a promising candidate for endangered species listing.[30] (In fact, in 1980 Atwood had conducted a gnatcatcher census for the California Department of Fish and Game and estimated its population at fewer than 2,000 breeding pairs. At that time, he had recommended adding the bird to state and federal ESA lists and halting development in CSS.[31])

Although Atwood published his research in the journal *Ornithological Monographs* in 1988, the gnatcatcher remained a relatively obscure bird until 1990, when some of Atwood's former UCLA classmates informed him that development in southern California threatened the gnatcatcher with extinction.[32] As environmental consultants to California developers, they felt they could not sound alarms about the bird and its disappearing habitat without jeopardizing their own livelihoods, but they encouraged Atwood, who now worked at the Manomet Bird Observatory in Massachusetts, to petition the U.S. Fish and Wildlife Service (FWS) to list the bird as endangered under the ESA. With the help of the Natural Resources Defense Council (NRDC), Atwood proceeded to gather data on and generate projections of southern California's growth prospects. He concluded that "nearly all areas where California gnatcatchers are currently distributed are expected to be destroyed within 20 years as a result of intensive urban development."[33] In December 1990, the Manomet Bird Observatory and the NRDC, backed by a seventy-two page status review of the bird and letters of support from the American Ornithologists' Union, the International Council for Bird Preservation, and the National Audubon Society, requested that the FWS list the bird under an emergency rule.[34] They sent a similar packet to the state of California and asked it to list the bird under the California Endangered Species Act (CESA) as well.

Developers React to Efforts to List the Gnatcatcher

The prospect that the FWS might list the gnatcatcher prompted some of southern California's most profitable and influential developers to begin seeking ways to avert the listing, which could temporarily derail construction on thousands of acres of prime real estate and block the installation of infrastructure from highways to water-reclamation projects to sewer lines. The region's developers were already intimately familiar with the ESA, having had two formative experiences in the 1980s—with the Least Bell's Vireo and the Stephens Kangaroo Rat—and having observed the conflagrations in the northern part of the state over the spotted owl.[35] Moreover, it was clear that not only the gnatcatcher but a host of other CSS-obligate species were candidates for listing, so the potential for regulatory delays was enormous.

One approach developers could adopt was to generate public opposition in hopes of intimidating the California Department of Fish and Game (CDFG) and the FWS so that they would refrain from listing the bird.[36] To this end, some builders launched a public relations campaign to frame the listing petition as an attack on private property rights and an effort by no-growth extremists to stymie all development in the region. In a handbill advertising informational lunches about the proposed listing in Orange County, the hard-line Building Industry Association of Southern California (BIA) characterized the gnatcatcher as "Your Worst Nightmare."[37] Portraying opponents of listing as moderates and advocates of balance, Mark Ellis Tipton of the National Homebuilders Association said: "There is a place in society for protecting the gnatcatcher, but it has to be with a proper relationship to mankind. I see people in California living in garages and cardboard boxes and abandoned cars. Now who's more important? These people and their children, or ecological preserves?" Defining quality of life in a way that stressed cornucopian, rather than environmental, values, Tipton argued: "When you destroy the quality of life to protect an endangered species, it doesn't make sense. You're going to stop water reclamation projects; you'll stop hospitals; you'll have lawsuits." The consequences of a listing, he claimed, would be cataclysmic: "When that lesser

quality of life shows up, you're going to have a revolution." Tipton characterized environmentalists as the elite and their policy goals exclusionary, saying:
"I look at most of the resumes of the Sierra Club, and they're doctors and
lawyers, and they have got great big houses and they don't want anybody else
to have them."[38]

The NCCP Process Gets Under Way

A more moderate group of landowners, including some of the largest holders of CSS, formed the Alliance for Habitat Conservation, however, and they
chose a different tack to head off the ESA listing.[39] In particular, the Irvine
Company—a massive and sophisticated developer[40]—hoped to capitalize on
a window of opportunity opened by the election of Governor Pete Wilson to
link a novel solution to the endangered species problem. Irvine vice president
Monica Florian acted as a policy entrepreneur, urging the newly installed governor to promote a state-level program that would facilitate conservation
planning by stakeholders based on principles developed by a scientific panel.
In theory, this approach would enable communities to set aside some acreage
for conservation while continuing to allow development according to specified rules. Because it would preserve enough land that species could persist,
proponents reasoned, no further regulations would be necessary.

This solution had political as well as practical appeal for developers: most
importantly, it would remove the grounds for invoking the ESA. Thus, collaborative, ecosystem-scale planning, Florian reasoned, would provide landowners and developers with greater certainty about what they could do with their
land while also making possible the kinds of ecosystem-wide reserves that
conservation biologists prefer.[41] Landowners and developers like certainty
because serial listings can delay or halt projects after substantial investments
have been made; it is hard to plan or finance construction when the regulatory
environment is in flux. Biologists were disillusioned with the reactive, species-
by-species approach to conservation embodied in the ESA, finding it ineffectual and inconsistent with ecological principles, which increasingly emphasized ecosystem-scale processes.

Governor Wilson perceived the program's political appeal, and in April
1991, he unveiled the Natural Community Conservation Planning (NCCP) program, the framework of which had been crafted by scientists from the (CDFG)
and the FWS, staff from the Nature Conservancy, and Irvine Company executives. In announcing the program, Wilson said that environmental problems for
too long had been stalled by the "tactic of confrontation." The NCCP, he said,
would inaugurate a "new era of consensus" based on "good faith efforts at
mutual accommodation."[42] The legislature was dubious about the program,
however, so to demonstrate its viability the state Resources Agency chose
Southern California for a test run.

The first step in the pilot project was to establish a panel of conservation
biologists, the Scientific Review Panel (SRP), to create scientific guidelines for

reserve design, species conservation, and adaptive management that cities and counties could use in developing their own long-range conservation plans.[43] The panel's more subtle purpose was to provide a credible underpinning for the program in order to avert the usual technical squabbles that so often derail regulatory efforts. To enhance the SRP's credibility, NCCP administrators staffed the panel with five eminent conservation biologists and geographers—Reed Noss, Dennis Murphy, Peter Broussard, Michael Gilpin, and John O'Leary—all of whom were both nationally known and familiar with the local ecology.

The SRP soon found itself deeply frustrated in its efforts to develop guidelines for building viable preserves, however. Developers who had information about species on their land obstinately refused to hand it over to government scientists, so the panel was limited to identifying potentially imperiled species (they found ninety-six) and providing a set of general tenets to guide reserve design. They came up with the following principles:

- Conserve target species throughout the planning area. Species that are well distributed across their native ranges are less susceptible to extinction than are species confined to small portions of their ranges.
- Preserve larger reserves containing large populations of the target species; they are better than small blocks containing small populations.
- Keep reserve areas close to one another.
- Keep habitat contiguous because less fragmented habitat is better.
- Link reserves with corridors. Such linkages function better when the habitat within them resembles the preferred habitat of target species.
- Make sure reserves contain a diversity of physical and environmental conditions.
- Protect reserves from encroachment by human disturbance.[44]

After concluding that it was "not able to produce scientifically defensible guidelines for long range planning purposes"[45] given the inadequacy of the existing database, the SRP strongly recommended that the state convene a new panel to study three target species: the coastal California gnatcatcher, the San Diego Cactus Wren, and the Orange-Throated Whiptail Lizard. The research program the panelists envisioned would entail six tasks: mapping the biogeography of coastal sage scrub; monitoring trends in biodiversity in the region; gathering information on the dispersal abilities of CSS species and landscape corridor use; conducting a viability analysis; collecting data on particularly sensitive CSS-associated species; and acquiring baseline data on genetic variability in target species. State resource agencies did not pursue these tasks.

The FWS Moves to List the Coastal California Gnatcatcher

As the SRP was embarking on its work, the FWS and the state of California were simultaneously reviewing the biological data on the coastal California gnatcatcher. On August 30, 1991, in a move that delighted developers and incensed environmentalists, the California Fish and Game Commission announced that it would not make the gnatcatcher a candidate for the California endangered species list. Designating the bird as a candidate would have afforded it temporary protection and, more importantly, spurred exhaustive studies of its status that could serve as the basis for advocacy to limit future development in the region.

The no-list decision, in which the commissioners disregarded the advice of their own staff, followed an impassioned plea by Undersecretary of Resources Michael Mantell, on behalf of Governor Wilson, against making the bird a candidate on the grounds that doing so would lead to more "polarization and confrontation between the two sides."[46] The commission's decision probably also was influenced by continuing efforts by some developers to frame gnatcatcher protection as a major economic risk; for example, a BIA-sponsored study released a week earlier projected that protecting the gnatcatcher would cost the region 212,000 jobs and $20 billion in business activity and earnings. Furthermore, developers had told the commission that more than 100 square miles of CSS was already protected as open space in the region (although commission staff recognized that much of that acreage was high-elevation and therefore unsuitable for the coastal California gnatcatcher).[47] Immediately after the commission announced its decision, the NRDC filed a lawsuit on the grounds that the panel did not follow the provisions of CESA and that its decision "virtually guarantee[d] that the California gnatcatcher [would] continue toward extinction."[48]

Unfortunately for developers, one week after the Fish and Game Commission's announcement, the FWS concluded that proposing the bird for listing as an endangered species under the normal (though not the emergency) procedures was warranted based on the available science: in 1990, Atwood had estimated that no more than 2,500 breeding pairs of coastal California gnatcatchers remained in the United States. Moreover, the FWS found clear evidence of the impending threats to gnatcatcher habitat: of about 19,000 acres of sage scrub below 300 meters in elevation in coastal Orange County, only 36 percent was preserved; another 21 percent was approved or proposed for development, and 43 percent was of uncertain status.[49] San Diego County in particular had lost much of its coastal sage scrub: between 1980 and 1990, San Diego's human population increased by 600,000, and most of this increase occurred on or near the coast, where CSS historically predominates.

The agency published a proposed rule on September 17, 1991, at which point an extended period of public comments began.[50] During the comment period, which the agency extended twice in response to political pressure, the FWS received a total of 770 comments, more than half of which opposed the listing. Because the decision makers were agency professionals, not elected officials, listing opponents needed more than a politically compelling causal story; they had to muster a sophisticated methodological critique of the scientific basis for concern about the bird and its habitat. Specifically, they argued that the coastal California gnatcatcher and its northern nominate subspecies were not valid taxa.[51] They based this assertion on Atwood's appendix to the listing petition, which amended the conclusions of his doctoral dissertation. In his 1990 status report, Atwood divided the California gnatcatcher into three subspecies rather than two, as he previously had, thereby making the condition of *Polioptila c. californica* appear even more dire. While this change was comprehensible to scientists—it was actually a return to an earlier classification scheme—it looked highly suspicious to developers.[52] FWS taxonomists independently evaluated Atwood's modification in response to these objections, however, and concluded that the coastal California gnatcatcher was a valid subspecies whose range extended only to Baja California, Mexico.

Opponents of the listing also criticized Atwood's statistical analysis, but here too the FWS found Atwood's procedures and methods "well within the norm for systematic/taxonomic reviews of geographic variation in birds." Independent scientific reviewers Banks and Gardner concluded that "all readily available pertinent specimen material was used, population samples were assembled properly, all important variable morphological characteristics were examined, and statistical treatments were appropriate."[53] The FWS was similarly unpersuaded by consultants' reports suggesting that scientists had underestimated the amount of available gnatcatcher habitat or that they had overestimated the loss of CSS habitat since 1940. (A study commissioned by developers put the figure at 65 percent since the turn of the century.)

In a last-ditch bid to get FWS to change its position, in November 1991, developers requested Atwood's data to assess whether his switch from two species to three was justified. When Atwood declined to turn over his data, developers insisted that the FWS halt the listing process until he complied. The FWS refused, so a coalition of developers and public transportation agencies filed suit in November 1992. The judge dismissed the suit, however, because the agency had not actually made a decision to list the bird.[54]

The FWS was particularly adamant because, notwithstanding assurances by developers that CSS already was adequately protected, local governments were continuing to approve construction projects in the face of FWS requests for greater scrutiny. Between 1989 and 1993, urban and agricultural development had destroyed 3,600 acres of CSS in Orange County and 2,400 acres in San Diego County, most of it located below 300 meters. Another 8,000 acres of gnatcatcher habitat was vulnerable to proposed or approved construction projects.[55] Not only was the gnatcatcher's habitat deteriorating rapidly, but there were no regulatory mechanisms in place that could protect it. It was not listed under the federal or California ESA; local and county ordinances did not have sufficiently stringent standards to protect the bird, or they were easily changed, or both.

Even areas that had been designated as open space were vulnerable to changing land-use decisions. The FWS documented numerous instances in which construction projects during the 1990s made no effort to mitigate habitat losses, and county agencies ignored the FWS's notifications that the projects they were approving failed to disclose the presence of gnatcatchers even though the birds were candidates for federal listing. In one incident, which occurred just prior to the FWS proposal to list the bird, the San Marcos City

Council allowed a San Diego developer to clear hundreds of acres of prime gnatcatcher habitat despite a FWS request to hold off until its own biologists could review mitigation measures ordered by the city. The city council approved the bulldozing of CSS even though it had not yet approved the final development plans.[56] Thus, by the early 1990s, with development interests clearly holding sway in local decision making, pressure was mounting on the FWS to list the gnatcatcher as endangered in the hopes of saving the last remaining fragments of CSS habitat.

The Marriage of the ESA and NCCP

While the FWS was working on its listing proposal, a process that ultimately took 18 months, the state of California moved ahead with the NCCP program. The stated goal of the NCCP Act, which the California legislature passed in October 1991, was to provide "for the regional or area-wide protection and perpetuation of diversity, while allowing compatible and appropriate development and growth."[57] The act created an approach in which developers, environmentalists, and local officials could meet, under the auspices of the Department of Fish and Game, to develop a regional wildlife preserve and accompanying development guidelines. In contrast to the ESA, the NCCP allowed for the creation of reserves before species were on the brink of extinction, and it was ecosystem- rather than species-based. The pilot project for NCCP divided the 6,000-square-mile coastal sage scrub region of southern California into eleven subregions, each of which was required to come up with its own plan.

Aside from generating conservation guidelines and a research protocol, however, the inchoate NCCP did not make much headway. It had little structure, no funding, and minimal support; it did not specify the criteria habitat reserves needed to meet, nor did it provide incentives for property owners to enroll their land, so it is hardly surprising that initially there was little enthusiasm for the program among the region's landowners and developers. By late 1993, only thirty-nine private landowners had enrolled in the program.[58] Federal agencies, which managed some of the most intact CSS habitat in the region, were unable to enroll their land in NCCP because there was no legal mechanism enabling them to do so. Governor Wilson's appointees, who were supposed to recruit the local officials that would implement the program, were not particularly sympathetic to environmental concerns and thus did not promote the program as effectively as they might have.[59] Even developers like the Irvine Company, which had originally backed the program, threatened to drop out of the NCCP if environmentalists pursued the gnatcatcher listing. Environmentalists refused to back down, however, concerned that in the absence of a listing they would have little leverage against developers.

In an effort to jumpstart the NCCP, in late 1993 the Wilson administration—whose appointees had lobbied aggressively to keep the gnatcatcher off state and federal lists—reversed itself and threw its support behind federal listing of the coastal California gnatcatcher.[60] The governor changed his position after working out an arrangement with the FWS to list the bird as threatened rather than endangered, as the agency had originally intended, and to issue a special rule allowing for a series of HCPs to be negotiated under the auspices of California's NCCP program.[61] Plans prepared under the NCCP differed from HCPs negotiated under the ESA in a couple of respects: HCPs were required for compliance with the ESA, whereas participation in the NCCP program was voluntary; HCPs were created to deal with listed species, whereas the NCCP program was designed to prevent listings.

The Special Rule for the Coastal California Gnatcatcher, published in December 1993, linked the two processes, however: it delegated authority for enforcement and development approval to the California Department of Fish and Game, and it specified that incidental take due to development activities in an approved NCCP plan would not be considered a violation of the ESA. Habitat plans devised under the special rule thus would serve as both NCCPs and HCPs (hereafter NCCP/HCP). In announcing the special rule for the gnatcatcher, Interior Secretary Babbitt underscored the imperative for such innovations with a slew of metaphors, saying: "We need to find common ground, to find parallel tracks that show the compatibility of environmental protection and economic development. . . . If we don't, we'll run ourselves right off a cliff."[62]

The marriage of the ESA and NCCP created several powerful new incentives for landowners to enroll in the program. First, the creation of an NCCP/HCP promised to streamline the regulatory process: once the FWS was satisfied that an NCCP/HCP would save enough habitat, it would issue a blanket permit allowing local governments to approve development on habitat outside the preserves. Without this rule, landowners would have to navigate a labyrinth of federal permitting and review procedures for each new housing development or road in gnatcatcher habitat. Once the rule was in place, landowners who chose to participate in NCCP would only have to go through a single permit application process, an advantage that was touted as "one stop shopping." Those who chose not to participate, however, would have to craft a separate HCP or undergo a Section 7 consultation and then demonstrate that the plan they formulated was consistent with NCCP/HCP. The special rule offered an additional incentive to landowners as well: participants were allowed to destroy 5 percent of CSS within each subregion during the NCCP/HCP development process. And a final feature made the NCCP process almost irresistible: once a plan was developed, even if species covered by it were later listed by the ESA, participating landowners were not responsible for any additional conservation requirements; instead, public authorities would have to finance measures not included in the original plan—a controversial feature that became known as the "no surprises" policy.

Although NCCP/HCPs promised to eliminate layers of regulatory review and compliance, the process of devising them promised to be arduous. Each separate subregional plan would have to be approved by a host of municipal and county officials; to implement a subregional plan each municipality would have to enact zoning changes, come up with ways to mitigate habitat loss, and create mechanisms for funding the acquisition of land. The prospect did not dampen the enthusiasm of the program's most vocal cheerleader, however: "It is admittedly going to be a long and complicated and sometimes frustrating process," Secretary Babbitt conceded."But the alternatives are all worse. The alternative is a train wreck that results in stalemate and no development, and a decade of litigation like we've had in the forests of the Pacific Northwest."[63]

The NCCP's objective of eliminating adversarial politics notwithstanding, advocates on both sides tried their luck in court, and in 1994 two lawsuits threatened to derail the NCCP experiment. In May, U.S. District Judge Stanley Sporkin ordered the FWS to remove the bird from its list of threatened species. Although its original lawsuit had been thrown out, the BIA of Southern California and the Orange County Transportation Agencies had reinstated their suit after the FWS made its final listing decision, on the grounds that the agency had failed to make public all the data it relied on in declaring the gnatcatcher threatened.[64] The ruling was only a temporary setback, however; Atwood immediately submitted his data to the FWS, and the agency made it publicly available. A second judicial ruling in 1994 threatened to unravel the program as well: California's Third District Court of Appeals found in favor of the NRDC, which had contested the state's refusal to list the gnatcatcher. The court ordered the Fish and Game Commission to reconsider its decision, a move that prompted outrage and threats to withdraw from the program among developers who wanted no more complications. Although environmentalists pressed the commission to list the gnatcatcher (concerned that the Republican Congress would dismantle the federal ESA and leave the bird unprotected), it again declined, and the NCCP process went forward.

The San Diego Multiple Species Conservation Plan

In December 1996, the FWS and the CDFG approved what the Clinton administration hailed as its showpiece plan: the 581,649-acre (900-square-mile) San Diego Multiple Species Conservation Plan (MSCP).[65] Adopted in March 1997 by the San Diego City Council and in October 1997 by the County Board of Supervisors, the MSCP carved out a 172,000-acre habitat preserve from a 582,000-acre portion of southwestern San Diego County. The plan purported to protect 62 percent of all CSS (70,700 of 117,500 acres) and 54 percent of all habitat in one of the most densely populated and fastest-growing areas of the U.S.; it was touted to benefit at least eighty-five species of animals and plants and twenty different habitats.[66]

Formulating the Plan. The original impetus for the San Diego MSCP actually preceded the NCCP program. The Clean Water Department (CWD) of the San Diego Metro Waste District initiated an HCP process in 1990, in response to a lawsuit by the EPA charging that the city was improperly treating its sewage. In order to get a permit under the Clean Water Act, the city needed to upgrade and expand its sewerage system, but doing so entailed construction in endangered species habitat. In consultation with the FWS, the CWD came up with the idea of pursuing an HCP to satisfy the mitigation demands that would be raised during the permitting process.[67]

In 1991, the department set up a small, industry-dominated citizen advisory committee to begin crafting an HCP, but quickly realized that it would need to broaden participation to include environmentalists if it wanted to have any credibility. The resulting group, which became the MSCP Working Group, had thirty-two members, including representatives of the FWS, the CDFG, the city of San Diego and other municipal jurisdictions, developers, environmentalists, and several special districts. Shortly into its deliberations, the Working Group recognized that it needed a chair that would be perceived as both neutral—that is, not affiliated with developers or environmentalists—and highly qualified. They settled on Karen Scarborough, the president of the San Diego-based Citizens Coordinate for the Century Three (C3), a nonprofit San Diego environmental group. Scarborough was a fortuitous choice: shortly after becoming chair of the Working Group, she took a position in Mayor Golding's office as a land-use and environmental policy analyst, which gave her even more clout and credibility as a leader.[68] Moreover, Scarborough turned out to be a committed and talented policy entrepreneur. The group also selected Jim Whalen, a moderate developer, to be its vice chair and hired environmental and financial consultants to enhance its technical capacity.

Early on, the CWD recognized that it would need a portrait of the region's biological resources as well as its political and private property boundaries to serve as a foundation for planning decisions. Led by the Ogden consulting firm, staff from various regional and municipal offices collected data gleaned from aerial photos, satellite images, field surveys, and existing maps and environmental impact reports. Biologists developed a model to evaluate the quality of the region's habitat depending on its vegetation, the presence of sensitive species, soil types, connectivity, and other features. Planners then used geographic information systems (GIS) to create habitat maps, as well as maps reflecting current and planned land uses, ownership and economic value. By overlaying the land-use maps on the biological resource maps, they were able to conduct a "gap analysis" to identify areas in the region that were most at risk of development.[69]

The mapping exercise revealed that the MSCP study area—which is bordered by Mexico to the south, national forest lands to the east, the Pacific Ocean to the west, and the San Dieguito River Valley to the north—contained 315,940 acres of undisturbed habitat, of which almost two thirds was privately owned. The gap analysis also revealed that only 17 percent of the 202,757 acres of biological core[70] and linkage areas was preserved for biological open space as of 1994, and that these areas were widely distributed and often unconnected. Existing general and community plans had designated much of the remaining habitat area in the MSCP study area for low density residential uses (39 percent) or as parks, preserves or open space (29 percent).[71] The task of the Working Group, then, was to devise a reserve that preserved as much of the core biological resource areas and linkages as possible, maximizing inclusion of public lands and lands already conserved as open space, while sharing costs equitably among landowners and not "unduly" limiting development.

The group considered three alternatives: a builder-initiated plan to focus exclusively on the gnatcatcher and protect 85,000 acres; an environmentalist-supported plan to set aside 179,000 acres; and a middle-ground plan to protect nearly 75 percent of the habitat in a 172,000-acre preserve.[72] Negotiations centered on: how much land to reserve; whether or not to draw a firm line around the habitat preserve; how many species to cover; what assurances to give landowners regarding the amount of land designated as preserve; how to allocate the financial responsibilities of involved parties; how to achieve equity between large and small landholders; and how to allocate the contribution of federal and state governments to land acquisition funds.[73] Negotiations were complex because so many landowners—and such inordinately valuable real estate—were involved; nevertheless, the Working Group's once-monthly meetings were generally "civil and friendly."[74] Over the course of resolving a series of issues, members of the group came to trust one another and became increasingly committed to the innovative effort to conduct ecosystem-scale planning.[75] This turned out to be vital because, in 1993, the city of San Diego prevailed in the lawsuit over its sewage treatment. Although this ruling eliminated the impetus for the MSCP, moderate Republican San Diego mayor Susan Golding remained firmly committed to the planning process. Along with the imprimatur of Interior Secretary Babbitt, Golding's backing was crucial to maintaining the plan's political momentum.[76]

Although trust developed among participants in the Working Group, the planning process did not alleviate the mutual suspicions of environmentalists and developers altogether. As the Working Group tried to reconcile the objectives of each of the subareas covered by the plan, several episodes provoked the ire of environmentalists. The cities of San Diego and Chula Vista each approved large-scale developments in critical habitat; in two cases, permits were issued over the objections of the FWS, which noted that the projects were inconsistent with the MSCP. The FWS threatened to reject the entire plan if the third project, the siting of a University of California satellite in Otay Valley, went forward, so the Working Group eliminated it from the reserve design. Moreover, environmentalists contended that once subarea plans had been incorporated into the MSCP, the level of habitat protection offered had been diminished considerably: buffer zones were narrower than some alternatives in the original plan had envisioned; several core habitat areas were also designated for low-density residential development; a future road was slated to run through the Otay area; and the list of species ostensibly covered by the plan had been raised from fifty-seven to eighty-five.[77]

Some environmentalists also expressed concern that the planning process was not sufficiently inclusive. From the beginning, Working Group meetings were public, with time reserved for public comment, but some found that forum intimidating, and few members of the public attended those meetings. Interested parties were more likely to attend public hearings that were held in the evening and on weekends. While these hearings were both better attended and more participatory than the Working Group meetings, it was not always clear whether or how public input was subsequently incorporated into Working Group decisions.[78] Moreover, some of the most delicate and potentially contentious decisions, such as whether or not to grant incidental take authorization for certain species, were made outside of the larger group in subcommittees or closed-door meetings between city and county representatives and resources agencies.[79] Finally, while representation in the group was broad, some environmental and private property rights groups felt marginalized.[80]

Approving the MSCP. After nearly four years of negotiations, the Working Group presented the MSCP for public review and comment. The 172,000-acre habitat preserve created by the MSCP was to be assembled through conservation of 82,200 acres that were already in public ownership, more than half of which was held by localities; private contributions of 63,000 acres to comply with development regulations and mitigate impacts of development outside the preserve; and public acquisition of about 27,000 acres of private land from willing sellers. (Local governments were to acquire half of that land, while state and federal governments would acquire the remainder.) The Working Group had decided on a "soft-line" reserve, known as the Multi-Habitat Planning Area (MHPA). Although the plan delineated the general boundary of the MHPA, it did not specify precisely which lands were to be preserved; instead, local jurisdictions were supposed make decisions about individual development projects in conformance with the plan's habitat protection guidelines.[81]

Emerging from a deliberative effort that had received little media coverage, the MSCP entered the arena of electoral politics, where rhetoric and framing assumed much larger roles. To enhance the prospects for the plan's approval, the city of San Diego launched a publicity blitz featuring public hearings and mass mailings in the spring of 1995. The state's largest bank, the Bank of America, threw its weight behind the plan, warning that unchecked urban sprawl would delay the state's economic recovery and destroy its quality of life.[82] Despite efforts to publicize the MSCP, however, the public didn't seem to understand it, so the officials and scientists who had developed the plan asked the Nature Conservancy to come up with a more effective sales pitch. In the fall of 1996, the Nature Conservancy—in collaboration with Stoorza, Ziegaus, and Metzger, California's biggest public relations firm—embarked on a campaign to gain public acceptance of the MSCP. Entitled the Naturelands Project, the public outreach and education effort was intended to tap into existing values in order to generate enthusiasm about the plan. Recognizing that the average Californian was no longer susceptible to the doomsday rhetoric traditionally employed by environmentalists, the project sought instead to ascertain what San Diegans did care about and craft a message that reflected those values.[83]

Decision Resources, the firm hired to acquire information on San Diegans' values, discovered that an overwhelming percentage of the region's residents—even those who did not consider themselves environmentalists—placed a high value on quality of life (an admittedly vague concept). More particularly, surveys suggested that San Diegans cared deeply about their chaparral- and sagebrush-covered hillsides and the region's other environmental features. In recognition of these findings, the Naturelands Project focused on building the equivalent of "brand loyalty" for quality of life in San Diego. The campaign involved billboards, public service announcements, and corporate co-marketing. To gain visibility, the Nature Conservancy wooed a host of celebrities, including Robert Redford, to serve on the project.[84]

Apparently, the campaign paid off: in March 1997, after a six-hour session before a standing-room-only crowd, the San Diego City Council unanimously approved the MSCP. Many at the meeting expressed satisfaction with the plan: the San Diego Office of the BIA, the San Diego Chamber of Commerce, the Sierra Club, the Audubon Society, and the League of Conservation Voters all endorsed it.[85] The plan was not without its detractors, however. Of continuing concern to many scientists and environmentalists was the "no surprises" clause that freed landowners from financial responsibility for additional conservation measures. Critics also lamented that even though it provided stronger development curbs than otherwise would have existed in the region's smaller municipalities, the MSCP supplanted the city of San Diego's stronger restrictions, a charge that the creators of the plan rejected.[86] Jim Peugh, former president of the San Diego chapter of the Audubon Society, did not believe the plan supported the recovery of endangered species. "Our grandkids are going to think we were really stupid at some point," he said, "and we'll work to make this stronger."[87] Skeptics also pointed out that the region was likely to have trouble raising the funding necessary to implement the plan fully.[88] And some elected officials, small landowners, and anti-tax advocates characterized the plan as a waste of money and an infringement on private property rights.

Despite these objections, the city's endorsement of the MSCP promised to pave the way for its adoption by the other subareas covered by the plan. With its outsized political clout, the city of San Diego had taken the lead in developing the plan, even though it controlled only one-third of the 172,000-acre preserve. It had spearheaded the process both because its sewer system was the impetus for the plan and because it controlled the most valuable land and faced the most contentious development battles. Thus, in gaining the city of San Diego's approval the MSCP had surmounted its biggest potential hurdle. Nevertheless, potential stumbling blocks remained, the biggest of which was that the approval of San Diego County was not assured. The chairman of the San Diego County Board of Supervisors, Bill Horn, had been outspoken in his opposition to the plan, dubbing it the "Multiple Stolen and Confiscated Property" plan.[89]

Implementing the Plan. In October 1997, the San Diego County Board of Supervisors voted 4–1 to approve the MSCP. The plan still faced a host of veto points, however; it awaited the approval of and, more importantly, implementation by ten local jurisdictions. To comply with the plan, each jurisdiction, or subarea, had to create a plan consistent with the MSCP that would then need to be approved by the CDFG and FWS.[90] (The MSCP itself is just a framework. It is the area plans, together with the Implementing Agreements, that are the basis for ESA take permits.) Each subarea plan needs to specify how the recipient of a take authorization will conserve habitat and contribute to the MSCP preserve using, in part, the existing land-use planning and project approval processes. Subarea plans also contain conservation targets, mitigation standards, and measures to ensure development is consistent with habitat preservation. Finally, they contain mechanisms to avoid or minimize project impacts on the preserve, as well as preserve management plans. Each local jurisdiction must then incorporate its subarea plan into its policies, land-use plans, and regulations; any project a local jurisdiction approves would have to be consistent with the subarea plan. The Implementing Agreement, a binding contract signed by the local jurisdiction (or other take authorization holder), CDFG and FWS, specifies the responsibility of each of the parties and the remedies to be imposed if participants fail to live up to the agreement.

In addition to preparing and enforcing subarea plans, local jurisdictions established a cooperative effort to find regional funding sources and coordinate the activities of all jurisdictions. For their part, the CDFG and FWS issue take authorizations, manage land, and coordinate biological programs. They also meet annually with authorization holders, provide technical assistance, provide funding for the implementation of the MSCP, and help jurisdictions develop regional funding and public outreach programs. While the MSCP itself did not create any new institutions, jurisdictions participating in the MSCP formed two coordinating committees: a Habitat Management Technical Committee and an Implementation Coordinating Committee.[91]

While subareas struggled to devise their plans, developers were finding that the MSCP had not really created regulatory certainty or eliminated project-by-project review because environmentalists continued to challenge individual projects on the grounds that they were inconsistent with the spirit of the MSCP. Even environmental groups that had supported the MSCP were increasingly critical as they watched individual development projects go forward. For instance, in 1998, the city of San Diego allowed Cousins Market Centers to bulldoze seventy acres of wetland habitat in the northern part of the city. Jim Peugh of the San Diego Audubon Society charged that local authorities abused their discretion in allowing the project to proceed. The land clearance destroyed sixty-five of the site's sixty-six rare vernal pools, which were habitat to dozens of small species including the San Diego fairy shrimp. Fourteen environmental groups sued the city of San Diego, the Army Corps of Engineers (which issued the permit), and the FWS over the Cousins decision, pointing out that the MSCP implementing agreement required the city to avoid vernal pool impacts "to the maximum extent practicable."[92] Michael Beck, a county planning commissioner and director of the Endangered Habitats League, responded that MSCP itself was not the problem; rather, the plan gave local elected boards such as the San Diego City Council tremendous discretion.[93]

OUTCOMES

As of the summer of 2001, the majority of the subareas covered by the MSCP either had not yet completed or had not yet received approval for their own plans (four of eleven subarea plans had been approved). The plan estimates that take authorizations could affect up to 44,230 acres of CSS; as of December 1999, 4,184 acres of CSS had been lost under the plan. It is difficult to estimate total land acquisitions under the MSCP because no single agency compiles such data for the entire program. However, the city of San Diego has conserved or obligated for conservation an impressive 83 percent of the 30,884 acres targeted for conservation under its portion of the MSCP.[94]

As expected, funding for the acquisition of private land necessary to maintain the ecosystem has been a key stumbling block to implementing the MSCP. Implemented over thirty years, the MSCP is expected to cost a total of $540–650 million, of which localities would bear $262–$360 million.[95] Since the passage of the NCCP, the state has appropriated a total of nearly $40 million for land acquisitions for the entire NCCP program.[96] On the other hand, in 2000, California voters approved Proposition 12, the Safe Neighborhoods, Clean Water, Clean Air, and Coastal Protection Bond Act, which includes $100 million that the legislature can appropriate to the Wildlife Conservation Board for acquisition of MSCP lands. It also provides $50 million to the Department of Parks and Recreation to acquire land for the state park system. In the 2000–2001 budget, the legislature appropriated the full $100 million to the Water Conservation Board and $10 million to the Parks Department.[97] In 1998, the MSCP also got $2.7 million from the federal Land and Water Conservation Fund and $2.75 million from ESA funds, and in 1999, the FWS provided another $5.6 million for land acquisition in Southern California. While the federal and state governments have pitched in, local governments have struggled to raise their share of funds. As of 2001, the local jurisdictions had yet to establish a dedicated funding source, and the longer they wait, the more expensive land acquisition will be. As a consequence, there is still a serious shortage of money for land acquisition as well as for management and monitoring.[98]

In May 1997, the NRDC, which has followed the NCCP/HCP process closely since its inception, released the first comprehensive assessment of the program. The study, entitled "Leap of Faith," identified a host of problems with the process, including inadequate scientific review of plans, poor and insecure funding to implement plans, and undefined or inadequately enforced regulatory standards. The NRDC recommended a series of reforms of the NCCP program, such as requiring independent scientific consultation and review of planning decisions and reserve design; setting clear standards for reserve design, including buffer zone specifications and infrastructure restrictions; scaling back blanket assurances to landowners; creating secure funding sources; and ensuring that the NCCP program does not interfere with enforcement of other environmental laws, such as the Clean Water Act. A study of 206 HCPs released in 1998 underscored the concern that HCPs did not follow consistent standards and concluded that even when good science was available, political or economic considerations often trumped science in decision making. The study recommended that the FWS institute basic standards for HCPs and require peer review of plans by independent scientific experts.[99] In 2000, the California legislature amended the NCCP to enhance both scientific oversight and public participation in NCCP development.

Even as the state and federal governments were trying to respond to these critiques of the NCCP and HCP processes, a new threat to California's program emerged in the fall of 2000, when the state's Coastal Commission insisted that it should have a formal role in the development of NCCP/HCPs. Developers reacted angrily to the proposal, saying it would add another layer of bureaucracy.[100] But the Coastal Commission insisted that plans that affect coastal resources must meet the standards of California's 1972 Coastal Act, the nation's strictest coastal protection law. Eventually, state agencies struck a deal to allow the Coastal Commission to review HCPs that could affect coastal wetlands and other coastal resources.

In another blow to the program, after seven years of legal battles, in October 2000, the FWS released court-mandated critical habitat designations for the gnatcatcher.[101] The designation, which comprised 513,650 acres of habitat, imposes an additional layer of government on major developments in the region. While the FWS grandfathered existing NCCP/HCPs, it could not exempt future HCPs, and developers contend that the designation eliminates incentives for them to participate in the NCCP process.[102] Further exasperating developers, environmentalists sued the FWS for exempting existing NCCP/HCPs from critical habitat designation. Working Group Chair Karen Scarborough concedes that the lawsuit is a setback. "We had hoped to change the environmentalist vs. builder paradigm," she says.[103]

CONCLUSIONS

According to conservation biologist Dennis Murphy, "The goal of the Endangered Species Act is unrealizable. Recovering species that only need public lands may be possible, but on private lands only heroic efforts will be able to sustain species that will inevitably decline. That's a reality."[104] Many environmental groups, including the Nature Conservancy, the World Wildlife Fund, and Environmental Defense, eschew Murphy's pessimism, however, and see NCCP/HCPs as a promising solution to the quandary of preserving species on private land. One observer eloquently suggests that

> although it will be some years before it is known whether the plans have been successful at sustaining the biodiversity of Southern California ecosystems, the plans faithfully incorporate the concepts that inspired their creation and offer a potent response to a difficult environmental challenge. They are unprecedented in breadth and scale, unique in approach and technique, and unsurpassed in their capacity to protect wildlife and natural habitats and to harmonize environmental and economic goals for the region.[105]

The potential advantages of NCCP/HCPs over more conventional regulatory approaches to habitat protection are evident. For landowners and developers, NCCP/HCPs promise to streamline the regulatory process and provide certainty. For conservation biologists, NCCP/HCPs promise to generate information about species and habitats and offer an ecosystem-level rather than a species-by-species approach to habitat conservation. For environmentalists, NCCP/HCPs promise to provide a mechanism for acquiring habitat that might not otherwise be protected and, in theory at least, establish funds for management and monitoring of habitat preserves. And for regulators, NCCP/HCPs promise to reduce regulatory conflict while facilitating more innovative, tailor-made solutions to the problems of individual regions.

Not surprisingly, however, in practice NCCP/HCPs have not achieved all that their boosters hoped. Above all, many environmentalists and scientists have serious doubts about the scientific basis for NCCP/HCPs. Enthusiasts point out that in a collaborative working group, scientists collect and interpret information jointly with citizens, who become quasi-experts by imitation.[106] However, critics of the NCCP/HCP process suggest that working groups have disregarded science when it was politically or economically inexpedient. They point out that while the state of California assembled a prestigious team of scientists to develop the overarching conservation principles to which NCCP plans would adhere, scientists subsequently played only a minor role in the process: they had little input into sub-regional decisions about where to draw boundaries, nor was a peer review panel formed to evaluate the final MSCP. Moreover, in his careful assessment of the MSCP, Daniel Pollak concludes, "it appears the decisions [to issue incidental take permits] did not employ a clear methodology or well-defined criteria, and relied on uncertain assumptions."[107] In any case, because collaboration promotes compromises that are dictated by nonscientific concerns, NCCP/HCPs are unlikely to be ideal from the perspective of wildlife and habitat protection.

Scientists and environmentalists are also dubious about the "no surprises" policy embedded in the MSCP.[108] Proponents of the policy insist that it constitutes a powerful incentive for developers to negotiate, noting that prior to the no surprises rule the FWS had approved only fourteen HCPs in the decade from 1983 to 1992. In contrast, as of summer 2001, more than 313 HCPs covering 20 million acres had been finalized, and another 200 were in development.[109] Defenders add that "no surprises" does not preclude additional mitigation measures but only ensures that "where additional requirements are needed, the financial burden of those requirements will fall on the public, not the private landowner or business."[110] Environmentalists and scientists respond that the biological world is inherently uncertain, as is our understanding of it, so we should not lock in plans for fifty years or more.[111] They contend that "no surprises" gives business the assurances it wants at the expense of government's ability to respond to new information.

A related worry concerns the extent to which the monitoring and adaptive management—that is, continuous collection of data on species and habitats, as well as refinement of management techniques in response to new information—will actually occur under the MSCP. The SRP made clear that "areas designated as reserves are . . . unlikely to be self-sustaining (that is, provide for natural, dynamic ecosystem processes) or to be capable of maintaining viable populations without active management."[112] The design of the MSCP's MHPA and the issuance of incidental take permits were premised on adaptive management; such practices are critical because the MHPA's designated reserves lie in the middle or on the fringes of densely populated urban and suburban areas. Yet the funding of both research and reserve monitoring and management remain tenuous; moreover, there is little, if any, coordination of those activities within or across MSCP jurisdictions.[113]

Critics have also expressed reservations about the policy consequences of devolving habitat preservation decisions to the local level. Environmentalists are concerned that for municipal officials, development—which generates prosperity in the short-run—is almost always a more attractive option than habitat preservation. This feature of local governments may undermine efforts to preserve habitat in the long run, especially if—as in southern California—local jurisdictions have primary responsibility for implementing plans. As one scientist commented after the Cousins Market incident: "Personally, I believe the [MSCP] is a setback because, as I understand it, you are basically handing the enforcement of the Endangered Species Act over to the San Diego city council, and they have no track record for conservation, in particular for vernal pools."[114]

Finally, although collaborative processes are intended to defuse conflict among stakeholders, questions about who is a stakeholder and how to incorporate "the public" into decision making remain; groups on both sides of the MSCP complain that they were excluded from the process. Moreover, it was the threat of litigation over ESA regulations, which could potentially have halted development altogether, that brought landowners and developers to the table in southern California. The lawsuits that have accompanied the implementation of the MSCP make it clear that the plan has eliminated neither conflict nor the fundamental value differences between environmentalists and cornucopians.

QUESTIONS TO CONSIDER

- Are Habitat Conservation Plans, the current mechanisms of choice for dealing with endangered species on private lands, likely to defuse conflict over preserving species habitats and landscapes? Why or why not?
- Are such approaches likely to accomplish their conservation goals? Or are they, as some environmentalists suggest, simply a way that developers can circumvent the strict requirements of the Endangered Species Act?

Notes

1. Reed F. Noss, Michael A. O'Connell, and Dennis D. Murphy, *The Science of Conservation Planning: Habitat Conservation Plans Under the Endangered Species Act* (Washington, D.C.: Island Press, 1997).

2. Oliver Houck, quoted in Daniel Pollak, *The Future of Habitat Conservation? The NCCP Experience in Southern California* (California Research Bureau, California State Library, June 2001), 4.

3. Quoted in Terry Rodgers, "City Affirms Plan to Save Area Wildlife, Interior Secretary Calls Large-Habitat Action Magnificent," *San Diego Union-Tribune*, March 19, 1997, A1.

4. Deborah S. Knopman, M. Susman, and Marc K. Landy, "Civic Environmentalism: Tackling Tough Land-Use Problems With Innovative Governance," *Environment* 49 (December 1999): 26.

5. Julia M. Wondollek and Steven L. Yaffee, *Making Collaboration Work: Lessons From Innovation in Natural Resource Management* (Washington, D.C.: Island Press, 2000), 23.

6. Dewitt John, *Civic Environmentalism: Alternatives to Regulation in States and Communities* (Washington, D.C.: CQ Press, 1994); Knopman et al., "Civic Environmentalism"; Philip Brick, Donald Snow, and Sarah Van De Wetering, *Across the Great Divide: Explorations in Collaborative Conservation and the American West* (Washington, D.C.: Island Press, 2001).

7. See, for example, Jacqueline Savitz, "Compensating Citizens," in *Beyond Backyard Environmentalism,* ed. Charles Sabel et al. (Boston: Beacon Press, 2000), 65–69; Matthew Wilson and Eric Weltman, "Government's Job," in *Beyond Backyard Environmentalism,* ed. Sabel et al., 49–53; and Steven L. Yaffee et al., *Balancing Public Trust and Private Interest: Public Participation in Habitat Conservation Planning* (Ann Arbor: School of Natural Resources, University of Michigan, 1998).

8. See, for example, B. C. Bingham and B. R. Noon, "Mitigation of Habitat 'Take': Application to Habitat Conservation Planning," *Conservation Biology* 11 (1995): 127–139; F. Shilling, "Do Habitat Conservation Plans Protect Endangered Species?" *Science* 276 (June 13, 1997): 1662–1663; and Peter Kareiva et al., *Using Science in Habitat Conservation Planning* (Washington, D.C.: American Institute of Biological Sciences, 1999).

9. See, for example, Lance H. Gunderson, C. S. Holling, and Stephen S. Light, eds., *Barriers and Bridges to the Renewal of Ecosystems and Institutions* (New York: Columbia University Press, 1995).

10. Jeffrey L. Pressman and Aaron Wildavsky, *Implementation*, 3d ed. (Berkeley: University of California Press, 1983).

11. Charles Mann and Mark Plummer, "California vs. Gnatcatcher," *Audubon*, (January–February 1995), 29–38, 100–104.

12. Ibid.

13. U.S. Fish and Wildlife Service (FWS), "Special Rule Concerning Take of the Threatened Coastal California Gnatcatcher," *Federal Register,* 58 FR 16742 (March 30, 1993).

14. Chaparral is a community of shrubby plants adapted to dry summers and moist winters. Riparian habitats are areas of stream- and riverside vegetation.

15. A. D. Dobson et al., "Geographic Distribution of Endangered Species in the United States," *Science* 275 (January 24, 1997): 650–653.

16. U.S. Fish and Wildlife Service (FWS), "Endangered and Threatened Wildlife and Plants: Determination of Threatened Status for the Coastal California Gnatcatcher," *Federal Register,* 50 CFR Part 17 (March 30, 1993).

17. Half of all ESA-listed species make their homes exclusively on non-federal land, most of which is privately owned. For listed species found only on private land, the ratio of declining to improving is 9:1, whereas the ratio is 1.5:1 for listed species found entirely on federal land. See Noss et al., *The Science of Conservation Planning.*

18. Critical habitat is defined as areas that contain "physical or biological features (I) essential to the conservation of the species, and (II) which may require special management considerations or protection." See P.L. 93-205, 16 U.S.C. 1531 et seq. § 4(b)(2). The 1978 amendments to the ESA allow the FWS to take economic considerations into account when designating critical habitat.

19. According to the FWS, fifty-three charges were filed against individuals or corporations for killing endangered species, destroying their habitat, or poaching for specimen collectors between October 1988 and September 1992. Thirty-three were convicted of criminal charges and six of civil charges. Fines and civil penalties totaled about $60,000, and offenders served 1,347 days in jail. See Maura Dolan, "Nature at Risk in a Quiet War," *Los Angeles Times*, December 20, 1992, A1.

20. In the first case, against Anderson and Middleton Logging Company of Washington, the FWS later dropped the charges and bought the threatened stand of 1,000-year-old trees for $3.5 million. In the second case, involving the Oregon Coast Range, the FWS fined the International Paper Company $92,000 for illegally clearcutting 300 acres of critical owl habitat between 1991 and 1996. In an out-of-court settlement, IP agreed to contribute $47,000 to the Nature Conservancy and $25,000 to help fund a database for tracking owls. The company admitted to no wrongdoing, however. See Kathie Durbin and Paul Larmer, "The Feds Won't Enforce the ESA," *High Country News*, August 4, 1997.

21. Dolan, "Nature at Risk."

22. Quoted in Durbin and Larmer, "The Feds Won't Enforce the ESA."

23. Dolan, "Nature at Risk."

24. Timothy Beatley, *Habitat Conservation Planning: Endangered Species Protection and Urban Growth* (Austin: University of Texas Press, 1994).

25. Ecologists believed that preserving 2,000 of the landowner's 3,500 acres would be sufficient to ensure the long-term survival of the two federally listed butterfly species.

26. Timothy Beatley, "Habitat Conservation Plans: A New Tool to Resolve Land Use Conflicts," *Land Lines*, September 1995.

27. Craig W. Thomas, *Bureaucratic Landscapes: Interagency Cooperation and the Preservation of Biodiversity* (Cambridge: MIT Press, forthcoming).

28. The coastal California gnatcatcher (*Polioptila c. californica*) was originally described in 1881 as a distinct subspecies. A subsequent analysis conducted in 1926 suggested that *P. californica* was actually three subspecies of the black-tailed gnatcatcher (*P. melanura*), which is widely distributed throughout the deserts of the southwestern United States and Mexico. In 1988, however, Atwood challenged the prevailing classification scheme, contending that *P. californica* was distinct from *P. melanura* based on differences in its behavior and its ecological niche. The American Ornithologists' Union Committee on Nomenclature adopted Atwood's scheme in 1989. See FWS, "Endangered and Threatened Wildlife."

29. FWS, "Endangered and Threatened Wildlife."

30. Under the ESA, the FWS may determine a species to be endangered or threatened if one or more of the following is true: its habitat or range is threatened with or undergoing destruction or curtailment; it is being overused for commercial, recreation, scientific, or educational purposes; it is experiencing high rates of disease or predation; existing regulatory mechanisms are inadequate to protect it; and/or other natural or manmade factors are affecting its continued existence.

31. Mann and Plummer, "California vs. Gnatcatcher."

32. Ibid.

33. Quoted in ibid., 24.

34. The FWS received similar petitions in September 1990 from the Palomar Audubon Society and the San Diego Biodiversity Project.

35. Thomas, *Bureaucratic Landscapes*.

36. Although the FWS is allowed to take only scientific considerations into account in deciding whether to list a species, in practice its decisions have reflected economic and political concerns. See Richard Tobin, *The Expendable Future: U.S. Politics and the Preservation of Biological Diversity* (Durham: Duke University Press, 1990).

37. Terry Rodgers, "Catching Gnats—and Flak," *San Diego Union-Tribune*, May 4, 1991, A1.

38. Quoted in David L. Coddon, "What Price Progress? Tiny Gnatcatcher Hatches a Conflict That Won't Go Away," *San Diego Union-Tribune,* September 6, 1991, F1.

39. In a letter to California Resource Agency head Douglas Wheeler, Irvine Company vice president Monica Florian made clear that the company's goal was to avert state or federal listing of the gnatcatcher. See Ralph Frammolino, "Irvine Co. Tries to Forestall Bid to Protect Bird," *Los Angeles Times,* April 25, 1991, A1.

40. The Irvine Company owns two hotels, eighteen shopping centers, 5.2 million square feet of industrial property, a six-square-mile technology center, and 62,000 acres of "amazingly valuable" real estate. See Mann and Plummer, "California vs. Gnatcatcher."

41. Thomas, *Bureaucratic Landscapes.*

42. Quoted in Mann and Plummer, "California vs. Gnatcatcher," 48.

43. NCCP established the SRP to give the program credibility. The law itself merely suggests the appointment of one or more "advisory committees" but does not specify their composition; nor does the law set substantive, procedural, or evidentiary standards for reserve planning. See Michael Jasny, *Leap of Faith: Southern California's Experiment in Natural Community Conservation Planning* (Washington, D.C.: Natural Resources Defense Council, 1997).

44. "Southern California Coastal Sage Scrub Natural Communities Conservation Planning: Draft Conservation Guidelines" (1993), 8–9.

45. Quoted in Pollak, *The Future of Habitat Conservation?,* 13.

46. Quoted in Marla Cone, "Endangered Status Denied for Gnatcatcher," *Los Angeles Times,* August 31, 1991, A1. The panel's vote was 3–1. The three against listing were all California businessmen appointed by former Governor Deukmejian. The dissenting vote was cast by a Wilson appointee and former director of the Nature Conservancy.

47. Drew Silvern, "Protected Status for Gnatcatcher Is Turned Down," *San Diego Union-Tribune,* August 31, 1991, A1.

48. Cone, "Endangered Status Denied."

49. FWS, "Endangered and Threatened Wildlife."

50. Federal agencies must publish proposed rules in the Federal Register and allow time for comments from the public. It has become standard practice for agencies to respond to those comments in the preambles of final rules.

51. If the bird is not a valid subspecies, then it is part of a larger group whose habitat extends over more territory. Such a finding, in turn, changes the calculus of whether the bird is endangered.

52. Mann and Plummer, "California vs. Gnatcatcher."

53. FWS, "Endangered and Threatened Wildlife."

54. The courts can rule only on a final decision.

55. FWS, "Endangered and Threatened Wildlife."

56. Drew Silvern, "Bird Loses More Land While Fate is Debated," *San Diego Union-Tribune,* October 13, 1991, B1.

57. The NCCP Act of 1991 (AB 2172). For a summary of the act's legislative history, see Daniel Pollak, *Natural Community Conservation Planning (NCCP): The Origin of an Ambitious Experiment to Protect Ecosystems* (California Research Bureau, California State Library, March 2001).

58. Marla Cone, "U.S. Begins Experiment to Save Songbird," *Los Angeles Times,* December 9, 1993, A3.

59. Thomas, *Bureaucratic Landscapes.*

60. Craig Thomas contends that the Wilson administration approached the FWS behind the scenes, in order to be able to deflect blame for the federal regulations while providing the necessary incentives to increase participation in NCCP. See Thomas, *Bureaucratic Landscapes.*

61. Under Section 4(d) of the ESA, the FWS can issue special regulations for a threatened (but not endangered) species that are deemed "necessary and advisable for

the conservation of the species." Section 6 allows the ESA to delegate enforcement of the rule to states.

62. Quoted in Michael Jasny, *Leap of Faith*, 4.
63. Quoted in Cone, "U.S. Begins Experiment."
64. David Handane and Faye Fiore, "U.S. Will Act to Keep Gnatcatcher Protected," *Los Angeles Times*, May 12, 1994, A1.
65. This was southern California's second NCCP/HCP. The first, approved in July 1996, was Orange County's Central-Coastal Plan, which set aside 37,380 acres out of a 209,000-acre planning area. See Noss et al., *The Science of Conservation Planning*.
66. Widlife experts believe there are more endangered species in the region covered by the plan than in virtually any other location in the country. See Frank Clifford, "San Diego OKs Conservation Plan," *Los Angeles Times*, October 24, 1997, A3.
67. Because of its origins, the boundaries of the MSCP reflect the boundaries of the Metropolitan Sewerage System.
68. Michael McLaughlin, Director of Land-Use Planning at the San Diego Association of Governments, personal communication, March 30, 2001.
69. Janet Fairbanks, "Room to Roam: Why the San Diego Region Is Considered a National Model for Habitat Conservation," *Planning* 60 (January 1994): 24–26.
70. Core areas are defined as "areas generally supporting a high concentration of sensitive biological resources which, if lost or fragmented, could not be replaced or mitigated elsewhere." See City of San Diego, "Multiple Species Conservation Plan," 29.
71. Multiple Species Conservation Program, "MSCP Plan" (August 1996), http://www.sannet.gov/mscp/.
72. Karen Scarborough, Chair of the MSCP Working Group, personal communication, May 20, 2001.
73. Jennifer Merrick, "The San Diego Multiple Species Conservation Plan," in *Improving Integrated Natural Resource Planning: Habitat Conservation Plans* (October 14, 1998), National Center for Environmental Decision-Making Research, http://www.ncedr.org/casestudies/hcp/sandiego/htm.
74. Ibid.
75. Scarborough, personal communication.
76. McLaughlin, personal communication; Scarborough, personal communication.
77. Raising the number of listed species covered reduces the likelihood of further conservation measures in the future. See Jasny, *Leap of Faith*.
78. Merrick, "The San Diego Multiple Species Conservation Plan."
79. Ibid.; Michael McLaughlin, personal communication.
80. Merrick, "The San Diego Multiple Species Conservation Plan."
81. Pollak, *The Future of Habitat Conservation?*
82. Emmet Pierce and Terry Rodgers, "Four Years of Biological Surveys and Quiet Negotiations by Builders, Conservationists, and Planners Are Nearing a Climactic Conclusion," *San Diego Union-Tribune*, June 11, 1995, H1.
83. Emmet Pierce and Terry Rodgers, "Environmentalists Will Try Soft Sell," *San Diego Union-Tribune*, November 14, 1996, A1.
84. Ibid.
85. Marla Cone, "San Diego Approves Broadest Conservation Plan in U.S.," *Los Angeles Times*, March 19, 1997, A1.
86. Scarborough, personal communication.
87. Quoted in Cone, "San Diego Approves."
88. Ibid.
89. Ibid.
90. Not only local jurisdictions but also special purpose agencies, regional public facility providers, and utilities were all preparing subarea plans.
91. Multiple Species Conservation Program, "MSCP Plan."
92. Pollak, *The Future of Habitat Conservation?*

93. Steve LaRue, "Environmental Groups in Region Assail Habitat Management," *San Diego Union-Tribune,* January 4, 1999, B3.
94. The reserve design included 22,083 acres already conserved and targeted an additional 30,884 for conservation in the city of San Diego. See Pollak, *The Future of Habitat Conservation?*
95. Ibid. Municipalities can raise money in a variety of ways, including a benefit assessment by a regional park or open space district, a habitat maintenance assessment, an ad valorem property tax, or a sales tax increase.
96. Ibid.
97. Pollak, *Natural Community Conservation Planning.*
98. The plan's management costs were estimated at $4.6 million per year for local governments and $2 million annually for federal and state governments. See Pollak, *The Future of Habitat Conservation?* Municipalities can raise money in a variety of ways, including a benefit assessment by a regional park or open space district, a habitat maintenance assessment, an ad valorem property tax, or a sales tax increase.
99. Deborah Schoch, "New Approach to Protecting Fragile Habitats Criticized," *Los Angeles Times,* July 20, 1998, A3. In response to these critiques, the Clinton administration proposed tightening oversight of HCPs and requiring specific goals spelling out how the plans benefit wildlife. Specific changes include requiring measurable biological goals and objectives; requiring a monitoring program based on science; and creating flexible systems of managing reserves that can adjust as more is learned.
100. Deborah Schoch, "Coastal Panel Seeks Wider Role in Plans to Conserve Habitat," *Los Angeles Times,* October 12, 2000, A1.
101. In May 1997, the U.S. Circuit Court of Appeals ruled 2–1 that the federal government violated the ESA by failing to designate critical habitat for the gnatcatcher.
102. Seema Mehta, "Wide Swaths of Southland Called Vital to Bird, Shrimp," *Los Angeles Times,* October 18, 2000, A1.
103. Scarborough, personal communication.
104. Quoted in Paul Larmer, "The Real Problem."
105. Marc J. Ebbin, "Is the Southern California Approach to Conservation Succeeding?" *Ecology Law Quarterly* 24 (November 1997): 696.
106. Charles Sabel, Archon Fund, and Bradley Karkkainen, "Beyond Backyard Environmentalism," in *Beyond Backyard Environmentalism,* ed. Sabel et al., 3–46.
107. Pollak, *The Future of Habitat Conservation?*
108. The FWS formally introduced the "no surprises" language in 1994, promulgated it as a rule in 1997, and finalized it in 1998.
109. For updated information on HCPs, http://endangered.fws.gov/hcp/index.html.
110. Noss et al., *The Science of Conservation Planning,* 63.
111. Jon Margolis, "Critics Say 'No Surprises' Means No Protection," *High Country News,* August 4, 1997.
112. Quoted in Pollak, *The Future of Habitat Conservation?* 46.
113. Ibid. Pollak notes, however, that the local agencies involved in the MSCP are implementing a centralized database for tracking habitat gains and losses.
114. Quoted in LaRue, "Environmental Groups in Region."

Recommended Reading

Mann, Charles, and Mark Plummer. "California vs. Gnatcatcher." *Audubon,* January-February 1995, 29–38, 100–104.
Noss, Reed, Michael A. O'Connell, and Dennis D. Murphy. *The Science of Conservation Planning: Habitat Conservation Plans Under the Endangered Species Act.* Washington, D.C.: Island Press, 1997.

Pollak, Daniel. *The Future of Habitat Conservation? The NCCP Experience in Southern California*. California Research Bureau, California State Library, June 2001.

Web Sites

http://www.dfg.ca.gov/nccp (California Department of Fish and Game site)
http://ceres.ca.gov/ (California Environmental Resources Evaluation System site)
http://www.ci.san-diego.ca.us/mscp/plansum.shtml (City of San Diego site)

Conclusions

Having read the preceding cases, you are probably beginning to think like a political scientist when you read or hear about an environmental policy controversy. You do not expect that just because someone has identified an environmental problem and even figured out how to engineer a solution, the government will necessarily address the problem or adopt the most "rational" solution. As the framework laid out in chapter 1 made clear, policymaking is not a linear process, in which government officials recognize a problem, deliberate based on the available information, and select the most appropriate solution. Rather, policymaking consists of a series of engagements among advocates trying to get problems addressed in the venue they believe will be most hospitable to their concerns and in ways that are consistent with their values.[1] Advocates of policy change struggle to create a context in which their definition of a problem dominates the debate, while awaiting a window of opportunity to push their preferred solution. Defenders of the status quo, on the other hand, have myriad ways to stave off change; it is much easier, in American politics, to prevent change than to enact it.

THE STRENGTH OF THE STATUS QUO

One of the features of the American environmental policymaking process that stand out most starkly in the preceding cases is the remarkable persistence of the status quo. The prevailing policy may be shielded by the president, well-situated members of Congress, or the agencies that administer the policy. The president can block change using a veto or veto threat or, more subtly, by failing to put forth a policy proposal and arguing instead on behalf of more research. Highly placed members of Congress can rebuff policy change as well: committee chairs can refuse to send a bill to the floor; majority leaders in either chamber can refuse to schedule a vote on a bill. In the Senate, a minority can filibuster legislation; in the House, the majority party can use multiple referral, amendment-friendly rules, and other parliamentary maneuvers to derail a bill. Agencies can weaken a legislative mandate by delaying implementation or interpreting a statute in ways that are inconsistent with the intent of Congress.

The strength of the status quo manifests itself most plainly in cases involving natural resources on public lands, where environmentalists have faced enormous resistance to reforms aimed at introducing their values into management practices. In natural resource policymaking, narrow, relatively homogeneous subsystems historically have been extremely difficult for competing interests to penetrate. While timber policy has become noticeably more environmentally protective in response to advocates' efforts, mining and grazing policies on public lands retain vestiges of century-old routines. Of course, the fact that existing policies resist change does not only benefit development interests; as the Arctic National Wildlife Refuge (ANWR) case makes clear, the tenacity of the status quo can work in favor of environmentalists as well. The important lesson is that history shapes current politics and policy, making some outcomes more likely and others less so.

The "power" of the status quo means not only that institutionalized interests have an advantage in policy debates, but also that policies tend to lag behind advances in the scientific understanding of the natural world. Many of the environmental policies passed in the 1970s, which continue to shape decision making, reflect ecological notions of stability and balance that were anachronistic among practicing scientists even then. For instance, the Endangered Species Act (ESA), the "pit bull of U.S. environmental laws," focuses on conserving individual species and their habitats, whereas conservation biologists now advocate preserving diversity at all levels of biological organization.[2] Critics also charge that, because of their initial design, many environmental laws are inefficient or counterproductive. Economists and public health professionals have criticized the Superfund Act, for example, for diverting millions of dollars to what most experts agree are relatively low-risk toxic dump sites. Although neither the ESA nor the Superfund Act is perfectly "rational" from most experts' point of view, both have been highly resistant to reform—not just because some organized interests benefit from the laws as written but also because environmentalists recognize that, once they are opened up for reconsideration, they are vulnerable to rollback.

THE IMPORTANCE OF BUILDING COALITIONS

Given the fragmentation of American politics—among levels of government and among the various branches of government—dislodging the status quo requires a formidable effort. As the backlash case reveals, one way that opponents of the status quo have tried to circumvent the arduous reform process is by attaching riders to appropriations and omnibus budget bills. More commonly, however, proponents of fundamental policy change must assemble a supermajority coalition.[3] To build such a coalition, advocates have learned they must join forces with groups that may have different values but similar objectives. Thus, environmentalists have allied with hazardous waste cleanup firms to resist changes in the Superfund law; gas, solar, and geothermal power companies, as well as insurance firms, are cooperating with environmentalists to press for cuts in greenhouse gas emissions; labor unions and municipal governments have taken the side of environmentalists in opposing legislation to compensate property owners when regulation reduces the value of their land because they believe such laws will severely compromise government's ability to protect public (and workers') health and safety.[4]

Keeping such disparate coalitions together is no mean feat. In particular, it is difficult to craft approaches that are palatable to mainstream interests without alienating the true believers that form a coalition's activist core.[5] Often, when the vague ideas and symbols needed to bind members of an alliance together are translated into practical policies, rifts and factions develop. Groups that opposed the North American Free Trade Agreement (NAFTA), for example, including the Sierra Club, Friends of the Earth, and Greenpeace, publicly charged those that supported the treaty, including the National Audubon Society and the National Wildlife Federation, with "selling off" the environment and becoming "too cozy" with corporate America.[6] More recently, a similar schism appeared during climate change negotiations at the Hague in 2000, where moderate environmental groups supported a plan to allow the United States to get credit toward its carbon dioxide (CO_2) emissions limits for forests, which absorb CO_2, but other environmentalists opposed such a deal because they felt it allowed the United States to evade its responsibility for cleaning up its share of pollution.

INFORMATION, PROBLEM DEFINITION, AND POLICY CHANGE

Key to advocates' success in building a coalition substantial enough to overturn the status quo is their ability to promote a compelling definition of the environmental problem. Although conventional tactics, such as lobbying legislators and donating money to political campaigns, remain important means of influencing policy, scholars increasingly have recognized the importance of strategically defining problems in determining the outcome of policy contests.[7] For environmentalists, those efforts entail generating scientific information and framing it in ways that emphasize the risk of inaction. When advocates succeed in translating the scientific explanation of a problem into a compelling causal story, as they did in the Everglades, spotted owl, and other cases, they are much more likely to attract support.

Among the features that emerge from the cases is the political potency of scientific predictions in problem definition. "If predictive science can improve policy outcomes by guiding policy choices," it is thought, "then it can as well reduce the need for divisive debate and contentious decision making based on subjective values and interests."[8] But scientific models, which have been critical elements of the Everglades, gnatcatcher, fisheries, acid rain, and climate change debates, are inherently uncertain because natural systems are not "closed" or static and therefore may respond to perturbations in fundamentally unpredictable ways. Moreover, the predictions that come out of such models reflect modelers' assumptions, which themselves hinge on experts' values. Nevertheless, scientific models—of climate, species populations, and other natural systems—lend credibility to environmentalists' arguments and legitimacy to political decisions.

Generating predictions is just one way advocates translate the complexity of the world into compelling political stories. As any experienced advocate will tell you, another crucial attribute of stories that succeed in garnering public (and hence political) attention is crisis. The cases of Love Canal and Rocky Flats illustrate the impact that dramatic events can have on the public, particularly if advocates manage to interpret those events to reinforce their policy position. In the case of Love Canal, advocates pounced on scientific studies identifying chemicals in the air and health effects to buttress their claims that their neighborhood was contaminated; the media were their allies in this endeavor because of their propensity to focus on human interest stories and health risks. In the Rocky Flats case, media revelations of government and contractor misappropriation of funds, errors and carelessness in disposing of waste, and concealment of waste management practices all contributed to building public anxiety about the plant. Opponents of the plant in turn drew on those stories to reinforce their definition of the plant as an environmental and public health threat rather than a critical building block of the national security edifice.

Further buttressing environmentalists' efforts to define a problem is the support of scientists, who may have identified the problem in the first place. Periodic scientific reports serve as focusing events, keeping media—and hence public and elite—attention trained on the issue. Individual scientists, acting as knowledge brokers, can be particularly compelling advocates of policy change.

Ultimately, for advocates of policy change to prevail, they must not only define a problem but also provide a solution that is consistent with their definition of the problem, as well as viable in terms of the budget and the political mood.[10] While awaiting the opening of a window of opportunity, policy entrepreneurs soften up their pet solutions; for instance, an emissions trading solution to acid rain was in the pipeline for more than two decades before it was finally enacted into policy. During that period, economists in particular were expounding on the virtues of incentive-based solutions to environmental problems in textbooks, classrooms, and scholarly and popular journals. Similarly, the Everglades restoration plan and San Diego MSCP reflect ideas about adaptive ecosystem-level management that had been circulating among conservation biologists for nearly a decade.

Recognizing the importance of problem definition for building the broad, cohesive coalitions necessary to enact policy change, opponents try to define problems in ways that hinder or fracture such alliances. For example, in the grazing case, ranchers used cowboy symbolism and the language of rugged individualism and government tyranny to weaken the force of environmentalists' claims. In the acid rain and climate change cases, opponents tried to undermine the science in which environmentalists' stories were rooted.

In addition, opponents of regulation shift attention to the costs of addressing environmental problems. Both the acid rain case and the spotted owl case illustrate the extent to which predictions of the cost of regulations can vary and are likely to exceed the actual costs. Other examples abound. In the late 1970s, the chemical industry predicted that controlling benzene emissions would cost $350,000 per plant, but by substituting other chemicals for benzene, chemical manufacturers virtually eliminated control costs. In 1993, carmakers estimated that the price of a new car would rise $650 to $1,200 per car as a result of regulations limiting the use of CFCs, yet in 1997, the actual cost was between $40 and $400. Prior to the passage of the 1978 Surface Mining Control and Reclamation Act, estimates of compliance costs ranged from $6 to $12 per ton of coal, but actual costs were in the range of $.50 to $1 per ton.[9] Cost projections, like scientific predictions of environmental outcomes, are unlikely to take into account the accidents and unexpected features of the future, technological innovations, or the market's response to regulation, and they are heavily shaped by modelers' assumptions. Nevertheless, cost projections, like scientific projections, are persuasive when interpreted as providing certainty about the future, particularly when—as in the owl case—they portend economic and social disaster.

LEADERSHIP

Even if advocates succeed in crafting a compelling problem definition and linking it to a viable solution, legislative majorities sufficiently large to enact policy change do not simply emerge and cohere spontaneously. Nor do agencies readily replace standard operating procedures with new approaches. Rather, one feature that emerges powerfully from the cases as a whole is the importance of individuals and, more particularly, of leadership, in bringing about policy change.

Just as well-placed individuals can block reform, talented leaders can induce change by facilitating coalition building, brokering solutions to apparently intractable conflicts, and shepherding solutions through the decision making process. For example, after nearly a decade of stalemate over acid rain, Senator George Mitchell's skillful and dogged micromanagement of negotiations over the Clean Air Act Amendments of 1990 proved indispensable to the policy's passage. By conducting negotiations in private, away from the glare of the media and the demands of special interests, Mitchell was able to wring concessions from holdouts and forge an agreement among parties that for a decade had refused to bargain. Similarly, the Clinton administration's highly publicized backing of the Everglades restoration and the San Diego MSCP elevated scientists and their beliefs, making it possible to enact far more protective solutions than might otherwise have been crafted. Compare the outcome of those cases with that of the ANWR case, where public squabbling among competing interests, unmediated by leadership, stymied efforts to pass a comprehensive energy policy bill. (Development advocates hope that George W. Bush will provide the leadership that has been lacking to move an energy bill with ANWR drilling provisions through Congress during his term.)

Leaders need not be "true believers." The stringency of the Clean Air and Water Acts of the early 1970s reflect the efforts of President Richard Nixon and presidential hopeful Sen. Edmund Muskie to trump one another and thereby gain the kudos of environmentalists. Twenty years later, presidential candidate Bush promised to be "the environmental president" in hopes of undermining support for Democrat Michael Dukakis, and one result is the Clean Air Act Amendments of 1990. Neither Nixon nor Bush were environmentalists; both were trying to garner political credit by capitalizing on the popularity of environmental protection, salience that advocates had worked hard to create.

Nor are political leaders the only ones who can make a difference in policymaking. Individuals outside the decision making process—policy entrepreneurs—are crucial as well: Ralph Nader's organization spurred Muskie to propose more ambitious clean air and water laws than he originally intended; Karen Scarborough's skilled facilitation of the San Diego Multispecies Conservation Plan yielded a plan that protects more coastal sage scrub habitat than might otherwise have been saved; without her, the process might have collapsed altogether. Dexter Lehtinen's flamboyant decision to launch a dubious lawsuit in the Everglades started in motion a chain of events whose result no one could have predicted. Ron Arnold, Alan Gottlieb, and other anti-environmental policy entrepreneurs employed powerful rhetoric to throw a wrench into the environmental juggernaut and thereby prompt a wholesale reevaluation of the movement's tactics and goals.

THE COURTS

Although observers tend to focus on legislative and administrative decision making, another avenue for major policy change in the American political system is the judicial branch. The courts have always been the forum for resolving intractable value conflicts; thus, it is not surprising that environmentalists and cornucopians find themselves so frequently making their cases before a judge. At the beginning of the modern environmental era, environmentalists filed lawsuits to force the newly formed Environmental Protection Agency (EPA) to write regulations under the Clean Air and Water Acts; they subsequently used the National Environmental Policy Act, the National Forest Management Act, and other laws in the spotted owl case to redirect federal land management priorities. Efforts to control overfishing of cod, flounder, and haddock in New England were failing until a lawsuit filed by the Conservation Law Foundation forced the National Marine Fisheries Service to institute more protective rules. Similarly, a lawsuit against the state of Florida spurred action in both the state legislature and Congress to restore the Everglades.

Lawsuits can have direct and indirect effects. They can prompt administrative policy change directly by narrowing the range of options an agency may consider and precluding the status quo altogether. They may have less immediate but equally potent impacts if they raise an issue's visibility and thereby facilitate reframing or result in the intervention of elected officials or their appointees.

Observing the success of environmentalists in court during the 1970s, those who oppose environmental regulations began resorting to litigation to achieve their ends as well. By the 1980s, it was common for both industry and environmental groups to sue the EPA over the same decision, with one litigant claiming the regulation was too strict and the other arguing that it was too lenient.[11] Property rights advocates made skillful use of the courts in the 1990s to revise the legal interpretation of the takings clause of the Fifth Amendment. Thus, in contrast with many other nations whose political cultures are less legalistic, jurisprudence—and the adversary relationships it fosters—has been a defining feature of American environmental politics.

In an effort to avert the wave of lawsuits that has accompanied every new environmental law or regulation, agencies have been experimenting with negotiated rulemaking, mediation, and other consensus-building procedures. Many advocates on both sides have endorsed collaborative environmental problem-solving as an alternative to more conventional, top-down regulatory decision making. However, critics of collaboration as a mechanism for resolving environmental problems point out that compromise is likely to be inconsistent with science and that collaborative processes may exclude stakeholders and thus fail to achieve their participatory ideals. More importantly, collaboration is not a panacea. As efforts to restore the Everglades show, there are myriad institutional barriers to cooperation among agencies. The gnatcatcher case reveals, in addition, that efforts to implement collaborative agreements can cause already tenuous efforts at habitat preservation to unravel. Finally, as long as fundamental value differences persist, advocates are likely to challenge the results of collaborative processes in hopes of bringing about an outcome more consistent with their preferences.

CONCLUSIONS

A key objective of this book is to identify patterns that help us understand the politics of environmental issues without obscuring the uniqueness of each case. I posited at the outset that two elements of American environmental politics remain relatively constant: advocates in environmental policy contests are almost always deeply divided over values; and how those values translate into political choices depends heavily on the way a problem is defined in terms of science, economics, and risk.

Direct discussions of competing value are rare in part because while its adversaries caricature environmentalism as an effort by elites to impose their values on society, public opinion polls suggest that most Americans are sympathetic with the general aims of the environmental movement. Even its critics concede that environmentalism is becoming "the lens through which we look at our relationship to nature."[12] At the same time, issues such as climate change expose the tensions latent in American environmentalism: while claiming to value the natural environment, most Americans appear unwilling to compromise their energy-consuming lifestyle—a fact that is underscored by the proliferation of SUVs, minivans, and pickup trucks in America's cities and suburbs. Although individual behavior is clearly at the root of many of our environmental problems, political stories that cast ordinary citizens as the villains have fared poorly in the American political context. Similarly, stories that suggest direct human health effects have galvanized the public more consistently than those involving ecological decline.

In short, the depth of Americans' commitment to environmental protection remains unclear, as does our willingness to sacrifice—in practice, not simply in theory—on behalf of the environment, this, in turn, enables opponents of environmental regulations to frame issues in a way that emphasize costs or inconvenience to individuals and thereby stymie protective policies. Thus, for some, the patterns that emerge from these cases may suggest that the prospects for genuine change in our approach to environmental protection are poor. But political science, like ecology, is not a predictive science; the patterns we identify are probabilistic and subject to change. New people, like new ideas, can affect the process in dramatic and unexpected ways. The lessons of past experience thus should not limit but rather should liberate both professional activists and concerned citizens who wish to challenge the status quo.

Notes

1. Deborah Stone, *Policy Paradox: The Art of Political Decision Making* (New York: Norton, 1997).
2. See, for example, Richard L. Hutto, Susan Reel, and Peter B. Landres, "A Critical Evaluation of the Species Approach to Biological Conservation," *Endangered Species Update* 4 (October 1987), 1–4.
3. Keith Krehbiel, *Pivotal Politics: A Theory of U.S. Lawmaking* (Chicago: University of Chicago Press, 1998).
4. For a critical view of such coalitions, see Jonathan H. Adler, "Rent Seeking Behind the Green Curtain," *Regulation* 4 (1996): 26–34; Michael S. Greve and Fred L. Smith, *Environmental Politics: Public Costs and Private Rewards* (New York: Praeger, 1992).
5. Jane Mansbridge, *Why We Lost the ERA* (Chicago: University of Chicago Press, 1986).
6. Walter A. Rosenbaum, *Environmental Politics and Policy*, 4th ed. (Washington, D.C.: CQ Press, 1998), 36.
7. Stone, *Policy Paradox*.
8. Daniel Sarewitz and Roger A. Pielke, Jr., "Prediction in Science and Policy," in *Prediction: Science, Decision Making, and the Future of Nature*, ed. Daniel Sarewitz, Roger A. Pielke, Jr., and Radford Byerly, Jr. (Washington, D.C.: Island Press, 2000), 17.
9. Eban Goodstein and Hart Hodges, "Polluted Data," *American Prospect*, November–December 1994; http://www.prospect.org.archival35/35goodfs.html.
10. John Kingdon, *Agendas, Alternatives, and Public Policies*, 2d ed. (New York: Harper-Collins, 1995).
11. Lettie M. Wenner, "Environmental Policy in the Courts," in *Environmental Policy in the 1990s*, ed. Norman J. Vig and Michael E. Kraft (Washington, D.C.: CQ Press, 1990), 189–210.
12. Charles T. Rubin, *The Green Crusade: Rethinking the Roots of Environmentalism* (Lanham, Md.: Rowman and Littlefield Publishers, 1998).

Index